THE PICTURES IN THE COLLECTION OF
HER MAJESTY THE QUEEN

RAPHAEL'S CARTOONS
AND THE TAPESTRIES FOR
THE SISTINE CHAPEL

BY JOHN SHEARMAN

PHAIDON

I. *St. Paul preaching at Athens.* Detail from Plate 39.

RAPHAEL'S CARTOONS

IN THE COLLECTION OF

HER MAJESTY THE QUEEN

AND THE TAPESTRIES

FOR THE SISTINE CHAPEL

BY

JOHN SHEARMAN

PHAIDON

© 1972 PHAIDON PRESS LTD · 5 CROMWELL PLACE · LONDON SW7

PHAIDON PUBLISHERS INC · NEW YORK
DISTRIBUTORS IN THE UNITED STATES: PRAEGER PUBLISHERS INC
111 FOURTH AVENUE · NEW YORK · N.Y. 10003
LIBRARY OF CONGRESS CATALOG CARD NUMBER: 72 79553

ISBN 0 7148 1450 4

MADE IN GREAT BRITAIN
TEXT PRINTED BY WESTERN PRINTING SERVICES LTD · BRISTOL
PLATES PRINTED BY BEN JOHNSON AND CO. LTD · YORK

CONTENTS

PREFACE

I CANNOT now remember how this book was originally conceived. At a certain point it became clear either to Sir Anthony Blunt or to myself, or perhaps to both of us in conversation, that the Catalogue of the Earlier Italian Paintings in the Royal Collection would look strangely unbalanced if it embraced, as logically it should, two monumental cycles, the *Triumphs* by Mantegna and Raphael's Cartoons. These cycles seemed to invite separate treatment, and it was decided to devote a volume to each; I was very happy to surrender the peculiarly difficult problems of Mantegna's *Triumphs* to Andrew Martindale.

It may very well be the result, at least in this case, that the volume is not obviously part of a series of catalogues. I have been entirely free to recast the material of a catalogue-entry, to expand its normal scope and to extend its length, so that it more resembles a monograph. Yet, in spite of appearances, I would claim to have remembered at least the spirit of a catalogue. Tangibly, but relatively trivially, this is evident in the 'Catalogue Notes' at the end, where it should be possible to find directly or by cross-reference the basic information one expects to find in a catalogue-entry. More fundamentally, I have interpreted my task as, in the first place, the collection, criticism and presentation of whatever material seemed relevant to an understanding of these great works: not to provide an understanding, but rather to set before the reader the materials with which, as I would hope, he may form his own.

As it happens—yet not quite accidentally—this intention conforms with my inclinations in general. I do not believe that the reader needs to be told that Raphael's Cartoons are beautiful, and I am fairly certain that I cannot explain why they are. Nor do I think that the reader wants to be told that his eye follows the composition from the bottom left-hand corner, or from the right, as the case may be; I know that my eye only needs to be given this sort of instruction for it to start doing something else. And if it is anybody's proper function to offer such analyses, as they are hopefully called, it does not seem to me to be the historian's. Secondly, I have found with this particular subject that the material requires discussion in the least assertive manner that is possible; and here I should like to make a brief comment on method. Nobody could ask for a richer subject for a book, but the richness imposes its own problems and first among these is the multiplication of possibilities. Inevitably I have exercised my judgement on the material that presented itself, but beyond a certain point it seemed to me unjustifiable to eliminate alternative interpretations, or bases even for contrary interpretations; and when I bear in mind the frequency of accidents that brought material or ideas to my notice I find it even less appropriate to endow the results with the appearance of finality. No doubt a touch of Ockham's razor would produce a neater job, but I am convinced that it would then be less representative of the reality of the situation. I certainly do not imagine that all the possibilities I have explored, particularly in footnotes, are valid—indeed some must be mutually exclusive; but I prefer to leave it to the reader to accept or reject what he will, if he sees more clearly than I do that some options should be closed.

I was first concerned with the problems of the Cartoons some twenty years ago and the initial results were eventually published in two articles, written in collaboration with John White, in *The Art Bulletin* of 1958; neither of us is now clear about the division of responsibility for the ideas in those articles, and to neither of us does it seem important. I have freely changed my mind on many points, and above all on the method of approach, but nevertheless I am conscious, however imprecisely, that to John White, and to Lee Johnson, who worked with us in the initial stages of that project, I owe a great deal.

The richness of the subject, referred to already, could never have come within my reach were it not for the resources of four superb institutions. I first began to assemble the material for this book while the guest of the Institute for Advanced Study at Princeton; that providential invitation I owed to Millard Meiss and the late Robert Oppenheimer. Then I have been so fortunate as to be repeatedly the guest of the Bibliotheca Hertziana in Rome, through the kindness of Wolfgang Lotz. And—although they may be so familiar as to be taken for granted—the Biblioteca Apostolica Vaticana and the British Museum Library must still leave a frequent visitor with a sense of profound gratitude for their existence and accessibility. In addition, Oliver Millar in the Surveyor's Office and Graham Reynolds in the Department of Paintings at the Victoria and Albert Museum put at my disposal all the accumulated material in their files, much of it unpublished, and answered my questions. One could scarcely ask for more.

Actually I did ask for more. I have probably pestered nearly all my colleagues at the Courtauld Institute with my problems at one time or another, and I recall with particular gratitude the specialist advice of Howard Burns, Robin Cormack, Julian Gardner, Michael Hirst, Christopher Hohler, Michael Kitson, Stephen Rees-Jones and George Zarnecki. And outside the Institute I have had guidance and information from a great many kind people, among whom I should mention, as collaborators in some degree: Norman Brommelle, Christoph Frommel, John Gere, Creighton Gilbert, Richard Krautheimer, Jane Langton, Susan McKillop, Jeremy Noble, Konrad Oberhuber, Giovanni Paccagnini, Dioclecio Redig de Campos, Mgr. José Ruysschaert, Frederick Sternfeld, Hugh Tait, Mrs C. van der Velde and John Ward Perkins. The typescript was much improved by the criticism of Anthony Blunt (the most tactful and encouraging of editors), Nicole Dacos, Ernst Gombrich, Michael Hirst, Martha McCrory, Oliver Millar, Father Heinrich Pfeiffer, and Ruth and Nicolai Rubinstein, each of whom undertook to read at least a part of it. In the last stages I have been grateful repeatedly to Dr I. Grafe at the Phaidon Press for his patience, but even more for his scholarly attention and criticism. And finally the reader and I are fortunate indeed that Rolf Quednau, who has an enviable flair for spotting imperfections of all kinds, volunteered to collaborate in checking the proofs; his meticulous standards have brought that sort of improvement that places in his debt anyone who should use this book, and I alone am responsible for the faults that remain.

Almost all the time I was at work on this project I enjoyed the inspiration and guidance of the late Johannes Wilde, and I was able to discuss with him in detail the subject—very near to his heart—of Chapter II; if I cannot express my debt to him, equally I cannot forget it.

It goes without saying that Jane, my wife, has suffered once again and borne it all cheerfully, for the most part—it goes without saying because if she had not the book would not exist; I cannot possibly thank her adequately, and I have already apologized.

JOHN SHEARMAN

I: Patron and Commission

Aliud est historia, aliud laudatio (Leonardo Bruni)

IN 1511 the Professor of Biblical Exegesis at Milan, the Carthusian Zaccaria Ferreri, became secretary to the schismatic Council of Pisa, and two years later—after the collapse of the revolt against Pope Julius II and the establishment of the legitimate Lateran Council—he found himself stranded at Lyon.[1] He was stranded because he had betrayed Julius, his former friend, and now the leading schismatic cardinals were making their peace with Rome. That they should be able to do so was due to the death of Julius in February 1513 and the election on 11 March of the young Giovanni de' Medici as Pope Leo X; it was calculated, accurately in fact, that the new papal policy would be conciliatory, and the pardon given to the leaders of the schism was characteristic of the new situation. Zaccaria Ferreri decided to take the same advantage in September and he had succeeded by the end of the year, but the manner of his approach was idiosyncratic. Before making a direct appeal to Leo he composed a remarkable—and at times beautiful—poem, the *Lugdunense Somnium*, which was published at Lyon on 13 September 1513.[2] In the *Somnium* time is cast back to March of the same year, to a dream in which the poet is transported to the celestial spheres where Dante becomes his guide, as Virgil was for Dante himself in the *Divine Comedy*. When Dante informs the outcast of the election of a new pope, and promises to lead him to Leo's throne, the visionary becomes intertwined with the real, and the exegetical with the prophetic, in a particularly fascinating way.

Ferreri follows Dante to Rome, and to the Mons Vaticanus with the Papal Palace surrounded by the Leonine walls; they cast a rapid glance over the rest of Rome, they explain (or perhaps invent) the symbolism of the Medici *palle*, they discuss the virtues of the Medici family and of the nine previous pontiffs of the name Leo, and digress further on the biblical texts in which Christ is characterized by the virtues of the lion and on the noble qualities of the king of beasts itself. Dante continues, with a striking conflation of two images of the Peace of Christ taken from the Epistles of Peter and Paul: ' "Indeed the great Father himself (that is Leo) builds for the Heavenly King an eternal temple of living stone, bringing the separate together into one; and as the corner joins what is divided, so he reunites the scattered;[3] with his healing hand he cures all ills; he transforms an age of iron into one of gold; he conciliates the fierce hearts of men, and spreads ambrosia and nectar throughout the world." As the sage is telling me this,' continues Ferreri, 'we make our way into the palace, and by lofty steps we enter its spacious halls. Golden walls and golden vaults are refulgent on every side; the creations of Apelles glow, the painted chambers shine and embroidered tapestries are resplendent.[4] The entrances are crowded with the people and the nobility; it is scarcely possible to pass through, so forcefully are we pressed and turned aside. We enquire where the Roman Pontiff may be found, and they, rejoicing in the *claviger pater*, reply that he is being carried towards the altar, to be placed upon the daïs and the lofty throne. We pass on, penetrate the countless throng on every side, and enter the holy place. The temple echoes with magnificent sound, like that of headlong waves that loudly murmur and deeply resonate as they recede from the rocks. We push on further, and now there appears a splendid crowd of patriarchs by the high altar, and

1. B. Morsolin, *Zaccaria Ferreri: episodio biografico del secolo decimosesto*, Vicenza, 1877, pp. 47 ff.; see also L. Pastor, *The History of the Popes*, vi, ed. F. I. Antrobus, London, 1950, pp. 385 ff., and viii, ed. R. F. Kerr, London, 1950, pp. 208 ff.; H. Jedin, *A History of the Council of Trent*, i, London, 1957, pp. 39 ff.

2. Zacharia Ferreri, *Lugdunense somnium de divi leonis decimi pontificis maximi ad summum pontificatum divina promotione*, Lyon, 1513 (unpaginated). In fact the presentation copy (see below, n. 7) is dated 'XV Cal. Aprilis MDXIII' (18 March 1513) at the end of the poem, but it seems clear that this is a false date and in effect a kind of flattery since it would imply that it was completed within a week of the pope's election; the poem is printed with a letter, addressed by Ferreri to Louis XII, which is dated 22 August. Leo's remarkably severe letter of absolution, dated 11 December 1513, is in C. Baronius and O. Raynaldus, *Annales ecclesiastici*, xx, Cologne, 1694, pp. 144–5.

3. 'Maximus ipse etenim pater immortalia tecta
    Construet aetherio regi de marmore vivo
    Efficiens utraque esse unum: divisaque sicut
    Angulus annectet, dispersaque colliget . . .'
cf. I Peter ii. 5 ff., and Ephesians ii. 11 ff. These and other texts on the same theme are discussed below in Chapter III, pp. 79 ff.

4. 'Auratus paries, testudo aurata refulgent
    Undique: apellaei rutilant monumenta
       laboris:
    Pictaque fulcra nitent, *aulaeaque barbara*
       splendent.'
Ferreri uses the same term in his *Itinerarium divi leonis decimi pontificis max.*, Rome, 1516, fol. 4v., of Leo's entry into Florence:
'Barbara de summis pendent aulea fenestris.'
I owe the translation of *barbara* as 'embroidered' to Ernst Gombrich, who suggested *Aeneid* xi. 777 as a parallel: 'pictus acu tunicas et barbara tegmina crurum'.

5. E. Albèri, *Relazioni degli ambasciatori veneti al senato*, Ser. 2, iii, Florence, 1846, pp. 96 ff.

6. 'superiorem partem testudineam pulcherrimis picturis et auro exornavit (Julius)'; for the whole text, see E. Steinmann, *Die Sixtinische Kapelle*, i, Munich, 1901, p. 136, n. 2.

7. Pastor, ed. cit. in n. 1, viii, pp. 208 ff. The presentation copy of the *Somnium*, acknowledged in the letter of absolution (see n. 2 above), appears (No. 5) in a list of books that entered Leo's private library in 1513–14: G. Mercati, 'Un indice di libri offerti a Leone X', *Il libro e la stampa*, ii, 1908, pp. 41 ff.; it is now in the Biblioteca Nazionale, Florence (Banco rari 158).

8. Biblioteca Apostolica Vaticana, MS. Vat. Lat. 3535, fols. 85r. ff., *Scripturus quae memoratu digna Romae et in Italia ab excessu Adriani. vj. Pont. Max. gesta sunt*, fols. 96v.–97r.; this MS. concludes with an account of the election of Clement VII, November 1523. The original of the text quoted, which appears to be unpublished, is as follows: 'a leva (of the Sala Regia) Xisti. 4.ti aliud sacellum conspicitur maxima impensa constructum (fuit enim Sistus in operibus publicis extruendis valde magnificus) . . . quod quidem sacellum Iulius. ij. opera Michaelis Angeli pingendi sculpendique scientia clarissimi admirabili exornavit pictura. quo opere nullum absolutius extare aetate nostra plerique iudicant. Moxque Leo X.mus ingenio Raphaelis Urbinatis architecti, et pictoris celeberrimi, Auleis auro. purpuraque intextis insignivit, quae absolutissimi operis pulchritudine omnium oculos tenent, animos in admirationem convertunt.'

9. Bibl. Vat., MS. Chigiana H. II. 22 (a seventeenth-century compilation from documents of the *fabbrica* of Saint Peter's), fol. 21v.: '1515. E più a dì 15 Junio deve dare duc. trecento di cam.a pagati per ord.e di Mons.r R.mo (Bibbiena) a Raphaele da Urbino per parte di pagam.to delli cartoni o disegni si mandano in Fiandra per li pani razza si fanno per la Capella, appare quitanza. d. 300.' This document, and the one in the next note, were first cited by C. Fea, *Notizie intorno Raffaele Sanzio da Urbino*, Rome, 1822, pp. 7–8.

10. MS. cit., fol. 22r.: '1516. E più a dì 20 decembre deve dare duc. cento trentaquattro di Cam.a pagati per ord.e di mons.r a m. Raphaele da Urbino per pagam.to delli cartoni ha fatto p. la Capella. Ne ho poliza d. 134' (from *Entrata e uscita*, fol. 39v.). The force of the words *ha fatto* is made clear in this summary of the two payments on fol. 2r. of the same MS.: '1515 15. Giug. Raffael da Urbino riceve d.i 300 per i Cartoni che si mandan in fiandra pe' panai di rassa della Capp.a 1516. e *pel residuo* di d.i cartoni a 20 d'Xbre ha d.i 134.' The second payment is briefly recorded in Archivio Fabbrica di San Pietro, Cod. II, fols. 12r., 14v. (K. Frey, 'Zur Baugeschichte des St. Peter', *Jahrbuch der königlich preuszischen Kunstsammlungen*, xxxi, 1910, Beiheft, pp. 27 n. 3, 29; a similar record of the first payment, in the same codex, fol. 3v., was apparently overlooked by Frey and published by V. Golzio, *Raffaello nei documenti . . .*, Vatican City, 1936, p. 38). The absence of further payments on this account is discussed below, p. 13. A. Springer, *Raffael und Michelangelo*, Leipzig, 1878, ii, p. 265, thought that the first payment implied that Raphael had begun work long before its date, but payments on account do not carry this implication. C. G.

a long succession of priests, some in purple and others in white surplices, engaged in the sacred rites. And we see the Medici Pope gleaming with jewels and gold, wearing the tiara shining with celestial light and seated to universal acclamation on the sublime throne.'

The poet undoubtedly knew the character of the new pope as well as he had come to know the Vatican during his sojourn there as *prelato del sacro palazzo* under Julius a few years earlier. There is nothing casual in this passage and we must notice the place of splendid tapestries in his coruscating vision of the Leonine *Maiestas papalis*. Nor is the hyperbole in the description of the approach to the throne as disproportionate as it seems; a very similar—and obviously sober—report to the Venetian Senate in April 1523 describes the visual magnificence, including tapestries, that struck the ambassadors as they passed through the Vatican Palace to the papal presence.[5] And because of this element of realism in Ferreri's dream it is worth noticing that the theatre of the enthronement is not intended to be Saint Peter's, which would not be approached by a visitor through the palace, but the Sistine Chapel; as we shall see, there would have been a good reason for that choice in 1513. Nevertheless the progress towards the throne follows no sequence that is intended to be exactly related to the topography of the palace, and even if, for example, the golden walls of the entrance halls were inspired by a memory of the lavishly gilded walls of the Sistine Chapel, or if the golden vaults were suggested by the description of Michelangelo's ceiling frescoes (which he had not seen) published by Albertini in 1510,[6] the vision retains the kaleidoscopic diffusion proper to a dream. It is characteristic, even so, of at least the artistic enterprises of Leo X that prophetic suggestion and reality have a distinct if subtle relationship; and the separate fragments of Ferreri's dream, brought into a new focus, will concern us surprisingly often when we turn to the interpretation of Leo's principal artistic contribution to the Sistine Chapel. But the situation is a complex one. Although Leo certainly admired Ferreri's *Somnium*,[7] it is not necessarily the case that it played a part in the pope's artistic decisions that was both effective and fully recognized. Its imagery was by no means uncommon in the first years of the Medici pontificate.

Ten years later an anonymous author returns to the description of the entrance to the Vatican Palace. After leading us up the grand staircase, the predecessor of Bernini's Scala Regia, and into the great hall of the Consistory, the Sala Regia, he continues in these terms: 'On the left appears the Chapel of Sixtus IV, built at enormous expense (for Sixtus was truly magnificent in the construction of public works) . . . and Julius II decorated this chapel with an admirable work of painting by Michelangelo, outstanding for his skill in painting and sculpture; and many judge that nothing in our age is more perfect than this. And soon afterwards Leo X enhanced the chapel, through the genius of the celebrated architect and painter Raphael of Urbino, with tapestries woven with gold and splendid colours; they hold everyone's attention by the incomparable beauty of the work and compel every mind to admiration.'[8] Few present-day visitors to the Sistine Chapel recall that below Michelangelo's vault-painting there once hung a work by Raphael that contemporaries judged its equal—or that the chapel once contained those now faded and lacerated tapestries which rank with the Sala di Costantino and the Medici Mausoleum in Florence as the greatest artistic initiatives of the first Medicean pontificate. But just as Leo-Augustus (to use an image of the period) succeeded Julius-Caesar on the throne of Saint Peter, so—and quite appropriately—the eloquence of Raphael once complemented the *terribilità* of Michelangelo in the first chapel in Christendom.

The major artistic contribution of Leo and Raphael to the Sistine Chapel (*Fig.* 1) was begun within three years of the completion of that of Julius and Michelangelo. The first recorded payment on account to Raphael is dated 15 June 1515, and it is probable that this date marks approximately the beginning of the project.[9] Only one other payment is known, dated 20 December 1516, and since this one is described as closing the account it undoubtedly marks the termination of Raphael's task.[10] This task entailed the production of ten large coloured cartoons, and with a natural and characteristic respect for the occasion he assumed entire responsibility for their design and himself painted the aesthetically significant parts—at least in the seven that survive. These seven entered the Royal Collection in 1623. The original set of ten was sent to Brussels, for at that time it was universally recognized that Flemish weavers were the best,[11] and there over the next three years or more the tapestries were woven in the workshop of Pieter van Aelst. It is not certain, but entirely possible, that Raphael saw the whole series in its intended place before his death on 6 April 1520; Pope Leo unquestionably had that satisfaction before his death on 1 December 1521.[12]

Paris de Grassis, the Master of Ceremonies of the *Capella papalis* under Julius II and Leo X, described the Sistine Chapel as 'ista cappella tam in maestate quam in structura . . . prima mundi'.[13] In spite of its immense scale, truly awe-inspiring when one stands beneath it in the Cortile Borgia, one might doubt that there is no chapel more outstanding structurally; but in the strict sense of the word *maiestas* it has no equal. Its proper titles are *Cappella palatina*, *Capella magna* (or *maior*) in the Vatican, which at this date was the only residence of the popes in Rome. It was, with the Basilica of Saint Peter, the setting for the principal liturgical ceremonies in the calendar of the papal court. The *Maiestas papalis* was more clearly displayed in the chapel than in the basilica since the former was designed specifically for the modern pontifical liturgy and functioned without the complications of other purposes and a long history of adapted usage which applied to the latter.

The present chapel is the second on this site. The first was built by Nicholas III (1277–80) and may well have been on the same outstanding scale;[14] its style and decoration may perhaps best be visualized on the basis of the surviving *Cappella palatina* of the Lateran, also built by Nicholas III and now known as the *Sancta sanctorum*.[15] The Sistine Chapel was erected soon after 1473, when the previous *Capella maior* was mentioned as still in use, and Pope Sixtus's new project may have been associated with the jubilee year of 1475. The principal dedication was to the Virgin of the Assumption and the dedication ceremony took place on the anniversary of that feast, 15 August, in 1483.[16] The chapel has undergone many modifications since that date— some almost immediately—and the reconstruction of its state in 1515 and thereabouts will concern us in the next chapter. In order to understand Pope Leo's commission we need to look more generally now at the pre-existing scheme of decoration.

Stridbeck, *Raphael Studies II: Raphael and Tradition*, Stockholm, 1963, p. 28, suggested that the commission might initially have been given by Julius II; I find his argument unconvincing, and the iconographical evidence seems overwhelmingly against this idea.

11. There is an apposite comment on this superiority in the *Relazione di Borgogna* by Vincenzo Quirini, 1506: 'In detto paese tre cose sono di somma eccellenza. Tele sottilissime e belle in copia in Olanda; tapezzerie bellissime in figure di Brabante; la terza è la musica, la quale certamente si può dire che sia perfetta' (Albèri, op. cit. in n. 5, Ser. I, i, Florence, 1839, pp. 11–12).

12. The history of the cartoons and tapestries is reconstructed below, pp. 138 ff.

13. Paris de Grassis, *Diarium*, 5 April 1518; as in all subsequent quotations I have used the copy in the British Museum, Add. MSS. 8440–4, in this case 8444, fol. 91r. No edition of Paris de Grassis's diary exists; a very small selection of extracts was published by P. Delicati and M. Armellini under the misleading title *Il Diario di Leone X di Paride de Grassi*, Rome, 1884, and these extracts are themselves frequently compressed without indication. Other extracts have been published in a number of specialized contexts.

14. F. Ehrle and H. Egger, *Der vatikanische Palast in seiner Entwicklung bis zur Mitte des xv. Jahrhunderts*, Vatican City, 1935, pp. 71 ff.; D. Redig de Campos, *I palazzi vaticani*, Bologna, 1967, pp. 26, 64. The deduction that the previous chapel was about as big can be argued from the fact that it already accommodated the cardinals' cells at conclaves (e.g. those of Pius II and Paul II: Nationalbibliothek, Vienna, MS. 6324, fols. 81v., 101v.).

15. The history of this building is given in detail by J. B. Gatticus, *De oratoriis domesticis et de usu altaris portatilis*, ed. J. A. Assemano, Rome, 1770, pp. 26 ff.; more recent information is to be found in C. Carletti, 'Il "Sancta Sanctorum" ', *Miscellanea Giulio Belvedere*, Vatican City, 1954, pp. 387 ff.

16. The latest summary of the evidence is in E. Camesasca's appendix to R. Salvini, *La Cappella Sistina in Vaticano*, Milan, 1965, pp. 123 ff.; Salvini himself, pp. 15 ff., has reopened the question of the attribution and has demonstrated that Vasari, who gave it to Baccio Pontelli, could be correct. D. Redig de Campos, 'L'architetto e il costruttore della Cappella Sistina', *Palatino*, ix, 1965, pp. 90 ff., comes to the same conclusion but for different reasons.

17. This problem is discussed by L. D. Ettlinger, *The Sistine Chapel before Michelangelo*, Oxford, 1965, pp. 15 ff.; he concludes that if Piermatteo d'Amelia, who certainly made a design, did indeed paint it, that was most likely to have been after this artist's stay in Orvieto, 1480–81; but it seems to me more likely that any painting would have been done from the same scaffolding from which the vault itself was erected, that is to say about 1477–79.

18. The most revealing discussion of the decorative system is by J. Wilde, 'The decoration of the Sistine Chapel', *Proceedings of the British Academy*, xliv, 1958, pp. 61 ff.

19. The tradition is, of course, much older; as will be explained below, p. 22, the area of the Sistine Chapel immediately inside the screen is, in liturgical origin, the *chorus*; the title *presbyterium*, by which it is generally known, should properly be reserved for the area, raised again, immediately round the altar. In several early mediaeval churches—such as San Clemente in Rome or Castel Sant'Elia—the enclosed *chorus* is one step higher than the floor of the nave.

20. Other examples come to mind—such as the Upper Church of San Francesco at Assisi—but they are less likely to provide an effective prototype; the decorative scheme at Assisi, in any case, is probably dependent on that of the Lateran chapel. Much earlier churches with painted hangings in the lowest zone are S. Maria antiqua and S. Urbano alla Caffarella.

21. 'Parata fuit Capella circumquaque de pannis': the description is by Pietro Amelio, and is quoted by F. Cancellieri, *Descrizione delle cappelle pontificie e cardinalizie*, Rome, 1790, p. 102. Also, 'Decem panni virides qui ponuntur in capella S.^mi d. nostri' are listed in the inventory taken at the death of Pius II, 1464 (E. Müntz, 'Les arts à la cour des papes', *Bibliothèque des écoles françaises d'Athènes et de Rome*, fasc. iv, 1878, p. 319).

22. Steinmann, op. cit. in n. 6, i, p. 553 n. 4, quotes a document which states that Sixtus 'Capellam Apostolicam paramentis pretiosissimis decoravit'. Sixtus's *paramenta* are in part traceable at a later date. The Sacristan of the Sistine Chapel in the period of Leo X and Clement VII, Gabriele d'Ancona, Bishop of Durazzo (c. 1450–1534), wrote an *aide-mémoire* on the duties of his post: *Instructio pro successoribus Sacristis Pape super Cappellis totius anni cum quibusdam pro Temporum varietate mutationibus observationibus* (Bibl. Vat., MS. Cappon. 187, dated 1529); he mentions (fol. 57v.) 'Pluviale sixti vel aliud rubrum', and a later

additional note (made, however, before 1555) refers to another 'Pluviale sixti cum floribus et postis et in aurifrigio sunt rose ex perlis' (fol. 52v.); from this description it is probable that to Sixtus was also due the 'palium cum floribus et postis' and the matching set of 'paramenta pro celebrante violacea cum floribus et circulis' which Gabriele, fol. 16r., prescribes for the second Mass 'in die Cinerum' in the Sistine Chapel. A number of vestments with the arms of Sixtus IV, some apparently identical to those mentioned by Gabriele, appear in the inventory of the treasury of the *Capella papalis*, 1547, published by X. Barbier de Montault in *Bulletin monumental*, Sér. v, No. 6, vol. xliv, 1878, Nos. 11, 22–24, 27. Sixtus's textiles for the chapel were completed by 18 *banchalia* (hangings for seat-backs, probably for the *quadratura* of the cardinals) and

three *spalliere*, paid for on 18 December 1483: Müntz, op. cit. in n. 21, fasc. xxviii, 1882, p. 262.

For the symbolism of the liturgical colours (white, green, red, purple and black) in relation to the feasts and seasons of the Calendar, see J. Braun, S.J., *Die liturgische Gewandung*, Freiburg-im-Breisgau, 1907, pp. 728 ff., and L. Eisenhofer, *Handbuch der katholischen Liturgik*, Freiburg-im-Breisgau, 1932, i, pp. 410 ff.

23. For example, under the date 24 December 1489 (J. Burchard, *Liber notarum*, ed. E. Celani, in *Rerum italicarum scriptores*, xxxii, Part I, i, Città di Castello, 1907, p. 286): 'Forerii . . . deposuerunt et amoverunt pannos virides ex capella ut chorum basilice sancti Petri pararent' (compare the *panni virides* of the previous chapel, inventory cited above, n. 21). In the

Michelangelo's frescoes of 1508–12 may or may not have been the first on the vault;[17] below them, however, the decoration of the side walls effected under the immediate stimulus of Sixtus in 1481–83 has not changed in principle to the present day. These walls are divided by two cornices into three zones, divided vertically by pilasters (painted pilasters in the middle and lowest zones) into a pattern resembling a façade of six bays.[18] Each bay in the uppermost zone contains a window which is flanked on either side by a portrait of one of the early popes set in a niche. The middle zone is occupied by a series of large history-paintings, with scenes from the Life of Moses on the left, and from the Life of Christ on the right. In the lowest zone are fictive tapestries, now heavily overpainted but still appreciable as astounding counterfeits in fresco of silver and gold hangings, richly 'woven' with the emblems of Sixtus IV. This scheme is continued over the entrance wall, where the frescoes—following a series of structural collapses—were substantially remade in the sixteenth century. It was formerly continued, too, over the altar wall, but no trace survived the imposition of Michelangelo's *Last Judgement* in 1536–41.

The space of the chapel is divided by a beautiful marble screen which separated the area reserved for the *Capella papalis*—in the corporate sense of the term—from that for the unprivileged laity. At this point the floor rises by one symbolic step. In this respect the Sistine Chapel follows a tradition that may be traced back to the *Cappella palatina* of the Lateran.[19] As in the Lateran chapel, too, the Sistine altar stood on two steps above the *presbyterium*, there are marble benches around the walls, and there is a marble inlay floor of the type loosely called Cosmatesque, or *opus sectile*. But for our purposes the most significant similarity between the Sistine and Lateran chapels lies in the decoration of the lower surfaces of the walls with fictive tapestries.[20] It is reasonable to suppose that the same feature had existed in Nicholas III's *Capella maior* in the Vatican; but however this may be, it is certain that in that building real tapestries had been hung on occasion over these lower surfaces, and that the Sistine Chapel was designed to follow *this* tradition. There is, for example, a description of the canonization of Saint Bridget of Sweden by Boniface IX, 1391, 'in magna capella sacri palatii', when 'the chapel was hung all round with tapestries'.[21] And in Sixtus's new chapel provision for such tapestries, to replace the fictive ones on feast days or in different seasons, was built into the structure, for the lower cornice is provided with closely-spaced rosettes, each containing a hook.

It is much less easy, however, to reconstruct Pope Sixtus's exact intentions with regard to tapestry-decoration. The evidence suggests that they would not have been the same as Leo's. Sixtus endowed the chapel with *paramenta*, that is to say a set of strictly liturgical textiles, hangings for the altar and vestments for the celebrants, and it seems that this set included alternatives of different colours symbolic of the feasts and seasons of the Church calendar;[22] such an endowment was normal practice for the founder of a chapel, and there is no reason to suppose that Sixtus took the exceptional step of ordering tapestries specifically designed to clothe the walls. But there is evidence from the late 1480s onwards that wall-hangings of some kind were normally in place; in the diary of Johannes Burchard, Paris de Grassis's predecessor as Master of Ceremonies, there are references to the removal of these hangings, and on one occasion they are specified as being green and as being used in Saint Peter's as well.[23] It is likely, therefore, that these hangings were simply taken out of the enormous store of tapestries in the papal wardrobe, which provided in this way for the needs of the *Capella papalis* wherever it was assembled; the *forrerii* were required, for example, to cope with such contingencies in S. Maria del Popolo and S. Maria sopra Minerva.[24] At all events these hangings seem to have been of one predominant colour and non-figurative, like the gold- and silver-painted tapestries of the Sixtine fresco-decorations.

In the Musée Condé at Chantilly there is a miniature (*Fig. 4*), cut perhaps from a choir-book, which helps us to visualize this Quattrocento tradition.[25] From the evidence of the liturgy it is clear that it represents accurately but compactly the *Capella papalis*, in the corporate sense; the positions of papal throne, *credenza* (table for the celebrant), processional cross, acolytes and *quadratura* of the cardinals are all correct. The Master of Ceremonies, in white surplice, instructs an acolyte in the *incensatura*. The style of the miniature is very close to that of the early work of Gherardo and Monte di Giovanni, who ran one of the most important Florentine manuscript workshops, and the most probable date for its execution is in the 1470s.[26] The painstaking papal portrait is not very obviously that of Sixtus IV, but on the other hand it can represent no other pope of the period and it is not irreconcilable with the head in the copy of the lost Perugino altarpiece of the Sistine Chapel (*Fig. 9*) or another in a Platina manuscript in the Vatican Library.[27] It is possible that the miniature was made either when the *Cappella palatina* of Nicholas III still existed (that is to say before *c.* 1475), or when the new chapel was being built (it may even be a fragment of one of Sixtus's endowments); but it cannot be in the exact sense a representation of either building. Literal portrayal should not be expected within the conventions of the genre, and the artist, in any case, may have had no more precise knowledge than the type of windows he should show or the subject of the altarpiece. Nevertheless, because of its accuracy in the liturgical sense we may extend its credibility to the tapestries shown on the walls, and these are of the type that documentary evidence would lead us to expect: with an abstract floreated pattern on a ground of one predominant colour.

It is from the pontificate of Leo that we have the first evidence of figurative tapestries being used in the Sistine Chapel. In an inventory of the tapestry wardrobe begun in 1518 there is a long list of forty-seven pieces, all acquired by Leo X and all used in the Sistine Chapel; twenty of this group represented scenes from the Passion, but they were of varying dimensions and were in no

Liber caeremoniarum of Agostino Patrizi Piccolomini, 1488 (ed. C. Marcellus, Venice, 1516, fol. ciii, v.—for this edition see below p. 21, n. 4), it is laid down that on Good Friday the chapel should be 'tota nuda, sedes nudae, altare nudum', and accordingly Burchard records that for *Tenebrae* on 23 March 1486 'nudata fuit tota capella pape per florerios adeo quod neque in parietibus neque in terra aliquis pannus remansit' (ed. cit., i, p. 141). See also Steinmann, op. cit. in n. 6, i, p. 578. In addition there are records of Innocent VIII's acquisition, 1488–90, of a number of *panni* and *drappi* of silk, gold and silver for use in the *capella pontificalis* or *capella palatii* (only the latter specifically indicates the Sistine Chapel): E. Müntz, *Les arts à la cour des papes*, Paris, 1898, pp. 124–6, 128; some of these are likely to have been wall-hangings.

24. On 14 March 1502, for instance, Burchard records that the 'locus capitularis de Populo' was scarcely ready in time 'quia forrerii pape non miserunt pannos et tapetes' until the last moment, and on 29 March, for Mass in S. Maria sopra Minerva, 'Chorus fuit paratus pannis aureis palatii pape et scamna cardinalium et prelatorum aliis pannis et bancalibus convenienter, et tapetes per terram strati per totum chorum' (*Liber notarum*, ed. cit., ii, pp. 322, 325).

25. The fragment is boxed with the collection of Italian drawings, and has not, so far as I know, been noticed by manuscript specialists.

26. Compare the documented *Messale di S. Egidio*, Florence, Bargello, Cod. 67, especially the *Consecration of S. Egidio by Martin V* (repr. M. Salmi, *Italian Miniatures*, London, 1957, Pl. xliiia); this codex is dated 1474 by M. Levi d'Ancona, *Miniatura e miniatori a Firenze dal xiv al xvi secolo*, Florence, 1962, p. 129.

27. Bibl. Vat., MS. Vat. Lat. 2044, repr. Steinmann, op. cit. in n. 6, i, p. 10. See also the relief bust of Sixtus attributed to Bregno in the Kunsthistorisches Museum, Vienna. The dating of the Chantilly fragment suggested in the text is tentative and for purposes of identification of the portrait it is necessary to allow a period from *c.* 1460 to *c.* 1490; however the predecessor and the successor of Sixtus, Paul II and Innocent VIII, looked much less like this portrait than he did. Comparison with the medals of Sixtus would certainly suggest that the head in the MS. fragment was not a good likeness, but on the other hand the indubitable portraits of Sixtus in other MSS., derived from the medals, show astonishing physiognomical deviations (for this material see R. Weiss, *The Medals of Sixtus IV*, Rome, 1961, passim).

sense a set, and the rest were made up of four lots of 'diverse histories'.[28] Again it appears that the collection was casual and its employment in the chapel *ad hoc*. Those that were used at any particular moment must have borne a chance dimensional relationship to the real and painted architecture of the chapel. Raphael's set, then, was in all probability intended to remedy this confused and unsatisfactory situation, and we may say with some certainty that they were the first designed for employment in this one place, so that the possibility of a tidy and intelligible relationship with the structure arose in them for the first time. Moreover, since any tapestries commissioned specifically for the chapel by Sixtus or intervening popes—if such a commission had occurred to them—would almost certainly have been non-figurative, for this reason also the project of Leo X must be related, not to recent practice but to a distant mediaeval tradition.

We tend quite naturally to think of the Gothic period as the great age of tapestry, which was effectively closed by Raphael's *Acts of the Apostles*. But our viewpoint is in one sense too wide, since its scope is European, and in another sense too narrow, since it is based upon surviving quantities that have been subject to the accidents of survival. A more relevant viewpoint is the Roman one around 1500, from which it would appear that the epoch of the Carolingian popes had been the heroic period; and in this case, as a student of Carolingian tapestry, Stephan Beissel, said rightly, Raphael's tapestries represent the final revival of that tradition.[29] The evidence for this distant heroic age was perhaps partly visible in surviving pieces, but it was above all accessible and very obvious in the widely read *Liber pontificalis*.[30] The picture that this book presents is at first sight astonishing, but it is amply confirmed by archaeological and liturgical research. Papal patronage in the eighth and ninth centuries provided the great Roman basilicas with tapestries in very large sets; the most extensive on record had ninety-six pieces, while there were several that had between forty and seventy.[31] Occasionally these hangings were of almost unimaginable size; Gregory IV (827–44), for

---

28. *Inventarium omnium bonorum existentium in foraria S.ᵐⁱ D. Leonis papae X . . . MDXVIII* (Archivio di Stato, Rome, Archivio Camerale I, 1557, filza 1), fols. 15r. and v.; first published by E. Müntz, 'Les tapisseries de Raphaël au Vatican', *Chronique des arts*, 1876, pp. 246 ff., and in *Histoire générale de la tapisserie en Italie*, ed. Guiffrey, Paris, 1879–84, ii, pp. 19 n. 3, 20 n. 3. Müntz stated that the words 'pro Servitio Cappellae Sixti' appeared alongside one group of six Passion tapestries in this list of Leo's acquisitions, but in fact the interpolation he saw belongs to the title of a much longer list of 'Tapezarie empte tempore S.ᵐⁱ D. N. Leonis X.ᵐⁱ p. servitio Cappell. Sixti'. Subsequently Müntz, in *Les tapisseries de Raphaël au Vatican*, Paris, 1897, p. 2, stated that a set of seven Passion scenes was hung in the chapel on ceremonial occasions, and that this may be deduced from inventories of Sixtus IV and of Leo X; I suspect that this was due to a lapse of memory; in *Chronique des arts*, 1876, p. 246, and *Histoire*, p. 20, Müntz had made the perhaps hazardous identification of the group of six, recorded *c.* 1518, with seven of the Passion listed, with the observation that they were used in the Sistine Chapel, in an inventory of 1608. The twenty Passion scenes in the Leonine inventory are made up of one group of 'quattuor cum passione ex quibus duo magni et duo parvi' (corrected to: 'quattuor mediocres Et duo magni'), and a second group of 'Quattuordecim alii panni magni et parvi cum historia passionis D. N. Iesu Xpi inter quos est unus cum resurrectione Lazari'.

29. S. Beissel, S.J., 'Gestickte und gewebte Vorhänge der römischen Kirchen in der zweiten Hälfte des viii. und in der ersten Hälfte des ix. Jahrhunderts', *Zeitschrift für christliche Kunst*, xii, 1894, p. 374.

30. One tapestry (blue, with images of Christ, the Virgin and Apostles), together with a *tunicella* and *paliotto*, of Leo III survived in the sacristy of Saint Peter's in the seventeenth century (F. M. Torrigio, *Le sacre grotte vaticane*, Rome, 1639, p. 485). An awareness of, or at least curiosity towards, Early Christian tapestry is suggested by the altar-frontal attributed to Saint Helena in the inventory of Philip the Good of Burgundy (F. Bock, *Geschichte der liturgischen Gewänder des Mittelalters*, Bonn, 1859, p. 134), and by the reputedly Constantinian *dossale* and *pallium* in the fourteenth- and fifteenth-century inventories of the sacristy of Saint Peter's (E. Müntz and A. L. Frothingham, *Il tesoro della basilica di S. Pietro in Vaticano*, Rome, 1883, pp. 13, 70). The edition of the *Liber Pontificalis* I have used is that by L. Duchesne, Paris, 1955, which will be cited as *L.P.*

31. Leo III 'Fecit autem in supradictam ecclesiam (sc: beati Petri) vela de stauracim atque de fundato, pendentes inter columnas maiores dextra levaque, numero lxv . . . Enimvero . . . vela de stauracim quae pendent in arcora argentea in circuitu altaris et in presbiterio, numero xcvi . . .' (*L.P.*, ii, p. 13); Leo IV gave to Saint Peter's 'vela de fundato, in circuitu autem de blata, numero xlv' (*L.P.*, ii, p. 111). Hadrian I (772–795) 'per universos arcos eiusdem apostolorum principis basilicae de palleis tyreis atque fundatis fecit vela numero lxv . . .', and for S. Paolo 'per diversos arcos . . . ex palleis quadrapolis fecit vela numero lxx' (*L.P.*, i, p. 499). It is worth noticing that the second text quoted here follows immediately upon the description of the miracle of the Fire in the Borgo, which Raphael would have had occasion to read in 1514.

32. *L.P.*, ii, p. 79.

33. The position and liturgical function of the tapestries has been studied by Bock, op. cit. in n. 30, pp. 4 ff., 181 ff., by Beissel, op. cit. in

n. 29, pp. 358 ff., and by H. Grisar, *Geschic[...]Roms und der Päpste im Mittelalter*, i, Freibur[...] im-Breisgau, 1901, pp. 375 ff.; the practic[...] aspects of hanging are elucidated by Mgr. Crostarosa, *Le basiliche cristiane*, Rome, 189[...] pp. 63 ff.   J. Croquison, 'L'iconograph[...] chrétienne à Rome d'après le "Liber Pon[...]ficalis" ', *Byzantion*, xxxiv, 1964, pp. 535 [...] deals with the striking iconography of the hangings.

34. *L.P.*, ii, pp. 54, 62, 111.

35. G. Milanesi, *Documenti per la storia dell'a[...] senese*, ii, Siena, 1854, p. 213; E. Müntz, '[...] tapisserie à Rome au xve. siècle', *Gazette [...] Beaux-Arts*, 2ᵐᵉ Pér., xiv, 1876, p. 174, and c[...] cit. in n. 21, fasc. iv, 1878, pp. 180, 326; the[...] does not seem to be any information on t[...] intended setting.

36. For example, the remodelling of S. Pie[...] in Vincoli, which he began as titular cardir[...] 1467–71; but the revival of interest in Ea[...] Christian basilicas is shown by other Quatt[...]

example, endowed San Paolo fuori le mura with a *cortina*—woven with the *Annunciation* and *Nativity*—to hang from the triumphal arch to the floor and to act as a screen for the *presbyterium*.[32]

The extensive sets of tapestries presented by the Carolingian popes were made to hang around the *presbyterium* of a basilica, on the *pergula* or columned screen, and in each intercolumniation of the nave; in the latter case they were suspended from rods embedded in the columns.[33] In other words these sets were made with a precise and predetermined relationship with the architecture. And while some of the sets were undoubtedly of abstract, patterned design or in plain colours, many were figurative, and moreover displayed narrative subjects, even cycles. Paschal I (817–24) gave to Saint Peter's two forty-six-piece sets, one with stories of the Acts of the Apostles, the other representing the Passion and Resurrection of Christ, and Leo IV (847–55) endowed the same basilica with eighteen golden tapestries of the Life of Saint Peter to hang in the *presbyterium*.[34] There is little doubt that Nicholas V consciously revived this tradition when he had made, in 1451, five golden tapestries likewise of the Life of Saint Peter.[35] Leo X and Raphael—the latter now directing the rebuilding of the basilica—could not have been unaware of their own position in the same tradition. But by the same argument it is clear that they must have been equally aware that they were imposing a feature of basilical decoration on the *Cappella palatina*, which appears to have had its own tradition of non-figurative tapestries; the reason for this adjustment will be discussed a little later. In the meantime it is worth emphasizing how precisely they reproduced an earlier situation in Saint Peter's, where tapestries of the Acts of the Apostles hung under two fresco-cycles, of the Old Testament on one side and of the New Testament on the other.

The chapel and its decoration were already distinguished from other Renaissance examples by conscious revival in form and symbolism of mediaeval and Early Christian usage. In this way it is characteristic of Sixtus IV's buildings[36] and in this way too it naturally stimulated the historical imagination of patrons and artists who made further contributions. It has been pointed out that the overall disposition and content of the Sixtine figurative frescoes follow a tradition established in the basilicas of Saint Peter and Saint Paul, S. Urbano alla Caffarella, S. Saba and S. Maria antiqua, and that the curious relation originally made between the choir-gallery (*cantoria*) and the screen (*cancellata*—itself of the *pergula* type erected in the seventh century in Saint Peter's) is derived from the ancient conjunction of screen and ambo.[37] We may add that the design of the floor, which has not received the attention it deserves, follows an ancient tradition too (*Fig.* 1); its general pattern is an adaptation of those of mediaeval Roman floors to the liturgy as it existed in the time of Sixtus and to the particular requirements of the *Capella papalis*.[38] But it contains one very significant element, a large porphyry circle immediately inside the entrance door; this is the *rota porphyretica* which is still to be found in such a position in earlier Roman churches, has a precise function in the conduct of the liturgy, and was considered of such importance in the case of Saint Peter's that it was replaced in the Baroque floor.[39] Current restoration of the historical cycles on the side walls has revealed a feature unexpected in Quattrocento frescoes: explanatory inscriptions in the frieze above each scene (*Fig.* 29); these were a revival of the *tituli* of early Roman mosaics and frescoes.[40]

The seven (now eight) beautiful candelabra on the screen (*Fig.* 3) are interesting too—not simply because they are there, as there were formerly

cento popes between Nicholas V and Alexander VI: see R. Krautheimer, 'S. Pietro in Vincoli and the Tripartite Transept in the Early Christian Basilica', *Proceedings of the American Philosophical Society*, lxxxiv, 1941, pp. 364 ff., and 'Some Drawings of Early Christian Basilicas in Rome', *Art Bulletin*, xxxi, 1949, p. 213.

37. F. X. Kraus, *Geschichte der christlichen Kunst*, II, ii, Freiburg-im-Breisgau, 1900, p. 447; Steinmann, op. cit. in n. 6, pp. 196, 227 ff., and Ettlinger, op. cit. in n. 17, p. 12.

38. See below, p. 22; there survives, in fact, no trace of the Ceremonial of Sixtus IV but its existence may be inferred from Burchard's disapproval of innovations made by Innocent VIII (e.g. 'Cantores cantarunt omnes prophetias, quia SS. D. N. ita voluit, qui noluit illas per cardinales cantari, prout Xystus alias ordinaverat', *Liber notarum*, ed. cit. in n. 23, i, p. 144); such modifications are, however, likely to have been matters of small detail, and the outlines of the original Sixtine liturgy, itself following earlier ones closely, may be envisaged from that of Innocent VIII, which is contained in the *Liber Caeremoniarum* of Agostino Patrizi. A passage in the selections from Paris de Grassis published by Delicati and Armellini, op. cit. in n. 13, p. 9, appears to provide evidence of an *ordo sixtinus*, but is, in this much compressed form, entirely misleading (contrast B.M., Add. MS. 8443, fols. 78 ff.).

39. See M. Andrieu, 'La "rota porphyretica" de la basilique vaticane', *Mélanges d'archéologie et d'histoire*, lxvi, 1954, pp. 189 ff., for extensive documentation of the rôle in the topography of ceremonies in Saint Peter's of this and other circular stones in the floor, and G. Beltrami, 'La "rota porphyretica" nella Basilica Vaticana', *Roma*, x, 1932, p. 571, for the decisions of 1649 on the placing of this relic. Grimaldi, in the early seventeenth century (quoted by Andrieu), thought that the floor of Old Saint Peter's was 'fortasse Constantiniani', and Renaissance observers probably also over-estimated the antiquity of this type. Very large porphyry circles are to be found just inside the entrance of a number of Roman churches, such as SS. Giovanni e Paolo and S. Gregorio Magno. In the period of Leo X that of Saint Peter's, at least, preserved its function: cf. Paris de Grassis, *Caeremonialium Regularum Supplementum et Additiones*, Bibl. Vat., MS. Vat. Lat. 5634/2 (dated 1515), fol. 342r., on the Mass of Corpus Christi in Saint Peter's: 'Pape autem ad porticum applicanti celebrans deposita mitra obviat cum Ministris suis extra portam et in Lapide porfiretico rotundo genuflectit . . .'

40. E. Steinmann, *Die Tituli und die kirchliche Wandmalerei*, Leipzig, 1891, deals with this

tradition down to the tenth century and points out that Giotto's *Navicella* conformed to it, but his book has to be consulted with caution. The *tituli* of the Sistine Chapel are listed below, p. 48.

41. These are the pair now in the Vatican Museum, Galleria dei candelabri III, 24 and 25; two more of the set, different in shaft-design, are also in the Vatican, and a fifth is in S. Agnese; see G. Lippold, *Die Skulpturen des vaticanischen Museums*, iii, 2, Berlin, 1956, pp. 249 ff., Pl. 15. In the Sistine candelabra one section of the shaft is omitted, but their design corresponds in other respects to the extent that their own variety allows.

42. *Ordo Romanus I*, ed. M. Andrieu, in *Spicilegium sacrum lovaniense*, fasc. 23, Louvain, 1948, pp. 82, 84, 107, and especially p. 85: 'tolluntur cereostata (septem) de loco in quo primo steterant, ut ponantur in una linea per mediam ecclesiam . . .' Paris de Grassis, *Caeremoniarum opusculum*, Bibl. Vat., MS. Vat. Lat. 5634/1, fols. 50v.–51v.

43. Innocent III, *De sacro altaris mysterio libri sex*, Leipzig, 1534, fol. 22r. (J. P. Migne, *Patrologiae cursus completus . . ., Series latina*, Paris, 1878 ff.—hereafter cited as *P.L.*—217, col. 804).

44. Several of these sources are quoted by P. Bloch, 'Siebenarmige Leuchter in christlichen Kirchen', *Wallraf-Richartz Jahrbuch*, xxiii, 1961, pp. 55 ff., and 'Der siebenarmige Leuchter in Klosterneuburg', *Jahrbuch des Stiftes Klosterneuburg*, N.F. ii, 1962, pp. 162 ff., to which the most important addition is the eighth-century description of the Gallican liturgy by Germanus of Paris; from our point of view the similar opinion of Durandus, papal *capellanus* (*Rationale divinorum officiorum*, I, i, 10) is especially relevant. A text from the pontificate of Leo X is in the *Oratio* of Bishop Maximus Corvinus at the twelfth session of the Lateran Council, March 1517: 'Quid candelabrum septem luminibus distinctum, nisi septifarium sancti Spiritus lumen? cujus fulgore Pontificum & sacerdotum lumina ita noctes & dies accenderentur, ut semper vigilare, semper insidias satanae intueri possint' (J. Hardouin, *Acta Conciliorum et epistolae decretales ac constitutiones summorum pontificum*, ix, Paris, 1714, col. 1854). E. Wind, 'Michelangelo's Prophets and Sibyls', *Proceedings of the British Academy*, li, 1965, pp. 47 ff., has suggested that the Seven Gifts of the Spirit are represented on the Sistine ceiling, but I do not find his hypothesis convincing.

45. E. Battisti, 'Il significato simbolico della Cappella Sistina', *Commentari*, viii, 1957, pp. 96 ff.

candelabra on the *pergula* of Saint Peter's, but also because in design they are based upon the reputedly Constantinian candelabra which at one time stood by the colossal Early Christian porphyry tomb of S. Costanza.[41] This connection must have been quite clear in Raphael's circle, for the representation—in fact a reconstruction—of the *pergula* of Saint Peter's in the *Donation of Constantine* fresco in the Sala di Costantino (1524) shows candelabra which are virtually identical with those of the Sistine Chapel, and yet are conceived, obviously, as Constantinian. The number of Sixtus's candelabra, seven, is proper to the pope alone, and they have their origin in the seven candlesticks which in the earlier liturgy were carried in procession before the pontiff and during the ceremony were placed around him or across the church. Paris de Grassis was quite clear that the screen-candles had this processional origin, which he traced still farther back to Roman Imperial custom, whence they came to the popes by the gift of Constantine.[42] According to Innocent III, from whom so much of the symbolic tradition inherited by Durandus and Paris de Grassis originates, they symbolized the Seven Gifts of the Holy Spirit (Isaiah xi. 2);[43] a well-documented tradition from at least the eighth century identifies seven lighted candles with the Seven Gifts, and frequently associates them with the Mosaic seven-branched candlestick, the *Menorah*, in the Temple of Solomon.[44]

Several other elements in the Sistine Chapel may be connected with the Temple. In this respect it is exceptional among Quattrocento buildings, but not in the total history of Christian architecture. The connections with the Temple—such as the dimensional one[45]—do not entail the final conclusion, which would be difficult to accept, that Sixtus's building was a reconstruction of Solomon's;[46] rather, they suggest that the origin of the Christian Church

46. Perhaps the most important evidence on this point is in Aegidius of Viterbo's *Historia viginti saeculorum* (c. 1517: Bibl. Angelica, MS. Lat. 351, fol. 312v.); he compares Julius's Saint Peter's with Solomon's Temple, but: 'Abstinuit a Templo etiam Sixtus: tametsi non nihil fundamenti iecisset Nicholaus David tamen imitatus duo sacella consecrat, alterum domi, ubi nunc sacra fiunt: alterum in magni templi latere ubi se moriens iussit sepelliri . . .'

47. 'Ab utroque, scilicet a tabernaculo (of Moses) et a templo (of Solomon), nostra materialis ecclesia formam sumpsit' (Durandus, *Rationale*, I, i, 5).

48. Blasius de Martinellis, *Diarium* (J. B. Gatticus, *Acta selecta caeremonialia sanctae romanae ecclesiae*, Rome, 1753, p. 444, and B.M., Add. MS. 8446, fol. 40r.): 'Sancta Sanctorum capellae (sc. palatii) reservabatur pro missis, Officiis et devotione Cardinalium, & a cancellis capellae est locus Laicorum, potius quam Clericorum . . .' (1534).

49. See Otto Nussbaum, 'Sancta Sanctorum', *Römische Quartalschrift*, liv, 1959, pp. 237–8, and the list of sources in J. M. Neale and B. Webb, *The Symbolism of Churches and Church Ornaments*, Leeds, 1843, p. lxiv, n.

50. 'Vesperae solemnes . . . in Cappella Pal tina, et non in Basilica S. Petri propter ruina illius, et propter frigora, et pluvias instant . . . Papa in fine iussit quod panni aurei, q solent estendi in tribuna Basilicae ponantur Cappella intra Cancellos, sed et reliqua pa Cappellae ultra Cancellos similiter panr ornetur' (B.M., Add. MS. 8443, fol. 91v an incomplete transcription in Delica Armellini, op. cit. in n. 13, p. 12).

51. Paris de Grassis, B.M., Add. MS. 8443, f 23v., Easter Sunday 1513: 'cum propter temp ruinam posita esset aulea circumcirca tribuna maioris Altaris S. Petri, et vento praevalen omnia lacerata fuissent . . . Papa statuit, qu in Cappella Palatina omne offitium ager tur . . .'; ibid., fol. 41v., Pentecost 1513: 'qu altare S. Petri erat discohopertum . . . vent ter, aut quater intra missam lumina alta extinxerit'; 8441, fol. 244v., All Saints' 150 'in Cappella Palatii sic manente Papa, ex quia Tribuna S. Petri, est nimis ventosa, frigida propter fabricam, quae ibi fuit basilica'.

52. The evidence for this date, and for th conception of the altar-house after Le accession, will be published in my article ' "tegurio" di Bramante in San Pietro', to appe in the Acts of the Bramante Congress, 1970.

in that of the Jews[47] was intended to receive symbolic expression in its forms. One instance of this continuity of tradition is significant for our purpose: the area of the chapel inside the screen was known as the *Sancta sanctorum*.[48] In this case the term is to be understood by reference not to the *Cappella palatina* of the Lateran which had acquired the same name, but to an unbroken tradition reaching back to the Early Christian period in which the *presbyterium* was acknowledged as the successor to the Holy of Holies of the Temple.[49]

The emphasis placed, in this and other ways, upon this area in the chapel was recognized in an instruction of Pope Leo's on Christmas Eve 1513. 'The Pope', says Paris de Grassis, 'ordered that the golden tapestries, which are normally hung in the *tribuna* of the basilica (of Saint Peter), should be placed in the chapel, within the screen, but that the remaining part of it outside the screen should also be decorated with tapestries.'[50] Gold is not one of the seasonal or festal liturgical colours, but symbolizes *maiestas*; the tapestries outside the screen could only have been of lesser value.

The occasion of this sumptuous decoration in 1513 is significant for the understanding of Pope Leo's commission to Raphael about eighteen months later, for it was one of many upon which ceremonies normally and properly held in Saint Peter's were transferred to the Sistine Chapel. Julius II had laid the foundation-stone of the new basilica on 18 April 1506, and the subsequent destruction of the earlier building progressively made the celebration of major feasts at its high altar more difficult. Various expedients were tried, but they were ineffective against the wind, cold and rain to which the ceremonies were exposed by the early removal of the western part of the roof. Tapestries were torn, candles were extinguished, and even Julius II had sometimes been unable to attend what had become, in effect, an open-air event.[51] Even after the erection of Bramante's Doric altar-house, designed to cope with this problem and completed in 1514,[52] the continuing exposure during the ceremonies of Pontifical Entrance and Exit and the dangerous condition of the old building made performance in the Palace Chapel from time to time a necessity;[53] the alternative, successful on some occasions, of conducting the Mass in the other Sistine Chapel near the left transept of Saint Peter's itself was often impossible for the same reasons and the penetrating cold. Thus from Epiphany 1508 onwards[54] these basilical ceremonies were held during inclement weather in the Palace Chapel of Sixtus, which thereby acquired a status still higher than that originally intended for it. Leo X, with his characteristic respect for proper form in matters of liturgy, instituted immediately after his election order instead of confusion in the face of what promised to be—and in fact was—a long-term problem, and he made the chapel as far as possible an acceptable substitute for the basilica.[55] The perfectionist Paris de Grassis was impressed; 'Truly', he wrote on Easter Sunday 1513, 'the *Maiestas papalis* shone again in the chapel in all respects as in Saint Peter's.'[56]

Pope Leo's contributions to the Sistine Chapel were by no means confined to the commission for tapestries, and a consideration of the others reveals to some extent the intention that lay behind Raphael's task. He took care that the chapel was kept in good condition, but most of these details of maintenance are of little interest.[57] Within four months of his election he began the replacement of some, at least, of the windows, and his new ones were probably, like Sixtus's, of stained-glass; by early September of 1513 he had provided a new set of the *panni virides* which, since the late Quattrocento, had served as occasional wall-hangings, and with them a new rose-coloured covering for the papal throne.[58] After the commission of the tapestries, but

53. For example, B.M., Add. MS. 8443, fol. 125r., All Saints' 1514: 'missam cantavit Grimanus Cardinalis ... in Cappella Palatii, non autem in Basilica ut est de more, sed propter pluvias non itum est ad S. Petrum ruinosum, et detectum ...'; MS. 8444, fol. 171v., All Saints' 1519: 'missa ... in cappella palatii eo quia porticus sancti Petri erat in ruinis ita, ut in Ecclesiam illam, nec tuto ob timorem maioris ruinae nec commode ire possemus ...'

54. B.M., Add. MS., 8441, fol. 179r.; this seems to be the first occasion.

55. The continuation of this problem in fact is illustrated by records of translation of ceremonies due to the weather in 1525, 1537 and 1538, by the successor to Paris de Grassis, Blasius de Martinellis (B.M., Add. MS. 8445, fol. 64r., 8446, fols. 210r., 243v.).

56. B.M., Add. MS. 8443, fol. 24r. (continuing the passage quoted in n. 51 above with a list of new arrangements necessary): 'Vere in Cappella illa refulsit omnimodo Maiestas Papalis cum in Sto. Petro, nonnisi difficulter appareat Maiestas, et melius esset semper hic celebratur quam in Sto. Petro propter angustiam illius loci Papa.'

57. Some documents describing work of this kind were published by K. Frey, op. cit. in n. 10, pp. 23, 30.

58. June 1513: 'E a dì decto ducati 25 di camera pagati per mano del Thesoriero al maestro di vetri per cominciare le finestre de la capella de papa Sixto' (A. Mercati, *Le spese private di Leone X*, 1928, p. 102). These were no doubt necessitated by the inefficiency of the original windows, which were, in any case, probably partly destroyed during the conclave in March 1513: 'fenestrae autem altae fuerunt diligenter cum tela, et stupa incollatae, ut ventus nullo modo intraret, duae autem fenestrae quae sunt supra sacristiam, idest super altari fuerunt muratae ... et etiam illa in Ingressu Cappellae ad sinistram fuit semimurata, et fenestrae parva (sic) ex choro cantorum ...' (Paris de Grassis, B.M., Add. MS. 8443, fol. 5v.). The previous windows of Sixtus IV on the altar wall were decorated with the arms of the pope (Steinmann, op. cit. in n. 6, p. 641) and Leo's were probably similar. None of the early windows survived an eighteenth-century remodelling of the chapel; their form may be visualized from the painted substitutes that remain on the entrance wall, mainly composed of discs of coloured glass. The present windows of plain glass were introduced by Leo XII (1823–29) to increase the quantity of light (E. Platner and C. Bunsen, *Beschreibung der*

Stadt Rom, II, i, Stuttgart-Tübingen, 1834, p. 245). The new hangings (which might, however, have been floor-coverings) are recorded in a payment of 12 ducats on 4 October 1513 (honouring a *mandato* of 6 September) to 'Magister Joh. paulo de Castiglione sutori pro manifactura et cusitura quatuordecim pannorum viridum pro usu cappelle sacri palatij et pro manifactura unius panni rosati pro coperimento apud sedem D.N. in dicta Cappella' (Archivio segreto vaticano, Camerali, Introitus et exitus 551, fol. 138r.). A later contribution deserves to be noted in view of the quality of the artist: 80 ducats 'de mandato sub die xvj huius Ioanni Barili lignarolo pro parte subselliarum (benches) et aliarum rerum factarum ad usum Capelle S.D.N.' (30 November 1519: Introitus et exitus 559, fol. 169r.).

59. 'Et mihi imposuit, ut sibi hoc ad partem recordarer, quia omnino volebat, quod maestas Papalis in re divina servaretur' (B.M., Add. MS. 8444, fol. 91r.). Gio. Fr. Poggio, *De veri pastoris munere* (c. 1516, addressed to Leo—see below, p. 75, n. 170), Bibl. Vat., MS. Vat. Lat. 3732, fol. 25r., advises that nothing is more worthy of Leo than the defence of the *Majestas Christi vicarii*. In Andrea Guarna's *Simia*, Milan, 1517 (unpaginated, written 1515), the angel in discussion with Peter characterizes Leo as follows: 'Nihil in eius Domo videas nisi Cultum: nisi grave: & quod maiestati Pontificiae Decorum possit afferre.' The wooden *pulpitum* of which Paris de Grassis spoke so scathingly was almost certainly the one provided by Julius II towards the end of 1511; there is a payment of 15 ducats on 9 January 1512 (back-dated to 28 December 1511) to 'Magister Jacopo de mirtina ad bonum computum pulpiti confecti in Cappella palatij' (Archivio segreto vaticano, Camerali, Introitus et exitus 550, fol. 136v.).

60. B.M., Add. MS. 8444, fol. 159r., Easter Monday 1519: 'fuit Cappella ordinaria, in qua presente Papa, Cardinalis de Medicis Vice Cancellarius celebravit, et habuit omnia nova tam pro altari, et credentia, quam etiam pro persona sua, et assistentes, et Diaconi, ac subdiaconi'. Leo had already presented one set of vestments, first used on 17 February 1518 (ibid., fol. 68v.). In the treasury of the Papal Chapel in 1547 there were pieces from at least five sets of Leonine vestments, one described as 'paramenti ricchi', another as 'paramenti poveri' (see the inventory published by Barbier de Montault, op. cit. in n. 22, Nos. 41, 52–8, 70–73, 118–21, 125–9, 157, 160, 175, 183–4 etc.). At this date the surviving vestments of Leo X were only equalled in number by those of the reigning pope, Paul III.

before their delivery, there was a discussion of other improvements, which were put into effect. An account is given by Paris de Grassis under the date Easter Monday 1518: 'I told the pope that in this chapel, as much in *maiestas* as in structure the first in the world, it now happens that it is befouled with spiders' webs and disgraced in every part in other shameful ways, so that it would be a good thing if two or more cleaners were appointed with the specific task of dealing with it once a month, and from top to bottom; and he approved. . . . Further, I said that the pulpit, or rather lectern, from which the *Prophetiae* are chanted was so unworthy, and in my opinion the wood so old and coarse, that His Holiness ought to replace it; and the pope said that I should do so. When he asked me what kind of lectern I would have made, and when the cardinals replied first that it would be quite suitable to make one of gilded wood and silk, or velvet, I said laughing that even I had one of that kind in my own house; and the pope enquired what I proposed. I replied that the whole thing ought to be of solid silver, and gilt . . . and the pope praised my judgement and charged me that one of his household should see that it was executed, so that everything should be ready a year hence. And when the pope, smiling, asked me whether I had in mind anything else that pertained to his honour, so that he could provide for it, I replied that it might be a good idea to make three different liturgical sets, for the three different degrees of rank, that is to say for priests, for cardinals, and for His Holiness, and that these different sets should not only be for the person, such as planeta, dalmatic, tunicella and so on, but also for the tables (*Fig. 4*); so that the priests' (table-sets, or plate) would be smaller than the cardinals', and the cardinals' smaller than the pope's, and that even in the statues (of the Apostles) on the altar, the candlesticks, and in fact in every respect, each set should be different from the others. And the pope, when he heard this, approved enthusiastically, saying that in all respects he wished to provide as above, and to melt down all the silver Apostles, the candlesticks and the rest of the silver plate, so that they should be different for each set . . . and he charged me to remind him, *for he desired, by all means, whatever sustained the* Maiestas papalis *in the liturgy.*'[59] Exactly a year later, indeed, when the Cardinal Giulio de' Medici celebrated Mass in the chapel, everything was new on the altar and the table, and there were new vestments for all those officiating.[60]

This discussion is interesting from a number of points of view. It appears to settle the fate, for example, of earlier sets of silver Apostles belonging to the altar of the Sistine Chapel, one reputedly in part by Verrocchio, another a gift of Julius II.[61] This destruction cannot be described as barbarous, within the conventions of the period, since we cannot guess the quality of the statuettes that replaced them. As it happens there survives at Chatsworth a set of drawings of twelve Apostles, worked up by Giulio Romano a little before

61. This very complex problem has not been properly investigated, and a solution is not necessary in this context. It should, however, be pointed out that the arguments by which Vasari's statements (*Vite*, ed. Milanesi, ii, p. 648, iii, p. 359) are dismissed by C. de Fabriczy, 'Andrea del Verrocchio ai servizi de' Medici', *Archivio storico dell'Arte*, Ser. 2, i, 1895, p. 164, and Steinmann, op. cit. in n. 6, p. 554, are inconsistent with the evidence. A fairer statement appears in G. Passavant, *Andrea del Verrocchio als Maler*, Düsseldorf, 1959, p. 22, but some unwarranted assumptions are made

there too. It seems generally to be overlooke[d] that (i) Vasari's consistent statements imply [a] date for the Paolo Romano-Verrocchio set i[n] the last years of the previous *Cappella palatin[a]*; (ii) in addition to this set and the one presente[d] by Julius II (probably formerly belonging [to] his relative, Cardinal Ascanio Sforza) a thir[d] also of gilt silver statuettes, was made for th[e] Sistine Chapel under Alexander VI, 1493–9 (Müntz, op. cit. in n. 23, pp. 232, 243), an[d] (iii) yet another set was made for Paul II[I] from models by Raffaello da Montelupo, 154[5–]1547 (X. Barbier de Montault, *Œuvres complète[s]*

II. *The Miraculous Draught of Fishes.* Detail from Plate 1.

this date from sketches by Raphael; they must have been made for some quite different purpose, but they remind us that the availability to Leo of such talent for the designs, and of silversmiths of the calibre of Raphael's friend Antonio da San Marino for the execution, could have produced worthy replacements. At all events Leo's silver Apostles themselves do not seem to have lasted for long. They are unlikely to have survived the pillage during the Sack of Rome, 1527, and it is possible that they had already been stolen in the sack of the Vatican Palace by the Colonna in 1526.[62] None of the liturgical plate made in 1518–19 can be identified positively, but an obvious possibility —which at least gives us a guide to its quality—is presented by the marvellous Leonine silver-gilt dish, inset with crystal, rubies and sapphires, now in the Schatzkammer at Munich (*Fig. 8*).[63]

Paris de Grassis's report provides above all a rare example of that kind of conversation which leads ultimately to the creation of a work of art, and something similar must have taken place before the decision to commission tapestries was made (unfortunately Paris de Grassis was on leave, so that there is a gap in the diary, for the early months of 1515,[64] when the idea was probably born). It is easier to imagine, of course, that a discussion was initiated in this case by observation on the scrappy results of *ad hoc* arrangements of hangings from the wardrobe, unworthy of the papal dignity, rather than by complaints about cobwebs. But it seems legitimate to be guided by the report of the closely related event in our interpretation of the motivation of the tapestry commission, and above all of the lavishness of the materials, silk, gold and silver. These were not in the first place signs of personal indulgence, or of Medici family ostentation—nor were they a purely decorative and meaningless extravagance. The richness of tapestries, solid silver lectern, and multiple sets of Apostles, liturgical vessels and vestments, touched upon the *Maiestas papalis*, which was very much Pope Leo's concern. The tapestry commission was itself the manifestation of an idea about the papacy in its setting; the subjects selected were, as we shall see, harmonious with this intention. And one further deduction seems legitimate when we remember that Sixtus IV had chosen for his permanent, fictive tapestry-decoration the colours silver and gold, symbolic in that context of *maiestas*. In this one fundamental sense, at least, Leo X's new endowment was not in conflict with the original intention of the founder of the chapel.

Leo's primary motive, then, was probably more exalted than personal aggrandizement and gratification, but also less sublime than tribute to the Glory of God; it makes sense in relation to a man who—in spite of inevitable gossip and perhaps appearances too—took his office seriously, and it makes sense in the context of the Papal Chapel. This is not to exclude, however, other considerations that are likely to have come to his mind. Two Della Rovere popes had made their mark on the chapel so prodigally that their *stemma*, the oak-leaf, was to be seen on all its surfaces and sculptured parts. Leo would have been less than human, and much less than a proud son of Lorenzo *il magnifico*, if he had not wished to leave, in this place above all, some sign of the remarkable family ascendancy that culminated in his succession to the throne of Saint Peter. Sixtus and Julius had left nothing undone in the chapel except what he did; and it may be assumed that the personal and family emblems appeared as prominently on his silver and furnishings as they did on his vestments and tapestries. The latter, in fact, removed from his sight the countless oak-leaves at eye-level on the fictive hangings.

The choice of tapestry for his principal artistic contribution was dictated by the principal opportunity. Leo, however, must have been conscious of a

i, Poitiers, 1889, pp. 315, 318); this set perhaps replaced Leo's of 1518–19, and may be the one —usually taken to be Sixtus IV's—which was stolen in the eighteenth century (Vasari, *Vite*, ed. G. Bottari, Rome, 1759, p. 456, n. 2).

62. The Colonna 'preseno il Borgo et poi il palacio, il qual tutto hanno sachizato, et del Borgo molte case, le cose del Papa, la sacrestia, li apostoli, li razi di papa Leon, et più spogliorno tutti si trovorono in Palazzo...' (letter from Rome, 21 September 1526, in *I diarii di Marino Sanuto*, xlii, Venice, 1895, col. 700); since this account does not state that the *apostoli* were removed from the sacristy of the *Cappella palatina* some doubt remains. Their fate in the Sack of Rome is not clear; on the one hand there are two reports that they were melted down by Clement VII for coinage with which to pay off the armies of Charles V (D. Orano, *Il sacco di Roma del M.D.XXVII, studi e documenti, I: I ricordi di Marcello Alberini*, Rome, 1901, pp. 313–14, and Sanuto, *Diarii*, ed. cit., xlvi, col. 135); on the other hand Gregory XIII is said to have added seven statuettes to six which had survived the Sack of Rome (H. Siebenhüner, 'Die Ausstattung von St. Peter in Rom', *Festschrift für Hans Sedelmayr*, Munich, 1962, p. 264).

63. H. Thoma and H. Brunner, *Schatzkammer der Residenz München*, Munich, 1964, No. 33.

64. From 11 January until April; on the Feast of the Ascension, 1515, Paris de Grassis complained to the pope of seating arrangements made in New Saint Peter's, contradicting dispositions of Innocent III, 'me ab urbe absente' (B.M., Add. MS. 8443, fol. 133r.).

Medicean tradition in tapestry patronage, distinguished not only by extensive purchases directly from Flanders[65] but also, it seems, by commissions of cartoons from indigenous artists of the stature of Botticelli and Leonardo.[66] The collaboration thus imposed, perhaps particularly by Lorenzo, between the most esteemed designers and executants, seems to offer the most exact precedent for the manner in which Leo proceeded in Rome. Then it must be remembered that even the conspicuously sumptuous set that he ordered had some competition from those of his cardinals; Domenico Grimani, for example, also purchased a set of figurative tapestries woven with gold and silver.[67] And finally we should allow one further motive in the case of this pope, so conscious of his name: the emulation of his predecessors Leo III and Leo IV, who had been among the most generous of the Carolingian tapestry-patrons. We can more conveniently look at the meaning of this emulation a little later, but perhaps it should be said now that such a parallel, drawn across seven centuries, need not have escaped an intelligent observer of the period. When Eugenius IV, for example, presented to Saint Peter's the bronze doors of Filarete, Flavio Biondo compared this gift with one by

65. E. Müntz, *Histoire générale de la tapisserie*, ed. Guiffrey, ii, Paris, 1878–84, p. 10, and *Les collections des Médicis au quinzième siècle*, Paris, 1888, pp. 20 ff., 58 ff., 106 ff.; A. Warburg, 'Flandrische Kunst und florentinische Frührenaissance', in *Gesammelte Schriften*, Leipzig, 1932, i, p. 187; R. de Roover, *The rise and decline of the Medici Bank*, New York, 1966, p. 144.

66. A tapestry after a design by Botticelli was published by Müntz; bibliography, discussion and reproduction can be found in G. Poggi, 'La giostra medicea di 1475', *L'Arte*, v, 1902, pp. 71 ff.; Poggi rightly questioned Müntz's assertion that it was executed for Lorenzo *il magnifico*, but that proposition is not unreasonable; see the discussion of iconography and date in A. Chastel, *Art et humanisme à Florence au temps de Laurent le Magnifique*, Paris, 1959, p. 263. Vasari (*Vite*, ed. Milanesi, iv, p. 23) knew a cartoon by Leonardo of Adam and Eve 'per una portiera, che si aveva a fare in Fiandra d'oro e di seta tessuta per mandare al re di Portogallo'; he placed it in Leonardo's early Florentine period, and although he did not say that it was a Medici commission that (provided that his date is correct) would seem very likely. A plaque in the Musée Cluny which seems to record this design was published by W. Suida, *Leonardo und sein Kreis*, Munich, 1929, p. 38; a derivative composition is probably Raphael's in the Stanza della Segnatura.

67. P. Paschini, *Domenico Grimani, Cardinale di S. Marco*, Rome, 1943, p. 159.

68. 'Leo quartus ... is Pontifex magnanimus ... magnamque suscipiens ipsius & basilice beati Petri curam, multa fecit ... (but) Sola re una videris (Eugenius IV) a Leone superatus: quod valvas ille argenteas tu eneas basilice dedisti ...' (Flavius Blondus, *Urbis romae instauratae ... Liber*, Rome, 1474 (?), fol. 11v. For Leo's gift see *Liber pontificalis*, ed. cit. in n. 30, ii, p. 127. Maffeo Vegio was another contemporary witness just as clear that Eugenius was restoring a gift of Leo IV (*De rebus antiquis memorabilibus basilicae S. Petri romae*, c. 1455–57, in *Acta sanctorum*, June, vii, ed. Antwerp, 1717, pp. 71, 84).

69. D. Gnoli, 'Secolo di Leon X?', in *La Roma di Leon X*, Milan, 1938, pp. 341 ff., is as wilful and polemical a piece of debunking as one would ever wish to read.

70. Pietro Aron, *Thoscanello de la musica*, Venice, 1523, dedication to Sebastiano Michiel: 'Leone. X. Pontefice, il quale benche fussi di molte virtù ornato, et studioso, di meno di niuna si è più dilettato, et niuna hebbe più

favorita, et essaltata che le Musica.' Anon., *Vita Leonis X^{mi} imperfecta* (c. 1523, far from adulatory), Bibl. Vat., MS. Vat. Lat. 3920, fol. 3v.: 'Bonarum artium haud quaquam ignarus fuit: sed musice praecipuam ac continuam operam dedit ... erat enim musice artis peritissimus: ac propterea eius professoribus.' See also Raffaello Brandolini, *Dialogus Leo nuncupatus* (c. 1513–14), ed. F. Fogliazzi, Venice, 1753, pp. 125–6; Stephanus Ioanninensis, *In mediceam monarchiam penthatheucus*, Ancona, 1524, fol. 98r.; and Pastor, op. cit. in n. 1, viii, pp. 144 ff.

71. A. Pirro, 'Leo X and Music', *Musical Quarterly*, xxi, 1935, p. 6, n. 84; H. W. Frey, 'Leo X', in *Die Musik in Geschichte und Gegenwart*, viii, Kassel, 1960, cols. 619 ff.

72. Pietro Martire d'Anghiera, letter of 20 April 1513, quoted by Pirro, op. cit., p. 6; see also: Cristoforo Marcello, *Ad Leonem X. Pont. Max. ... Oratio* (1513), Bibl. Vat., MS. Vat. Lat. 3646, fols. 16r. ff. (with the interesting reflection that the discipline of *consonantia*, inducing *concordia*, is an excellent training for a pope elected at this moment); Raffaello Brandolini, *De musica et poetica opusculum* (dedicated to Leo), Rome, Bibl. Casanatense, MS. 805, fol. 18v.; Sebastiano Compagni, *Terreni orbis descriptio generalis*, 1519, Bibl. Vat., MS. Vat. Lat 3844 (presentation copy), fol. 1r.

73. This we learn from Paris de Grassis's account of the occasion—which annoyed him—when Leo X ordered a special *Missa solemnis* for the visit of the Duchess of Bari in November 1520: 'Missa per cantores elegans, et mirabilis propter cornua musicale' (B.M., Add. MS. 8444, fol. 201r.); and it seems that we should

interpret in this way his account of the ceremonies of Thursday in Holy Week, 1516: 'Cantores hodie inceperunt cantare psalmum miserere mei Deus partim cum canto figurato, et simphonia ...' (Add. MS. 8443, fol. 178r.); for the reorganization, see Frey, loc. cit. in n. 71.

74. Andrea Adami, *Osservazioni per ben regolare il coro dei cantori della Cappella Pontificia*, Rome, 1711, p. xix; Pirro, op. cit. in n. 71, pp. 11 ff. E. Lowinsky, 'A newly discovered Sixteenth-Century Motet Manuscript ...', *Journal of the American Musicological Society*, iii, 1950, p. 178; idem, *The Medici Codex of 1518*, Chicago, 1968, pp. 28 ff. Leo's endowments of the Sistine Chapel were naturally completed by a number of sumptuous choir-books, for which see the 1547 inventory published by Barbier de Montault, op. cit. in n. 22, Nos. 439–41, 447, and J. M. Llorens, *Capellae Sixtinae codices musicis notis instructi*, Vatican City, 1960, Nos. 10, 16, 34.

75. One of the fools whom Leo suffered gladly was a quack musical theorist called Evangelista Tarascono Parmigiano; he was thought half-mad because he believed that acoustics were improved by *removing* tapestries from the walls (Paolo Giovio, *Vita di Leone*, ed. L. Domenichi, Florence, 1549, p. 296). For the abstention from *cantus figuratus* (with the exception of Thursday in Holy Week), see Paris de Grassis, *Ordo Romanus*, in E. Martène, *De antiquis ecclesiae ritibus*, iii, Antwerp, 1737, col. 614.

76. Paolo Giovio, *Vita Leonis decimi*, Florence, 1548, p. 105; the same figure is given by Panvinio in his additions to Platina, *Vite de' pontefici*, Venice, 1685, p. 495. It should be noted that no charge of luxury would be

Leo IV—unfavourably only in the matter of materials, for Leo IV's doors had been of silver.[68]

It may seem accurate today to describe Raphael's tapestries as Leo's most splendid gift to the Sistine Chapel, and if it does it is essential to register the objection that the pope himself may have thought otherwise. No amount of scepticism can detract from Leo's status as a discriminating and ambitious patron of the visual arts,[69] but it is probable that his appreciation of literature was still keener and certain that his greatest passion was for music.[70] He was himself a composer, and according to some accounts he had been the pupil of Heinrich Isaac.[71] As a cardinal he had already acquired a reputation as an expert in musical science; his election to the papacy was greeted by one observer with the statement 'We have an erudite but musical pontiff— Habemus pontificem eruditum, sed musicum',[72] and it was celebrated by Isaac with a six-part motet.

Much as he loved music as recreation in his private apartments, there is no doubt that his patronage and preference were chiefly directed to the music of the liturgy, and in consequence the Sistine Chapel in his pontificate passed through one of the finest moments in its unique musical history. He revolutionized the organization of the choir, and enriched its sound— remarkably, in this a cappella tradition—with wind instruments.[73] The composers whose music was heard there included Josquin, Isaac, Mouton, Brumel and Pierre de la Rue—that is to say all the outstanding contemporary polyphonists—and the performers were the best that money and influence could obtain.[74] The quality of the chapel's music was certainly not inferior to that of its decoration, and it is worth remembering the musical complement of Raphael's tapestries in order to see the latter in just proportion within Leo's total patronage in the chapel. The tapestries owed their existence in the first instance to extra-aesthetic considerations, and so did a beautiful and impressive setting of the Mass. Polyphony and tapestry in the *Capella papalis* were alike in another sense, that they were both regarded as 'luxuries' the use of which was symbolically suspended in Holy Week. And it is a possibility to be borne in mind that one of the functions of tapestry in the chapel uppermost in Leo's mind was in fact dependent upon his musical sensibility, for Paolo Giovio tells us that the beneficial acoustical properties of tapestry were well known at Leo's court.[75]

Paolo Giovio is also the author who retails the story that the great expense of the tapestries was met by the improper diversion of funds collected for the crusade and for the rebuilding of Saint Peter's. Characteristically he cannot resist this piece of post-Lutheran gossip, but he says he does not himself sympathize with it and eventually he muddles through to approximately the right answer: 'they were dedicated to the Chapel of Sixtus for the greater honour of the altar and the sacred mysteries'. The story had in any case been improved in the telling, for the total expenditure in this version was put at fifty thousand ducats,[76] whereas an apparently informed statement by Marcantonio Michiel, an eyewitness to the exhibition of the first tapestries to arrive, indicates a total of sixteen thousand ducats, one thousand of which had been spent on the Cartoons.[77] The cost reported by Michiel sounds enormous, and it was, but it should be seen in relation to other expenses touching the *Maiestas papalis*. It is a little less than the accumulated salaries of the choristers of the Sistine Chapel over the same period, 1515–21.[78] The tiara of Leo X was valued in 1521 at 17,785 ducats, the tiara of Julius II at 62,430 ducats, and one individual settlement of Leo's coronation expenses had amounted to 57,692 ducats.[79]

attached to Leo in his own period on account of these tapestries; the attitude of an austere reformist—Vincenzo (Pietro) Quirini—indicates that sumptuous hangings were appropriate to the Divine Office, for he recommended to Leo in the summer of 1513 'che tutti li drapi di oro et di setta che sono nelle sale, nelle stanze, et per le letta di V.S. siano levati et dedicati al culto divino …' (H. Jedin, 'Vincenzo Quirini und Pietro Bembo', *Miscellanea Giovanni Mercati*, iv (Studi e testi 124), Vatican City, 1946, p. 423).

77. Michiel states that Raphael received 100 ducats for each cartoon, and that material and manufacturing costs on each tapestry amounted to 1500 ducats; he quotes Leo's own estimate of 1600 a piece, and says that it is being spread abroad that they are worth 2000 (for the text, see below, p. 38); 2000 ducats was the cost for each piece quoted to a visitor to Brussels in 1517 (see below, p. 42). This is exactly the figure given by Paris de Grassis: 'In die Sancti Stephani (26 December 1519), fuit missa Papalis solita in Cappella presente papa cum triginta Cardinalibus eam missam cantavit Cardinalis de valle. Hodie Papa jussit appendi suos pannos de rascia novos pulcherimos, et pretiosos, de quibus tota cappella stupefacta est in aspectu illorum, qui ut fuit universale judicium sunt res, qua non est aliquid in orbe nunc pulchrius, et unumquodque petium est valoris ducatorum 2000' (B.M., Add. MS. 8444, fol. 177v. collated with MS. Vat. Lat. 5636, fol. 295r.; this text was already known to Fea, op. cit. in n. 9, p. 82). In the Vienna MS. the last phrase reads: 'et unumquodque petium est valoris undecim milium ducati auri in auro' (Nationalbibliothek, MS. 6309, fol. 553r.); this improbable figure is perhaps a corruption from a MS. reading 'ii milium'.

78. This figure is calculated from the monthly *provisioni* of about 250 ducats (Archivio segreto vaticano, Camerali, Introitus et exitus 554 ff., passim).

79. The tiara valuations, largely based on cost-prices of individual jewels, are taken from an inventory of 6 December 1521 in Archivio di Stato, Rome, Camerale I, 1552, filza 2. The item for coronation expenses, paid to Leonardo Bartolini on 4 August 1513, is recorded in Archivio segreto vaticano, Camerali, Introitus et exitus 551, fol. 117v.; the detailed account is in A.S.R., Camerale I, 1488. Giovio's account of the source of the money spent on the tapestries is neither proved nor disproved by the very small charge on the *fabbrica* of Saint Peter's attested by the two known payments to Raphael (see above, ns. 9, 10); it may be that they were chiefly funded from another account,

since in the much earlier biography of Leo by Francesco Novello the commission for the tapestries is listed separately from the public works in a description of his private activities: *Vita Leonis. X. Max: Pont: per Franciscum Novellum Romanum. I. V. professorem*, dedicated to Clement VII, Bibl. Vat., MS. Barb. Lat. 2273, fol. 18v.: 'Sacellum a sixto quarto aedificatum, et a Iulio II.° max: Pont: pictura egregia decoratum, pulcherrimis auleis sirico et auro intertextis ex flandria advectis ornavit.'

80. Stephanus Ioanninensis, op. cit. in n. 70, fol. 110v.: 'Primo namque in vaticano testudineam illam templi partem quae ad levam eiusdem augustissimo opere fabrefactam conspicimus: porfireticis: atque lapideis lateribus opulentissimo opificio fabrefecit.' It is probable that this passage contains some rhetorical *amplificatio* and its detail may be more conventional than trustworthy; but in that case the terms selected are, for our purpose, just as revealing.

81. This famous indiscretion is recorded in a letter by the Venetian orator in Rome, Ser Marin Zorzi, of 17 March 1517—that is, some time after the event—and he makes it clear that it is hearsay: '. . . *disse* "Quando il Papa fo fato, diceva: Juliano, godianci il papato, poichè Dio ce l'ha dato" ' (Sanuto, op. cit. in n. 62, xxiv, col. 90); see the comments of Pastor, op. cit. in n. 1, viii, p. 76.

82. F. Nitti, *Leone X e la sua politica*, Florence, 1892, p. 9.

83. Novello, MS. cit. in n. 79, fol. 2v.: 'patre Laurentio Tuscie primario: et patriae patre: . . . nostrae aetatis viro, in quo dum vixit quies totius Italiae pendere videbatur'; Brandolini, op. cit. in n. 70, pp. 108–10. See also: Pietro Crinito, *De honesta disciplina* (Florence, 1504: quoted by F. Gilbert, 'Bernardo Rucellai and the Orti Oricellari', *Journal of the Warburg and Courtauld Institutes*, xii, 1949, p. 120—and Rucellai himself, quoted p. 121); Filippo Beroaldo, *Ode ad Bononienses de Jo. Medice Car.ʰ legato* (1511: B.M., Harley MS. 3462, fol. 50v.); Aldus Manutius, *Supplicatio* to Leo X (preface to Marco Musurus's *Omnia Platonis opera*, Venice, September 1513); G. B. Gargha, *Oratio*, 17 December 1513 (see below, n. 106); Filippo Beroaldo, dedication to Leo of Tacitus, *Opera*, 1515 (?), fol. 3r.; Aegidius of Viterbo, *Libellus de litteris hebraicis* (presented to Cardinal Giulio de' Medici, 1517: MS. Vat. Lat. 3146, fol. 23v.; *Scechina*, ed. F. Secret, Rome, 1959, i, p. 29). These ideas have their origin in a Quattrocento rhetorical tradition of praising the Medicean *Aurea pax*: see E. H. Gombrich, 'Renaissance and Golden Age', *Journal of the Warburg and Courtauld Institutes*, xxiv, 1961, pp. 306 ff.

Undoubtedly Leo X enjoyed spending money, and just as certainly his personal taste was inclined towards material splendour. Typically, the part of Saint Peter's that he erected was notable for its porphyry and opulent marbles.[80] His inclination to luxury was surely intimately bound up with his conception of the dignity of his office. An enormous and ugly epicurean, gentle, bejewelled and weak-sighted, he is a little too ridiculous, too complicated, and perhaps also too reasonable, to become a twentieth-century hero like Julius II. His reputation will probably never recover from the rumour of an aside that he may not in fact have made to his brother: 'Giuliano, let us enjoy the papacy since God has given it us.'[81] With the clarity of hindsight we are tempted to see in him a latter-day Nero, playing on his expensive Neapolitan alabaster organ—perhaps in the *Stanze*—while Lutheran flames swept through the Church of Rome. But that would be a grossly unfair judgement. By all accounts he was a pious man whose frivolity was superficial, and he was also firm in his decisions but liked to make them slowly: too slowly in the Lutheran case, for death intervened. There remains an element of ambiguity in his policies in his later years, above all in the Urbino war, but it is important for our purpose that we distinguish these from the earlier part of his reign, up to the period of Raphael's work on the Cartoons, when it seemed that all those high expectations aroused by his election were to be fulfilled.[82]

There is an astonishing amount of information, all of it consistent, about what was expected of the young Cardinal Giovanni de' Medici when he was made pope on 11 March 1513: peace in the Christian world, the reunion of the Church, and the restoration of dignity to the Church, with a generous patronage of the arts as a consequent benefit. The pressure for the last, which has received too much emphasis, was a natural result of the magic of the Medici name; it is less well known now that the son of Lorenzo was expected to follow his father in the rôle of universal peacemaker. In Francesco Novello's *Vita Leonis*, Lorenzo is remembered as 'the man of our time upon whom seemed to depend, while he lived, the peace of the whole of Italy', and in Raffaello Brandolini's dialogue *Leo*, written immediately after the election, the peace and prosperity of Medici rule in Florence are recalled, and the peace of Italy, which Lorenzo had established and which had vanished with his death, is confidently anticipated in the new pontificate.[83] The myth of Lorenzo the peacemaker—if it was a myth—was not, however, a Leonine invention. One of the laments for the dead Lorenzo, composed by Poliziano in 1492 and set to music by Isaac, has the title: *Quis dabit pacem populo timenti?* And the expectation that Lorenzo's son would pursue a policy of peace was undoubtedly one of the principal reasons for his election; all the cardinals at the Conclave of 1513 signed Election Capitulations which bound the future

84. For the Election Capitulations I have used the copy in the British Museum, Harley MS. 3462, fol. 33r. ff.; the first of the *Capitula publica* provides for the propagation of the Crusade; the next of a political nature was precisely fulfilled by Leo: 'Item quod statim post assumptionem suam omnibus viribus per legatos, et nuncios procurabit pacem, et concordiam inter principes Christianos inter se dissidentes.' The Isaac motet is in *Liber selectarum cantionum quas vulgo mutetas appellant . . .*, ed. L. Senfl, Augsburg, 1520, fols. 1, v. ff., and

it is described in A. W. Ambros, *Geschichte der Musik*, ed. O. Kade, iii, Leipzig, 1893, pp. 395 ff.; I am very grateful to Professor Frederick Sternfeld for his help in identifying it.

85. D. Gnoli, 'Pasquino pedagogo', in *La Roma di Leon X*, Milan, 1938, p. 178.

86. For example in Aegidius of Viterbo's letter (accompanied by an olive-branch) to Leo, welcoming his election, in E. Martène and U. Durand, *Veterum scriptorum et monumentorum . . .*

pope to the immediate conciliation of the Christian powers. The burden of these expectations could not be better illustrated than by the contribution of Isaac, again, which is his six-part motet *Optime Pastor* celebrating Leo's election; for in this work the polyphony sets off with four concurrent texts, all invoking the Good Shepherd, the *Medicus* who will heal the wounds of his flock and give them *pax aurea*, over a double *cantus firmus* on the words *Da pacem Domine in diebus nostris* and *Sacerdos et pontifex et virtutum artifex bonus pastor*.[84] The praise of Leo as the man of peace was a commonplace of the Pasquinades of 1513, and of course these have to be read as spontaneous if not strictly just reaction and relief after the exceptionally strife-ridden pontificate of Julius II.[85] The succession was compared, on a more sophisticated literary plane, with that of Numa Pompilius after Romulus,[86] or of Augustus *pacator orbis* after Julius Caesar,[87] but the difference was not always expressed by secular analogies; in 1512 Aegidius of Viterbo, General of the Augustinians, had flattered Julius by comparing him with Moses, the maker of war for God's people, whereas immediately after his election Leo in his turn was compared by Pietro Delfin, General of the Camaldolese, with Moses the very gentle ruler[88]—a case which illustrates the necessity of identifying the specific mythology of these pontificates before we interpret their images.

Leo came to the throne between the fifth and the sixth sessions of the Fifth Lateran Council, which had been summoned by Julius in 1511 to crush the schismatic Council of Pisa. As cardinal, Giovanni de' Medici had already acquired a great reputation for diplomacy in this matter while detained by the French after his capture at the battle of Ravenna, 11 April 1512,[89] and as pope he swiftly increased this reputation by healing the schism through the application of gentleness, rather than of force. The reunification of the Church was recognized as his achievement, and its maintenance became one of the principal aims of his policy; it may have, as we shall see, much to do with the thematic structure of his tapestry-cycle. At the opening of the sixth session of the Council, the first over which Leo presided, the chosen Gospel text began *Pax vobis* (John xx. 19 ff.), and at the closure of the eighth session, in December 1513, the Peace Bull *Ad omnipotentis* expressed the same intention even more clearly: 'We . . . desiring from the depth of our heart, and as a duty of our pastoral office, the peace and unity of the whole Christian people . . .'[90] The *Acts* of the Council were published at the end of Leo's pontificate by Cardinal Antonio del Monte, who described in his preface the pope's greatest achievements: the extinction of the pestilence of the schism, and above all the preservation and increase of the dignity of the Roman Church.[91]

We are not of course concerned with the justice of this propaganda, nor with the reality of the contrast between the policies of the two popes, but with their public presentation; for our purposes the myth, in so far as it deviates from reality, is both more interesting and more relevant. Nevertheless, and from a certain point of view, there was truth in the contention that by the end of Julius's reign the dignity of the Church was in need of some attention. The oration of Bishop Simon Begnius at the first Leonine session of the Council, 27 April 1513, ends with an impassioned appeal for peace, 'to restore to its pristine *maiestas* our Christian republic'.[92] In this case policy and Leo's personal taste for ceremony reinforced each other to produce certain practical effects. Francesco Novello and Paolo Giovio agree that he cultivated the ritual of the Divine Office with a devotion and diligence exceptional among popes,[93] and Paris de Grassis, who was hard to please,

amplissima collectio, iii, Paris, 1724, col. 1258; and in Giovanni Poggio, *De veri pastoris munere* (c. 1517), Bibl. Vat., MS. Vat. Lat. 3732 (Leo's presentation copy), fol. 9r.: 'Tu vero Numa Pompilio iustior, sanctiorque Orbem pacabis.'

87. *Egidii Viterbensis Historia viginti saeculorum*, Biblioteca Angelica, Rome, MS. Lat. 351, fol. 357r. This long text was compiled 1513–18 (G. Signorelli, *Il Cardinale Egidio da Viterbo*, Florence, 1929, p. 215, n. 25). Julius II, after the conquest of Bologna, 1506–7, had a medal struck with the inscription: IVLIVS. CAESAR. PONT. II.; for this and similar texts of the period, see R. Weiss, 'The Medals of Julius II', *Journal of the Warburg and Courtauld Institutes*, xxviii, 1965, pp. 163, 180, and J. W. O'Malley, S.J., 'The fulfillment of the Christian Golden Age under Julius II: text of a discourse of Giles of Viterbo, 1507', *Traditio*, xxv, 1969, p. 269, n. 13.

88. Aegidius of Viterbo, *Oratio prima synodi Lateranensis*, Rome, 1512; *Petri Delphini Veneti, Oratio ad Leonem X. Pont. Max.* (Bibl. Laur., MS. Plut. XLVII. 17, presentation copy, 13 March 1513, fol. 134r.), in Martène–Durand, op. cit. in n. 86, iii, col. 1213: '. . . sicut de Moyse legitur, mitissimus es super omnes homines qui morantur in terra'.

89. See, for example, Brandolini, op. cit. in n. 70, p. 85.

90. Hardouin, op. cit. in n. 44, col. 1721; the Bull was also published separately as *Bulla sive cedula materiam universalis pacis & destinationis legatorum de latere . . .*, Rome, 1513. Compare the letter of Francesco Vettori, Florentine ambassador in Rome, to Machiavelli, 20 August 1513: 'L'ufficio suo (sc: del papa) è non si intricare in guerre, ma mettersi di mezzo et conporre et sedare quelle che son nate fra i principi; et questo egli ha fatto dal principio che fu creato papa insino ad hora . . .' (*Lettere familiari di Niccolò Machiavelli*, ed. E. Alvisi, Florence, 1883, p. 280). Further sources are set out in Chapter III, p. 76.

91. '. . . schismate pestifero extinguendo . . . conservandaque amplificandaque Romanae ecclesiae dignitate maxime . . .' (Hardouin, op. cit. in n. 44, ix, col. 1563).

92. Hardouin, op. cit. in n. 44, ix, col. 1687.

93. Novello, MS. cit. in n. 79, fol. 17v.: 'semper . . . Christianam religionem coluit: et observavit, et rebus divinis diligens et curiosus extitit, Ceremoniisque maxime studiosus: et deditus'; Giovio, op. cit. in n. 75, p. 333:

'Celebrò sempre & fece tutti gli uffici delle ceremonia con singolar maiestà; di modo che col vero si diceva che non fu mai alcuno de passati pontefici, il quale ne più honoratamente ne con maggior riputatione di lui sacrificasse'; also Cristoforo Marcello, MS. cit. in n. 72, fol. 7r.; *P. Matthaei her. Encomion in Leonem X. Pont. Max.*, Bibl. Ambrosiana, MS. H. 35 inf. (4), fols. 78v., 100r.; Cardinal Sforza Pallavicino, *Istoria del Concilio di Trento*, Rome, 1656, p. 86; and W. Roscoe, *Vita e pontificato di Leone X*, ed. L. Bossi, Milan, 1816, iii, pp. 18–19.

94. B.M., Add. MS. 8444, fol. 91r.; see also the passages quoted by Pastor, op. cit. in n. 1, viii, pp. 78–79.

95. Erasmus, *Dialogus, cui titulus Ciceronianus*, Paris, 1528, fols. 115r. ff.: 'Sed quid haec ad Iulium Christianae religionis antistitem, Christi vices gerentem, Petri et Pauli successorem?' The sermon (Good Friday, 6 April) was perhaps by Tommaso Inghirami (P. de Nolhac, *Érasme en Italie*, Paris, 1888, pp. 65, 76).

96. Paris de Grassis, 1 January 1514: B.M., Add. MS. 8443, fol. 94v. In fact Leo was enforcing an earlier ruling (of Eugenius IV and Calixtus III) that all sermons should be submitted for the prior approval of the *Magister sacri palatii apostolici* (G. Moroni, *Dizionario di erudizione storico-ecclesiastica*, xli, Venice, 1846, p. 202), but the terms appear to be stiffer and more specific.

97. 'Aurea pax revocabitur, dicemusque cum Isaia, & cantabimus: Exsulta satis filia Sion, quia ecce Salvator tuus veniet tibi' (a free rendering of Zechariah ix. 9).

98. This identification already in Saint Ambrose *In apocalypsin expositio* (*P.L.*, 17, col. 808).

99. Nicolaus de Lyra, *Postilla super actus apostolorum, super epistolas canonicales, et super apocalypsin*, Mantua, 1480, and *Biblia latina cum postillis Nicolai de Lyra*, Venice, 1489 (both unpaginated): 'per seniores intelliguntur ecclesie prelati, et ideo videtur melius quod iste senior fuerit petrus . . . Aperire librum, idest manifestare ecclesie decursum a deo preordinatum'. See also Johannes Annius Viterbensis, *Glosa super Apocalypsim de statu ecclesie* (Gouda, 1481?).

100. 'Sed ne fleveris, filia Sion, quia ecce venit Leo de tribu Juda, radix David: ecce suscitavit tibi Deus Salvatorem, qui salvabit te de manibus vastantium, & populum Dei de manu persequentium liberabit. Te, Leo beatissime, salvatorem venturum speravimus . . .' (loc. cit. in n. 92).

would concur, with the sole reservation that Leo was rather frequently late.[94] A reform of Leo's in the Sistine Chapel is much to the point here. There is a diverting account by Erasmus of a sermon that he had heard addressed to Julius in the chapel in 1509, full of Ciceronian intricacies, mythological illustrations, and flattery, and of great length; Erasmus asked the perfectly serious question: what did all this have to do with Julius, the High Priest of the Christian religion, the Vicar of Christ, and the successor of Peter and Paul?[95] Within a year of his accession Leo issued an order, with the penalty of excommunication, that all Sistine sermons should be submitted beforehand in writing, that all irrelevant matter and all flattery or allusions to himself must be excised, and that no preacher might occupy the pulpit for more than half an hour.[96]

Bishop Begnius concluded his appeal for peace with a striking prophecy: 'The peace of the Golden Age shall be revived and we shall proclaim and sing with Isaiah, "Rejoice greatly O daughter of Zion, for thy Saviour cometh unto thee."'[97] The analogy between Leo and Christ is scarcely veiled, and is perfectly explicit in another case earlier in the same oration: 'Weep not, O daughter of Zion, for behold the Lion of the Tribe of Juda, the Root of David.' The fulfilment in the new pope of the prophecy *Ecce vicit Leo de tribu Juda, radix David* (Revelation v. 5), enjoyed a great success that was not

101. 'Quem ubi tandem, opitulante Domino, tuo apostolatui subegeris, factumque fuerit unum ovile et unus pastor, de te passim praedicetur: Vicit leo de tribu Juda' (loc. cit. in n. 88).

102. In a letter to Leo from London, 29 April 1515 (*Epistolae . . . ad diversos, et aliquot aliorum ad illum . . . collectae*, Basel, 1521, p. 71).

103. MS. cit. in n. 87, fols. 316r., 357r., 381r., 386r. and v., and especially 357v.: (comparing the epochs ending with the coming of Christ and the election of Leo X) 'uterque itaque Iulius extremus fuit: ille humani imperii cui successit divinum: hic noni saeculi: quod decimum est secutum: illi Leo de tribu juda: huic ille successit Leo: *qui statim in numismate scribi jussit*: Vicit Leo de tribu juda: divini spiritus opera: ille homo factus: hic Pontifex creatus. Excisus sine manibus Lapis: Testimonio Danielis: absque corruptione sacerdos summus: is ortus tanquam ex Deo Deus: hic a deo vocatus tanquam Aron. Uterque decimo saeculo dedit: is finem: hic initium. Ille decimam dragmam servaturus: hic decimi cognomen obtenturus . . .' The important notice of Leo's *immediate* order for the new coin (see below) suggests the probability that this imagery came from the mind of Leo himself and not, for example, from Bishop Begnius.

See also the serio-comic account of a sermon on the Epiphany by Aegidius in S. Agostino in Rome, January 1517, in Sanuto, op. cit. in n. 62, xxiii, cols. 486–7 ('. . . questo è quel leone serenissimo che dice San Zuane in L'Apocalipse,

veniet leo de tribu Juda; questo è quel Leone che vinzerà il nemico nostro di la fede di Cristo . . .'). The significance of this text from Revelation was also rooted in recent eschatological speculations, and expectations of the millennium; see below, p. 75.

104. Giovanni Poggio, MS. cit. in n. 59, fol. 9r. ('In adventu pacifici Regis omnia novabuntur'); Aegidius of Viterbo, MS. cit. in n. 87, fol. 17v.; Erasmus, op. cit. in n. 102, p. 70. The meaning of this title (derived from the Messianic text I Chronicles xxii. 9–10) is defined by H. Windisch, 'Friedensbringer—Gottessöhne', *Zeitschrift für die neutestamentliche Wissenschaft*, xxiv, 1925, pp. 247 ff., who may also be consulted, pp. 254 ff., for the background of the similar circle of ideas: Leo-Christ-Augustus, as *pacator orbis*.

105. These sources are collected in Chapter III, pp. 77–8, ns. 185–8. The conceit was a reapplication to Leo of one already used in the time of his father Lorenzo; see Ficino, dedication to Lorenzo of *De vita*, in *Opera omnia*, Basel, 1576, i, p. 493, and dedication to Cardinal Giovanni himself of Dionysius the Areopagite, *De mystica theologia*, ed. cit., ii, p. 1013; also Leonardo, Conte di Nogarola, dedication to Lorenzo of *De immortalitate animae*, quoted by E. Garin, *La cultura filosofica del rinascimento italiano*, Florence, 1961, p. 124. Aegidius of Viterbo, in 1517, described the pacifying rôle of the 'clarissima Medicorum familia' as *medicamenta* (loc. cit. in n. 83); see also, in similar vein, Petrus Alcyonius, *Medices legatus de exsilio*, Venice, 1522, fol. aiiii, r.

simply due to the ingenious pun. It had a serious topical meaning at the Council in April 1513; for it was at the council of the archetypal prelates of the Church, the meeting of the four-and-twenty Elders before the Throne, that one of them—identified as Saint Peter—hailed the Lion of Juda, who alone could loose the Seven Seals of the Book, that is Christ,[98] who alone could effect the fulfilment of the Church.[99] Just so the new Lion arose for the succour of the daughter of Zion, the Church, at the sixth session: 'The Lord has raised up for you a Saviour', continued Begnius, 'who will rescue you from all your enemies, and will free God's people from their persecutors. We put our trust in you, most blessed Leo, as the coming Saviour.'[100] The same prophecy is invoked in an oration by Pietro Delfin,[101] by Erasmus,[102] and repeatedly in the *Historia viginti saeculorum* of Aegidius of Viterbo.[103]

The deliberately Messianic, even soteriological, allegorizing of the election of Leo was presented in other ways. Leo was packaged, so to speak, as the *Rex pacificus*, a title of Solomon as well as of Christ,[104] for reasons that will now be obvious. And the irresistible play upon words produced just as naturally the equation between the Medici pope and *Christus medicus*, Who healed the wounds of His people.[105] But the compliments of the panegyrists, whose sincerity was not necessarily compromised by the conventions of their art-form, had a relationship with the pope's own ideas that was not entirely simple. There is little doubt that these apostrophes inspired in Leo the ambition to fulfil such high expectations, and that his policies were to some extent shaped by the pressures that they expressed. On the other hand there is some evidence—but of course not very much—that Leo himself inspired (in a different sense) the imagery of the panegyrists. This is particularly to be suspected in the case of the oration delivered by Giovanni Battista Gargha at the opening of the eighth session, 19 December 1513, which contained an appeal for peace, the observation that the weapons of the army of Christ were not the breastplate, shield and sword, but piety, religion, integrity, innocence and chastity (a contrast of Julian and Leonine attributes), and an apostrophe to the *medicus* sent from heaven. In the preface to the printed version issued in Rome in 1514, Gargha confessed that for advice about what he should say he had consulted the pope's cousin and confidant, Giulio de' Medici.[106] There is every reason to suppose that Giovanni de' Medici had inherited the family flair for inventing a mythology of their rule.

One of the most revealing facets of Leo's personality was his preoccupation with Fate,[107] and his remarkable life had certainly been marked by such reversals of fortune and such coincidences as to make them reasonable objects of his attention. When pope he took the opportunity to manipulate Fate and thus to produce further coincidences. The sequence of events following his capture at Ravenna is a case in point. That event had marked one of the lowest points in his fortunes, and his escape was read at the time as a result of divine intervention.[108] Within a year the Medici had been restored to power in Florence and he had been elected pope, and at his election he took his motto from Psalm cxx: 'In my distress I cried unto the Lord, and he heard me';[109] with his brother Giuliano he shared the device GLOVIS, in reverse SIVOLG, which seems to have been a reference to the turn of Fortune.[110] He rearranged the date of the procession in which he took possession of the Lateran so that it fell on 11 April 1513, the anniversary of his capture, and symbolically he rode then the same white horse that he had ridden at Ravenna.[111] On one of the triumphal arches erected for this procession the eight principal events of Leo's life were depicted, with a Latin verse which claimed that they had all occurred on the eleventh of the month.[112] It is not

106. The *oratio* is reprinted by Hardouin, op. cit. in n. 44, cols. 1728 ff.; a copy of the pamphlet of 1514 with its preface is in the British Museum. The passage in question reads: 'In quo orandi munere ut in omnibus nostrae religionis negotiis Reveren̄. Cardinalis Iulius Medices nostri Ordinis ingens praesidium mihi opem & favorem impendit.'

107. He was elected 'in giorno di Venerdì, il quale giorno diceva egli di haverlo trovato molto felice, et favorevole, affermando ch'ogni sua prosperità, et grandezza gli era accaduta nel giorno di Venerdì sino dal principio della sua vita . . .' (from an anonymous description of the conclave of 1513 in B.M., Add. MS. 28464, fol. 5r.).

108. Paris de Grassis, B.M., Add. MS. 8442, fols. 217r. ff.; Brandolini, op. cit. in n. 70, p. 89; *Ruinagiae iurisconsulti et oratoris placentini Oratio* (1513–14: presentation copy, Bibl. Laur., MS. Plut. XIII. 14, fol. 31r.); Marcello, MS. cit. in n. 72, fol. 24v.

109. O. Raynaldus, *Annales ecclesiastici*, xx, Cologne, 1694, p. 135; J. von Hefele and J. Hergenröther, *Conciliengeschichte*, viii, Freiburg-im-Breisgau, 1887, p. 552.

110. Paolo Giovio, *Dialogo dell'Imprese militari et amorose*, Rome, 1555, p. 45, gives this explanation, but states that it was the *impresa* of Giuliano de' Medici alone; this is certainly not the case, since the device is to be found on a great number of Leonine objects, such as the Sistine choir-books, and in the *Stanze*. It should be noted that Moroni, op. cit. in n. 96, xxxviii, p. 45, gives an alternative decoding: GLOria, VIta, Salus; he gives no source, but is unlikely to have invented it.

111. In fact the pope should properly ride a white horse for the Lateran *possesso*: see *Ceremonie in coronatione Summi Pontificis*, B.M., MS. Harley 3462, fol. 154v., and H.-W. Klewitz, 'Die Krönung des Papstes', *Zeitschrift der Savigny-Stiftung für Rechtsgeschichte*, Kan. Abt., xxx, 1941, pp. 117 ff.

112. F. Cancellieri, *Storia de' solenni possessi*, Rome, 1802, p. 81.

113. The dates are examined below, p. 84.

114. J. Shearman, 'Raphael's unexecuted projects for the Stanze', *Walter Friedlaender zum 90. Geburtstag: Eine Festgabe ...*, Berlin, 1965, pp. 170 ff.

115. Reproduced and discussed by E. H. Gombrich, 'The Early Medici as Patrons of Art', in *Norm and Form: Studies in the Art of the Renaissance*, London, 1966, p. 49. The new equestrian group in the fresco is also clearly inspired by the pope's appearance at his *possesso*; compare the little-known woodcut of the latter which serves as a frontispiece to Giovanni Giacomo Penni, *Cronicha delle magnifiche & honorate Pompe fatte in Roma per la Creatione & Incoronatione di Papa Leone. X. Pont. Max.*, Rome, 27 July 1513 (the text reprinted by Cancellieri, op. cit. in n. 112).

116. Pastor, op. cit. in n. 1, vii, p. 31. In fact the papacy had been predicted in Florence as early as 1489, at the time of the first promise of the cardinalate; see the contemporary poem reprinted in W. Welliver, *L'Impero fiorentino*, Florence, 1957, p. 198.

117. Leo IX had taken the name in imitation of *Magnus Leo*, i.e. Leo I: W. Ullmann, 'Leo I and the theme of Papal Primacy', *Journal of Theological Studies*, N.S. xi, 1960, p. 47.

118. In greatest detail by Ferreri, op. cit. in n. 2, and by Aegidius of Viterbo, MS. cit. in n. 46, passim; but see also Brandolini, op. cit. in n. 70, p. 112; Delfin, *Oratio*, ed. cit. in n. 88, col. 1213; Marcello, MS. cit. in n. 72, fol. 29v.; Erasmus, loc. cit. in n. 102; Baptista Spagnuoli (Mantuanus), *De sacris diebus*, Poitiers, 1525, Bk. IV (first ed. 1518).

119. P. Künzle, 'Zur obersten der drei Tiaren auf Raffaels Disputa', *Römische Quartalschrift*, lvii, 1962, pp. 226 ff., 240 ff.

120. Compare the subjects of the frescoes executed during his pontificate in the Sala Regia.

121. On 10 January 1518 Leo X had the *arca* of Leo III opened (it was not opened again until 1903), and the rest of the relics in the treasury identified and inventoried (H. Grisar, S.J., *Die römische Kapelle Sancta Sanctorum und ihr Schatz*, Freiburg-im-Breisgau, 1908, pp. 61, 143, and P. Stanislao dell'Addolorata, *La Cappella Papale di Sancta Sanctorum*, Grottaferrata, 1919, pp. 111 ff.). In the same year, on 14 March, Leo X carried the sacred icon of the *Sancta sanctorum* in procession through the streets of Rome to invoke divine aid against the Turk;

in order to spoil the game that we must notice that these dates were obtained by adjusting history,[113] but in order to be clear that there was at work a process (which might be called undecimalization) that was another aspect of image-making. For the question that arises is whether the Romans were really so quick to see, unprompted, the point of the date of the procession, or whether in fact the iconography of this triumph was in part controlled by the Medici. In any case Leo had arranged a double coincidence, for the revised date was also that of the feast of Saint Leo, and it is in this fact that the real—and typical—coincidence occurs, since the pope stepped into the title rôle of Raphael's fresco in the second of the Vatican *Stanze*, *Leo and Attila* (*Fig.* 12), the subject of which had already been chosen by Julius. Raphael had to adjust a design already fully prepared,[114] and the new equestrian group, with the portrait of Leo X upon the portrait of the white horse, was clearly inspired by a recollection of Benozzo Gozzoli's group with Piero de' Medici—also on a white horse—in the procession of the Magi in the chapel of Palazzo Medici in Florence.[115] Whose recollection? It is as likely to have come to Leo's mind as to Raphael's, since Gozzoli's group was more than an artistic precedent. Questions like these remind us that we have to deal with a patron who was intensely, even self-consciously, aware of his actions and his lineage, and of their projection in a public image.

We come, then, to the choice of the name Leo. It was remarked that no pope had borne it for several centuries, and its egregiousness predictably provoked a good deal of thought and exegesis. At first sight some of the explanations offered are too complicated to inspire belief, and some are indeed highly improbable. But the Cardinal Giovanni had had time and cause to think about his choice—often a matter of considerable significance—since he had been reckoned *papabile*, that is tipped for the papacy, as early as 1511.[116] It seems most likely that the defeat at Ravenna on the feast of Saint Leo, and its consequences, acted as the final trigger to his thoughts, and that the fundamental concept is the one most often invoked by his contemporaries, that in Leo X were to be summarized all the qualities and attainments of the

in this he was following the example of Leo IV, who had done the same to rid Rome of the pestilence of a dragon (P. G. V. Giannini, *Notizie istoriche ... della ven. antichissima immagine del SS.*ᵐᵒ *Salvatore ...*, Rome, 1798, p. 7); the symbolism of this revival probably depends upon the idea (e.g. in Aegidius of Viterbo, MS. cit. in n. 87, fols. 376r., 397r.) that the pope was the *Leo* who would defeat the *Maumetiis bestiam*, that is the Turk, adumbrated in Revelation xvii.

122. C. Fea, *Parallelo di Giulio II con Leone X*, Rome, 1822, p. 69, quotes the Bull of 1514 that makes this provision, together with two chaplaincies with the obligation to celebrate the anniversaries of Leo X and all other Medici who should die in Rome.

123. In the decree *Pastor Aeternus*, promulgated at the eleventh session of the Lateran Council, December 1516, the pope compares his action in abrogating the Pragmatic Sanction with that of 'Leo Papa. I. praedecessor noster, cujus in

hoc libenter, quoad possumus, vestigia imitamur', who revoked at the Council of Chalcedon the *gesta* of the second Synod of Ephesus (Hardouin, op. cit. in n. 44, col. 1828); see also Ullmann, op. cit. in n. 117, p. 51, n. 2. Contemporary authors were quick to exploit the comparison, for example: Filippo Donato, dedicatory preface of Girolamo Donato's *De processione Spiritus Sancti*, Bibl. Vat., MS. Vat. Lat. 4326, fol. 2r., and Zanobi Acciaioli, *In libros Theodoriti: quorum tittuli Curatio graecarum affectionum* (ded. to Leo X), Bibl. Vat., MS. Ottob. 1404, fols. 1v., 156r.

124. This is aesthetically the finest of many Leonine coins with this subject and inscription; cf. A. Cinagli, *Le monete de' Papi descritte in tavole sinottiche*, Fermo, 1848, pp. 76 ff. The type has been taken to refer to the expulsion of the Della Rovere from Urbino in 1516 (E. Martinori, *Annali della zecca di Roma*, fasc. vii, Rome, 1918, p. 10), but some examples, including the *Leone* illustrated here, bear the mark of the Fugger control of the Roman mint,

previous bearers of the name.[117] It is, in fact, surprising how comprehensively the concept could be filled in,[118] partly, no doubt, because the material was readily available in the *Liber pontificalis* and even predigested in Platina's *Historia de vitis Pontificum Romanorum*. Leo I was a Tuscan, champion of councils, exceptional in vigilance, innocence, piety, integrity and doctrine; Leo II, a musician himself, gave music a new rôle in the liturgy, triumphed over Ravenna, and was a Greek and Latin scholar; Leo III was pious, wise, generous and forgiving, and patient in adversity; and so on until we reach Leo IX, who was replete with all virtues, was released from captivity and had a triumphal entry into Rome. Only the fifth and seventh of the name left a little to be desired. To this catalogue of paradigms there is to be added, of course, the animal itself, of legendary *pietas*, magnanimity towards the humble and fortitude against the proud.

The preoccupation of popes with their predecessors in name is not uncommon; it had happened with Sixtus IV and Julius II,[119] and it happened again with Gregory XIII.[120] In Leo's case it amounted, however, to an obsession. He displayed a unique curiosity in the treasury of Leo III in the *Sancta sanctorum*,[121] and he provided for a chapel in the University of Rome with the striking dedication to Saints Leo and Fortunatus.[122] But the point is nowhere clearer than in the choice of subjects for Raphael's frescoes in the third of the Vatican *Stanze* (1514–17, contemporary with the tapestry cartoons) which are historical events from the pontificates of Leo III and Leo IV applied as allegories to the present. It is very probable that his patronage of the visual arts was inspired as much by the example of these two predecessors as by that of his Medici forebears; the donations of the Carolingian Popes Leo, of great opulence and quantity, are set out in the *Liber pontificalis*, and they included, as we have seen, many tapestries. The doctrinal example of Leo I will be a natural object of enquiry when we consider the iconography of the tapestries, for Leo X remarked upon its value to himself as a precedent.[123]

This excursus into the ideas set in motion when Cardinal Giovanni became pope must be completed by some examples of those ideas translated into public images that are thematically related to the tapestries. They are to be found in the insufficiently explored field of coinage. Three reverses of new Leonine coin-designs are significant as statements of policy, and they are significant as works of art, since they exemplify the considerable increase in sophistication in the papal coinage of the early sixteenth century. The most beautiful of the new coin-designs of Leo X is a *Giulio*, also known as a *Leone* (*Fig.* 5), with a lion in profile crowned by a Victory and with the inscription VICIT LEO DE TRIBU JUDA; the date is 1513, and there can be no doubt that it refers to the pope's emergence during the Lateran Council to resolve, like Christ, the problems of the Church.[124] A second, which is of the same date and refers as obviously to Leo's triumphant policy of peace, is the *Triplice Giulio* with a representation of Christ addressing His Apostles and the inscription PACEM MEAM DO VOBIS (John xiv. 27). Unusually, there exist two versions of this coin, the first being undistinguished in design and crude in technique[125] while the second (*Fig.* 6) is of far higher quality pictorially and numismatically;[126] the revised version is in fact strikingly Raphaelesque in design, and brings to mind a number of Raphael's drawings of this period, including one for the *Charge to Peter* (*Fig.* 47).[127] No evidence has yet been produced to show a connection between Raphael and the papal mint, but it is known that a few years later he was considered for the design of coinage for Lorenzo de' Medici, Duke of Urbino.[128]

which terminated in January 1515; and it seems to me unlikely, in any case, that such purely temporal political events would be reflected in Leonine imagery. A reference to these coins by Aegidius of Viterbo, quoted above, n. 103, seems to imply that the first were struck immediately after the election in 1513. In a description of the Lateran procession of 11 April 1513 in *Petrosanti Sansonii . . . Papalogus Elegeiacus* (c. 1514, ded. to Leo), Bibl. Laur., MS. Plut. XXXVII. 23, fol. 83r., it is stated that coins with this design were thrown to the crowd after the enthronement. Different texts from Aegidius were already quoted in explanation of a variant design by C. du Molinet, *Historia summorum pontificum a Martino V ad Innocentium XI*, Paris, 1679, p. 37, with approximately the correct conclusion: '. . . sicut Christus . . . venit in mundum pacem mittere non gladium; sic ipsum alloquens Leonem Pontificem Christi vicarium'.

125. C. Serafini, *Le monete e le bolle plumbee pontificie del medagliere Vaticano*, i, Milan, 1910, p. 178, Pl. xxviii. 7.

126. Serafini, op. cit., Pl. xxviii. 8. Martinori, op. cit. in n. 124, p. 4, suggested that the first version was struck to commemorate peace with Louis XII in December 1513, and was made by Piermaria Serbaldi; and (p. 13) that the second should be attributed to Camelio (this is open to doubt, however, since Camelio was not appointed to the mint until June 1515, whereas both versions appear to bear the Fugger stamp). Cinagli, op. cit. in n. 124, p. 78, Nos. 23–24, suggested that the coins referred to the peace established between the Colonna and the Orsini, but it is unlikely that their significance would be so limited. The meaning may perhaps be better sensed from a comparison with Aldus Manutius's *Supplicatio* to Leo X, 1513 (ed. cit. in n. 83): 'Tu modo Beatus Pater qui Iesu Christi . . . locum tenes, cuique commissa est cura populorum, curabis pro viribus, quae tua est probitas, tua prudentia, tua Pietas PACEM, quam solam moriturus Christus tanquam testamento reliquit hominibus . . .'

127. Compare also the drawings of 1513–14 for the *Christ in Limbo* and *Doubting Thomas* (repr. M. Hirst, 'The Chigi Chapel in S. Maria della Pace', *Journal of the Warburg and Courtauld Institutes*, xxiv, 1961, Pls. 31b, 32a), and (of the same date) for the *Doctrine of the Two Swords* (A. E. Popham and J. Wilde, *Italian Drawings at Windsor Castle*, London, 1949, No. 797r.). C. du Molinet, op. cit. in n. 124, preface, already suggested that Raphael may have designed some of the coinage of Leo X, but he offered no particular examples.

128. Golzio, op. cit. in n. 10, p. 63.

129. Serafini, op. cit. in n. 125, i, Pl. xxviii. 11, etc.; Martinori, op. cit. in n. 124, pp. 9 ff. (dated 1513–14, and attributed to Serbaldi); the architectural implications are discussed by H. Geymüller, *Die ursprünglichen Entwürfe für Sanct Peter in Rom*, Vienna-Paris, 1875, p. 259.

130. '. . . leo apertis oculis dormit; sic et tu, sic quiesce sopitus a mundo, ut pervigiles semper oculos habere perseveres in Domino'; the lion is a type of Christ, for three days after it is born dead the father breathes life into it . . . 'et hoc modo, qui catulum leonis de tribu Juda die tertia suscitaverat' (St Peter Damianus, *De bono religiosi status, et variarum animantium tropologia, Cap. III: De natura leonis*, in *P.L.*, 145, col. 768).

    'Lumina aperta Leo tenet, & vigilare videtur Quum dormit . . .' (Ferreri, op. cit. in n. 2, listing the virtues of the animal). Compare A. Alciati, *Emblemata libellus*, ed. Venice, 1546, fol. 31v., and P. Valeriano, *I ieroglifici*, ed. Venice, 1625, pp. 3–4.

131. *Oratio obedientie illustrissimi domini Guglielmi Marchionis Montisferrati apud Leonem decimum* (Rome?), December 1513, and Mantuanus, op. cit. in n. 118, Bk. IV.

A third coin, a *Giulio* again (*Fig. 7*), is perhaps the most interesting symbolically.[129] It shows a lion, apparently asleep, on the Mons Vaticanus at the foot of New Saint Peter's. This lion is a symbol of vigilance, since lions were believed to sleep with their eyes open, and for this reason is the guardian here, as in front of so many mediaeval churches, at the door of the basilica.[130] The church, however, is the same Bramante project that had appeared on Caradosso's medal, and on the reverse of this coin, inscribed PETRE ECCE TEMPLUM TUUM, Pope Leo kneels before Saint Peter and offers him the altar-house (*tegurio*) as a pledge. The conceit seems to be that Leo will be the vigilant champion of the new church in the structural sense, like a new Solomon, as well as the vigilant guardian of the Church in the corporate sense, like a new Christ. These were two of the expectations that Leo encountered, or perhaps promoted, at the beginning of his pontificate, and it is typical of the complexity of Leonine imagery that the legendary vigilance of the lion was thought to be an attribute of this Pope Leo and of Leo the Great.[131]

II: Reconstruction

IT is a principle of historical analysis that we do not rush into the formal or iconographical appreciation of works of art before we have satisfied ourselves that we are seeing them, in imagination if not in fact, in the state and environment that the artist intended. We seldom do so. Frequently, of course, this principle cannot be applied, for we may be frustrated by a total lack of information; but even in these cases the enquiry is not valueless if it reminds us of the probable impoverishment, or indeed inaccuracy, of our conclusions. When a result is obtainable there can be no reason for neglecting it.

In the present case we have to deal, in the first place, with movable works that manifestly were invented for specific positions: the Leonine tapestries which now hang in glass cases in the Pinacoteca of the Vatican Museum but which, as we have seen, were commissioned for the decoration of the Sistine Chapel. Moreover they were designed by an artist who was exceptionally sensitive to the environment of his works, and to the relationship between the parts of a single scheme; and their subjects were selected and arranged in an age—and in a papal court—in which a casual approach to the problem is in the highest degree improbable. Thus, if our ultimate task is to understand as fully as possible the Cartoons that are now in the Victoria and Albert Museum, we must first attempt a reconstruction of Raphael's intentions for the tapestries. In this chapter we shall examine the problem of the physical reconstruction, that is of the precise position in the Sistine Chapel intended for each tapestry. Upon the solution to this problem will depend the subsequent analyses of their meaning and design.[1]

Of the two components that have to be brought together, the tapestries and the chapel, the latter (*Figs.* 1, 3) has itself undergone a number of changes, and so it is necessary to reconstruct with the greatest possible precision the state, in the years 1515–16 when the Cartoons were made, of the lowest zone where the tapestries could have been hung. We need to know the exact shape of the wall-areas available and the positions of all obstacles that Raphael had to negotiate. This reconstruction has been undertaken before, notably by Steinmann, but some significant mistakes have been made and a number of issues remain in doubt. On the other hand there exists a quantity of evidence that has not been used, especially in the diaries of the Masters of Ceremonies, Johannes Burchard (1483–1506)[2] and Paris de Grassis (1504–21),[3] and in liturgical sources of the period. This kind of information is very precise and allows substantial documentation of virtually all necessary details, but its interpretation necessarily entails a prior understanding of the terminology and functions of the various parts of the chapel.

The chapel was divided—and still is, but not at the original point—by a screen (*cancellata*). It is customary to say that this divided the area nearer the entrance, for the use of the laity, from that containing the altar, which is the *presbyterium*. These statements are not in fact correct.[4] A considerable number of the lay-congregation were admitted inside the screen: members of the papal household, the *Oratores* (ambassadors), and the *Barones, Conservatores, Senatores* and Prefect of the city of Rome; in addition—to judge from Erasmus's experience—a visitor with the right connections seems to have had little difficulty in finding a position near the papal throne.[5] The *presbyterium* proper

1. A similar reconstruction has already been proposed in J. White and J. Shearman, 'Raphael's Tapestries and their Cartoons', *Art Bulletin*, xl, 1958, pp. 193 ff.; although the result has not changed in any major respect the argument has been rearranged and some corrections have been made. It now seems possible to provide better documentation of the reconstruction, and more precise explanations of problems that arise. The same article contained a survey of earlier solutions, which need not be repeated.

2. I have used the edition by E. Celani, *Johannis Burckardi Liber Notarum*, in L. A. Muratori, *Rerum italicarum scriptores*, xxxii, Part I (2 vols.), Città di Castello, 1907 ff., to which I shall refer as: Burchard-Celani, 1 or 2, p. xx etc. Another edition by L. Thuasne, *Johannis Burchardi ... Diarium sive rerum urbanarum commentarii*, 3 vols., Paris 1883–85, is much less reliable; for examples of its inaccuracies, see F. Ehrle, *Gli affreschi del Pinturicchio nell'appartamento Borgia del Palazzo Apostolico Vaticano*, Rome, 1897, p. 8, n. 1, D. Gnoli, *La Roma di Leon X*, Milan, 1938, p. 109, n. 4, and Celani's preface.

3. As in Chapter I, references will be made to the British Museum copy, Add. MSS. 8440–4, unless otherwise stated. The extant MSS. of the papal diaries from the fifteenth to the seventeenth century are listed in L. Caetani, 'Vita e diario di Paolo Alaleone', *Archivio della R. società romana di storia patria*, xvi, 1893, pp. 7 ff. and A. Pieper, 'Das Original des *Diarium Burchardi*', *Römische Quartalschrift*, vii, 1893, pp. 387 ff.

4. The most complete descriptions of the layout and seating arrangements of the chapel in the period *c.* 1500 are contained in two sources: (i) Christophorus Marcellus, *Rituum ecclesiasticorum sive sacrarum cerimoniarum SS. romanae ecclesiae libri tres*, Venice, 1516 (dedicated to Leo X); this is in fact an edition of the *Liber caeremoniarum* MS. compiled by Burchard and Agostino Patrizi for Innocent VIII in 1488 (Bibl. Vat., Vat. Lat. 4738); see J. B. Gatticus, *Acta selecta caeremonialia sanctae romanae ecclesiae*, Rome, 1753, p. 1, R. Avesani, 'La biblioteca di Agostino Patrizi Piccolomini', *Mélanges Eugène Tisserant*, vi (*Studi e testi* 236), Vatican City, 1964, pp. 19–20, C. Vogel, *Introduction aux sources de l'histoire du culte chrétien au moyen âge*, Spoleto, 1966, pp. 211 ff., and J. Nabuco, *Le*

cérémonial apostolique avant Innocent VIII, Rome, 1966, pp. 31 ff. Paris de Grassis was much offended by the printed edition of 1516; he rightly said that it was no longer accurate, and he held the view that the books of papal ceremonial were not for public reading; for his reactions, early in 1517, see B.M., Add. MSS. 8443, fols. 212v., 224r., and 8444, fol. 2r. ff. (a copy of a letter to Leo X). (ii) Paris de Grassis, *Caeremoniarum opusculum*, Bibl. Vat., MS. Vat. Lat. 5634/1, passim, but especially fols. 53v. ff. This important MS. brings the *Liber caeremoniarum* of Burchard and Patrizi up to date and contains a quantity of additional information; the sequence of chapters follows no premeditated plan, but represents the response to and record of a series of contingencies. A passage near the beginning, fol. 23v., can be dated 1510–11 (it refers to Julius II's *capella* at Bologna, *nuper*); for other datable passages see below, ns. 92, 93. A passage from this MS. has been quoted (inaccurately, and with a misleading interpretation) by E. Camesasca, appendix to R. Salvini, *La Cappella Sistina in Vaticano*, Florence, 1965, pp. 264 ff.; the passage, which he takes to be a description of the Sistine Chapel, is, rather, a set of general principles for the *Capella* wherever it convenes.

Visual records of the *Capella papalis* in the Sistine Chapel, with detailed notes on seating etc., but after some changes, are given in a print by Lorenzo Vaccari, 1578 (E. Steinmann, *Die Sixtinische Kapelle*, Munich, i, 1901, Pl. XXXIV) and another in F. Cancellieri, *Descrizione storico-critica delle Sale Regie e Ducale e delle Cappelle Paoline e Sistina del Vaticano e del Quirinale*, i, Rome, 1790, p. 108; these are useful for the interpretation of the earlier texts.

5. See above, Chapter I, p. 16, n. 95.

6. 'aditum, sive presbyterium, sic enim nostri vocant, aream, sive planitiem illam gradibus elevatam, qua altare, & abbachus (i.e. *credenza*, table), & faldistorium hinc, & inde, solium ... comprehenduntur ...' (Paris de Grassis, MS. Vat. Lat. 5634/1, fol. 23v.—from a description of arrangements made at Bologna in 1510, reproducing as closely as possible those in the Sistine Chapel; see also *Diarium*, second Sunday in Advent, 1510, B.M., Add. MS. 8442, fols. 66v. ff.).

7. Marcellus, op. cit. in n. 4, fols. cxxii, v. ff.; Paris de Grassis, MS. Vat. Lat. 5634/1, fols. 19r., 25r.

8. Marcellus and Paris de Grassis, loc. cit., talk of the *postergale* of the *sedilia* of the cardinals decorated with 'pannis quos vocant Attrabatentes' (sc: *Arazzi*) and 'tapetibus auleis, & pannis vulgo rasseis dictis'; this situation may be

was the raised area at the altar end of the space inside the screen;[6] it bore not only the altar itself but also, on a projection on our left side, the daïs for the throne (*Fig.* II, p. 25).

The space between the *presbyterium*-steps and the screen was largely taken up by the *quadratura* (or *saepta*), that is the seating for the cardinals arranged symmetrically around three sides of a square, the fourth side towards the altar being left open.[7] The original *quadratura* has long since been removed; it was a wooden bench with a high back covered with tapestry, and a step in front.[8] It seems clear that it was exactly related to, and in fact determined the shape of, the mosaic floor-pattern of the area inside the screen.[9] In the centre of the side nearest and parallel to the screen there was an opening, corresponding to the door in the screen, and the passage through into the *quadratura* was called the *ambulacrum*; nearer the altar, between the *quadratura* and the *presbyterium*, was an open space, the *vestibulum*,[10] which stretched laterally from the papal throne across to the right wall. The main elements of the floor-pattern of this part, a series of rectangles, reflect the function of this area, which was to provide seating space (on the floor) for minor members of the *Capella papalis*, including secretaries, arranged in rows at right angles to the steps to the *presbyterium*. The pulpit, which was portable, was also placed in the *vestibulum*. The remaining spaces inside the screen, but outside the *quadratura*, were passage-ways, but it is certain that there were also wooden benches (*sedilia*) between the cardinals and the right wall for prelates of various orders, and probable that there were more on the left.[11] In the lateral space immediately inside the screen there was standing room for those who could claim some connection with the ambassadors or the prelates. Outside the screen movement was only limited by two rows of men-at-arms who kept clear the passage between the entrance to the chapel and the door of the screen for the processions of Pontifical Entrance and Exit (each enacted twice during the Mass); the floor-pattern is once more related to the liturgy where the sequence of six spirals leads from the *rota porfiretica*[12] by the entrance up to the screen.

The first important problem to be resolved is the original height of the *presbyterium*. It is now approached up a flight of four steps, but according to

visualized from Pinturicchio's representation of the *quadratura* in the *Congress of Mantua* fresco in the Piccolomini Library, Siena.

9. Paris de Grassis (MS. Vat. Lat. 5634/1, fol. 25r.) arranged the *quadratura* at Bologna, 1510 (see n. 6) round a square with internal dimensions of 3 *canne* (6·7 m.); the inner square on the Sistine floor has this dimension, and is framed by a strip-pattern, without major motifs, of a total width of 68 cm. which was probably designed to be hidden by the cardinals' benches and step.

10. 'Vestibulum ... pars illa anterior, quae est inter presbyterii gradus, & Cardinalium consessum, idest, directè ante solii conspectum, quantum se ipsius solii gradus extendunt, ubi Epistola, Evangelium, & huiusmodi recitari solent' (Paris de Grassis, MS. Vat. Lat. 5634/1, fol. 24r.); this area is derived from the *chorus*

or *schola cantorum* of the earlier liturgy—cf. th Pontifical of Durandus, Bk. III, ii, 53, ar xxv, 4 (published by M. Andrieu, in *Studi Testi* 88, Vatican City, 1940, pp. 571, 654 and J. Braun, S.J., *Der christliche Altar*, Munich, 1924, pp. 656 ff.

11. The stone wall-bench at either side, runnir from the *presbyterium* to the screen, is calle *comercium* by Paris de Grassis (B.M., Add. M 8440, fol. 331r.); it was properly reserved f archbishops and clerical ambassadors (on th right) and secular ambassadors (on the le MS. Vat. Lat. 5634/1, fol. 61r.) but the latt frequently encroached on the steps of th throne. A passage in Burchard-Celani, 2, 462, seems to imply that the ambassadors al occupied the stone bench against the scree itself.

12. See above, Chapter I, p. 7.

Steinmann and all subsequent scholars it was initially raised on one.[13] That something has been changed is clear from the evident conflict at every point between the lowest step of the present flight and the floor-pattern (*Fig.* 1); the former seems to overflow, as it were, on to a design calculated for a less extensive flight. Even more obviously the stone bench against the left wall has been crudely cut back to accommodate the present steps. Steinmann's conclusion that the *presbyterium* has been appreciably raised was based upon his interpretation of a stone slab against the first bay on the left side, that is between the throne and the altar-wall; he took this to be the top of a bench, similar to the stone benches at the foot of the walls in most other parts of the chapel, and from its supposed submergence during a raising of the floor he calculated, reasonably, that this area could have been raised only on one step originally. Steinmann was led from this conclusion to its corollary, that the mosaic floor of the *presbyterium* has been re-set, and he went so far as to suggest a reconstruction of the first pattern.[14] The floor-pattern that he designed, however, is unconvincing stylistically and is less sensibly connected with liturgical movements in front of the altar than the present one;[15] furthermore the present one shows the same kinds of restoration as the rest of the chapel and no signs of re-setting. The hypothetical bench-top has a projecting moulding on its outer edge which is angular, like that of the original steps surviving in other parts of the chapel, and it is not of the rolled form provided (as a concession to comfort) for the stone benches. There is no reason to suppose that it was ever anything but a step, and its height above the floor, seventeen centimetres, is reasonable if that is the case. However, in the papal diaries of the period that concerns us there is no reference either to a bench or to a step in this position, but some fairly clear indications that there was no obstruction at the base of this wall. It seems probable that the step in question was added at a date long after the commission for the tapestries;[16] while its moulding is comparable in angularity with those of the original steps in the chapel, it is not in fact consistent with them in style.

The arguments for the raising of the *presbyterium* therefore depend only upon the conflict between the present steps and the floor-pattern of the *vestibulum* and the stone wall-bench on the left. As it happens there is in the papal diaries and liturgical sources an almost unmanageable quantity of evidence about the original steps which arises from discussions about seating and precedence. It should be explained that normally the steps around the projection on the left for the papal throne provided sitting or standing room for princes of inferior rank, Senators, Conservators and Barons of Rome, and occasionally ambassadors, between whom there were infinite possibilities for dispute over precedence, while the steps running across the chapel and leading up to the *presbyterium* were occupied by minor clerics of the papal household. There are very numerous references to these steps in the plural ('scalae', 'gradus marmoreos per quos ascenditur ad Presbyterium', and so on),[17] there are as many references to the 'top step', the 'bottom step', and the 'second step'; and Paris de Grassis records that on one occasion the *Praelati officiales*, because of overcrowding, had to sit on the first, second and third steps.[18] In another place he states unequivocally that there were three.[19] There can, then, be no doubt that there were, in this period, three steps to the *presbyterium* and throne-platform; and this conclusion is consistent with the evidence of a dozen or more situations on record where the papal throne or the whole apparatus for the *Capella papalis* was provided, the most informative of which is the occasion at Bologna in 1510 when Paris de Grassis was required to

13. Steinmann, op. cit. in n. 4, i, pp. 159 ff.; there would be little purpose in a list of those scholars who have followed him on this point, but it includes myself in the article cit. in n. 1, p. 199.

14. Op. cit. in n. 4, Pl. IX.

15. Steinmann allowed only two patterned squares in front of the altar where there are now three; at a number of points in the liturgy three positions are defined in front of the altar.

16. See below, n. 28.

17. A selection from many such references, spread over the period: Burchard-Celani, i, pp. 245 (1488), 311 (1490), 352 (1492), 581 (1495); Paris de Grassis, B.M., Add. MSS. 8440, fol. 135r. (1505), 8441, fol. 257v. (1508), 8443, fol. 39v. (1513), 8444, fols. 11v. (1517), 198v. (1520). See also Marcellus, op. cit. in n. 4, fol. civ.

18. Easter Sunday, 1513: 'Barones multi replerunt gradus solii sedentes, ita quod fuit necessarium Praelatis Officialibus sedere super primo, secundo et tertio gradu, sicut assistentes Praelati in Sto. Petro' (B.M., Add. MS. 8443, fol. 24r.).

19. MS. Vat. Lat. 5634/1, fol. 227r.: 'In capella palatina, atque alibi communiter, tres tantum gradus solio supponemus, praeter id, quod duos gradus scabellorum suppedalium adiungemus'; on fol. 232r. he explains that in Saint Peter's the throne is raised on seven steps (six *gradus* and one *scabellum*), like Solomon's, but 'in Capella palatii . . . solium non maius, nec altius est altare, sed ambo illa, idest altare, & solium in aequalitate posita sunt'. The only text I have found which appears to conflict with this clear statement is in a passage from the *Liber caeremoniarum* of Burchard (quoted by Steinmann, op. cit. in n. 4, i, p. 659) in which it is explained which secular members of the *Capella* occupied each of *four* steps to the throne; *magni principes* were on the fourth step. But there is in fact no contradiction here; *magni principes* had the right to stand beside the pope on the *solium*—that is on the step of the throne itself in distinction to the *planum solii*. This confusion, arising from a loose use of terms, is clarified by another passage from Paris de Grassis: 'solium, quod appellamus illum quartum gradum quadrangulare super gradibus' (B.M., Add. MS. 8442, fol. 67r.). For the Canonization of S. Francesco da Paola, 1 May 1519, Paris de Grassis arranged in Saint Peter's a *suggestum* 'cum tribus gradibus . . . et sub solio magno . . . unum gradum sicut in cappella Palatii' (B.M., Add. MS. 8444, fol. 142v.).

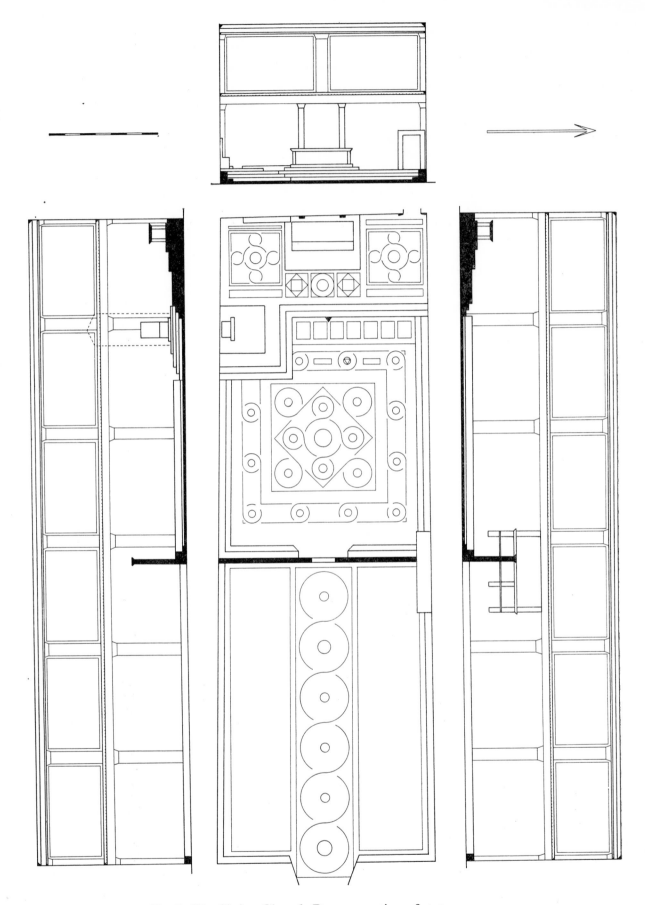

Fig. I. The Sistine Chapel: Reconstruction of state c. 1515

FINDING OF MOSES   NATIVITY OF CHRIST

STONING OF STEPHEN   ASSUNTA   MIRACULOUS DRAUGHT

CIRCUMCISION

MOSES IN EGYPT

CROSSING OF RED SEA

ADORATION OF GOLDEN CALF

CONVERSION OF SAUL

CONVERSION OF PROCONSUL

SACRIFICE AT LYSTRA

P. IN P.

PAUL AT ATHENS

ALTAR

PRESBYTERIUM

SOLIUM

SOLII

PLANUM

VESTIBULUM

QUADRATURA

AMBULACRUM

CANTORIA

CHARGE TO PETER

HEALING OF LAME MAN

DEATH OF ANANIAS

BAPTISM OF CHRIST

HEALING OF LEPER

CALLING OF APOSTLES

SERMON ON MOUNT

Fig. II. The Sistine Chapel: Reconstruction of the original hanging order of the tapestries, and identification of the parts

20. 'Ascendebatur autem ad presbyterium gradibus quatuor, eo computato, qui planitiem liminarem presbyterii faciebat' (i.e. four, counting the level of the *vestibulum* as the first: MS. Vat. Lat. 5634/1, fol. 24r.); compare the passage from B.M., Add. MS. 8442, fol. 67r., in the previous note, which refers to the *solium* steps on the same occasion. Typical of the other situations are the temporary *apparatus* erected in the Consistory on 18 August 1504, when the Sistine Chapel was under repair (Add. MS. 8440, fol. 50v.), the arrangements for the Lateran Council in 1512 (Add. MS. 8442, fol. 177r. and the woodcut frontispiece to *Oratio habita per Antonium Puccium . . . in Nova Sacrosancti Lateranensis concilii Sessione*, Rome, 1514 (?)), and the Canonization ceremony of 1519 mentioned in the previous note. The number of steps to the *presbyterium* is unlikely to be casual, and it is probable that there is some symbolism involved; but in any case the architect of the Sistine Chapel had to take account of liturgical tradition, and at this point specifically of the transition from the *schola cantorum* (see above, n. 10) to the *presbyterium*, which in Pontificals is by steps, in the plural, and in surviving examples like San Clemente or Castel Sant'Elia is by a flight of three.

21. The floor-pattern leaves no room for a bench or step in either case. On Easter Sunday 1513 Paris de Grassis arranged for robing (an exceptional case) a second throne directly against the wall on this side, 'ad latus epistolae parieti adhaerens' (Add. MS. 8443, fol. 24r.; he did exactly the same on 18 December 1517, Add. MS. 8444, fol. 47v.). His terms are extremely precise; on the same occasion in 1513 he describes the unusual position of the papal *mensa* on the left of the altar as 'ad cornu evangelii posita *quasi* parieti adhaerens, sicut altare . . .' (for the distinction, see below). On 4 May 1513 his own foot-stool was given a new position 'apud parietem credentiae' (i.e. against the right wall of the *presbyterium*), displacing the pope's *faldistorium* which went 'apud parietem, quod est inter Ostium Sacristiae, et Cornu epistolae altaris' (Add. MS. 8443, fol. 39v.).

22. E. Steinmann, 'Cancellata und Cantoria der Sixtinischen Kapelle', *Jahrbuch der K. preuszischen Kunstsammlungen*, xviii, 1897, pp. 24 ff.; also White-Shearman, op. cit. in n. 1, p. 213, and Camesasca, op. cit. in n. 4, p. 128.

23. F. Ehrle and H. Egger, *Die Conclavepläne (Studi e documenti per la storia del Palazzo Apostolico Vaticano*, fasc. 5), Vatican City, 1933, Pls. I and II.

24. Steinmann, op. cit. in n. 4, i, Pl. XXXIV; a passage from the *Diarium* of F. Mucantius,

reproduce in the papal residence a chapel-arrangement conforming as closely as possible to that of the Sistine Chapel.[20]

If, then, the original steps were three there would seem to be little point in raising the level by one more, a gain of about fifteen centimetres, which would have entailed the considerable task of re-setting the floor—something, in any case, that does not appear to have taken place. The simpler and more probable solution is that the *presbyterium* level has never been altered, and that the steps have been increased from three (each of about 20 cm.) to four (of about 15 cm.) for other reasons: either because the first steps were inconveniently high or—more probably—in order to provide additional area for seating; the circumstances in which this would have been necessary and the likely date can better be considered later. Three steps, each of the width of the present ones, would allow a perfect relationship with the pattern of rectangles on the floor of the *vestibulum* (*Fig.* I, p. 24). The only point at which difficulty arises is in the relationship between the steps on the left, leading up to the throne, and the pattern near the *quadratura*, which would still have been interrupted (but less brutally than at present); this interruption may have been unavoidable.

The present and, if we are right, original floor-level of the *presbyterium* is within one centimetre the same as that of the top of the stone wall-benches flanking the remaining area inside the screen. It is certain that there were no such benches at the right end of the *presbyterium* or against the wall to the right of the altar;[21] we have seen that at the left end, next to the throne, there was similarly no obstruction, and it will appear presently that there was a low stone bench, perhaps more like a step, against the wall to the left of the altar. Therefore with the last exception it can be established that the base-line of the wall-areas of the *presbyterium* available for tapestries was the same as that of the rest of the wall-areas—above the stone benches—in the chancel.

at the end of 1573 (Steinmann, i, p. 161, n. 1), tells us that the chapel had recently been enlarged and this probably refers to the moving of the *cancellata*; but since it was the duty of the Master of Ceremonies to have a long memory the meaning of 'recently' may be a little elastic. One would expect to find some record of such an important rearrangement in the papal diaries at the moment when it was made; I have been through the British Museum copies from Paris de Grassis to 1572 without finding one; however there is a gap, 1551–55, in the two copies of Ioannes Franciscus Firmanus's (Add. MSS. 8435, 8447), and these years correspond with one of the possible moments for the change, suggested by the 1555 Conclave plans of Marcellus II and Paul IV (repr. Ehrle-Egger, op. cit. in n. 23), which show the screen in the new position (contradicted, however, by a plan identified by Ehrle-Egger, Pl. VI, as that of the Conclave of Pius V, 1565–66, where the screen appears about half-way down the chapel; but this may not be significant since in that Conclave there were no cells in the chapel and its details were of no importance to the draughtsman). A date in the early fifties, on the other hand, would not be easy to understand in relation to Paul IV's project for enlargement cited in n. 26.

25. A comparison between the lists of t[ ]households of Leo X and of Pius IV (156[ ]excluding in each case the lower grou[ ](*Officiales*), shows an increase of about on[ ]third; cf. A. Ferrajoli, 'Il ruolo della corte Leone X', *Archivio della R. società romana storia patria*, xxxiv, 1911, pp. 363 ff., and von Sickel, 'Ein Ruolo di famiglia des Paps[ ]Pius IV', *Mittheilungen des Instituts für oest[ ]reichische Geschichtsforschung*, xiv, 1893, pp. 571[ ]

26. Letter of Scipione Saurolo, 6 Septemb[ ]1561, to Cardinal Carlo Borromeo: 'Paulo [ ]ad ogni modo voleva provederlj (sc: t[ ]problem of Michelangelo's fresco) havendo animo di agrandir la Capella tirandola dentro nella Sacristia . . .' (A. Sala, *Docume[ ]circa la vita e le gesta di S. Carlo Borromeo*, [ ]Milan, 1861, p. 90).

27. *Diarium* of Cornelius Firmanus, B.M., Ad[ ]MS. 8448, fols. 164v., 165v. (1571).

28. MS. cit., fol. 181v., and *Electio Pape Leo[ ]Decimi, Anno M C. Tredecimo. Ordo Mansion[ ]Reverendorum dominorum Cardinalium in Concla[ ]existentium . . .*, Rome, 1513. The general e[ ]pansion of membership of the *Capella papa[ ]would reasonably also require, at about t[ ]

The chancel, however, has been enlarged. On this point there is little that need be added to the evidence provided by Steinmann.[22] The screen is now about two-thirds of the way down the chapel (*Fig.* 3), whereas its original position on a step just a little over half-way down the chapel is clearly marked by an inset marble strip on the floor. In this position it abutted on to the *cantoria*, and its removal has led to the insertion of new sections into the balustrade of the gallery, and the provision of a new section of its entablature, together with a new pier at the right end of the screen and an additional (and symbolically superfluous) candlestick on top. The moving of the screen is especially significant for the placing of tapestries on the walls. Because the side walls of the chapel converge slightly towards the altar, the screen at its original and narrower point would have been bonded into the wall, and indeed the carving of its extremities, now visible, is unfinished for this reason. At the left side, therefore, no tapestry could have been hung across the fourth bay, counting from the altar end; on the right the greater part of the fourth bay is already occupied by the choir-gallery.

The date of the moving of the screen is not yet clear, except within rather broad limits. In a plan prepared for the Conclave of Julius III (1549) it is clearly shown in its original position,[23] whereas in the engraved view of the interior of the chapel by Lorenzo Vaccari, 1578, it is equally clearly shown in its new and present position.[24] Its moving is probably connected with the considerable increase in the membership of the *Capella papalis* during the century.[25] An alternative expedient proposed by Paul IV (1555–59), to demolish the altar-wall (including the *Last Judgement*) and to extend the building in that direction, was perhaps considered too drastic.[26] It seems sensible to relate the moving of the screen to two other changes in the area it encloses: the provision of an extra step to the *presbyterium*—which, as we have seen, would produce additional seating—and the enlargement of the *quadratura* of the cardinals, which by the time of Vaccari's engraving was no longer a square in the centre of the chancel but had been extended down the chapel and asymmetrically across to the left wall. By 1570 the number of cardinals attending Mass in the chapel had risen well above forty,[27] and the fifty-one who attended the Conclave of Gregory XIII (1572) may be contrasted with the twenty-nine who were present for the election of Leo X (1513).[28]

We must now turn to the controversial problem of the original appearance of the altar-wall. It will be as well to begin with the altar itself, about which we are well informed by the diarists. It stood on two steps (*scabella, suppedanea*), like the present ones except that they were wooden;[29] it is probable that the upper one was optional, according to the stature of the celebrant.[30] The altar had columns, but their number is nowhere stated.[31] It is clear, however, from details recorded by chance, that the altar was of the table-type; at the Conclave of Paul III (1534) the security precautions included a search for gate-crashers *under* the altar, and at the Conclaves of Innocent VIII (1484) and of Leo X the wooden doors of the screen were removed and placed beneath the altar.[32] The original Sixtine altar may perhaps be visualized on the basis of the beautiful Doric table-altar of about the same date in S. Maria dei Miracoli in Venice. But the practice of placing the doors beneath also helps us to determine limits for the altar's width. It may be assumed that the original doors, like the present ones, were 3·35 metres in length, and thus we are given, indirectly, a minimum width for the altar (allowing for columns and overhangs) approaching four metres, which is about the size of the eighteenth-century altar now in the chapel.[33] If, on the

date, the additional step to the left of the throne in the *presbyterium* discussed above, p. 23, and shown in the print by Lorenzo Vaccari, 1578 (see n. 4).

29. Paris de Grassis, Good Friday 1512: 'Ipse celebrans erravit ante gradus ligneos Altaris . . .' (B.M., Add. MS. 8442, fol. 172r.); see also Add. MSS. 8440, fols. 161r., 172v., 8442, fol. 12v., 8444, fol. 48r., Burchard-Celani, 1, pp. 140, 262, and Marcellus, op. cit. in n. 4, fols. lxxii, r., lxxxix, v.

30. Paris de Grassis, Saturday in Holy Week, 1505, distinguishes between two positions, 'super scabello sive suppedaneo altaris' and 'in gradu altaris' (Add. MS. 8440, fol. 177r.); his description of the equivalent arrangement at Bologna, 1510, is particularly informative: '. . . altare duos habebat gradus, unum, scilicet, lapideum imobile, & alterum ligneum quidem mobilem, ut sic pro modulo, & statura cuius vis super eo celebraturi attolli, deprimive posset' (MS. Vat. Lat. 5634/1, fol. 24r.); he also gives dimensions, in *canne*, for the permanent step, which would be: 4·8 m. wide, 3·4 m. deep, 15 cm. high.

31. Paris de Grassis, Saturday in Holy Week, 1505: 'Cereus fuit in inferiori plano, ubi manent Cubicularii, adhaerens cum pede triangulari gradibus (sc: to the *presbyterium*) directè ante Columnam altaris in cornu epistolae' (Add. MS. 8440, fol. 174v.); the same Feast, 1506, revising this position: 'Locum ubi poni debet cereus videlicet ante altare, non praecisè ante columnam altaris, sed quidem ante cornu epistolae, praecisè autem cum duobus ex tribus pedibus tangens ultimum gradum scalarum, et cum tertio super lista marmorea per lungum Cappellae directae, magis ad medium altaris, quam ad columnam parietis in dicto cornu' (8440, fol. 330v.); for an interpretation of this passage, see below n. 33, and *Fig.* I, p. 24, where I have marked the position of the tripod in 1506.

32. Blasius de Martinellis, B.M., Add. MS. 8446, fol. 46r. (this passage also printed in Gatticus, op. cit. in n. 4, p. 325); and Burchard-Celani, 1, p. 23 (also Gatticus, p. 284), Paris de Grassis, Add. MS. 8443, fol. 5v.

33. Paris de Grassis (MS. Vat. Lat. 5634/1, fol. 24v.) gives the dimensions (in *canne*) of the equivalent altar at Bologna, 1510, which would have been 3·57 m. wide, 1·45 m. deep, and 1·22 m. high (without the top step). The passages quoted in n. 31 above, describing the placing of the candelabrum-tripod, may also be applied to this problem. The position selected

in 1506 placed the front foot on the white marble strip in the *vestibulum* nearest to the centre-line of the chapel (the sixth from the right); the position in 1505 would have been farther to the right, in line with the triangle-in-circle pattern on the framing of the *quadratura* (probably the position for the tripod intended by Sixtus IV) and in line with the end-column of an altar slightly shorter than the present one. E. Wind, 'Maccabean Histories in the Sistine Ceiling', *Italian Renaissance Studies* (ed. E. F. Jacob), London, 1960, p. 320, n. 1, mistakenly supposes that the altar of the chapel is of the so-called 'papal privilege' type, that is orientated with the celebrant facing the congregation. There is in fact no doubt on this question; the altar is 'apud parietem', 'adhaeret parieti', 'quasi parieti adhaerens' (Marcellus, op. cit. in n. 4, fol. cxxii, v.; Paris de Grassis, Add. MS. 8440, fol. 222v., Vat. Lat. 5634/1, fol. 142v., Add. MS. 8443, fol. 23v.); in Vat. Lat. 5634/2, fol. 35r., Paris de Grassis specifically contrasts the altar of the Sistine Chapel with the reversed type found in Saint Peter's.

34. Vasari, *Vite* (ed. Milanesi), iii, p. 579. This arrangement, with altar detached from the wall, is exemplified among contemporary monuments now surviving by the Della Rovere Chapel in S. Maria del Popolo; the type is analysed by Braun, op. cit. in n. 10, ii, p. 286.

35. F. Wickhoff, 'Ueber einige Zeichnungen des Pinturicchio', *Zeitschrift für bildende Kunst*, xix, 1884, p. 59 (as Pinturicchio's original drawing for the altar-piece).

36. J. Wilde, 'The decoration of the Sistine Chapel', *Proceedings of the British Academy*, xliv, 1958, pp. 69 ff.; see also Camesasca, op. cit. in n. 4, p. 174.

37. This point, also made by Wilde, may seem too baroque, if it recalls for example the view of the *Cathedra Petri* that Bernini planned through the columns of the *baldacchino* in Saint Peter's; but it must be remembered that Bernini's idea has a mediaeval precedent, and possibly an effective one, in Innocent III's statement (quoted by Paris de Grassis, 1515, B.M., Add. MS. 8443, fol. 133r.) that the papal throne in the apse of Saint Peter's should be raised on steps so as to be visible over the High Altar and thus through the ciborium. A parallel for the Sistine Chapel situation would be provided by the view, so obviously planned, of Titian's *Assunta* through the opening of the choir-screen in the Frari in Venice.

38. L. D. Ettlinger, *The Sistine Chapel before Michelangelo*, Oxford, 1965, pp. 23 ff.

39. J. Wilde, 'Der ursprüngliche Plan Michelangelos zum Jüngsten Gericht', *Die graphischen Künste*, N.F. i, 1936, p. 8.

40. J. Q. van Regteren Altena, 'Zu Michelangelos Zeichnungen', *Stil und Überlieferung in der Kunst des Abendlandes*, ii, Berlin, 1967, p. 177.

41. A. Ghidiglia Quintavalle, *Gli affreschi del Duomo di Modena*, Milan-Modena, 1967, Pl. 31.

42. The height of the bottom of the first cornice from the *presbyterium*-floor is 4·26 m., from which we should subtract about 1·45 m. for the permanent step and altar-table, leaving a maximum height of about 2·8 m. for the

other hand, we are right in assuming that the floor of the *presbyterium* has not been re-set, a maximum width for the altar-steps is suggested by the distance between the complete patterns to right and left, which are about 4·8 metres apart; the width of the altar is likely to have been a little less.

The altar was placed against, or more probably very close to, the wall ('quasi parieti adhaerens'), and on the wall were a frescoed altar-piece, the *Assumption of the Virgin*,[34] and two history-paintings in the second zone beginning the cycles of the Lives of Moses and of Christ: the *Birth of Moses* (or the *Finding of Moses*) on the left, the *Nativity* on the right. The composition and proportions of the altar-piece are known from a copy in Vienna (*Fig.* 9).[35] The relationship of these three frescoes is in dispute and the issue is an important one in our context. In one reconstruction, by Wilde, a small altar-piece is fitted beneath the first cornice, which allows the two history-paintings to be of the same size as those on the side-walls, and to be separated like them by a painted pilaster; this arrangement would have reflected that of the entrance-wall, with the altar-piece in place of the door.[36] It would also produce an altar-piece of such dimensions that it would be exactly framed by the opening of the *cancellata* when viewed from the entrance door.[37] In the second reconstruction, recently proposed by Ettlinger, an enormous altar-piece nearly six metres in height inside its frame would rise to the second cornice, thus dividing the histories and reducing their proportions almost to square; the altar-piece, with its frame, would be about five metres wide, and would have diminished the areas of the lower zone available for tapestries significantly more than would an altar of the width we have calculated.[38]

There is little doubt that the first reconstruction is correct. It was originally supported by Michelangelo's preliminary drawing in the Casa Buonarroti for the *Last Judgement*, which clearly shows the frame of a small altar-piece which at that stage it was his intention to retain.[39] Recently another drawing has appeared, a copy of an earlier project by Michelangelo, which demonstrates the same intention;[40] its proportions are evidently not calculated, since the total field is rather taller than the end wall itself, but there is no question that it records the smaller altar-piece. Michelangelo's initial idea, in which some of the figures of his composition were supported on the altar-piece frame, was inspired by the altar-wall of the Carafa Chapel in S. Maria sopra Minerva, where Filippino Lippi had similarly painted his great *Assumption* fresco around the frame of a small frescoed altar-piece; and

painting. If we assume that the top of the altar-piece frame (see below) was the cornice itself, and if we allow framing pilasters (like those of Filippino's Carafa altar-piece) that would add about one-third to the painting width, the result (applying the proportion derived from the Albertina copy) would be total width of 3 m. This represents a maximum. A visualization in which the pilasters supported an independent entablature below the cornice or one which included some sort of *predella* must produce a lesser width.

43. For the text see above, n. 31. The *columna parietis* is probably identical with the 'column

another precedent that may have been in his mind is provided by the altar-wall of the first chapel on the right in the Duomo at Modena, where a *Last Judgement* was painted in fresco, about 1480, around an altar-piece.[41] The evidence of Michelangelo's projects is important for our purposes, since it follows from the choice of the reconstruction with the smaller altar-piece that the width of the latter (about three metres with its frame) would have been *less* than that of the altar itself.[42] This conclusion can be supported by a passage from the diary of Paris de Grassis in which the *columna altaris* is distinguished from the *columna parietis*, presumably the altar-piece frame, in such a way that the latter must be nearer the centre-line than the former.[43] The result that concerns us is this: if the altar of about four metres was attached to the wall, the extent of uninterrupted wall to either side would have been about 4·7 metres;[44] but if, as seems from the limited evidence more likely, the altar stood a little removed from the wall, the areas available for tapestry-hanging would have been delimited by the altar-piece rather than by the altar itself and therefore a little wider, about 5·1 metres (*Fig.* I, p. 24).

It has been denied that Sixtus IV provided a sacristy for his chapel,[45] but in fact it is quite certain that he did so, for it is mentioned in a description of the Conclave at his death (1484).[46] At that date it was entered through a door to the left of the altar; the present door in this position is, however, of the early eighteenth century. Some time after 1489, at which date the door was still on the left,[47] the sacristy-entrance was moved over to the right; it is first mentioned in this position in 1505,[48] and the door-frame bears the arms of Alexander VI (1492–1503). It was certainly through this door that the sacristy was entered throughout the pontificate of Leo X; the former door on the left had probably been walled up. This sacristy door occupies part of an area of wall otherwise available for tapestries, and so we must ask whether or not a tapestry could be hung over it. If access to the sacristy were necessary during the Mass—as might be the case for robing and for fetching the Sacrament —it is unlikely that it would be covered. The liturgy of the Sistine Chapel in this period, however, is exceptional in two respects. Firstly the elaborate ceremony of the robing of the pope was performed in the *Camera del papagallo* (between the private apartments and the Consistory-rooms); the vesting there of Leo X is represented in the frontispiece of a beautifully decorated manuscript of 1520 now in New York, *Praeparatio ad missam pontificalem*.[49] Secondly the Sacrament was fetched by a procession which formed in the *quadratura*, passed through the screen and out of the main door and then crossed the Sala Regia to the *Capella parva*, or Chapel of Saint Nicholas, where the Sacrament was kept.[50] The sacristy itself served no purpose in this liturgy, and the several references to its use all record contingencies;[51] its designed purpose was to serve as a repository for service-books, relics, plate and vestments, and to be a lodging for the sacristan.[52] Thus it seems that there would be no objection to hanging a tapestry over the sacristy-door during major ceremonies, and it might well be thought desirable to do so since an asymmetrical feature could thereby be concealed.

There is one remaining feature of the altar-wall that must be mentioned, since it put a permanent limitation upon the wall-space available to the left of the altar; there was a low stone bench that ran from the altar up to the opening of the earlier door in the left corner. This bench was moved when Michelangelo cut back the lower part of the altar-wall before painting the *Last Judgement*, and then at some later stage it was replaced by the present somewhat narrower step. But its presence is indicated by a crude re-paving and by the contraction of the floor-pattern on this side, compared with the

quadraturae altaris extra picturas' (B.M., Add. MS. 8440, fol. 117r.) already interpreted by Wilde (op. cit. in n. 36, p. 69, n. 5) as referring to the altar-piece.

44. The width of the altar-wall is 13·35 m.

45. First by Steinmann, op. cit. in n. 4, i, pp. 134, 142, who based his argument on the statement in Albertini's *Opusculum*, 1510, that the sacristy was founded by Innocent VIII (1484–92); perhaps Albertini drew his own conclusions from the presence of this pope's arms on the exterior which must, however, signify his completion of Sixtus's sacristy.

46. Burchard-Celani, I, p. 22 (talking of the *camerae* erected in the chapel): 'ultima ad sinistram intrantis capellam, quae erat prope ostium, quo intratur ad cameram sacriste in cornu evangelii altaris'; cf. Marcellus, op. cit. in n. 4 (i.e. 1488), fol. i, v.: 'in capite huius capellae ad sinistram intranti camerae sunt, in quibus sacrista palatii Apostolici habitat'.

47. Compare two descriptions of the Feast of the Purification of the Virgin, 2 February: 1486 'Papa benedixit candelas ad sinistram suam in angulo, ubi . . . assistentes sedere solent, positas', and 1489 'paratis . . . candelis juxta ostium mansionis sacriste' (Burchard-Celani, I, pp. 137, 250).

48. Paris de Grassis, B.M., Add. MS. 8440, fol. 159r.; cf. 8443, fol. 39v. (1513).

49. In the style of Attavante degli Attavanti; see *Books and Manuscripts from the Heinemann Collection*, Pierpont Morgan Library, New York, 1963, p. 13.

50. See the precise accounts in Burchard-Celani, I, pp. 112, 140, 143, 188–9, 227–8 (1485–88), and 2, p. 214 (1500); also Paris de Grassis, B.M., Add. MSS. 8440, fols. 163v., 173r. (1505), 8443, fol. 221v. (1517).

51. For example: resting-place for a chaplain who fainted; emergency latrine; papal breakfast and lunch; occasional conservation of the Golden Rose; and irregular robing.

52. 'Item prima auleta et camera parva sacristie, in qua paramenta et libri capelle sunt reposti, dimisse sunt libere pro conclavi' (1484: Burchard-Celani, I, p. 23); see also Marcellus, op. cit. in n. 4, fol. cxxxii, and Albertini, *Opusculum*, 1510, quoted by Steinmann, op. cit. in n. 4, i, p. 136, n. 2. Burchard's account of the death of the sacristan, 1501, makes it clear that the latter did actually live in these rooms (Burchard-Celani, 2, p. 302).

53. Paris de Grassis, MS. Vat. Lat. 5634/1, fols. 25v., 59v.; he himself, after being made bishop in December 1513, was seated at the end of the row (B.M., Add. MS. 8443, fol. 84v.).

54. Marcellus, op. cit. in n. 4, fol. cxii, v.; Paris de Grassis, MS. Vat. Lat. 5634/1, fols. 53v.–54r. The *solium* itself was removed when the pope 'sedit in sede parva camerali' (e.g. Papal Vespers on the Eve of the Feast of the Baptist, 23 June 1517: Add. MS. 8444, fol. 18r.).

55. MS. Vat. Lat. 5634/1, fols. 53v.–54r.; the papal throne 'ornatum esse debet velis, sive ... postergali ex colore reliquis rei divinae paratibus congruo, sed cum nullo prorsus velo, idest, umbraculo, sive, ut vulgo dicunt baldachino desuper caput extenso tam in hac Capella ...', which is improper during the Mass but correct (as a symbol of the Vicariate) in 'consistoriis publicis, processionibusque, & sessionibus'; but this rule is often broken (he adds) by the 'florerii' who do put up the *baldacchino* over the throne for the Mass. There is a particularly interesting report in the diary of Ioannes Franciscus Firmanus, 1535 (B.M., Add. MS. 8447, fol. 21v.): 'Papa (sc: Paul III) venit ad Cappellam, fecerat enim prius apponi baldacchinum super sedem suam propter aerem, qui ipsum offendebat, et post-modum dixit, quod etiam Alexander Sextus utebatur Baldacchino eodem modo ...'

56. The position of this throne was inaccurately reconstructed by Steinmann, op. cit. in n. 4, i, Pl. IX, directly in line with the pilaster.

57. The present door in the last bay of the left wall (the first counting from the entrance) is already described in G. P. Chattard, *Nuova descrizione del Vaticano*, ii, Rome, 1766, p. 44, and is said by Camesasca, op. cit, in n. 4, p. 133, to be mentioned by Burchard, but he gives no reference; it seems likely that he misread the passage in the *Liber notarum* that refers to the sacristy door (see above, n. 46). I have found no fifteenth- or sixteenth-century source that describes a door in the last bay. L. Pastor, *The History of the Popes*, VIII, ed. R. F. Kerr, London, 1950, p. 304, says that galleries for ladies were erected by Leo X to left and right of the entrance, and he cites in evidence Armellini's extracts from Paris de Grassis (see above, Chapter I, n. 13); but neither this nor any other part of Paris de Grassis's diary says anything about them.

58. E. Müntz, 'Les tapisseries de Raphaël au Vatican', *Chronique des arts*, 1876, p. 262; for a summary of the discussion see White-Shearman, op. cit. in n. 1, p. 216, n. 72. To this account I should now add that the earliest evidence

pattern on the right of the altar, to accommodate it (*Fig.* I, p. 24); it is also referred to by Paris de Grassis,[53] and its purpose was to provide seating for the sacristan and *assistentes Papae*. We can only guess how high it stood above the floor, but it probably made the height of free wall-space on the left of the altar between fifteen and thirty centimetres less than that on the right.

The remaining problem concerning the wall-space inside the screen arises from a movable object, but one that could scarcely be ignored: the papal throne. The rectangular *planum solii* projected from the *presbyterium* on the left side, as we have seen, and it was reached in the same way by three steps. Above this was a broad and semi-permanent platform, the *solium* proper (or *magnum scabellum*), then a readily removable step (*parvum scabellum*), and finally the throne itself, which had a high back normally covered with a *postergale*.[54] It is also clear from an important passage in the *Caeremoniarum opusculum* of Paris de Grassis that—although he disapproved on principle— the *forrerii* often put up a *baldacchino* over the throne;[55] and since this feature was proper to Consistories it may be visualized like a consistorial *baldacchino* of the period with a vertical hanging below the canopy and behind the throne. Just such a *baldacchino* is shown in the illuminated fragment at Chantilly which shows the *Capella papalis* at an earlier date (*Fig.* 4). The significance of this detail is considerable since it would have provided an uncertain obstruction—sometimes present and sometimes not, customary but controversial—to the view of any tapestry hanging in the same wall-space. The position may be defined since channels for rods by which the *baldacchino* was suspended still survive; it would have overlapped the painted pilaster dividing the first and second bays on the left wall and a strip a metre or so wide of the second bay.[56] A blank triangular area, corresponding to its canopy, in the bottom right-hand corner of Botticelli's *Moses in Egypt* fresco (*Fig.* 22) in the second bay of the second register, demonstrates that the presence of the *baldacchino* was allowed for in the original Sixtine decoration.

On the right side of the chapel the *cantoria*, as we have seen, occupies the greater part of the fourth bay of the lowest zone. To be more precise: it eliminates the pilaster between the third and fourth bays, so as to present an obstacle at the immediate limits of the third painted tapestry; and it runs outside the screen to the extent of two-thirds of the part, that is the wider part, of the fourth bay that projects outside the chancel on this side (*Fig.* I, p. 24). With this exception there was, during the period in question, no interruption on the side walls in the outer part of the chapel until the aperture of the entrance door was reached.[57] Nor was there any disturbance of the lower datum-line given by the stone bench, which continued along these walls like the one inside the screen but at a lower level, since these benches are not raised on a step and there is in addition a difference in floor-level at the screen. Any tapestries designed to hang outside the screen should therefore be of uniform height, which would be a little more than that of any tapestries made to hang in the chancel.

We can now turn our attention to the other part of the equation, the tapestries themselves. It should be made clear at once that the ten pieces now exhibited in the Pinacoteca of the Vatican Museum are the only ones that concern us. Of the small number of additions that have been proposed the only one to be taken seriously—since it was made after a design by Raphael —is a *Coronation of the Virgin* which, according to an eighteenth-century inventory, was used in the Sistine Chapel. But this tapestry bears the arms of Paul III (1534–49)[58] and Raphael's drawing was made originally for a different purpose,[59] and so the *Coronation* cannot have been envisaged by

Leo X. It may have been used, and even intended, as an occasional altar-piece after the destruction of Perugino's by Michelangelo; such a practice still continues (*Fig.* 1).

A complete Leonine tapestry (*Fig.* 25) is much more than the translation to another medium, and reversal, of one of the Cartoons now in the Royal Collection (*Pl.* 39). The picture-field, which corresponds more or less accurately to the Cartoon, is surrounded on all sides by a porphyry-coloured frame described, illusionistically, as having a depth about equal to its breadth; its inner surfaces are visible and its front face is decorated with a running *guilloche* design and rosettes at the corners.[60] Below this is a fictive bas-relief, bronze-coloured,[61] of a length equal to that of the 'frame' rather than that of the 'picture' itself. A vertical figured border, equal in height to the framed 'picture' and the 'relief' together, stands to right or left. These borders have been cut in some cases, moved and re-sewn, and their present arrangement is misleading; some, furthermore, are lost. But it seems clear from the rather small number of designs surviving in the Leonine set or reflected in later sets, that only one border separated each 'picture' in the series.[62] Beneath the bas-relief and vertical border runs a blue key- or *grecque*-pattern; and finally each complete tapestry is edged with a narrow strip of dark blue.

In four cases some comment is necessary on the present state of the Vatican tapestries. The least important is that of *Paul preaching at Athens* (*Fig.* 25); after the tapestries were stolen during the Sack of Rome, 1527, the fictive bas-relief, part of the *guilloche* frame and the lower half of the border on the left were cut off.[63] The restoration made in the middle of the century was based upon a partial knowledge of the original in the border, but not at all in the relief. In the same course of events, damage that was obviously considered irreparable was done to the *Blinding of Elymas* (*Fig.* 27); little more than half of the 'picture' survived, and the original composition must be reconstructed from the version (*Fig.* 23) in the set at Mantua, which seems to have have been made from the same Cartoons. The surviving Cartoon itself (*Pl.* 26) is insufficient in this instance since a substantial part has been cut from this too. There is no trace of the design of the 'relief' from this tapestry.

The *Stoning of Stephen* and the *Conversion of Saul* present a more complicated problem (*Figs.* 18, 20). In neither case does the Cartoon survive; but in both cases it appears—from comparison with other early sets like that at Mantua (*Figs.* 19, 21)—that the Cartoon was wider by about 27–28 centimetres than the 'picture' woven in the Leonine set, and in its wider format the figure-composition of each is certainly more satisfactory. The two Leonine tapestries in question also differ from the rest of the series in their *guilloche* frames, which lack the fictive 'inner surface' and are thus slightly narrower than those in the rest of the set. The amount by which these compositions were diminished in weaving corresponds to the combined widths of two of these narrower framing elements. An examination of the 'reliefs' throughout the series suggests what probably happened in the making of these two tapestries. Each 'relief' obeys a sculptural convention in which the design is closed on all sides not only by the termination of the figure-design but also by a notional return to the front plane in the form of a narrow framing strip. The cartoons for these 'reliefs', which must have been made separately, could not be extended by the weavers without an inventive initiative. The designers in Raphael's workshop, on the other hand, had to remember, when calculating the length of each 'relief'-cartoon, to add two frame-widths to the

known to me for the use of the *Coronation* tapestry in the Sistine Chapel is of 1703: V. Vittoria, *Indice dell'opere di Rafaello*, Royal Library, Windsor, MS. H.H.-C., p. 88. Less plausible additions to the set are listed in White-Shearman, op. cit., p. 196, n. 12.

59. J. Shearman, 'The Chigi Chapel in S. Maria del Popolo', *Journal of the Warburg and Courtauld Institutes*, xxiv, 1961, p. 159.

60. The frames of the *Stoning of Stephen* and the *Conversion of Saul*, however, have no visible recession, and lion-masks replace rosettes in the corners.

61. With the exception of the one below the *Healing of the Lame Man*, which is pink.

62. The problem of the original arrangement of the borders is discussed below, p. 43.

63. See below, p. 141.

64. This calculation has to be made with particular care. The Mantuan tapestry, which is convincing as a reproduction of the original figure-design, is an accurate guide to the proper width of the lost cartoon but not to its height. The Vatican *Stoning of Stephen* is appreciably less in height than the rest of the series and its weavers could have had no reason for compressing the design vertically; an explanation for this peculiarity will appear later. When other sets of tapestries were made from these cartoons, however, uniformity of height was natural and achieved in the case of the *Stoning of Stephen* by raising the heavenly group on the right.

65. Any tapestry intended for the altar-wall would be provided, on the side nearest the altar, with a real vertical frame—the pilaster of the altar-piece; additional tapestry-borders at this point seem unlikely.

66. The original system of the Chiostro dello Scalzo must be reconstructed too; see J. Shearman, 'The Chiostro dello Scalzo', *Mitteilungen des kunsthistorischen Institutes in Florenz*, ix, 1960, pp. 207 ff.

67. An instruction may be imagined similar to that of Gabriele d'Ancona to the sacristan of the Sistine Chapel (see above, Chapter I, p. 4, n. 22).

length of the 'picture'-cartoon. It would not be surprising if they forgot the addition twice and supplied 'relief'- and 'picture'-cartoons of the same length; nor would it be surprising if the weavers, faced with the cartoons so delivered, decided to trim the 'picture' (but by the minimum, adopting a thinner frame that would seem uniform with the rest), rather than to extend the 'reliefs'. No other set of tapestries made from the main Cartoons included the 'reliefs', so the trimming never had to be repeated.

Even if this interpretation is not correct it is clear that Raphael's intentions must be judged from the design—the whole design—for the principal Cartoons for each tapestry, which means that we must reconstruct the widths that he calculated for these two on the basis of the later sets. This adjustment has the practical effect of reconstructing the intended *Stoning of Stephen*[64] with proportions (but not dimensions) identical with those of the *Miraculous Draught of Fishes*, that is to say a little over square, and the intended *Conversion of Saul* with a length equal to those of five others in the series.

A preliminary glance at the tapestry-set makes clear three points about their intended relationship to the decoration of the chapel. The first is deduced from their dimensions. There are small but not insignificant variations in their height, but very wide variations in their width, and it is obvious that each piece was designed for a specific and predetermined position. The second point places a limitation upon these positions. The vertical borders, one between each 'picture', must have been intended to replace the painted pilasters which, in the Sixtine decoration, separate the fictive Della Rovere tapestries; when the tapestries were in place, then, the vertical system by which the walls were articulated would still be continued in the lowest zone. An uncertainty in the implementation of this principle occurs only in the corners of the chapel where, in the original decoration, before Michelangelo cut back the end wall for the *Last Judgement*, painted half-pilasters met at the angle (*Fig.* I, p. 24). A reinterpretation of this situation in tapestry is somewhat unlikely to have been made by hanging a single border round the corner, and improbable too is a solution that placed a border on one wall and not the other. It is likely that in such a case the 'pictures' would have been separated by two borders, one closing each wall.[65]

The third point concerns the 'reliefs', which are equal in height to the seat-backs of that part of the peripheral stone bench that runs across the inner side of the screen. These vertical surfaces of uncarved stone would normally be covered by textile hangings (*spalliere*). The tapestry 'reliefs' must have been intended to continue on the same level and to serve the same function above the wall-benches, with the additional practical purpose of lifting the 'pictures' into uninterrupted view above the rows of seated prelates. In principle the system of Raphael's decoration is similar to that of Andrea del Sarto's fresco-cycle in the Chiostro dello Scalzo in Florence, begun about 1510–11; for in each case pilaster-borders rose from a stone bench and separated the narrative scenes, beneath each of which was a fictive relief-*spalliera*.[66]

It is probably safe to assume that the location of each tapestry was written down in the form of an instruction to the *forrerii* whose duty it would be to take them from, and return them to, the papal *guardaroba* as occasion demanded.[67] But neither this nor any other text exists which can provide a starting point for the reconstruction. The next steps can only be taken by interpreting further visual evidence in the tapestries themselves and by considering the conventions within which Raphael may have worked. In this situation it is helpful to retreat a little way from the particular problem and to judge what, in general terms, we have a right to anticipate. And then it seems that we should demand four conditions of a reconstruction of the intended hanging. The first and most obvious is that it should work in the dimensional sense within the limitations described above—taking account, that is, of all obstacles present on the walls in 1515 and conforming reasonably well to the structural system of the existing decoration; there must be a complete explanation in these terms of the many variations in height and width. The second condition is that the narrative sequence of the events in the Gospels and the Acts of the Apostles should be respected unless there is some very compelling reason to suppose otherwise. Exceptions to this rule can be seen on the walls and ceiling of the Sistine Chapel itself, and in the Chiostro dello Scalzo, but in such cases the reason is a contingency momentarily modifying a principle, and the principle is seen to be the same.

The adherence to convention is of course functional in all narrative cycles since it facilitates reading and instruction. And for the same reason we may expect that Raphael would conform to the conventions of disposing narrative cycles in Christian buildings. There are two traditions that might apply, and both options must remain open until we find a reason for closing one of them. If the ten tapestries formed one continuous series, tradition would lead us to expect it to start on the right of the altar (as we look at it) and then to unfold from left to right, clockwise, around the walls. If, however, the tapestries were conceived as two series in parallel, then we should expect one to begin on the right of the altar and to run left to right down the right wall towards the entrance, and the other, mirror-wise, to begin on the left of the altar and to run right to left down the left wall; this tradition is already represented in the Sistine Chapel by the two history-cycles of the Lives of Moses and of Christ.

Finally it is certainly legitimate to demand a fourth condition of the reconstruction of any monumental scheme of decoration designed by Raphael—or indeed by almost any thinking artist of his period: we may anticipate that the direction of the light represented as falling within the 'pictures', on the 'frames' and on the 'reliefs', will correspond to the direction of the real light in the chapel-space. It is true of course that the movement of the sun seems to give some latitude of choice, here as in other chapels, but in fact there was unanimity among all artists who worked in this one. On the ceiling and on the walls, in figurative scenes and on fictive reliefs, frames and tapestries, the notional light was always identified with that which originally came from the two windows in the altar-wall, which in this case is to the West.[68] The choice was probably equally influenced by considerations of practical convenience (a side-light being desirable on the longer walls) and by those of meaning (the light from the altar being a symbol of Divine Grace). In any case Raphael was in no position, and had no evident incentive, to make a different choice; and his own earlier practice, as well as his words, demonstrate that he could not have been oblivious of the point.[69]

It may seem natural to suggest another condition of the reconstruction: that the subjects of the tapestries should bear some meaningful relationship to those of the Sixtine historical frescoes. The *Charge to Peter* tapestry, for example, may seem to assume its natural place beneath Perugino's *Donation of the Keys*. But anticipation along these lines is extremely unwise, for two reasons. Firstly the meaning of any individual tapestry—its meaning, that is, beyond illustration of a text—is in no case unequivocal, and the various possibilities can best be controlled after we know the context. And secondly

68. The existence of these windows, rightly stressed in the reconstructions by Steinmann, op. cit. in n. 4, i, p. 141, and Wilde, op. cit. in n. 36, p. 65, is proved by (i) a passage from Paris de Grassis, 1513, quoted in Chapter I, p. 9, n. 58, (ii) a ground-plan of the early Cinquecento in the Uffizi (UA 287), and (iii) an unnoticed exterior view of the West end of the chapel in an engraving, *c.* 1530–35, *The Worship of Psyche*, by the Master of the Die (B. xv, p. 213, No. 40).

69. In the *Stanze* Raphael had already made the natural choice of the southern windows as the notional source for his painted light. When he was asked in 1515 to paint a picture for Isabella d'Este he wrote to Castiglione to ascertain 'la mesura del quadro et il lume' (V. Golzio, *Raffaello nei documenti . . .*, Vatican City, 1936, p. 37).

the diversity and richness of exegetical comment on the texts in question, combined with that kind of human resourcefulness which seems particularly inspired by iconographical problems, makes it possible to draw a connection in virtually any juxtaposition. A random allocation would, one assumes, be less illuminating than the right one, but we cannot anticipate the degree or quality of illumination that Raphael and Leo X, or his aides, intended. That has to be deduced from the reconstruction and is one of the principal reasons for making it.

Our problem, in any case, can be solved by applying the four conditions already imposed. It is simplest to consider first the variations in the described direction of light. In four tapestries—the *Miraculous Draught of Fishes*, the *Charge to Peter*, the *Healing of the Lame Man*, and the *Death of Ananias*—the light in the 'pictures', the 'reliefs' and the frames is from the left, and there can be no doubt that they were to be placed on the right of the altar, as we look at it. In the remaining six—the *Stoning of Stephen*, the *Conversion of Saul*, the *Blinding of Elymas*, the *Sacrifice at Lystra*, *Paul in Prison* and *Paul preaching at Athens*—the light which comes from the right attests their location on the left of the altar. In one of these, the *Conversion of Saul* (*Fig.* 20), the 'picture' itself is uninformative, since the described light, in exact illustration of the text, radiates from the central apparition of Christ; but the framing and 'relief' of this tapestry conform with the group which must go on the left side. A second distinction separates the tapestries into the same groups; in the first four the winding of the *guilloche* frames above and below runs from left to right, and in the other six its direction is reversed. This is a small detail, but an interesting one which demonstrates the care that was taken in planning and manufacture.

The division produced by these considerations coincides with an iconographical one; the four tapestries to be placed on the right of the altar are concerned with the story of Saint Peter, while the six on the left, including the *Stoning of Stephen*, illustrate the story of Saint Paul. This gives us a clear indication that of the two traditions to which the tapestries may be expected to conform (our third condition), only one applies; the tapestries were conceived as two complementary and parallel series. We may therefore take the next step, and arrange the Petrine set so that it reads from left to right in narrative order (our second condition) and ask where, on the right side, these tapestries will fit the available wall-spaces (our first condition). The Petrine set includes three tapestries of standard proportions, a long rectangle the length of which is about equal to that of the fictive tapestries between painted pilasters on the side walls. One, however, the *Miraculous Draught*, is significantly shorter and must be the first (the text is Luke v. 3–10), at the left end of the sequence. A comparison between this sequence and the wall-surfaces of the chapel restored to their condition in the Leonine period (*Fig.* I, p. 24) offers one possibility for their positions, and only one. The *Miraculous Draught*, with one border on its right, is of exactly the right width (5·1 metres) to hang on the altar-wall, covering the sacristy door, and the *Charge to Peter* (John xxi. 15–17), the *Healing of the Lame Man* (Acts iii. 1–11) and the *Death of Ananias* (Acts v. 1–11) could follow in the three uninterrupted bays on the right side of the chancel, from *presbyterium* to *cantoria* (*Fig.* II, p. 25).

An element of proof appears when we test this arrangement, for it will be seen that the landscape is continuous between the *Miraculous Draught* and the *Charge to Peter* (*Figs.* 13, 14), and that this continuity is calculated so as to allow for their separation by one or two vertical pilaster-borders, but by no wider interval. In other words these two tapestries were intended to be adjacent and in the sequence deduced, that is with the *Miraculous Draught* on the left of the *Charge to Peter*. The whole Petrine set clothes the available wall-area so accurately (*Fig.* II, drawn to scale) that even the elimination of the fourth pilaster by the *cantoria* is accounted for. There remains one possibility for error, arising from an assumption not yet justified, that the four Petrine tapestries were intended to hang in succession, without later additions between the second and the third, or between the third and the fourth; there could be no objection on grounds of dimensions, lighting or narrative sequence, to a position outside the screen for the *Healing of the Lame Man* or the *Death of Ananias*, and hypothetical intervening subjects, such as *Pentecost*, come readily to mind. Such a speculation, however, would entail the conclusion that an incomplete series was ordered in a peculiarly fragmentary way; and it is rendered in the highest degree improbable by an examination of the Pauline set.

The Petrine story was designed to unfold on the right side of the chapel from left to right like the Sixtine Christ-cycle above, and like the Christ-cycle it was to begin on the altar-wall. Clearly we should now test the self-evident corollary, that the Pauline story was to be disposed in the reverse sequence, beginning on the altar-wall and unfolding from right to left, in both respects like the Moses-cycle above. The first tapestry, the *Stoning of Stephen* (Acts vii. 54–60), was intended, as we have seen, to have the same proportions as the first of the Petrine set but also to be a little smaller; it would fit comfortably on the left of the altar, and the reasons for its shorter dimensions can be reviewed later. The *Conversion of Saul* (Acts ix. 1–7), in its planned format, the *Blinding of Elymas* (Acts xiii. 6–12) and the *Sacrifice at Lystra* (Acts xiv. 7–18) would then occupy the first three bays of the left wall in the same manner as the Petrine set on the right wall. These should be followed by *Paul in Prison* (Acts xvi. 23–26); and this very narrow tapestry would fit into the part of the fourth bay that projects inside the screen—in other words into that part of the wall-area which is obstructed on the right side of the chancel by the *cantoria*. And as on the right wall so on the left, these tapestries in these positions will exactly clothe the length of the wall up to the permanent obstruction which, on this side, is presented by the screen (*Fig.* II, p. 25). There remains the last of the Pauline set, *Paul preaching at Athens* (Acts xvii. 15–34), which is precisely of the length required to fill the longer part of the fourth bay outside the screen. The way in which the irregular dimensions of the last two tapestries are accounted for by the interruption made by the screen guarantees, it seems, that they are in the right positions; and from this guarantee there follows a reasonable confidence that the rest of the Pauline set are rightly placed and that it was never intended to insert, at some later date, additional subjects between the ten initially ordered.

Between the first two tapestries of the Pauline set there is again a continuity of landscape background (*Figs.* 18, 20); this is certainly not as obvious as the one between the first two Petrine tapestries, but it was just as carefully contrived since beyond the wooded hill on the right of the *Conversion of Saul* there appears the continuation of the white, apparently snow-covered, slope that is so prominent on the left of the *Stoning of Stephen*. Elements of proof for the reconstruction in this pattern can, furthermore, be found in other details. The design of the *Blinding of Elymas* is one of these. The position suggested for this tapestry, in the second bay, also places it where a strip down its right side would be behind the papal throne; and we saw that this throne could be completed by a *baldacchino*, the presence of

70. In the Appendix below, p. 166, the dimensions of the Cartoons and tapestries are set out with a reconstruction, where possible, of those intended by Raphael; it will be seen that the weavers took liberties with vertical dimensions in the Pauline set, and that the intended height of *Paul preaching at Athens* cannot be established because its 'relief' has been replaced.

71. These two tapestries are 4·50 m. and 4·90 m. high respectively.

72. I have in mind such practicalities as the placing of the processional Crucifix in the left corner, for which some wall-fixture may have been provided.

which was, however, controversial and unpredictable. The *Blinding of Elymas* (*Fig.* 23), surely as a result of this unpredictability, is unique among Renaissance historical compositions in that there is a narrow vertical section on the right—the pier with niche, statue and herms—which is, so to speak, optional; it may be read either as an element in the space of the narrative or as a frame to it, and the composition would be complete and intelligible whether this strip was visible or eclipsed by the *baldacchino*. The brilliance of Raphael's response to a strange problem is illustrated by the fact that few if any observers of the Cartoon (*Pl.* 26)—where the 'optional' section is missing—are aware of the loss of about one-fifth of the original composition.

After four and a half centuries of use (and abuse) the tapestries, not surprisingly, vary in their vertical dimension, and the inevitability of uneven stretching should warn us against attaching too much importance to such discrepancies.[70] Nevertheless one outstanding case is worth notice: the *Stoning of Stephen*, which is appreciably the shortest in the vertical dimension; when hung with the rest its lower edge would not only be above that of the rest of the Pauline set but also above that of the tapestry proposed as its pendant on the altar-wall, the *Miraculous Draught*.[71] It seems clear that this irregularity was necessitated by the low wall-bench for the *assistentes* which, as we have seen, was an obstruction that existed only on the left of the altar. The presence of that bench presented Raphael, if we are right so far, with a problem with alternative solutions. His desire to disguise the asymmetry as far as possible may be taken for granted, and he could do so either by making the pendant tapestries for the altar-wall of equal lateral dimensions but necessarily of different proportions, or by making their proportions the same and accepting inequality in both dimensions. He chose the latter. Whether he was right to do so we cannot judge, since the choice may have been influenced by practical considerations of which we have no knowledge.[72] And he may well have been influenced by the solution that had been evolved by the original designer of the *opus sectile* floor (*Fig.* I, p. 24). For the projection of the bench by some 35 centimetres had led necessarily to the compression of the floor-pattern in the left part of the *presbyterium*; the necessity, however, concerned only the longitudinal, or East–West, dimension, and it was by choice that the designer applied a proportional compression on the altar side with the result, evidently considered visually acceptable, of shifting the centre of the pattern nearly 20 centimetres nearer the centre-line of the chapel than that on the right. It is not easy to follow the floor-designer's thinking—which again might have been determined by exigencies now unknown—but it is clear that Raphael was presented with a precedent for his own slight lateral asymmetry when he came to consider the same corner of the chapel (*Fig.* II, p. 25).

The reconstruction of the tapestry-sequence proposed so far implies that he made another choice when an obstacle prevented a neat solution. The three tapestries on the right wall, when each is assumed to include one lateral border, do cover the wall-surface up to the *cantoria*; but since the latter eliminates the painted pilaster that would otherwise have closed the third bay, the vertical border on the right of the *Death of Ananias* would be out of alignment with the painted pilaster in the register above (*Fig.* II, p. 25). It may at first sight seem odd that he should not avoid this misalignment by the simple expedient of omitting a closing border. But a glance at his problems and apparent solutions on the opposite side of the chapel suggests a practical reason for a decision to include it; for the gap between the screen in its original position and the fictive pilaster closing the third bay of the left wall could not have been more than about 75 centimetres, and a figurative tapestry of exactly these dimensions is beyond the bounds of serious consideration. He seems to have solved that problem by expanding the width of *Paul in Prison* to make a practical (but still difficult) proportion,[73] thereby displacing the border that separated it from the *Sacrifice at Lystra* by about the width of the painted pilaster it replaced. It was this displacement on the left side of the chapel that was exactly mirrored on the right.

At this point we should consider the effect of this reconstruction upon the sequences of subjects represented in the 'reliefs'. These, unlike the principal subjects, are grouped into three sequences, a separate one for each wall, but each sequence reads in its correct order.[74] On the altar-wall are shown the two principal events in the patron's career in the Church. On the left of the altar is the entry into Florence of the young Cardinal Giovanni after his investiture at Fiesole, 1492 (*Fig. 18*); the direction, from left to right, is continued on the right of the altar in two scenes, the entry into Rome for the Conclave of 1513 and the election to the papacy (*Fig. 13*). On the right wall, reading again from left to right, are scenes illustrating the reversals of the secular fortunes of the patron and of his house: beneath the *Charge to Peter* the sack of Palazzo Medici in Florence and the flight of the cardinal, 1494 (*Fig. 14*); beneath the *Healing of the Lame Man* the capture of the cardinal, then papal legate, at the battle of Ravenna and his escape to Mantua, 1512 (*Fig. 16*); and beneath the *Death of Ananias* the recall of the Medici to Florence by *parlamento* and the triumphant re-entry, both later in 1512 (*Fig. 17*). In fact the two events shown beneath the second tapestry are arranged in the wrong order. No error occurred in the painter's or the weaver's workshops in the reversal of the cartoon for this 'relief', because the direction of the light is consistent with the rest of the tapestry and all appropriate gestures are right-handed. It is probable, however, that a different error was made. In some cases the 'reliefs' are woven integrally with the main scene (as in the *Death of Ananias*); in others the 'reliefs' were woven separately (or cut at some later date and re-sewn), and this is the situation in the *Healing of the Lame Man*. In fact the 'relief' is itself in three parts, stitched together, and it would be natural if there had been three separate cartoons since the two historiated sections are divided by a central heraldic motif. We may suppose, therefore, either that the instructions to the weavers were inadequate (or misunderstood), or that a 'relief' initially properly composed was later cut and wrongly re-assembled.

The 'reliefs' on the left wall are reduced to two by the loss of those below the *Blinding of Elymas* and *Paul preaching at Athens* (a third remains under *Paul in Prison*, but its subject has not been satisfactorily explained); it is clear, nevertheless, that the sequence represented events in the life of Saint Paul complementary to the main scenes above, and that like them they were to be read from right to left. Under the *Conversion of Saul* is a sarcophagus-like frieze showing Saul persecuting the Christians (*Fig. 20*, Acts viii. 3), while beneath the *Sacrifice at Lystra* there are two episodes from the principal event following that at Lystra, the disputation on the circumcision of the Gentiles at Jerusalem, between Paul and Barnabas and the Apostles and Elders, and the departure in peace of Paul, Barnabas, Judas Barsabas and Silas on their now-approved mission to the Gentiles (*Fig. 24*, Acts xv. 4–21, and 22). Thus the sequences of 'reliefs' on left and right of the chancel begin and end with symbolic acts of persecution and reunion, on the one hand between Paul and the Church, on the other between the Medici (or Cardinal Giovanni personally) and Florence. It seems that no permutation of the

73. The width of this piece is now 1·3 m. It is also possible that another practical consideration entered Raphael's mind and reinforced this decision—that of controlling the distortion of the tapestry by giving it the greatest possible lateral dimension; that this could well have been in his mind is particularly suggested by the fact that the border between this piece and the *Sacrifice at Lystra* seems to have been attached to the right of the former and not, as would apparently be more regular, on the left of the latter. This detail is dependent upon observations of the *grecque* patterns at the base of each piece which, in their present state, may be either closed in a manner that is clearly planned or cut in a manner that is equally clearly unintended. All deductions based on this evidence are subject to a possible error, since the *grecque*-strips were woven separately and could have been moved and re-sewn. If those under the two pieces in question have not been moved, the implications are that the *Paul in Prison* was originally woven with a border on its right (the *grecque*-pattern is cut on this side), whereas the *Sacrifice at Lystra* was woven without a border on either side (the *grecque* is closed at both ends). The implications for the remaining tapestries are as follows: *Miraculous Draught*: border only on right; *Charge to Peter*: border on both sides; *Healing of Lame Man*: left side indeterminate, border on right; *Death of Ananias*: border only on right; *Stoning of Stephen*: see below; *Conversion of Saul*: no border on either side; *Blinding of Elymas*: *grecque* missing. The *Stoning of Stephen* seems to be an example where the *grecque* has been re-sewn; as at present arranged it is closed on the left but open on the right. However a peculiarity in this tapestry suggests that there was once a border on the left; the outer blue edging, which normally encloses a complete tapestry, survives on the left in this case but has outside it fragments of red, cut and turned over, which seem to be the remains of the red beaded 'moulding' that frames a vertical border. I cannot suggest why there should be no border woven on either side of the *Conversion of Saul*, unless their absence had something to do with the papal throne; I assume that free-hanging borders were provided.

74. The identifications and significance of these subjects are discussed in the next Chapter, p. 84.

positions of the ten tapestries can produce another result that makes sense simultaneously of the narrative sequences in principal and subsidiary events. The reconstruction thus receives a confirmation independent of earlier arguments.

The suggested disposition of the tapestries cannot be deduced, as we have seen, from any document; but once made, it can be compared with a document that demands, and now receives, an explanation. The first exhibition of the tapestries, on 26 December 1519, was witnessed by the intelligent and artistically critical Venetian, Marcantonio Michiel, who recorded that 'the pope put on display in the chapel seven pieces of tapestry, since the eighth had not arrived'.[75] Later in the same passage he tells us which the seven were, and he puts them in order: the *Miraculous Draught*, the *Charge to Peter*, the *Healing of the Lame Man*, the *Stoning of Stephen*, the *Conversion of Saul*, the *Blinding of Elymas* and the *Sacrifice at Lystra*. If the reconstruction is correct it is intelligible that he thought that only one more was due (the *Death of Ananias*), for the tapestries he lists would leave only one other gap, a very narrow one that could easily be overlooked, for the *Paul in Prison*; unless specifically told he could not have reckoned for one more large tapestry outside the screen, *Paul preaching at Athens*. The order in which he lists the seven that had been delivered is significant because in several cases he gives wrong titles for tapestries, which remain, however, identifiable;[76] he records, then, the order in which he saw them and not that in which he reasoned that they ought to be listed. And so it would seem that he looked to right and then to left in the chancel, at a hanging corresponding to this reconstruction.

The reconstruction, nevertheless, has two significant features against which immediate objection is natural. Firstly, it places the Petrine set on the right wall, that is to say on the left from the point of view of the altar and its Crucifix, when the opposite might be anticipated. And secondly it leaves us with one tapestry, *Paul preaching at Athens*, hanging alone outside the screen. Each of these features requires discussion.

The question whether Saint Peter or Saint Paul should be placed on the right (our left) of the Crucifix or altar is a *cause célèbre* which is, however, difficult to examine because its history is still to be written. It is difficult, too, because the problem has a number of discrete contexts among which the appropriate one may not be immediately identifiable. One context, naturally, is the visual one: what could be seen that would constitute authoritative

---

75. 'Adì 27 dicembre 1519. Roma. Queste feste di Natale il Papa messe fuori in Capella 7 pezzi di razzo perchè l'ottavo non era fornito fatti in ponente ...' The text is most easily accessible in V. Golzio, *Raffaello nei documenti...*, Vatican City, 1936, pp. 103–4, but this version omits a passage which is not insignificant and which is here italicized: Michiel says that the tapestries were 'giudicata la più bella cosa, che sia stata fatta in eo genere a nostri giorni, benchè fussino celebri *li razzi di Papa Giulio de l'anticamera*, li razzi del Marchese di Mantova del disegno del Mantegna ...' etc. Julius's tapestries were perhaps also figurative; I think that they do not survive, but were probably among the 'Paramenta facta sive empta pro ornatu Camerae Pont. tempore fe. me. D. Iulii', listed in the 1518–21 inventory (see above, p. 6, n. 28), fol. 7. The Mantegna tapestries were probably those, now lost, referred to in Gonzaga documents of 1465–9 (P. Kristeller, *Andrea Mantegna*, Berlin-Leipzig, 1902, pp. 524–6; I owe this suggestion to Michael Hirst).

76. 'Le historie di detti razzi erano, la Conversione di Santo Andrea, et San Iacomo nelle barche pescatorie; la consegnatione, che fa Christo a S. Pietro delle Chiavi; la conversione di Santo ... nel Tempio di Salomone, per el sanare di alcuni storpiati, che fa Christo; la lapidatione di Santo Stefano; la Conversione di S. Paulo; la Conversione di Sergio Consule per lo illuminar di un cieco, che fa S. Paulo; la resistenza che fa S.P. di sacrificare nel Tempio di Marte agli Idoli.'

77. It is, however, doubtful whether it would be justified by a really close view of the problem. According to J. Kollwitz, 'Christus als Lehrer und die Gesetzübergabe an Petrus', *Römische Quartalschrift*, xliv, 1936, p. 56, the earliest (mid-fourth-century) groups show Peter on Christ's right, and he attributes the general reversal in the fifth century to the influence of the *Traditio Legis* subject; a contrary view is expressed by E. von Dobschütz, *Der Apostel Paulus*, ii, Halle, 1928, pp. 5 ff. The greater number of Early Christian gilt glass portraits of the Apostles show Peter on Paul's right. From our point of view it is significant that in the 'Boldetti medallion' in the Vatican, almost certainly a sixteenth-century fake intended to conform with what was thought to be ancient usage, Paul is on the right of Peter (E. Dinkler, 'Die ersten Petrusdarstellungen', *Marburger Jahrbuch für Kunstwissenschaft*, xi, 1938, p. 11).

78. Flavio Biondo, letter to Gregorio Lolli Piccolomini, 30 September 1461: 'In absida ... Sancti Petri superimposito Salvator medio in loco musivo est pictus Dominus Deus noster et hinc Petrus inde Paulus musivo pariter sunt depicti, in eaque trium imaginum figuratione Petrus, sicut in altari et plumbeo, adeuntibus inspicientibus dexter, sinister Paulus est positus': *Scritti inediti e rari*, ed. B. Nogara, Rome, 1927, p. 207, Lett. 20; cf. also Lett. 19, to the same: 'sicut est in altari Sancti Petri', in which he makes it clear that the statues on the altar were so disposed. In that case there is an ambiguity in his statement since the High Altar was reversed with the celebrant facing the nave, not the apse; it seems to me probable that he meant that Saint Peter appeared on the right as one looked at the front of the altar, rather than at its back. A *dossale* for the High Altar is described in a fourteenth-century inventory 'cum nostra domina in medio et a dextris eius sanctus Paulus ... et a sinistris sanctus Petrus' (Müntz and A. L. Frothingham, *Il tesoro della Basilica di S. Pietro in Vaticano*, Rome, 1883, 14).

79. The composition is known from a number of copies; see, for example, W. Oakeshott, *The Mosaics of Rome*, London, 1967, pp. 67 ff., and Fig. 29; another is used by A. Schiavo, *S. Pietro in Vaticano*, Rome, 1960, Pl. II. The mosaic probably corresponded fairly accurately to the original Constantinian decoration; see P. Künzle, 'Bemerkungen zum Lob auf Sankt Peter und Sankt Paul von Prudentius', *Rivista di storia della chiesa in Italia*, xi, 1957, p. 309, and C. Ihm, *Die Programme der christlichen Apsis*

precedent. But the instant result of this line of enquiry is impeccable authority for either disposition. From the point of view of Paris de Grassis, as we shall see, there was an 'old' tradition in which Saint Paul was found on the right of Christ (our left). It is exemplified (and the epithet is to this extent justified)[77] by the greater number of Early Christian mosaics in Rome, by papal seals of all periods down to Leo X, and by individual cases in sculpture and painting far into the sixteenth century. A list of examples would be pointless because it would also be endless; but it would include Michelangelo's frescoes in the Pauline Chapel. A singularly authoritative sequence of this kind was the one presented to the visitor to Saint Peter's: first Filarete's bronze doors of Eugenius IV, then the High Altar itself,[78] and finally the apse-mosaic of Innocent III.[79] However the same visitor had previously passed the colossal statues of the two Apostles placed the other way round by Pius II on the steps leading up to the basilica.[80] There is an enormous number of examples of this disposition too, which Sixtus IV also favoured and which seems to have become the rule in the later sixteenth century.[81] Protests, however, continued to be made and curiosity in the problem continued.[82]

It is Paris de Grassis, once again, who comes to our aid—providentially, and only because he was intensely irritated. His first comment comes in 1510 in a passage in the *Diarium* in which he is discussing Feasts on papal name-days: '... Paul II (1464–71) established that the image of Saint Paul should be placed once more *ad locum antiquum apud crucem*, that is to say on the right of the Crucifix, and that the image of Saint Peter should be placed on its left'; he suspects Pope Paul of partiality and condemns the practice 'for the image of Saint Peter ought to be placed, *tanquam dignioris*, on the right, not the left, of the Crucifix ... and popes should place Saint Peter on the right ... for they are his successors, and Vicars'.[83] In order to understand this passage it is necessary to distinguish two issues in these disputes. The first, which had bedevilled the location of Pius II's statues, was simply what was meant by right and left; from the internal position of Paris de Grassis this problem had been resolved once and for all by Innocent VIII (1484–92): right and left were defined with respect to the object or image in question, not to the view of the spectator.[84] There remained the second issue: what privileges or other considerations determined the allocation of the one position or the other? Paris de Grassis must have known very well that he was over-simplifying the problem by insisting upon the Primacy of Peter as the decisive point. A little later he wrote a marvellously disingenuous document in which he shows that he could be just as obtuse as he was observant (his successors generally called him 'Crassus').

In the form in which this document is preserved it is a fifteen-page *tractatus* entitled *Utra ex statuis Apostolorum Petri, an Pauli in capella palatina, & alibi sit alteri ritè praeferenda, qualiterve locanda*, incorporated into (but not in the first place written for) his *Caeremoniarum opusculum*.[85] The title particularizes but the text generalizes, and it is clear that he is concerned with the wider issue of the placing of all images of the Apostles. He begins by saying that he thinks it is quite obvious that the image of Saint Peter should be given precedence 'non modo in sacra aula palatina (i.e. the Sistine Chapel); sed semper, & ubique' (in fact the rule in the Sistine Chapel, to the contrary, was that the statue of Saint Paul should be placed on the right of the Crucifix).[86] He then launches into the proofs of the *Primatus Petri*, which do not for the moment concern us, and returns to the dispute by way of an historical sketch of recent events. Nicholas V had called for an enquiry before decorating his chapel in the Vatican Palace,[87] so had Pius II in connection

lerei, Wiesbaden, 1960, pp. 22, 128; for contrary views, see C. Davis-Weyer, 'Das Traditio-Legis-Bild und seine Nachfolge', *Münchner Jahrbuch der bildenden Kunst*, Ser. 3, xii, 1961, p. 16.

80. The discussions about this location, controversial at the time, are collected by R. O. Rubinstein, 'Pius II's Piazza San Pietro and Saint Andrew's Head', *Essays in the History of Architecture presented to Rudolf Wittkower*, London, 1967, pp. 27 ff.

81. One of the most important texts is that of Francesco Mucanti (a successor of Paris de Grassis), *De sanctorum apostolorum Petri et Pauli imaginibus*, Rome, 1573; the work was commissioned by Gregory XIII so that some clarification could be introduced into the chaos of custom. A polemical work produced at the same moment is Antonius Georgius, *Statua divi Pauli a dextris divi principis ecclesie Petri non removenda*, Rome, 1573. An anonymous tract, *Cur in Bulla summi Pontificis, et in plurimis vetustissimis templis Paulus ad dextram Petrus ad sinistram ponitur*, is bound with the MS. of Mucantius's text in Bibl. Vat., MS. Barb. Lat. 2624.

82. E.g. Cardinal Bellarmino, *De romani pontificis ecclesiastica hierarchia* (c. 1600), Bk. I, cap. xxvii, in J. T. de Rocaberti, *Bibliotheca maxima pontificia*, xviii, Rome, 1698, p. 508 (cf. p. 49, n. 25); P. G. V. Giannini, *Notizie istoriche ... della ven. antichissima immagine del SS.mo Salvatore ... Coll'aggiunta delle ragioni, e motivi, per cui l'Immagine di S. Paolo si trova situata mano alla destra di S. Pietro*, Rome, 1798, pp. 17 ff.; and F. Cancellieri, *Memorie storiche delle sacre teste dei santi apostoli Pietro e Paolo e della loro solenne ricognizione nella Basilica Lateranense*, 2nd ed., Rome, 1852 (with a long bibliography, p. 48, n. 2). This literature tends to be repetitive.

83. B.M., Add. MS. 8442, fol. 39v.

84. *Liber caeremoniarum* of Burchard-Patrizi, 1488, ed. Marcellus, cit. in n. 4, fols. cxxiv, r., cxxxvii, v.

85. Bibl. Vat., MS. Vat. Lat. 5634/1, fols. 39r. ff.

86. Paris de Grassis, *Caeremonialium Regularum supplementum: et Additiones*, Bibl. Vat., MS. Vat. Lat. 5634/2 (dated 1515), fol. 34r.: 'ponantur S. sancti pauli ad dextram crucis: et sancti Petri ad eiusdem crucis sinistram. Quoniam sic ex consuetudine capellae apostolicae semper locari ...'

87. Neither Apostle appears in Fra Angelico's decoration; perhaps he is referring to a lost altar-piece.

88. The occasion is not clear. He made this choice for the decoration of the apse of the Cappella Sistina in Old Saint Peter's; other contingencies demanding discussion were the location of the reliefs on the new ciborium over the High Altar of Saint Peter's, and the decoration of the end wall of the Sistine Chapel where, in the upper zone between the windows, it is probable that a figure of Christ was painted in the centre with Saint Peter on His right (our left) and Saint Paul on His left (Wilde, op. cit. in n. 36, p. 70). I think it is less likely that any problem would have arisen with Perugino's Sistine altar-piece (*Fig.* 9), for the placing of Saints Peter and Paul in that case was conditioned by the necessary introduction of the pope by Saint Peter to the Virgin on her right hand.

89. E.g. Innocent III, *Sermo iii in communi de Evangelistis, P.L.,* 217, col. 608; Durandus, *Rationale,* VII, xliv, 6; and cf. Mucanti, op. cit. in n. 81, p. 8.

90. Petrus Damianus, *Opusculum de picturis principum apostolorum, P.L.,* 145, cols. 589 ff. (a letter to Abbot Desiderius, explaining the location of Paul on the right of Peter 'in imaginibus picturarum per universas adjacentes Romae provincias', which he believes is the ancient custom introduced by Constantine and Silvester). For the title of Benjamin, cf. Genesis xxxv. 18. The text of Petrus Damianus is quoted by Mucanti, op. cit. in n. 81, p. 4.

91. I have not found the text of this Bull, which is cited by Durandus, loc. cit. in n. 89, who describes its contents, and by Mucanti, op. cit. in n. 81, p. 8, who attributes it to Innocent III; it decreed that the head of Paul should be placed on the right of the Crucifix, that of Peter on its left. It was probably connected with the relics of San Giovanni in Laterano, which were set up in new busts in these positions by Urban V in 1369, under the ciborium of the High Altar; see especially Cancellieri, op. cit. in n. 82, and I. Machetti, 'Orafi senesi', *Diana,* iv, 1929, p. 44; the busts in these positions are shown in a drawing by Borromini, *c.* 1650, reproduced in *Francesco Borromini, disegni e documenti Vaticani,* Biblioteca Apostolica Vaticana, October 1967, Pl. II, No. 36. The inscriptions on the busts were related closely to the ideas of Petrus Damianus. It should be noted that the Bull attributed to Innocent III would be consistent not only with the apse mosaic of Saint Peter's which he restored but also with the locations assigned to the Apostles on the silver cover of the Pantocrator ikon of the *Sancta sanctorum* presented by the same pope (C. Cechelli, 'Il tesoro del Laterano: III', *Dedalo,* vii, 1926–7, 2, p. 309.

with the statues in front of Saint Peter's, and so had Sixtus IV;[88] the implication is that all these authorities stood in favour of his thesis, and towards the end he returns most insistently to the precedent set by Sixtus IV, a theologian, he claims, unsurpassed in his century. He continues, however, with an admission of the merits of Paul, *vas electionis, praedicator doctorque gentium,* which do not in his view, however, approach those of Peter, *princeps apostolorum* and Head of the Church in every sense. His discussion becomes more interesting when he denies any precedence to Paul on the grounds that the latter was called by Christ in spirit while Peter was called by Christ in flesh; he makes the valid point that Peter also was appointed effectively by Christ in spirit, the promise of the Keys (Matthew xvi. 19) being fulfilled in the Charge to Peter (John xxi. 15–17), that is after the Resurrection. When he faces this aspect of the problem he shows that he is aware of a complex mediaeval argument which had been used to justify the placing of Paul on the right.[89] But this is also where he is disingenuous; for he must have known too that this position for Paul was arguable on the symbolic level, for Saul was of the tribe of Benjamin, *filius dexterae,*[90] and he suppresses authorities whom in any ordinary circumstances he would have welcomed, Petrus Damianus and a Bull of Innocent III.[91] He merely takes the opportunity to abuse his predecessor Durandus, who was persuaded by these authorities. He turns finally to consider early church decoration, and specifically the apse-mosaic of Saint Peter's, together with apostolic seals, and blames the *paulistae* for what he regards as a grave error.

Paris de Grassis's little treatise might be allowed to pass by as a compilation requiring no particular explanation if he did not at one point go well away from the beaten track to consider the episode of the Sacrifice at Lystra. The point he wishes to make is that Paul was ranked below Barnabas, as is evident from the sacrifices offered, a ram to the former as Mercury, a bull to the latter as Jupiter. The deduction, however, is no more eccentric than the reference to this subject in the first place, and it is natural to wonder whether the whole outburst has something to do with the tapestry-commission; almost certainly it has.

Utra ex statuis is written as if with wounded pride, and with a good deal of false humility; one senses all the way through that its author has been overruled. The text belongs to a manuscript that was compiled piecemeal over a long period of time, according to no overall plan but at random, as occasion demanded the reformulation or definition of ceremonial lore. Within certain limits the text can be dated, for it appears a few pages after a comment on an event on the Feast of the Ascension, 1515,[92] but about two hundred and fifty pages before an aside on the publication of Cristoforo Marcello's *Rituum* which he must have made early in 1517.[93] In the introduction to the argument he makes it clear that he is repeating the form and arguments of a letter he has sent recently (*nuper*) to his brother, Bishop of Bologna, from whom perhaps he expected support or consolation.[94] However, Francesco Mucanti, writing on the same subject but more objectively in 1573, knew what was evidently the same argument in the form of a letter addressed by Paris de Grassis to Leo X,[95] and so the text of *Utra ex statuis* should properly be compared with the indignant letter he wrote to Leo when Marcello published the *Rituum.*[96]

It is difficult to imagine what Paris de Grassis was protesting about in the present case if it was not a decision, taken without or against his advice, to place Petrine tapestries on the altar's left in the *Capella papalis,* and Pauline tapestries on its right. So far as we know there was no other occasion of the appropriate date that could have given rise to a dispute on this principle—new statuettes for the altar, for example, were commissioned three years later—and the range of date to be allowed for the original letter to Leo X coincides with that which is most probable for the tapestry-commission, the first half of 1515. Paris de Grassis was absent on leave for much of that period, and he may have returned to find a decision made in this matter of which he disapproved, just as he disapproved of modifications made in Saint Peter's while he had been away.[97] In some respects his frame of reference seems to be a deliberate and polemical exploitation of subjects chosen for the tapestries—the appointment of Peter compared with that of Paul, the Sacrifice at Lystra, and in general their different rôles in the foundation of the Church—and his insistence on the precedent set by Sixtus IV, now, it seems, to be set aside, would be a shrewd reaction in this situation.

However, the connection between this text and the tapestry-commission remains hypothetical and it is not essential to accept it before we draw two conclusions which are, in fact, more important. The first is that at the appropriate date, and in the immediate context of the commission, authority did indeed favour the location of images of the two Apostles that corresponds to our reconstruction. The second is that the choice must have been made, with conscious awareness, not on the doctrinal basis of the *Primatus* which would have led to the result favoured by Paris de Grassis,[98] but upon the argument *ab antiquitate* or upon symbolism (*per mysterium*); Leo X was a pope intellectually disposed to favour each of these lines of approach. In addition to the established arguments for the 'old' location—Paul as *filius dexterae*, appointed by Christ in spirit—the point had also been made that Peter and Paul exemplify, respectively, the *vita activa* and the *vita contemplativa* which, as the pope would surely know, were associated with the left and the right of the body.[99] Moreover the choice, even if it were made solely *ab antiquitate*, could be justified by the result in this particular case, which would be to place Saint Paul below Moses in the Sixtine decorative scheme, and Saint Peter below Christ; the first coupling would seem reasonable since in Quattrocento philosophy Moses and Paul were cited as instances of inspiration through *furor divinus*, and in theological terms the rôle of Moses as *Doctor populi* was a clear precedent for that of Paul as *Doctor gentium*,[100] while the second coupling would underline the juristic descent of papal authority directly from Christ.[101] Since Leo X was himself educated in philosophy and law, neither justification need be dismissed as irrelevant. And finally it could have been sufficient—if none of these ideas was decisive—to draw the normal (if not entirely clear) association between, on the one hand, Peter, the Apostle who founded the Church *ex judeis*, and the Epistle side of the altar (left, our right), and, on the other hand, Paul, who founded the Church *ex gentibus*, and the Gospel side (right);[102] the choice of subjects for the tapestries does particularly distinguish between the rôles of the two founders.

Thus the proposed reconstruction cannot be objected to on the grounds that it does not place Peter and Paul on the sides we expect; on the contrary when the reconstruction is tested in its proper context—proper, that is, in time and place—it receives some additional support and is seen to represent a choice with certain implications. The second objection, that this reconstruction places one tapestry eccentrically and alone outside the screen, cannot be answered so satisfactorily. The pursuit of this problem, however, suggests that we may be asking the wrong question; what is really a matter of doubt is perhaps not the reconstruction but the completeness of the commission.

92. *Utra ex statuis* begins on fol. 39r.; on fol. 30v. he had discussed the height of the papal throne above the High Altar in Saint Peter's, saying that his citation of the rules laid down by Innocent III had convinced Leo X to make alterations *novissime*; this refers to his complaint entered in his diary on the Feast of the Ascension, 1515 (see above, Chapter I, p. 11, n. 64).

93. On fol. 165v. the *Rituum* is noted as published *hoc anno*; the publication date is in fact given in the first edition as 21 November 1516, but the papal privilege is dated 17 December 1516 and Paris de Grassis notes its appearance in his diary on 11 March 1517 (B.M., Add. MS. 8443, fols. 212v. ff.).

94. '. . . aliter non dicam, quam in quadam mea epistola ad R.ᵐⁱᵘᵐ D. Achillem de Grassis Car.ˡᵉᵐ Bononiensem germanum meum nuper à me desuper iudicium exigentem . . .'

95. Op cit. in n. 81, p. 4; against his summary is the marginal note: 'Paris Crassus in Epistol. quadam ad Leonem X' (similarly in the MS., cit. in n. 81, fol. 83r.).

96. For this letter, see B.M., Add. MSS. 8443, fol. 224r., 8444, fols. 2r. ff.

97. See above, Chapter I, p. 11, n. 64.

98. Petrus Damianus, op. cit. in n. 90, col. 593: 'Ut ergo ad id unde coepit sermo recurrat, cum B. Petrus ad dexteram ponitur, primatus ejus, quem inter caeteros est sortitus apostolos, honoratur. Cum vero Paulus ejusdem dextri lateris occupat locum, in Benjamin, cujus est filius, mystice figurae redolet sacramentum'; and Mucanti, op. cit. in n. 81, p. 4.

99. Petrus Damianus, loc. cit.; Mucanti, op. cit. in n. 81, p. 10.

100. E. Panofsky, *Studies in Iconology*, New York, 1939, p. 140, and A. Chastel, *Marsile Ficin et l'art*, Geneva, 1954, p. 168. For the titles of Moses and Paul see below, p. 69.

101. W. Ullmann, 'Leo I and the theme of Papal Primacy', *Journal of Theological Studies*, N.S. xi, 1960, p. 38.

102. These associations are standard in Early Christian mosaics; see Ihm, op. cit. in n. 79, pp. 14, 34, 98. The ultimate reasons for the reading of the Gospel from the right side of the altar (our left) are much disputed; a reasonable summary of the arguments is given by J. A. Jungmann, S.J., *The Mass of the Roman Rite*, i, New York, 1951, pp. 110, 413 ff. Particularly relevant is the interpretation of Petrus Damianus,

op. cit. in n. 90, col. 590: 'Non ergo immerito filius dexterae Paulus vocatur, per quem omnis gentium multitudo, quae ad dexteram Dei ponenda est, ad fidei sacramenta colligitur' (this point is repeated by Mucanti, op. cit. in n. 81, p. 10).

103. A further suggestion, that this tapestry was an addition, or afterthought, made as a kind of memorial to Inghirami, was put forward by P. Künzle, 'Raffaels Denkmal für Fedro Inghirami auf dem letzten Arazzo', *Mélanges Eugène Tisserant*, vi, Vatican City, 1964, pp. 499 ff.; my reasons for not accepting this argument are set out below, pp. 61, 71.

104. Antonio de Beatis, 30–31 July 1517, quoted from L. Pastor, *Die Reise des Kardinals Luigi d'Aragona*, Freiburg-im-Breisgau, 1905, p. 117: 'Lli (sc: Brussels) papa Leone fa lavorare xvi panni de razza, secondo dicano per la cappella de Sixto quale è nel palazzo Apostolico de Roma, per la magior parte di seta et d'oro; consta il pezzo MM ducati d'oro. Fuimo al loco ad vederli lavorare, et un pezzo de la demostratione quando Christo donò le chiavi ad san Pietro, che è bellissimo, il vedimo fornito; dal quale el signore fe juditio che saranno de più belli de Christiani.'

105. A third interpretation might appear convenient: that the pope intends, in the end, to have sixteen made ... But it should be noted that this is not what the text says, and is nowhere within the bounds of its ambiguities; we lose the right to use it at all as soon as we imply that the diarist meant something other than what he did say.

106. See above, p. 8, n. 50.

107. Leo X, undoubtedly, commissioned twenty pieces (the so-called *Giuochi de' putti*) for the *basamento* of the Sala di Costantino; this is made clear in the letter of Tommaso Vincidor to Leo X, 20 July 1521 (published by E. Müntz, in *La revue de l'art*, vi, 1899, p. 335). The same letter also mentions the design for a 'bed' (*leto*) for the pope, which was in fact another tapestry designed by Raphael (see O. Fischel, 'Ein Teppichentwurf des Thomas Vincidor', *Jahrbuch der K. preuszischen Kunstsammlungen*, lv, 1934, pp. 89 ff.; Raphael's drawing is at Oxford, No. 564). The 'bed' was almost certainly the Consistorial throne; compare the prescriptions for the papal *thalamus* in Pontificals, and the payment (1418) 'per fattura del letto della sala del Concistoro', published by Müntz, 'Les arts à la cour des papes: nouvelles recherches', *Mélanges d'archéologie et d'histoire*, iv, 1884, p. 280. A series of grotesque tapestries was also ordered by Leo X

In the first place one very simple point must be made: the available lengths of tapestry are, in any event, insufficient to clothe the whole chapel, and yet too great in extent to be placed wholly within either part of it. It is also obvious that the part outside the screen would not be decorated with these extremely rich hangings at the expense of the chancel; and from this it follows that even if all our earlier calculations are wrong, the *Paul preaching at Athens*, because it is the last in narrative sequence, must have hung somewhere outside the screen, on one side or the other. There is no wall-space in this part of the chapel in which the tapestry will fit as well as the one to which we have assigned it, and so it seems that we have to try to understand the decision to extend the tapestry-decoration by one extra piece in the area frequented by the unaccredited laity. There are probably three ways of doing this, but it may be artificial to distinguish too sharply between them. In the first place its subject could have had a special meaning to the patron, to the laity, and with respect to the relationship between them, and it will be shown in the next Chapter that this was almost certainly the case. Secondly it could have been judged that the projection of the greater part of the *cantoria* beyond the screen on the right side required to be balanced on the left; this possibility makes sense when we remember that the *cantoria*, when in use, was itself a colourful object decorated with woven hangings. Thirdly it should be allowed that the tapestry-set of ten pieces may have been intended to be supplemented, at some later date, by additional pieces to complete the clothing of the chapel down to the entrance door.[103]

The full clothing of the chapel would in fact entail the addition of six new tapestries, or seven if we include the narrow strip of the fourth bay on the right not occupied by the *cantoria*; since a comparable narrow strip inside the screen on the left was provided, it seems, with a separate tapestry (*Paul in Prison*), this possibility cannot be ignored. At this point a puzzling document—the only one relating to the manufacture of the tapestries—must be introduced. Late in July 1517, the Cardinal Luigi d'Aragona visited the weaver's workshop in Brussels, and his secretary made this note in his diary: 'Here (in Brussels) Pope Leo is having made XVI pieces of tapestry, it is said for the Chapel of Sixtus which is in the Apostolic Palace in Rome, for the most part of silk and gold; the price is two thousand gold ducats a piece. We were on the spot to see them in progress, and one piece of the story of the *Donation of the Keys*, which is very fine, we saw complete, and from it the cardinal estimated that they would be among the richest in Christendom.'[104] This text, at first sight, seems to support the supposition that Leo X intended to decorate the whole chapel. However a little thought on the matter produces new difficulties. Raphael had not produced sixteen Cartoons, but ten, and ten tapestries were made, not sixteen, and so if the text is taken to mean that the weavers were working on sixteen pieces like the *Donation of the Keys* (that is, the *Charge to Peter*), it is incorrect and valueless in this argument. The diarist, however, seems to be making rather careful statements ('it is said for the Chapel of Sixtus . . .'), and there is in fact one way in which his report could be exactly correct. With the technique of the executed tapestries in mind it is natural to interpret the phrase 'for the most part of silk and gold' as referring to the material composition of each of sixteen pieces; but the somewhat loose construction of the report allows an alternative reading: that the greater part of the sixteen (ten, for example) were of precious materials, silk and gold, with the implication that the remainder were of inferior quality.[105] This reading recalls the pope's instruction, on Christmas Eve 1513, that the golden tapestries from the *tribuna* of Saint Peter's should be hung in the chancel of the Sistine Chapel and that the rest of the chapel should be decorated with other tapestries.[106] And if a further six non-figurative and materially inferior pieces were in fact made in the Brussels workshop to complement those designed by Raphael it would be understandable if they were not listed with the latter in the Leonine tapestry-inventory of 1518–21, but elsewhere and unrecognizably.

This expedient would resolve most of the questions that come to mind when we consider the position suggested for *Paul preaching at Athens*; its subject is sufficient to explain why it should be the only figurative piece in the area of the laity, and its unique richness there could be planned as a balance to the *cantoria*. However the problem cannot be considered closed. Ideally, as we have seen, seven more pieces are required rather than six; and the solution depends upon an ambiguous document which has been interpreted in the more unnatural sense. In any case, whether the interpretation is right or (as is more likely) wrong, the question remains whether it was the intention to complete the figurative set at a later date, perhaps when more funds were available. In many ways this is a logical supposition. There is only one fact to be registered against it: Leo X and Clement VII, his Medicean successor after the brief but austere intervening pontificate of Adrian VI, did indeed commission a number of expensive tapestry-sets but did not, so far as we know, contemplate the extension of Raphael's.[107] It seems impossible to go beyond this point. We cannot, for example, make assertions by analogy with narrative cycles elsewhere that certain additional subjects are necessary—such as the Imprisonment of Peter, or the Martyrdoms of the Apostles—because an examination of other cycles shows that no subject is predictable,[108] and because it is a serious mistake to assume iconographic comparability between the Papal Chapel and any other building. Furthermore the decision was unquestionably made that more than the chancel alone should be decorated with the Leonine set. It might be imagined that a project eventually to be completed would be divided as the chapel is divided, by the screen. Therefore, any argument which justifies the extension of a supposed 'first phase' by the one extra piece outside the screen can be used with equal force to justify a supposed complete project of the same extent.

In the present state of our knowledge it seems essential to preserve, in all further discussion of the Cartoons and tapestries, an open mind on this question—whether the set is complete in itself or a fragment of a larger project—even (or especially) when the uncertainty inhibits interpretation. It does not seem necessary, however, to deduce from the exceptional position given to the *Paul preaching at Athens*, that the reconstruction of the Leonine arrangement is itself at fault. The real insufficiency in the reconstruction is that no convincing locations can be deduced for the vertical borders; this impossibility arises from the operation upon the argument of too many variables, including uncertainty over the number of designs provided by Raphael.[109] Five borders from the original Leonine set survive today: the *Fates*, the *Seasons*, *Time*, *Hercules*, and the *Theological Virtues*. The *Hercules* border is integrally woven with *Paul preaching at Athens*, on the left side (*Fig.* 25), the *Fates* is woven on the right of the *Charge to Peter* (*Fig.* 14), and the *Theological Virtues* is similarly woven on the right of the *Death of Ananias* (*Fig.* 17). But in the last case the lighting of the border (from the right) conflicts with that of the rest of the tapestry (from the left) and it is clear that a mistake was made at some point; and from this mistake, in turn, it is clear that little reliance can be placed upon the correctness of the positions of the

the cartoons being made by Giovanni da Udine (see A. M. L. E. Erkelens, 'Rafaëleske grotesken op enige Brusselse wandtapijtseries', *Bulletin van het Rijksmuseum*, x, 1962, pp. 115 ff.). In addition the scanty evidence on the commission for the so-called *Scuola nuova* tapestries (for the Consistory) allows the possibility that it was initiated by Leo X; there is no doubt that the confirmation of the commission was one of the first acts of Clement VII (see C. Hope, *The Tapestries of the Scuola Nuova in the Vatican Museum*, unpublished M.A. thesis, Courtauld Institute, 1968, p. 2). And there is an English tradition, which could be correct (see below, p. 143), that the gold and silver set of the *Acts of the Apostles* formerly in Berlin was presented to Henry VIII by Leo X. It would be difficult to argue that the 'completion' of the Leonine set was held up by lack of funds. The alternative supposition that a delay was imposed until Raphael had more time is hardly more plausible; Raphael undertook many less important tasks after 1516.

108. The *Imprisonment* or *Release of Saint Peter*, for example, is missing from the mosaic cycle formerly in the Oratory of John VII in Saint Peter's, the twelfth-century fresco-cycle at Idensen, and from Cimabue's cycle in the Upper Church of San Francesco at Assisi; A. Weis, 'Ein Petruszyklus des 7. Jahrhunderts im Querschiff der vatikanischen Basilika', *Römische Quartalschrift*, lviii, 1963, pp. 259 ff., gives a useful check-list of Petrine cycles which can be supplemented from the files of the Index of Christian Art at Princeton.

109. I now feel compelled to abandon the precise reconstruction argued in the appendix to art. cit. in n. 1, pp. 219 ff. It appears to me now that the argument was wrong in at least three respects: (i) the number of borders required (then nine, now eleven—see above, p. 32; the higher number is also suggested by the physical examination of the *Miraculous Draught* and the *Charge to Peter*, which seem to have been separated by two borders, as explained in n. 73); (ii) the lighting of the *Hours* or *Time* from the right is unassertive but not indecisive, and this border cannot have been intended for the right side of the chapel—from this objection it follows that the substantial reliance placed upon the location of designs in the Mantuan set (where the *Time* border flanks the *Healing of the Lame Man*) was unjustified; (iii) the relevance of Hercules to Leo X (see below, p. 89) was not appreciated, and thereby a second *Hercules* border was unnecessarily rejected.

110. These borders are reproduced in art. cit. in n. 1, p. 203, Fig. 16. The number of Muses was not reduced for lack of space; one group of three is accompanied by Jupiter, the other by Minerva. It seems to me more probable that these two designs were adapted from some separate source in which three borders had been required. Two grotesque borders, very probably designed by Giovanni da Udine, are at present hung with the Leonine tapestry-set in the Vatican; they are Leonine too, but it is certain that they do not belong to the Sistine Chapel project—they are, for example, framed in blue and not in red.

Hercules and the *Fates*. The most that can be asserted is that *Hercules*, *Time*, and the *Theological Virtues* (all lit from the right) were to be interspersed among the Pauline set, and the *Fates* and the *Seasons* (lit from the left) among the Petrine set.

The most probable number of the original borders was eleven; this figure is reached by allowing two borders to intervene between the corner-tapestries (*Fig.* II, p. 25). Now there is no difficulty in finding a sufficient number of additional Raphaelesque border-designs among later sets of tapestries such as those at Mantua and Madrid; the difficulty lies in determining which of these are really convincing as inventions of Raphael's studio, since a certain competence in Raphaelesque invention is displayed in the horizontal borders of these sets which replace the Leonine 'reliefs'. Any additions made from these sources are subject to another complication since several of them appear in alternative, reversed, directions. This duplication was made because each tapestry in these sets was provided with a vertical border on either side. The result is that it is far from clear which is the 'Raphaelesque' direction, either of figural composition or of light. Four designs in these sets seem comparable in quality with the five surviving Leonine borders and are likely to reproduce lost companions to the latter; these four represent the *Cardinal Virtues*, the *Elements*, and, in two borders, the *Liberal Arts* (*Figs.* 28b–e). A second *Hercules* design (*Fig.* 28f) is a possible addition, and this would bring the total to ten. The later sets also include, however, two designs each with three *Muses*; these are notably the weakest in invention and are unlike the other borders (which are striking in the variety of invention displayed) in that the architectural framework is exactly repeated. And the *Muses* are also unimaginable in this form in a Leonine set because their number is limited to six; there should be nine of them, or they should not be there at all.[110]

Beyond this point—listing the subjects of nine or ten Leonine borders—little progress seems possible. One perhaps helpful detail is that the later reproductions of the *Cardinal Virtues* (*Fig.* 28d) are unique among all known border designs, for the lowest part is without meaning and looks like a rather feeble extension (in fact adapting a motif from the *Theological Virtues*, *Fig.* 17); this suggests that the original cartoon was unusually short, and it may, therefore, have been intended to frame the *Stoning of Stephen* in the left corner. The *Theological Virtues*, which can be expected in close proximity, was certainly intended for this side of the chapel and may also have been intended for the left corner, on the right of the *Conversion of Saul*. Subsequent discussion of the Cartoons and tapestries must retain, then, a second flexibility, with regard to the subjects and positions of the lateral borders.

III: Meaning

Soli tamen petro dicitur: Duc in altum—
hoc est in profundum disputationum.
(Ambrose).

IT is not necessary to accept all the conclusions or tendencies of modern iconographical research to allow the general proposition, overwhelmingly implied by such studies, that Raphael's Cartoons and tapestries would be exceptional among comparable works of the period if they did not carry a meaning on more than one level. The practical problem, however, is not to discover possibilities, but to limit the multitudinous possibilities that arise; for without restraints or controls of any kind the number of hypotheses that come to mind is in direct proportion to the amount of related literature consumed, such is the wealth of association and interpretation in the exegetical tradition. In our particular position a number of controls suggest themselves.

First it seems clear that in the pontificate of Leo X and in the first chapel in Christendom—above all when it has assumed some of the functions of the basilica of Saint Peter's—we should expect ideas to be rigorously traditional, authoritative and orthodox. We may anticipate, in other words, that if our interpretation contains any real surprises it is almost certain to be wrong.

Second, the sources thus suggested may be controlled again if we demand evidence of one kind or another that they were widely accessible and generally consulted in the time and place within which the Cartoons were produced, and if we demand that every idea we wish to extract from them was given circulation in the same context. It is not good enough, in other words, to pluck out of the air a text from, say, Rabanus Maurus unless we can also show that both the text and the way in which we wish to use it were familiar, or ought to have been familiar, to a member of the *Capella papalis*. Without this control we risk the dubious proposition that the tapestries were designed to communicate meanings that would not have been understood.[1]

Third, a limitation of another kind is applied by the physical context of each tapestry, established in the previous Chapter, if we demand—as we should, for reasons that will appear later—that its interpretation should take account of its position, of its relation to its neighbours, and of the total thematic structure of the tapestry-cycle. This is simply to insist on the importance, in this problem of interpretation, of one more aspect of the context of the work of art.

Fourth, we need, in this investigation above all, the keenest scepticism—not only to satisfy ourselves, but also to satisfy the standards of the period to which the Cartoons belong, in which can be found admirable examples of ridicule of over-abstruse interpretation.[2] However, the process of iconographical investigation engenders not only scepticism but also pessimism. In a case like this, when there is no contemporary written evidence to provide a foundation for the edifice of interpretation, it is easy enough (and much easier than it looks) to erect an imposing pile of texts from the exegetical literature alongside the work of art and to claim that the one illuminates the other; but at best there exists no proof that we have chosen the right texts and have thereby hit upon the intended illumination. The closest approach to proof comes in those rather rare situations in which we can seize upon some oddity in the design or conjunction of themes that seems to demand

1. The ancient tradition that sacred histories in churches instruct and inspire the faithful was very much alive in the period of the Cartoons; a remark in this sense which is specifically directed to the decoration of the Sistine Chapel appears in Paolo Cortese, *De cardinalatu*, Castro Cortese, 1510, fol. liii, v.; for a collection of such texts from Saint Gregory to Durandus, see L. Gougaud, 'Muta praedicatio', *Revue Bénédictine*, xlii, 1930, pp. 168 ff.

2. For example: Filippo Beroaldo, *Comentarii . . . conditi in Asinum Aureum Lucii Apulei*, Bologna, 1500, fol. 95v., and especially the pungent common sense of G. B. Giraldi, *Discorso intorno al comporre de i romanzi*, Venice, 1554, pp. 77–82 (ed. Milan, 1864, pp. 89–93).

3. Published without place or date, dedicated to Sigismund of Poland; a date not later than 1516 is indicated by a reference, fol. 4r., to the Pragmatic Sanction as still in existence. Benetus was in Rome 1509–22, Professor of Theology at the Sapienza, and chaplain to Domenico Jacobazzi; see J. Klotzner, *Kardinal Dominikus Jacobazzi und sein Konzilswerk* (*Analecta Gregoriana* xlv), Rome, 1948, pp. 40, 195 ff.

4. 1444–1527; Rector of the Sapienza from 1505, Cardinal in 1517; a detailed biography in Klotzner, op. cit. in n. 3. His brother Andreas was an outstanding Greek and Hebrew scholar.

5. 1468–1533; also known as Gaetano or Cajetanus; Professor of Philosophy and Biblical Exegesis at the Sapienza, General of the Dominican Order from 1508, Cardinal in 1517; for a modern survey of the literature, see R. de Maio, 'Savonarola, Oliviero Carafa, Tommaso de Vio e la Disputa di Raffaello', *Archivum fratrum praedicatorum*, xxxviii, 1968, pp. 150 ff.

6. 1469–1532; General of the Augustinian Order from 1506, Cardinal in 1517, close personal friend of Leo X and of the sacristan of the Sistine Chapel, Gabriele d'Ancona (see above, Chapter I, p. 4, n. 22). The monograph by G. Signorelli, *Il Cardinale Egidio da Viterbo*, Florence, 1929, is in part superseded by J. W. O'Malley, S.J., *Giles of Viterbo on Church and Reform*, Leiden, 1968; the study by F. X. Martin, O.S.A., 'The Problem of Giles of Viterbo: a Historiographical Survey', *Augustiniana*, ix, 1959, pp. 357 ff., and x, 1960, pp. 43 ff., is indispensable for bibliography of all periods.

7. H. Jedin, *A History of the Council of Trent*, i, London, 1957, p. 158. I have not made an exhaustive analysis of the sources most frequently consulted by Leonine theologians; but it seems right to accept the lead given by their references towards the kind of sources that are most likely to have been familiar in the period, and I have followed these general indications towards the sources quoted in this Chapter. I had not anticipated, for example, that the sermons of Ambrose, Augustine, the Beatus Maximus, Leo the Great and Bede, would have been among the most often cited texts.

a specific explanation, and when we can erect a text-pile that, uniquely, fulfils the requirement.

The problems of text-usage are in any case compounded with the natural ambiguity of visual evidence. The capacity of works of art to sustain a plurality of interpretations is on the one hand one of the realities that the artist may exploit; in fact it is taken for granted in any hypothesis that seeks to add any other meaning to the literal one. On the other hand plurality of interpretations on our part is limited by nothing except our imagination and experience. Attention to detail, a feeling for the period, and a sense of proportion may save us from some traps, but in the end there is no solution to the dilemma unless it is to be exactly aware of what we are doing. It would be a failure to understand works of art (and ourselves) if we pretended that our conclusions were anything other than hypotheses. Hypotheses, however, are the only alternative to not trying at all and art-history is in this respect no different from any other kind of history.

A fifth limitation is suggested by the reflection that the tapestries were to hang in a space that was not private, but public, even international, and thus their message—or at least their main message—would be ineffective unless it were universal, familiar and direct. It is reasonable to suppose that the same reflection was in the minds of those who drew up the programme and also, since Raphael was always very sensitive to the function of his works, in the mind of the artist who translated the ideas into images. Moreover it must have been clear to all concerned that the medium of tapestry entailed a considerable time-lag (in the event nearly five years) between commission and delivery, and this realization alone would have eliminated ideas contingent upon the moment, and would have encouraged themes that were enduring, or that appeared so.

Restraints of this kind are effective, but perhaps not as much as might be expected. In a moment of reaction we may recall that Migne's compendious and elaborately indexed *Patrologia* had not yet been published. But that reaction is to some extent artificial. We are dealing with a period in which a surprising amount of the *Patrologia* was already available in printed editions, and in addition it may be assumed that the author of Raphael's programme had access to the manuscript collection of the papal library. Let us consider a specific example of what this means. One of the slighter doctrinal studies of these years is the twenty-four-page *Tractatus de autoritate Romanae Ecclesiae* by Cyprian Benetus,[3] a minor theologian in Leonine Rome; yet in this work we find citations from thirty-four authorities, most of whom are represented by more than one work. The field of reference of one of the really significant scholars—Domenico Jacobazzi,[4] Thomas de Vio,[5] or Aegidius of Viterbo[6]— is enormously greater. One aspect of the historical context of the Cartoons is intensive and profound study of the sacred texts, the Church Fathers, and the entire mediaeval exegetical and ecclesiological traditions.[7]

8. The *Historia scholastica* is a very natural source for consultation; but in this case its particular relevance may be inferred from the fact that it was already one of the major sources used in the Sixtine fresco-cycle (first demonstrated by A. Groner, 'Zur Entstehung der sixtinischen Wandfresken—Erklärung des Wand-Historienzyklus', *Zeitschrift für christliche Kunst*, vii, 1906, cols. 193 ff.). An illustrated

MS. ('Historia scholastica Petri Commestoris figurata') appears in the Vatican Library inventory of 1518 (Bibl. Vat., MS. Vat. Lat. 3948, fol. 29r.).

9. *Collectio antiquorum Christianorum poetarum*, 3 vols., Venice, 1501–4.

10. *Aratoris Cardinalis Historia Apostolica cum*

commentariis Arii Barbosae Lusitani, Salamanca, 1516; the text is followed by two apologetic verses, the first confessing that the author is a humanist, not a theologian, and the second excusing his prolixity. Arias Barbosa (Arius Lusitanus), *c.* 1470–1530, had been a pupil of Poliziano in Florence at about the same time as Leo X, but was already teaching Greek at Salamanca by 1495; he was subsequently

Knowledge, then, was one effective substitute for Migne's *Patrologia*. But there was another. A surprising number of the compilations or predigestions of patrology were already in print: the extensive biblical glosses of Nicolaus de Lyra, for example, or the *Catena aurea* of Thomas Aquinas; Petrus Comestor's *Historia scholastica* existed in many editions,[8] the several versions of the *Homeliarius* made a significant collection of the great sermons widely available and also testify to their relevance and popularity, while the Early Christian poets had been collected in a beautiful edition by Aldus Manutius.[9] The British Museum has twenty-five editions of the *Sententiae* of Petrus Lombardus published before 1515. This kind of material made it possible, to cite one concrete example, for a non-specialist such as Arias Barbosa to produce, in 1516, an elaborate and convincing gloss[10] upon the sixth-century *De actibus apostolorum* by Arator.[11] And it is easy to understand in these terms how even Paris de Grassis could produce, in 1515, a polemical tract, *Utra ex statuis*, on Saints Peter and Paul,[12] which can be rated as a very passable piece of do-it-yourself theology.[13]

It must be stressed that what concerns us is not the background of theological scholarship of a period in the general sense, important as that is, but rather the foreground against which the tapestries were to be set—that is the specific level of theological competence of those many individuals who would, in the normal course of events, find themselves in the Sistine Chapel. This is easily assessed in the case of the clerical members of the *Capella papalis*; it appears to have been very high indeed. More surprising, but just as well documented, is the competence of the non-specialists, such as the ambassadors, displayed by their readiness to produce in letters or orations an apt biblical quotation. The protonotary Caracciolo, for example, wrote to Isabella d'Este a letter of optimistic predictions on the election of Leo X woven round two appropriate quotations from John x.[14] And when at Christmas 1522 the architrave of the entrance door of the Sistine Chapel collapsed, killing a Swiss guard and narrowly missing the pope (Adrian VI), the Venetian Girolamo Negro interpreted the event as an ill omen, recalling the text 'Et petrae scissae sunt' (Matthew xxvii. 51).[15] The particular sophistication of the congregation, in other words, is yet another aspect of the reconstruction of the context of the tapestries. Our judgement of what kinds or levels of meaning could have been intended in and understood from Raphael's designs must take account of this aspect of their unique setting, and the result seems to be (unfortunately, in a certain sense) that there is virtually nothing tolerably orthodox that can be excluded on the grounds that it would have been beyond the grasp of the spectators.

The assistance we could gain from another potentially limiting factor— the Sixtine fresco-cycle immediately above the tapestries—would be more effective if the iconography of that cycle were entirely clear. There is a good *prima facie* case for the proposition that the tapestry- and fresco-cycles would bear a vertical thematic relationship, if only because a vertical formal relationship is calculated and visible, and this proposition is confirmed by experiment. However, the experiment also suggests some revisions to current interpretations of the frescoes, so we must begin by looking briefly at these. It is not necessary to attempt a comprehensive survey, since this has recently been made by Ettlinger,[16] nor is it necessary to challenge his principal conclusion, which seems most convincing, that Sixtus's frescoes illustrate, on the allegorical level, the history, powers and functions of the priesthood and the papacy. But it is necessary to suggest two amendments, one of which substantiates his main argument.

Professor of Rhetoric, and of Grammar, there. Bibliography: L. Marineus Siculus, *Epistolarum familiarium libri XVII*, Valladolid, 1514, fols. 87r., 88r.; N. Antonio, *Bibliotheca hispana*, Rome, 1672, i, p. 132; A. M. Bandini, *Specimen literaturae florentiae saeculi XV*, i, Florence, 1747, p. 208; P. Verrua, *La prima fortuna del Poliziano nella Spagna*, Rovigo, 1906, pp. 1–7; M. Bataillon, *Erasmo y España*, Mexico City, 1966, p. 19; both J. de Carvalho, *Estudos sobre a cultura Portuguesa do século XVI*, Coimbra, 1948, ii, pp. 18 ff., and Luis de Matos, *Dicionario de História de Portugal*, i, Lisbon, 1963, pp. 297 ff., have several other references. It is, obviously, tempting to speculate that Barbosa remained in contact with Leo X and might have sent a MS. of his commentary in time to be of use in the tapestries, but I do not think this was the case. The commentary is valuable, nevertheless, as an intelligent and straightforward reading of the poem, as indebted to Augustine in its expansions as Arator himself had been, and it probably represents the way in which any careful scholar of the period would have interpreted Arator. At all events its publication testifies to an interest in Arator at the date of the Cartoons.

11. Read first in Saint Peter's and again in S. Pietro in Vincoli in 544; the *editio princeps* appears to be Salamanca, 1500 (Bataillon, op. cit. in n. 10, p. 27), and the second is in Manutius, op. cit. in n. 9, ii, 1502; there is another of *c.* 1505, published without place or date, and the Barbosa edition followed in 1516. A MS. copy appears in the Vatican Library inventory of 1518 (MS. Vat. Lat. 3948, fol. 16r.). There is a modern critical edition by A. P. McKinley in *Corpus scriptorum ecclesiasticorum latinorum*, lxxii, 1952.

12. Bibl. Vat., MS. Vat. Lat. 5634/1, fols. 39r. ff.; see above, Chapter II, p. 39.

13. A contemporary example of the use of compilations, or handbooks, rather than primary sources, is provided by the analysis of Giovanni Gozzadini's *De electione romani pontificis* (1510–11), by H. Jedin, 'Giovanni Gozzadini, ein Konziliarist am Hofe Julius' II.', *Kirche des Glaubens, Kirche der Geschichte*, Freiburg-im-Breisgau, 1966, ii, pp. 48–9.

14. A. Luzio, 'Isabella d'Este ne' primordi del papato di Leone X', *Archivio storico lombardo*, xxxiii, 2, 1906, p. 115; see below, p. 81.

15. Letter to Marcantonio Michiel, 29 December 1522, in *Lettere di principi*, ed. G. Ziletti, Venice, 1564, i, fol. 93v.

16. L. D. Ettlinger, *The Sistine Chapel before Michelangelo*, Oxford, 1965.

17. *Electio Pape Leonis Decimi, Anno MC. Tre-decimo. Ordo Mansionum Reverendorum dominorum Cardinalium in Conclavi existentium: assignatarum secundum Prophecias in Capella pontificia figuratas* (no place or date, but presumably Rome, 1513; there are copies in the Biblioteca Vaticana and the British Museum). The *tituli* ('Propheciae') on the end walls are not given. Between those given for the left wall and the newly recovered and restored inscriptions the variations are minor matters of epigraphy. On this subject see now the study by D. Redig de Campos, 'I "tituli" degli affreschi del Quattrocento nella Cappella Sistina', *Rendiconti della pontificia accademia romana di archeologia*, xlii, 1970, pp. 299 ff., but already (as Rolf Quednau has pointed out to me) O. Clemen, 'Zur Papstwahl Leos X', *Historische Vierteljahrsschrift*, x, 1907, pp. 506 ff., who had seen the essential point.

18. J. Wilde, 'The Decoration of the Sistine Chapel', *Proceedings of the British Academy*, xliv, 1958, pp. 68 ff.

19. Augustine, *Quaestiones in Heptateuchum*, II, x (*P.L.* 34, cols. 598–9), quoted in the *Glossa ordinaria* (*P.L.* 113, col. 196); for a contemporary text (in fact adapting the interpretation of Nicolaus de Lyra) see Paris de Grassis, MS. Vat. Lat. 5634/1, fol. 41v.: 'Moises fuit in administratione major, Aaron autem in consecratione sacerdotali ...', etc., which is especially relevant since it occurs in a discussion of the *Primatus Petri*; in a similar context Torquemada (*Summa ecclesiastica*, ed. Salamanca, 1560, p. 217) had already juxtaposed the priesthood of Aaron and the *Pontificatus* of Peter in Matthew xvi. 18–19, as they are juxtaposed in the Sistine Chapel: 'Aaron simul factus est sacerdos, & episcopus: ergo similiter, & multo magis Petrus, qui per Aaron fuit figuratus.' Compare Angelo da Vallombrosa, *Epistola ... Iulio Papae. ii. contra Generalem ordinis praedicatorum*, n.p., 1512: 'Aaron nostri figura summi sacerdotii, figuraque Ro. pontificis ...'

20. The arch of the Florentine merchants (F. Cancellieri, *Storia de' solenni possessi de' sommi pontefici*, Rome, 1802, p. 77).

21. E. Steinmann, 'Sandro Botticellis Tempel-scene zu Jerusalem in der Sixtinischen Kapelle', *Repertorium für Kunstwissenschaft*, xviii, 1895, pp. 1 ff.; idem, *Botticelli*, ed. London, 1901, pp. 47 ff.; idem, *Die Sixtinische Kapelle*, i, Munich, 1901, pp. 245; I am unable to follow Ettlinger's statement (op. cit. in n. 16, p. 78) that this interpretation 'has no textual or iconographic evidence to support it'.

22. The latter was Ettlinger's unexplained substitution (op. cit. in n. 16, p. 79) for the former, which has been the traditional identification.

23. H. P. Horne, *Sandro Botticelli*, London, 1908, p. 98.

24. *Commentaria in evangelium S. Matthaei* (*P.L.* 26, col. 118); a printed edition in the *Opera divi Hieronymi*, Venice, 1497–8.

Present restoration has revealed unexpected inscriptions, or *tituli*, in the frieze above each of the Sixtine histories; at the time of writing only those on the left wall have been uncovered. However a list of the inscriptions of both side-walls was published in 1513, as it happens in a pamphlet setting out the distribution of the cardinals' cells for the Conclave of Leo X.[17] This list demonstrates two significant points about the thematic structure of the history-cycles. The first is a rigorous coupling of opposite frescoes that relates the two walls in a system that is indeed typological, but without exact precedent. For example, where the *Baptism* on the right wall faces the *Circumcision* on the left, the *tituli* are, respectively, *Institutio nove regenerationis a Christo in baptismo* and *Observatio antique regenerationis a Moyse per circumcisionem*; the last pair, over the *Last Supper* and the *Testament of Moses*, are *Replicatio legis evangelice a Christo* and *Replicatio legis scripte a Moyse*.

The second point to be made about the list of *tituli* is that within each sequence there is a special relationship between the second and fifth. On the right wall these are *Tentatio Iesu Christi latoris evangelice legis* and *Conturbatio Iesu Christi legis latoris*, and on the left they are *Tentatio Moysi legis scripte latoris* and *Conturbatio Moysi legis scripte latoris* (*Figs.* 22, 29). And so this was at once a very singular thematic structure and one which, because of the exceptional presence of *tituli*, would have been immediately obvious.

It will be noticed, when we look at the four frescoes beneath *these* inscriptions, that in all cases this ideal scheme links the minor rather than the major events represented; for example, the stoning of Christ in the background of Perugino's *Donation of the Keys* is the *Conturbatio Iesu Christi*. Nevertheless the pattern of ideas is very revealing, and is clearly reinforced visually. As Wilde has pointed out,[18] the pictorial organization of the side walls depends upon their division—corresponding to the spatial division made by the screen—into units of three bays each, the centre bay being accentuated in a number of ways: by silver instead of gold fictive tapestries in the lowest zone, by emphatic centrality and tripartite design in the history above, and by the commission of these frescoes from the two major artists, Perugino and Botticelli; these are aesthetic factors that give special emphasis, on each six-bay wall, to the second and fifth histories. The relationship between these four particularized histories can be demonstrated further in the case of the second and fifth on the left wall, which were both designed by Botticelli; for it is impossible to explain the narrow strip of architecture framing the *Punishment of Corah and the Sons of Aaron* on its left (*Fig.* 29) without reference to the equivalent feature on the right of *Moses in Egypt* (*Fig.* 22).

There can be no doubt that there is a relationship, similar to those revealed by *tituli* and design, between the major themes of these particularized frescoes. In fact this is made clear by a disjunction between the *tituli* and the main subjects that is peculiar to these four. The *tituli*, referring to the secondary episodes, carry the burden of continuity of the Moses and Christ stories in typological parallel, while another theme is introduced in the principal episodes.

The major theme illustrated by the various scenes in the *Moses in Egypt* (*Fig.* 22) is the *Principatus* of Moses; but the same texts from Exodus also indicate the division of authority in the Old Covenant[19] by which the

Meaning MEANING

Pontificatus was entrusted more particularly to Aaron, and that authority is the major theme of the fifth fresco (*Fig.* 29), a fact that is made quite clear by an inscription within it. The two frescoes are connected because *Principatus* and *Pontificatus* are combined in the heirs of Moses and Aaron in the New Covenant, Saint Peter and his successor the reigning pope. For example, one of the triumphal arches erected for Leo X's Lateran procession, 11 April 1513, had two representations of the pope, with the inscriptions *Tamquam Moyses* and *Tamquam Aron*.[20]

The transmission of plenary authority in the New Covenant to Peter is the major theme of the fresco in the fifth bay of the right wall, the *Donation of the Keys*. The real problem, to which no satisfactory answer has yet been given, concerns its equivalent within the screen, the second in sequence, in which the *Tentatio Christi* appears in the background (*Fig.* 15). I am convinced by Steinmann's chapter-and-verse confrontation with Leviticus xiv,[21] and by the consequent title, the *Healing of the Leper*. I am also convinced that the Temple of Jerusalem in the centre background is represented metaphorically as Sixtus IV's Hospital of Santo Spirito and not as Old Saint Peter's.[22] It has been observed, however, and rightly, that Santo Spirito was not a leper-colony.[23] The solution to this apparent difficulty is to be found in Saint Jerome's commentary on the text (Matthew xvi. 18–20) of the fifth fresco, the *Donation of the Keys*.[24] Saint Jerome enlarges on the power of the priesthood that is symbolized by the Keys, and when dealing with that which is later defined as *Potestas ordinis*, that is the capacity to distinguish between sinners and innocent, he specifically compares it with the power of the priesthood in the Old Covenant in distinguishing between the clean and the unclean: 'Legimus in Levitico de leprosis . . .' In the same way, says Saint Jerome, the priest of the New Covenant is given, in Matthew xvi, the knowledge of who should be loosed and who bound. The reasoning depends upon the interpretation of leprosy as a metaphor of sin, which is one of the constants of Christian exegesis.

The point made by Saint Jerome in his *Commentary on Saint Matthew*—which itself is not an obscure text—was given wide circulation in the discussion of Matthew xvi; his interpretation was followed by Nicolaus de Lyra, and the whole passage was quoted in the *Sententiae* of Petrus Lombardus, the *Glossa ordinaria* and the *Catena aurea* of Thomas Aquinas.[25] And it is because of the common acceptance of the doctrinal link between Leviticus xiv and Matthew xvi that a Leonine theologian such as Cyprian Benetus could speak metaphorically of one of the judiciary powers of the Vicar of Christ as the divination of the leprous. In so doing, however, Benetus was repeating the formulation of Gratian's definition, in the *Decretum*, of the nature of the two keys given to Peter; and through Gratian's formulation, derived from Saint Jerome, the latter's juxtaposition of the two texts Matthew xvi and Leviticus xiv was given still wider circulation and discussion among the canonists.[26]

The healing of the Leper is a figure of the Sacrament of Penance,[27] and for Bede it is particularly a type of the purification by the Holy Spirit.[28] Sixtus IV's Bull of 1477 re-instituting the Confraternity of the Hospital of Santo Spirito perhaps explains Botticelli's metaphor of the Temple;[29] the hospital, says the Bull, fulfills the pope's pastoral and apostolic duty, proclaimed by Christ's words after the Resurrection, *Accipite Spiritum Sanctum*—the text (John xx. 22–23) which was accepted as marking the moment of transmission to the priesthood generally of the power of the remission of sins promised in Matthew xvi, because here too the Apostles are empowered to

25. Nicolaus de Lyra, e.g. in *Biblia latina cum postillis*, Venice, 1489, and in several other collections. Walafrid Strabo (attr.), *Glossa ordinaria* (*P.L.* 114, col. 142). Petrus Lombardus, *Sententiarum libri quatuor*, IV, dist. xviii (*P.L.* 192, col. 887); this source was quoted, in turn, by Thomas de Vio, *De divina institutione Pontificatus Romani Pontificis . . .* (*ed. princeps* Milan, 1521, dedicated to Leo X), cap. v, in his discussion of the Keys (reprinted in J. T. de Rocaberti, *Bibliotheca maxima pontificia*, xix, Rome, 1699, p. 538). Thomas Aquinas, *Glossa continua super quatuor Evangelistas* (*Catena Aurea*), Nuremberg, 1475 (cf. also *Summa theologica, Additiones*, Quaestio xxi, art. iv—ed. Thomas de Vio, Lyon, 1564, iv, p. 452). For a rich collection of other mediaeval theologians who follow Jerome, see P. Anciaux, *La théologie du Sacrement de Pénitence au xiie siècle*, Louvain-Gembloux, 1949, pp. 38 n. 2, 41 n. 4, 284 n. 2; to these we may add, from the period immediately before the Sixtine decoration, Torquemada, *Summa*, ed. cit. in n. 19, p. 160, from whose discussion of the Keys it would appear that in fifteenth-century theology the whole issue turned upon the authority of Jerome's exegesis.

26. *Tractatus de autoritate Romanae Ecclesiae* (see above, n. 3), fol. 5v.: 'Tria quippe distinguit Iudicia (sc: Christi Vicarius) . . . Ultimum inter lepram & lepram, per quod ecclesiasticum & criminale notatur.' Gratian, *Decretum*, Part I, dist. xx. 2: 'Christus . . . prius dedit sibi claves regni coelorum: in altera dans ei (Petro) scientiam discernendi inter lepram et lepram, in altera dans sibi potestatem ejiciendi aliquos ab ecclesia, vel recipiendi . . .' (*P.L.* 187, col. 112). The implications of this text are exhaustively discussed, for example, by Torquemada, *Commentaria . . . super totum Decretum*, ed. Lyon, 1519, fols. 81r. ff.; see also the mediaeval canonists quoted by Anciaux, op. cit. in n. 25, pp. 546 ff.

27. *Glossa ordinaria*, on Leviticus xiv (*P.L.* 113, col. 336).

28. *Quaestiones super Leviticum*, cap. xi (*P.L.* 93, cols. 391–2).

29. Sixtus's Bull *Illius qui pro dominici salvatione gregis* (P. de Angelis, *L'Ospedale di S. Spirito in Saxia*, ii, Rome, 1962, pp. 104, 648 ff.) was confirmed and re-issued by Leo X, immediately after his election, as *Salvator dominus noster* (*Bullarium sive collectio diversarum constitutionum multorum Pontif.*, ed. D. Laertius Cherubinus, Rome, 1586, pp. 172 ff.).

30. E.g. *Summa, Additiones*, Quaestiones xviii, xx.

31. Origen, *In Leviticum homilia VIII* (*P.G.* 12, col. 492).

32. Christ is the *medicus humilis*, according to Augustine, Who cures mankind of Pride; see R. Arbesmann, O.S.A., 'The Concept of "Christus Medicus" in Saint Augustine', *Traditio*, x, 1954, pp. 9 ff.

33. *Belone belone* (*Aguglia comune*, or Gar-fish); *Raja radula* (*Razza scuffina*, or Sandy Ray); *Torpedo narke* (*Torpedine occhiata*, or Cram Ray); *Galeorhinus galeus* (*Canesca*, or Tope); see A. Palombi and M. Santarelli, *Gli animali commestibili dei mari d'Italia*, Milan, 1953, pp. 15, 197, 187, 168. I cannot resist the suspicion that the fish alongside the boat (the one that might have got away, so to speak, but did not) is intended to be the one still known in Italy as San Pietro, but I am doubtful of the identification.

34. C. W. King, 'The Emerald Vernicle of the Vatican', *Archaeological Journal*, xxvii, 1870, pp. 181 ff.; G. F. Hill, *The Medallic Portraits of Christ*, Oxford, 1920; G. Habich, 'Zum Medaillen-Porträt Christi', *Archiv für Medaillen- und Plaketten-Kunde*, ii, 1920–21, p. 75 (whose solution to the problem of the origin of the type seems the most convincing). Several of these medals, and a number of paintings apparently derived from the same source, carry inscriptions recording the provenance of the emerald and the circumstances of the gift; the date of the latter is unknown, but it is likely to be close to that of the same Sultan's gift of the relic of the Sacred Lance to Innocent VIII in 1492. It is worth noting that at that date Lascaris, a friend of Leo and Raphael (see below, p. 61), was ambassador of Lorenzo de' Medici to Bajazet in Constantinople (B. Knös, *Un ambassadeur de l'hellénisme, Janus Lascaris*, Paris-Uppsala, 1945, p. 34).

35. Inventory of John, Lord Lumley, at Lumley Castle, 1590 (E. Milner, *Records of the Lumleys*, London, 1904, p. 333, cited by Hill, op. cit. in n. 34, p. 30); in the same collection there was a portrait of Raphael.

36. H. C. Marillier, *English Tapestries of the Eighteenth Century*, London, 1930, pp. 98 ff.; they were made by J. C. Le Blon by a patent process of mass-production. A number survive, for example in the London Museum, Pembroke College, Cambridge, and Warwick Castle. The one illustrated here was *c.* 1850 in the collection of Sam Bagster, London (A. Way, note in *Archaeological Journal*, xxix, 1872, p. 113), passed with the Meyrick Collection to the British

loose and to bind. Thomas Aquinas, moreover, repeatedly uses the analogy of *medicina* to explain the Sacrament of Penance and the remission of sins.[30]

The connection between the healing of the Leper and the *Tentatio Christi*, which is the title of the fresco, need not be obscure, but it might well be a little strained as a result of the difficulties in achieving perfect reconciliation between the two patterns in the total thematic structure. Interpretations of the various biblical texts on the healing of lepers make it clear that the priest himself does not effect the cure; he recognizes the cure performed by God. In the Homilies of Origen on Leviticus—quoted, for example, in the *Sententiae* of Petrus Lombardus—the leper of Leviticus xiv, that is the sinner, receives his cure in fact from the *Christus medicus*.[31] And thus the foreground scene is interlocked with the background where Christ is the protagonist against sin, particularly the sin of Pride.[32]

The interpretation of the *Healing of the Leper* as a type and clarification of the *Donation of the Keys* will be invoked and perhaps confirmed when we consider the tapestry designed to be placed beneath, the *Healing of the Lame Man* (*Fig.* 16); an association at the most superficial level is implied by the repetition of the theme of healing. We might reasonably suspect that the thematic structure of the Sixtine history-cycle (indicated, inescapably at this date, by the *tituli*) would be reflected in that of the tapestry-cycle, and so we shall look again for close parallels between opposite tapestries and for a special emphasis upon the central tapestry in each group of three on the side walls, that is, the *Healing of the Lame Man* on the right and the so-called *Blinding of Elymas* on the left (*Fig.* 23). An inscription in this last tapestry makes it clear that that is not the main subject; before we attempt to interpret any of them it would be as well to look closely at each in turn and to define what is represented.

The subject of the first tapestry (*Fig.* 13) is the earlier of two miraculous draughts of fishes described in the Gospels (the text in this case is Luke v. 3–10); the same text is one of three which illustrate the calling of the first Apostles. Raphael follows Saint Luke very closely. Christ sits in Peter's boat, which is overloaded with fish; his companions in the other boat come to his aid and soon they will be as low in the water as he is; in the distance is the crowd on the shore to whom Christ has been preaching. Christ had instructed Peter: 'launch out into the deep (*Duc in altum*), and let down your nets for a draught'; and it can scarcely be by accident, but, rather, by the artist taking thought, that all the identifiable fish collected in such a remarkably accurate still-life in Peter's boat are, normally, inhabitants of deep water.[33] Consistent with this precision of representation is the fact that the head of Christ is in the strictest possible sense a portrait. The type is derived from the *Vera effigies* on the emerald cameo from the Treasury of Constantinople, and reputedly of great antiquity, that was given by the Sultan Bajazet II to Innocent VIII; the cameo, which also bore the portrait of Saint Paul, has been lost, but it was reproduced in a number of bronze medals of the end of the Quattrocento and one of these may have been Raphael's model (*Fig.* 31).[34] But Raphael's connection with the emerald portrait may have been more direct and more interesting; fragments of the evidence for such a conclusion seem to survive in two curious facts. The first is that Cardinal Pole brought to England, probably in the 1550s, an object that was inventoried later in the century as a 'speciall picture of Christ Cast in mould by Raphael de Urbino'.[35] The second is that a group of tapestries made in Chelsea about 1720 (*Fig.* 30) reproduces the bust of Christ from the *Miraculous Draught of Fishes* with an inscription, however, that identifies its model, in the same manner as do those on the medals, as Bajazet's emerald.[36] It seems more probable that the identification made in these tapestries was based upon a tradition preserved in some Raphaelesque representation in England than that it was produced by historical research.[37]

It is much less easy, but perhaps just as important, to identify the topographical portrait that appears on the farther shore of the lake (*Figs.* 33, 34). With some degree of certainty we may recognize, near the left margin of the tapestry, the Western tract of the Leonine wall that rises over the summit of the Mons Vaticanus and overlooks the Vallis inferni.[38] The form of these immense and distinctive round towers, two of which survive, is closely reproduced, and so is their orientation, for the view is taken from a little South of West and the light that falls on them from the left, and therefore from the West, is—most clearly in the Cartoon—the low pinkish light of sunset. The view is unfamiliar today, and is indeed substantially blocked by the fortifications of Pius IV and Pius V and by modern apartment blocks, but early in the sixteenth century it would have been well known since it was that of the visitor to Rome who entered on the Via Aurelia.[39]

From this point the topographical portrait begins to enter the realm of fantasy, but to what extent it is hard to say. The tapestry is not easy to read in this area, and the Flemish weavers may not have understood what they were required to reproduce; moreover the equivalent detail in the Cartoon is not entirely trustworthy because it has been repainted, as we can see from a comparison with early tapestries.[40] It is obvious, nevertheless, from the interpolation, within the Leonine wall, of the Torre de' Conti, that we are not presented with a straightforward view of the remainder of the buildings on the Mons Vaticanus. The nearest group of houses with a Doric gate is not shown on the early maps of Rome, but these maps certainly omit much that lay outside the walls. This group has a distinctly authentic appearance, and it may have stood in this position, in the area known as the Borgo delle fornaci; it is certainly a kiln or oven of some kind that smokes so prominently to the right of the gate.

Let us now start again from the other side of the problematic *veduta*, that is from the right in the tapestry and from the left in the Cartoon. If the identification of the Leonine wall and the consequent orientation of the view are correct, then the group of churches which appears low against the background of a mountain occupies the position of the city of Rome itself. It is clear that we are not presented with an accurate townscape, nor even with a conventionally selective view of its most famous landmarks; on the other hand the buildings are not fantasies either, for we can identify the three principal new Roman churches of Sixtus IV, each in its original Sixtine form characterized by *bifore*-windows. On the right (in the tapestry) stands the large domed octagon of S. Maria della Pace in about the right position with respect to the viewpoint of the Leonine wall; in the centre is a somewhat schematic rendering of the octagonal lantern and clustered apses of S. Maria del Popolo with its polyconical campanile alongside the façade, seen from the appropriate orientation but transposed into visibility from its proper position behind the hill; and on the left, at the foot of the reverse slope of the Mons Vaticanus and partly hidden by it, the octagonal lantern of S. Spirito appears just about where it ought to be.[41] It seems, therefore, to be a highly selective view of Rome, dominated by the churches of Sixtus IV, and this conclusion demands an explanation; but first it should encourage us to look with more interest at the structures on the Mons Vaticanus, inside the wall and behind the foreground group with the Doric gate.

Museum in 1878, whence it was transferred to the Victoria and Albert Museum in 1935 (T. 155-1935). The relationship between this type and Raphael's Cartoon, noticed by King, op. cit. in n. 34, p. 181, was in fact realized at the moment of their manufacture. The gift of the version still owned by the Spalding Gentlemen's Society (repr. Marillier, op. cit., Pl. 39a), is recorded in the Society's minutes of 1723 and 1730 with this information ('a fine specimen of Our Saviour's head from the image in Raphael's cartoon of ye Boat'—Marillier, loc. cit.); see also George Vertue's comments in his Notebooks, 1733 (*The Walpole Society*, xxii, 1934, p. 69). Another version, now at the Mormon Tabernacle, Salt Lake City, is reproduced by G. P. Woeckel, 'Christusdarstellungen von Ignaz Günther', *Das Münster*, xx, 1967, p. 373, with the mistaken assumption of a sixteenth-century date but a good discussion of its relation to the emerald prototype and other derivative 'portraits of Christ'.

37. In this connection it may be significant that a group of sixteenth-century paintings of Christ, derived ultimately from the same prototype, and incorporating the inscription recording the latter's provenance, appears to be English; one of these, belonging to Professor George Zarnecki, is reproduced by Woeckel, loc. cit. in n. 36.

38. Compare the photograph of one of these towers, the Torre di Leone IV, in C. Cechelli, *Il Vaticano: La Basilica, i Palazzi, i Giardini, le Mura*, Milan-Rome, 1927, Pl. 442, and the engraving in A. Nibby, *Le mura di Roma*, Rome, 1820, Pl. XXXI; also the views of the wall from the North-West in H. Egger, *Römische Veduten*, 2nd ed., Vienna, 1932, Pls. 49, 52. For a description and history, see E. Platner and C. Bunsen, *Beschreibung der Stadt Rom*, Stuttgart-Tübingen, 1832, ii, 1, p. 34. This tract of the walls includes the Porta Pertusa which, according to G. P. Chattard, *Nuova descrizione del Vaticano*, Rome, 1767, iii, p. 222, was rebuilt by Leo X—but I think he must have misread the arms of a later Medici pope, Pius IV.

39. In fact the viewpoint seems to be on the present Via di Villa Alberici, near the junction with Via Aurelia.

40. For example, the third tower on the wall, which appears in all early sets of tapestries, is no longer visible in the Cartoon.

41. The lantern of S. Spirito is in fact rather too tall, the campanile of S. Maria del Popolo should not be polygonal but square, and the dome should not be conical; there are also

minor liberties in the case of S. Maria della Pace. However the drums of both churches did originally have *bifore*, as in the tapestry; compare, respectively, the engravings of Silvestre and the drawing of 1656–58 in V. Golzio and G. Zander, *L'Arte in Roma nel secolo XV*, Bologna, 1968, Pl. XLV. 2.

42. See especially the passage from Stephanus Ioanninensis quoted in Chapter I, p. 14, n. 80.

43. This assertion has been made by F. Castagnoli, 'Raffaello e le antichità di Roma', in *Raffaello: l'opera, le fonti, la fortuna*, ed. M. Salmi, Novara, 1968, ii, p. 581. G. Becatti, in the same volume, p. 511, identifies this view with a corner of the Foro Romano near S. Francesca Romana.

44. Compare the early views of this area assembled in G. Fiorini, *La casa dei Cavalieri di Rodi al foro di Augusto*, Rome, 1951, Figs. 8, 17.

45. H. Belting, 'Das Fassadenmosaik des Atriums von alt St. Peter in Rom', *Wallraf-Richartz-Jahrbuch*, xxiii, 1961, p. 42.

46. The detail is reproduced by T. Hofmann, *Raffael in seiner Bedeutung als Architekt*, i, Dresden, 1900, Pl. XXXIV.

These buildings near the summit include, as we have seen, the Torre de' Conti, which has no topographical right to be there. To its left is the top of a conically-capped turret which would be in about the right position for the one that stood at the North end of the mediaeval loggia of the Vatican Palace. To its right is a large broken mass which is topped by a crane as if it were under construction or demolition. This mass stands in the position of the West end of Saint Peter's but it is clearly not the new basilica, which by this date had been advanced as far as the erection of the arches over the crossing; nor is it the Rossellino-Bramante choir, which might also have been completed. What it could be is the Western end of the Constantinian church, which is shown with similar heavy cornice and broken profile—but naturally in a more advanced state of demolition—in a drawing from the early 1530s by Marten van Heemskerck (*Fig.* 35). Providentially the Heemskerck drawing was made from approximately the same angle as the one that concerns us, but from a very much closer viewpoint. It suggests that we could then interpret the curved wall under scaffolding as the Southern exedra of the new basilica under construction—the Southern transept had been begun by Julius II but its progress was the particular preoccupation of Leo X.[42] The Cartoon has been totally repainted at this point (an X-ray photograph shows a large hole in the paper), and there the curved wall seems a simple rustic construction; but in the tapestry it is a regular piece of architecture with fragments of columns. If it existed in isolation one would never be tempted to identify it with the exedra shown in a more advanced state by Heemskerck. But it does not stand in isolation, nor without a topographical reference-point, and next to it stands a small circular temple in the position of S. Maria delle febbre; this again could not be identified, if it stood alone, with the building shown by Heemskerck and its recognition can only be based upon its position and upon the presumption that Raphael has restored it to an ideal Early Christian condition.

This landscape-view presents a formidably difficult problem. The easiest and certainly the most tempting solution is to dismiss it as something meaningless, and that might even be the right solution. However, it would be a facile one if we had not first attempted and failed to make some sense of the view; and the failure, as it turns out, need not be complete. The way into an understanding of the problem is through the realization that Raphael's standards of topographical accuracy were as different from Heemskerck's as were his purposes. An apposite illustration of this point is provided by the background of the little *Esterházy Madonna* in Budapest (*c.* 1508), for the structures shown there are not, as has been supposed, a random and picturesque invention of ruins,[43] but they represent, in rearrangement and with only partial accuracy, a corner of the Forum Nervae topped by the campanile of the Convento dei Basiliani;[44] the whole group has been set—arbitrarily, from the topographical standpoint—on the far side of a strip of water, and thus it affords a parallel to the situation we face in the tapestry. A similar understanding is necessary of the view across the Piazza San Pietro in the *Fire in the Borgo* (1514–15), in which some parts—notably the façade of the atrium—are highly accurate while others are ideal.[45] Another case occurs in the *Battle of Constantine*—painted, probably, in the second half of 1520 but after Raphael's design—where a view of the Villa Madama, in part inaccurate, is placed upon and identifies Monte Mario.[46] These cases establish the extent of tolerance that may be allowed in the interpretation of the view in the *Miraculous Draught of Fishes*. But if they then encourage us to take that view seriously the analogies also clarify an important point, for in them Raphael did not choose a perverse view of his subject; so, if we are shown in the tapestry what would be an odd but nevertheless the first view of Saint Peter's under construction, the artist's primary intention manifestly was not the portrayal of the basilica, but of its site. For no one would choose this angle (even supposing his *veduta* were entirely accurate) if his purpose was to represent the basilica so that it should be recognized; but on the other hand this is the natural angle from which to take a view of the Mons Vaticanus, as impressive an eminence from the West as it is imperceptible from the East, and it would be just as natural to identify it most clearly by its crowning feature, the Leonine Wall.

The background of the *Esterházy Madonna* has no meaning that we can guess, unless it has some connection with Raphael's unknown patron. But from the more nearly analogous cases in the *Fire in the Borgo* and the *Battle of Constantine* it may be inferred that the topographical portraits are likely to carry a meaning associated with the principal subject and with the patron. In the first the view of Saint Peter's locates the Borgo (and the spectator) very precisely and flatters the Medici, who had contributed to the façade of the old basilica;[47] the ideal tower to the right is indirectly a compliment to Leo X since it is a reconstruction (as its inscription implies) of the original campanile erected by Leo IV. The portrait of Villa Madama in the second is a reference point for the Milvian Bridge below Monte Mario, where the battle occurred, and it is again, of course, a discreet compliment to the Medici who commissioned both the building and the mural from Raphael. Similarly the portrait of Sixtus IV's hospital of S. Spirito in the *Healing of the Leper* in the Sistine Chapel was a compliment to the patron of both buildings and an essential part of the subject (*Fig.* 15). The specific challenge of the view in the *Miraculous Draught* is, then, to see if it is possible to make sense of it in a similar way: with reference to the patron and to the main subject.

If Raphael's other uses of topography allow us to take a generous view of the identifications of the structures suggested above—the conditional must be preserved—then it is possible to offer such an interpretation. The Mons Vaticanus is not represented as it was but *sub specie aeternitatis*. The Constantinian basilica under demolition is shown without the new structures that would have obscured it because it is important as a symbol of that continuity implied by the notion of *Instauratio*, reconstruction; the continuity of the site is shown with maximum clarity by the juxtaposition of this detail and the new exedra where Leo (and Raphael, as his architect) carried on the rebuilding that had been begun by Julius II. It is to be noted that Flavio Biondo selected Innocent III as the type of the papal builder and that the sole example he chose was the Torre de' Conti; it was Innocent III who founded S. Spirito, which was rebuilt by Sixtus IV;[48] and the next important additions to S. Spirito were made by Leo X, whose personal interest in this foundation is further attested by his re-issue or confirmation of Sixtus IV's Bull of 1477 immediately after his election.[49] Leo had also had a long association with S. Maria del Popolo since his earliest days as cardinal. And a particularly suggestive possibility arises from the most conspicuous of the churches in the tapestry, S. Maria della Pace, which was popularly known as the Temple of Peace; for this was a votive church erected in thanksgiving for the peace in Italy, and especially the reconciliation between Sixtus and Leo's own father Lorenzo, which followed the Pazzi Conspiracy of 1478.[50] Without that reconciliation, indeed, Sixtus could hardly have acquired the services of the overwhelmingly Florentine team which decorated his new *Cappella palatina*. Thus it may be that the *veduta* should be interpreted, with

47. G. Vasari, *Le Vite*, ed. G. Milanesi, Florence, 1906, ii, p. 443, *Vita* of Michelozzo: 'Per la facciata ancora di San Pietro di Roma mandò il disegno per sei finestre, che vi si feciono poi con l'arme di Cosimo de' Medici.' The 'Anchises' in the foreground of the same fresco, in the group that I take to be a symbol of the *Pietas leonis* (a common image of the pontificate), has the features of Cosimo (taken from a medal); this was pointed out to me by Johannes Wilde.

48. For the first point see Flavio Biondo, *Additiones correctionesque Italiae illustratae*, in B. Nogara, *Scritti inedite e rari (Studi e testi* 48), Vatican City, 1927, p. 238 (the context is his praise of Pius II's initiatives at Pienza, for which he finds precedents in Septimius Severus, Marcus Aurelius and Innocent III); for the second, see his *Romae instauratae . . . Liber*, Rome, 1474 (?), I, xlii.

49. See H. Brockhaus, 'Das Hospital Santo Spirito zu Rom im 15. Jahrhundert', *Repertorium für Kunstwissenschaft*, vii, 1883–84, p. 443; and above, n. 29.

50. P. Tomei, *L'Architettura a Roma nel Quattrocento*, Rome, 1942, pp. 129–30, from which I take this quotation from Sixtus's Bull of October 1483: 'Deo dicavimus et in memoriam huiusmodi pacis et concordiae templum Pacis nuncupari voluimus.' Raphael, who was currently at work on the Chigi Chapel there, would hardly need instruction on the meaning of the church's name. *Templum Pacis* is the popular title given to the church in, for example, Andrea Guarna, *Simia*, Milan, 1517 (unpaginated; written 1515).

respect to the patron, as a symbol of continuity or *concordia* between the Medici and the Della Rovere popes, just as the tapestries themselves are symbols of the same continuity in the *Cappella palatina*. It remains to suggest an interpretation of the Mons Vaticanus in relation to the subject of the *Miraculous Draught of Fishes*. This can very easily be done, and it may help to explain the apparent reference to Innocent III, but it is best introduced later in the context of the ecclesiological significance of the tapestry as a whole.

It must be stressed that we have not, in fact, made very much progress. If it is possible to make some sense of the identifications upon which the hypothesis rests, it remains true that those identifications are nonetheless, and in different degrees, suspect. The *veduta* is surely sufficiently provoking to require some explanation of its presence if the identifications should be correct; but the doubt that persists is also sufficient to ensure the collapse of any weighty edifice of interpretation that is built upon it. It is unfortunately true that this is the assessment to be made of several of our observations upon the tapestries and the Cartoons, and this limitation is another result of the potential ambiguity of visual evidence.

The birds so prominent in the foreground of the *Miraculous Draught of Fishes* (*Pl.* 4) are not, as Fuseli thought, 'herons' introduced 'for popular amusement';[51] they are cranes,[52] and their prominence within the scene suggests that we should read them as the common symbols of vigilance or *custodia*, as we find them interpreted by Saint Ambrose and frequently thereafter. The symbol is used in this sense in papal imagery of the early sixteenth century, for example in a woodcut published, in 1535, with a poem celebrating the election of Paul III (*Fig.* 38).[53] The flock of ravens that wanders aimlessly and, it seems, unnaturally over the water cannot fail to provoke a similar speculation; and ravens, too, are familiar symbols. The origin of their symbolism is to be found in that raven which Noah sent out from the Ark and which—unlike his dove—did not return (Genesis viii. 6–9). The Ark of Noah being normally interpreted as a figure of the Church, it followed naturally that ravens became symbols of sin and apostasy.[54] In the period of the Cartoons the image was used by Aegidius of Viterbo, and by Domenico

51. *The Life and Writings of Henry Fuseli*, ed. J. Knowles, London, 1831, ii, p. 235.

52. *Grus cinerea*, or *Grus grus grus*, the type normally seen in Italy; see G. Martorelli, *Gli uccelli d'Italia*, 3rd ed., Milan, 1960, p. 266.

53. Ambrose, *Hexaemeron*, Bk. V, cap. xv (*P.L.* 14, col. 227); Isidore, *Etymologiae*, Bk. XII, cap. vii (*P.L.* 82, col. 460); Rabanus Maurus, *De universo*, Bk. VIII, cap. vi (*P.L.* 111, col. 244); Hugo de St. Victoire, *De bestiis*, Bk. I, cap. xxxix (*P.L.* 177, col. 41). See also P. Valeriano, *I ieroglifici*, ed. Venice, 1625, pp. 3–4, and G. de Tervarent, *Attributs et symboles dans l'art profane, 1450–1600*, i, Geneva, 1958, cols. 206–7. The woodcut is used at the end of I. Santa Fiore, *Al divo colleggio delli reverendissimi Signori Cardinali ... In la Creatione di Paulo III ...*, Rome, 9 January 1535; it was presumably not made in the first place for this hurried publication but re-used from some earlier one, like the papal arms at the front to which Farnese lilies have been added on a new block.

54. Hilary, *Tractatus in CXLVI Psalmum* (*P.L.* 9, col. 874); Ambrose, *De Noe et arca*, cap. xvii–xviii (*P.L.* 14, cols. 390–2); Augustine, *Quaestiones in Heptateuchum*, Bk. I, cap. xiii (*P.L.* 34, col. 551); idem, *In Joannis Evangelium*, Tr. VI, cap. i, 1, 19 (*P.L.* 35, cols. 1425, 1434); idem, *Annotationes in Job*, xxxviii. 41 (*P.L.* 34, col. 880); idem, *Sermones LXXXII, CCXXIV* (*P.L.* 38, cols. 512, 1095); Petrus Damianus, *Expositio libri Geneseos*, viii. 6–10 (*P.L.* 145, col. 848), etc. It may be relevant to remember that there is a strong tradition identifying Noah's Ark as a prefiguration of Peter's boat in Luke v; see Ambrose, *Sermo XI* (in the collection published Milan, 1490; *P.L.* 17, col. 675 ff., as No. XXXVII); the passage in question was cited, as a proof of the *Primatus*, by Christoforo Marcello, *De authoritate summi Pontificis ...*, Florence, 1521, Bk. I, cap. vii. It may, therefore, be by design that the wandering ravens seem to turn away from the fishing-boats. But see also below, n. 192.

55. Aegidius of Viterbo, letter to Leo X after the election, accompanying an olive-branch (E. Martène and U. Durand, *Veterum scriptorum et monumentorum ... amplissima collectio*, iii, Paris, 1724, col. 1259); Domenico Jacobazzi, *De concilio tractatus* (1512 ff.), quoted by Klotzner, op. cit. in n. 3, p. 51, n. See also Raphael Maffeius Volterranus, *Commentariorum urbanorum libri octo et triginta*, Rome, 1506, fol. ccclxvi, r.

56. Rabanus Maurus, op. cit. in n. 53, col. 245; Hugo de St. Victoire, op. cit. in n. 53, col. 51.

57. Ambrose, op. cit. in n. 53, cols. 214–15; Hugo de St. Victoire, op. cit. in n. 53, col. 108.

58. Ambrose, op. cit. in n. 53, col. 212: 'Noli igitur, o bone piscis, ... timere Petri retia, cui dicit Jesus: Duc in altum ...'; idem, *Expositio seu explanatio ... in corpus evangelii sancti Luce evangeliste*, ed. Augsburg, 1476, Bk. IV (on Luke v. 1–10): 'Et bene apostolica instrumenta piscandi retia sunt: que non captos perimunt: sed reservant. Et de profundo ad lumen extrahunt & fluctuantes de infernis ad superna perducunt.'

59. E.g. Bede, *In Lucae evangelium expositio*, v (*P.L.* 92, col. 381); Jacques Lefèvre d'Etaples, *Commentarii initiatorii in quatuor evangelia*, Meaux, 1522, fol. 187r.

60. Antonio de Beatis, describing the manufacture of the tapestries in Brussels, July 1517: 'quando Christo donò le chiavi à San Pietro' (L. Pastor, *Die Reise des Kardinals Luigi d'Aragon* Freiburg-im-Breisgau, 1905, p. 117); Marcantonio Michiel, describing the first hanging, 2 December 1519: 'la consegnatione, che Christo a S. Pietro delle chiavi' (V. Golzio, *Raffaello nei documenti ...*, Vatican City, 193 p. 104); contrast, however, the entry in the 1518–21 Leonine inventory (cf. Chapter I, 6, n. 28): 'Inprimis un panno della Navicell ... El secondo pasce oves meas ...'

61. Beatus Maximus, *Sermo II in natali b. Pet & Pauli* (also attr. Leo I: *P.L.* 57, col. 397 Petrus Comestor, *Historia scholastica: In Evangeli* cap. lxxxv (*P.L.* 198, col. 1581); Torquemada *Summa ecclesiastica*, Bk. II, cap. xxix, xxxii (ec cit. in n. 19, pp. 216, 219); Petrus à Monte, *L primatu papae* (c. 1450), in Rocaberti, op. ci in n. 25, xviii, p. 102. For the same point view in the period and context of the Cartoons Thomas de Vio, *Commentarii in quatuor Evangel et Acta Apostolorum*, Venice, 1530, fols. 39r

Jacobazzi, who took the raven as the type of the corrupt priest.[55] We should also notice that there is a group of swans on the water below the ravens; if they seem to require explanation we may recall a proverb on the difficulties of conversion used by Aegidius: 'One might as well try to make ravens white, or swans black . . .'; alternatively, they appear in the standard collections of zoological symbolism as figures of pride or deceit.[56] In ordinary circumstances the shell-fish stranded in the foreground could be taken for granted as appropriate detail in such a scene and it would be absurd to attribute to them any symbolic significance; in this case, however, when other animal symbols of vice and virtue seem to be present it is as well to remember—and to go no further—that the genus *cancer* is taken by Ambrose and others as the type of the devious, insidious and avaricious man.[57] It may be that Raphael intended a contrast between the 'good fish', or the 'saved', as Ambrose calls them, who come in such quantity and variety into Peter's net[58] and these cancerous fish who seem to have been picked over by those other fishermen, the vigilant cranes. It may also be, however, that we should allow complete scepticism in these matters; and certainly it would be unwise to build anything substantial on these potential symbols except in the case of the cranes, and perhaps the ravens.

Between this tapestry and the next, the *Charge to Peter* (*Fig.* 14), there is a continuity of landscape which, on the literal level, is to be understood as an illustration of the conventional identification of the Lake of Gennesaret of the first text and the Sea of Tiberias of the second as geographically the same.[59] But the boat and fishing tackle on the left margin, recalling the second Miraculous Draught that preceded the Charge to Peter, implies a thematic continuity as well. The text for the principal event is from the last chapter of Saint John's Gospel; there is no possibility of confusion since Christ carries the Stigmata and wears the white robes of post-Resurrection events, and these robes, in the tapestry, glisten with silver. Nevertheless the subject is not quite straightforward. According to Saint John there were only seven Apostles present on this occasion, not eleven, and he makes no reference to the keys. The keys are so obviously important in this design that it is not surprising that in the earliest reference to it, in 1517, and repeatedly until the present day, it is called the *Donation of the Keys*;[60] it does indeed seem as if Christ commits the keys to Saint Peter at the same moment as He commits the care of His flock. The subject, then, is a conflation of the texts Matthew xvi. 17–19 and John xxi. 15–17, which corresponds to and expresses the orthodox interpretation of the second as the moment of fulfilment of the *promise* contained in the first: 'Et tibi *dabo* claves regni caelorum.'[61] This concept had been represented in earlier paintings, manuscript illuminations and sculpture,[62] and was shown just as clearly by Rubens in his painting in the Wallace Collection. However, it should be borne in mind that although the juxtaposition of the two texts is common and widespread, a conflation of them, in the strict sense, occurs with surprising frequency in the discussion of one specific doctrinal point—the *Primatus Petri*—to which we shall return.[63] For the moment it may be sufficient to notice that in the late Baroque decoration of Saint Peter's the central circular relief in the apse, directly over the *Cathedra Petri*, illustrates the same two texts and that its figural design is very clearly derived from Raphael's tapestry.

There is no textual problem in the next tapestry, the *Healing of the Lame Man at the Beautiful Gate of the Temple* (*Fig.* 16), but there is still need for definition of what is represented. The structure has been taken to represent the Temple itself, and the resulting reconstruction of the building supposedly

211v.; idem, *De comparatione auctoritatis Papae et Concilii* (1511), in Rocaberti, op. cit. in n. 25, xix, p. 446; Domenico Jacobazzi, *De concilio* (1512 ff.), ed. C. Jacobazzi, Rome, 1538, pp. 666, 675; Giovanni Francesco Poggio, *De potestate papae et concilii* (1511–12), Rome, 1517(?), fols. 43r., 60r.; Paris de Grassis, *Utra ex statuis* (c. 1515), in Bibl. Vat., MS. Vat. Lat. 5634/1, fol. 43r.; Silvestro Mazzolini (Prierias), *De iuridica, et irrefragabili veritate Romanae Ecclesiae* (1520), in Rocaberti, op. cit. in n. 25, xix, p. 232; idem, *De papa et eius potestate*, Rocaberti, xix, p. 369. For similar modern opinions: E. Florit, *Il Primato di S. Pietro negli atti degli Apostoli*, Rome, 1942, p. 6; P. Gaechter, S.J., 'Das dreifache "Weide meine Lämmer" ', *Zeitschrift für katholische Theologie*, lxix, 1947, p. 328.

62. For example, a relief on the ninth-century Ciborium of Arnulphus in the Schatzkammer, Munich (repr. H. Thoma, *Kronen und Kleinodien*, Munich, 1955, Fig. 5), and an illustration in the Verdun MS. *Prayers and Meditations of St. Anselm* (repr. C. G. Stridbeck, *Raphael Studies II: Raphael and Tradition*, Stockholm, 1963, Fig. 28). A closely related exegetical tradition, in which the *Pontificatus* is conferred on Peter by Christ at the moment of His Ascension (immediately after the Charge to Peter) is reflected in representations of the Donation of the Keys at the Ascension; see the discussion of Donatello's marble relief in the Victoria and Albert Museum and its iconographical prototypes in J. Pope-Hennessy, *Donatello's Relief of the Ascension*, London, 1949, pp. 5 ff.; an important precedent, to be added, occurs in the *antependium* for the High Altar of Saint Peter's presented by Leo IV (*Liber pontificalis*, ed. L. Duchesne, Paris, 1955, ii, p. 130). Donatello's relief is clearly one of the formal prototypes of Raphael's *Charge to Peter*.

63. The type of Christ in this tapestry is an adaptation to three-quarter view of the same 'vera effigies' followed by Raphael in the *Miraculous Draught*; I cannot agree with Stridbeck's opinion (op. cit. in n. 62, p. 65) that the type is derived from the *Apollo Belvedere*. I am also unable to follow Stridbeck's observation (p. 64) that in the tapestry and in its preliminary study (repr. here, *Fig.* 47) Peter's hands are covered with a cloth—a detail which, if true, would have the considerable significance he attaches to it. The background buildings in this scene, among which the mediaeval (Rhenish?) church is remarkable, elude identification; the circular temple in the centre of the Cartoon resembles the one now known by the title Minerva Medica, but the resemblance seems to be due to an accident of restoration since the building that appears in the tapestries is quite different.

64. M. Ermers, *Die Architekturen Raffaels in seinen Fresken, Tafelbildern und Teppichen*, Strassburg, 1909, pp. 86 ff., Pl. XVIIa.

65. *Historia scholastica: Liber III Regum*, cap. xiv–xvii (*P.L.* 198, cols. 1360 ff.); cf. also his comments *In Actus Apostolorum*, cap. xvii (*P.L.* 198, col. 1655).

66. Compare Leviticus xii. 6–8.

67. This group of copies is discussed below, Chapter IV, pp. 97 ff.

68. J. Ward Perkins, 'The Shrine of Saint Peter and its Twelve Spiral Columns', *Journal of Roman Studies*, xlii, 1952, pp. 21 ff.; E. Kirschbaum, S.J., *Die Graeber der Apostelfürsten*, 2nd ed., Frankfurt-am-Main, 1959, pp. 55, 154, 163, 166; I. Lavin, *Bernini and the Crossing of Saint Peter's*, New York, 1968, p. 15, n. 70.

69. An inscription to this effect was placed around the base of one of the twelve, the *Colonna santa*, by Cardinal Orsini, 1438. The legend is repeated by: Giovanni Rucellai, 1450 (G. Marcotti, 'Il giubileo dell'anno 1450, secondo una relazione di Giovanni Rucellai', *Archivio della R. società romana di storia patria*, iv, 1881, p. 567); William Brewyn, c. 1470 (C. E. Woodruff, *A XVth Century Guide-Book to the Principal Churches of Rome*, London, 1933, p. 33); Arnold von Harff, 1496 (A. Reumont, 'Viaggio in Italia ... del Cav. Arnoldo di Harff di Colonia sul Reno', *Archivio Veneto*, xi, 1876, p. 138); Luca Pacioli, 1509 (*Divina proportione*, ed. C. Winterberg, Vienna, 1896, p. 149); Bernardo Portinari, c. 1515 (*Disputationes II de daemonibus*, Laurenziana MS. dedicated to Leo X, quoted by L. Thorndike, *A History of Magic and Experimental Science*, v, New York, 1941, p. 85); Fra Mariano da Firenze, 1517 (*Itinerarium urbis romae*, ed. P. E. Bulletti, Rome, 1931, pp. 80, 82). It was also accepted implicitly by Fouquet (K. Escher, 'Die columnae vitineae in St. Peter in Rom im Werke eines französischen Künstlers', *Monatshefte für Kunstwissenschaft*, ii, 1909, pp. 413 ff.). It should be remembered, however, that the legend was probably of no great antiquity; in the twelfth-century *Descriptio basilicae vaticanae* of Petrus Mallius (R. Valentini and G. Zucchetti, *Codice topografico della Città di Roma*, iii, Rome, 1946, p. 384) the columns are said to have been brought by Constantine from Greece; this alternative, derived from the *Liber pontificalis*, was revived by F. M. Torrigio, *Le sacre grotte vaticane*, Rome, 1639, p. 283. An attempt by A. Busiri-Vici, *La Colonna Santa del Tempio di Gerusalemme ...*, *notizie storiche*, Rome, 1888, to reconcile the two provenances is ingenious rather than convincing.

intended does violence to the visual evidence and insults Raphael's intelligence.[64] The *Porta speciosa* of the text (Acts iii. 1–11) cannot be confused with the Temple. The most accessible and helpful analysis of its location and function comes in Petrus Comestor's *Historia scholastica*.[65] He places it with perfect clarity between the second of the peripheral courts around the Temple, the *atrium mundorum*, and the third, the *atrium mulierum*. Passage through the *Porta speciosa* was allowed to healthy Jewish men at all times, and also to women for the offering of sacrifices at the gates of the innermost court, the *atrium sacerdotum*. The women in Raphael's tapestry are offering, among other things, the sacrifice of purification after childbirth, and this explains the presence of the three children.[66] The activity of the women and children is important because it informs us of Raphael's reasoning on the subject. The preparatory drawings for this design are all lost, but copies of preliminary compositional drafts exist (*Figs.* 55–59); they show with more emphasis than the final design the lateral movement of the figures into the inner court and towards the Temple, which in the tapestry direction would have been from right to left towards the altar of the Sistine Chapel. And the copy that appears to record, however miserably, the earliest stage (*Fig.* 55) shows a significant step, like that of the Sistine Chapel at the *cancellata*, corresponding to Petrus Comestor's distinction of levels between the two courts.[67]

Raphael shows us, then, a cross-section of the *Porta speciosa* which by implication extends further outwards so that we, the spectators, may feel that we also stand within it. There remains, however, a problem posed by the columns. At first glance it seems obvious why Raphael used the distinctive type of the twelve twisted Salomonic columns that formerly stood in a double row before the *Confessio* of Saint Peter's and formed the screen of the sanctuary:[68] partly because their familiar function as *cancello* in the basilica would clarify the situation depicted and partly because no one at the time

70. Contrast, for example, the reconstruction of the *Porta speciosa* in Luca Pacioli, *Divina proportione*, ed. cit. in n. 69, pp. 130, 143, 157 (with diagram).

71. The *Colonna santa*; these healing powers are referred to in the 1438 inscription and by Giovanni Rucellai, Brewyn, von Harff, Luca Pacioli, Bernardo Portinari, and Fra Mariano da Firenze (references in n. 69), and also by Maffeo Vegio, *De rebus antiquis memorabilibus basilicae S. Petri romae* (c. 1455–7), in *Acta Sanctorum*, June, vii (ed. Antwerp, 1717, p. 70).

72. For example: Augustine, *Sermones CCLXXVIII, CCLXXXIX Pro solemnitate conversionis S. Pauli*, and *CCCXVI, CCCXVII In solemnitate Stephani martyris* (*P.L.* 38, cols. 1269, 1275, 1433, 1435). In representations of the story of Saint Paul the Stoning of Stephen finds its natural place at the beginning: for example in the series of reliefs on the important reliquary bust of 1369 formerly in S. Giovanni in Laterano (see above, Chapter II, p. 40, n. 91, and Machetti, loc. cit.). It should be noticed that

the brief life of Paul in Platina's *Liber de Christi ac pontificum omnium* (ed. *princeps* Ven[ice] 1479—the source for the list of early po[pes] represented in the upper register of the Sist[ine] Chapel) is very similar, in selective empha[sis] to the Pauline set of tapestries: Stoning [of] Stephen, Conversion of Saul (and appointm[ent] as *Vas electionis*), Conversion of the Procons[ul] preaching in various places with Barnabas ([and] at Lystra), election by the other apostles [as] preacher specifically to the Gentiles (the [Blinding?] 'relief': see below, p. 88).

73. Cap. xiv, *De passione sancti Stephani pr[oto]martyris*:

'(Stephen) ... per vulnera sacra vocatus
Sanguine fecit iter, cupiensque in praemi[a] victor
Hac properare via, nivei metitus honore[m]
Callis, ad excelsi pergit fastigia regis.
Et per tot lapides petrae coniungitur uni .

Compare the commentary by Barbosa, ed. in n. 10, fols. lxv, r. and v.: '*nivei callis*: id[est] viae candidae ... ideo niveus callis &[c.]'

seems to have doubted the legend that they came from Solomon's Temple.[69] However, if we assume, as I think we must, that Raphael was informed either by his own reading or by expert advice about the topography and function of the Beautiful Gate we must also conclude that he drastically and quite consciously revised its form, for according to the texts it was not composed of a screen of columns but of doors of Corinthian brass. From such texts Raphael would also have learnt that the *Porta speciosa* of Acts iii was not the one built by Solomon. Furthermore he followed the design of one group of the Salomonic columns carefully, yet changed them materially to massive silver. From these observations it follows that the *form* of the Gate in the tapestry is not a reconstruction.[70] The meaning of the columns cannot, therefore, be literal but must be symbolic—either of the miraculous healing powers associated with one of them,[71] or of Solomon himself, *Rex pacificus*, or perhaps of both.

The fourth tapestry, the *Death of Ananias (Fig. 17)*, presents the sequence of events in Acts v. 1–11 in a perfectly straightforward way. At this point we need only notice that to either side of the main event are references to its sequels, the punishment of Sapphira, which did not, in fact, occur before an interval of three hours, and the distribution of the common goods of the Church, for which purpose the office of Deacon was instituted; Stephen was one of these Deacons. The *Death of Ananias* thus leads naturally to the next tapestry, which is the first of the Pauline series, the *Stoning of Stephen (Fig. 18)*.

In earlier reconstructions of the hanging of the tapestries the *Stoning of Stephen* was thought to belong to the Petrine set, so perhaps it is not obvious that it introduces Saint Paul. The point may be sufficiently well proved by the connections which are so frequently drawn by the Church Fathers[72] between this scene and the next, the *Conversion of Saul (Fig. 20)*, across an intervening chapter in Acts in which the narrative returns to the story of Peter. But the tapestry itself is specific in one detail: Saint Stephen kneels. A moment is defined, after Stephen commits his soul to Christ, when he kneels and prays: 'Lord, lay not this sin to their charge' (Acts vii. 60). The immediately succeeding verses (Acts viii. 1–3) are the text for the fictive relief below the *Conversion of Saul*.

The tapestry that shares the altar-wall of the chapel with this one also represents a specific moment. The point in the narrative of the Miraculous Draught of Fishes at which Peter kneels before Christ is that at which he, too, prays: 'Depart from me, for I am a sinful man, O Lord' (Luke v. 8). The coincidence, especially of the subject of sin, cannot be accidental, and entails a strong presumption of a thematic parallel between the two tapestries.

Another detail of the *Stoning of Stephen* requires a symbolic rather than a literal interpretation. In the left background of the tapestry in the Mantuan set *(Fig. 19)*, which more accurately reflects the lost Cartoon, a high plateau stretching from the wooded hill to the frame is white, as if covered with snow. In the Vatican tapestry, in which a narrow strip on the left is omitted, the snow is transferred to the wooded hill; and this implies that its significance was real and understood. So far as I can discover there is only one text by which this can be explained: Arator's *De actibus apostolorum*. In his chapter on the Martyrdom of Saint Stephen Arator uses, as a metaphor for the path of the martyr, the expression *niveus callis*, a snowy mountain-slope.[73] By 1515 Arator's poem was readily accessible in three printed editions, and a manuscript is listed in the Vatican Library inventory of 1518.[74] We could expect that its highly figured Latin would be most sympathetic to the taste of Leo X. The apparently exact reference in the *Stoning of Stephen* thus encourages the

candida martyrium hic appellatur: quia ut Ambrosius & Augustinus in cantico nobili dixerunt. Te martyrum candidatus laudat exercitus ...' It cannot be supposed that Raphael or his advisers expected many of their audience to recognize the reference to Arator, but perhaps to read the snow, rather, in the same sense but less specifically, as the common symbol of *candor iustitiae* (e.g. Rabanus Maurus, *De universo*, Bk. XI, cap. xvi: *P.L.* 111, col. 326). The admission should be made that the appearance of snow in these tapestries could be due to an accident, the fading of fugitive dyes in the thread; but such an explanation would not seem to me to fit the facts of the case, particularly the repetition with translation between the Vatican and Mantuan versions; nor do threads normally fade to white. In the background of this scene there is, quite clearly, another 'topographical portrait' of a hill-town. I am convinced that this is a view of Nepi from the South-West, the conspicuous bridge being that which led to the old Porta Romana. The character of the landscape, with the tree-lined *fossoni* and outcrops of *tufo*, is compellingly true in the tapestry, but the identification of the town itself must be made by reading Antonio da Sangallo's plans of the town (especially Uffizi, 953A, 956A) in conjunction with the present situation, much altered by the new fortifications and demolitions carried out by Sangallo for the Farnese 1538–45 (see G. B. Ranghiasci-Brancaleoni, *Memorie istoriche della città di Nepi e suoi dintorni*, Todi, 1845, pp. 140 ff., and G. Giovannoni, *Antonio da Sangallo il giovane*, Rome, 1959, pp. 343 ff.). I cannot see that Nepi has anything to do with the main subject of the tapestry; but its introduction here might in one way be compared with that of the Della Rovere buildings in the *Miraculous Draught* (see above, p. 54); for Nepi was above all a Borgia-Medici town and it could stand as another symbol of continuity or *concordia*. Rodrigo Borgia had not only rebuilt the *rocca* after his appointment as Governor in 1456 but also, as Pope Alexander VI, had successively invested Lucrezia, Cesare and Giovanni Borgia with its *signoria*; Cesare took refuge there on the death of Alexander in 1503 (Ranghiasci-Brancaleoni, op. cit., pp. 120 ff., and P. de Roo, *Material for a History of Pope Alexander VI*, iv, Bruges, 1924, p. 60). Leo X paid fairly frequent visits to Nepi, principally for hunting, from 1514, and in that year gave the *investitura* to Alfonsina Medici-Orsini; in 1516 the city appealed to the pope for aid in restoration-works, particularly of its seven bridges (D. Gnoli, *La Roma di Leon X*, Milan, 1938, pp. 245 ff., and Ranghiasci-Brancaleoni, op. cit., pp. 134 ff.).

74. See above, n. 11.

75. E. Steinmann, *Die Tituli und die kirchliche Wandmalerei im Abendlande vom v. bis zum xi. Jahrhundert*, Leipzig, 1892, p. 29; and *Die Sixtinische Kapelle*, Munich, 1901, i, p. 227.

76. Cap. xiii, *De eo ubi ab apostolis septem diaconi ordinati sunt*, and xiv, *De passione sancti Stephani protomartyris*. Cap. ii, *De allocutione petri, & mathiae*, begins with the Miraculous Draught and passes to the Charge to Peter; it should be noted that there is an intervening reference to the Donation of the Keys ('Ad clavem est translata manus (sc: Petri)'): cf. Barbosa's commentary, ed. cit. in n. 10, fols. xvii, v. ff.

77. Compare the commentary by Barbosa, ed. cit. in n. 10, fols. lxv, v. ff.; this passage continues the one with the *niveus callis*: see above, n. 73. Arator's antithesis appears to be developed from Augustine, *Sermo CCCXVII, De Stephano martyre*: '(Stephen) Petris lapidabatur, qui pro Petra moriebatur; dicente Apostolo (I Cor. x. 4), *Petra enim erat Christus*' (*P.L.* 38, col. 1437).

78. Bibl. Vat., MS. Urb. Lat. 2, fol. 250r.; E. von Dobschütz, 'Die Bekehrung des Paulus', *Repertorium für Kunstwissenschaft*, 1, 1929, pp. 100 ff.

79. Origen, *Commentarii in Epistolam S. Pauli ad Romanos, Praefatio* (*P.G.* 14, col. 836); Jerome, *De viris illustribus*, cap. v (*P.L.* 23, col. 615); *Glossa ordinaria*, Acts xiii. 9 (*P.L.* 114, col. 455). It should be noted, however, that there is an equally authoritative tradition which states that *Paulus* is derived from the Apostle's own remark: 'Ego enim sum minimus Apostolorum' (I Cor. xv. 9): see, for example, Augustine, *Sermones LXXVII, CCXCV* (*P.L.* 38, cols. 484, 1352.)

80. Arator, cap. xxv: *De eo ubi Saulus qui et Paulus apud proconsulem paulum praedicavit in papho*; Petrus Comestor, *Historia scholastica*, cap. lxvii: *Quod Paulus et Barnabas converterunt Sergium proconsulem* (*P.L.* 198, col. 1690).

81. H. Mattingly, *Coins of the Roman Empire in the British Museum*, iv, London, 1968, pp. xxvi, lvii, lxvi, and 799, No. 556; repr. Pl. 106(i); Mattingly intreprets the inscription *SALUS* in the exergue as *Salus publica* (the inscription that was placed on the 'Pazzi Conspiracy Medal' of Leo's father, Lorenzo: G. F. Hill, *A Corpus of Italian Medals of the Renaissance before Cellini*, London, 1930, No. 915). The *sestertius* was presumably not as obscure as it seems, since it was copied on two later Cinquecento medals (G. F. Hill and G. Pollard, *Renaissance Medals from the Samuel H. Kress Collection*, London, 1967, Nos. 398, 409). It should be added that a very similar design appears on a Roman bronze medallion of Faustina the

supposition that it may be one of the principal sources for the whole cycle, which is intrinsically plausible since Arator divides the Acts of the Apostles into a sequence of separate 'pictures', to the extent that Steinmann once thought that he was describing an actual narrative cycle.[75] There are, indeed, some resemblances between the structure of Arator's poem and that of Raphael's tapestry-cycle. For example, at the beginning of the chapter on the Martyrdom of Saint Stephen he refers back to the appointment of Deacons that followed the Death of Ananias; and, more strikingly, Arator, like Raphael, begins the story of Peter in Acts with an introduction from Luke v, the Miraculous Draught of Fishes, and John xxi, the Charge to Peter.[76]

When dealing with the Martyrdom of Saint Stephen, Arator allegorizes the stones:

'Et per tot lapides petrae coniungitur uni',

by all these other stones he, Stephen, is joined to *the* stone, that is the Cornerstone, Christ.[77] Since the Cornerstone is embodied as symbol in the altar or its crucifix, and since in the Sistine Chapel the altar would stand immediately to the right of this tapestry and in the direction of Stephen's prayer, it seems that Arator's stylish antithesis was in Raphael's mind. We shall return later to the meaning of the Cornerstone; but it may be suggested now that in the category of potential symbols there is in this tapestry a contrast between good and evil stones (familiar in the imagery of the building of the spiritual Church) like that between the good and evil fish in its companion, the *Miraculous Draught*.

As if to stress the continuity of theme the landscape background of this tapestry is continued into the next, the *Conversion of Saul* (*Fig.* 20), including an extension of the snowy mountain. In this second tapestry of the Pauline set Raphael adds nothing else of importance to the text, except that he found there no reference to Saul falling from a horse; this reasonable interpretation, however, had been made in several earlier representations, and Raphael's model was most probably the illumination in the Urbino Bible (*Fig.* 84).[78] The rather peculiar background of a Gothic Damascus in the latter reappears in the tapestry, as do a number of other details.

The *Blinding of Elymas* is not a good title for the next tapestry (*Fig.* 23); it is the only one with an explanatory inscription—a *titulus*—as if it were Raphael's concern that we should not misplace the emphasis: 'Through the preaching of Saul, Sergius Paulus, Proconsul of Asia, embraces the Christian Faith.' What matters, then, is not what happened to Elymas, but what happened to Sergius Paulus—not what Paul did to a Jew, but what he did to a Gentile; the blinding of Elymas is instrumental, only, in effecting the

Younger (F. Gnecchi, *I medaglioni romani*, Milan, 1912, ii, p. 39, No. 3, Pl. 67.3). For an interpretation of the roundel in the tapestry, see below, p. 80.

82. The suggestion that this head might be a portrait was first made by my colleague, Michael Hirst; it was a late addition to the design, after the *modello* (*Fig.* 65—see p. 102, below). The most complete 'portrait gallery' of the Leonine court is in Vasari's frescoes of the *Entry of Leo X into Florence, 1515* and the

Creation of the Cardinals, 1517 in Palazzo Vecchi[o] Florence; Vasari himself identifies them (*R[a] gionamenti*, ed. Milanesi, viii, pp. 140 ff.). Amo[ng] these there is only one head that resembl[es] although in profile, the one in the Cartoo[n] that of Silvio Passerini on the extreme left of t[he] *Creation of the Cardinals*; Passerini was a cl[ose] friend of Leo and a member of the Roman cou[rt] from 1514 (A. Ferrajoli, 'Il ruolo della corte [di] Leone X', *Archivio della R. società romana [di] storia patria*, xxxiv, 1911, p. 370). But th[e] identification, however attractive, must

III. *The Charge to Peter.* Detail from Plate 6.

conversion of the Proconsul. The distinction then separates two possible interpretations; we are not, as might be imagined, concerned primarily with metaphors of blinding and enlightenment, continuing those latent in the conversion of Saul himself, but with the Apostle's preeminent position in the evangelizing of the Gentiles and his adoption of a Gentile name, Paul, from the Proconsul's.[79] The chapter-headings to this incident in Arator's *De actibus apostolorum* and in Petrus Comestor's *Historia scholastica* both refer to the conversion, not to the blinding.[80]

On the right of the tapestry, but within the picture-frame, is a pier with a statue which may be intended to represent Venus, the titular goddess of Cyprus, where the event took place. The statue is, however, of a matronly type and severity of feature that hardly bring Venus to mind; its lack of attributes suggests that no particularization was intended, and that it stands instead as a generalized symbol of the sin of the Gentiles, idolatry. The circular relief between the herms, on the other hand, is closely imitated (in reverse) from a Roman coin, specifically a *sestertius* of Commodus, which represents a personified *Salus* feeding the serpent sacred to Aesculapius.[81] This figure is identified by an inscription on the coin (but not in the tapestry) and the reference so painstakingly made is most unlikely to be casual; a potential meaning for it can best be introduced later in the argument.

On the other side of this tapestry we should notice that a portrait appears among the heads in the background; the same head, probably made even from the same drawing, reappears in a similar context in a contemporary fresco in the Stanza dell'Incendio, the *Oath of Leo*, but I can find no convincing evidence for its identification.[82] It seems very probable, however, that the head of the mature Paul in this and the following tapestries should be read as a portrait of the Apostle in the same way, and for the same reasons, as the *Vera effigies* of Christ in the *Miraculous Draught of Fishes* and the *Charge to Peter*; for Raphael's Paul-type conforms to that of the medals of Paul that were copied from the same ancient emerald from the Treasury of Constantinople (*Fig.* 32),[83] and contrasts with the bald-headed type that had become conventional. Another portrait appears on the extreme left of the *Sacrifice at Lystra*; it is cut and damaged in the Cartoon, very much worn in the Vatican tapestry, and is best read from the version at Mantua (*Fig.* 36). The features and expression are distinctive, but again it seems impossible to suggest a positive identification; all that can be said is that of the major personalities at Leo's court whose physiognomies we know the only one who seems a possible candidate is Cardinal Lorenzo Pucci who, as a friend of both artist and patron, might very well be included.[84]

The main scene of the *Sacrifice at Lystra* (*Fig.* 24) offers no ambiguities that need explanation, and every detail follows from the text (Acts xiv. 7–18). The inhabitants of Lystra identified Paul and Barnabas with Jupiter and Mercury because these were their local gods who had been expected to return; Paul was thought to be Mercury because of his great eloquence. We see, therefore, the beginnings of sacrifices to these gods; the archaeological and liturgical aspects of the sacrifices do not require discussion here, but in the next Chapter.

The *Release of Paul from Prison* (*Fig.* 26) is the tapestry that closes the Pauline series within the screen; it is a gap-filler, and it seems that its didactic purpose was limited in somewhat the same way. All its details, including the slightly comic personification of the earthquake, follow an uncomplicated reading of the text (Acts xvi. 23–26). Far more problematic is the tapestry that alone hung outside the *cancellata*, *Paul preaching at Athens*

doubted when the head is compared with the three-quarter portrait over Passerini's tomb in S. Lorenzo in Lucina. It is perhaps relevant to this problem that in the *Oath of Leo* the head looks fixedly at the pope; it was the duty of the Master of Ceremonies to keep his eyes always on the pope (Christophorus Marcellus, *Rituum ecclesiasticorum . . .*, Venice, 1516, fol. cxxxiv, v.); it is thus a possibility, for which there is no other evidence, that the head is that of Paris de Grassis, of whom no certain portrait, to my knowledge, exists. The conventional identification with him of the figure to the left of the pope in the *Repulse of Attila* (most recently in A. Haidacher, *Geschichte der Päpste in Bildern*, Heidelberg, 1965, p. 280) is unlikely to be correct since that frescoed head is too young. A precise birth-date for Paris de Grassis does not seem to be known, but since he was Doctor of Law and Governor of Orvieto before joining the papal court in 1501 a date not later than *c.* 1470 might be reasonable; in his *Diarium*, 1512, he remarks that he has known Rome for forty years (B.M., Add. MS. 8442, fol. 245r.). It is worth remembering that Michelangelo included a portrait of a later Master of Ceremonies, albeit ironically, in the *Last Judgement*.

83. Hill, op. cit. in n. 81, Nos. 900a, 902, 904. See above, p. 50, n. 34.

84. Compare the frontal portrait, possibly painted by Sebastiano del Piombo a few years later, in the Abercorne Collection (formerly attributed to Raphael) and the medallic profile, also a few years later, repr. Hill, op. cit. in n. 81, No. 1187. Lorenzo Pucci was made cardinal by Leo X on 23 September 1513 (the pinkish-violet robes of the figure in the Cartoon could be those of a cardinal), and was a close friend of Raphael too (L. Pastor, *The History of the Popes*, ed. R. F. Kerr, London, 1950, vii, pp. 82 ff., viii, p. 92). O. Fischel, 'Ritratti raffaelleschi poco conosciuti di Leone X', *L'Illustrazione vaticana*, ix, 9, 1938, p. 361, remarked of a stucco in the *Logge* in which Leo is seen receiving a kneeling, bearded cardinal: 'a quell'epoca pochi dignitari della corte papale usavano portare la barba lunga. La figura . . . potrebbe essere Lorenzo Pucci, che probabilmente è accommiatato per una missione oppure riceve il Breve per una delle iniziative artistiche del Pontefice, per le quali quell'uomo abile soleva curare le spese e superare gli ostacoli.' W. Trull, *Raphael Vindicated by a Comparison between the Original Tapestries . . . of Leo X and the Cartoons at Hampton Court . . .*, London, 1840, p. 44, noted that the head in the Cartoon was 'said to be that of Socrates', which is clearly not the case. This head was a late addition to the design (cf. *Fig.* 68), like the portrait in the *Conversion of the Proconsul*.

85. Trull, op. cit. in n. 84, p. 41, quotes the opinion to this effect of an unnamed Raphael specialist in Rome; see also A. Luzio, *Gli arazzi dei Gonzaga restituiti dall'Austria*, Bergamo, 1919, p. 11.

86. P. Künzle, 'Raffaels Denkmal für Fedro Inghirami auf dem letzten Arazzo', *Mélanges Eugène Tisserant*, vi, Vatican City, 1964, pp. 499 ff.

87. Künzle, however, believed that the squint was evident, and also that Leo was not stout (op. cit. in n. 86, pp. 518–19); on the latter point, and for other evidence of Leo's appearance, see V. Cian, 'Su l'iconografia di Leone X', *Scritti varii di erudizione e di critica in onore di R. Renier*, Turin, 1912, pp. 559 ff., esp. p. 563.

88. This drawing has also been attributed to Sebastiano del Piombo and Giulio Romano; it is normally held to be the cartoon for the head of Clement I (Leo I) in the Sala di Costantino, but even the advocates of this view have to admit that the measurements do not in fact correspond (e.g. P. Marconi, in *Bollettino d'Arte*, xxviii, 1935, p. 484, and Fischel, loc. cit. in n. 84). I have no doubt that it was re-used as a model for that fresco, but I believe (against the denial by Fischel) that it was originally made for the colossal statue of Leo X commissioned by the Conservatori di Roma and now in S. Maria in Aracoeli (cf. the reproduction in Cian, op. cit. in n. 87, Pl. IV, from about the right viewpoint); the progress of the protracted execution of the statue, by Domenico Aimo, indicates a critical date of revitalization of the project in February 1520 (Cian, p. 571). The head in the Cartoon (*Pl.* 46) seems to have been painted first with a red cap with short ear-flaps, in fact the papal *camauro* (cf. the *Logge* stucco portrait of Leo X, repr. Fischel, p. 361); the final extravagant extension of these flaps seems to have been inspired by the head-dress of a somewhat similar figure in Dürer's *Christ before Pilate* (Small Engraved Passion, B.7, 1512).

89. The one reproduced here is in the Ambrosiana series, Milan; I am indebted to Sig. Lamberto Vitali for his assistance in obtaining the photograph; there is another in the Uffizi series, No. 587 (174, Inv. 1890). These, like the engraved versions, carry the title *Joannes Lascaris*; Janus, however, signed his name in this way and there is no possibility that his obscure brother Joannes would have been of interest to Giovio (L. Dorez, ' "Joannes" Lascaris, frère de "Janus" Lascaris', *Revue des bibliothèques*, v, 1895, pp. 323 ff.). An independent portrait of Lascaris appears in Vasari's group of Lorenzo *il magnifico* among his

scholars in the Sala di Lorenzo Vecchio in Palazzo Vecchio (*Ragionamenti*, ed. cit. in n. 82, viii, p. 117), but this is unhelpful since the sitter was too young for useful comparison.

90. Knös, op. cit. in n. 34, p. 120.

91. Janus Lascaris, *Epigrammata* (published with his edition of Polybius, *De romanorum militia*), Basle, 1537, p. 85, and *Jani Lascari rhyndaceni epigrammata*, Paris, 1544, fol. 12r. I owe the following translation to Ekaterini Samaltanou:

'Hephaestos, seeing your works, Raphael,
Images of Gods having the appearance of
    men, said:
You cannot create these without inspiration
From the Goddess Aphrodite and Grace.
In spite of the fact that my wife, Aphrodite,
As well as Grace, have both come to you,
I will not make nets in revenge
Nor will I create laughter and mockery
Among the Gods and men on earth.
Instead, the destructive fire of fever will
    destroy you.
Let my wife and Grace stay with me.
Thus he spoke: the revenge of the Gods is
    swift;
The flame of your creative imagination
    which had
Entered your soul has left your body.
Excellent among painters, may the glory of
    your wisdom
And the gentleness of your soul never perish.'

The date and context of the epigram are discussed in Miss Samaltanou's *Knowledge of Greece among Artists in Rome in the Early Sixteenth Century*, unpublished M.A. Thesis, Courtauld Institute, 1969, p. 14. I first came across a reference to the epigram in Knös, op. cit. in n. 34, p. 143, where it is given the unreasonable date 1514. The third possible portrait in this tapestry is the figure sitting with these two behind Paul; the type seems particularized, but I have no suggestion to make except that this could be the same (unidentified) person, clearly an intimate friend of Raphael, who appears with him in the double portrait in the Louvre (the so-called 'Fencing-Master').

92. *Sermones in natali beatissimorum Petri et Pauli apostolorum, I–VI*, of which I–V are attributed in a number of collections to Leo I (see Migne's *Admonitio* at the head of each in *P.L.* 57, cols. 391 ff.); *Sermo* IV is also attributed to Bede, and V also to Ambrose and Augustine. III and

V were commonly included in the *Homeliari* collections as sermons for the Feast of SS. Pet and Paul (29 June), attributed to the Beat Maximus. For a striking example of t influence of this group on a contempora sermon delivered in the Sistine Chapel of Sai Peter's, see Christophorus Marcellus, *Oratio Julium II Pont. Max. in die Omnium Sanctorum Capella habita*, separately printed without pla or date (for the date of this sermon, All Sain 1511, and its place of delivery, see Paris Grassis, B.M., Add. MS. 8442, fol. 142r.).

93. Paris de Grassis records that a sermon Leo I, *Salvator Noster*, was read in the Sisti Chapel on Christmas Eve, 1504 (B.M., Ad MS. 8440, fol. 119v.). Leo's sermons are fr quently cited in theological works from To quemada to Benetus and Poggio; his remarkab (and in our context relevant) authority expressed in the Preface to the *editio prince Leonis Magni opera*, Rome, 1470, addressed Paul II by Giovanni Andrea de' Bossi, Bish of Aleria: 'divina viva nimirum Evangelii tu & prope electionis vas alterum . . . eloquent nemini cedens: multos excedens sapienti brevitatis magister: & pene unicus artifex . Hic est Leo certe ecclesiastice dictionis Tulliu Theologie Homerus. Rationum fidei Aristot les. & ut omnia unico absolvam verbo Petrus pontificio throno: Paulus in pulpito Christia . . . Is igitur sit noster in terris instructor. celis apud omnipotentem deum intercessor.'

94. For contemporary statements see, for e ample, the *Oratio* of Marcellus delivered in 15 (op. cit. in n. 92), and Erasmus, quoted abov p. 16. Tommaso Giustiniani and Vincen Quirini, *Libellus ad Leonem X* (June–July 1513 in J. B. Mittarelli and A. Costadoni, *Annal Camaldulenses ordinis Sancti Benedicti*, ix, Venic 1773, col. 631, hasten to remind Leo that holds the position of both Apostles; Jerome celebrated remark to Heliodorus, 'Non est faci stare in loco Petri et Pauli' is quoted by Benetu *De autoritate romanae ecclesiae*, and Poggio, potestate papae et concilii*, fol. 8v. (see ns. 26, 6 The succession of the popes from the tv *Principes apostolorum* was symbolized by the tv portraits on papal lead bulls, and by the ritu at the Coronation in the Lateran, during whic the pope was placed successively on tv porphyry thrones, the one on the right signif ing the 'principis apostolorum Petri primatu the one on the left the 'doctoris gentium Pau

discussion of portraits with the observation that there seem to be two more, perhaps three, in this tapestry in the group behind Saint Paul. Each of these figures is particularized in a way that sets them apart from the wide repertory of Raphaelesque types that forms the remainder of the Athenian audience.

In the case of the portly figure wearing a cap (*Pl.* 40), two suggestions have already been made; in the nineteenth century this was believed to be Leo himself,[85] and more recently he has been identified as Tommaso Inghirami.[86] In the choice that we make—and there seem to be no other plausible candidates to be added—we are spared one of the normal obstructions to identification since portraits of Leo and Inghirami exist by Raphael himself; and in my judgement the comparative material makes it clear that the head is indeed that of the pope. The portly stature was common to both men, but only Leo had the dark, flushed complexion of this figure, and its deeply furrowed features; on the other hand the head in the Cartoon, while seeming to be characterized by weak eyesight, appropriately for Leo, notably lacks the squint that disfigured Inghirami.[87] We may compare this head not only with the one in the Uffizi portrait of 1517–18 (*Fig.* 2), but also with the most intensely realized (and the last) of all Raphael's portraits of Leo, the monumental black-chalk drawing at Chatsworth in which the gaze is similarly directed upwards (*Fig.* 39).[88] The bearded figure standing next to Raphael's patron and listening with equal concentration to Paul's sermon (*Pl.* 40) seems most likely to be the greatest Greek scholar of the period, Janus Lascaris, mutual friend of pope and artist. The identification in this case is more problematic because we have to rely on one likeness of Lascaris, evidently made at a later date, which found its way into Paolo Giovio's portrait-collection and was thus reproduced in a number of copies (*Fig.* 37).[89] It is true that these show Lascaris with a shorter beard, but on the other hand at an earlier date the Greek's beard, since it was particularly remarked upon,[90] must have been rather impressive, and it does seem that the features, and above all the severe expression, of the heads in the Cartoon and in the Giovio portraits are compatible. The close association between Raphael and Lascaris is attested by an epigram of the latter in praise of the artist which appears to have been written on his death, and which has been overlooked by Raphael scholars.[91]

Let us now return to the consideration of the whole series, leaving aside for the moment *Paul preaching at Athens.* It must surely be clear that these tapestries do not represent, in any precisely meaningful sense, the Acts of the Apostles. The inclusion of the Miraculous Draught of Fishes and the Charge to Peter, and the exclusion of such events as Pentecost, leave no doubt on that score. The structure of the literal reading of the two cycles resembles nothing so much as one of the great sermons for the Feast of the two Apostles, attributed now to the Beatus Maximus of Turin but in some early collections to Saint Leo.[92] This resemblance is probably not accidental. Such sermons were still in use in the *Capella papalis*,[93] and Leo X, as we have seen, had a special reverence for the first pope of the name.

By way of introduction we should bear in mind (once more) that these tapestries were to hang in the pope's chapel, that the pope is successor to both Peter and Paul,[94] and that at this date the preeminence of the Roman Church is derived in great part—at least in argument—from its foundation jointly by the two Princes of the Apostles and from its consecration by their joint Roman martyrdom.[95] Leo himself endowed the Sistine Chapel with a sumptuous Missal for the Feast of Saints Peter and Paul.[96]

In the *Miraculous Draught of Fishes* the humble and sinful fisherman is

praedicatio' (*Pontificale romanae curiae*, ed. M. Andrieu, in *Studi e testi*, 87, Vatican City, 1940, pp. 282, 538–9, and 88, 1940, p. 88; *Ceremonie in coronatione summi Pontificis*, B.M., MS. Harley 3462, fol. 156r.; G. de Novaés, *Il sacro rito antico e moderno della . . . Elezione del Sommo Pontefice . . .*, Rome, 1769, p. 216).

95. See especially Leo I, *Sermo in natali Petri et Pauli I* (1470 ed., cit. in n. 93; LXXXII in *The Letters and Sermons of Leo the Great*, ed. C. L. Feltoe, Oxford, 1895, p. 194; included in the *Homeliarius* for the Feast of SS. Peter and Paul), and Beatus Maximus (or Leo I), *Sermones in natali Petri et Pauli I*, *IV*, and *V* in the group listed above, n. 92 (*P.L.* 57, cols. 396, 402, 405). For other early sources, see the collection by L. F. J. Meulenberg, 'Der Primat der römischen Kirche im Denken und Handeln Gregors VII.', *Mededelingen van het Nederlands Historisch Instituut te Rome*, xxxiii, 2, 1966, pp. 20, 29; K. Adam, 'Neue Untersuchungen über die Ursprünge der kirchlichen Primatslehre', *Theologische Quartalschrift*, cix, 1928, pp. 197 ff.; E. Caspar, 'Primatus Petri . . .', *Zeitschrift der Savigny-Stiftung für Rechtsgeschichte*, xlvii, Kan. Abt. xvi, 1927, p. 269; C. Ihm, *Die Programme der christlichen Apsismalerei vom vierten Jahrhundert bis zur Mitte des achten Jahrhunderts*, Wiesbaden, 1960, p. 22. For sources closer to Raphael: Torquemada, *Summa ecclesiastica*, ed. cit. in n. 19, p. 228; Platina, *Liber de vita Christi ac Pontificum omnium* (ed. 1685, p. 8); Aegidius of Viterbo, *Oratio* at formal opening of Lateran Council, 3 May 1512, separately printed Rome, 1512; also in J. Hardouin, *Acta Conciliorum et epistolae decretales ac constitutiones summorum pontificum*, ix, Paris, 1714, col. 1580; Benetus, op. cit. in n. 26, fol. 1, v.; Giustiniani-Quirini, *Libellus ad Leonem X*, ed. cit. in n. 94, col. 617. One of Leo X's new coins is a *Doppio Giulio* with busts of SS. Peter and Paul *all'antica*, inscribed: *FUNDATORES ROMAN. ECCLESIAE* (C. Serafini, *Le monete e le bolle plumbee pontificie del medagliere Vaticano*, i, Milan, 1910, p. 178, No. 17, Pl. XXVIII. 9). Modern theologians do not argue the Primacy of the Roman Church from any dependence upon Peter's presence or death in Rome (W. Ullmann, 'Leo I and the theme of Papal Primacy', *Journal of Theological Studies*, N.S. xi, 1960, p. 28); it is essential to remember that in the Renaissance this argument was strongly supported, and just as strongly attacked by anti-papal interests; for a masterly survey of this controversy see R. Baümer, 'Die Auseinandersetzungen über die römische Petrustradition in den ersten Jahrzehnten der Reformationszeit', *Römische Quartalschrift*, lvii, 1962, pp. 20 ff.

96. X. Barbier de Montault, 'Inventaire de la Chapelle Papale', *Bulletin monumental*, Sér. v,

No. 7, vol. xlv, 1879, p. 267: 'Un messal grande, dove è una messa ad longum dei SS. Pietro e Paolo, coperto di broccato in filo rosso, con 4 scudi d'argento indorato, dove son rilievi et intagli, cioè quattro teste de leone con 4 diamanti con lettere Suave gloviis, con 4 fibbie d'argento indorate'; I have been unable to trace this MS.

97. This paragraph is based upon Sermons I, III and IV in the group listed in n. 92.

98. *Sermo III*: 'Quantum igitur meriti apud Deum suum Petrus erat, ut ei post naviculae parvae remigium totius Ecclesiae gubernacula traderentur?'; cf. Ambrose, *Sermo de mirabilibus* (1490 ed. XI; *P.L.* 17, cols. 675 ff., as No. XXXVII); idem, *Expositio ... in corpus evangelii Sancti Luce evangeliste*, on Luke v. 3, which is included as a sermon in the *Homeliarius* collections for the fourth Sunday after Pentecost, for which the Gospel is Luke v. It may be convenient to relate here the other texts of the tapestries to the *Missale Romanum*: Donation of Keys/Charge to Peter: Gospels for Feasts of Cathedra Petri (22 February) and Eve and Feast of SS. Peter and Paul; Stoning of Stephen: *Lectio* for Feast of Saint Stephen; Conversion of Saul: *Lectio* for Feast of Conversion of Saul (ed. Venice, 1509, fols. 142v., 169v. ff., 164r., 11r.). The text for the Healing of the Lame Man ('Argentum et aurum non est mihi: quod autem habeo, hoc tibi do', Acts iii. 6) was in this period spoken by the newly elected pope at his Coronation (MS. cit. in n. 94, fol. 156r.).

99. Cf. Ambrose, *Sermo* cit. in n. 98, and *Expositio ... in corpus evangelii Sancti Luce evangeliste*, Augsburg, 1476, Bk. IV; Augustine, *Sermo CCXLVIII* (on the Miraculous Draught: *P.L.* 38, col. 1159).

100. Cf. Jerome, *Commentaria in Evangelium S. Matthaei* (*P.L.* 26, col. 117); Augustine, *Sermo CCXCV* (*P.L.* 38, cols. 1348 ff.); Bede, *Homilia XVI, in natali Petri et Pauli* (*P.L.* 94, col. 221); idem, *Expositio in Matthaei Evangelium* (*P.L.* 92, col. 78); *Glossa ordinaria* (*P.L.* 114, cols. 141 ff.).

101. *Sermo I*, in the group listed in n. 92 (LXVIII in *P.L.* 57, col. 394).

102. Prudentius, *Dittochaei*, xlvii, *Vas electionis*:

'Hic lupus ante rapax vestitur vellere molli:
Saulus qui fuerat, fit adempto lumine Paulus.
Mox recipit visum, fit apostolus ac populorum
Doctor et ore potens corvos mutare columbis.'

Cf. also: Augustine, *Sermones CCLXXIX, CCCXVI, CCCXVII* (*P.L.* 38, cols. 1275, 1433, 1435); Arator, *De actibus apostolorum*, cap. xvii, xxxii; Petrus Comestor, *Historia scholastica: in*

selected by Christ to be a fisher of men;[97] the oarsman of the little boat is chosen to be the helmsman of the great ship of the Church, to occupy, that is, the position of *gubernator* for the moment held by Christ (Raphael is precise on this point).[98] When he obeys Christ's command to launch out into the deep and let down his nets he preaches and converts by divine and profound doctrine; the nets are broken only by heretics.[99] The profundity of Peter's faith is tested and proved twice in the conflated events shown in the second tapestry, the *Charge to Peter*. Through the inspiration of the Holy Spirit, and not by earthly knowledge, he recognizes Christ, the Son of the Living God; because of this faith, superior to that of the other Apostles, he is Simon Bar-Jonah, Son of the Dove, and he is now Petrus, after Petra, the Stone, which is Christ Himself.[100] This firm faith is to be the foundation of Christ's Church, and it is proof against all heresy. To Simon, now Peter, are promised the Keys and the office of *Janitor coeli* with the power of the remission of sins. The faith of Peter is tested a second time in the threefold question: 'Simon ... lovest thou me more than these?'; and it is rewarded with the threefold command: 'Feed my sheep.' Christ is the True and Eternal Shepherd, not Peter; but to Peter is given the care of the flock. 'So that those whom Christ's mercy should redeem, will be preserved by the strength of Peter's faith', as the Beatus Maximus says; 'and rightly did the Son of God commit to him the duty of tending and feeding His sheep, in whom He confirmed that there was lacking neither care nor faith for the raising of the Lord's flock.'[101]

The Pauline story begins in a very similar way, and we can continue with a passage from the same sermon: 'What should I say of the most glorious Paul, in whom the Lord confided His faith while he yet persecuted that

Actus Apostolorum, cap. xlii (*P.L.* 190, col. 1671); Thomas Aquinas, *Commentaria super epistolas S. Pauli*, Bologna, 1481 (unpaginated: Galatians i. 11–14); Nicolaus de Lyra, *Expositiones morales secundum sensum mysticum super totam Bibliam*, Mantua, 1481 (unpaginated: Acts ix. 3–8). This concept also crops up in the context of the Cartoons; see, for example, Baptista Spagnuoli (Mantuanus, d. 1516), *Fasti* (*De sacris diebus*, ded. Leo X), Bk. XII, *De Sancto Stephano*: 'Ecce Lupus de gente rapax Isacidae Saulus' (ed. Poitiers, 1518).

103. This event seems always to be taken as coincidental with the conversion: Augustine, *De videndo Deo*, cap. xiii (*P.L.* 33, col. 610); Arator, loc. cit. in n. 102 (cf. commentary by Barbosa, ed. cit. in n. 10, fol. lxxv, v.); *Glossa ordinaria* (*P.L.* 114, col. 448); Aquinas, op. cit. in n. 102 (on II Cor. xii. 2); Nicolaus de Lyra, *Postilla super actus apostolorum ...*, Mantua, 1480 (on Acts ix. 3–8). For texts contemporary with the Cartoons: Mantuanus, op. cit. in n. 102, Bk. I, *De conversione sancti Pauli*, and Jacobazzi, *De concilio*, ed. cit. in n. 61, p. 668.

104. These titles are very commonly paired in this way: for example on the mosaic formerly on the façade of S. Paolo fuori le mura where Paul, on Christ's right (our left), and Peter on His left, were accompanied by the inscriptions:

VAS ELECTIONIS ET DOCTOR GEN- TIUM and *PRINCEPS AP(OSTO)L (RUM) ET PASTOR OVIUM* (J. Wilpert *Die römischen Mosaiken und Malereien der kirchliche Bauten vom iv. bis xiii. Jahrhundert*, Freiburg-im Breisgau, 1916, ii, pp. 627 ff.). For the histor of these titles, and the distinctions of functio that they imply, see the rich collection of sources in P. J. Ficker, *Die Quellen für d Darstellung der Apostel in der altchristlichen Kuns* Altenburg, 1886, pp. 7–21.

105. *Sermo III* in the group cit. in n. 92 (LX in *P.L.* 57, cols. 397–400).

106. For other texts relating the *Miraculo Draught* and the *Stoning of Stephen*, see Ambros *Hexaemeron*, Bk. V, cap. vi (*P.L.* 14, col. 212 idem, *Expositio ... in corpus evangelii Sancti Lu evangeliste* (ed. Augsburg, 1476, Bk. IV, o Luke v. 3); Augustine, *Sermones CCLII* (on th Miraculous Draught) and *CCCXVI* (on Sai Stephen: *P.L.* 38, cols. 1173 ff., 1432). For relation between the Charge to Peter and th Conversion of Saul, see, e.g., Nicolaus de Lyr *Expositiones morales*, ed. cit. in n. 102 (on Ac ix. 3–8: 'deus ... saulum lupum atroce fecit ovium pium pastorem'). In Augustine *De videndo Deo* the revelation to Peter in Ma thew xvi. 16 and that to Paul at his conversic are discussed and implicitly compared

faith? Who, while he laid waste the Christian Church like the harshest persecutor, as Christ's enemy yet found Him to be a friend in his heart; and even as he forced Christians into submission (the 'relief', *Fig.* 20), was himself seized to eternal grace (the *Conversion*, *Fig.* 20); from a wolf he was suddenly turned into a shepherd, from a robber into a watchman, and from an enemy into a defender.' One point needs explaining here. Saul, who came from the Tribe of Benjamin, was very widely identified with the *Benjamin lupus rapax* of Genesis xlix. 27: the ravenous wolf of whom Jacob prophesied, 'In the morning he shall devour the prey, and at even he shall divide the spoil' (that is, he shall begin as a persecutor and end as a friend). Thus the *lupus rapax* who persecutes Stephen and—as in the 'relief' below the *Conversion* (*Fig.* 20)—the Church generally, becomes both sheep and shepherd.[102] He is at the same time revealed as Christ's chosen vessel, the *Vas electionis*, another of Paul's most common titles (e.g. *Fig.* 32); and while temporarily blinded to earthly things at his conversion, was 'caught up even to the third heaven' (II Corinthians xii. 2) and instructed in the most profound secrets.[103]

Thus Paul is appointed by divine revelation and grace to be the *Doctor* or *Magister gentium*, as Peter, in the opposite tapestry, is appointed to be *Princeps apostolorum et Pastor ovium* on the strength of his divine revelation.[104] It is a feature of the sermons by Leo the Great or the Beatus Maximus that this kind of comparison is frequently drawn. We may take from another, for example, this conjunction: 'How great were the merits of Peter in the eyes of God that he was promoted from the oars of his little boat to the helm of the ship of the whole Church? Or how much should we believe Paul to have been esteemed by Christ for the preaching of His Gospel when even as persecutor he satisfied Him so entirely?'; the same sermon continues with a comparison between the revelation to Saul at the moment of his conversion and the consignment of the Keys to Peter.[105] The first two tapestries in each set form particularly striking pairs in the same manner as do the Sixtine frescoes.[106]

The two cycles each continue with a pair of tapestries illustrating the complementary powers and fields of action of Peter and Paul. The *Healing of the Lame Man* is the first of Peter's miracles described in Acts, as the *Conversion of the Proconsul* is the first of Paul's, and they were performed among Jews and Gentiles respectively. As Paul sets out most clearly in Galatians ii. 7–9, and as was always acknowledged, the care of the Church and the preaching of the Gospel among the Jews were especially committed to Peter, those among the Gentiles especially to himself,[107] although each did in fact operate in the other's territory. In the final pair of tapestries, the *Death of Ananias* and the *Sacrifice at Lystra*, the Apostles confront the sins of the two peoples, that of the Jews being obstinacy or disobedience,[108] and that of the Gentiles idolatry. This particular emphasis is not implied in the group of sermons in question, and was perhaps inspired by the pairing of the Sixtine frescoes, among the *tituli* of which is the unexpected *Conturbatio* of the Old and New Covenants.[109]

It is precisely because the structure of the cycle, when read in the historical or literal sense, is sermon-like that we may anticipate and justify further readings in other, moral, senses in the manner of sermons.[110] It is particularly clear from the combination of subjects in the Petrine set that there is a reading to be made in the doctrinal or ecclesiological sense.

The text for the *Miraculous Draught of Fishes* (Luke v) has a long and consistent history as one of the principal proofs of the *Primatus Petri*. More important, perhaps, than a massive text-pile from the Church Fathers[111] is a series of references to their doctrine in tracts on the *Primatus* from the period

successive chapters (xii, xiii: *P.L.* 33, col. 610). In the *Missale Romanum* (ed. Venice, 1509, fol. 164) the *Lectio* for the Feast of the Conversion of Saul is Acts ix. 1–20 (including the text for the tapestry), the second *Oratio* refers to the Donation of the Keys. The two 'elections' are frequently compared or contrasted in tracts of Raphael's period: for example in Jacobazzi's *De concilio*, ed. cit. in n. 61, p. 668. It is worth recalling Michelangelo's first project for the Cappella Paolina: 'due storie una di San Pietro e l'altra di San Paulo, l'una dove Christo dà le chiavi a Pietro; l'altra la terribile conversione di Paulo' (G. Vasari, *Vite*, Florence, 1550, p. 987).

107. E.g. Ambrose, *Commentaria in epistolam ad Galatas* (*P.L.* 17, col. 349): '(Paulus) Petrum solum nominat, et sibi comparat; quia primatum ipse acceperat ad fundandam Ecclesiam: se quoque pari modo electum, ut primatum habeat in fundandis gentium Ecclesiis ... plana auctoritas Petro in Judaismi praedicatione data dignoscitur, et Pauli perfecta auctoritas in praedicatione gentium invenitur ...'; Jerome, *Commentaria in epistolam ad Galatas* (*P.L.* 26, cols. 336–7): Peter and Paul were sent to Jew and Gentile 'ut Christo ex cunctis gentibus Ecclesiam congregarent'.

108. The fault of the Jews is generally expressed by the metaphor 'durissima cervix', stiff-neck, e.g. by Maximus, *Sermo VI in natali Petri & Pauli* (LXXIII in *P.L.* 57, cols. 407 ff.); it is defined as obstinacy by Giustiniani-Quirini, *Libellus*, ed. cit. in n. 94, col. 622, and by Thomas de Vio, *Oratio ... in secunda sessione Concilii Lateranensis* (16 May 1512), separately printed, Rome, 1512 (also in Hardouin, op. cit. in n. 95, ix, col. 1620).

109. In fact the rebellion of Ananias is specifically compared with that of the sons of Aaron by Petrus Comestor, *Historia scholastica: in Actus Apostolorum*, cap. xxii (*P.L.* 198, col. 1659) in the sense that these events demonstrated the rigour of nascent law in the primitive Synagogue and Church.

110. H. Caplan, 'The four senses of Scriptural Interpretation and the mediaeval Theory of Preaching', *Speculum*, iv, 1929, pp. 282 ff.: a survey of the systems of plural interpretation (up to eight) in preaching that only began to fall into disrepute with the Reformation.

111. H. Rahner, S.J., 'Navicula Petri: zur Symbolgeschichte des römischen Primats', *Zeitschrift für katholische Theologie*, lxix, 1947, pp. 1 ff., is a comprehensive study.

112. Poggio, *De potestate papae et concilii* (1511–1512), ed. Rome, 1517 (?), fols. 42v. (quoting Bede), 61r. (Ambrose); Marcello, *De authoritate summi Pontificis* (loc. cit. in n. 54, quoting Ambrose); Angelo da Vallombrosa, *Oratio pro concilio Lateranensi contra conventiculum pisanum* (Sept.–Oct. 1511), ed. R. Maiocchi, in *Rivista di scienze storiche*, iv, 1907, pp. 344–5 (quoting Chrysostom); Paris de Grassis, *Utra ex statuis . . .*, MS. Vat. Lat. 5634/1, fol. 39v. The importance of the nautical metaphor of papal power can hardly be overrated. From the early period the extended image in the *Apostolic Constitutions* attributed to Clement I is probably the most important text; Leo I calls himself *Gubernator Ecclesiae* (*Sermo I*, in *Opera*, Rome, 1470). The concept is expressed in papal coins of the fifteenth and sixteenth centuries, and in the texts of Papal Bulls of the period of the Lateran Council. Typical of the applications to Leo X is this passage from a congratulatory letter from Pietro Delfin, 13 March 1513 (*Epistolae*, ed. Jacobus Brixianus, Venice, 1524, Bk. XI. i; O. Raynaldus, *Annales ecclesiastici*, xx, Cologne, 1694, p. 135): 'laborasti per multos annos in remigando (i.e. as cardinal, Legate, etc.); nunc ad clavum naviculae suae posuit te Dominus: sperant omnes non defuturum per gubernatoris sapientiam & studium, quin felici stante desuper aura, post multas tempestates et procellas in portum tutissimum deducatur' (which may be compared with the passage from Maximus/Leo, *Sermo III*, quoted in n. 98 above; but the letter is at this point closely related to the *Oratio* of Aegidius of Viterbo at the opening of the Lateran Council, 3 May 1512: Hardouin, op. cit. in n. 95, col. 1577). For Leo's own frequent use of the image see, for example, his letters of 17 March, 4 April, 10 July 1513, in P. Bembo, *Epistolae Leonis Decimi . . . nomine scriptae*, Lyon, 1538, pp. 7, 26, 75.

113. *Epistolae*, Bk. VII. cciii (*P.L.* 215, col. 512): 'Navis ergo Simonis est Ecclesia Petri, quae benedicitur una, quia catholica Ecclesia una est, quam Christus commisit Petro regendam, ut unitas divisionem excludat . . . (Christus) sedens docebat de navicula turbas, quia extunc fecit Petrum stabilem sedem habere, sive in Laterano, sive in Vaticano.'

114. *Oratio* at opening of Lateran Council (Hardouin, op. cit. in n. 95, ix, col. 1577): 'universa ecclesia . . . in altissimis apicibus ac sanctissimis montibus . . . fundata est. *Fundamenta enim ejus in montibus sanctis.* Unitas nempe mons Dei nuncupatur, quod in una dumtaxat Dei essentia sit atque natura: & ut unitatem illam non solitariam, non sterilem, sed uberrima fecunditate praeditam cogitemus, ideo mons pinguis adjicitur.' For his identification with the

Mons Vaticanus, see J. W. O'Malley, S.J., 'Giles of Viterbo: a Reformer's thought on Renaissance Rome', *Renaissance Quarterly*, xx, 1967, pp. 9–11, and idem, op. cit. in n. 6, pp. 122, 124, 162 n. 2, 190. Also, for another aspect of the mystique of the Mons Vaticanus 'concretized and symbolized' in the basilica see idem, 'The Fulfillment of the Christian Golden Age under Pope Julius II: text of a discourse of Giles of Viterbo, 1507', *Traditio*, xxv, 1969, p. 272. The prophecy from Psalm lxxxvii is quoted by Cyprian Benetus, *De prima orbis sede, de consilio, & ecclesiastica potestate . . .* (ed. *princeps* dated 1512, but with revised dedication to Leo X), in Rocaberti, op. cit. in n. 25, vii, p. 763, in a slightly different sense: the *fundamenta in montibus sanctis* are the Apostles collectively, from whom Peter is particularly selected by Christ (*Tu es Petrus . . .*, Matthew xvi. 18); this is closely similar to another interpretation of the prophecy by Thomas de Vio, *Oratio*, 16 May 1512 (cit. in n. 108; Hardouin, ix, col. 1621). The identification of the Mons Vaticanus with Mount Zion is also, however, clearly implied in Leo's Bull *Posteaquam ad universalis ecclesiae curam* (5 May 1514, ninth session of Lateran Council, in Hardouin, ix, col. 1742): 'ex summo statim Apostolatus apice, tamquam ex vertice montis Sion'; see also Poggio, *De potestate papae et concilii*, Rome, 1517(?), fol. 39r. A little later, in the *Oratio* of Stephanus de Taleazis, Archbishop of Patras, at the tenth session, 4 May 1515 (Hardouin, ix, cols. 1784 ff.), the Apostolic Throne is compared with the *Mons sanctus* of two other biblical texts; he begins by quoting Psalm xlviii. 1: 'Magnus Dominus, & laudabilis nimis, in civitate Dei nostri in monte sancto ejus . . .', and explains: 'Dicat propheta: *In civitate Dei*, in sancta utique immaculata ecclesia Dei, & quod fortius et dignius est, *in monte sancto* Apostolicae Sedis ejus; de quo Isaias (ii. 2): *Et erit in novissimis diebus mons praeparatus in domo Domini super verticem omnium montium*, qui est potestas plenitudinis Christi ejus in Sede Apostolica, per legem immaculatam super omnia regna mundi sedens . . .'; he returns later to the 'mons sanctus Apostolicae Sedis'. It should be noted, furthermore, that Andrea Fulvio, *Antiquaria urbis*, Rome, 1513, fol. 34r., had remarked that on the Mons Vaticanus, ancient seat of oracles, now stood rightly the temple of Peter, supreme fisherman, on whom rose firm the Roman Church; and that this was the seat of apostolic, universal authority, where now Leo was enthroned. Following this line of (public) thought it is clear that a representation of the Mons Vaticanus in the tapestry could well be read by a contemporary as a figure of papal authority. But an alternative approach to the 'topographical portrait' is sufficiently remarkable and circumstantial to be mentioned,

although I can find no echoes of it in Leo pontificate. The *Naumachia* (or *Stagnum*) *Neron* was believed, in the fifteenth century, to hav been to the South of the Mons Vaticanus, tha is, where the stretch of water (*stagnum* in Luk v. 2) in the tapestry is located (e.g. by Flavi Biondo, *Romae instauratae . . . liber*, Rome, 147 (?), I, xliv, and in Alessandro Strozzi's map c Rome, 1474, repr. J. M. Huskinson, 'Th Crucifixion of Saint Peter', *Journal of the Wa burg and Courtauld Institutes*, xxxii, 1969, P 14b). Maffeo Vegio, op. cit. in n. 71, p. 66 discussing the *site* of the Vatican basilica unde the rubric *Naumachia Neronis* (cedit) Petro, say that Peter was appointed our protagonist in th Miraculous Draught so that the 'shipwrecked human race should be saved from its enemie 'quasi in hac mundi naumachia pugnanti ill ac omnibus successoribus, ad id *eodem in loc* electis Pontificibus, committeret'.

115. Cf. again, for example, the importan sermon of Ambrose, *De mirabilibus* (ed. 149C XI; *P.L.* 17, cols. 675 ff., as XXXVII): 'Han igitur solam ecclesiae navem ascendit dominus in qua petrus magister est constitutus dicent domino: Super hanc petram aedificabo eccle siam meam.' Arator, *De actibus apostolorum*, cap ii, links the Miraculous Draught directly wit the Donation of the Keys and the Charge t Peter (see also Barbosa's commentary, ed. cit in n. 10, fol. xvii, v.).

116. Torquemada, *Summa*, Bk. II, passim. Fo contemporary sources, see especially: Thoma de Vio, *De comparatione auctoritatis Papae & Concilii*, cap. i (1511: Rocaberti, op. cit. in n 25, xix, p. 446); idem, *De romani pontific institutione* (ed. *princeps* 1521: Rocaberti, xix, p 526—'duo sunt praecipui textus, scilicet Matth 16 & Ioann. ult.'); Angelo da Vallombrosa *Oratio* (1511), cit. in n. 112, p. 345; Bernarde Zane, *Oratio* at Lateran Council, first session (1512: Hardouin, op. cit. in n. 95, ix, col 1604); Giustiniani-Quirini, *Libellus ad Leoner X* (1513: ed. cit. in n. 94, col. 616); Benetus *De prima orbis sede* (1512: Rocaberti, vii, p 763); Jacobazzi, *De concilio* (1511 ff.: ed. cit in n. 61, p. 666); Silvestro Mazzolini, *De pap et eius potestate* (Rocaberti, xix, p. 369); Par de Grassis, *Utra ex statuis* (c. 1515: MS. Vat Lat. 5634/1, fol. 39v.); Petrus Galatinus (chap lain to Cardinal Lorenzo Pucci), *De republic christiana* (c. 1519, dedicated to Leo, Bibl. Vat. MS. Vat. Lat. 5578, fol. 87r.).

117. Jacobazzi, *De concilio*, ed. cit. in n. 61, p 664; *Ioh. Poggii Florentini ad Leonem X.P.M. D veri pastoris munere liber*, MS. Vat. Lat. 3732 fol. 15r. (c. 1516); also, idem, op. cit. in n. 61 fols. 16v., 37v. The conflation appears i Sacramentaries of the eighth–tenth centurie in the *Collectio* for the Feast of Cathedra Petr

of the Cartoons—for example in Giovanni Francesco Poggio's *De potestate papae et concilii*, in Christoforo Marcello's *De authoritate summi pontificis*, or in the *Oratio pro Concilio Lateranensi* of Angelo da Vallombrosa; even Paris de Grassis cites the event in this sense.[112] It is a commonplace of these interpretations that Peter and his boat, each selected by Christ, are figures of the Church. Typical is a conspicuous letter of Innocent III in which the text is taken to mean, by extension of the figure, that Christ appointed Peter to supremacy 'so that unity should exclude schism'; when Christ sat in Peter's boat, he explains, it signified that 'Peter was given a firm throne, whether in the Lateran or the Vatican'.[113] This is one way in which the inclusion of a view of the Mons Vaticanus in this scene might be interpreted. To Aegidius of Viterbo the Mons Vaticanus fulfilled the prophecy of the *Mons sanctus Dei* in a number of Old Testament texts, notably Psalm lxxxvii: *Fundamenta enim ejus in montibus sanctis*; it was the new Mount Zion, the eternal centre of orthodoxy, grace and Petrine authority.[114] And the identification of the Mons Vaticanus with Mount Zion became well established, for we find inscribed on Bernini's colonnade, by the entrance to the Scala Regia: VENITE ASCENDAMUS IN MONTEM DOMINI ADOREMUS IN TEMPLO SANCTO EIUS. For Aegidius it was a symbol of *unitas*, and significantly Innocent III's letter celebrated the re-unification of the Church. To this aspect of the tapestry we shall return. For the moment it must be insisted that on the doctrinal level of interpretation it is uniquely in the sense of Petrine authority that the Miraculous Draught is the logical introduction to the Donation of the Keys and the Charge to Peter.[115]

We saw before that these two subjects are assimilated in the second Petrine tapestry. It is in the context of the *Primatus Petri*—and, so far as I know, only in that context—that the two texts from Matthew xvi and John xxi are not only juxtaposed on innumerable occasions,[116] but also frequently conflated. As examples from the immediate context of the Cartoons we may take a passage from Domenico Jacobazzi's *De concilio tractatus*, 'dicente domino pasce oves meas & quodcumque ligaveris super terram &c.', or another from Giovanni Francesco Poggio's *De veri pastoris munere*, 'Potestas haec sola a Christo est Petro et successoribus nullo mediante concessa dicente, Tibi dabo claves regni caelorum, Et pasce oves meas.'[117] Separately, also, the two texts are, of course, normally cited as the clearest proofs of the *Primatus*;[118] the point of the juxtaposition is that the second clarifies, and removes a slight ambiguity from, the first.[119] It is beyond doubt, I think, that

---

ejusque successores vicarios suos instituit' (Hardouin, op. cit. in n. 95, ix, col. 1826).

118. Caspar, op. cit. in n. 95, pp. 255 ff.; Meulenberg, op. cit. in n. 95, p. 26; E. Dinkler, 'Die ersten Petrusdarstellungen', *Marburger Jahrbuch für Kunstwissenschaft*, xi, 1938, p. 66; M. Maccarone, *Vicarius Christi: storia del titolo papale*, Rome, 1952, pp. 16 ff. For a detailed analysis of these texts in the period of the Cartoons, see Jacobazzi, *De concilio*, ed. cit. in n. 61, pp. 663–7; it is perhaps unnecessary to cite further references, which are very numerous. It is, however, relevant to mention the use made of the two texts, as sources of pontifical authority, in the Bull *Unam Sanctam* of Boniface VIII, confirmed by Leo X in December 1516 (Hardouin, op. cit. in n. 95, ix, col. 1830), and in Leo's own Bulls: *Nos qui pontificatus dignitate*, 3 September 1513 (Raynaldus, *Annales*, ed. cit. in n. 112, p. 159); *Supernae dispositionis arbitrio* (the Reform Bull of 5 May 1514: Hardouin, ix, col. 1747); *Supernae maiestatis praesidio* (December 1516: Hardouin, ix, col. 1806); and *Lex supernae* (11 October 1521, appointing Henry VIII *Defensor fidei*: *Bullarium*, ed. cit. in n. 29, p. 273). In the last case Leo was responding to Henry's *Assertio septem sacramentorum adversus Martinum Lutherum*, London and Rome, 1521, in which the Donation of the Keys is (almost ritualistically) cited as proof of papal authority; a probable gift from Henry to Leo of about this date is recorded in the inventory of the sacristy of the Cappella Paolina, 1547: 'una pianeta figurata tutta, e riccamata d'oro, dove Xpo dà le chiave a San Piero, con l'arme del re d'Inghilterra' (Barbier de Montault, op. cit. in n. 96, No. 6). It is also worth remembering the quotations and paraphrases of Matthew xvi and John xxi in the inscriptions around the dome and in the frieze of Saint Peter's, and that the *Donation of the Keys* and the *Charge to Peter* are set as reliefs in the *Cathedra Petri* of Bernini.

G. P. Kirsch, 'Le Feste degli Apostoli S. Pietro e S. Paolo nel martirologio Geroniamo', *Rivista di archeologia cristiana*, ii, 1925, pp. 56 ff.); the tradition is perhaps to be traced back to Cyprian's *De catholicae Ecclesiae unitate* (A.D. 251: cf. J. Chapman, O.S.B., 'Les interpolations dans le traité de S. Cyprian sur l'unité de l'Eglise,' *Revue Bénédictine*, xix, 1902, pp. 50–1). An example from the later mediaeval period is in Matteo da Aquasparta's *Sermo de potestate papae* (preached before Boniface VIII, 1302: text, ed. G. Gál, in *Bibliotheca Franciscana ascetica medii aevi*, Florence, 1962, p. 186); the address on the same subject by John of Montenero at the Council of Florence, 1439, provides another (J. Gill, S.J., *Personalities of the Council of Florence*, Oxford, 1964, p. 272); and the same formula in the same context is used by Torquemada (*Summa*, Bk. II, cap. vi: ed. cit. in n. 19, p. 187). However, this formula seems to appear with the greatest frequency in the period of the Cartoons; in addition to the sources quoted above, see also: Benetus, op. cit. in n. 116, pp. 752, 763; *Petrosanti Sansonij . . . Papalogus elegeiacus* (c. 1514, dedicated to Leo), Bibl. Laur., MS. Plut. xxxvii. 23, fols. 17v. ff.; an epigram addressed to Leo by Faustinus Buturinus Veronensis, Bibl. Vat., MS. Ottob. Lat. 1519, fol. 32r.; and Marco Girolamo Vida, *Christiados*, Cremona, 1535, Bk. VI (commissioned by Leo X). It is fundamental to the opening of the greatest of Leonine Bulls, *Pastor Aeternus*, 19 December 1516: 'Pastor aeternus gregem suum usque ad consummationem saeculi nunquam deserturus . . . migraturus vero ex mundo ad Patrem, *in soliditate petrae Petrum*

119. The ambiguity in Matthew xvi alone (which could be, and was, exploited by antipapal interests) arises from Matthew xviii. 18 (and to a lesser extent John xx. 23), in which Christ appears to confer the power of the Keys on all the Apostles, not Peter specifically; the Charge to Peter in John xxi, when read with Matthew xvi, removes this difficulty: see Torquemada, *Summa*, ed. cit. in n. 19, p. 187; Jacobazzi, *De concilio*, ed. cit. in n. 61, pp. 665 ff., and Poggio, op. cit. in n. 61, fol. 16v. In Raphael's Cartoon the second Miraculous Draught, which precedes the Charge to Peter (John xxi. 1–11), is clearly recalled in the boat and nets drawn up on the shore; this event was also adduced as a proof of the *Primatus*: for example by Torquemada, *Summa*, ed. cit., p. 197.

120. For example by Innocent III in the letter to the Patriarch of Constantinople that amounts to a classic *tractatus* on the *Primatus*: 'Hic (sc: Petrus) inter discipulos, curando claudum, primus fuit miraculum operatus; et in Ananiam et Saphiram uxorem ipsius, tanquam primus et praecipuus inter eos, quia mentiti fuerant Spiritui Sancto, mortis sententiam promulgavit' (*Epistolae*, Bk. II. ccix: *P.L.* 214, col. 761; the letters of Innocent III were an authoritative source frequently consulted by Leonine theologians). For the Healing of the Lame Man as a proof of the *Primatus*, see also Poggio, op. cit. in n. 61, fol. 42v.; for the Death of Ananias, Torquemada, *Summa*, ed. cit. in n. 19, p. 185 ('in qua re maxime primatus Petri ostenditur') and Mazzolini, *De iuridica et irrefragabili veritate romanae ecclesiae* (Rocaberti, op. cit. in n. 25, xix, p. 233). This interpretation of the miracles of Peter in Acts seems to originate with Ambrose. The study by E. Florit, *Il Primato di S. Pietro negli atti degli Apostoli*, Rome, 1942, is both slight and polemical; but cf. p. 8 for the Death of Ananias.

121. Stridbeck, op. cit. in n. 62, pp. 34 ff., mistakenly separates powers of 'loosing' and 'binding' and assigns them respectively to the *Healing of the Lame Man* and the *Death of Ananias*. It must be stressed that in all periods the *potestas clavium* was indivisible and singular, from the beginning of this doctrine in Ambrose, *De poenitentia*, Bk. I (*P.L.* 16, cols. 467 ff.). The exceptions to this rule are rare and unorthodox, and are treated as such (see Anciaux, op. cit. in n. 25, pp. 544 ff.). On the other hand Stridbeck has drawn attention to a passage in Tertullian's *De pudicitia* that requires comment, since Tertullian takes the examples of the Healing of the Lame Man and the Death of Ananias to illustrate his views on the *potestas* of loosing and binding; in fact the correspondence between this passage in Tertullian and the tapestries in the chapel is even more striking than Stridbeck has observed, since it includes the Blinding of Elymas, and he cites the Healing of the Leper as a clarification of the *disciplina* of the remission of sins. But I have not found the *De pudicitia* to be a familiar source in the period, and I doubt that Tertullian's point—challenging the papal power of decision over the remission of sins—would recommend itself to Leo (the *editio princeps* is in the *Opera*, ed. Jean Gagny, Paris, 1545, and MSS. seem to be rare; the passage in question is: *De pudicitia*, Ed. G. Rauschen, in *Florilegium patristicum*, x, Bonn, 1915, pp. 91–5).

122. Petrus Lombardus, *Sententiae*, Bk. IV, dist. xviii (*P.L.* 192, cols. 885 ff.); Thomas Aquinas, *Summa*, *Additiones ad tertiam partem*, Quaestiones xvii–xxii (ed. cit. in n. 25, iv, pp. 445 ff.).

the theme of the Primacy of Peter is continued in the remaining pair of tapestries. In the literature of this problem the miracles of Peter in Acts are taken as secondary proofs, in particular his first miracle at the *Porta speciosa* and the punishment of Ananias.[120] However it seems probable that these scenes also, and perhaps principally, illustrate the doctrine of the Two Keys; in that sense they follow just as logically after the Charge to Peter.

The doctrine of the Keys in this period is not easy to grasp, partly because a definitive formulation seems not to have been achieved. This much, however, was established: that the power of remission of sins, which the Keys symbolize, was not divided as between loosing and binding, which are indivisible aspects of the same power, but between two degrees of remission.[121] First there is the capacity of *knowledge* of who should be loosed and who bound, and secondly the capacity of *performing* the loosing or binding; the second is the more reserved, being granted only to the higher degrees of priesthood. Petrus Lombardus defined the Keys as *Clavis discernendi scientia* and *Clavis potentia judicandi*; Thomas Aquinas separated them in exactly the same way, and also as *Clavis ordinis* and *Clavis iurisdictionis*.[122] According to Aquinas the second was given to Peter alone; and he specifies the Death of Ananias, a figure of excommunication, as an example of the *Clavis iurisdictionis*, the authority to administer punishment.[123]

The definition of Thomas Aquinas is also essential to the understanding of the *Healing of the Lame Man* as an example of the *Clavis ordinis*. This tapestry was designed to hang in the central position on the right side of the chancel, beneath Botticelli's *Healing of the Leper* (*Figs.* 15, 16). According to Aquinas the Keys of the Church are not like the powers of the priests of Leviticus, which admit only to the earthly tabernacle; 'the priests of the Old Covenant', he says, 'had the *potestas discernendi & iudicandi*, but not that of admitting the sinner, once judged, to Heaven' as do those of the New Covenant.[124] In another passage he is more precise: the power of the priest of the Old Testament, which he contrasts with the powers conferred with the Keys, was 'discernendi inter lepram et lepram'.[125]

We have seen already, by following a canonical passage in Saint Jerome's commentary on Matthew xvi, that the *Healing of the Leper* is a type of the *potestas ordinis*. To appreciate the full richness of meaning in the juxtaposition of the tapestry below we have to take account of a tradition of interpreting the Healing of the Lame Man, from Arator and Bede into the *Glossa ordinaria*, in which the lame man represents Israel, introduced by Peter into Christ's Church. The *Porta speciosa* is the gate to the Celestial Jerusalem.[126] Thus in a very specific sense Peter acts as *Claviger coeli*, particularly for the Jews, in the two tapestries that follow the one in which he receives that appointment.

Petrus Lombardus quotes Ambrose, *De poenitentia*; see also Augustine, *De doctrina christiana*, cap. xviii (*P.L.* 34, col. 25); idem, *Sermo CCLXVIII* (*P.L.* 38, col. 1273); Beatus Maximus, *Sermones LXVIII, LXXII* (*P.L.* 57, cols. 392–3, 403—I and V in the group discussed above, n. 92); Bede, *In Matthaei Evangelium expositio*, xvi (*P.L.* 92, col. 79); idem, *Homilia XVI* (*P.L.* 94, col. 222); Nicolaus de Lyra, *Biblia latina cum postillis*, Venice, 1489 (Isaiah xxii. 20–24, and Matthew xvi). For the origin of the imagery of the Keys, see W. Köhler, 'Die

Schlüssel des Petrus', *Archiv für Religionswissenschaft*, viii, 1905, pp. 214 ff.; and for a thorough study of the growth of the doctrine in the early Scholastic period: L. Hödl, 'Die Geschichte der scholastischen Literatur und der Theologie der Schlüsselgewalt', *Beiträge zur Geschichte der Philosophie und Theologie des Mittelalters*, xxxviii, 4, 1960, pp. 1 ff.

123. *Summa*, *Additiones*, Quaest. xxi, art. iii (ed. cit. in n. 25, iv, p. 452); the Ananias story is the only example he gives (text below, n. 182)

Finally it must be made clear that the doctrine of the Keys was familiar in the circle of Leo X and at the Lateran Council; for it is referred to by Jacobazzi, Poggio, Aegidius of Viterbo and others in essentially the same Scholastic terms.[127]

However, the operation of the powers of the Two Keys in these cases is susceptible of yet more particular definition, and it would perhaps be wrong to overlook a distinction that applies especially in Canon Law, partly because Leo X was trained in that discipline and partly because it seems to conform to the most obvious visual distinction between the two tapestries in question. The juridical distinction is between the operation of the power of loosing and binding in the *forum internum* and in the *forum externum*. The *forum internum*, which is also called the *forum poenitentiale* or *forum conscientiae*, has as its scope matters between man and God, and the *potestas ordinis* can in this case give direct access to Heaven, as in the Healing of the Lame Man. The *forum externum*, which Aquinas also calls the *forum publicum* or *forum exterius*, is the sphere of jurisdiction between man and the Christian society, and excommunication belongs to it; the crime of Ananias would properly be dealt with—through the power of the Keys—in the *forum externum*.[128] Thus Raphael's *Death of Ananias* may have its action cast in an open setting with some, at least, of the features of a Roman forum because in that design he makes concrete a metaphor of the theologians and canonists. And his *Healing of the Lame Man* may be treated contrastingly as an interior scene (which was certainly not necessary and perhaps not even natural as an illustration of any biblical text) because he gives formal expression thereby to the concept of the *forum poenitentiale*. This additional interpretation should perhaps be held in reserve in the category of potential meanings if it seems less necessary than the simpler distinction between *Clavis ordinis* and *Clavis iurisdictionis*.

The metaphorical, juridical, meaning of Botticelli's *Healing of the Leper* would have been clear, as we have seen, to a relatively minor member of Leo's court such as Cyprian Benetus. An understanding of the non-literal message here suggested for the *Healing of the Lame Man*, and in fact for the whole Petrine set, would also have been within the grasp of most of those, laymen or churchmen, who were privileged to pass the *cancellata*, and it would also have been within the range of their expectations for the decoration of that unique chancel. (It is interesting to interpolate here the contrast with Perugino's *Donation of the Keys* in the area outside the screen, where the expression of the *Primatus Petri* is theologically much less sophisticated: simpler in one sense, less carefully defined in another.) Further, the special emphasis placed upon the central fresco and central tapestry on the right wall of the chancel, and the striking correspondence of the conventional metaphorical reading of their texts, bring us as near to the conditions of proof of interpretation as we are likely, in the circumstances, to attain: proof not only of *this* interpretation, but also that a metaphorical interpretation is indeed required. There is one other point, concerning the *Charge to Peter*, that confirms this conclusion.

The preparatory drawing (*Fig. 46*) for the *Charge to Peter* is very directly related to the Cartoon except in the gesture of the figure that would become Christ; the difference here is so marked that we should allow and examine the possibility that the subject is not in fact the same. It will be seen that Peter holds the Keys just as prominently. But both the original fragment of the drawing in the Louvre and the offset at Windsor (*Fig. 47*) are cut at such a point that we cannot tell whether or not the lowered arm of the Christ-

124. *Summa, Additiones*, Quaest. xix, art. 1 (ed. cit. in n. 25, iv, p. 448).

125. *Summa, Additiones*, Quaest. xx, art. 1 (ed. cit. in n. 25, iv, p. 450); cf. Nicolaus de Lyra, op. cit. in n. 122, on Matthew xvi.

126. Arator, *De actibus apostolorum*, cap. vi; Bede, *Expositio super acta apostolorum*, iii (*P.L.* 92, col. 951); *Glossa ordinaria*, Acts iii. 2 (*P.L.* 114, col. 434). This concept is almost certainly Augustinian in origin, but may be derived from Augustine's idea of the Church of Peter generally (analysed by S. J. Grabowski, 'Saint Augustine and the Primacy of the Roman Pontiffs', *Traditio*, iv, 1946, p. 93). In this sense the *Healing of the Lame Man* is very accurately an illustration of the *clavis ordinis* 'quae se extendit ad ipsum coelum, immediate removendo impedimenta introitus (i.e. lameness) in coelum per remissionem peccati' (Aquinas, *Summa, Additiones*, Quaest. xix, art. iii: ed. cit. in n. 25, iv, p. 448). Compare also another Scholastic definition, No. 493 in the *Collectio sententiarum* (quoted from Anciaux, op. cit. in n. 25, p. 284, n. 2): 'Claves iste sunt scientia et potentia. Scientia autem est illa discretio, qua discernunt, quos debeant in templum recipere, quos ut leprosos abicere'; and Gratian, *Decretum*, quoted above, n. 26.

127. Jacobazzi, *De concilio*, ed. cit. in n. 61, pp. 131, 282 ff., 666; Poggio, op. cit. in n. 61, fols. 61r. ff.; for Aegidius's formulation, see O'Malley, op. cit. in n. 6, p. 120, n. 3. See also: Thomas de Vio, *De romani pontificis institutione*, cap. v (Rocaberti, op. cit. in n. 25, xix, pp. 537, 539); idem, *Commentarii in quatuor evangelia et acta apostolorum*, Venice, 1530, fol. 39r.; Arias Barbosa, op. cit. in n. 10, fol. xvii, v.; Jacques Lefèvre d'Etaples, *Commentarii initiatorii in quatuor evangelia*, Meaux, 1522, fol. 66v. (Lefèvre, however, modifies the formula towards an anti-monarchic position).

128. See, for example, Aquinas, loc. cit. in n. 126, and especially *Additiones*, Quaest. xxii, art. i; this terminology was kept in use by, e.g., Torquemada, *Commentaria super toto Decreto*, ed. cit. in n. 26, pp. 81 ff., and *Summa*, ed. cit. in n. 19, pp. 160 ff. (where, however, the dualities are also pursued beyond this point in a manner bewildering to a layman). I have relied particularly upon the sources and surveys given by P. Capobianco, O.F.M., 'De notione fori interni in iure canonico', *Apollinaris: Commentarius iuris canonici*, ix, 1936, pp. 364 ff., and F. Russo, S.J., 'Pénitence et excommunication: Etude historique . . .', *Recherches de science religieuse*, xxxiii, 1946, pp. 256 ff.

129. A characteristically unbeautiful engraving by Giulio Bonasone (*Fig.* 80: B. xv, p. 17, 6) must be considered at this point. It is obviously more closely related to the Cartoon than to the Louvre and Windsor chalk-drawings, and it might be dismissed as an arbitrary variation on the former (or a tapestry). However, in the print the Christ is fully clothed, as in the Louvre *modello* (*Fig.* 51), and this detail seems to guarantee that Bonasone was following some stage in the preparatory process. The alternatives are: (a) that the engraving follows the Louvre *modello*, with arbitrary modifications (in favour: the two upward-pointing gestures which, if reversed in a tapestry, would be left-handed); (b) that it follows a first *modello* with the subject suggested in the text and perhaps rejected by the patron (in favour: the repetition of the upward-pointing gesture from the chalk-drawings, which Bonasone is unlikely to have known in addition to the Louvre *modello*).

130. Such a conflation would account for one difficulty raised by a reading of Christ's gesture as the invocation of the Holy Spirit: that the events of John xx. 19–23 took place indoors, whereas the drawing clearly shows a landscape setting. The latter would be appropriate to Matthew xvi; it could also, of course, have been added in the process of adaptation to a new subject, the Charge to Peter. The alternative conflation of the texts suggested here would, of course, fit perfectly with the rest of the Petrine sequence without the necessity of other changes, since they too introduce the Doctrine of the Keys and are frequently coupled in that context (e.g. Aquinas, *Summa, Additiones*, Quaest. xviii, art. i; xviii, art. iii; xix, art. v; xx, art. i; ed. cit. in n. 25, iv, pp. 445, 447, 449, 450). In relation to the theme of the *Primatus Petri* the sense would probably be close to that of a much-quoted sermon of Bede (*Homilia XVI, P.L.* 94, cols. 222 ff.): although the *officium* of loosing and binding is given to the whole Church (John xx), 'beatus Petrus . . . specialiter claves regni coelorum et principatum judiciariae potestatis accepit . . .' (Matthew xvi). H. Grimm, *Raphael und das Neue Testament*, Berlin, 1883, p. 15, already suggested a change of subject between drawing and Cartoon, but his alternative text for the drawing was John xxi. 19, *Sequere me* (after the Charge to Peter).

131. For examples of John xx. 21 quoted in the Conciliar sense in this period, see Giovanni Gozzadini, *De electione romani pontificis* (*c.* 1511), quoted by Jedin, op. cit. in n. 13, pp. 17 ff., 33, and Lefèvre, op. cit. in n. 127, fol. 66v. Thomas de Vio acknowledges this argument and then answers it in the monarchist sense in *De romani pontificis institutione* (Rocaberti, op. cit. in n. 25, xix, p. 536). The moment of the

figure was intended to point to a flock of sheep. And the raised arm evokes no command suggested by the text of the Charge to Peter, but rather the one in Christ's previous appearance to the Apostles in John xx. 22–23: 'Receive ye the Holy Ghost.'[129] We are in no position to insist on this interpretation, but we should consider it as an alternative; as such it entails a related but subtly different meaning. At this meeting with the Apostles Christ speaks to them all, in the plural: '*Accipite spiritum sanctum.* Whose soever sins ye remit, they are remitted unto them; and whose soever ye retain, they are retained.' This text also is taken as a fulfilment of the promise in Matthew xvi, but the conflation of these texts[130] signifies the transmission to the Church generally of the power of loosing and binding in the first of them, whereas the eventually chosen conflation of Matthew xvi and John xxi, *Pasce oves meas*, addressed to Peter alone in the presence of the other Apostles, signifies the transmission of the power to the Vicar of Christ, and through him to the Church; it underlines, in other words, the monarchical powers and position of Peter and his successors.

If, therefore, there has been a change in subject it entails an important shift of emphasis, from a doctrine that could have been interpreted as comforting Conciliar views, as they are called, on the descent of authority[131] to a doctrine that must be read unambiguously as a demonstration of the monarchical institution of the papacy. If, on the other hand, there has not been a change of subject—if, that is, we read the lowered arm of Christ in the drawing as an amputated gesture already implying the presence of sheep —the change in the whole figure is still significant and still entails a shift of emphasis in the monarchical direction. The final position and gestures of Christ, pointing simultaneously at the Keys and the sheep, far more effectively isolate Peter from the other Apostles, in their presence, as the sole direct recipient of authority. The first drawing, or the first subject if it was indeed different, could well have been criticized for the kind of ambiguity that would be most inappropriate in the Sistine Chapel.

It is much less certain that the same doctrinal level of meaning is sustained throughout the Pauline cycle as well, but the possibility is worth exploration. It is essential that we recall at this point that the *Primatus Petri* cannot be the main theme of the whole tapestry-sequence; had that been the intention the Petrine set would have been placed on the left wall, on the right from the point of view of the altar and the Crucifix, the point of precedence overriding all other considerations.[132] The chosen arrangement strongly suggests, on the contrary, a balance and equal division of powers. In fact in a famous sermon attributed variously to Ambrose, Augustine, Leo the Great and the Beatus Maximus, it is said that the *Clavis scientiae* (probably to be considered identical with the *Clavis ordinis*) was given also to Paul.[133] The healing of the lame man in the *Sacrifice at Lystra* (*Fig.* 24) could therefore be intended and interpreted in the sense applied to the similar subject in the Petrine set; and Arator and Bede, in fact, compare the two miracles of healing as the collection, by Peter and Paul, of the Jews and Gentiles into the Church of Christ.[134] But it does not seem that this extension to Paul of the power of the Keys was generally followed.[135]

We have found that the central tapestry on the right wall, the *Healing of the Lame Man*, like the fresco above it, has a particularly complex and significant symbolism. The corresponding tapestry in the Pauline set, the *Conversion of the Proconsul* (*Fig.* 23), seems to be similar in depth of meaning, in the meaning itself, and in the close relation to the fresco above. The collection of events in the latter, which we call *Moses in Egypt* (*Fig.* 22), represents the appointment of Moses as *Princeps* of the Jews, as Petrus Comestor has it, or *Doctor populi* as in the *Glossa ordinaria*.[136] In the *Conversion of the Proconsul* the beginning of the ministry of the *Doctor gentium* is shown or, as Petrus Comestor says, the beginning of the *Magisterium gentium*.[137] In the opposite tapestry the *Porta speciosa* is the threshold of the *Ecclesia ex Judaeis*; in this one, I suggest, the building represents the *Ecclesia ex gentibus* to which Paul gives entry (it is worth noting that this pair of tapestries flanked the *vestibulum* of the chapel). The seat of justice itself implies that this building is a basilica, and Raphael must have been fully conscious of the point, not only because he was an architect, and a student of the history of architecture, but also because one of the lictors on the steps is taken from Sebastiano del Piombo's *Judgement of Solomon*, where there can be no question of the building's classification. The basilica, then, in the tapestry is remarkable for the stones of which it is built; most beautifully painted in the Cartoon, and most subtly coloured, they seem to be semi-precious. And when set against the material splendour of the *Porta speciosa* in the opposite tapestry, they recall vividly the lapidary prophecy of the expansion of Christ's Church in Isaiah liv, which so significantly begins: 'For thou shalt break forth on the right hand and on the left; and thy seed shall inherit the Gentiles (also) . . . O thou afflicted, tossed with tempest, and not comforted, behold I will lay thy stones with fair colours, and lay thy foundations with sapphires. And I will make thy windows of agates, and thy gates of carbuncles, and all thy borders of pleasant stones.'[138] (This text, of course, anticipates the vision of the Celestial Jerusalem in Revelation xxi. 10–27.) The prophecy continues: 'And all thy children shall be taught of the Lord; and great shall be the peace of thy children.' This prophecy of the *plenitudo gentium* concerning stones and peace may be, as we shall see, significant on a third level of meaning.

At this point we should consider again the two tapestries that extend the Pauline series beyond symmetry with the Petrine series. The *Release of Paul from Prison* (*Fig.* 26) is obviously unlikely to introduce any major theme. When read in the literal sense the text (Acts xvi. 23–26) may be understood as continuing Paul's confrontation with the Gentiles in the *Sacrifice at Lystra*. The capacity of this gap-filler to sustain further meaning is clearly minimal; Raphael's treatment of the event is serious, but at the same time, exceptionally, humorous, and perhaps we should read it as the dramatic painter's equivalent to the tragedian's device of the comic scene.

Very different, however, are the problems presented by the tapestry that was designed to hang outside the *cancellata*, *Paul preaching at Athens* (*Fig.* 25). It is here that we must face again the question of completeness: whether the ten pieces commissioned from Raphael and Pieter van Aelst were all that were intended by Leo X, or whether they were the first stage of a project to be continued at a later date. Some aspects of this problem have been considered in the previous Chapter; now it must be reviewed from the iconographical standpoint. One observation is worth repeating: that the necessity of a continuation cannot be argued from the absence of certain scenes such as the *Imprisonment of Peter*, for there is on the one hand no consistency in the tradition of Petrine cycles (nor, for that matter, in Pauline ones) sufficient to justify such assertions, and on the other hand those scenes that were chosen for the executed tapestries would not have been predictable on such a basis.[139] Above all, the pope's chapel must be treated as something unique.

Nevertheless it remains true that every argument that seems to make sense

commission of the Cartoons is not one of the most critical in the history of the struggle between pope and Council; it is, rather, a moment of recent victory for the former. Nevertheless the issue was a sensitive one and its implications could not have been overlooked in the decoration of the pope's chapel; for this subject, see Jedin, op. cit. in n. 13, and idem, op. cit. in n. 7, i, pp. 39 ff. In our context it is interesting to look again at the *Oratio pro concilio Lateranensi* of Angelo da Vallombrosa, 1511, who admits that the Keys appear to be given to all the Apostles, but asserts the *Primatus Petri*; opponents of the proofs of the *Primatus* are, he says, 'hi qui se clavium moderatores nuncupant' (ed. cit. in n. 112, p. 345).

132. See Chapter II, p. 41.

133. *P.L.* 57, col. 401 (cf. Migne's *Admonitio* for attributions); one of the group discussed above, n. 92, and included in the *Homeliarius* collections for the Feast of SS. Peter and Paul; No. LXVII in the collection of *Epistolae, sermones . . .*, etc., of Ambrose, Milan, 1490.

134. Arator, *De actibus apostolorum*, cap. xxvii (see especially the paraphrase and clarification by Barbosa, op. cit. in n. 10, fol. cxv, v.); and Bede, *Expositio super acta apostolorum*, xiv. 7 (*P.L.* 92, col. 975).

135. Gregory VII, however, seems to continue this line of thought when he defines the 'auctoritatem, quam Deus beato Petro tibique (sc: Paulo) in coelo et in terra ligandi atque solvendi tribuit . . .' (quoted from Meulenberg, op. cit. in n. 95, p. 20).

136. Petrus Comestor, *Historia scholastica: in Actus Apostolorum*, cap. xxxvi (*P.L.* 198, col. 1666); *Glossa ordinaria*, Exodus iii. 4 (*P.L.* 113, col. 191).

137. Op. cit., cap. lxvii (*P.L.* 198, col. 1690). For a comparison of Moses and Paul in this sense in the period of the Cartoons, see G. F. Pico della Mirandola, *De rerum praenotione*, Bk. II, cap. viii (*Opera omnia*, Basle, 1601, ii, p. 292: 'ille Judaeorum, hic Gentium doctor').

138. Thomas Aquinas, however, interpreted this text as a prophecy of the foundation of the Church on the Apostles: 'Fundabo te in saphyris. idest in celestibus viris' (*Comentaria super epistolas sanctissimi gentium doctoris pauli apostoli*, ed. Petrus de Bergamo, Bologna, 1481, on the crucial text Ephesians ii. 14: *Ipse enim est pax nostra*, discussed below, p. 79).

139. The occasional additions made to later sets of tapestries do not include subjects such as

the Martyrdoms; for these additions, see J. White and J. Shearman, 'Raphael's Tapestries and their Cartoons', *Art Bulletin*, xl, 1958, p. 196, n. 13.

140. M. Dibelius, *Studies in the Acts of the Apostles*, ed. H. Greeven, London, 1956, p. 28.

141. Jonathan Richardson, *A Theory of Painting*, in *Works* . . ., Strawberry Hill, 1792, p. 42, already noticed that the background of this scene carried a meaning: 'it is expressive of the superstition St. Paul was preaching against'.

142. Arator, *De actibus apostolorum*, cap. xxxii:

'O lupe pauli rapax. dedit hoc benedictio iacob
Nomen habere tibi. Quid iam remanebit in orbe
Quod non ore trahas? postquam solertia graia
Cessit: & invictas in dogmate vincis athenas', etc.

cf. the commentary by Barbosa, op. cit. in n. 10, fols. cxxv, r. ff.

143. See, most recently, H. Conzelmann, 'The Address of Paul on the Areopagus', *Studies in Luke-Acts*, ed. L. E. Keck and J. L. Martin, London, 1968, p. 219; also Dibelius, op. cit. in n. 140, pp. 67–8.

144. Abbot Hilduin, *Passio sanctissimi Dionysii*, *P.L.* 106, col. 26; *Glossa ordinaria*, *P.L.* 114, col. 460 (quoting Rabanus Maurus and Bede); Petrus Comestor, *Historia scholastica*, cap. lxxxvi (*P.L.* 198, col. 1702); Nicolaus de Lyra, *Postilla super actus apostolorum* . . ., Mantua, 1480 (on Acts xvii. 15–34). This interpretation is followed by E. Curtius, 'Paulus in Athen', *Gesammelte Abhandlungen*, Berlin, 1894, ii, pp. 528 ff.; B. Keil, *Beiträge zur Geschichte des Areopags* (*Sächsische Akademie der Wissenschaften, Berichte, Phil.-hist. Klasse*, lxxi, 8, 1919), Leipzig, 1920, p. 60; K. Lake and H. J. Cadbury, *Commentary on the Acts of the Apostles* (*The Beginnings of Christianity*, ed. F. J. Foakes Jackson and K. Lake, iv, part 1), London, 1933, p. 212. Dibelius, op. cit. in n. 140, p. 68, while taking the opposite view, rightly sees that Raphael's Cartoon conforms to this tradition. Other authors, however, have read the Cartoon as if Paul were represented on the Hill of Mars (for example, *The Life and Writings of Henry Fuseli*, ed. J. Knowles, London, 1831, ii, p. 174, and Pastor, op. cit. in n. 84, viii, p. 313). It is of some importance that this is not the case; if it were, then it would be natural to relate the subject-matter to *Moses on Mount Sinai* in the fresco above, and to *Christ's Sermon on the Mount*

of the ten tapestries as a complete project may also be used to explain why it should have been decided (if such were the case) to end the first part of a larger project at just this point. The continuity of theme between the last Petrine tapestry, the *Death of Ananias*, and the first of the Pauline set, the *Stoning of Stephen*, is ambiguous in exactly this way, and so is the closure of the set with the *Preaching at Athens*.

The relationship, in the literal sense, between this subject and its predecessors is a perfectly natural one, since it is perhaps the most striking illustration of Paul fulfilling his special mission to the Gentiles; his sermon at Athens is in fact the only one recorded in Acts that was addressed to the Gentiles, with the exception of the brief expostulation at Lystra,[140] and the calibre of his audience made this the supreme test and proof of the power of preaching. It is a perfect climax to the *Magisterium gentium*. At the same time this tapestry continues Paul's confrontation with idolatry, deliberately emphasized by Raphael in the counterpoise of the Apostle against the bronze statue and the temple of Mars, and justified by the revelation in the sermon that the Living God 'dwelleth not in temples made with hands; Neither is worshipped with men's hands . . . the Godhead is (not) like unto gold, or silver, or stone, graven by art and man's device'.[141] When the tapestry hung in its place in the Sistine Chapel this revelation was inescapably compared with the wrath of Moses in the fresco above, the *Worship of the Golden Calf*; and perhaps it was also intended that Paul's gesture should embrace, in its warning, the splendours of the chapel itself.

This climax to the *Magisterium gentium* may therefore be seen as an epilogue to the rest of the series, and in this connection it is particularly interesting to read the chapter on this event in the poem by Arator, which we have found in other cases to bear a definite relationship, above all structurally, to the tapestry-series. In Arator's version the triumph at Athens (which is not, in the Bible itself, so decisive) closes the cycle begun in the Stoning of Stephen and the Conversion of Saul. The *lupus rapax*, says Arator, who began as antagonist but ended as protagonist, and the *Vas electionis*, are at this point wholly manifest, and Paul is the perfect model and guide of the faithful.[142] There is a perceptible pause at the end of Arator's chapter, very different from the breathless continuity in Acts; but of course Arator does go on to complete the narrative up to the martyrdom of the two Apostles, so that even if we could be satisfied that his poem was a major source of inspiration, his pause, and reflection back on the beginning, could as well justify a pause in the project at this point as its termination there.

The problem of completion or non-completion becomes important when we take account of aspects of the subject-matter of *Paul preaching at Athens* that are unrelated to the doctrinal or ecclesiological themes of the tapestries inside the *cancellata*. It is understandable that this tapestry, which hung in a separated space and was addressed to a different group of onlookers, should carry a meaning that is different in kind. But so long as the possibility remains that it may have been planned as part of a second series we must be aware of the implication: an unknown context, that of the unexecuted scenes, could clarify its meaning to the same extent that each tapestry set within the screen makes more sense in context than in isolation. We must accept, then, an additional limitation upon our capacity to interpret this tapestry; and for the same reason we should not be surprised if it is more difficult to make a choice between a number of potential meanings.

As it happens there is an ambiguity in the text itself that requires explanation, without which Raphael's tapestry makes no sense at all. Modern theology does not in itself concern us, but it is essential to realize that on two important points it differs in this case from the interpretations accessible to Raphael. In the first place the location of Paul's sermon, 'in the middle (ἐν μέσῳ, *in medio*) of the Areopagus', is now often taken to mean 'on the Hill of Mars' in Athens,[143] whereas by Raphael's time it had never been questioned that it meant 'before the court of the Areopagus', which assembled in the Agora.[144] Secondly, the whole tenor of the sermon has been altered by an adjustment, now conventional, of punctuation. It has been remarked that early readings, in which the recipients of this sermon were assumed to be identical with the Epicureans and Stoics mentioned in the preceding passage, give the event the character of an oral Ph.D. examination, or of a *disputa*, in a way that Luke probably did not intend; it is more likely that he meant that Paul addressed the Athenians generally.[145] In fact the exegetical comments on this episode that were available to Raphael constantly stress Paul's contradiction of the philosophies of both Stoics and Epicureans, and in consequence the main theme of the sermon was taken (as now it is not)[146] to be the Resurrection, of body and soul.[147] Thus a literal reading of the tapestry in the Leonine period could have brought two, perhaps three, ideas to mind: the power of preaching, immortality, and the relation between theology and philosophy.

This group of ideas is somewhat different in kind from those concerned with the institutions and history of the Church illustrated by the tapestries that were hung inside the *cancellata*. Certainly the theme of preaching continues the story of the *Magisterium gentium*—complementing, specifically, the confrontation with idolatry in the *Sacrifice at Lystra*—so logically that the tapestry *Paul preaching at Athens* can hardly be supposed to be an afterthought;[148] and this element of continuity is neither surprising nor in conflict with the differences we have noticed, since it must always have been anticipated that the tapestry would be seen by some who did pass the screen as well as by others who did not. But it is this theme of preaching above all that is so exactly suited to the position just outside the screen. When the tapestry was hung there it must have seemed that Paul was the bearer of the divine message (the *praeco datus fidei*, as Arator and others describe him, like a second Moses *legis lator* in the frescoes above), a message from the *Sancta sanctorum*, and that the half-circle of his pictorial audience was completed in reality by the spectator. The point is clarified if we recall the liturgical origin of the screen, or Durandus's comment on the division into two parts of Moses's tabernacle and Solomon's Temple: 'From both of these . . . our material church takes its form. In its outer part the laity offer their prayers and hear the word.'[149] In this more specific sense, too, this tapestry-episode would seem a counterpart to the *Promulgatio*, as the *titulus* defines it, in the fresco above.

However, all three ideas that this tapestry would have brought to mind were topical at the time of Raphael's commission, and it is unlikely to be accidental that this is so. Leo X, as we saw in Chapter I, took immediate and drastic steps towards the reform of preaching within the Sistine Chapel itself, and the reform of preaching generally was dealt with under his direction at the Lateran Council. At the end of the tenth session, on 15 December 1515, the Bull *Supernae majestatis* was read publicly, and in this document, devoted to the qualifications and responsibilities of preachers, we find Paul (perhaps predictably) given the title Prince of Preachers.[150] Leo's interest in this problem may have been spontaneous, or it may have been induced by the pressures of advice and circumstances; for example Vincenzo

in the opposite bay, in terms of the divine message delivered, in each case, from a height.

145. Lake-Cadbury, op. cit. in n. 144, p. 211. Acts xvii. 18 ff. reads, in the Vulgate: 'Quidam autem Epicurei et Stoici philosophi disserebant cum eo; et quidam dicebant: Quid vult seminiverbius hic dicere? . . . Et adprehensum eum ad Ariopagum duxerunt . . .' The point at issue is whether the second 'quidam' refers to the Epicureans and Stoics, which with this modern punctuation would not be the case. See below, n. 147.

146. See particularly Conzelmann, op. cit. in n. 143, and the other modern studies he cites, p. 230.

147. Augustine, *Sermo CL* (on Acts xvii. 18–34: *P.L.* 38, cols. 808 ff.); Arator, *De actibus apostolorum*, cap. xxxii: *De eo ubi Paulus cum Epicureis stoicis philosophis decertavit*; Bede, *Expositio super acta apostolorum* (*P.L.* 92, col. 979); Petrus Comestor, loc. cit. in n. 144. Nicolaus de Lyra, loc. cit. in n. 144, is worth quoting as an illustration of this tradition of exegesis and of the point about punctuation made above: '*quidam autem epicurei & stoici philosophi disserebant cum eo*: de felicitate hominis quam epicurei dicebant consistere in corporis voluptatibus. Stoici vero in animae virtutibus tamen in presenti vita. nam utrique . . . negabant resurrectionem & per consequens aliam vitam. Paulus autem asserebat eam esse in anima & corpore & hoc in vita futura.' Cf. also the Preface of the monk Ambrosius to the translation of the works of Dionysius (ed. J. Lefèvre, Paris, 1498): 'Cumque enim apostolus Paulus athenas petiisset, atque cum philosophis tum epicureis tum stoicis verba fecisset, Christumque ipsis dominum nostrum, mortuorum resurrectionem, et generale iudicium predicasset.' For a contemporary discussion of Epicureans, Stoics, and the *Summum bonum*, see G. F. Pico della Mirandola, *Examen vanitatis doctrinae Gentium, et veritatis Christianae disciplinae*, Bk. I, cap. xvii (*Opera omnia*, Basle, 1601, ii, pp. 527 ff.).

148. As argued by Künzle, op. cit. in n. 86.

149. *Rationale*, I, i, 5.

150. 'Paulus Apostolus praedicatorum princeps'. The proper date for the Bull is that of its approval at session eleven, 19 December 1516 (Hardouin, op. cit. in n. 95, ix, col. 1809; *Bullarium*, ed. cit. in n. 29, p. 206; for the first reading see Hardouin, ix, col. 1801).

Quirini and Tommaso Giustiniani, whose *Libellus ad Leonem X* of the summer of 1513 was the most far-sighted reform tract of the period, had told the young Leo that 'the pope's primary duty is to broadcast, sow and nurture the seed of the Divine Word'.[151] Their metaphor is another exegetical constant in a long tradition based upon biblical texts; conspicuous in this tradition is Augustine's *Sermon on Preaching*, in which it is explained that Christ sent harvesters to the Jews, sowers to the Gentiles, and that among these Paul is the prototype *seminator*—rightly, therefore, did the Athenians ask 'Who is this sower of words?'[152] The rôle of Paul at Athens is frequently cited as that of the 'Seminator verborum in agro Dei',[153] and thus to Leo and his court Paul's *Magisterium gentium*, culminating in the evangelization of the Athenians, could be read as a type of papal responsibility in the modern world, complementary to that which was offered by Peter. In this sense it is easy to understand why a portrait of Leo might be included in this tapestry, in the public part of the chapel, and why he might seem to pay such rapt attention to Paul's example. But there may be other reasons.

The Immortality of the Soul, which Paul preached to the philosophers at Athens, was one of the most lively controversial issues of the period of the Cartoons,[154] and for some time afterwards, and this also was a matter on

151. *Libellus*, ed. cit. in n. 94, col. 643: 'Pontificis praecipuum munus (est) semen Divini Verbi spargere, plantare, atque irrigare ...' For the date (June–July 1513) see H. Jedin, 'Vincenzo Quirini und Pietro Bembo', *Miscellanea Giovanni Mercati*, iv (*Studi e testi* 124), Vatican City, 1946, p. 410, n. 18.

152. *Sermo CI*, on Luke x. 2–6 (*P.L.* 38, cols. 605 ff.), included in the Amerbach edition of the Sermons, part vii, Basle, 1495.

153. E.g. Ambrose, *Sermo CL*, on Acts xvii. 18–34 (*P.L.* 38, cols. 807 ff.); Arator, *De actibus apostolorum*, cap. xxxii.

154. For the background of this controversy, and its continuation into the 1520s, see E. Gilson, 'Cajetan et l'humanisme théologique', *Archives d'histoire doctrinale et littéraire du moyen-âge*, Année xxx, 1955, pp. 112 ff.; idem, 'Autour de Pomponazzi', ibid., Année xxxvi, 1961, pp. 173 ff.; G. di Napoli, *L'Immortalità dell'anima nel rinascimento*, Turin, 1963, pp. 178 ff.; O'Malley, op. cit. in n. 6, pp. 41 ff.

155. Hardouin, op. cit. in n. 95, ix, cols. 1719 ff.; *Bullarium*, ed. cit. in n. 29, pp. 170 ff. The most thorough study of this Bull is by S. Offelli, 'Il pensiero del concilio lateranense V sulla dimostrabilità razionale dell'immortalità dell'anima umana', *Studia patavina*, ii, 1955, pp. 3 ff. It should be noted that Pietro Pomponazzi's *Tractatus de immortalitate animae*, which is sometimes said to be the object of refutation in this Bull, was not published until 1516 (MS. completed 24 September). The context and authorship of the Bull have been studied by F. Gilbert, 'Cristianesimo, umanesimo e la bolla "Apostolici regiminis" del 1513', *Rivista storica italiana*, lxx, 1967, pp. 976 ff., who suggests convincingly the participation of Quirini and Giustiniani; I should only question his assumption of a certain resistance on Leo's part to the ideas expressed in the Bull, in view of the pope's earlier interest in the subject (see below).

156. Petrus Alcyonius, *Medices legatus de exsilio*, Venice, 1522, a dialogue, in which Giulio de' Medici addresses Cardinal Giovanni, fol. d. i, r.: 'Eodem sanè modo harum disciplinarum usus nunc tibi constabit, quo superioribus mensibus constitisse animadverti, cum de immortalitate animorum, atque etiam de Principis Dei vi, ac numine te disputantem in Xysto audiebamus. Tum enim omnes, qui aderamus, in disputatione tua acquievimus ... liberati sumus magna suspicione, quam controversiae propositae à quibusdam novis Philosophis de immortalitate animorum, & de potestate Dei, attulerant. Omnem igitur operam, & studium ad te audiendum conferimus, & maiorem

aliquam levationem aegritudinis animorum nostrorum à te expectamus, quae magna, & gravi fortunae iniuria commota est.' The *disputa* is one of those mentioned more generically by Paolo Giovio, *De vita Leonis Decimi*, Florence, 1548, p. 34. It was considered sufficiently well known and important to be represented on a triumphal arch in the Lateran procession of 1513 (Cancellieri, op. cit. in n. 20, p. 78). From internal evidence the date of the *disputa* must be shortly before Giovanni de' Medici's appointment as Papal Legate to Bologna and the Romagna, 1 October 1511—therefore shortly after the completion, 25 February 1509, of Thomas de Vio's *In libros Aristotelis de anima*. Alcyonius, who clearly writes with a good deal of hindsight, refers to the *aegritudo animorum* in such a way as to suggest that he saw a connection between this *disputa* and the text of the Bull *Apostolici regiminis* (see below, p. 77). Leo's continued interest in this theme is demonstrated by Agostino Nifo's *De immortalitate humanae animae*, Venice, 1518, dedicated to and commissioned by the pope.

157. Offelli, op. cit. in n. 155, pp. 4–9. After the reading of the Bull at the Lateran Council Thomas de Vio (who had recently had second thoughts about the philosophical demonstrability of the Immortality of the Soul) objected to the second part, the instructions to philosophical faculties in universities, because he held it to be no part of the duties of Professors of Philosophy to teach the articles of Christian Faith; a cardinal present at the Council also expressed reservations: Hardouin, op. cit. in n. 95, ix, col. 1720; Di Napoli, op. cit. in n. 154, pp. 220–4; Offelli, op. cit., pp. 10–14.

158. This is the understanding of Stridbeck, op. cit. in n. 62, pp. 38 ff.

159. For example, Augustine, *Sermo CL*, on Acts xvii. 18–34 (*P.L.* 38, col. 809): 'Appetiti igitur beatae vitae philosophis Christianisque communis est'; see also Curtius, op. cit. in n. 144.

160. Acts xvii. 28: 'In ipso enim vivimus, e movemur, et sumus: sicut et quidam vestrum poetarum dixerunt'; as O'Malley, op. cit. in n. 6, p. 19, points out, this was one of the texts fundamental to the Renaissance concord of Christian and pagan teaching. Paul's quotation comes from the *Phaenomena* of Aratus, and there is also a similar verse in a hymn to Zeus by the Stoic Cleanthes (Dibelius, op. cit. in n. 140, p. 51). Paul's Platonism and the positive attitude of Cleanthes to the immortality of the Soul were both well understood in the period; see Petrus Galatinus, *Ad divum Leonem X ... in obitu ill.^{mi} principis Laurentij Medicis Duci Urbini* (1519), Bibl. Vat., MS. Vat. Lat. 3190 fols. 3v. ff.

161. Cf. Ficino, *De christiana religione*, cap. x 'Dionysius Areopagita philosophorum Atheniensium praestantissimus ...', and *In orationem Dionysii de Trinitate*: 'Dionysius Areopagita Platonicae disciplinae culmen, & Christianae Theologiae columen ...' (*Opera omnia*, Basle 1576, pp. 13, 1013).

162. Leo's stoicism is abundantly evident in his attitude, as cardinal, to his exile from Florence recorded in the dialogue of Alcyonius (op. cit in n. 156), as more generally in his fascination

which Leo defined a precise doctrine at the Lateran Council. The Bull *Apostolici regiminis*,[155] which was confirmed at the eighth session, 19 December 1513, established not only a clear doctrine in the face of current peripatetic speculation but also the manner in which the subject was to be taught at universities; it opens with a reference to the controversy, to pernicious errors sown 'in agro Domini'. But the issue was more personal to Leo than the Bull alone suggests. This pope was trained in Canon Law, and he was not a theologian like Sixtus IV with a bibliography in his own right. There is only one theological problem on which he is known to have collected and expressed his views, and that was the Immortality of the Soul; as cardinal, about 1511, he had conducted in Rome a *disputa* on this theme.[156] There could have been this specific and personal motivation for Leo's desire to have himself represented as a witness of Paul's sermon at Athens.

The Bull of 1513 on the Immortality of the Soul defined, in passing, the relationship between theology and philosophy, which was another issue of some (although milder) contentiousness in the period,[157] and this is the third idea that the tapestry inevitably brings to mind. It is important that the text illustrated here was not, as has been said, about a conflict between the two faculties that could be enlarged into a general conflict between Humanism and Christianity,[158] but it was, rather, about their essential harmony.[159] Paul quoted to the Athenians a passage from the Greek poets to demonstrate the compatibility of his message and their philosophy;[160] he revealed to them the identity of their Unknown God, and through his preaching—this is the foreground incident in Raphael's composition—the Platonist and Areopagite Dionysius embraced the Faith.[161] It is probably in this aspect of the subject that we should see the third justification for the presence in Paul's audience of Leo X, who was Stoic in philosophy, Epicurean in mode of life and Christian in spirit.[162]

Finally there is yet a fourth aspect of this tapestry that Leo's contemporaries could hardly have overlooked: the Athenian setting itself. For only recently Leo's establishment of a Greek Academy in Rome had been celebrated as the foundation of a new Athens on the Tiber, by Marco Musurus, and more obliquely and pertinently as that of a new *Stoa* by Zaccaria Ferreri.[163] The line of thought that could have led to the inclusion of a portrait of the Director of the Greek Academy, Janus Lascaris (if that identification is correct), next to that of his patron, Pope Leo, is fairly clear. But to be more precise the initiative of Leo and Lascaris was the refoundation in Rome of the *Athenae alterae* that had previously flourished in Florence under the patronage of Leo's father, Lorenzo; Lascaris had been distinguished in that Medicean Athens too.[164]

This discussion of the *Paul preaching at Athens* has led us a step beyond our survey of the other tapestries to consider aspects of meaning that apply to the present in which the Cartoons were made and also to the patron. It may not be obvious that such speculation is legitimate or necessary in the case of those other tapestries, so let us reflect, for a moment, on progress so far. The interpretations of the individual tapestries, and to some extent of their grouping, that have been advanced so far may be more or less convincing as explanations of what could have been intended to be read from them in the period and in the highly particularized context of the Sistine Chapel. But they do not answer the question: why were these subjects chosen? Why, for example, should the *Primatus Petri* be included, but in such a way that it cannot be the principal theme? It is true, of course, that the demonstration of the *Primatus* is particularly associated with Leo the Great, and that this

with fate (see below, pp. 89 ff.); his epicureanism scarcely needs comment.

163. Marco Musurus, prefatory poem addressed to Leo X, in his Greek edition of Plato, *Omnia Platonis opera*, Venice, September 1513; there is a somewhat loose English translation in W. Roscoe, *The Life and Pontificate of Leo the Tenth*, 5th ed., London, 1846, i, p. 425. The passage in Ferreri's *Lugdunense Somnium de divi Leonis Decimi*, Lyon, 1513 (also published in September), reads (under the rubric 'papa doctus in omni scibili'):

'O fauste antistes: cui tellus paret, & aether
Dulciter aspirat: sophiae cui maxima cura:
Cui noctu atque die lac porrigit attica pallas:
Cui nunc Stoa novos dat: nunc Academia
     census:
Cui graiae & latiae praestantia maxima
     lingua . . .'

The inclusion in the tapestry of a *Stoa*, in the architectural sense, is discussed below, p. 125. The first practical steps towards the foundation of the Academy were in fact taken on 5 August 1513 when Leo wrote, via Bembo, to Musurus requesting him to enlist young scholars from Greece (V. Fanelli, 'Il ginnasio greco di Leone X a Roma', *Studi romani*, ix, 1961, p. 380). The foundation and nature of the Academy are discussed in detail by Samaltanou, op. cit. in n. 91, pp. 7 ff.

164. The concept of Laurentian Florence as a new Athens (in the cultural sense rather than the political one, which is much older) appears to have been established *c.* 1505; see F. Gilbert, 'Bernardo Rucellai and the Orti Oricellari', *Journal of the Warburg and Courtauld Institutes*, xii, 1949, p. 121, but also the fragments of a lecture delivered in Florence *c.* 1475 by Lascaris, quoted by Knös, op. cit. in n. 34, p. 26. This concept is in fact recalled by Aldus Manutius in his *Supplicatio* to Leo X, published with Musurus's poem in the 1513 Plato edition; he remarks that as Ficino had dedicated his Latin Plato to Lorenzo, who had favoured scholars in each language 'ut Florentia & esset, & haberetur, vivente Laurentio, Athenae alterae', so the Greek Plato is now dedicated to Leo, whose *Academia* in Rome revives similar hopes. Likewise Filippo Beroaldo *il giovane*, in his dedication to Leo of Tacitus's *Opera*, 1515(?), compares Laurentian and Leonine patronage of Greek studies, and in each case of Lascaris.

165. Ullmann, op. cit. in n. 95, pp. 25 ff.; also Maccarrone, op. cit. in n. 118, pp. 14, 18; Caspar, op. cit. in n. 95, pp. 329 ff. Leo IX (1049–54) based his title to universality on the writings of Leo I (Meulenberg, op. cit. in n. 95, p. 34, n. 17). Leo the Great's sermons on this subject were quoted at the Council of Florence, 1439, in support of the primacy of the Bishop of Rome (Gill, op. cit. in n. 117, pp. 269 ff.), and frequently in the same context by Torquemada (*Summa*, Bk. II, esp. cap. xv), and in the Leonine period by Jacobazzi (*De concilio*, ed. cit. in n. 61, pp. 665 ff.), Benetus (*De autoritate Romanae Ecclesiae*) and Poggio (*De potestate papae et concilii*).

166. Ettlinger, op. cit. in n. 16, pp. 58, 60, 72, referring to three of the Moses scenes. In addition the first scene in the Christ-cycle, the lost *Nativity* by Perugino, is also conventionally read as the dawn of peace between Jew and Gentile. Compare the reference to Gentiles in the tapestry beneath, the *Miraculous Draught* (below, p. 79).

167. For a restatement of this point of view at the moment of Raphael's commission, see Lactantius, *Divinae institutiones*, Bk. II, cap. xiii, ed. Marco Musurus and Aldus Manutius, Venice, 1515, fol. 70r. It is possible that the histories on the ceiling were planned to end with this subject so as to provide a continuity with the references to reconciliation between Jew and Gentile in the first of the Moses and Christ scenes in the Sixtine cycle (see preceding note)—this in addition to the significance of Noah's drunkenness as a prefiguration of salvation and the remission of sins, and of Noah and his Ark as figures of the pope and Church (Ambrose, *Hexaemeron*, Bk. III, cap. xvi: *P.L.* 14, cols. 186–7; idem, *De Noe*, cap. xxix: *P.L.* 14, cols. 410–11; the Bull *Unam sanctam*; and the sources quoted by Rahner, op. cit. in n. 111, pp. 16 ff., and by E. Wind, 'Michelangelo's Prophets and Sibyls', *Proceedings of the British Academy*, li, 1965, p. 61, n. 2).

168. The Ciborium was perhaps completed by the Jubilee Year of 1475, but it did not remain in position until 1592, as is usually said, but was removed earlier at a date still to be established (H. Siebenhüner, 'Die Ausstattung von St. Peter in Rom', *Festschrift für Hans Sedelmayr*, Munich, 1962, p. 263); the reliefs are now shown in the Grotte Vaticane. Leo III endowed the High Altar with an *antependium* representing the Donation of the Keys and the martyrdoms of SS. Peter and Paul (corresponding to three of Sixtus's four reliefs); after the Saracen sack it was replaced by another, given by Leo IV, with the same subjects (*Liber pontificalis*, ed. L. Duchesne, Paris, 1955, ii, pp. 8, 130). The martyrdoms recur on Giotto's Stefaneschi

was appreciated at the time;[165] but Leo's respect for and emulation of his greatest predecessor in the name is unlikely to have provided more than a secondary motivation for the restatement of the theme in modern terms. And why is this theme balanced against that of the *plenitudo gentium*?

The tapestry-cycle, in its balanced emphasis on the Founders of the Church among Jews and Gentiles, is specifically related to the existing decoration of the Sistine Chapel. The original Sixtine histories of Synagogue and Ecclesia, of the eras *sub lege* and *sub gratia*, already contain secondary references to the Gentiles.[166] More important is the theme of parallel revelation to Jews and Gentiles expressed in the Prophets and Sibyls of Michelangelo's recent ceiling-frescoes; and perhaps it is especially significant that the last event in

polyptych, also made for the High Altar. This iconographical tradition must be related to the remarkably persistent but in fact erroneous legend that both Apostles were buried under the High Altar (E. Kirschbaum, S.J., *Die Graeber der Apostelfürsten*, Frankfurt-am-Main, 1959, pp. 219, 249, n. 65. Paris de Grassis sometimes uses the title 'Basilica Apostolorum Petri & Pauli' (e.g. in his *Ordo romanus*, in E. Martène, *De antiquis ecclesiae ritibus*, iii, Antwerp, 1737, col. 607). Stridbeck, op. cit. in n. 62, pp. 41 ff., has argued that an iconographical precedent for the Petrine tapestries was to be found in Raphael's day in a mosaic cycle in the apse of Old Saint Peter's, but it seems that he was much confused. Firstly the list of subjects he used was based on nothing more than an admitted speculation on the part of Wilpert, op. cit. in n. 104, i, pp. 367 ff.; and secondly, the mosaics to which Wilpert (and before him, Grimaldi) referred were not in the apse, but on the North side of the Western wall (the limited possibilities of reconstruction are demonstrated by A. Weis, 'Ein Petruszyklus des 7. Jahrhunderts im Querschiff der Vatikanischen Basilika', *Römische Quartalschrift*, lviii, 1963, pp. 230 ff.).

169. This change of emphasis may be a response sensitive to attacks on those arguments that would derive the authority of the Roman Church from apocryphal texts; contemporary theologians give the impression of skating over very thin ice in these cases. It would be unthinkable that the Roman Church in this period should surrender its claim to authority from its joint foundation by SS. Peter and Paul (see above, pp. 61 ff.); but on the other hand it could well have been thought advisable to avoid provoking controversy in the public forum of the Sistine Chapel by illustrating the disputed subjects. It had already been observed, for example, that there is no evidence in the New Testament for Peter's presence in Rome; the best available answer (first produced by Eusebius and Jerome) was that Peter meant 'Rome' when he conveyed the greetings of the Church at 'Babylon' (I Peter v. 13; e.g. in Torquemada, *Summa*, Bk. II, cap. xxxvi: ed. cit. in n. 19, p. 228, in this case refuting

Ockham). On the other hand a reaction in this sense by the compilers of the 'programme' for the tapestries would in fact anticipate by a few years the sharpest controversies of this kind which began with Ulrich Velenus's attack in 1519 (see Baümer, op. cit. in n. 95). Also, we must remember once again the possibility of an intended extension of the cycle, which in that case could have concluded with the two martyrdoms.

170. This is unfamiliar material, and some examples should be quoted. Bishop Begnius (*Oratio* at the opening of session six of the Lateran Council, 27 April 1513: Hardouin, op. cit. in n. 95, ix, col. 1688), began with the identification of Leo with the Lion of Juda, quoted in Chapter I, p. 16, and ended with an appeal for peace: 'Aurea pax revocabitur dicemusque cum Isaia, et cantabimus: Exsulta satis filia Sion, quia ecce Salvator tuus veniet tibi' (Isaiah lxii. 11; also Zechariah ix. 9) Aegidius of Viterbo compared the dawn of peace at the election of Leo with the same at the birth of Christ: 'Pacis, te duce, cultores evasimus: videmus te Leone principe fieri quae fecit cum se terris ostendit Leo de tribu Juda (Revelation v. 5): In Messia enim ortu cecinere numina: in altissimis gloriam: et in terris pacem (Luke ii. 14): prius in altissimis et in divinis numeris: rerum principiis: Leo et Taurus quos vidit Ezechiel (i. 10): una in gloria coiere unoque consensu conspiravere statimque orto principe qui fecit pacem in superis: hebrei ac gentes: prius inimicissimi ad angularem se lapidem coniunxere (Ephesians ii. 14–20) . . . Numquam tam terra marique parta pax: quam cum exorto in terris Leone de tribu Juda sub Augusto Caesare: quando Princeps pacis ut Isaias inquit (ix. 6–7) apparuit . . . orta est iustitia et abundantia pacis . . . Nunc vero te principe id Pacis apparuit gentibus: ea Lux: quam . . . nullis umquam saeculis vidit (for example) Urbs Roma . . .' (*Historia viginti saeculorum*, Bibl. Angelica, MS. Lat. 351, fols. 386r. and v.; for this work see Chapter I, p. 15, n. 87). Giovanni Francesco Poggio addressed Leo in similar terms: 'In adventu pacifici Regis omnia novabuntur . . . Tu ille

IV. *The Healing of the Lame Man.*

the main sequence of histories on the ceiling, the drunkenness of Noah and the derision of his son, represents the moment of the original separation of the Gentiles from the Chosen People,[167] to be reunited by Peter and Paul in the Church of Christ. Nevertheless such considerations do not provide a motivation for the choice of subjects in the tapestries that can be expressed as the completion of an iconographical scheme for the Chapel, since it cannot in fact be said that the iconography is really completed, nor even that this was the only natural way in which it could be extended.

Since the tapestries illustrate the sources of authority of the Bishop of Rome it can be argued with some cogency that the choice of subjects was related to the new functions of the Sistine Chapel that followed from the uncertain practicability in the foreseeable future of the High Altar of Saint Peter's for the celebration of major feasts. In Chapter I it was suggested that the exceptional nature of the commission of figurative tapestries was probably related to these new functions. The histories of Peter and Paul do in fact represent an expansion of the traditional iconography of the High Altar of the basilica, most recently expressed in the reliefs of the Ciborium of Sixtus IV;[168] in one of those reliefs the Donation of the Keys is brought together with the Healing of the Lame Man, and it is difficult to escape the conclusion that this illustration of the *Potestas clavium* was as much a doctrinal precedent for the Petrine tapestries as it was so clearly an artistic precedent for Raphael's designs for them. Sixtus's Ciborium had recently been enclosed in Bramante's Doric altar-house and, although still accessible to visitors, was eclipsed as a public monument. Yet there remains in the tapestries an important shift of emphasis, away from the apocryphal and martyrdom scenes that were shown in three of the four Ciborium reliefs, towards the balanced episodes from the Gospels and the Acts of the Apostles that illustrate the complementary responsibilities, powers or missions of the twin Founders of the Roman Church.[169] The precedent in the basilica does not provide a wholly satisfying explanation of the iconography of the tapestries.

The examination of *Paul preaching at Athens* led us to consider not only the implications of the scene that would have appeared timeless, but also those that would be related to the present and to the patron. For this reason, and because we seem frustrated elsewhere, it is reasonable to look in this direction for an explanation of the overall programme of the cycle; and this investigation may even be thought obligatory if we believe that it is always dangerous to ignore a well-documented imagery that characterizes the source of patronage.

The accession of Leo X was accompanied, as we saw in Chapter I, by a great deal of comment with a strong Messianic tendency.[170] However much we aim off, as it were, for the wind of eulogy and rhetoric this comment remains remarkable, and in character unique, among those normally high and normally disappointed expectations that were voiced of other Renaissance popes. To dismiss it would be either a wilful blindness to evidence or an unjustifiable demotion to triviality of the sincerity and seriousness of so many responsible contemporary witnesses; it would be scepticism misplaced. The commentary was both plentiful and consistent in tendency because it assimilated three things: an already existing Medicean imagery, universal awareness of the exceptional purity of the young Leo's life, and eschatological speculation, beginning late in the Quattrocento, on the birth of a new millennium, a new era of peace.[171] The catalyst could well have been the identification made by Augustine of the *Leo* of biblical texts as Christ.[172]

es Beatissime Pater, quem dudum pro Christianorum quiete Prophetae nunciarunt esse venturum . . . Tu ille es (ut credimus) angelicus pastor coelitus demissus, nobis longo tempore praedicatus. Tu solus is es, qui in ovile Christi per ostium non per fenestras intrasti (John x. 1 ff.), vocatus a deo tanquam Aaron . . . Tu solus ecclesiam Dei reformaturus a Deo nobis es datus, ac sine ulla criminis macula pius, clemens, et iustus . . .': *De veri pastoris munere*, Bibl. Vat., MS. Vat. Lat. 3732, fols. 9r.–10r.; this is the presentation copy with a splendid illuminated title-page (*Fig.* 10): Leo is enthroned with Christ and God the Father above, and the Dove over his head carrying the inscription: HIC PASTOR VERE EST. ET SINE LABE PIUS. HUNC HABITABO QUONIAM ELEGI EUM; beneath is the text: VENIENT AD TE QUI DETRAHEBANT TIBI ET ADORABUNT VESTIGIA PEDUM TUORUM (Isaiah lx. 14). Vincenzo Quirini and Tommaso Giustiniani to Leo, 1513: '. . . ad Te, qui ejus (sc: Dei) in Terra vices geris, semel scribere ausi sumus, cum maxime Te precibus eorum omnium, qui consolationem Israel expectant . . .' (*Libellus ad Leonem X*, ed. cit. in n. 94, p. 614). See also the letters addressed to Leo by Pietro Delfin (*Epistolae Petri Delphini*, ed. cit in n. 112, Bk. XI. i and ix); Zaccaria Ferreri, quoted in Chapter I, p. 1, and the sources on the Lion of Judah and *Rex pacificus* quoted p. 16, ns. 100–4.

171. E.g. Johannes Viterbiensis, *Glossa super Apocalipsim de statu ecclesiae*, Genoa, 1480 (frequently reprinted), esp. on cap. xxi: 'omnes occurremus in unitatem fidei et agnicionis filii. *quia tunc intrabit plenitudo gentium. et omnis Israhel salvus fiet.* et idem apostolus predixit. quia secundum christum tunc in toto orbe predicabitur evangelium. *et fiet unum ovile et unus pastor.*' Cf. also the *Oraculum de novo saeculo*, Florence, 1496, by Giovanni Nesi, and the *Propheticae solutiones*, Florence, 1497, of Giorgio Benigni, quoted by E. Garin, *La cultura filosofica del Rinascimento italiano*, Florence, 1961, pp. 181, 225; for the context of these and other works, and their continuity in Aegidius of Viterbo, see O'Malley, op. cit. in n. 6, p. 115. It is characteristic of this situation that Leo should have been identified as the long-awaited *Papa angelicus*; see, most recently, C. Vasoli, 'Temi mistici e profetici alla fine del Quattrocento', in *Studi sulla cultura del Rinascimento*, Manduria, 1968, pp. 188, 222, and Poggio, cit. in n. 170.

172. E.g. *Tractatus in Joannis Evangelium* (*P.L.* 35, cols. 1728, 1735).

173. An example of the 'specific mythology' of Julius II may illustrate the point: the medal, attributed to Serbaldi, with the *Conversion of Saul* (Hill, op. cit. in n. 81, No. 866), inscribed: CONTRA STIMULUM. NE. CALCITRES (cf. Acts xxvi. 14). The reference, which is clearly political, may be to the temerity of Alfonso d'Este in 1510 (C. du Molinet, *Historia summorum pontificum a Martino V ad Innocentium XI*, Paris, 1679, p. 32), or to that of the Baglioni or Bentivoglio in 1506 (R. Weiss, 'The Medals of Julius II', *Journal of the Warburg and Courtauld Institutes*, xxviii, 1965, p. 178). But however this may be, such an interpretation of the Leonine tapestry would be unthinkable, so much had the political climate and imagery changed. For another example, see Chapter I, p. 15.

174. Above, Chapter I, p. 17.

175. Quoted from Caplan, op. cit. in n. 110, p. 284.

176. Giovanni Rucellai was, at the time of Raphael's commission, very close to Leo and in a good position to observe his preoccupations; he describes them in a letter to Giangiorgio Trissino, 5 November 1515, as 'la pace universale e la impresa contra agli infideli ... altra causa particolare non lo muove, se non l'unione della Christianità ...' (*Le opere di Giovanni Rucellai*, ed. G. Mazzoni, Bologna, 1887, p. 246); this is a private letter between friends, and there is no reason to take it at anything but its face-value. There is also, to my mind, no reason to doubt that Leo's own statements of these ideals were sincere and intensely, if complicatedly, motivated; in addition to the sources quoted in Chapter I, p. 15, see his letters of 1513 (ed. Bembo, cit. in n. 112, Bk. I. v, viii, xix, etc.), and particularly his private letter to Isabella d'Este, immediately after his election, begging her to pray that his reign may serve to the Glory of God 'et extirpationem heresum ac pacem et quietem populi christiani ...' (Luzio, op. cit. in n. 14, p. 117). For the Beauvais tapestries see M. Crick-Kuntziger, 'A Fragment of Guillaume de Hellande's Tapestries', *The Burlington Magazine*, xlv, 1924, pp. 225 ff.; G. L. Hunter, a letter, ibid., xlvi, 1925, p. 194; and P. Verlet, in *Il libro degli arazzi*, ed. J. Jobé, Milan, 1965, p. 66 (with reproductions of all eight surviving pieces).

177. F. Cabrol and H. Leclercq, *Dictionnaire d'archéologie chrétienne et de liturgie*, xi, Paris, 1933, p. 157: 'Le Christ médecin'; Arbesmann, op. cit. in n. 32; A. S. Pease, 'Medical Allusions in the Works of Saint Jerome', *Harvard Studies in Classical Philology*, xxv, 1914, pp. 73 ff.

I believe that Raphael's tapestries cannot be fully understood without reference to the highly particularized mythology of this pontificate.[173] There is positive evidence, as we have seen,[174] that Leo himself contributed to the invention of this mythology, which is to say that he had inherited the Medicean propensity, even genius, for image-making. Characteristic products are two of the new coins issued in the first year or so of his reign, useful in this context because their circulation was so wide that there must have been the expectation that their imagery would be readily understood; these are the *Leone* (*Fig.* 5), inscribed *Vicit Leo de Tribu Juda* (Revelation v. 5), and the *Triplice Giulio* (*Fig.* 6), Raphaelesque in design, so significantly inscribed *Pacem meam do vobis* (John xiv. 27). In each of these Leo is a new Christ (the idea, among popes, is no more novel than it is blasphemous), but a Christ in certain clearly defined rôles which we have already isolated; and the same choice of imagery is to be found in his titles in letters, orations and panegyrics (*Rex pacificus*, for example), in many applications of biblical texts to his person and policies, and of course in the *impresa* that he had, in fact, already adopted before his election (and which was earlier on a medal of his great-grandfather Cosimo, *Pater patriae*), the Yoke with the motto *Suave*, extracted from the text 'My yoke is easy and my burden is light' (Matthew xi. 30).

Gregory the Great was one of those who favoured a threefold interpretation of sacred histories; 'First we lay the foundations in history,' he said, 'then by following a symbolical sense, we erect an intellectual edifice to be a stronghold of faith, and lastly, by the grace of moral instruction, we as it were paint the fabric in fair colours.'[175] This is an encouragement for the use of the imagination in the third level of meaning, but not for irresponsibility. And it is undoubtedly at this point that the methodological problem of interpretation is most difficult. Such is the richness of the exegetical history of the texts on the one hand, and of Leonine imagery on the other, that apparent conjunctions automatically and accidentally present themselves. The game, in other words, is too easy. Such conjunctions of exegesis and imagery will only be credible if we reduce, even if we cannot eliminate, the possibility of accident by demanding that they apply not only to individual cases but also to the whole cycle. Satisfying this demand leaves us two concepts for consideration—I do not see on what grounds we can advance to the point of advocacy—which are both reasonable and both full of meaning. They satisfy another requirement in that they refer not to contingencies, or quickly outdated political events, but, like the coins, to the common expectations of this pontificate and the declared aspirations and permanent policy of the pope: the healing of the Church and the recovery and maintenance of its peace and unity, two aspects, obviously, of the same ideal through which the fulfilment of the Church could be attained. The real justification, in fact, for considering these suggestions is that if, indeed, Pope Leo wanted *any* political ideals expressed in these public works and in this public forum, the evidence suggests that these would be by a long way the most obvious and the most naturally to be anticipated. It needs, perhaps, to be added that the notion of a tapestry-cycle as a vehicle for the particular meaning now suggested would not be without conspicuous precedent. For one of the most famous tapestry-cycles of the fifteenth century, that of the Cathedral of Beauvais (1460), which Cardinal Giovanni de' Medici might

178. *In Leviticum homilia VIII* (*P.G.* 12, col. 492); a little later (ibid., col. 500) Origen, on the basis of the prophecy in Jeremiah xxxiii. describes the *Medicina Dei* in the healing of t[

even have seen on his youthful journey through France, is devoted to subjects from the lives of Saints Peter and Paul, and is liberally sown with small banderoles inscribed *Pace* or *Pax*; it seems, in fact, to have been commissioned to celebrate the end of the Hundred Years' War.[176]

Let us first consider the tapestries as an illustration of the healing power of *Christus medicus*, a concept (depending always upon the metaphorical identification of sickness and sin) that is discussed with remarkable frequency by Augustine but is also common enough in Origen, Jerome and Ambrose.[177] As we have already seen, for Origen the Healing of the Leper is an example of the power of the *Christus medicus*, and so it seems likely that the idea was already implicit in Botticelli's fresco in the chapel (*Fig. 15*). But Origen says, in the same breath, that the same power is displayed in the purification after the birth of the male child, which appears as a subsidiary theme in the tapestry beneath, the *Healing of the Lame Man*.[178] The main subject of this tapestry refers to healing not only in the obvious literal sense, but also and more importantly in the metaphorical sense. Petrus Lombardus, discussing the *Potestas clavium*, defines the rôle of priests in the Sacrament of Penance as that of doctors of souls, and Thomas Aquinas, under the same rubric, constantly compares the remission of sins with *medicina*.[179] Ambrose, in a famous sermon on the Miraculous Draught of Fishes, reads the whole of that event as *medicina salutis* and the doctrine of Peter as *cura animarum*.[180] For Augustine there was no clearer case than the Conversion of Saul; *Christus medicus* selected such a great sinner 'so that, after the performance of such a miraculous cure, no sinner need despair of obtaining forgiveness'; Augustine made this point on five separate occasions.[181] Rather in the opposite sense, of 'tough medicine' so to speak, the Death of Ananias, and by extension excommunication, are *medicina* once more for Thomas Aquinas.[182] The healing of the lame, by Peter at the *Porta speciosa* and by Paul at Lystra, are brought together by Arator and Bede as examples of the curing of sin among Jews and Gentiles.[183] And indeed the selection of these two healing scenes, one for each Apostle and Founder of the Church, must be remarked, for it gives a particularizing bias to the miracles that each performs and one that is distinctly unusual. It is easy to read the whole cycle as an illustration of the *medicamentum* applied to Mankind at the coming of Christ and the institution of His Church. Even the tapestry hung outside the screen, *Paul preaching at Athens*, may have been intended to sustain this reading, since the Leonine Bull *Apostolici regiminis* of 1513, which sets out the doctrine on the Immortality of the Soul, begins with a reference to the apostolic duty of the cure of the *animarum languores*.[184]

From the other side it is not difficult to discover what this might have meant in the period of the Cartoons. With extraordinary frequency we come across the concept, expressed in the tracts, orations, letters and panegyrics of the period, that Leo was the new *medicus* who would cure the ills of the Church. Obviously the success of this image depended partly upon the happy coincidence that the pope was a Medici. But, just as in the case of the Lion of Judah, the pun was chiefly a success because it had a serious and topical meaning in the context of reform and at the Lateran Council. It represents the convergence of earlier ideas with the Messianic (more accurately, soteriological) expectations of the new pontificate; for at the Lateran Council Cristoforo Marcello had already addressed Julius II in these terms, 'Tu enim pastor, tu *medicus*, tu gubernator, tu cultor, tu denique alter Deus in terris' (every epithet is worth reflection),[185] and the conceit had already been applied to Leo's father, Lorenzo *il magnifico*.[186] In this way the image

leper, figuratively of the soul, as a *Manifestatio Pacis*.

179. Petrus Lombardus, *Sententiae*, Bk. IV, dist. xviii. 2, *De clavibus*: 'sacerdotes . . . medici sunt animarum' (*P.L.* 192, col. 889); Aquinas, *Summa, Additiones*, esp. Quaest. xviii and xx (ed. cit. in n. 25, iv, pp. 447, 450).

180. *Sermo de mirabilibus* (1490 ed., No. XI; *P.L.* 17, cols. 675 ff., as No. XXXVII).

181. These sources are quoted by Arbesmann, op. cit. in n. 32, pp. 18–19.

182. *Summa, Additiones*, Quaest. xxi, art. iii, *De excommunicatione*: 'Petrus Ananiam & Saphiram pro defraudatione pretii agri sententia mortis damnavit: ergo & Ecclesia licet pro temporalibus damnis excommunicare . . . poenae medicinae sunt' (ed. cit. in n. 25, iv, p. 452). It was also said more generally that the powers of the Keys included the *animae cura*, for example by Baptista Mantuanus in a hymn to Saint Peter (*Hymni divini ad Leonem X. Pont. Max.*, Bibl. Laur., MS. Plut. xxxiv. 54, fol. 118r.).

183. Arator, *De actibus apostolorum*, cap. xxvii (see especially the exposition by Barbosa, ed. cit. in n. 10, fol. cxv, v.); Bede, *Expositio super acta apostolorum*, xiv. 7 (*P.L.* 92, col. 975).

184. 'Apostolici regiminis solicitudo nos assidue pulsat, ut medendis animarum languoribus, quarum nos ex alto Omnipotens auctor curam habere voluit, iis potissimum qui instantius fideles nunc urgere cernuntur, salutifero olei & vini medicamine ad instar Samaritani in evangelio solicitam operam impendamus, ne nobis illud Jeremiae (viii. 22) objiciatur: Numquid resina non est in Galaad, aut medicus non est ibi' (Hardouin, op. cit. in n. 95, ix, col. 1719). The medical metaphor is deliberate, being prepared in the *Oratio* at the opening of this session by Giovanni Battista Gargha, in which the pope is hailed as the new *Medicus* (see below, n. 187). Cf. Petrus Alcyonius's summary of Cardinal Giovanni's *disputa*, n. 156 above.

185. *Oratio* at session four of the Lateran Council, 10 December 1512; Hardouin, op. cit. in n. 95, ix, col. 1651.

186. See Chapter I, p. 16, n. 105.

187. Aegidius of Viterbo, MS. cit. in n. 170, fols. 358v., 367r. (a specific comparison between the *Medicus Pontifex Maximus* and Christ, each 'ad nostram medicinam vulnerandus'); Erasmus, letter to Leo, 29 April 1515, in *Epistolae ... ad diversos ...*, Basle, 1521, p. 71 ('Medici certe debemus remedium', etc.); Giustiniani-Quirini, *Libellus* (1513), ed. cit. in n. 94, col. 622 ('Te, qui animarum omnium languentium vere medicus es', etc.). See also: Pietro Delfin, letter to Giuliano de' Medici, 12 March 1513, on Leo's election, in *Epistolae*, ed. cit. in n. 112, Bk. X. c ('... ut haud temere Cardinalis olim de Medicis facile futurus sit totius Christianae rei publicae languentis medicina' —an obvious case of the re-application of earlier Medicean imagery); idem, *Oratio ad Leonem X*, 13 March 1513 (Bibl. Laur., MS. Plut. xlvii. 17, presentation copy, fol. 131v.; Martène-Durand, op. cit. in n. 55, iii, col. 1211); Pietro Bembo, letter to Leo, 13 March 1513 (M. Sanuto, *I diarii*, xvi, Venice, 1886, col. 41); G. J. Penni's description of the arch at the Casa de' Sauli in the Lateran procession, 11 April 1513 (Cancellieri, op. cit. in n. 20, p. 80); Ferreri, op. cit. in n. 163 (unpaginated); the text of Isaac's motet (1513?—see above, p. 14, n. 84: 'Optime pastor ovili tandem qui laceri medicus gregis ulcera sanes . . .'); Marcellus Palonius, *De clade Ravennati*, Rome, 1513, Bk. II; Giovanni Battista Gargha, *Oratio* at session eight of the Lateran Council, 17 December 1513 (Hardouin, op. cit. in n. 95, ix, col. 1729); *Oratio obedientiae ... Guglielmi Marchionis Montisferrati apud Leonem decimum* (12 December 1513—the pamphlet publ. n.p. or d.); Naldo Naldi, *Carmina ad Sanctissimum D. Nostrum Leonem. X. Pont. Max.* (Bibl. Laur., MS. Plut. xxxv. 43, presentation copy, 1513–14, fols. 11r. ff., with a specific comparison with *Christus Medicus*, the anticipation of universal *salus* and of the *unum ovile* under *unus pastor*); Sansonius, MS. cit. in n. 117, fol. 5v.; Buturinus, *Quae vitia in terris*, epigram addressed to Leo X (MS. cit. in n. 117, fol. 33r.); M. Antonio Casanova, a poem *Ad Leonem decimum* (Bibl. Vat., MS. Vat. Lat. 2834, fol. 71r.); Fra Zanobi Acciaioli, *In libros Theodoriti: quorum tittuli Curatio graecarum affectionum* (Bibl. Vat., MS. Ottob. Lat. 1404, fol. 2v.); Guarna, op. cit. in n. 50 (unpaginated, written 1515); Egidio Pontano, *Oratio et versus* addressed to Leo (Bibl. Vat., MS. Vat. Lat. 6284, fols. 221v., 224r.); P. Matthaei her. *Encomion in Leonem X. Pont. Max.* (Bibl. Ambrosiana, MS. H. 35 inf. (4), fols. 90v., 97r.); Poggio, MS. cit. in n. 117, fol. 9v.; Cristoforo Marcello, *Dialogi de animae sanitate* (Bibl. Vat., MS. Vat. Lat. 3647, presentation copy to Leo, 1518, fol. 5v.); Galatinus, MS. cit. in n. 116, fols. 103v. ff.); Janus Vitalis Castalius, poem celebrating the Lateran procession, in W. Roscoe, *Vita e pontificato di Leone*

came readily to the entirely serious minds of Aegidius of Viterbo, Erasmus, Vincenzo Quirini and Tommaso Giustiniani and several others.[187] We might take as typical this passage from a letter of the dedicated reformist Gasparo Contarini, June 1514: 'our Supreme Pontiff . . . was raised to this dignity by the Holy Spirit, as if the latter had consigned the ailing Church of Christ *ad optimo medico*'.[188] In this sense, then, the examples of the *medicina Dei* in the tapestries could be read as allegories of the achievement and continuing aspiration of Leo X, *alter Deus in terris* and successor to Peter and Paul. It would have been as easy for a contemporary spectator of the tapestries to comprehend the *medicamenta* in the sense suggested as to interpret the *Miracle of the Fire in the Borgo*, painted at the same date in the Vatican Stanze, as an allegory of Leo's extinction of the flames of war. 'Pestilence' was as natural and common a metaphor for the Schism (to take a specific case), now among other ills in the Church healed by Leo, as that of 'Conflagration' for contemporary wars, as natural, indeed, as our metaphor of the 'ills' of society.

The second concept for consideration, that of peace and unity in the Church, is only a more precise definition of the *medicina Dei*, expressed in what might be called the architectural and pastoral formulae. Summarizing an extremely complex situation we may say that there is in the appropriate exegetical material a circle of ideas on peace and unity that intersects with the themes of the tapestries, and that the same circle of ideas was drawn around the pontificate of Leo X. Two very familiar texts are fundamental to these ideas. The first is Paul's classic statement of the 'architectural' peace-formula in Ephesians ii. 14: 'For he (Christ) is our peace, who hath made

X, ed. L. Bossi, Milan, 1816, v, p. 233; G. F. Pico della Mirandola, *De reformandis moribus oratio ... ad Leonem X*, in *Opera omnia*, Basle, 1601, ii, p. 886; Baptista Spagnuoli, op. cit. in n. 102, Bk. IX, *De SS. Cosma e Damiano*; and already the Pasquinades of 1513 (D. Gnoli, 'Pasquino pedagogo', in *La Roma di Leon X*, Milan, 1938, p. 178).

188. Contarini to Quirini, 13 June 1514: 'Cominciai a considerare a la election di questo nostro Summo Pontefice el qual, contra el pensier de tuti, da el Spirito Sancto era stato assumpto a questa dignitade, quasi che la languida Chiesia di Christo ad optimo medico per lui fosse stata commessa . . .' (H. Jedin, 'Contarini und Camaldoli', *Archivio italiano per la storia della Pietà*, ii, 1959, p. 94).

189. See, for example, the opinions collected by Petrus Lombardus, *Commentarium in Psalmos* (*P.L.* 191, col. 1038).

190. Jerome, *Commentaria in epistolam ad Ephesos*, ii. 15 (*P.L.* 26, col. 473); Aquinas, *Comentaria super epistolas ... pauli*, Bologna, 1481, Eph. ii, 14–19; Augustine, *Tractatus in Joannis evangelium*, x. 16 (*P.L.* 35, col. 1735); Bede, *In S. Joannis evangelium expositio*, x. 16 (*P.L.* 92, col. 768).

191. Hill, op. cit. in n. 81, No. 903.

192. *Sermones CCXLVIII, CCLII* (*P.L.* 38, cols. 1159, 1173); idem, *Tractatus in Joannis evangelium*, xxi. 1–11 (*P.L.* 35, col. 1963); Arator, *De actibus apostolorum*, cap. xxvii; Bede, *In Luce evangelium expositio*, v (*P.L.* 92, col. 382); *Glossa ordinaria*, Luke v (*P.L.* 114, col. 256); Aquinas, *Catena Aurea*, ed. cit. in n. 25, on Luke v; Nicolaus de Lyra, *Expositiones morales secundun sensum misticum super totam Bibliam*, Mantua, 1481, on Luke v (the last three quoting Bede); Jacques Lefèvre, *Commentarii initiatorii in quatuor evangelia*, Meaux, 1522, fol. 187v. In this connection it is important to notice that the ravens in this tapestry may (and perhaps ought to) be interpreted by an alternative symbolism to the one mentioned above, p. 54; this alternative is derived from the texts about ravens in Psalm cxlvii. 9 and Job xxxviii. 41 ('Quis praeparat corvo escam suam, quando pulli ejus clamant ad Deum, *vagantes* eo quod non habeant cibos?'), which are taken to adumbrate the conversion of the Gentiles by preaching: Hilary, *Tractatus in CXLVI Psalmum* (*P.L.* 9, col. 874); Augustine, *Enarratio in Psalmum CXLVI* (*P.L.* 37, col. 1911); Gregory, *Moralium*, Bk. XXX, cap. ix (*P.L.* 76, cols. 539 ff.); Rabanus Maurus, *De universo*, Bk. VIII, cap. vi (*P.L.* 111, col. 252); Hugo de St. Victoire, *De bestiis*, Bk. I, cap. xxxv (*P.L.* 177, cols. 31 ff.). This tradition is not in conflict with the other, but rather particularizes the raven-sinner as the Gentile. Gregory lays special

both one, *Ipse est enim pax nostra, qui fecit utraque unum.*' Paul was talking of the rejoining of Jews and Gentiles in Christ, and a few verses later he explains the metaphor by another, the joining of the two sides in the Cornerstone, Christ. Paul was extending a prophecy in Psalm cxviii. 22: 'The stone which the builders refused is become the head stone of the corner' and another in Isaiah xxviii. 16: 'Behold I lay in Zion for a foundation a stone, a tried stone, a precious corner stone, a sure foundation.' Christ himself described His coming as the fulfilment of these prophecies (Matthew xxi. 42), and this identification was followed in a sermon of Peter (Acts iv. 11) and again in the First Epistle of Peter, ii. 6; it became another constant in the exegetical tradition.[189] The second fundamental text, which is frequently quoted with the first because it carries the same meaning, comes from the Parable of the Good Shepherd (John x. 15–16): 'I lay down my life for the sheep. And other sheep I have, which are not of this fold: them also I bring, and they shall hear my voice; and there shall be one fold, and one shepherd, *Et fiet unum ovile, et unus pastor.*' The 'other sheep' in this text were always taken to be the Gentiles, who must also be collected into the Church of Christ. Jerome and Thomas Aquinas quote this passage in explanation of Ephesians ii. 14, and Augustine and Bede vice versa.[190] The two texts appear together on one of the versions of the Medal of Christ which Raphael used in the Cartoons.[191]

To illustrate the relevance of these texts to the tapestries we may turn to Augustine on the Miraculous Draught of Fishes. Like many others, Augustine took the two boats to represent the separated peoples, Jews and Gentiles, who were joined together in the Church of Christ.[192] 'To which two peoples, as if two walls,' he says, 'the Lord is become the Cornerstone, so that He unites them, coming from different sides, in Himself.' The tapestry with this subject was to hang beneath the *Nativity of Christ* fresco and it should be noticed that this subject was commonly interpreted in exactly the same way —by Augustine, for example,[193] and by Innocent III. The latter's commentary is striking: at the Nativity peace was reestablished between God and Man, between Angel and Man, and between the separated Jew and Gentile, 'but when the True Peace came He made both one, and destroyed their cause of enmity, joining the two walls coming together in Himself, the Cornerstone, so that there should be one flock, and one shepherd'; Jew and Gentile are represented by Shepherds and Magi, by ox and ass at the manger.[194] It seems very possible, as in the case of the placing of the *Healing of the Lame Man* beneath the *Healing of the Leper*, that such a thematic connection was deliberately drawn between fresco and tapestry, exploiting a meaning latent in the former; and this connection would be comprehensible above all on the altar-wall, for the symbolism of the Crucifix between two candles on the altar is exactly the same: the Cornerstone joining the two peoples. The Mons Vaticanus in the tapestry could be interpreted by a contemporary, as we saw earlier, as a figure of *Unitas*, and the more distant buildings as a figure of *Concordia.*

It is probably in this sense, too, that we should understand the demonstration of the *Primatus Petri*. Its meaning during the period of the Lateran Council, as at other times in the history of the Church, was an insurance of unity.[195] In the Introit for the Feast of *Cathedra Petri*, on the other hand, the *Primatus* is called Christ's *Testamentum pacis*.[196] The Bull *Unam Sanctam* (reissued by Leo X in 1516) is one of those texts that draws together the Charge to Peter, *Pasce oves meas*, and the prophecy of the one flock and the one shepherd, as the divine commitment to unity in the Church under the pope.[197]

stress, in this context, on the rôle of Paul, *Magister Gentium*, in this conversion. Following this line of thought, then, the *plenitudo* of the whole of Christ's Church could be seen to be foreshadowed in the first tapestry, the conclusion of the cycle in its beginning.

193. *Sermones in Epiphania Domini CXCIX–CCIV* (*P.L.* 38, cols. 1026 ff.).

194. *De sacro altaris mysterio*, ed. Paris, 1517, Bk. II, cap. xvi, fol. xxii; ed. Leipzig, 1534, Bk. II, cap. xx, fol. 25v.

195. Julius II's Bull, *Salvator Dominus*, 13 April 1512, summoning the Lateran Council; Bernardo Zane, *Oratio* at first session (Hardouin, op. cit. in n. 95, ix, col. 1604); Thomas de Vio, *Oratio* at second session (Hardouin, ix, col. 1621); Aegidius of Viterbo, letter *c.* 1512, quoted by O'Malley, op. cit. in n. 6, p. 167; Poggio, *De potestate papae et concilii* (1511–12), ed. cit. in n. 61, fol. 29; Mazzolini, *De iuridica et irrefragabili veritate Romanae Ecclesiae* (Rocaberti, op. cit. in n. 25, xix, pp. 229 ff.); the Bull *Pastor Aeternus*, 1516 (Hardouin, ix, col. 1830). For earlier sources, see Cyprian, *De ecclesiae unitate* (Chapman, op. cit. in n. 117, pp. 250–1); Optatus, *De schismate Donatistorum*, Bk. VII (*P.L.* 11, cols. 1087–8); Augustine, e.g. *Sermo XLVI* (*P.L.* 38, col. 287), and the texts collected by P. van Wavre, *Privilegium S. Petri ac successorum ejus ex S. Augustino assertum*, Louvain, 1719, pp. 6 ff.); Bede, *Homilia in vigilium Petri et Pauli* (*P.L.* 94, col. 218); Innocent III, *Epistola CCIII* (*P.L.* 215, col. 512); Aquinas, *Catena Aurea*, ed. cit. in n. 25, on Matthew xvi, also quoting the *Glossa ordinaria*; Torquemada, *Summa*, Bk. II, cap. v (ed. cit. in n. 19, p. 183).

196. *Missale Romanum*, ed. Venice, 1509, fol. 169v.: 'Statuit ei (sc: Petro) dominus testamentum pacis: & principem fecit eum ut sit illi sacerdotii dignitas in eternum.'

197. 'Ecclesiae unius et unicae unum corpus, unum caput ... Christus scilicet, et Christi Vicarius Petrus, Petrique Successor, dicente Domino ipsi Petro: Pasce oves meas ... (whoever denies Peter's authority is not of the Lord's flock ...) dicente Domine in Joanne: unum ovile, et unum unicum esse pastorem.' The association is already made by Augustine, e.g. *Sermo XLVI*, *De pastoribus* (*P.L.* 39, col. 287); for examples in the Leonine period: Poggio, *De potestate papae et concilii*, ed. cit. in n. 61, fol. 37r., and Mazzolini, *De iuridica et irrefragabili veritate Romanae Ecclesiae* (Rocaberti, op. cit. in n. 25, xix, pp. 232, 240); Mazzolini also quite logically takes together, in a kind of conflation, John x and Matthew xvi, saying that the Church is of necessity under one governor 'quod principalis Dominus ordinavit, dicens:

Et super hanc petram aedificabo Ecclesiam meam; & erit unum ovile, & unus pastor' (*De papa et eius potestate*, in Rocaberti, xix, p. 369).

198. E.g. Augustine, *Enarrationes in Psalmos*, lxxxvi (*P.L.* 37, cols. 1101 ff.), specifically quoting I Peter ii. 5. Notable is his insistence, which is very characteristic, 'Ne itaque putarent Gentes non se pertinere ad Sion (i.e. the Celestial Jerusalem) ... Dicit fortasse aliquis, Si angularis lapis est Christus Jesus, in illo quidem duo parietes in unum de diverso venientes: sic et populi duo ex circumcisione et ex praeputio, ad pacem Christianam sibimet convexi in una fide, una spe, una charitate ...' This line of thought would suggest the reading of the *Healing of the Lame Man* and *Conversion of the Proconsul* as complementary in the fulfilment of the Church and of the Peace of Christ, as suggested above, p. 69.

199. *Oratio* at second session (Hardouin, op. cit. in n. 95, ix, cols. 1618 ff.), which is apparently much influenced by Augustine, e.g.: 'Quod autem Jerusalem pacisque nomen, verum nostrae civitatis nomen sit ... Illorum est haec sanctissima Jerusalem, quae ex vivis lapidibus construitur, de qua David loquitur, & cujus portarum ferae ac claustra a Domino confortantur. Haec est illa Jerusalem ... in qua ... rex pacificus pacem relinquit nobis, pacem suam dat nobis ...' etc. This *Oratio*, separately printed in 1512, was probably in the minds of Quirini and Giustiniani when they addressed Leo in summer 1513: '... per tranquillissimam in Terris pacem ad aeternae Beatudinis felicitatem, omnes pariter homines perduceres. Hoc, Beatissime Pater, proprium, praecipuumque Pontificis munus esse ... credimus; ... tuae ... amplitudinis munus (est), si Christi vestigia imitari; ejusque beneplacitis in hac ab eo Tibi tradita potestate inhaerere volueris ... tuis manibus Christo Domino puros commissarum tibi ovium animos offerre, ut illa citius perficiatur Ecclesia, quae in Coelis vivis, aeternisque construitur ex lapidibus' (*Libellus*, ed. cit. in n. 94, col. 618). It should be noted that an argument of this kind would provide, for Leo, a very particular meaning for the sequence *Charge to Peter—Healing of the Lame Man*, directly opposite his throne.

200. Arator, *De actibus apostolorum*, caps. vi, xvii; Bede, *Expositio super acta apostolorum*, iii (*P.L.* 92, col. 951). For the origins of the concept of Solomon, *Rex pacificus*, as a type of Christ, see Chapter I, p. 16, n. 104. The sequence Solomon-Christ-Leo *Rex pacificus* ought to be borne in mind in the case of the decorations of the Leonine Loggia ('Raphael's Bible'), the thematic structure of which concludes so remarkably with two bays dedicated to Solomon and Christ.

Since the *Porta speciosa* of the Temple is a figure of the threshold of the Church, the *Healing of the Lame Man* represents, metaphorically, the reception into the New Jerusalem, of which Christ is the Cornerstone and the citizens those 'living stones' of the First Epistle of Peter.[198] The New Jerusalem, of which Peter is both foundation and *janitor*, was the theme of the oration of Thomas de Vio at the Lateran Council, 7 May 1512, in which he explained it at length as a figure of peace.[199] But the same interpretation could be reached by a different route, for as Arator and Bede explain (almost superfluously) the Temple of Solomon in this story which is entered by the lame man, once healed, is the Temple of the new *Rex pacificus*, Christ, to which Peter admits Israel.[200] The Salomonic columns of this portal can be symbols of *Christus medicus*, since the healing powers of the *Colonna santa* (one of those that formerly stood in front of the *Confessio* in Saint Peter's) were reputedly derived from Christ, or they can be symbols of *Rex pacificus*, or perhaps both.[201] And we may also interpret the *Death of Ananias* and the *Sacrifice at Lystra* in relation to unity and peace, since the disobedience of the Jews and the idolatry of the Gentiles were the *obstacula* against peace overcome by Christ.

The *Salus* roundel in the *Conversion of the Proconsul*, which would appear, in fact, immediately next to the papal throne, has not yet been interpreted; and indeed an interpretation is difficult, not because there are too few biblical texts that might apply but because there are too many. It happens, however, that the one that is probably the most familiar appears immediately after the text for the main scene in this tapestry. In the next episode (Acts xiii. 47) Paul warns the Jews of the divine promise of the *plenitudo gentium*, quoting Isaiah xlix. 6: 'I will also give thee for a light to the Gentiles, that thou mayest be my salvation—*ut sis salus mea*—unto the end of the Earth.' In 1513 Pietro Delfin, in an oration addressed to Leo X, had used this text as an image of the repacification and reunification of the Church.[202]

But these individual examples, even if interpreted correctly, are not convincing as they stand; it is, rather, the whole tapestry-cycle as a metaphor of peace and unity that is more compelling. The architectural formula of Saint Paul, like Christ's metaphor in Matthew xvi, 'upon this rock I will build my church', is based upon the idea that the material church is an allegory of the spiritual Church. Thus Arator called Peter and Paul the 'first architects' of the Church of Christ. This idea was still very much alive in the Renaissance period. It is characteristic, for example, that in the fresco of the *Donation of the Keys* in the Sistine Chapel the two architects, or the architect

201. It is worth noting that in the most circumstantial (but erroneous) account of the provenance of the columns in this period, that given by Fra Mariano da Firenze, *Itinerarium urbis romae*, 1517 (ed. cit. in n. 69, p. 82), they were said to have been removed from Solomon's Temple by Titus and Vespasian and installed in the *Templum Pacis* in Rome, whence they were removed to Saint Peter's by Constantine.

202. The passage from Delfin's *Oratio* is quoted below, n. 215.

203. Arator, *De actibus apostolorum*, cap. xxvii, on the Sacrifice at Lystra (see also the extended commentary by Barbosa, ed. cit. in n. 10, fol.

cxiv, v.). Durandus, *Rationale*, I, i. 8 and ii. 31 perhaps it should be stressed again (cf. Chapter I, p. 8) that this book had a special relevance to the *Capella papalis*, and was frequently consulted by e.g. Paris de Grassis. The passage on the altar is almost identical to one in Innocent III's *De sacro altaris mysterio*, Bk. II, cap. xxi where the same formula is used; Innocent III's writings were also at the finger-tips of Paris de Grassis, whose *Caeremoniarum opusculum* (Bibl. Vat., MS. Vat. Lat. 5634/1) is as informative on the continuity of symbolism as on that of ritual.

204. 'Primitiva illa ecclesia in angulari petra a Salvatore nostro Jesu Christo fundata

and *capomaestro*, who erected it are portrayed as witnesses of Christ's words, 'thou art Peter, and upon this rock I will build my church'; and it is perhaps worth remembering that when Raphael designed the Cartoons he had already assumed responsibility for the 'new Temple' on the 'new Zion', Saint Peter's, symbol of the Roman Church. 'The material church', as Durandus said, 'symbolizes that Holy Church that is built in Heaven of living stones'; Durandus then quoted Ephesians ii (Paul's 'architectural' peace-formula) and explained that the walls built upon these foundations, with Christ as the Cornerstone, signified the Jews and Gentiles. And he returned to Ephesians ii to explain the altar; the Crucifix is placed between the candlesticks 'because Christ stands in the Church, the Mediator between two peoples. For He is the Cornerstone, Who hath made both one.'[203]

Now it so happens that Raphael's tapestries are uniquely architectural in character, with vertical borders and *basamenti* that take the place of pilasters and *spalliere*, and they form two walls, or visually replace two walls, that come together at the altar like allegories of those spiritual walls of Jews and Gentiles that converge from different sides in Christ, the Cornerstone. 'Ipse est enim pax nostra, qui fecit utraque unum.' The example of Perugino's *Donation of the Keys* should warn us against dismissing this formulation as beyond the range of symbolic thinking in this period and context. Yet the idea does not need to be expressed, and need not have been realized, so concretely for the cycle to constitute a figure of peace and unity. What really matters is that the notion of the two peoples collected and reconciled by Peter and Paul in the Church of Christ is a familiar expression of peace and unity restored (after the schism implied at the end of the history-cycle on the ceiling); and that this approach to the series does account for the subordinate place within it that is given to the *Primatus Petri* and the deliberated balance that is struck in the illustration of the complementary rôles of the two Apostles. The tapestry-cycle illustrates the ideal of the 'Primitive Church' as it was described at the Lateran Council in 1516, 'founded on the Cornerstone by our Saviour Jesus Christ, brought to fruition by the teaching of the Apostles, consecrated and enriched by the blood of the martyrs'.[204] It remains to be shown that this concept was widely understood, with a particular meaning in relation to Leo X and the condition of the Church, in the period in which the Cartoons were commissioned.

The text 'Et fiet unum ovile, et unus pastor', the 'pastoral' peace-formula with a similar but more specifically eschatological meaning, had already been used in appeals to popes for peace and reunion in the Church. Ficino, for example, quotes this text as the corollary of the Charge to Peter, *Pasce oves meas*, in a letter to Sixtus IV which is a remarkably frank admonition to peace in Christendom;[205] Angelo da Vallombrosa does exactly the same in his *Oratio* addressed to Julius II in 1511.[206] The topicality becomes explicit in Cristoforo Marcello's *Oratio* to Julius in 1512: 'take care that the flock committed to your charge is nourished with good spiritual food . . ., take care that the flock shall be one, *ut ovile unum fiat*, for it is to some extent divided into separate parts' (the divided flock is, clearly, the Church split by the schismatic Council of Pisa).[207] Immediately after Leo's election Pietro Delfin returned to this metaphor in a congratulatory letter, hailing Leo as the *pastor bonus* who tends the Lord's flock, scattered and torn apart.[208] The protonotary Caracciolo, whose letter to Isabella d'Este written two days after the election was cited at the beginning of this Chapter as an example of the textual expertise of the non-specialist in the *Capella papalis*, also looked forward with confidence to peace and unity; Leo, he said, is the Good

Apostolorum praeconiis elata, martyrumque sanguine consecrata et aucta . . .', the opening of the *Schedula* read at session eleven, December 1516 (Hardouin, op. cit. in n. 95, col. 1810); incorporated in the Bull *In eminenti*, defining the concordat with Francis I (*Bullarium . . .*, ed. cit. in n. 29, p. 207).

205. *Epistole Marsilii Ficinii Florentini*, Venice, 1495, Bk. VI, fol. cxii, r.: *Oratio christiani gregis ad Pastorem Sistum Suadens ut ovibus suis dicat Pax vobis*, which is strongly eschatological in its imagery; see also his second letter, 25 December 1478, ibid., fol. cxiv, v., congratulating the pope on his conversion to peace, in which the same text is quoted.

206. *Oratio pro concilio Lateranensi . . .*, ed. cit. in n. 112, p. 345: 'Crediderim insuper Deum meum Jesum Christum, ut sue Ecclesie unitatem denotaret, unum illi summum ac maximum voluisse preesse pastorem . . . Scriptum quoque in libro invenio: *Erit unum ovile et unus Pastor*.'

207. *Oratio* at session four, 10 December 1512 (Hardouin, op. cit. in n. 95, ix, col. 1651): 'Cura, ut grex tibi commissus optimis ac spiritalibus alimentis alatur & vivat . . . Cura, ut Ovile unum fiat, quod modo est in partes divisum . . .'; the same text is invoked again in the midst of a long appeal for unity and peace in the *Oratio* of Archbishop Giovanni Maria de Monte, session five (Hardouin, ix, col. 1667).

208. 13 March 1513: 'Benedictus Deus, qui benedictionem omnium gentium dedit tibi: & testamentum suum confirmavit super caput tuum . . . ut datus sit nobis pastor bonus: qui dissipati et dilacerati gregis dominici pia solicitudine curam gerat: qui vexato discordiis ac bellis contrito benedicat populo tuo in pace . . .' (*Epistolae*, ed. cit. in n. 112, Bk. XI. i); the same idea, more specifically applied to peace in Italy, appears in the *Elogia ad Leonem X* of Janus Damianus (in N. Reusner, *Selectissimarum orationum . . . de bello turcico . . . volumen secundum*, Leipzig, 1596, p. 183). See also Naldo Naldi, MS. cit. in n. 187, fol. 14v.; Bernardo Lavignete, MS. text cit. below in n. 217; Blosio Palladio, *Oratio in praestatione obedientiam Rhodiorum Leoni X. Pont. Max.* (Bibl. Vat., MS. Ottob. Lat. 2413, fol. 89v.); Girolamo Bordoni da Sermoneta, *La exortatione de la cruciata . . .*, publ. n.p. or d. (c. 1517), addressed to Leo, fol. 3v.

209. *Oratio* at session eight, 19 December 1513 (Hardouin, op. cit. in n. 95, ix, cols. 1729 ff.); the very remarkable imagery of this *Oratio* was probably 'inspired' by Leo himself, through Cardinal Giulio de' Medici (see Chapter I, p. 17).

210. *Oratio* at session nine, 5 May 1514, by Antonio Pucci: 'Quid enim flagrantius nobiscum simul optare debent, qui modo erant in ecclesia Dei hospites atque advenae, quam ut nunc fiant cum aliis per morum instaurationem Sanctorum cives & domestici Dei, superaedificati supra fundamentum Apostolorum & prophetarum, in ipso summo angulari lapide Christo Jesu, in quo omnis aedificatio crescit in templum sanctum ... Jam ecclesia Dei in integrum fidei, spei, caritatisque vinculum est restituta ... Jam universum illius corpus uni capiti, hoc est, tibi subditum esse conspicitur...', etc. (Hardouin, op. cit. in n. 95, ix, col. 1763); a MS. copy of this work was presented to Leo in 1514 (G. Mercati, 'Un indice di libri offerti a Leone X', *Il libro e la stampa*, ii, 1908, pp. 41 ff., No. 23). *Oratio* at session ten, 4 May 1515, by Stephanus, Bishop of Torcello (Hardouin, ix, cols. 1787–8).

211. The Latin text in Chapter I, p. 1, n. 3.

212. Under the rubric *Papa reformator ecclesiae*:
'Quo duce relligio toto reparabitur orbe:
Atque per eoas procul amplificabitur oras.
Quas ibi vidisti, quinque in consortia nymphae
Atque sodalitii foedus iungentur, & unum
Sub pastore uno late consurget ovile.
Ipse pedo minabit oves ad pascua laeta
Pastor, & exertis languentes colliget ulnis.'

213. MS. text quoted in n. 170.

214. Delfin was reflecting on the meaning of the name Leo: 'sanctum & terribile nomen tuum. Sanctum utique fidelibus, terribile infidelibus, venerandum & adorandum populo Christiano, formidolosum atque tremendum populo barbaro. Quem ubi tandem, opitulante Domino, tuo apostolatui subegeris, factumque fuerit unum ovile & unus pastor, de te passim praedicetur: Vicit leo de tribu Juda' (*Oratio ad Leonem X*, 13 March 1513, in Martène-Durand, op. cit. in n. 55, iii, col. 1213).

215. *Oratio ad Leonem X*, loc. cit. in n. 214: 'Utinam, pater sancte, id mihi hac aetate contingat, ut, te auctore, compositis Christianorum dissidiis, ac reddita tandem fidelibus pace, etiam gentes ac nationes barbarae subjiciantur tibi: ut illud in te propheticum impleatur: Dedi te in lucem gentium, ut sis *salus mea* usque ad extremum terrae' (Isaiah xlix. 6); see above, p. 80.

Shepherd, 'È intrato per ostium con ogni sincerità come vero pastore' (John x. 1), and 'se potrà dire in Italia erit unum ovile et unus pastor'. By the end of 1513 Leo X was addressed in the Lateran *Oratio* of Giovanni Battista Gargha as the *medicus* who had healed the infirmities of the Church and as the *optimus pastor*, for the Schism had by then been cured; he urged, as the next step, that the Christian Princes should be pacified, 'and your dispersed sheep collected in the holy sheepfold, *quo unum sit ovile, sicut unus est pastor*'. Gargha then introduced the 'architectural' metaphor, encouraging Leo towards unity and reform, and 'to watch over the fragments of your people brought together again ... *in angulum*'.[209] The Cornerstone metaphor reappears in two more of the Lateran orations in 1514 and 1515.[210]

However the credit for first applying the formulae in this sense probably belongs to Zaccaria Ferreri, whose poem, the *Lugdunense Somnium*, was published in September 1513; in the passage which was our original point of departure he comments circuitously but unambiguously on Leo's achievement in the healing of the Schism. Leo 'builds for the Heavenly King an eternal temple of living stones, bringing the divided together into one; and as the corner joins what is divided, so he reunites the scattered; with his healing hand he cures all ills ...'[211] Ferreri also uses, in another passage, the 'pastoral' metaphor of the 'one flock' more explicitly.[212]

For Zaccaria Ferreri, as also, a little later, for Aegidius of Viterbo,[213] Leo has become the new Cornerstone, *Pax nostra, qui fecit utraque unum*, and, as we have seen, Leo himself seems to have sanctioned the image and to have given it circulation at the Council through the *Oratio* of Gargha. On the same occasion he had promoted the ideal of the *unum ovile* and *unus pastor*, perhaps taking it from the existing tradition but more probably directly inspired by the *Oratio* of Pietro Delfin in which the *unus pastor* had been identified with the Lion of Judah.[214] The proposition, then, is that the subject-matter of the tapestries carried, apart from its doctrinal meaning, essentially the same message as Leo's new coinage. A people tired of strife could not have mistaken the meaning of the *Triplice Giulio, Pacem meam do vobis* (*Fig. 6*), and the more sophisticated observers in the Sistine Chapel, churchmen, ambassadors, Senators of Rome and the rest, would be well prepared to read the establishment of peace and unity in the Primitive Church as an allegory of the present and future policy of the new Prince of Peace, the policy that he regarded as the duty laid upon the Vicar of Christ in eternity.

Out of the Council rose the new Lion of Judah, who alone could effect the fulfilment of the Church (*Fig. 5*). But what, more precisely, could that fulfilment mean? It could simply mean the healing of the Schism, certainly a great event in itself, or it could mean the establishment of peace in the whole *Respublica christiana*, no less of a triumph and no less of an eternal ideal. But it should not be forgotten that there was a contingent idea in the air that

216. They specifically compare Leo's duty 'totum humanum genus, omnes scilicet gentes, populos, nationes, quae sub Coelo sunt, tuae subditas esse potestati, tuisque nutibus regenda humana omnia, atque tuo arbitrio moderanda' with Christ sending His apostles 'ad Evangelium omnibus Creaturis in universo orbe praedicandum ... non solum in Jerusalem, Judaea, & Samaria; sed usque ad ultimum Terrae ... Te enim vere hodie constituit Dominus super gentes, & Regna ... non enim angustissimae hujus Italiae modo, aut etiam non satis lata Europae solum, sed longe etiam ampliora potentioraque Africae, Asiaeque, totius scilicet Universi Regna, & Imperia omnia tua subiecit potestati, tuaeque fidei commisit ...' and, again, the pope's duty is 'ex universarum gentium diversitate, unam Christi Ecclesiam congregare ...' (*Libellus ad Leonem X*, summe 1513, ed. cit. in n. 94, cols. 615, 617, 620; se also col. 622). When they turn to the rejoining of those Christians divided from the Church

might explain the emphasis on the *plenitudo gentium* in the tapestries; this was the extension of the *Respublica christiana* to the whole world, including not only those parts then under Turkish rule but also the New World, coming together into one, and in one flock under one shepherd. This task was recommended to Leo with all seriousness by Delfin,[215] Quirini and Giustiniani,[216] and by Aldus Manutius, who—remarkably—envisaged Leo sending out *his* 'Apostles to preach the Gospel' to the entire universe.[217]

This question is not, unfortunately, the only one that comes to mind. It is a matter for individual judgement whether or not there exists sufficient evidence for the proposition that this is in principle one way in which those who had access to the chapel were intended to read the tapestry-cycle. The contemporary sources are mostly public ones, the greater part (perhaps all) of the orations at the Lateran Council were instantly circularized in pamphlet form, and the demands that it would make upon exegetical resources are not really very taxing when measured by the standards of the appropriate context. The accessibility of the material in the context, and the preparation, by repeated exposure to the principal ideas, of the members of the *Capella papalis* are essential to the argument. But if this point can be conceded it must, nevertheless, be recognized as not being the point that matters above all; for there still remains a lack of any proof that the tapestries were intended to be so interpreted. The sources that have been quoted, however relevant they may be, must not be misconstrued so that they support that contention. All that they can do is to give potential validity to an hypothesis.

It is partly because the different ways in which the tapestry-cycle might be read seem compelling in different degrees—the literal sufficiently, the metaphorical-doctrinal partially, the political-personal least—and partly because a certain schematization is necessary for exposition, that this analysis has been developed on three levels. There is, of course, a patent absurdity in the idea of the Sistine congregation making in unison a kind of three-ply reading of the tapestries. But it is not absurd to imagine that the choice of subjects, sequence, position and internal details was made deliberately so as to allow, and even encourage, two other readings, beyond the literal, along the lines suggested. In other words that ambiguity of visual images, that capacity that they have to sustain a plurality of meanings which is for us the fundamental methodological embarrassment, could indeed have been exploited so that the thoughts of the congregation would be guided towards the reminiscence of familiar metaphors, some members towards one train of thought, others towards another. It should be said, parenthetically, that ceremonies such as Pontifical Mass, which could last several hours, gave ample occasion for trains of thought. But the realistic consequence of the supposition that the choices were made with this intention is that it would have been impossible to invent a scheme that was consistently perfect in these several ways. If some tapestries, such as the *Healing of the Lame Man*, seem particularly eloquent on the three levels of meaning, and in relation to their neighbours and the fresco above, while others seem less so, this inconsistency, which might certainly arise from our failure to find the right key to their interpretation, might also be the real and unavoidable imperfection in the scheme. Reconsidering, for example, the Petrine set in relation to the Sistine histories above, we find that some of the parallels are more obvious than others. The *Miraculous Draught of Fishes* and the *Nativity of Christ* can be read together, as we have seen, in more than one way (and also in one more, which we have yet to consider). The *Charge to Peter* beneath the *Baptism* brings together the formal institutions of the ministries of Peter and of Christ (a point that would have

they use four times, more or less obliquely, the 'architectural metaphor' of Ephesians ii. The implications of this appeal, and the practical recommendations for its implementation, are discussed by H. Jedin, 'Ein Vorschlag für die Amerika-Mission aus dem Jahre 1513', *Neue Zeitschrift für Missionswissenschaft*, ii, 1946, pp. 81 ff.; he points out that the evangelizing of the New World had not hitherto been regarded as a papal responsibility, and that Quirini, in particular, knew what he was talking about. Jedin seems unaware, however, of Delfin's and Manutius's similar appeals in the same year. G. Moroni, *Dizionario di erudizione storico-ecclesiastica*, xlv, Venice, 1847, p. 243, who usually speaks with good authority, says that Leo did, in fact, send missionaries to America.

217. 'Additur & illud, quod maximi faciendum est, tantum terrarum, tantum maris, tot varios populos ante vel Romanis illis rerum dominis, nedum nobis incognitos, inveniri aetate nostra, & subiici Christianis regibus, ita, ut te rectore Romanae Ecclesiae sperandum sit, unum futurum Ovile sub uno pastore eodemque optimo, & pientissimo ...'; when Leo has restored peace among Christians, 'afflictis ... populis succurreris restituta pace ... curabis homines, ubicunque terarum (sic) incogniti lateant, disquirendos, ad eosque subactos mittes Apostolos tuos ad praedicandum illis Evangelium, ut sacris Romanae Ecclesiae instituti, soli Deo nostro serviant. En potes iam ab indis incipere. potes ab aliis populis, quos in oceano occidentali Hispani superioribus annis invenere' (*Supplicatio* to Leo X, preface to *Omnia Platonis opera*, ed. Marco Musurus, Venice, September 1513). The same idea appears in *Bernardi Lavignete Vasconis de questionibus quibusdam in philosophia et theologia* (Bibl. Laur., MS. Plut. xiv. 13, presentation copy dedicated to Leo, fols. 122 ff.), in an interesting list of the achievements of this pope at the Lateran Council: (i) The reunification of the *Corpus mysticum Christi* (ii) Suppression of all animosities (iii) Expulsion of errors from the Church (iv) The collection of the 'alias oves, quae non sunt de hoc ovili' (John x. 16) (v) Promotion of the Crusade (vi) With cross-reference to (iv), sending preachers to the heathen 'qui eis suos errores ostendent, et Sanctae fidei Catholicae veritatem aperient ... Et hoc tenetur facere de iure, *quem ad modum Christus fecit, Mittendo Apostolos* ad praedicandum per totum universum. Nam Christus est principium fidei nostrae, Et Tua Sanctitas eius vicarius et medium coniunctionis inter nos & infideles penes deum esse debet.'

218. The relationship may also exist on a more symbolic level; in Matthew xvi. 17, Christ recalls Peter's name, Simon Bar Iona, Son of the Dove, that is, guided by the Holy Spirit (cf. *Glossa ordinaria*: *P.L.* 114, col. 141, but the sense is common). If the suggestion made above is correct, that the first project for this tapestry had a different subject, or conflation of texts (*Accipite spiritum sanctum*), the connection would then have been still more pointed. Furthermore the text for the *Baptism* fresco, Matthew iii. 13–17, ending 'Hic est filius meus dilectus, in quo mihi complacui', foreshadows the manner of Christ's choice of Peter, and also of Paul in the opposite tapestry, *Vas electionis*.

219. *Congregatio populi* in these inscriptions is a term with the specific meaning of *Ecclesia*, particularly *ex Judaeis* (cf. Petrus Comestor and Durandus).

220. White-Shearman, op. cit. in n. 139, p. 200, and K. Langedijk, *De Portretten van de Medici*, Amsterdam, 1968, p. 31; the entry is described in a letter of Pietro Delfin, 11 March 1492 (*Epistolae*, ed. cit. in n. 112, Bk. III. xxvi; A. Fabroni, *Laurentii Medicis magnifici vita*, Pisa, 1784, p. 305).

221. This convincing identification for the rider in armour *all'antica* was made by O. Fischel, 'Porträts des Giuliano de' Medici, Herzogs von Nemours', *Jahrbuch der K. preuszischen Kunstsammlungen*, xxviii, 1907, p. 129. For the characterization of Appenino, compare the description of his *carro* in Giovanni Jacopo Penni, *La magnifica & sumptuosa festa facta dalli S. R. per el Carnovale MDXIII*, Rome, 1513.

222. This building has been identified by Castagnoli, op. cit. in n. 43, p. 581, as 'una immagine assai accurata della tomba di Annia Regilla' (that is, the so-called Tempio del Dio Redicolo just outside Rome), but it seems to me to lack all the peculiar characteristics of that building.

223. W. Roscoe, *The Life and Pontificate of Leo the Tenth*, Liverpool, 1805, i, p. 172, gives 9 November; the same date is implied by the Signoria's announcement on that day of the flight of all three Medici brothers (G. L. Moncallero, *Il Cardinale Bernardo Dovizi da Bibbiena (Biblioteca dell' "Archivum Romanicum"*, Ser. 1, xxxv), Florence, 1953, p. 137 n. 56); however G. B. Picotti, *La giovinezza di Leone X*, Milan, 1927, p. 589, gives 10 or 11 November, and from a report in a Bolognese diary (Moncallero, op. cit., p. 147 n. 89) that Cardinal Giovanni arrived in Bologna on 11 November, the day after Piero, it would seem reasonable to believe that he had also fled Florence later than his brothers.

been clear when the *titulus* over the second read *Institutio nove regenerationis . . .*),[218] and the ties of meaning between the *Healing of the Lame Man* and the *Healing of the Leper*, from the literal and obvious to the metaphorical and sophisticated, are perhaps strongest of all. By contrast the placing of the *Death of Ananias* beneath the *Calling of the First Apostles* seems to have little point; at best the discipline of the Primitive Church might seem to have some kind of connection with the emphasis of the *titulus* upon the *Congregatio populi legem evangelicam recepturi*.[219]

In the previous Chapter the question of the reconstruction of the hanging was approached, in the first instance, by considering the main scenes alone; confirmation of the answer that they provided was found later in an independent examination of the 'reliefs' in the zone of the *spalliere*. A re-examination of these 'reliefs' from the iconographical standpoint, necessarily brief, is to some extent helpful in a similar way in our present problem of trying to understand all the nuances of the main scenes. It is, in any case, an obligatory step in this question too, because the disposition of the 'relief'-subjects would undoubtedly have provoked such curiosity when the tapestries were hung in the chapel. In the previous Chapter the subjects of these 'reliefs' were defined, but a further analysis is necessary now in order to clarify some important aspects of those that were located on the altar-wall and on the right, all concerned with the history of the patron.

The 'relief' below the *Stoning of Stephen* (*Fig.* 18) does not represent, as has been stated many times, the entry of Cardinal Giovanni into Florence as Cardinal-Legate on 20 May 1492, nor an entry into Rome, but his first ceremonial entry into Florence on 10 March 1492 after the investiture with the cardinalate at the Badia of Fiesole on the previous day;[220] this identification is clear in the tapestry itself in which the hill-god is to be identified as Appennino, and is clearer still in the several versions of the preliminary drawing (*Fig.* 54) in which the two peaks of Fiesole are visible, the farther one crowned by the monastery of San Francesco, and the gates of Florence are more accurately mediaeval. The presence of Giovanni's brother, Giuliano (in the tapestry but not in the drawings), is appropriate only to this entry.[221] The two river-gods, which must be Arno and Mugnone, indicate an arrival from Fiesole, and not from Rome, and the classical façade outside the gates is probably intended to be Lorenzo's church of San Gallo, destroyed in the siege of 1529–30.[222] The second 'relief' on the altar-wall, the one beneath the *Miraculous Draught of Fishes* (*Fig.* 13), has never been misunderstood; it shows the entry into Rome for the Conclave and the election, 11 March 1513.

A new sequence begins in the 'relief' under the *Charge to Peter* (*Fig.* 14). On the right is the flight of Cardinal Giovanni, disguised as a Franciscan monk, which followed the expulsion from Florence of his brothers Piero and Giuliano on 9 November 1494. Florentia, who had welcomed the cardinal in the first 'relief' and had sent him with good grace to Rome in the second, here sits mournfully at the city gate. Only two points remain in doubt in this case; the first is the date of Giovanni's flight, which is not clear from the sources but was perhaps on the day following his brothers',[223] and the second is the identity of the palace being sacked on the left, which is probably Palazzo Medici in Via Larga but could also be the cardinal's own house at Sant'Antonio, which was also pillaged.[224] Under the *Healing of the Lame Man* there are two scenes, separated by a pair of lions (*Fig.* 16); as we saw earlier these two scenes are now, for one reason or another, in the wrong order. The capture of the cardinal by the French at the Battle of Ravenna should come next in sequence, on the left, and the date of that event was 11

April 1512. The scene which should follow, on the right, has been identified with obvious correctness as the escape from captivity and safe arrival in Mantua, personified by the nymph Amymone and further identified by the Virgilian fountain;[225] in fact the cardinal evaded the French on 4 June 1512 and reached Mantua on 13 June.[226] These two events do exactly illustrate the moment of change in Giovanni's fortunes, as is appropriate to their median position in the series on the right wall. The escape from captivity was reckoned miraculous at the time, and the brief rest in the haven of Mantua, although often omitted from the story, was in Leo's superstitious mind particularly significant. For at that moment a Franciscan fortune-teller had prophesied the return of the Medici to Florence and the election of Giovanni to the papacy; and at his election Leo observed that he was wearing robes presented to him, destitute, in Mantua by the Marchese Francesco Gonzaga.[227] At the Battle of Ravenna, on the other hand, the cardinal was, as Paolo Giovio put it, 'beyond all doubt reserved for the papacy by Divine Providence', and even in that catastrophe anticipated his pastoral duties by standing firm, when he could have escaped, to comfort the victims and recommend their souls to God.[228]

Beneath the *Death of Ananias* the 'relief' is once more divided by a pair of lions (*Fig.* 17); this docile pair, resting on their haunches like those in the Sala dei Gigli in Palazzo Vecchio, should probably be interpreted as the emblematic lions of Florence, *Marzocchi*, significantly acting as heraldic supporters of the weightless Medici Yoke. The cardinal revived this *impresa* on the Medicean restoration of 1512 (as a gesture of reconciliation) and two episodes in this restoration are represented flanking the *Marzocchi*. The first, on the left, is an historical curiosity. The setting is clearly the *ringhiera* of Palazzo Vecchio, on which stands Michelangelo's *David*. The event has been interpreted as the public allocution of the Republican Gonfaloniere Soderini, or as that of his successor Giovanni Battista Ridolfi; but the first made his speech inside the Palazzo Vecchio, in the Sala del Gran Consiglio, while the second is not recorded, so far as I can discover, as making any public speech at all in this period.[229] The scene, in any case, has all the appearance of a *parlamento* in Piazza Signoria, that is an extraordinary gathering of the citizens of Florence in front of the *ringhiera*, as if to imply that the return of the Medici was brought about by popular demand. In the other part of the 'relief', on the right, the return of the cardinal himself is greeted by the populace and by Florentia, whom we last saw grieving at his exile by the same gate. The sequence of events was in fact as follows: 31 August 1512, fall of Soderini; 1 September, entry of Giuliano; 8 September, election of Ridolfi; 14 September, entry of Cardinal Giovanni; 16 September, *parlamento*—which, however, was called to approve the setting up of a *balìa* for instituting reforms in the government, not to recall the cardinal.[230] Thus if our interpretation of the scenes is correct, they represent history considerably idealized.

An idealization of history has, in any case, been effected in a different and in this context more significant sense. There can be no doubt that the 'reliefs' of the story of Cardinal Giovanni are designed to illustrate the legend that everything important in his life happened on the eleventh of the month, in spite of the fact that only two of these events (the capture at Ravenna and the election) actually did so; the rest, with the possible exception of the Flight from Florence, certainly did not. But the proof of this apparent paradox lies in the exact repetition in these 'reliefs' of six subjects represented on one of the triumphal arches erected for the Lateran pro-

224. Picotti, loc. cit. in n. 223.

225. W. Kemp, 'Eine mantegneske Allegorie für Mantua', *Pantheon*, xxvii, 1969, pp. 12 ff.

226. For the first date see P. Ravasio, 'Memorie e cimelii inediti di Pieve del Cairo Lomellina circa la liberazione del Cardinale de' Medici dalla prigionia dei Francesi', *Archivio storico lombardo*, x, 1883, p. 384; for the second, the letter from Francesco Gonzaga to Julius II, quoted by Luzio, op. cit. in n. 14, p. 102.

227. D. Gnoli, *La Roma di Leon X*, Milan, 1938, p. 69; Luzio, op. cit. in n. 14, p. 114. See also Leo's friendly reminiscences in a letter to Francesco, 15 March 1513, in Bembo, op. cit. in n. 112, p. 6. The Mantuan episode is referred to in *Diario romano di Sebastiano di Branca Tedallini*, in L. Muratori, *Rerum italicarum scriptores*, xxiii, 3, appendix, Città di Castello, 1907, p. 333, and by Paolo Giovio, *Vita Leonis decimi*, Florence, 1548, p. 60, but ignored by Ravasio, op. cit. in n. 226.

228. *Vita di Leon decimo*, ed. L. Domenichi, Florence, 1549, p. 143; cf. Pietro Delfin, letter to Leo, 13 March 1513 (*Epistolae*, ed. cit. in n. 112, Bk. XI. i): 'Paulo ante pene abductus in servitutem mox coelesti munere miraculose ereptus es: ut fieres paulo post servus servorum Dei: & universalis pater ac Dominus ...', and also Marcellus Palonius, *De clade Ravennati*, Rome, 1513. The reputedly miraculous nature of the escape from captivity was the point of a representation of this episode, in which an angel was seen to intervene, on the arch in Piazza di Parione in the Lateran *trionfo* of 11 April 1513 (Cancellieri, op. cit. in n. 20, p. 78).

229. For Soderini's speech see especially Francesco Guicciardini, *Storia d'Italia*, Bk. XI, ed. G. Rosini, Florence, 1835, p. 436, and Filippo de' Nerli, *Commentari*, ed. Trieste, 1859, p. 173.

230. Luca Landucci, *Ein florentinisches Tagebuch*, ed. M. Herzfeld, Jena, 1913, ii, pp. 230 ff.; Bartolomeo Masi, *Ricordanze*, ed. G. O. Corazzini, Florence, 1906, pp. 99 ff.; Iacopo Nardi, *Istoria della città di Firenze*, ed. Florence, 1842, ii, pp. 7 ff.; Nerli, *Commentari*, ed. cit. in n. 229, pp. 184 ff.; Guicciardini, *Storia*, ed. cit. in n. 229, pp. 439 ff.; Giovio, *Vita*, ed. cit. in n. 228, pp. 183 ff.; and the letters of Cardinal Giovanni, dated 15 and 16 September, copied in Sanuto, op. cit. in n. 187, xv, cols. 101, 105 (the first of these letters seems, like Guicciardini, to date the *parlamento* to 15 September, in contradiction to the other sources).

231. A set of octagons on the arch of Messer Ioanni Zincha, as described in the letter by Giovanni Giacomo Penni, published in Rome, 1513; this now very rare publication is re-printed by Cancellieri, op. cit. in n. 20, p. 81; see also Moroni, op. cit. in n. 216, xix, p. 315, xxxvii, p. 36. On the arch there were two additional scenes, the birth of Giovanni on 11 December 1475 (correctly dated), and the Lateran procession itself, 11 April 1513.

232. For this location see *Electio Pape Leonis . . .*, cit. in n. 17.

233. *Scripturus quae memoratu digna Romae et in Italia ab excessu Adriani. vj. Pont. Max. gesta sunt*, Bibl. Vat., MS. Vat. Lat. 3535, fol. 97v.; public interest along these lines probably accounts for the publication of the location of the cardinals' cells in *Electio Pape Leonis . . .*, cit. in n. 17.

234. The altar of the Sistine Chapel has, in fact, a special significance in this period in the ritual of pontifical election; immediately after the confirmation of the votes the new pope was symbolically enthroned *on* this altar. In the case of Leo X, see Paris de Grassis, *Diarium*, B.M., Add. MS. 8443, fol. 17r.; and for the ritual in general, de Novaés, op. cit. in n. 94, pp. 95 ff.

235. See above, p. 56, n. 73; the best possibility of an extension of the parallel lies in the symbolic snowy landscape of the main scene, referring, probably, to the path of the martyr or more generally to *Candor iustitiae*, which may have been intended, and indeed introduced, to point the analogy with the unspotted reputation and sanctity of the Deacon Giovanni, the subject of frequent comment; for a characteristic appreciation of the 'ante actae vitae incredibilis sanctitas, morum candor' of Leo, see Filippo Beroaldo *il giovane*, dedication of the *Opera* of Tacitus (1515?).

236. See above, Chapter I, p. 20, for the interpretation of this coin, and vigilance as an attribute of Leo X. It is appropriate to notice at this point that Pietro Delfin, discussing Leo's absorption in his responsibilities, plucked a nice text out of Isaiah xxi. 8, that relates rather precisely the *custodia* of the lion and the crane: 'Et clamavit ut Leo. Super speculam Domini ego sum stans iugiter per diem: & super custodiam meam ego sum *stans totis noctibus*' (letter to Leo, 25 November 1513, in *Epistolae*, ed. cit. in n. 112, Bk. XI. ix). It is possible that with this text we come very close to the precise interpretative 'key', the one that was in fact in Leo's mind (or those of his advisers); the reason is that Delfin's letter to Leo seems to explain the reference to the same text in the Lateran

cession of 11 April 1513, which were accompanied by an explanatory verse claiming the coincidence of the dates.[231]

Let us now return to the *Entry from Fiesole*, 1492 (*Fig.* 18), and to consider Leo's superstitious self-awareness in greater depth. The *Stoning of Stephen*, to which this 'relief' belongs, clothed the left side of the altar-wall, and this tapestry, like the *Conversion of Saul*, which also hung on the wall enclosing the left half of the *presbyterium*, differs from all the rest in the set in its framing; lion-masks replace the rosettes normally found in each corner of the red *guilloche* border (*Figs.* 18, 20). This peculiarity is best explained by the fact that this corner of the chapel had a special significance for Pope Leo, since it was the location of his cell at the Conclave in which he was elected.[232] At the previous Conclave the position of the cell of Cardinal Giuliano della Rovere beneath the *Donation of the Keys* was read as an augury;[233] in Leo's mind the position of his, elevated in the *presbyterium* next to the altar, must have seemed an augury too.[234] And then it is to be noticed that while Saint Stephen was the first Deacon, Giovanni de' Medici, at the time of his election, was the senior Cardinal-Deacon. It can scarcely be casual that the creation of the Cardinal-Deacon in 1492 is represented below the calling of the first Deacon-Martyr, while his election to the papacy is represented below the selection of Saint Peter in the *Miraculous Draught of Fishes* (*Fig.* 13).

The vertical relationship between 'reliefs' and main scenes may go no further than this in the case of the *Stoning of Stephen*,[235] but there is little doubt that it was more extensive in the *Miraculous Draught*. In the first place we must pick up again two prominent symbols in this tapestry, the cranes that signify vigilance or *custodia*, and the Mons Vaticanus or *Mons sanctus Dei*, and relate them to a third new Leonine coin as witness of the expectation, at least, of common understanding—the *Giulio* inscribed *Petre ecce Templum tuum* (*Fig.* 7). We have already seen that the lion asleep on the Mons Vaticanus on the obverse of this coin is a figure of Leonine vigilance in the building of the material and spiritual Church of Rome;[236] the potentiality of the same meaning in the complete tapestry cannot be questioned, and it amplifies the obvious analogy, in main scene and 'relief', between the respective promotions of Peter and Leo from the oars to the helm of the Church (another metaphor applied commonly to this papal election, as to others).[237] This interpretation of the superimposition of the *Miraculous Draught of Fishes* over the election of the Cardinal Giovanni to the throne of Peter may be compared with the combination (*Fig.* 83), in Piero Cattaci's *Genealogia medicea*, of a portrait of Leo and the inscription 'Ingressus operatus sine macula ascendentem iustitiam in montem domini: he who has toiled at righteousness has entered, without fault, upon the Lord's hill' (a conflation of Psalms xv. 1–2 and xxiv. 3).[238]

Oratio by Giovanni Battista Gargha, 19 December, the imagery of which appears to have been dependent upon papal instruction (see above, p. 17); and in that *Oratio* the vigilance-text from Isaiah is paraphrased between assertions of the *primatus* and of the providential nature of Leo's ascent to the papal throne, just as, in the tapestry, the vigilance-symbols appear between the selection of Peter and the election of Leo in the 'relief': 'tibi . . . (Christus) . . . ligandi & solvendi potestatem dedit. Tu in specula Domini pervigil fortiter adstans, cuncta in rectum tramitem rediges. Tibi ergo

omnium ecclesiarum praesides & totius orb Christiani principes parere affectant. O qua divina & salutifera fuit haec tua ad summ Pontificatus apicem assumptio . . .' (Hardoui op. cit. in n. 95, col. 1729). But an alternati framework for the interpretation of t 'election' relief in relation to the symbols the main scene is provided by a passage Cristoforo Marcello's *Ad Leonem. X. Pont. Ma . . . Oratio* (1513: Bibl. Vat., MS. Vat. La 3646, fol. 30r.) in which the principal duties the pope are defined as the *erectio*, *custodia* a *salus* of the Church, followed by univers

The two 'reliefs' placed on the altar-wall are, however, dominated by the two processional entries, and there is probably a good reason for this. Each entry has the characteristic features of classical representations of the Imperial Epiphany, the *Adventus regis pacifici* or the *Adventus Augusti*; these features are the meeting with the personified *Natio* (Florentia and Roma, in these cases), a temple, indications of the point of departure as well as that of arrival, and the welcome by the citizens (omitted in the case of Roma). The imagery of the Imperial *Adventus* had been absorbed into the ritual of papal entry in the mediaeval period, and even into that of a cardinal's entry by the fifteenth century, and a recent example which points to the continued recognition of its soteriological implications is provided by the decision of Julius II to delay his triumphal entry into Rome, after the conquest of the Romagna, until Palm Sunday, 28 March 1507.[239] It is unlikely that it was by accident that the two 'entry-reliefs' were placed upon the altar-wall, traditionally reserved in church-decoration for Epiphany-scenes;[240] this tradition was already observed, in the Sixtine fresco-cycle, in the locations of the *Finding of Moses* and the *Nativity of Christ*, and was probably remembered again in their replacement by Michelangelo's *Last Judgement*, Christ's Second Coming.[241] This line of thought leads to the conclusion that the Epiphany or *Adventus* of Giovanni de' Medici in the 'reliefs' should be seen in vertical relationship extended at least through the *Miraculous Draught of Fishes* to the *Nativity of Christ*, Prince of Peace; we should recall Leo's titles, *Rex pacificus* and Augustus, the frequent analogies with Christ in this particular sense, and the specific formulation of Aegidius of Viterbo, comparing the dawns of two eras of peace: 'Ille (Christus) homo factus: hic (Leo) Pontifex creatus.'[242]

It would probably be beyond human ingenuity to invent a programme for the tapestries in which all the 'reliefs' were placed in vertical relationship with the main scenes and the frescoes above; in any case it does not seem to have been attempted in the rest of the series, and the natural alternative, that of relating the 'reliefs' of opposite walls, was exploited instead. In the second Chapter we saw that an understanding of this situation was inevitably reduced by the loss of two of the Pauline 'reliefs' and by the obscurity of the one below Paul in Prison,[243] but that there was, nevertheless, a clear parallel in the evolution from persecution to reconciliation represented in the Medicean and Pauline sequence. The clues to understanding the parallel are to be found in the subjects of the 'relief' below the *Sacrifice at Lystra* (*Fig.* 24). In this case two episodes are separated, once more, by a pair of lions which, differentiated from the others by standing over globes with raised paw, appear to be particularized as the Lion of Judah (compare *Fig.* 5). Between them stands the Medicean symbol of the diamond-ring and feathers, and they are flanked by two Yokes. A proper interpretation of these emblems requires that they be read together with the one in the opposite relief, under the *Death of Ananias* (*Fig.* 17); for the complete Leonine *impresa*, as it is found, for example, on the floor of the Stanza della Segnatura and in innumerable manuscripts (*Fig.* 11), consists of the *corpi* of Yoke and Ring and the *anime* of *Suave* and *N*, explained by the text *Anulus nectit iugum suave*,[244] which is itself a declaration of the ideal of reconciliation ('the ring unites, the yoke is easy'). In the tapestries the *N* appears below the Yoke supported by *Marzocchi* on the right wall, the Ring between the Lions of Judah on the left wall directly opposite.

The scene to the right of the 'relief' below the *Sacrifice at Lystra*, corresponding to the *parlamento* on the opposite wall, is the disputation at Jerusalem (Acts xv. 4–21) over the contentious and potentially divisive issue of the

peace. For other texts of the period in which the rebuilding of the *templum materiale* is taken as a symbol of that of the *templum spirituale*, see for example *Johannis Antonii Menavini . . . Liber de rebus et moribus turcarum*, Bibl. Corsiniana, MS. 389, fols. 1r. ff. (preface, dedicated to Leo), and Petrus Galatinus, *De angelico pastore*, Bibl. Vat., MS. Vat. Lat. 5578, fol. 26r.

237. See above, p. 64, n. 112 and Andrea Fulvio, cit. in n. 114.

238. Bibl. Laur., MS. Med. Pal. ccxxv, fol. 5v.; Langedijk, op. cit. in n. 220, p. 36.

239. For the foregoing see E. H. Kantorowicz, 'The "King's Advent" and the Enigmatic Panels in the Doors of Santa Sabina', *Art Bulletin*, xxvi, 1944, pp. 207 ff. For the application of the term *adventus pacifici regis* to Leo, see above, Chapter I, p. 16, n. 104.

240. A list of references in Ihm, op. cit. in n. 95, p. 2, n. 5.

241. This point has been made independently, and in a slightly different form, by S. Sinding Larsen, 'A Re-reading of the Sistine Ceiling', *Institutum Romanum Norvegiae, Acta ad archaeologiam et artium historiam pertinentia*, iv, 1969, p. 156.

242. See above, Chapter I, p. 16, esp. n. 103; also Aegidius of Viterbo, cit. p. 74, n. 170; it is obviously less likely that the Epiphany theme was extended across the *Stoning of Stephen* to the *Finding of Moses*, but it is worth remembering that Leo was compared not only with Christ but also with Moses, 'mitissimus . . . super omnes in terra' (above, p. 15), if only to appreciate the possible range of 'accidental' conjunctions.

243. It has been suggested that this relief (*Fig.* 26) illustrates Paul's vision in which he was summoned to Macedonia (Acts xvi. 9), with which I can see no connection. The best suggestion I can make is that it illustrates, in fact, no text but rather an idea that would round off the Pauline sequence inside the screen: a contrast between the pride of the young Saul and the humility of the mature Paul; this contrast, etymologically based on *Saulus* and *Paulus*, appears frequently in the exegesis of Acts (e.g. Petrus Comestor, *Historia scholastica*, on the Conversion of the Proconsul: *P.L.* 198, col. 1690).

244. Moroni, op. cit. in n. 216, xxxviii, p. 45.

245. E.g. *Glossa ordinaria* (*P.L.* 114, col. 573) and Aquinas, *In omnes S. Pauli apostoli epistolas commentaria* (ed. Turin, 1929, p. 541), on Galatians ii. 9. It may be questioned whether the two herms represented in this relief, the heads of which are in no way distinguished from those of the apostles, do not allude to the same text, in which Paul says that the apostles 'videbantur columnae esse'. It is unlikely that they are without some meaning; in the opposite relief (*Fig.* 17) a pair of herms are particularized as laurels putting out new shoots, an unmistakable symbol of Medicean rebirth. For a rich collection of classical citations on the *dextrarum conjunctio* (as symbol of *concordia*, reconciliation, etc.) see John Bulwer, *Chirologia, or the Naturall Language of the Hand*, London, 1644, pp. 109 ff.

246. Cancellieri, op. cit. in n. 20, pp. 71 ff.

247. F. X. Kraus, *Geschichte der christlichen Kunst*, II, ii, Freiburg-im-Breisgau, 1908, pp. 457 ff.; also White-Shearman, op. cit. in n. 139, p. 210.

248. There is an unpublished contemporary analysis of the iconography of the Florentine *Entrata* in the British Museum, MS. Harley 3462, fols. 194 ff. An arch was devoted to each of the seven Virtues, and on the eighth the Cardinal Virtues were supporters of the papal throne, and the Theological Virtues appeared above holding the tiara. Each virtue is related in detail to the person of Leo X.

249. Cancellieri, op. cit. in n. 20, pp. 78–82.

circumcision of the Gentiles. This episode has considerable ecclesiological significance, related to the main themes of the tapestries; but it also carried a particular meaning for the Medici pope. It is remarkable, first, that in this disputation Peter refers to the circumcision demanded by the Pharisees as 'a yoke upon the neck of the disciples'; but even more striking is the reference (vss. 7, 14) to God's visitation to the Gentiles 'to take out of them a people for his name', that is, to the prophecy in Jeremiah xii. 14–15 of the exile and return of the House of Judah: 'Behold I will pluck them out of their land, and will pluck out the house of Judah from among them. And it shall come to pass, after that I have plucked them out I will return, and have compassion on them, every man to his heritage, and every man to his land.' Leo X, surely familiar with all texts relating to the House of Judah, could not have been blind to the relevance of this one to his family's fortunes, and the allusion to the prophecy thus seems to connect the disputation at Jerusalem rather specifically with the Medici restoration of 1512 represented on the opposite wall. The prophecy of Jeremiah, however, is linked in the same passage with another in Amos ix. 11–12, foretelling the rebuilding of the tabernacle of David from its ruins so that it should include also the Gentiles —a text for the *plenitudo gentium* which may be readily interpolated into the meaning of the tapestry-cycle in general and one which is likely to have special significance for a pope in Leo's historical position, whether he referred it to the rebuilding of the spiritual Church or to that of the material church, Saint Peter's (the distinction being, in fact, somewhat artificial).

The brief text for the left-hand section of the 'relief' (Acts xv. 22) describes, nevertheless, another important episode, the confirmation by the Church in Jerusalem of the mission to the Gentiles, and it has to be read with Paul's amplification in Galatians ii. 9 (a continuation, in fact, of the fundamental text defining the separate rôles of Peter and Paul). The giving of the 'right hands of fellowship' at this moment, described only in the second text, was normally interpreted as a symbol of *unitas* and sets the seal, as it were, on the reconciliation between Paul and the Church.[245] In the last Medicean 'relief', directly opposite, the reconciliation between Giovanni de' Medici and Florence is symbolized and sealed in a similar way as the citizen leading the welcoming group reaches out with his right hand to grasp the cardinal's. Among the attributes of Leo's pontificate represented in the additions that Raphael made for him to the ceiling of the Stanza d'Eliodoro in 1514, is the giving of the right hands, apparently a token of *unitas* or *concordia* (as on Roman coins).

The examination of the 'reliefs' in some cases suggests that it may not be a mistake to interpret the cycle of the principal scenes in an alternative way that relates them to the ideals of the patron. It has also brought us to consider their relation to an already flourishing Leonine visual imagery, in particular that of the Lateran procession of 11 April 1513. In the interpretation of works of art we generalize at our peril, and the most fruitful results are obtained by re-inserting them in their specific context, the unique intellectual nest in which they were born. Leonine imagery is such a context, highly particularized and richly documented, by texts and by works of art. It has not yet been adequately studied, and this is no place even for a survey, but its importance for the Cartoons and tapestries is second only to that of the context of the Sistine Chapel itself. It is clearly relevant, for example, that the first triumphal arch in the Lateran procession had a representation (predictably) of the *Donation of the Keys* and was crowned with the particularizing inscription: LEONI. X. PONT. MAX. UNIONEM ECCLESIAS-

TICAM INSTAURANDI, CHRISTIANOSQUE TUMULTUS SEDANDI STUDIOSO, while the second was inscribed: LEONI X. PONT. OPT. MAX. PACIS RESTITUTORI FELICISSIMO.[246]

It is to this context that we should turn, finally, for an understanding of the vertical borders. These have been wrongly interpolated, by generalizing, into the mediaeval encyclopaedic tradition;[247] it is of considerable importance that they would have been recognized by a contemporary spectator in a particular way which would have encouraged the reading of the whole tapestry-set with a Leonine bias, for he would have encountered their subjects before, in such displays of Leonine imagery as the Lateran procession, or the triumphal entry into Florence in 1515.[248] For example, on the same arch of 1513 on which were represented the events in Leo's life that happened (with some adjustments) on the eleventh of the month, there also appeared the Liberal Arts and the Virtues; and it is only by referring to the exhibition on this occasion of the two antique *Satyrs* in the Della Valle Collection that we can understand their inclusion in the tapestry borders, below the *Fates* (*Fig.* 14).[249] The *Seasons* and *Time* (or, the *Units of Time*, Figs. 14, 13) refer, on a superficial level, to the familiar Medicean preoccupation embodied in Lorenzo's device, also used by Leo, *Le tems revient*;[250] but this line of thought inevitably leads to another, a meditation upon Fortune in which the *Fates* (*Tres Fortunae*, Fig. 14) have a natural place. The detailed iconography of the borders deserves a specialized study, which is not appropriate here; but in my view the overall theme would appear to be the stoical one, very characteristic of Leo,[251] of the triumph of *Virtù* over *Occasio*, which would be in harmony with the selection of episodes from his life represented in the 'reliefs'.

The incompleteness of the set of borders, and uncertainty about their proper disposition, prevent any further progress in the relation of this theme to the main subjects of individual tapestries, and perhaps there was none intended. To conclude this survey it is instructive to examine in more detail the border which seems, at first sight, the least predictable, *Hercules* (*Figs.* 25, 28a), because it turns out to be the most pertinent. It must surely appear odd that Hercules, who slew the lion and indeed wears its skin in this border, should appear at all in such a context, yet we find him again with the same trophy in the Leonine parts of the vault of the Stanza d'Eliodoro. The key to this paradox is provided by Aegidius of Viterbo, who explains that Hercules is a type of Leo X since he was the Tuscan hero who first bore the *insignia leonis*.[252] In fact the Leo-Hercules in the centre of this border bears the burden of Atlas, and this episode should probably be interpreted in the sense provided by Raffaello Brandolini in the Preface to his dialogue *Leo* (1513): the pope bears with ease the great weight of the Universe now placed upon his shoulders.[253] This meaning is consonant with the interpretation of the Herculean Labour, as a demonstration of his devotion to religion, favoured in the most relevant of all commentaries, the *Herculis vita* of Lilio Gregorio Giraldi, completed in the Vatican Palace in October 1513.[254] Below the Atlas scene there was in the original border before it was cut, as in the replica in the Mantuan series (*Fig.* 28a), the defeat of the Centaur; the interpretation of this episode as a symbol of the triumph over base instincts is a commonplace of the commentaries. And just as straightforward is the appearance of Fame above, explained by Fulgentius, etymologically, as the meaning of the Greek name Herakles.[255] Thus the border of *Hercules* should indeed be read in the conventional way, as an *exemplum virtutis*,[256] but also, in this way, with specific reference to the patron; and therefore this border, so far from standing apart from the rest of the set, provides the key to understanding all of them.

250. On this device see G. B. Ladner, 'Vegetation symbolism and the Concept of Renaissance', *De artibus opuscula*, ed. M. Meiss, New York, 1961, pp. 315 ff.; it is found in a variety of forms among the multitudinous *imprese* of Leonine MSS. See also the account of the Medicean carnival in Florence, February 1513, in J. Shearman, 'Pontormo and Andrea del Sarto, 1513', *The Burlington Magazine*, civ, 1962, pp. 478 ff.; the same preoccupation recurs, of course, in Michelangelo's Medici Chapel (the comparison is made by Langedijk, op. cit. in n. 220, p. 33).

251. Compare the dialogues recorded by Petrus Alcyonius, op. cit. in n. 156; Marcello, MS. cit. in n. 236, fols. 19v. ff.; Galatinus, MS. cit. in n. 160, fols. 8r. ff. It should be noted that Valeriano, who was probably well informed, said that Leo's personal interpretation of the emblem Yoke-*Suave* was that it stood for the Virtue of Patience, and that with it he would often quote Virgil (*Aeneid* V): 'Superanda omnis fortuna ferendo est' (I. P. Valeriano, *Hieroglyphica*, ed. Lyon, 1602, p. 519).

252. MS. cit. in n. 170, fol. 6v.; also fols. 36r., 316r.

253. Raffaello Brandolini, *Dialogus Leo nuncupatus*, ed. F. Fogliazzi, Venice, 1753, p. 69. The sign of Leo, not unnaturally, appears in the centre of the celestial globe in the tapestry.

254. *Opera omnia*, Basle, 1580, i, p. 555 (following Macrobius); the *Herculis vita* is dated in the colophon: 'Romae ex Vaticanis Pontificis Max. aedibus, mense Octobri MDXIII'.

255. See F. Gaeta, 'L'Avventura di Ercole', *Rinascimento*, v, 1954, p. 238, for the diffusion of this idea; also Sebastiano Erizzo, *Dichiaratione di medaglie antiche*, ed. Venice, 1559, p. 357.

256. Especially Giraldi, *Herculis vita*, ed. cit. in n. 254, p. 545. The lion-skin itself, *insignia leonis*, is interpreted as a *signum virtutis* by Boccaccio, *Genealogia deorum gentilium*, ed. Venice, 1472, fol. 197v. For the theme of Hercules in relation to Fortune in this period, see R. Wittkower, 'Chance, Time and Fortune', *Journal of the Warburg Institute*, i, 1937–8, pp. 319 ff. It should be noted that if the Hercules border is correctly woven to *Paul preaching at Athens*, the texts I have cited, especially Giraldi's, provide ample material for establishing a particular relationship between Hercules, symbol of *vis humanae sapientiae* and curator of the soul, and the theme of Paul's sermon. In Chapter II, p. 44, the possibility of a second Hercules border was discussed.

257. The sketch for this sonnet accompanies others for the *Disputa* on a sheet at Oxford, No. 546. The complete text can be read in V. Golzio, *Raffaello nei documenti* . . ., Vatican City, 1936, p. 183, or in E. Camesasca, *Raffaello Sanzio: Tutti gli scritti*, Milan, 1956, p. 80. Both these editors regard the source of the simile as a passage in Pulci's *Morgante maggiore*, a poem which Raphael is known to have read at an earlier date; but in my view neither the passage in question (L. Pulci, *Morgante magiore*, Venice, 20 March 1507, canto xxiv, 108–9: 'Et se paulo gli vide arcana dei/fu per gratia concesso a qualche fine'), nor its context, provides the meaning of the tiny scrap of theology which Raphael uses, and I think he must have found it in some other source, perhaps one of the handbooks.

There remain, finally, two related questions that require to be posed even if no answer is at present obtainable. The first concerns the authorship of the 'programme' of the series, the second concerns Raphael's ability to understand and give expression to the several ideas that have been suggested. A negative answer to the second question would naturally invalidate the entire hypothesis. There is no evidence whatever that can be brought to bear upon the first question. The contemporary sources that can be used to demonstrate the availability of the necessary points of interpretation have no particular bias, nor do they suggest an individual. This result is comprehensible in two distinct ways. The iconography of the tapestries has no positive tendency that can be isolated as Augustinian, Dominican or Franciscan, for example, because Leo X—unlike Sixtus IV or Julius II—derived no such inclinations from the circumstances of his own career. And no individual, or group, is indicated for the very reason that the fundamental ideas in the hypothesis were made so public that they became common property; as their expression could be interpreted by virtually any member of the *Capella papalis* who kept his eyes and ears open, so they could as easily be assembled. If it is true, for example, that at some points we rely on the written or recorded word of an individual such as Aegidius of Viterbo, it is also true that the thinking of such a man was not done in private; and if he turns up rather frequently in the footnotes, that may be because he was more articulate than most. In any case it is improbable, in my view, that the occupations of men of such major intellectual stature as Aegidius, Domenico Jacobazzi, or Thomas de Vio, included the composition of programmes for works of art—a view that does not preclude, however, their expert advice or criticism on particular issues. I think it is more probable that the work was done by secondary characters such as Giovanni Francesco Poggio, Cyprian Benetus or Zaccaria Ferreri, whose competence was certainly sufficient. The only more explicit suspicion that seems legitimate is that the *spiritus rector* of the scheme was Leo X himself, just as there is reason to believe that he stood behind much of the choice of imagery in the Lateran triumphal procession.

Was Raphael, however, competent to participate in some sort of sub-committee charged with this responsibility? The evidence in this matter is not conflicting, but virtually non-existent. There are only two points to be made. The first is that an examination of Raphael's other mature Roman works—the *Santa Cecilia*, for example, or, in another field, Villa Madama—inspires the conviction that he was a literate man of deep and independent intelligence, and that there were no limitations upon his ability to grasp and give substance to complex and, when occasion demanded, esoteric ideas. The second is that this intelligence did embrace theology. The only written evidence in this respect is, by chance, relevant to the theme of one of the tapestries, the *Conversion of Saul*. It comes in one of his sonnets, composed several years earlier, about 1509, when his mind was only at the earliest stage of that extraordinary expansion which seems to be the direct result of the stimulus of residence in Rome. Looking for a simile for the secrecy of his romantic feelings he recalled Paul's vision of divine secrets when 'caught up to the third heaven' at his Conversion (II Corinthians xii. 2–4)—the revelation of the *arcana verba* 'which it is not lawful for a man to utter':

'Como non podde dir d'arcana dei
paul, como disceso fu dal celo,
così el mio cor d'uno amoroso velo
a ricoperto tuti i penser mei.'[257]

IV: Design

Raffaello, allevato presso la verità, cercava la verità in sè stesso,
e la trovava unita all'espressione (Anton Raphael Mengs)

I T is only in very rare cases that the iconography of a work of art may be studied independently from its form without distortion in the understanding of each part. In fact it is necessary to question the assumption that these really are separable constituents, like threads that can be unwoven from the fabric of the work of art, each retaining in the process a self-sufficient identity unmodified by the other. At least it is clear that this separation is destructive when it is applied to works from the High Renaissance when content and form became as intimately fused in the inventive process as at any other time in the history of art.

The justification for separating the material of this chapter from that of the previous one rests, in the first place, upon the verifiable principle that classification is a necessary part of understanding. The separation is justifiable, in the second place, when it is clear what it is that is separated. 'Meaning', in the previous chapter, is restricted to programmatic meaning. But there are other dimensions of meaning that reside in the associative value of forms, textures, colours, movements and so on. While it may be doubted that there can ever be such a thing as an abstract work of art, it is certain that, in the kind with which we are concerned, what remains when we have isolated—brutally—the programmatic element is very far from abstract. Thus in this chapter we shall continue to pursue meaning while we concentrate upon the technique with which Raphael gave formal expression to the programme, just as, in the previous chapter, it was necessary to examine design even while concentrating upon programmatic meaning.

There is, however, another complex problem which may be illustrated by an example from Raphael's history-painting contemporary with his work upon the Cartoons: the *Coronation of Charlemagne* in the Stanza dell'Incendio. In modern judgements of this fresco the general and appropriate distaste for the quality of execution has been balanced by admiration for the novel 'invention' of the diagonally disposed banks of prelates which forms an unusual pattern in space and on the surface.[1] What seems to be overlooked is that this disposition *represents* something quite particular, the *quadratura* of the *Capella papalis* in session, which would have been familiar to Raphael at Mass, in Consistory, or at the Lateran Council, and which would have been intelligible, and meaningful, to the contemporary spectator.[2] The realistic thinking which produces this fundamental decision is then followed through to its natural conclusion, for the diagonal view of the *quadratura* was a logical consequence of the intrusion into the fresco-field of a door on its left which ruled out the possibility of symmetry. And the equally consequential lateral displacement of the enthroned pope to the right of the fresco is clearly related to his displacement to the left of the opposite fresco, the *Battle of Ostia*. The lateral displacement of the pope in each case, moreover, is so designed as to place him along the line of the gaze of Christ and of God the Father, respectively, in the *tondi* above, both of which are parts of Perugino's pre-existing ceiling decoration. This example demonstrates therefore more than the impoverishment of understanding that follows a too-abstract and compartmented approach to formal and iconographical problems. It also introduces and clarifies the issue of artistic free-will. For certain formal

1. S. J. Freedberg, *Painting of the High Renaissance in Rome and Florence*, Cambridge (Mass.), 1961, pp. 307 ff.; K. Oberhuber, 'Die Fresken der Stanza dell'Incendio im Werk Raffaels', *Jahrbuch der kunsthistorischen Sammlungen in Wien*, lviii, 1962, pp. 55 ff.; J. Shearman, 'Raphael's Unexecuted Projects for the Stanze', *Walter Friedlaender zum 90. Geburtstag*, Berlin, 1965, p. 176.

2. We should all have paid more attention to the description of this fresco by Vasari (*Vite*, ed. 1550, pp. 662–3): '. . . tutti i Cardinali, Vescovi, Camerieri, Scudieri, Cubicularii, sono in pontificale a' loro luoghi, a sedere ordinatamente come costuma la cappella . . .'. Gaspare Celio, *Memoria . . . delli nomi dell'Artefici delle pitture . . . di Roma*, Naples, 1638, p. 117, simply calls this fresco *il Concistorio*. For the appearance of the sessions of the Lateran Council, see now N. H. Minnich, S.J., and H. W. Pfeiffer, S.J., 'Two woodcuts of Lateran V', *Archivum historiae pontificiae*, viii, 1970, pp. 179 ff.

3. A more extended discussion is given in Shearman, op. cit. in n. 1, pp. 166 ff.

constraints were forced upon Raphael by his own habits of thinking realistically, and by the configuration and actions inherent in what he represents; yet, on the other hand, the solution is part of an effort of aesthetic organization, in this case the overall structure of the room's decoration, by which old and new are united.

At this point there are two qualifications to be made. Certainly his mind enjoys freedom of action, but it is most nearly complete at a remoter distance from the individual creative invention, during the formation of his particular approach to history-painting. We are not driven to accept a simple kind of determinism in our assessment of the situation but rather to the recognition of an individual's habits of mind, influenced in the normal way by environmental conventions and by the necessity, that he happens to feel, to communicate. Secondly, he does, of course, retain a measure of free-will even in the working-out of individual creative problems. The realistic and rationalizing approach, which is so characteristic of his history-painting, is never the master of his aesthetic judgement but is normally, on the contrary, shaped and reshaped by the latter. The evolution of the *Mass at Bolsena*, 1511–12, is an illustration of this point.[3] In the preliminary draft for this fresco (recorded in a set of three copies at Oxford) the disposition of liturgy and architectural forms is remarkably logical and could be interpreted quite realistically from experience of Mass in such a building as San Martino ai Monti, in its original form (*Fig.* 81); very ingeniously, such a mediaeval arrangement of lateral steps, altar-platform and apse is adapted to the problem raised by the intruding window in such a manner that the latter takes the place of the opening to the crypt beneath the altar. A compromise between realism and exposition is, however, already made at this stage, for the altar is unrealistically turned so that its length lies on the axis of the basilica for the better exhibition of the all-important action of the celebrant. In the final fresco-design the compromise is controlled more specifically and more radically by aesthetic will, for the architectural forms and the grouping of the figures that Raphael eventually chooses more effectively express the dramatic action and more clearly focus attention upon what is essential, while at the same time harmonizing more perfectly with the total picture-field; in the process the situation depicted becomes perceptibly more ideal and is to be construed less intelligibly in terms of real experience. Nevertheless it would be as great an error to overlook the remaining limitations placed upon Raphael's freedom of action by his habits of mind (which include, in many cases, the exploitation of precedent and ancient authority) as it would be to over-react to this thought by assuming a degree of passiveness that would amount to forgetting that he was an artist.

The problem of assessing the extent and operation of artistic free-will is just as acute when we come to examine the design of the Cartoons, but it is complicated by another factor. The freedom of action of the artist may be constricted not only by his habitual thought-processes, but also by decisions that he takes at the first moment of conception of a work of art; as the musician's product may be conditioned by the conscious decision to adopt, for example, the rhythm and structure of a certain dance-form, so the artist's composition may also be conditioned by a decision to work within a certain formula. The decision may be made with complete freedom (sometimes it is not), but once made it restricts freedom; for if discipline is not properly maintained that meaning which resides in the formula is obscured. The truth that the voluntary surrender of freedom of form can be as frequently a spur to real creation as it is in other cases a kind of structural safety-net is obvious from our experience of music, or indeed literature. That this also applies to the visual arts is always clear in the case of architecture; the choice of basilica-form, for example, may or may not be a free one, and even when it is it may have positive or negative qualitative results. And the further application of the same truth to the figurative arts is nowhere clearer—and the results nowhere more positive—than in the Cartoons. To anticipate with one example: the intelligent, reasonable and above all meaningful synthesis of the formulae of *acclamatio* and *immolatio* in the *Sacrifice at Lystra* (*Pl.* 38) was an intensely creative decision, based upon Raphael's exceptional visual literacy. But the decision, once made, left him little room for manœuvre; for what was not surrendered at that point was then constricted still further by the very intelligence and seriousness of purpose that made possible the decision, as it was followed through to its logical consequences. Deviation from the self-imposed discipline would have led to a loss, or at best a blurring, of meaning. To this extreme degree, then, 'meaning' and 'design' are indivisible. And when we take account of another self-imposed discipline, the formation of Cartoon-compositions with respect to the intended context of each single tapestry in the series and in the Sistine Chapel's decoration—the latter affecting, even, some detailed aspects of their style—we can begin to appreciate to what extent the appearance of the Cartoons was conditioned in advance, as it were, by the personality of the man who made them.

These preliminary reflections may seem superfluous but unfortunately they are not. Few would now assert that Raphael would have had any real freedom in the initial choice of subjects for the tapestries; and few, perhaps, would now dare to discuss their formal aspects without laying some sacrifice upon the altar of iconography. But there still persists, it seems, a false compartmentalization of form and content, too little effort directed towards the definition of their relationship in specific cases, and there persists also too little thinking upon the problem of artistic free-will and upon how—or on what different levels—it operates. In extreme cases this over-simplification amounts to the assumption that Raphael's mind, at the moment when his chalk or pen were poised above the paper, was a *tabula rasa*. The real, if inconvenient, complexity of the situation is the subject of this chapter. But it is natural and imperative to begin with a survey of the surviving drawings and of all other records of the creative process.

The most natural thing that could have happened to Raphael's drawings is their destruction, and it is only by a succession of miracles that each fragment has now reached this or that collection. Thus it is not odd that the accidents of survival have left us with some trace of the creative process of all but one of the ten original Cartoons—the exception is the *Stoning of Stephen* —while, on the other hand, providing us with evidence of different stages in the progress of each and in no case providing a satisfactory sequence. We can piece together the fragments of the evidence by interpolating in the lacunae of one case, by analogy, the examples of others; this in itself is not particularly difficult, but the technique rests upon an assumption that should not be too readily accepted, that the creative process was, in each case, the same. There is some evidence that it was not.

The fragmentary documents of the process with which we have to proceed do, in any case, require the greatest care in their interpretation. Not many of them are autograph drawings by Raphael. Some of them are copies of his designs made in his workshop, and the function of these copies is not always clear. They may be facsimiles made for purposes of learning the master's

4. Black chalk, pen and brown ink, cool sepia wash, white heightening; 203 × 340 mm. A. E. Popham and J. Wilde, *Italian Drawings at Windsor Castle*, London, 1949, No. 808, p. 315, as a copy after Raphael; for the attribution to Penni (already suggested by J. A. Crowe and G. B. Cavalcaselle, *Raphael: his Life and Works*, London, 1885, ii, p. 275n.) see P. Pouncey and J. Gere, *Italian Drawings ... in the British Museum: Raphael and his Circle*, London, 1962, p. 56. The first reference to this drawing appears to be by Richard Dalton (the Royal Librarian), 'Remarks on the whole number of the Sacred Historical Designs of Raphael d'Urbino', *The Gentleman's Magazine*, lvii, Part 2, 1787, p. 854, who accepted that it was Raphael's original study for the Cartoon as did A. Springer, *Raffael und Michelangelo*, Leipzig, 1878, ii, p. 511, and E. Müntz, *Les tapisseries de Raphaël au Vatican*, Paris, 1897, p. 11. J. D. Passavant, *Rafael von Urbino*, Leipzig, 1839, ii, p. 237, seems to have been the first to doubt it; Oberhuber, *op. cit.* in n. 1, p. 32, accepts the attribution to Penni and describes the drawing as 'etwa das Modello'.

I do not intend to give complete bibliographies of the drawings to be discussed, most of which are being catalogued concurrently by Dr. Oberhuber; but I shall mention untraced drawings of which I have found records in order to stress the limitations to be placed upon the interpretation of those that are known. There are, or were, at least three copies of this drawing: (i) Oxford, Ashmolean 665a (ii) Florence, Uffizi, 1223E (engr. Scacciati-Mulinari, ii, 1744, No. 118) (iii) Untraced, from the Banks Collection, 1827 (*Annals of Thomas Banks*, ed. C. F. Bell, Cambridge, 1938, p. 206). Another drawing, of uncertain appearance, but considered possibly the original, was the property of Alexander Dyce in 1865 (W. W. Lloyd, 'The Sistine Chapel and the Cartoons of Raphael', *The Fine Arts Quarterly Review*, iii, 1865, p. 260). In addition there is a pen-drawing in Berlin (No. 493) which was considered by G. F. Waagen, *Treasures of Art in Great Britain*, London, 1854, ii, p. 391, as an original by Raphael; it seems to me a product of the 'calligraphic forger' (to be added to the list of his works in Pouncey-Gere, *op. cit.*, p. 48; Mr. Gere concurs in this attribution), and I believe it to be derived from the woodcut mentioned below.

The Windsor drawing is inscribed on the *verso*: *siculo* (no other reading is possible); the number of ways in which this may be interpreted is, naturally, large. There are several contemporary or earlier scholars and theologians known as Siculus whose opinions might have been consulted for the programme; in addition there is a painter Jacopo Siculo who is sometimes said to have been in Raphael's

technique of drawing, or they may be records for posterity of the creative process, itself now considered a subject of sufficient interest; Gianfrancesco Penni seems to have been charged—or seems to have charged himself—with this responsibility. Other drawings, however, may themselves occupy a place within the creative process, being 'fair-copies' of lost and perhaps untidy drafts by Raphael requiring a purely mechanical clarification; it is worth remembering that by the date of the Cartoons Raphael had taken charge of the architectural drawing-office of Saint Peter's, where this system was in operation. In other instances the copy may be remote in time and place—even in style—from Raphael's workshop, and furthermore it may transpose the evidence of a lost drawing to another medium; such a transposition makes it difficult to conceive the character of the original, and for that reason more difficult to define the place of the original in the creative process.

These problems, in their most confusing form, confront us when we try to interpret the fragments of evidence for the genesis of the *Miraculous Draught of Fishes* (*Pl.* 1). The most significant drawing is the one at Windsor (*Fig.* 41) now attributed—I would think rightly—to Penni.[4] It includes in its black chalk underdrawing variations which are rejected in the final definition in pen and ink and wash, and in addition there is a correction of the horizon to a lower level in red chalk. Two reasonable interpretations of the drawing may be made and it is for the moment unwise to reject one in favour of the other. It may be, on the one hand, a facsimile of a lost compositional draft by Raphael and thus a record of a stage in the creative process; on the other hand it may be a fair-copy by Penni making concrete a more sketchy draft by Raphael, in which case it is no record but a real and functional part of the process. Each solution entails difficulties, perhaps even improbabilities. The first assumes that the facsimile will record *pentimenti*; this may indeed happen in such copies,[5] but these *pentimenti* have the convincing appearance of decisions taken in this particular drawing. The second solution, which that judgement would then favour, leads inevitably to the conclusion that Penni took decisions—some of them major decisions, such as the inflation of the curvature of Christ's robe—which were then accepted by Raphael for inclusion in the Cartoon. Since our knowledge, such as it is, of the practice of Raphael's studio is almost entirely assembled from a number of judgements upon individual problems of exactly this kind it is clearly inadmissible to assert that Raphael would do no such thing. There is, however, one other possible interpretation of the drawing that ought to be rejected as unreasonable: that Penni himself was the inventor of the design *ab initio*. Such a conclusion would need to be reconciled with the fact—it surely is a fact—that Raphael himself executed a large part of the eventual Cartoon, and it is hard to see how this can be done without departing from the sane principle that Raphael was master in his own shop.

Let us look more closely at the *pentimenti* recorded, or truly effected, in the Windsor drawing, and in particular at the rejected pattern of folds falling in steeply diagonal tubular folds from Christ's shoulder and at the swirl of folds first drawn just above the knee of the second Apostle, presumably Andrew. The sequence of development seems to follow a yet earlier stage

workshop and who certainly knew drawings from that source (J. Shearman, 'The Chigi Chapel in S. Maria del Popolo', *Journal of the Warburg and Courtauld Institutes*, xxiv, 1961, p. 157); and it is worth noticing Antonio Sicul dealer in tapestries and MSS. employed by th Grimani (P. Paschini, *Domenico Grimani, Ca dinale di S. Marco*, Rome, 1943, p. 159).

represented in the background of a drawing in the Albertina (*Fig.* 44) attributed to Giulio Romano,[6] and still more exactly, in the case of Christ's robe, a variant of the Albertina composition recorded in an etching (*Fig.* 45).[7] In each of these the second Apostle is standing more upright and the swirl of the lower edge of his robe is naturally related to his movement as he steers Peter's boat with a long oar; and it is as if a relic of this motif remained in the first draft in chalk on the sheet at Windsor, and was then rejected because it bore no similarly natural relationship to the new posture of Andrew.

At this point the problem becomes considerably more complicated. It would seem logical to assume that either the Albertina drawing as a whole or the etching—the relationship between the two is uncertain—represents an early stage in the evolution of the Cartoon. The subject is the same (*LVC:5* is inscribed in the lower right corner of the drawing) and the difference between this conception and that of the Cartoon lies in the exchange, between background and foreground, of the group in the boats and the congregation to whom Christ had been preaching. Our interest, and perhaps confidence, in the conception is increased by a drawing in Munich (*Fig.* 43), corresponding to one of the women in the foreground; it is not by Raphael himself, but it is more convincingly a facsimile of a lost drawing by him than either the etching or the Albertina drawing can be.[8] And the two conversing figures standing to one side of the latter are just as convincing as inventions of Raphael's. Moreover lighting and gesture in the Albertina drawing are appropriate for reversal in the tapestry. Nevertheless there are two observations upon this composition that should make us hesitate. Firstly the great ecclesiological significance of the action in the boats makes it hard to understand how Raphael could have approached the problem of representing this subject by giving the greater prominence to the coincidental and trivial activities of the crowd from whom Christ has departed. Secondly it is perhaps important that whereas in the foreground groups of the Albertina drawing there are *pentimenti* so extensive that some figures adumbrated in chalk are rejected altogether (the point of departure is Michelangelo's *Flood* on the Sistine ceiling), the groups in the boats are not at the same initial and exploratory stage of invention. Thus while no assertions are appropriate it is possible that the groups in the boats in the Albertina drawing are dependent, like the Windsor drawing as a whole, upon some other prior study of these groups alone, and that that prior study was Raphael's first idea for the Cartoon.[9] This solution recommends itself, furthermore, because it eliminates the suggestion—otherwise implicit in the Albertina drawing—that Giulio played the major part in the invention of the Cartoon; but it does not account for the Albertina drawing itself, nor does it account for Raphael's contribution, to this or a similar composition, which seems implied by the copy at Munich.

Several possibilities come to mind which could rescue us from these hypotheses, but only by replacing them with others. It is conceivable, for example, that the chalk-drawing on the Albertina sheet, in which so many forms are suggested but not selected for further definition, is by Raphael himself; that is not an attribution I am prepared to make, but if it were right the selection for reworking—by Giulio—could then again have been made by Raphael in drawings like that recorded on the Munich sheet. A reconstruction along these lines will leave control essentially in Raphael's hands; and it is permissible to speculate, when facing the problem of the relegation of the boats to the background, that Raphael might have experi-

5. For example, Louvre Inv. 4050, a copy by Penni of a draft for Raphael's *Saint Michael* of 1517–18; this seems to me a case where the '*pentimenti*' are not even deceptively genuine.

6. R.85 *recto*; sepia paper, black chalk, sepia wash, pen and sepia ink, white heightening; 227 × 330 mm.; from the Crozat Collection (1741 Sale, No. 120). P. J. Mariette, *Notes manuscrites . . . Les grands peintres I: Ecoles d'Italie*, ed. D. Wildenstein, Paris, 1969, p. 137 (who was perhaps the first scholar to take the design seriously); Passavant, op. cit. in n. 4, ii, p. 237; Waagen, op. cit. in n. 4, ii, p. 392; H. Grimm, 'Raphael und das Neue Testament', *Preussische Jahrbücher*, li, 1883, p. 13; Crowe and Cavalcaselle, op. cit. in n. 4, ii, p. 275n.; Müntz, op. cit. in n. 4, p. 10; A. Venturi, *Raffaello*, Rome, 1920, p. 200, all as Raphael's first sketch for the Cartoon; wrongly related by Wickhoff to a grisaille in the Stanza dell'Incendio (see O. Fischel, *Raphaels Zeichnungen: Versuch einer Kritik*, Strassburg, 1898, p. 101, who himself follows Morelli's attribution to Giulio Romano). F. Hartt, *Giulio Romano*, New Haven, 1958, p. 20, deduced from this drawing, which he calls a *modello*, a degree of responsibility for the design on the part of Giulio which seems to me and to Oberhuber extravagant (my comments in a review, *The Burlington Magazine*, ci, 1959, p. 457; Oberhuber, op. cit. in n. 1, p. 29). A copy after this drawing is in the Louvre, R.F. 3952, attributed to Girolamo da Carpi, and there is an engraving by G. B. Franco (B. xvi, p. 124, No. 14).

7. Attributed to A. Fantuzzi; C. Ruland, *The Works of Raphael . . . in the Raphael Collection . . . at Windsor Castle*, Weimar, 1876, p. 244, No. 20.

8. Inv. 6235; pen and brown ink; 102 × 140 mm.; from the Crozat and Mariette Collections. The style of the original must have been very close to that of Raphael's pen-study for Cupid and Psyche in the Albertina (J. Shearman, 'Die Loggia der Psyche . . .', *Jahrbuch der kunsthistorischen Sammlungen in Wien*, lx, 1964, p. 91, Fig. 92; I would now withdraw my doubts as to the originality of this sheet, having subsequently noticed a faint stylus underdrawing). Dr. Oberhuber has kindly informed me of a copy similar to the one at Munich in Madrid, Biblioteca Nacional, Dib. 7563.

9. It should be noted that this cannot be the study of these groups on the *verso* of the Albertina drawing (repr. Hartt, op. cit. in n. 6, ii, Fig. 3), for this—although more 'sketchy' than the *recto*—must follow it, as is clear from its *pentimenti*.

10. A. Reichel, *Die Clair-obscurschnitte des XVI., XVII. und XVIII. Jahrhunderts*, Zürich, 1926, p. 57, and K. Oberhuber, in the Albertina exhibition catalogue: *Graphik: italienische Renaissance*, 1966, No. 193, each with further bibliography. Prints from the same blocks were re-issued by Andrea Adriani in Mantua, 1609.

11. Pen, bistre and water-colour; 320 × 420 mm.; from the Colbrandini, Brigeleben and Goldschmidt Collections; Sotheby's Sale 7–10 December 1920, No. 348, as a sheet from Vasari's *Libro di disegni* (which is not impossible: compare the framing of the fragments by Andrea del Sarto in the Louvre: *Giorgio Vasari, dessinateur et collectionneur*, Cabinet des dessins, 1965, No. 71). This drawing is at present untraced, and its status must be assessed with reserve; I have discussed it with Mme Nicole Dacos-Crifò, who shares my doubts that it is autograph. The cranes, in particular, are somewhat less convincing anatomically than those painted in the Cartoon. It should be noted that the drawing (or its prototype) was not made for the Cartoon in the first place but was put to use there in such a manner that the directions correspond to those of the tapestry; it perhaps exemplifies the comment by Vasari on Giovanni's earliest relationship with Raphael in Rome: 'Ma sopratutto si dilettò (Giovanni) sommamente di fare uccelli di tutte le sorti, di maniera che in poco tempo condusse un libro tanto vario e bello, che egli era lo spasso ed il trastullo di Raffaello ...' (*Vite*, ed. Milanesi, vi, p. 550). The two fragments of an *Annunciation* mounted with this study clearly reflect a much later phase of Giovanni's style.

12. Red chalk; 257 × 375 mm. Popham-Wilde, op. cit. in n. 4, No. 802, with earlier literature. It should be noted that the statement rather frequently made that the offset has been reworked by Raphael cannot be correct, for the counter-proof of the stylus-lines of the original is at no point overlaid with new strokes.

13. Inv. 3854; stylus and red chalk; 254 × 134 mm. (irregular). Crowe-Cavalcaselle, op. cit. in n. 4, ii, p. 289n. (emphatically as Raphael); Fischel, op. cit. in n. 6, p. 102 (with earlier literature: attributed to Giulio; Fischel, however, later reversed this decision, calling it 'the only certainly authentic study for the ... Cartoons'—see *The Vasari Society*, Ser. 2, xi, 1930, Nos. 5–6, also *Raphaels Zeichnungen*, i, Berlin, 1912, p. 22 and *Raphael*, London, 1948, p. 365, as Raphael, but on p. 256 as a stylus-drawing by Raphael worked-up by pupils). The attribution to Raphael has more recently been generally accepted, except by Hartt, op. cit. in n. 6, pp. 20, 286, who put it back in the Giulio dustbin.

14. Stylus and red chalk; (i) 84 × 116 mm. (ii) 67 × 116 mm. I owe my knowledge of these fragments to John Gere, and I am most grateful to the present owner for permission to publish them here. They show that the original drawing was somewhat wider than the Windsor offset, which has been slightly trimmed on the left. I think they may be identical with the following, seen in the Crozat Collection by Jonathan Richardson Jnr., *An Account of the Statues, Bas-reliefs, Drawings and Pictures in Italy, France, etc.*, London, 1722, p. 13: 'Seven of the Heads in the Carton of giving the Keys; that of St. John divine! and much as the Carton. Red ch.' (the discrepancy in the number of heads is in this case negligible); and in that case they would be part of Lot 110 in the 1741 Crozat Sale: 'de belles Etudes des têtes d'Apôtres du suject des Actes, représentant Jésus-Christ donnant les clefs à S. Pierre ...'

15. Above, p. 67.

16. A drawing for a *Venus* in the British Museum (Pouncey-Gere, op. cit. in n. 4, No. 27) is an example of a drawing which dissatisfied Raphael to the extent that he pasted on it a new piece of paper on which he supplied, in this case, a revised lower part of the figure.

17. It should be noted, however, that as the fifth 'Apostle' in the *bottega*-study is moved nearer the fourth he is also separated from the sixth.

18. Inv. 3863; sepia-tinted paper, squared in black chalk, black chalk underdrawing, pen and brown ink, warm bistre wash, white heightening; *pentimenti* in the keys and some draperies; 207 × 353 mm.; from the collections of J. Stella, Duc d'Orléans, Coypel (1753 Sale, No. 228: see P. J. Mariette, *Abecedario*, in

mented with an alternative opening to the series in which the major Petrine theme was introduced in a minor key. As an experiment it is plausible; as a first idea it is less so, and the character of the background group in the Albertina drawing, more advanced along the inventive process, still makes it seem likely that that group was from the beginning the focal *concetto*. The modification was then made, probably, in a new drawing for Andrew alone, and the function of the Windsor drawing (*Fig.* 41) would be the proper reconciliation of this new posture with the rest of the group; it was in this secretarial way that Penni seems to have made himself so useful in Raphael's shop. It is clear that at this stage the city-view in the distance was already decided upon, but the drawing is cut above at such a point that the inclusion of the Mons Vaticanus cannot be assumed. A woodcut by Ugo da Carpi (*Fig.* 42)[10] follows either the Windsor drawing, or a later one of the figures and boats alone (the background has nothing to do with Raphael except in its general cadence); it must be very close to the missing *modello* but is unlikely to record it since there still remains to be effected the compression in the group in the second boat that is seen in the Cartoon (*Pl.* 1). At some point close in time to the *modello*, but not necessarily before it, a considerable series of studies must have been made for the fish in the boats and the cranes in the foreground, studies of the same supplementary nature as the topographical drawings that were made for, or used in, the background. Of these there survives, by chance, a drawing (or an accurate copy of one) on which two of the cranes were studied (*Fig.* 40), from which it is very evident, but no surprise, that this supplementary work at least was done by Giovanni da Udine.[11]

The problems posed by the *Charge to Peter* (*Pl.* 6) ought to be considerably easier since there are four drawings for it by Raphael himself; they do not, however, illuminate the obscurities of those for the first Cartoon, for they represent stages of creation that are not even hinted at in that case. At Windsor there is an offset (*Fig.* 47)[12] of a red chalk drawing of which three fragments survive. The largest of these fragments is a well-known study in the Louvre for the figure that is intended to be Christ (*Fig.* 46);[13] there are two smaller unpublished fragments of the heads and shoulders of eight of the Apostles in a private collection in Paris (*Figs.* 48, 49).[14] Taken together, the offset and the original fragments are documents of Raphael's personal responsibility for a stage in the process after the production of the compositional draft (of which no trace survives); the latter, perhaps resembling the Windsor drawing for the *Miraculous Draught* (*Fig.* 41), was necessarily made prior to these, which represent a moment when the inventive faculty is momentarily at rest, or nearly so, and the definitive process begins. The invention is checked against reality, and the postures previously drawn out of the head are now re-drawn from the life. Raphael had pursued this technique since his earliest active years, and these fragments are very characteristic, in appearance and function, of what are called his *bottega*-studies. Their objectivity is so complete that we become familiar with the physiognomies of his models.

The thought may not be pleasant to contemplate, but it may have been Raphael himself who mutilated the drawing which we see reflected very nearly complete in the offset. This possibility is suggested when we consider the relation between the red chalk life-studies and the Cartoon. We have already seen, in the previous Chapter, that the substantial revision in the pose of Christ may be occasioned by a more or less drastic revision of the subject.[15] In the offset (*Fig.* 47) the continuity of the figurative relief is beautifully judged; there is an expressive caesura between Christ and the Apostles, yet His raised arm fills the void above Peter. The revised posture of Christ—frontal, pointing with equal emphasis to keys and sheep—needed, obviously, to be submitted to the same test against reality, and one may assume that a new life-study was made, which could be attached to those already made for the Apostles.[16] However, the Apostle-group, too, required modification: first by the insertion of a new figure, standing between and behind Peter and John, which in the relief-pattern compensates for the lowering of Christ's arm; and second by a slight complementary compression between precisely those sub-groups of Apostles that are divided in the two smaller fragments (*Figs.* 48, 49)—complementary because the newly-invented Apostle brings a greater density to that part of the whole group which is nearest Christ.[17]

Together with the *bottega*-studies there must also have been made a series of drapery-studies appropriate to the characterization of the Apostles, and all this preparation was subsumed in the *modello* which survives in the Louvre (*Fig.* 51).[18] The very high quality of the drawing, in striking contrast to Giulio's in the Albertina (*Fig.* 44), makes the attribution to Raphael compelling. It should be noted that, whereas the *modello* almost exactly prefigures the Cartoon in its summary indications of landscape, the sheep on one side and the fishing-boat on the other, and also the foreground vegetation, are all missing. Moreover the *modello* does not quite terminate the inventive process even in the figure-group itself. A decision was taken later to eliminate Christ's undergarment, and at the same time the compression between the two sub-groups of apostles, already begun between the *bottega*-study and the *modello*, was taken a stage farther (it is simplest to follow the movement of the hand of the sixth Apostle across the shoulder of the fifth). A more subtle change affects the alignment of heads; those of John and of the fifth Apostle, which in the *bottega*-study and the *modello* were inclined, respectively, away from and towards the viewer, are seen in the Cartoon in almost strict elevation.[19]

The existence of the original *modello* for the *Charge to Peter* helps to make some sense of the copies of stages in the design of the next Cartoon, the *Healing of the Lame Man* (*Pl.* 12); for there exists a facsimile-copy (*Fig.* 56)[20]

Archives de l'art français, viii, 1857–58, p. 298, and E. Dacier, 'La vente Charles Coypel', *Revue de l'art*, lxi, 1932, p. 135); published, while in the Orléans Collection, by P. Robert with woodblocks by Nicolas Le Sueur. Fischel, op. cit. in n. 6, p. 103 (summary of earlier literature; dismissed as a copy and model for an engraving by Ghisi); Crowe-Cavalcaselle, op. cit. in n. 4, ii, p. 290n., Freedberg, op. cit. in n. 1, p. 274 and A. Marabottini, 'I collaboratori', in *Raffaello: L'opera, le fonti, la fortuna*, ed. M. Salmi, Novara, 1968, p. 278, n. 28, all as Penni; Hartt, op. cit. in n. 6, pp. 20, 286 and A. Forlani-Tempesti, in *Raffaello*, cit., ii, p. 429, n. 165, as Giulio; Shearman, loc. cit. in n. 6 and Oberhuber, op. cit. in n. 1, p. 29, as Raphael. There is a workshop facsimile of the Louvre *modello* in the Uffizi (1216E; 229 × 363 mm.), engraved in Scacciati-Mulinari, i, 1766, No. 80; the scale is precisely that of the original and it shows that the latter has been cut, especially below. An apparently similar drawing was in the collection of Jonathan Richardson Snr. (*Traité de la Peinture et de la Sculpture*, Amsterdam, 1728, i, p. 73); he acknowledged that it was not autograph. One of these versions was engraved by Diana Ghisi (B. xv. 434.5). In the 1528 inventory of Cardinal Marino Grimani, fol. 5r., is 'Uno quadro disegno di christo a pietro pasce oves meas'; the previous drawing in the list is by Raphael, and the inference is that this one is too (P. Paschini, 'Le collezioni archeologiche dei Grimani', *Rendiconti della pontificia accademia romana di archeologia*, v, 1928, pp. 149 ff.).

19. At this point we must reconsider the engraving by Bonasone (B. xv. 17.6, repr. here *Fig.* 80); as we have seen already, p. 68, there is something to be said for the hypothesis that this is an ungracious record of a stage in the evolution of the Cartoon, and as much to be said against it; L. Bianchi, 'La fortuna di Raffaello nell'incisione', in *Raffaello*, cit. in n. 18, ii, p. 670, writes in its favour. Its place, if it had one, would have to be between the *bottega*-study and the *modello*; the variations do not hold a natural place in a simple evolution between the surviving drawings, and at best it would be an alternative and rejected experiment in regrouping.

20. Pen and brown ink, brown wash, white heightening; 220 × 125 mm.; from the collection of Countess Adelheid Lanckoronska; Christie's Sale, 25 June 1968, No. 134. It should be noted that the vertical dimension is about the same as that of the Louvre *modello* before it was cut— see above, n. 18; but this copy is not by the hand that made the Uffizi *modello*-copies 1216E (above, n. 18) and 1217E (below, n. 57).

21. B. xii. 78.27 and B. xvi. 9.7; etching supplemented by two wood-blocks. Vasari (*Vite*, ed. Milanesi, v, p. 423) said that it was made from the tapestry; Passavant, op. cit. in n. 4, ii, p. 241, and K. Oberhuber, exhibition catalogue, *Parmigianino und sein Kreis*, Albertina, Vienna, 1963, Nos. 45–46, more correctly state that it was based on a preliminary drawing, which they do not more closely define; see also Bianchi, loc. cit. in n. 19, and n. 23 below. Oberhuber, 'Parmigianino als Radierer', *Alte und moderne Kunst*, viii, 1963, No. 68, p. 36, revises the opinion expressed in his catalogue in favour of one originally proposed by Johannes Wilde: the print is by a pupil, after a drawing by Parmigianino after Raphael.

22. Germanisches Nationalmuseum, No. 12097. This drawing was kindly brought to my attention by Dr. Oberhuber.

23. B. xvi. 124.15. This engraving, and the 'Parmigianino' prints, were taken seriously by earlier scholars (e.g. Mariette, ed. cit. in n. 6, p. 137, and Passavant, op. cit. in n. 4, ii, p. 241) as records of lost drawings.

24. Inv. 3988; black chalk, sepia wash, white heightening; 267 × 414 mm.

25. See above, p. 56.

of the left part of a drawing for this Cartoon, the lost original of which must have been identical in character to the Louvre drawing, and must, therefore, have been a *modello* too. Furthermore the copy-fragment corresponds very closely to the equivalent part of a print attributed to Parmigianino (*Fig.* 58), which is presumably a record in reverse of the whole of the lost *modello*,[21] even to the extent of showing only one column given spiral form; it is entirely credible that Raphael did this, but the inference would not be that the introduction of the Salomonic form was an afterthought, rather that he wished to save himself trouble and felt that one example was enough. Another drawing, at Nürnberg (*Fig.* 57), appears to be a copy of the central part of the lost *modello*;[22] it conforms well enough to the Parmigianino print, but its technique is remote from that of Raphael and it cannot be in that sense an exact reproduction of one of his drawings.

An engraving by Battista Franco (*Fig.* 59) is more difficult to interpret.[23] It may also be a copy of the lost *modello*, and if this were the case it would not be hard to understand why the engraver straightened the single twisted column so that it matched the rest, and why he added a column-base to complete the foreground sequence; in some respects the engraving conforms more exactly to the copy-fragment of the *modello* (*Fig.* 56) than does Parmigianino's woodcut (for example in the spacing of the groups with the children). On the other hand there are two additional heads in the background, to right and left, and several other variations, which might suggest that it follows a slightly different and perhaps earlier design. It seems best to treat it as an unreliable witness, which adds nothing to our knowledge or understanding.

A drawing in the Louvre (*Fig.* 55),[24] which looks at first sight to be appallingly unreliable, turns out, on careful inspection, to be much more interesting since it cannot be a copy after the tapestry, the Cartoon, the prints or the *modello*. It has most in common with the latter, including the division between open landscape and dark background at or about the centre and the turning of the mother's head on the right into profile (compare, for both points, the Parmigianino print, *Fig.* 58); but the original of this drawing included what the *modello*, apparently, omitted, that is the receding rows of columns behind the central pair, which Raphael surely always intended; and heads are placed between them, to the left of centre, as they are in the Cartoon. There are many variations in secondary figures, and the boy on the extreme left does not yet carry a pair of doves; above all, the group on the right is raised on a step, which is not an arbitrary revision, for a change of level at the *Porta speciosa* is described in the literary sources available to Raphael.[25]

In general the Louvre drawing is convincing as a clumsy record of the earliest traceable stage in the evolution of this design and it may in fact follow the lost preliminary draft, made before the life-studies. And if that is the right interpretation it demonstrates that in Raphael's initial idea the figures were moving through the gate with a more positive lateral impetus towards the Temple, and turning back more clearly on the right to look at the miracle. In the final Cartoon (*Pl.* 12) there is a greater measure of stability, contributed above all by the shift of level and emphasis that ties the kneeling beggar on the right and the children on the left into a broad triangle of forms which unites the triptych. The progressive application of this discipline is most impressive; it is seen, for example, in the movement of the diagonal forms in the central section of the triptych in the Louvre copy, regrouped already in the *modello*-copies (*Figs.* 55, 57), to final positions in the Cartoon which, like the newly-introduced pediment above, are aligned with the overall triangular structure.

In this case the fragments of the evidence suggest that Raphael again made considerable changes between the *modello* and the Cartoon. If it is reasonable to suppose that although the receding central rows of columns were omitted from the *modello* he always intended them, then the new head behind Peter's was introduced in the Cartoon to clarify and more exactly to integrate the spacing of figure-group and columns. The same process can be seen on the right where heads that had been in front of the columns in the *modello* are placed between them in the Cartoon, and one large head is in fact replaced by two smaller ones farther back. A more interesting change compensates for the loss of meaning in the initial lateral movement towards the Temple (which, when reversed in the tapestry, would have been towards the *presbyterium* of the Sistine Chapel)—the loss consequential upon the more deliberated equipoise of the figural structure. It seems that at the stage of the *modello* the intended background to the columns was to be largely open, and only partially blocked by architectural structures which may have been, as in the Louvre copy, at some distance to the rear. An X-ray photograph of the head immediately to the left of John's in the Cartoon shows that its background was originally painted as a landscape, and so the intention shown by the drawings was followed in the initial stages of the full-scale work. In the completed Cartoon, however, the intimate association of the foreground colonnade with a side wall bearing a blind tabernacle gives this part a specific and appropriate architectural form, that of a *vestibulum*. This final characterization of the colonnade is unlikely to be a casual or even unconscious modification since Raphael includes such a form, with its title, in his project for the Villa Madama a year or so later.[26] The type is best represented, in executed buildings, at Villa Imperiale, Pesaro, which was built towards 1530 and much influenced by Raphael's projects for Villa Madama (*Fig.* 52). The definition of the foreground colonnade in the Cartoon in this way distinguishes it from the one seen to the rear in the left part of the triptych, which must be read as a *stoa* peripheral to the *atrium mulierum*.[27] This restatement of the idea of entrance was motivated, probably, by second thoughts about the relation of the whole design to its context on the wall of the chapel, inducing a stricter symmetry, and can be considered in this light at a later point; but it is worth remembering now that the *Healing of the Lame Man* was to flank the *vestibulum* of the chapel, and worth noticing this further example of the indivisibility of form and meaning.

The preparation of the *Healing of the Lame Man* offers one particularly rare example of the re-use of a drawing made earlier for another purpose. In the Horne Museum in Florence is a study (*Fig.* 53) made in 1509–10 for the head of a muse in *Parnassus*.[28] Clearly Raphael used it again for the young mother on the right of the Cartoon (*Pl.* 20). But more interesting than the fact is the result, a comprehensive revision of style which may be observed here under exceptionally precisely controlled conditions. In the Cartoon the head is fuller and heavier, less imitative of the morphological detail on the surface of antique sculpture but more successfully emulating its qualities of substance and balance. In the drawing the detail is superficial to a basically simple form (and the same point is even more obvious in the painted head in *Parnassus*), whereas in the Cartoon the detail is integral with the shaping and movement of a total form, which becomes thereby more complex and more coherent as an expressive unit.[29]

The problems concerning the preparation of the *Death of Ananias* (*Pl.* 21)

26. See his own description—*vestibulo amodo et usanza antiqua*—in the letter published by P. Foster, 'Raphael on the Villa Madama: the text of a lost letter', *Römisches Jahrbuch für Kunstgeschichte*, xi, 1967–68, p. 309, which is to be read in conjunction with the first (in fact previous) plan, Uffizi 273A. Compare also the designated *vestibulo* on Antonio da Sangallo the Younger's plan for a royal palace, Uffizi 999A (G. Giovannoni, *Antonio da Sangallo il giovane*, Rome, 1959, Fig. 30).

27. Compare the *stoa*-colonnades surrounding the Temple in Raphael's first draft for the *Expulsion of Heliodorus*, a copy of which is in the Albertina (Shearman, op. cit. in n. 1, pp. 167 ff. and Fig. 9).

28. Black chalk; 262 × 207 mm.; Fischel, *R.Z.*, No. 254. It seems certain that for the figure of Paul in the *Conversion of the Proconsul* (*Pl.* 30) Raphael similarly re-used a now-lost study for the head and neck of the remarkably Pauline figure standing in the left foreground of the *Disputa*.

29. This survey of the drawings for the *Healing of the Lame Man* should be supplemented by a notice of the following, untraced: F. Basan, *Catalogue du Cabinet de M.ᵣ Neyman*, Paris, 1776, No. 683: 'Saint Pierre guérissant le boiteux près du temple; au bistre, rehaussé de blanc; connu par l'estampe: 14 pouces sur 9 de haut; il a été restauré par Rubens' (bt. Fourvell); this was perhaps the *modello* or a copy of it.

30. Müntz, op. cit. in n. 4, p. 14 reproduces a woodcut from the *Epistole et Evangelii volgari hystoriade*, Venice, 1512, which he accepts as a copy of a lost preliminary study by Raphael for this Cartoon (with further bibliography); E. Tietze-Conrat, 'Dürer and Raphael in a Venetian Book of 1512', *Print Collector's Quarterly*, xxiv, 1937, pp. 283 ff. (with futher bibliography) attempts, in my view unsuccessfully, to argue that the publication date of the book is correct, against the opinion of Kristeller, who assembled convincing arguments that it was a misprint for 1522. The woodcut remains a problem to be resolved and it may indeed be a record of a lost drawing.

31. B. xii. 46.27. Passavant, op. cit. in n. 4, ii, p. 243, and Bianchi, in *Raffaello*, cit. in n. 18, ii, pp. 669–70, as a copy of a preliminary drawing; see also Reichel, op. cit. in n. 10, p. 57 (facsimile reproduction, Pl. 32), with further bibliography. The first state bears the date and a long inscription claiming papal and Venetian privileges, and the one reproduced here is the second state. Vasari (*Vite*, v, p. 421) was presumably referring to this print when he said that Ugo da Carpi 'fece ... la storia di Simon Mago, che già fece Raffaello nei panni d'arazzo della già detta Cappella'; his confusion over the subject may have been caused, even subconsciously, by a recognition of Raphael's source for the figure of Ananias in the Sixtine Ciborium relief (see below, p. 121). Two drawings in the Louvre, Inv. 3989, 3990, appear to be copies after Ugo's print.

32. B. xiv. 47.42. Mariette, ed. cit. in n. 6, p. 78, believed that the plate was begun by Agostino and finished by Marcantonio; Passavant, op. cit. in n. 4, ii, p. 243, believed the opposite. I hesitate to express an opinion, but it seems to me to lack Marcantonio's finesse altogether and to be even a degree less competent than Agostino's print after the *Conversion of the Proconsul*, dated 1516 (see below, n. 41), and notably less so than his prints after the *Four Evangelists* of 1518 (B. xiv. 83.92–95); it may be Agostino's first work for Raphael. It should be noted that this print, compared with Ugo da Carpi's, shows the composition extended above and on both sides; a similar extension is found in Marcantonios print after the *modello* for *Paul preaching at Athens* (see below, n. 57); but in this case the 'completion' of the column-cum-tablet on the left is particularly unconvincing and it seems best to assume that Ugo's limits are more accurate.

33. The same process of centralization of the viewpoint may also be seen in the evolution of two compositions in the Stanza d'Eliodoro (1511–14), the *Mass at Bolsena* and the *Release*

are only simpler because we have no drawings at all and nothing in the way of records of drawings except two independent prints after what appears to have been the *modello*.[30] The first of these is a beautiful woodcut by Ugo da Carpi (*Fig.* 60), one version of which is dated 1518;[31] the second is a somewhat coarse engraving from the school of Marcantonio (*Fig.* 61), perhaps by Agostino Veneziano, which may be as early as 1516.[32] There are very slight differences between these prints, but in general they are consistent on all the essential points on which they differ from the Cartoon. The most obvious of these is the treatment of the background on the left (on the right in the case of the Cartoon); one may regret the elimination of this interesting glimpse of an antique city with arch, pyramid and obelisk and its substitution by a rather barren rectangle of landscape, but Raphael may have felt that these details—and particularly the curious column, tablet and statue—would conflict with the *stoa* on the right of the neighbouring tapestry, the *Healing of the Lame Man*, or simply that they were distracting from the main event. There are also several minor changes in details such as headdresses, the elimination in the Cartoon of the bowl held by one of the women at the side and of a foot which, on the left of the prints, appears between the legs of the trousered man alongside Ananias—the foot which belongs to a background figure bearing a sack and which was presumably judged to be a confusing repetition of that of the young man who points upwards above Ananias's head (its elimination may be another example of Raphael's sacrifice of strict realism in favour of aesthetic order). But the principal and really interesting change is a consistent revision of viewpoint. In the prints it is clear from the perspective of the *rostra* and of the architectural background (which at the *modello*-stage included pilasters framing the Apostles) that the vanishing-point was offset to the right, as it would also have been in the tapestry. It may be that this was calculated for the viewpoint of a spectator who had just passed the *cancellata* in the Sistine Chapel and looked at this tapestry, the first on the right. Between *modello* and Cartoon the decision was taken to reduce the architectural elements of the background and, in compensation, to establish the viewpoint by an emphatic pavement-pattern like that of the *Disputa*. This pavement-pattern, in the finished Cartoon, is precisely centralized, with its vanishing-point coincidental with the figure of Peter. But it is remarkable that on closer inspection one finds that it was first painted (not only drawn) with a vanishing-point far to the left, centred on the young deacon—probably Stephen—distributing the goods of the Church. Thus even after the means of spatial definition had been revised the intention remained for a moment the same as that which is shown, in reverse, in the prints.

of Peter; in each case the preliminary drafts show viewpoints offset slightly to the right (Shearman, op. cit. in n. 1, pp. 167–70).

34. This changing relation between subject and spectator is consistent with the evolution of Raphael's ideas of history-painting that may be watched—extended over a longer period—in the Stanze (a fuller analysis in Shearman, op. cit. in n. 1, pp. 170, 172).

35. A pen-drawing in the Albertina (No. 211, R. 76; Oberhuber, op. cit. in n. 1, p. 29, Fig. 24) of the *Stoning of Stephen* has been described by several scholars from Passavant, op. cit. in n. 4, ii, p. 240, to, most recently, Oberhube as a study for the Cartoon. In spite of t partial weaknesses in the drawing I believe th the attribution to Raphael (Mariette Sa catalogue, 1775, No. 693) is correct. But the are three reasons why I feel that it cannot be study for the Cartoon: firstly because t gestures make it clear that the design was n planned for reversal (all Raphael's knov studies for the tapestries are made in t direction of the Cartoon); secondly because t direction of light is from the left, whereas th in the tapestry is from the right; and third because the style of the drawing would pla it, in my judgement, c. 1510–12 (G. Grona

The reasoning behind Raphael's second thoughts during the execution of the Cartoon is a matter for speculation. It is clear that the final solution provides a focus on Peter, and Raphael may not have appreciated the force of the pavement-pattern—not anticipated in the *modello*—until he had begun to paint it. But the centralization of the viewpoint also brings the design into conformity with that of the opposite tapestry, the *Sacrifice at Lystra*, and moreover the first intention with the viewpoint offset to the right of the tapestry would have had the effect of detaching the *Death of Ananias* from the rest of the Petrine set, and it seems very probable, therefore, that the total context of the design in the rest of the series was a determining factor in the revision. At the same time, however, the shift of viewpoint has implications for the reading of the design in isolation. In the first place it is an act of formalization akin to the progressive imposition of formal symmetry in the *Healing of the Lame Man*.[33] Secondly it has subtle effects upon the relation between the subject and the spectator. In the initial, spatially asymmetrical idea, the implied lateral displacement of viewpoint to the right would have given the clear impression that Ananias fell to the left; the spectator would then have felt that he stood a little to one side of the axis of action and reaction between Peter and Ananias. The more emphatic indication of viewpoint by pavement-pattern begun in the Cartoon would surely have accentuated this effect of psychological detachment. The eventual centralization of viewpoint, on the other hand, places the spectator squarely before Peter and it is as if Ananias fell dead at his feet; he is, in fact, more than spectator now, no longer standing aside from the action but involved in it as if the punishment consequent upon the denial of divine authority (a figure, as we have seen, of excommunication) could indeed be extended to him too.[34]

The *Stoning of Stephen* (*Fig.* 18) is the only tapestry for which there remain neither drawings nor reliable records of drawings.[35] The lack of such evidence lends no support to the contention that the tapestry was not designed by Raphael but by Giulio Romano[36]—a contention that has been made from time to time and is quite unjustified. The case with the *Conversion of Saul* (*Fig.* 20), the design of which has also been attributed to Giulio, is different again but no less singular, for there exist at Haarlem and Chatsworth (*Figs.* 63, 64) two very fine versions of a chalk study for the group of soldiers on the right of the tapestry.[37] The confrontation of these two studies teaches us a sharp lesson, and it would be perfectly natural to react with the embarrassment so well expressed in an admittedly different context in *The Beggar's Opera*:

> How happy could I be with either,
> Were t'other dear charmer away!
> But while ye thus tease me together
> To neither a word will I say.

But although the Haarlem drawing has had many distinguished supporters there can be no reasonable doubt that the more damaged and superficially less attractive one at Chatsworth is the primary version, for there is an argument to be applied that does not depend upon personal assessments of quality. From the start of his career Raphael had been in the habit of beginning his more definitive chalk studies by mapping out on the paper the composition of forms with a stylus,[38] a convenient and characteristically economical line of attack since it left him free to change his mind, even drastically, without disfiguring the final result; the only residual effect in

Aus Raphaels Florentiner Tagen, Berlin, 1902, pp. 42 ff., placed it even slightly earlier). There is a very good replica of this drawing in the Louvre (Inv. 4125). Müntz, op. cit. in n. 4, p. 14, was one of those who agreed with the attribution of the Albertina drawing to Raphael (specifically contesting Wickhoff's attribution to Penni), and who thought that it was a study for the tapestry; he deduced from this example that Raphael began the creative process with studies of the nude; it is important that this is not the case. One must record, as an oddity, the conclusion of Grimm, op. cit. in n. 6, p. 20, that the drawing is a fake. Ruland, op. cit. in n. 7, p. 247, No. 4, clearly doubted that it had anything to do with the tapestry.

The best possibility of a record of Raphael's drawings for the Cartoon seems to me a pen-drawing in the Teyler Museum, Haarlem (K. 1), a product of Raphael's workshop which appears to be a compilation from drawings by Raphael in which a Saint Stephen kneels before the Virgin and Child; the figure of Stephen is convincing as a copy of a study by Raphael, in a posture very close to that of the tapestry but seen from a slightly different viewpoint. It should be noted that in this drawing the lighting of the figure of Stephen is from the right (as in the tapestry) whereas that of the Virgin and Child is from the left.

36. The extreme formulation of this view is that the design was added to the set by Giulio after Raphael's death: W. Kelber, *Raphael von Urbino*, 2nd ed., Stuttgart, 1963–64, ii, p. 57 and F. Filippini, 'Tommaso Vincidor da Bologna scolaro di Raffaello . . .', *Bollettino d'Arte*, N.S. viii, 1929, p. 318; these scholars might have noticed that the tapestry was among those delivered in 1519 (see above, p. 38).

37. Haarlem, Teyler Museum, A. 78; red chalk; 247 × 242 mm.; from the collection of Christina of Sweden. For bibliography see the catalogue, *Drawings from the Teyler Museum, Haarlem*, Victoria and Albert Museum, London, 1970, No. 77. Chatsworth, No. 905; stylus and red chalk; 325 × 247 mm.; the attribution to Raphael (but not the correct identification) already in J. H. Pollen, *The Chatsworth Raphaels*, London, 1872, No. xv; Ruland, op. cit. in n. 7, pp. 249–50, No. 5, and Crowe-Cavalcaselle, op. cit. in n. 4, ii, p. 281n., as Raphael's original study for the Cartoon; H. Dollmayr, 'Raffaels Werkstätte', *Jahrbuch der kunsthistorischen Sammlungen des allerhöchsten Kaiserhauses*, xvi, 1895, p. 266, as Penni.

38. That is, a metal-point which on unprepared paper would leave no mark other than an indentation which, when the paper was fresh, was presumably visible enough for his immediate purposes.

39. Naturally these stylus-lines need critical attention, since they could also arise from a copying-process; the question to be asked is whether or not they indicate a real process of creation and discovery on the sheet, and in these cases I have no doubt that they do. The horse is in fact more complete in the stylus-drawing than it is in the final chalk.

40. On the other hand it is also to be noted that where the Chatsworth drawing is summary in its indications (for example in the left hand of the running figure) the draughtsman of the Haarlem version is at a loss to interpret it. I believe that the copy was made in Raphael's studio—the artist may be Giulio—and it is not difficult to reconcile the rejection of this study on the *recto* with the acceptance for Raphael (which I would make) of the beautiful wash-drawing on the *verso* for the figure of the pope in the *Mass at Bolsena*, 1511–12.

41. Popham-Wilde, op. cit. in n. 4, No. 803; grey prepared paper, silver-point, white heightening, brown wash, pen and brown ink; 270 × 355 mm. The first certain reference is by Dalton, 1787 (loc. cit. in n. 4), who believed it to be a study by Raphael for the Cartoon; Passavant, op. cit. in n. 4, ii, p. 246, summarily dismissed it; Müntz, op. cit. in n. 4, p. 16, avoided a decision on the grounds of unsatisfactory condition; additional early bibliography is in Fischel, op. cit. in n. 6, p. 105. More recently the drawing has been attributed to Giulio by Hartt, op. cit. in n. 6, i, pp. 21, 286, and to Raphael by Freedberg, op. cit. in n. 1, p. 274, who agrees, however, with Popham's suggestion that the perspective constructional lines were prepared by an assistant, which I do not feel to be the case. This drawing appears to have been the direct model for Agostino Veneziano's engraving, B. xiv. 48.43, dated 1516; Passavant, loc. cit., mentions a woodcut by Ugo da Carpi which I have not seen. The Windsor drawing has been identified with one of this subject seen by Nicodemus Tessin the Younger in the collection of Christina of Sweden in Rome (see the exhibition catalogue: *Christina of Sweden*, Stockholm, Nationalmuseum, 1966, No. 1090), and this could be correct. A larger drawing, also attributed to Raphael, appears in the Jabach inventory of 1670–71, No. 98: 'Un Sainct Paul qui guérit un possedé, où il y a grand nombre de figures entières, à la pierre noire, rehaussé de blanc sur du papier brun, de 18 pouces ½ de longeur sur 13 pouces de hault' (P.-L. Lacroix, 'Inventaire des dessins de Raphaël qui faisaient partie de la collection Jabach', *Revue universelle des arts*, i, 1855, p. 122).

the finished drawing was a network of faint lines which appear white against the chalk where the latter traverses the tiny furrow made by the stylus. Such stylus-lines appear, for example, on the studies for the *Charge to Peter*, and even on the offset at Windsor (*Figs.* 46–49), and of the two drawings in question now they appear only on the one at Chatsworth (Fig. 63).[39] The Haarlem version must therefore be a copy, and it is noteworthy that this copy reproduces those small *pentimenti* that were made in the original in chalk.[40] And so the full lesson to be learnt from this case is that if by connoisseurship alone we had concluded that the Haarlem drawing was not by Raphael, and if the Chatsworth version were unknown, we might so easily have fallen into a trap which the accidents of survival often set for the unwary, deducing that some other artist played a major part in the design of this work. We are still left with a judgement to make upon the primary version. It would seem very eccentric to see a hand at work different in its capacities and habits from the one that made the drawings for the *Charge to Peter*.

The Chatsworth drawing is a life-study of the same kind, and from the same creative stage, as the chalk-drawings for the *Charge to Peter*. It is clear, for example, that the central horseman was a model sitting on something other than a horse, and that the light outlines of the latter were added by Raphael from his imagination. Between this study and the missing Cartoon he must have drawn a new helmet for the horseman, added the sword and the longer tunic of this figure and of the running foot-soldier, and applied a slight compression to the relationship between these two figures. But the most interesting point is the survival, in the Cartoon and tapestry, of the character of the studio-models' features, which is comprehensible in this case where no different and specific characterization was required as it would be for a major personality such as an Apostle.

Three drawings by Raphael for the *Conversion of the Proconsul* (Pl. 26) provide evidence that his design-technique was not as simple or consistent as we might expect. The most important of these is one at Windsor that appears to be the *modello* (Fig. 65).[41] The fact that this drawing contains major *pentimenti*, the most drastic in the background architecture,[42] is not in itself surprising; nor is the fact that a number of changes were made in the Cartoon, principally in the generally more specific characterization of dress and feature (which, in the drawing, are still close to those of studio-models), but also by the insertion of an extra head, a portrait, in the group on the right.[43] The oddest quality of the drawing is its technique, distinct from that of the other surviving *modelli*, for it was at first a silver-point study on grey prepared paper, self-sufficient except that the white heightening was very probably executed at this stage and always intended. This technique, which we know from other drawings of the period,[44] was then comprehensively reworked with a delicate brown wash,[45] and then a reinforcement of outlines with pen and ink was begun but not taken very far—happily, since this stage is a little clumsy and is perhaps the work of an assistant. In other words the silver-point and white heightening technique began to be converted into that of the other *modelli*. The issue is complicated by the existence in the eighteenth century of a drawing now untraced, the technique of which did indeed conform to that of the other *modelli*;[46] it could be the case that this other drawing, perhaps a workshop product, was the true and final *modello*, *en suite* with the rest, and that the Windsor drawing is a proto-*modello*, of a kind not preserved but conceivably made for the other Cartoons. The reworking in pen and wash would then represent an abandoned attempt to transform the silver-point study into a *modello* of the usual kind. But this interpretation is hazardous, based as it is upon the assumption that the lost drawing was not a later copy. There is, in any case, another possibility to be considered. We have no right to assume that the creative technique was uniform throughout the series, for it might have been subject to a process of evolution through experience or even to vagaries of temper from one day to the next. The elaborate and painstaking silver-point drawing, incorporating very precise perspective construction, might, for example, represent Raphael's first solution to the production of *modelli*, superimposing on one sheet creative stages from space- and posture-definition to chiaroscuro-distribution that were to be separated and simplified in later examples. There is other evidence, to be considered shortly, of inconsistency of creative approach and there is also reason to believe, as we shall see, that the *Conversion of the Proconsul* Cartoon was one of the first to be begun. Present evidence seems to favour an alternative interpretation of this kind; the abandonment of the reworking in pen may be due to no cause more complicated than Raphael's feeling that his secretary was making a mess of his text, already sufficiently explicit.

A second silver-point drawing, in the Ashmolean Museum (*Fig*. 66), corresponds very closely with the statue of the unidentified goddess in the niche of the pier on the right of the tapestry (*Fig*. 23).[47] The drawing is made in the direction of the Cartoon, but nevertheless it was not made in the first place for that purpose; the figure is defined in the drawing as a caryatid and is almost certainly to be connected with the fictive statues of this form in the *basamento* (*c*. 1514–15) of the Stanza d'Eliodoro, each of which has echinus and abacus of the same proportion, and also a similar base. It is very characteristic of Raphael that he never wastes an invention, and in the context of his habits over his whole career the eventual adaptation of this design to the tapestry is no surprise, particularly when the quality of the invention is appreciated; for in spite of its convincing classicism the figure is not an imitation of any known antique statue, nor is it even the synthesis of motifs from several, but it is essentially novel and a demonstration of Raphael's deep penetration of the principles of classical figural composition. It has in this respect a purity that the caryatids of the Stanza d'Eliodoro do not possess, each being cast into a posture expressive of its characterization, and so the drawing probably represents not so much a rejected idea for one of them as an ideal archetype from which the series was developed. On the *verso* of the Oxford drawing is a hasty and admittedly unprepossessing pen-study of a herm (*Fig*. 67), probably made for the one to the right below the statue-niche in the tapestry; the direction is once more that of the Cartoon. Raphael's most informal and exploratory jottings in pen are, in fact, as casual as this one and there is no need to look for any other attribution.[48] This apparently insignificant study is important at least in one respect, that it represents a creative stage earlier than that of any other surviving auto-graph study for the Cartoons, and thus allows us to visualize the exploratory sketches with which Raphael must have begun in each case. And it helps to justify the rôle attributed to Penni in such a case as the Windsor drawing for the *Miraculous Draught* (*Fig*. 41), which is nothing if not legible.

Two drawings illustrate the stage of the *garzone*-studies in the evolution of the *Sacrifice at Lystra* (*Pl*. 38). The first to be considered is a silver-point study at Chatsworth by Raphael himself for the irate Paul (*Fig*. 69); clearly the drawing was made from a studio-model posed in suitable robes and the figure was not characterized in feature as the Apostle.[49] Another significant

42. The three columns in echelon were preceded in this drawing by a tabernacle drawn also in receding perspective.

43. It was the lack of this head in the drawing which originally led me (op. cit. in n. 6, p. 457) to agree with Fischel's conclusion (op. cit. in n. 6, p. 106) that it was made *for* Agostino's engraving (see above, n. 41), while disagreeing with his rejection of Raphael's authorship.

44. Compare, for example, Popham-Wilde, op. cit. in n. 4, No. 801, a landscape drawing of about the same date which is also grey (not buff) prepared paper, silver-point and white heightening; also the Chatsworth study for the *Sacrifice at Lystra* (*Fig*. 69, and below, n. 49).

45. The quality of this wash is disturbed by restorations; a confident attribution of the unrestored areas is inappropriate, but I see no reason why the wash should not be by Raphael.

46. M. Cochin, *Voyage d'Italie*, Paris, 1758, ii, p. 85: 'Florence . . . chez M. Martin, peintre Anglois . . . Elymas . . . frappé d'aveuglément par Saint Paul . . . lavé au bistre, ou avec un encre qui a jauni. Les contours sont tracés à la plume avec une belle fermeté' (attributed to Raphael). Passavant, op. cit. in n. 4, ii, p. 246, mentions another drawing of this subject 'grau in Grau' formerly in the collection of Ant. Rutgers.

47. Acquired 1965 and uncatalogued; silver-point on pale pink prepared paper; 146 × 98 mm. I have no doubt that the attribution to Raphael is correct. The connection between this study and the tapestry was kindly pointed out to me by Hugh Macandrew.

48. The scarcity of compositional studies in pen from these years necessitates some reserve; but the confused studies for the *Resurrection* altarpiece of *c*. 1513 on Ashmolean 559 *verso* (repr. by Forlani, in *Raffaello*, cit. in n. 18, ii, p. 401) offer several passages for comparison; perhaps the most convincing parallels are to be found in the architectural sketches for Saint Peter's, to be dated to the summer of 1514, on Uffizi 1973F (repr. K. Oberhuber, 'Eine unbekannte Zeichnung Raffaels in den Uffizien', *Mitteilungen des kunsthistorischen Institutes in Florenz*, xii, 1966, pp. 225 ff.). The Oxford sketch is in fact worked in two distinct inks, but I can see no reason to distinguish two hands.

49. Chatsworth, No. 730; pale violet-grey prepared paper, silver-point, white heightening; 228 × 103 mm.; from the Lely Collection. First described, so far as I know, by J. D.

Passavant, *Kunstreise durch England und Belgien*, Frankfurt, 1833, p. 250, with the correct identification; Crowe-Cavalcaselle, op. cit. in n. 4, ii, p. 306n. (as Raphael but, like Passavant, with a faulty description of the technique); S. A. Strong, *Reproductions of Drawings by Old Masters ... at Chatsworth*, London, 1902, p. 8, as Penni; omitted by Fischel, op. cit. in n. 6, but included in his 1948 monograph, cit. in n. 13, i, pp. 255, 269, 364 as Raphael, which now seems to be the unanimous opinion.

50. Santarelli Collection, No. 128; pen and brown ink, white heightening; 236 × 293 mm.; unpublished.

51. This *pentimento* was noticed by R. H. Smith, *Expositions of the Cartoons of Raphael, illustrated by photographs printed by Negretti and Zambra*, London, 1860, p. 74.

52. It would be rewarding to be able to trace the drawing seen by the younger Richardson (op. cit. in n. 14, p. 13) in the Cabinet Crozat: 'S. Paul tearing his garment, a sketch only; on the Rev. is a drawing of Alb. Dürer.' There is no inherent improbability in these attributions, since 1515 was the year in which Raphael sent a group of his drawings as a present to Dürer. The drawing formerly in the Praun Collection, Nürnberg (Passavant, op. cit. in n. 4, ii, p. 247; engraved by Prestel) is now in Budapest (67.66; buff paper, pen and black ink, grey wash, white heightening; 327 × 270 mm.); it is a copy, probably of the second half of the sixteenth century, apparently made after a version of the tapestry. A drawing by Perino del Vaga exhibited by E. Schickman, New York, 1968, No. 23 *verso*, was catalogued as a copy after a study for the arms of the *popa*; but in fact it is a copy after a lost life-study for the Louvre *Saint Michael* of 1517–18.

53. Grey prepared paper, silver-point, white heightening; 115 mm. diameter; from the collections of the Richardsons and Reynolds; included in several exhibitions of the Scholz Collection, but see especially *Drawings from New York Collections I: The Italian Renaissance* (catalogue by F. Stampfle and J. Bean), New York, 1965, No. 50. The same drawing appears to have been the model for the facsimile in C. Rogers, *A Collection of Prints in Imitation of Drawings ...*, London, 1778, i, No. 46. Passavant, op. cit. in n. 4, ii, p. 250, said that the drawing reproduced by Rogers was subsequently in the Roscoe Collection; but since he described the medium of the Roscoe drawing as pen and wash, and gave considerably larger dimensions (c. 203 × 216 mm.), it seems clear that he was in fact talking of a different one. His confusion was repeated by Ruland, op. cit. in n. 7, p. 253, Nos. 2–3, who put together a

difference between the study and the figure in the Cartoon is the omission from the latter of that part of its robe which, thrown over the left shoulder, falls quite naturally, if not necessarily, into view behind the right arm; no doubt Raphael felt that these folds would confuse those of Barnabas standing behind Paul, and no doubt, also, we have another example here of his willingness to sacrifice a point of realism for an aesthetically more satisfactory solution.

The second drawing, in the Uffizi, is only a copy and is, moreover, by an artist whose style was somewhat remote from Raphael's; nevertheless it is of great interest since it records, probably quite faithfully, a lost drawing for the whole of the right half of the Cartoon (*Fig.* 68).[50] Its status and veracity are established in the first place by the fact that the figures are a group of studio-models, and hence one may envisage an original drawing like that for the *Charge to Peter* (*Fig.* 47—but it cannot be assumed that Raphael's drawing was in this case also in chalk). Secondly, and conclusively, its status is confirmed by the principal postural difference between this group and the completed Cartoon which is in the foremost kneeling figure, the *victimarius*, intended at this stage to hold the horn of the bull in the left hand rather than the right; the sharply bent left arm seen in the drawing is also to be seen in the underdrawing of the Cartoon but was then cancelled and replaced by the straighter arm in one of the most important *pentimenti* to be made in the whole set.[51] There remain, of course, all the lesser differences that we should expect between this drawing and the Cartoon—differences of characterization and of detail in costume. But there are two major changes of considerable interest: one is the insertion, in the Cartoon, of a new head on the extreme right, which is the one that appears to be a portrait, perhaps of Cardinal Lorenzo Pucci, and the other is the lateral compression of the whole group, which is a process we have already observed at this evolutionary stage in others of the set. And in addition the change in the position of the second bull's head in the crowd, from three-quarter to side view, is worth noticing, partly because its first position seems more convincingly to allow for the existence of its body (the change was probably related to the late introduction of architecture immediately behind this group); but the change is interesting too because in this case the first position was more directly related to the probable prototype among antique reliefs, to be discussed later, and the same is true of the changing manner in which the kneeling *victimarius* grasps the bull's horns. These changes warn us once more against underestimating the flexibility of Raphael's mind, and his reasoning was indeed likely to have been complex. The first adjustment has all the appearance of one made for aesthetic reasons alone. But the second change, while having the obvious effect of bringing the representation of the ritual into line with the majority of ancient sculptural precedents, also has compositional implications; the earlier, raised, position of the arm would have been associated, in the whole composition, with a diagonal leading through the figure with the axe (the *popa*) towards Paul's head. No doubt this line of emphasis was intended by Raphael, but when he began to paint

photograph of the drawing now belonging to Janos Scholz and the Rogers facsimile, saying that both were made from a pen and wash drawing then (1876) in the Royal Collection at Dresden; since Ruland should have known the source of the photograph, the Scholz drawing may once have been in that collection, but

Müntz, op. cit. in n. 4, p. 18, also mentions a pen-drawing of this figure at Dresden (with an implied attribution to Giulio), while Fischel op. cit. in n. 13 (1948), p. 266, speaks of a 'detailed, not quite certain drawing from the Grahl Collection' (part of which, at least, was formerly in Dresden) and A. P. Oppé, 'Righ

the Cartoon he felt, perhaps, that he had misjudged its effect; and the misjudgement, in that case, was probably a consequence of the exclusion of the *popa* from the lost *garzone*-study.[52]

There exists only one traceable drawing related to the penultimate tapestry, *Paul in Prison* (*Fig.* 26); it is in the collection of Janos Scholz, New York, and it corresponds to the figure personifying the earthquake (*Fig.* 70).[53] The technique is the same as that of the Chatsworth study for Paul in the *Sacrifice at Lystra*, and there can be no doubt that the two drawings were made by the same hand at about the same time, but the function of the Scholz drawing is less clear. The figure is drawn from the antique, specifically from the *Coelus* or *Ouranos* in the *Judgement of Paris* relief of Villa Medici in Rome,[54] and Raphael's drawing preserves a detail from this source that is omitted in the tapestry and is inappropriate to the personification of the earthquake: the cloth or veil held over the head, symbolic in the relief of the vault of heaven. He drew with a ruler a base-line below the torso that is related neither to the antique relief's limits nor to those of the tapestry (but it could, perhaps, reflect an early idea for the relation of the figure to the lower frame); and even as he drew from the antique he had in mind another figure that holds a cloth between its raised hands, Michelangelo's *ignudo* to the right of Daniel on the Sistine ceiling. Thus the drawing is not a straight copy from the antique, nor was it demonstrably made for the lost Cartoon; it is, however, in the direction of that Cartoon, and it is certain that it was put to use there. The retention of doubt about its original purpose is only important because Raphael's creative process should not be forced into a pattern of greater simplicity than the evidence necessitates.[55]

Two drawings survive for the final composition, *Paul preaching at Athens* (*Pl.* 39). These are a red chalk *garzone*-study for several figures, and the *modello*, and our material is therefore similar in kind to that which survives for the *Charge to Peter*; the deductions to be drawn from it, however, are quite different. The *garzone*-study for the *Charge to Peter* is incomplete, but because it is cut in the form in which we know it most comprehensively, that is the offset at Windsor (*Fig.* 47), and not because any gaps are left in the figure-group. The *garzone*-study for *Paul preaching at Athens*, which is in the Uffizi (*Fig.* 71),[56] is incomplete in a different way. It is clear from a framing-line drawn with the stylus that the drawing prefigures the whole breadth of the composition intended for the Cartoon (*Pl.* 39), yet just as clear that the six figures could never have been conceived as the whole of the intended figure-group; they are, rather, selected 'anchor-figures' to which others will be added later. The creative technique recalls that which Raphael had used, about 1509, in the development of the *Massacre of the Innocents*, when certain anchor-figures were fixed at an early stage and in later drawings further figures were invented to unite them. One must suppose that the Uffizi drawing was similarly followed by studies in which the supplementary figures were invented to fill out the whole group. This additive process is unusual for Raphael as late as 1515–16; by that date it appears to be more usual for him to start with a rough sketch in which an entire figure-group is drafted. It must be said, however, that these drafts are extremely rare and the assumption that Raphael always made them in his later years would be unjustifiable. The Uffizi drawing seems to prove that there was no such consistency in his approach, even to the several parts of a single commission.

The relationship between the six figures seen in the Uffizi drawing is not radically changed in the final Cartoon except that the proportion between

and Left in Raphael's Cartoons', *Journal of the Warburg and Courtauld Institutes*, vii, 1944, p. 90, said that the Grahl drawing was in the direction of the Cartoon. It is difficult to make sense of these references, but they do seem to testify to the existence of a second, now untraceable, drawing for the same motif.

54. Springer, op. cit. in n. 4, ii, p. 270; E. Loewy, 'Di alcune composizioni di Raffaello', *Archivio storico dell'arte*, N.S. ii, 1896, p. 244; G. Kauffmann, 'Zu Raffaels Teppich "Paulus im Gefängnis" ', *Münchner Jahrbuch der bildenden Kunst*, Ser. 3, xv, 1964, p. 123; G. Becatti, 'Raffaello e l'antico', in *Raffaello*, cit. in n. 18, ii, p. 540.

55. Kauffmann, op. cit. in n. 54, publishes a large drawing (black chalk and white heightening) at Gosford House, in the collection of the Earl of Wemyss, which he believes to be by Giulio Romano; the drawing is, however, in the direction of the tapestry, and in my view Kauffmann has not satisfactorily explained the rôle it should play in the production of the Cartoon. Like him, I have not seen the drawing; but I do not believe in the attribution to Giulio and I think that this piece should be compared with the putative 'cartoon' for the *Transfiguration* at Badminton, which seems to be a late-Baroque imitation.

56. Uffizi 540E; red chalk over stylus (with which the figures are in part drawn nude); 276 ×419 mm.; the composition is reduced, inside these limits, to 254 × 388 mm. by stylus-lines on either side and below, presumably indicating the format required for the Cartoon; now classified as 'Scuola di Raffaello', but in my opinion autograph. For earlier judgements see Fischel, op. cit. in n. 6, p. 106, who himself believed it to be by a pupil of Andrea del Sarto; P. Kristeller, 'Marcantons Beziehungen zu Raffael', *Jahrbuch der K. preuszischen Kunstsammlungen*, xxviii, 1907, p. 206, as a copy after Raphael; Springer, op. cit. in n. 4, ii, p. 287, Müntz, op. cit. in n. 4, p. 18, Oberhuber, op. cit. in n. 1, p. 60, and A. Forlani-Tempesti, in *Raffaello*, cit. in n. 18, ii, p. 428, n. 163 (with less enthusiasm) as Raphael; see also P. Künzle, 'Raffaels Denkmal für Fedro Inghirami auf dem letzten Arazzo', *Mélanges Eugène Tisserant*, Vatican City, 1964, vi, p. 520. The three left-hand figures from Uffizi 540E were engraved in facsimile by Scacciati-Mulinari, ii, 1744, No. 74.

57. Inv. 3884 *recto*; buff paper, black chalk, pen and brown ink, brown wash, white heightening, squared in black chalk; the whole sheet 270 × 401 mm., the composition itself 252 × 325 mm. The background architecture is drawn upon pouncing, presumably transferred from another, now lost study. Early bibliography in Fischel, op. cit. in n. 6, p. 106, who himself classified it as a copy made for Marcantonio's engraving (B. xiv. 50.44—but it should be noted that there are many variations in the engraving, which must have been made from a different model; there is a careful analysis of this problem in Kristeller, op. cit. in n. 56, p. 206). On the *verso* of the Louvre drawing is a copy, by the same hand, of a lost study by Raphael for the *Disputa* (Fischel, *R.Z.*, No. 268). Uffizi 1217E (254 × 321 mm.) is a facsimile of the *modello* on the Louvre sheet (but omitting the white heightening and the squaring), *en suite* with 1216E which is a copy of the *Charge to Peter modello* (Louvre Inv. 3863); published by Scacciati-Mulinari, v, 1782, No. 42; correctly assessed by Kristeller, loc. cit.; Freedberg, op. cit. in n. 1, p. 274, accepted the two Uffizi copies, together with Louvre 3863, as originals by Penni but overlooked Louvre 3884, thus introducing considerable confusion.

58. I have made this calculation allowing for the cropping of the edges of the Cartoon (see below, p. 168); the measurement for the *palmo romano* that I have used is 233 mm. It may be noted that the same unit is marked on a similar vertical scale at the side of the first surviving study for Raphael's Baglione altarpiece of 1507: Ashmolean 529.

59. Stella, Duc d'Orléans, Coypel; see Mariette, ed. cit. in n. 6, p. 78; idem, *Abecedario*, iv, p. 298; and Dacier, op. cit. in n. 18, p. 135.

60. Already noted by Mariette, loc. cit.

figures and spatial intervals is revised, with the result that the absolute scale of the figures is considerably smaller in the Cartoon than the one envisaged in the drawing. And it is the drawing which is in this respect more similar to the other Cartoons, particularly to the *Conversion of the Proconsul* (Pl. 26). This detail is not insignificant since there is reason to believe, as we shall see later, that *Paul at Athens* is the later of these two Cartoons. The dispersion and diminution of the figures in *Paul at Athens*—and their supplementation by others to produce a richer, more complex grouping—is connected with a revision of the spatial structure; for the evidence of the Uffizi drawing, although incomplete, is sufficient to suggest that at that point Paul's platform was to be raised only one step above the level upon which the other figures stood, as in the *Sacrifice at Lystra* (Pl. 38) and also, more significantly, as in most of the antique reliefs of the *Adlocutio* type, which was not unnaturally Raphael's point of departure. In this initial configuration the confrontation between Paul and the Athenians would have been more immediate and more informal, the conversion of Dionysius a more emphatic part of the subject. In the final composition the dispersion of the figures into a spatial unit of greater amplitude and complexity isolates and emphasizes Paul more effectively and, while reducing the conversion of Dionysius to marginal significance, concentrates the meaning of the whole upon the theme of preaching. The evolutionary direction towards concentration upon the action of the Apostle is in principle like that which we observed in the case of the *Death of Ananias*, where the final result was focused more single-mindedly upon the theme of retribution and the marginal incident, the distribution of the goods of the Church, was less pointed than it would have appeared in the *modello*.

There is evidence, however, that the evolution of *Paul preaching at Athens* was not straightforward, but that the dispersion and spatial amplification were taken (in Raphael's judgement) too far in the *modello* and were re-adjusted in the Cartoon. The *modello* is a drawing in the Louvre (*Fig. 72*) which has not, hitherto, been taken very seriously;[57] but the fact that this drawing, in technique like the *modello* for the *Charge to Peter* (*Fig. 51*), did hold a real place in the creative process seems demonstrable from the evident signs of invention and use: *pentimenti* between the black chalk underdrawing and the finishing in pen, the marking out of the perspective construction along the lateral edges, and a scale on the right (also applied with compass-points along the top), the units of which, when enlarged to the dimensions of the Cartoon, would be *palmi romani*.[58] Moreover this drawing has the same provenance[59] as the *modello* for the *Charge to Peter*. Nevertheless there is an undeniable contrast in quality between the two drawings,[60] and the one for *Paul at Athens* could not be attributed to Raphael himself; it is probably by Penni. But the conclusion should not be that this drawing is a copy, but rather that not all the original *modelli* were made by Raphael himself. And this conclusion is not without interest, for one sees that one of the few perspectival faults in the Cartoons, the failure to turn the capitals of the Doric temple with its annular entablature (a fault unimaginable as originating in the mind of a practising architect), is made in the *modello*.

There are several minor changes between the *modello* and the final Cartoon, such as the omission of the figures on the balcony of the temple and the introduction of a column seen through the arch behind Paul's head. But the principal change is the one already mentioned, the slight reduction, once more, of the amount of described space. This adjustment is effected partly by trimming the composition on the right, and proportionally a little less below, and partly also by shifting to the right the whole group (including the statue of Mars) in front of Paul and his steps. And by thus eliminating the open space on the right the adjustment corrects an impression inescapable in the *modello*, that Paul's address was rather poorly attended.[61]

It is obvious that the graphic evidence that happens to survive is insufficient in quantity for a coherent and detailed analysis of the creative technique applied to Raphael's unusual task. If it allows one conclusion, however, it is that the technique was not consistent throughout. This is not in itself a disturbing conclusion. The creative mind does not aspire to the same virtues as the historical—that is to say, reconstructive—mind, and the latter usually operates most erroneously, and most ahistorically, when it fails to observe the distinction. We aspire to consistency and tidiness; but unprejudiced observation of artists at work suggests that few of them share our interest and (as in the present case) there is no reason for them to do so. The general rule to be deduced from the best documented cases is that the onus of proof lies upon the historian who wishes to reconstruct a tidy situation. Raphael's pragmatism in the invention of the Cartoons, strongly implied by this survey of the drawings, is, however, more than a proof of this negative point. The positive implication is that we have to deal not with a production-line but with the master's pervasive and persistent intervention, modifying, improvising, exercising judgement upon opportunities and results as they arose. This study of the drawings suggests, furthermore, a fresh approach to a somewhat vexed question, which is the chronological sequence of the Cartoons.

The problem of sequence has been approached so far, it must be admitted, in a rather unsophisticated manner; and it is probable that the question that has been asked and answered is an unreal one. Different techniques of stylistic analysis have produced slightly different sequences; to do them justice it must also be added that these recent arguments have been presented tentatively. In one the yardstick, inspired by a phenomenon observable in Michelangelo's Sistine ceiling, was increasing scale of figures, both absolutely and in relation to the space in which they are placed.[62] The result was to place the *Miraculous Draught* (*Pl.* 1) near the beginning of a series and the *Conversion of Saul* near the end (*Fig.* 20), with *Paul preaching at Athens* and the *Conversion of the Proconsul* (for example) in between and in that order. It is not very obvious that this argument works, even within its own rules; and the example of the Sistine ceiling is of doubtful value since chronology in that case is not a unique explanation of changing scale, uncomplicated by other considerations such as a planned effect over the length of the ceiling always envisaged by Michelangelo. In any case there is one indication that the argument, when applied to the Cartoons, is fallible, and another that the result is in fact wrong. As we have already seen, the development during the evolution of *Paul at Athens* was towards a lesser density of figures in relation to space, and towards a smaller absolute scale. And the *priority* of the *Conversion of the Proconsul* over *Paul at Athens* is indicated by a detail only observable in X-ray photographs. The portrait finally painted in the first of these two Cartoons—the head in the rear of the group on the right (*Pl.* 28) —was initially very differently characterized (*Pl.* 33); the displaced portrait, however, reappears in the underpainting of *Paul at Athens* (*Pl.* 46) and is developed into the head which may or may not represent Leo X (*Pl.* 40)— the identification does not matter in this context. The direction of the translation of this head seems quite clear and it is in fact one of the very few clues that we have to the reconstruction of an order of execution.

Another set of stylistic criteria produced a somewhat different result. A

61. A number of untraced drawings should be noted: (i) a drawing attributed to Raphael, formerly in the collection of Christina of Sweden, later in that of Pope Clement XI (V. Vittoria, *Indice dell'opere di Raffaello*, 1703, Windsor MS. H.H.C., p. 15) (ii) Another (without attribution) in the inventory of the Earl of Arundel, Tart Hall, 1641 (Lionel Cust, 'Notes on the Collections formed by Thomas Howard, Earl of Arundel', *The Burlington Magazine*, xx, 1911–12, p. 234) (iii) One brought from Italy to France in 1754, and acquired by the Duc de Tallard; damaged, but Mariette (*Abecedario*, iv, p. 302) thought it superior to Louvre 3884 *recto*; later acquired by Silvestre (iv) A wash-drawing, with white heightening, formerly in the collection of Giulio Cesarei, Perugia (B. Orsini, *Guida . . . per . . . Perugia*, Perugia, 1784, p. 244) (v) Another, without heightening, formerly in the Neyman Collection, Amsterdam (1776 Sale Catalogue, cit. in. n 29, No. 681): 'Saint Paul prêchant à Ephèse: de même grandeur que l'estampe de M. Antoine; à la plume & au bistre' (acquired by Basan).

62. J. White and J. Shearman, 'Raphael's Tapestries and their Cartoons', *The Art Bulletin*, xl, 1958, pp. 321–2; see also L. Dussler, *Raffael: kritisches Verzeichnis der Gemälde, Wandbilder und Bildteppiche*, Munich, 1966, p. 116 (English edition, London and New York, 1971, p. 106).

63. Oberhuber, op. cit. in n. 1, pp. 52–53.

64. Forlani-Tempesti in *Raffaello*, cit. in n. 18, ii, pp. 411–12. The scepticism of L. Becherucci, ibid., i, p. 180, about these 'chronologies' should not go unrecorded.

65. It should, perhaps, be explained that the Viennese parody included a refinement that does not apply in our case: that the beads are punctuated at regular intervals by Paternosters, or Major Works.

66. Shearman, op. cit. in n. 1, esp. pp. 165, 172.

more complex analysis of drapery-style, light, colour and spatial construction led to the conclusion that the *Death of Ananias* and *Paul at Athens* were among the earliest Cartoons and the *Miraculous Draught* and the *Conversion of the Proconsul* among the latest.[63] This result, like the first, is in conflict with the evidence of the X-rays. The weakness of the argument seems to be derived from unstated but underlying assumptions that the appearance of works of art is conditioned only, or perhaps predominantly, by the passage of time and that each should be placeable in an autonomous, unidirectional and predictable stylistic development. This is an illusion that may have the appearance of truth in the case of poorly documented artists, but not otherwise. When we know a lot of facts we find the logic of a stylistic development much more difficult to define, and we are forced to acknowledge that what we call style, in this sense, is conditioned by factors additional to the passage of time—in a case like ours, for example, by subject-matter, position, and the diversity inherent in several formal prototypes.

A third approach to the problem, by distinguishing an 'early' group of naturalistically more descriptive Cartoons from a later group, more grandiose in the classical sense, led to the result that the *Death of Ananias* was among the latest, but this attempt was consistent with the others in placing the *Conversion of the Proconsul* after *Paul at Athens*; and for this reason, like the others, it seems to have failed.[64] The criteria leading to this decision are open to the same objections as are those of the second argument, and seem, additionally, to be somewhat more arbitrary.

All these approaches to the problem are based upon what used to be known in Vienna as the Rosary Fallacy: that is, the assumption that an artist's works follow each other in orderly sequence like beads on a string, each complete before the next is begun.[65] This is another illusion which functions rather well for the artists we know least about. The reality is rarely, if ever, like this. We have to adapt our techniques, once more, to the probability of a more untidy situation in which the thinking about, and execution of, separate and even several works overlap. It would seem, on reflection, that this is particularly to be anticipated in the case of the Cartoons, and that here an orderly production-line is the least likely of all processes. There is some reason to suppose that when Raphael had to produce sets of frescoes for the Vatican Stanze he made compositional drafts for the whole set before defining the invention and completing the execution of any one.[66] The good sense in such an approach is even more obviously applicable to a problem such as the composition of the ten Cartoons.

We cannot, of course, prove that Raphael worked up each of these compositions in drawings concurrently, nor do we need to work upon that extreme assumption. It is only necessary to remember that the design-process of several of them probably overlapped, which is in fact a more cautious hypothesis than the notion of a sequence of insulated creative acts—it is only necessary to remember this to realize that such a process will, effectively, eliminate much of the evidence of style-change subject to time upon which sequences have been argued, changes in spatial design, for example, or in figure-scale. If such elements in Raphael's style really were subject to unidirectional development, which may be doubted, their metamorphosis would become so confused by even a limited amount of concurrent work that we should have no hope of recognizing it.

The technical factor which forced Raphael, in the frescoes of the Stanze, to complete the execution of one part before beginning the next would not apply to the Cartoons which, like oil-paintings, could be begun, and laid on one side, taken up again and reworked at will. We have noticed enough significant *pentimenti* in the Cartoons to be able to assert that the inventive process, at least in its latest stages of modification and correction, was continuous between the drawings and the Cartoons; and nothing is more probable than the prompting of these modifications by the comparison of one Cartoon with another. Once again, we do not need the extreme assumption, imagining Raphael and his breathless pupils moving rapidly over ten enormous sheets of paper, adding a touch here and a touch there, working up the whole set at once; it is not certain, for example, that he had space in which he could do so. We need only to avoid that other frame of mind in which we imagine him proceeding from the invention to the completion of any one of them before beginning another; and then we see that it was almost certainly a mistake to pose the question of sequence in the first place. It is unlikely that there is anything so simple as an order to be worked out.

This conclusion does not mean that the passage of time—at the least about eighteen months, which in the flight of Raphael's career is a long stretch—had no effect on the appearance of the Cartoons. It means, on the contrary, that there are few ways in which we should expect to be able to discern that effect. It is possible to imagine certain types of style-change that could survive a moderate degree of overlapping work; they are unlikely to be matters normally settled in the design-stage, such as figure-scale or spatial character, but plausibly those associated with the execution in paint, particularly, for example, changes of formal definition or techniques that might reflect a maturing response to the unaccustomed task of designing for tapestry. We shall see, in another context, one such variation in approach which can be interpreted in relation to the passage of time. But the very process of deciding what, in principle, we might reasonably anticipate is itself sufficient to reveal the fragility of any resulting chronology, and to suggest that the whole exercise is better left in abeyance until some real evidence appears. It is not, in fact, a very important issue.

Among the less familiar of Raphael's problems when designing the Cartoons was the eventual reversal of the compositions in the tapestries, a reversal necessitated by the weaving technique then in use in Brussels.[67] But the novelty of the problem is easily over-stressed. Raphael, in fact, had valuable experience with two other media that posed the same problem: engraving, of course, and mosaic. He had probably been designing compositions to be engraved for about five years before he began the Cartoons. In many cases, certainly, he had made his drawings in the direction of the finished print and had left the problem of reversal to the engraver; but in the case of one of the most distinguished of his engraved designs, the so-called *Morbetto*, which may also have been his most recent when he began the Cartoons, it seems that the drawings were made in reverse.[68] The mosaics for the cupola of the Chigi Chapel in S. Maria del Popolo were made by a technique that entailed the reversal of the cartoons, probably by setting the tesserae face-down on the cartoon which was then peeled off when the mosaic was set in position; the process is not entirely clear, but at all events the point essential for our purpose is guaranteed by the existence of preparatory drawings in both directions. In addition to these experiences Raphael had made experiments with reversal that played an effective rôle in his inventive processes even for paintings—for *Madonnas* particularly—since about 1506.

At this point it should be made clear that in the case of the Cartoons the problem of reversal is in fact composed of three issues, distinct in kind and in difficulty of analysis. First there is the simple matter of ensuring that right

67. In this technique the weaver worked, looking through the horizontal warps at the Cartoon, upon that side of the tapestry which was destined to be the back.

68. B. xiv. 314.417; an undoubtedly autograph drawing at Windsor (No. 801), corresponding to the landscape, is in reverse; a drawing in the Uffizi, 525E, which might well have been the *modello*, is also in reverse, but its condition scarcely allows an assertion on its authorship (in the better-preserved parts I can see no reason to contradict the attribution to Raphael). The problem is additionally complicated by the loss of a drawing, attributed to Raphael, formerly in the collection of Christina of Sweden and later in that of Clement XI (Vittoria, MS. cit. in n. 61, p. 28). In my opinion the composition of the *Morbetto* should be dated 1514–15, and not earlier.

69. The former error led H. Wölfflin, 'Das Problem der Umkehrung in Raffaels Teppich-kartons', *Belvedere*, ix, 1930, p. 65, to the conclusion that the *Conversion of the Proconsul* was the only design more satisfactory in the Cartoon direction; another interpretation is suggested below, p. 132. The non-reversal of the *titulus* is also discussed below, p. 137. There are, so far as I can see, only two other unambiguous errors in the tapestries, in the 'relief' below the *Death of Ananias* (Fig. 17), where Michelangelo's *David* comes out the wrong way round, and in the 'relief' under the *Miraculous Draught* (Fig. 13), where the personified *Roma* wears her sword on the wrong hip. One may wonder about the gesture of the nearer soldier in the *Release of Paul* (Fig. 26), about the man on the left of the *Conversion of Saul* (Fig. 21) who beats the runaway horse with his left hand, and about the priest (*popa*) who swings the axe over his left shoulder in the *Sacrifice at Lystra* (Fig. 24), but it cannot be asserted that any of these actions is unnatural. In the *Sacrifice at Lystra* the placing of the knives on the right hip of the *victimarius* is illogical in a strictly realistic sense but amply justified by their consequent visibility; the same 'error' is committed, for the same reason, in some of the antique sacrificial reliefs. In the Vatican *Conversion of Saul* tapestry (Fig. 20) Saul's sword appears to be attached to his right hip, but in fact it is not; it lies detached on the ground, and the visibility of the attribute is again sufficient justification for its position. It is not possible to assert that the relationship of Christ and God the Father in the *Stoning of Stephen* (Fig. 18) contradicts Acts vii. 55–57 ('vidit ... Iesum stantem a dextris Dei'), since that text refers to the episode previous to the stoning, before Stephen was even taken out of the City.

70. For an extended discussion of the effects of reversal upon the Cartoon designs, and earlier bibliography on this problem, see Wölfflin, op. cit. in n. 69, and White-Shearman, op. cit. in n. 62, pp. 307 ff. I do not wish to disguise the fact that I now react against the perhaps too rigid analysis of appearances set out in our article; on the other hand I feel that Freedberg, op. cit. in n. 1, p. 275, over-reacts when he says that 'The belaboured problem of reversal between the Cartoons and Tapestries seems rather an invention than a problem of real historical or aesthetic significance' (it would be convenient if that were true, but I think it is not). I continue to think that the problem is a real one in both senses, but I now see it as being much more complex and I have less confidence in the possibility of a definitive solution.

71. In the article cit. in n. 62, pp. 309–10, we pointed out the dangers in a direct confronta-tion of a Cartoon with the corresponding tapestry, especially those arising out of the interpretations of the Cartoon by the weavers which introduce certain distortions of Raphael's intentions. The point still seems to me in general a valid one, but now I think that this issue, too, is more complex since some of the changes made by the weavers could have been foreseen by Raphael (see below, pp. 134 ff.).

72. A suggestion by Freedberg, op. cit. in n. 1, p. 274, should be recorded here: 'It may only be assumed, but the assumption seems reasonable, that the first *invenzioni* were in the sense of the Tapestries; counter-proofs of these, or tracings, would then have become the bases of detailed studies toward the Cartoons.' This suggestion is not irreconcilable with the evidence of any of the graphic material dis-

and left, under such headings as gesture, dress or lighting, are correctly resolved in the tapestry, which is the kind of success that depends upon concentration. And it is interesting, and perhaps satisfactory, that Raphael's concentration did occasionally lapse, as when he allowed Paul, in the *Conversion of the Proconsul*, and God the Father, in the *Stoning of Stephen*, to make their gestures with the left hand (*Figs.* 23, 18).[69] Second there is the necessary attention to the construction in reverse of all compositional or iconographical relationships to be established between each tapestry and its context; since each of these relationships could not have been made with anything less than complete awareness it is not surprising that he made no mistakes of this kind. More problematic is the third issue, assessing the psycho-physio-logical effects of reversal upon the way in which compositions are read—effects not only of shifting emphasis operative upon all formal elements in the work of art but also of modifying the dynamics of movement and ex-pression, and hence especially significant when applied to history-scenes. It is perfectly easy to demonstrate that reversal of a work of art does induce notable changes of this kind, to the extent that an artist may well prefer the mirror-image of his work, not necessarily because it is in any objective sense better but because it seems a fresh work. It is easy to observe differences, a little less easy to agree what those differences are (except when we deal with unsophisticated diagrams), and in most practical cases impossible to account for them.[70]

Again it may be helpful to identify three distinct issues. First it must be admitted that the texture of a work of art like one of Raphael's Cartoons is so rich and so dense that no technique of analysis can be sufficiently sophisticated to explain the effects of reversal upon it. Second it is impossible, probably, to isolate objective or universal effects from subjective or personal ones; and the psychology of reversal is much concerned with the experience and visual habits of the beholder. It would be in the highest degree impru-dent to assume that Raphael's reaction to the reversal of one of his Cartoons was the same as that of any one of us. Third there is an acute problem pro-duced by historical distance. Even if we could produce an analysis of such reversal that is convincing to us and agreeable between us, that analysis itself would have been much influenced by techniques, particularly psycho-logical techniques, that have been developed in the last hundred years. We cannot guess what terms of reference Raphael would have used in discussing the problem; we can only be certain that if he had any they would have been different from ours (it is important to put the point in this way since there is in fact no reason to suppose that he could have formulated any coherent ideas on the subject).

It may be that an admission of defeat in the face of these problems saves us from committing a serious error. Just as there may be no chronology to be worked out so, to be strict, there may be no reversal-technique which could properly be analysed. Raphael, as we have seen, was not an innocent in this matter. But the probability is that he exercised his judgement on an instinctive and empirical level, rather than a reasoning one, until he reached what was in his eyes the optimum result in formal and expressive terms. There can be little doubt that that optimum result was the one that appeared in the direction of the tapestry. It is perfectly legitimate to express a preference for the appearance of a Cartoon—legitimate but unimportant, unless it is believed that Raphael's effects were calculated to show to their best advantage in the contingent and provisional product rather than in the final one; but that belief would be so eccentric in relation to his outstanding sense of purpose and fitness to purpose that it would need powerful proof before it prevailed over common-sense, and such proof is altogether lacking. His intentions are surely accurately read in a mirror-image of the Cartoon.[71]

From this assumption it may seem natural to anticipate that he would take the safest route to that result, which would be by making all preliminary drawings in the direction of the tapestry and by reversing only the Cartoon. But all the preparatory drawings of which we have any record were made in the direction of Raphael's own product, the Cartoon. It may be that the decision to do so was influenced by a practical advantage, that the studies would then be of greater use to the painter, not always himself; and the decision could also be based on the confidence acquired in tackling successfully in this way, a year or so earlier, the design of some of the compartments of the Chigi cupola. He may then have checked the effects of reversal as he went along by making offsets from chalk-drawings, like the one for the *Charge to Peter (Fig. 47)*; this assumption, however, is not logically justified by that single piece of evidence, since there exist several offsets of other drawings that were made for paintings in which no reversal was entailed. It would seem, in any case, that what he most needed to check was the final *modello*, the technique of which did not, in any case that we know, allow reproduction in reverse in this way. He may simply have used a mirror at this stage and at all others.[72]

This problem, like several others, is interlocked with one which can no longer be evaded, that is the extent of Raphael's participation in the execution of the Cartoons. It has, of course, been much discussed, and it is probably true to say that all estimates that might be made in the abstract have, at one time or another, been made (and not infrequently as if they *were* made in the abstract); and it is encouraging to observe that the most extreme judgements have also been the least informed.[73] Recent opinion seems to have settled upon a moderate liberalism, that is to say a policy that allows Raphael a generous share of the work, but not too much. It must be stressed that such a conclusion is supported by very slight textual evidence—it is possible to exploit in this cause a near-contradiction between two statements by Vasari, one to the effect that Raphael painted all the Cartoons with his own hand, the other that Penni was very useful to him in painting a great part of the Cartoons, particularly their borders.[74] The conclusion is also often influenced, probably rightly, by another consideration independent of the actual appearance of the work, that is the great significance, in different respects, of the commission itself. But it is, and must always be, formed in the end by judgements of quality derived from a scrutiny of the works themselves. It is at this critical point that the apparent consensus of modern opinions turns out to be illusory, for each is in fact composed of separate judgements on particular Cartoons, or parts of Cartoons, that can astonish another observer. It would be vain to hope for a consensus at this level of particularization, and it is wrong in principle to put the question in such a

cussed above (except perhaps the pen-sketch for a herm at Oxford, *Fig.* 67, which must rate as an *invenzione*—but only of a detail); this is an hypothesis that deserves to be kept in mind, but it can hardly be the basis of an argument until some evidence for it appears.

73. E.g. Dollmayr, op. cit. in n. 37, pp. 253 ff. (who said they were entirely by Penni, with perhaps a little help from Giulio), who was rightly castigated by E. Gerspach, 'Les Actes des Apôtres: tapisseries d'après Raphaël', *Revue de l'art chrétien*, 5me série, xii, 1901, p. 100, with the observation that Dollmayr had not seen the Cartoons (a fact which, however, Dollmayr had admitted); Gerspach's own conclusion, hardly more helpful, was that they were so much repainted that attributions were arbitrary and in any case of little importance. Dollmayr's solution appears to be the basis for the oddly inadequate appreciation by H. Wölfflin, *Die klassische Kunst* (5th ed., Munich, 1912, pp. 108 ff.). One finds, however, the view that Raphael had nothing to do with the Cartoons, except to provide sketches, already in E. Platner and C. Bunsen, *Beschreibung der Stadt Rom*, II, ii, Stuttgart-Tübingen, 1834, p. 391. The opposite view, that they were entirely painted by Raphael, appears in one of the Vasari passages cited in the next note, but Vasari had not seen the Cartoons either; it is repeated occasionally by eighteenth-century writers, particularly by Englishmen such as Benjamin Ralph, who perhaps had a limited knowledge of Raphael's other work (*A description of the Cartons of Raphael Urbin in the Queen's Palace*, London, 1764, p. 1).

74. *Vita* of Raphael: 'Raffaello fece in propria forma e grandezza tutti di sua mano i cartoni coloriti, i quali furono mandati in Fiandra a tessersi . . .'; *Vita* of Penni: 'fu di grande aiuto a Raffaello a dipingere gran parte de' cartoni dei panni d'arazzo della cappella del papa e del concistoro, e particolarmente le fregiature' (the 'arazzi . . . del concistoro' are those known as the *Scuola nuova*, with scenes from the Life of Christ, with which Raphael was not directly connected). So far as I know the first equivalent assertion of Giulio's participation occurs in Edward Norgate's *Miniatura, or the Art of Limning* (MS. datable 1648–50), ed. M. Hardie, Oxford, 1919, p. 44: 'those incomparable Cartoni . . . soe rarely invented by the Divine Raphael d'Urbino, and done in water colours by him & Julio Romano'.

75. These X-rays were made by my colleague Stephen Rees-Jones, and I am much indebted to him for several discussions upon them. We hope to be able to reproduce the whole set in a separate publication.

76. It did confirm that the *Charge to Peter* is significantly the most damaged of the set, a judgement already expressed in 'A Description of the Cartoons at Hampton-Court' (Jonathan Richardson's notes re-worked), in *A Catalogue of the ... Pictures of George Villiers, Duke of Buckingham ...*, ed. H. Walpole, London, 1758, p. 68.

77. For this point I am indebted to the 1966 report of the restorers at the Victoria and Albert Museum, led by Norman Brommelle. Mr. Brommelle will shortly publish a detailed account of the restoration, and of the technical evidence then assembled, in *Studies in Conservation*, and the reader is referred to that account. But two points are necessary in this discussion and Mr. Brommelle has kindly allowed me to anticipate the publication of his findings: (i) the medium may be likened to a gouache or distemper, in that the pigments are bound with an animal glue or size, and (ii) there is no evidence of an underpainting in a different technique such as the supposed brown wash so often mentioned in earlier descriptions of the Cartoons.

78. Early restorations of the Cartoons are noted in Chapter V, below, pp. 147, 149. Another kind of flaking is due neither to the thickness of impasto nor to damage by creasing or folding of the paper, but to the failure of the underpaint to adhere to the painted lines with which background architecture was first marked out (perhaps with some acidic or greasy medium); an example illustrated here is the head ('Leo X') from *Paul preaching at Athens* (*Pl.* 46). The same characteristic is to be found in the *Death of Ananias*.

79. For example the highlight on the nose of the right-hand beggar in the *Healing of the Lame Man*; here the light comes from behind the head and in the underpainting the face, including the nose, was cast in shadow with the light catching only the projection of the eyebrow.

way that it invites simple answers, as if there were insulated areas of responsibility that could be identified and classified. The texture of the works is again, in this sense, too complex for that approach. What can usefully be attempted is a demonstration that there is visual evidence of collaboration, and then an approximate assessment of its nature. This attempt is particularly justified, and even mandatory, because there is a quantity of visual evidence that has not yet been used, because it is entirely new.

The new material now available for a review of this problem is provided by a set of some sixty X-ray photographs taken during a recent restoration campaign.[75] It must be stressed that, although this material is rich as to quantity and superb in quality, in no case does it cover even so much as ten per cent of a Cartoon, and that, although the selection of details for radiography does provide revealing evidence for our problem, it was not in fact made with that purpose in mind. The survey covered, in the main, a characteristic selection of heads and its primary purpose was to document condition.[76] There is only incidental coverage of drapery and limbs, virtually none of architecture or landscape, and none at all of animals. Thus when we use this material we are in the position of a statistician interpreting a sample, which is, moreover, a sample from a survey directed at a question different from his. There is one other introductory point to be made. The biggest surprise lies in what these X-rays do not show: not the repainting of restorers (probably because their pigments had no constituent of the radiographically-opaque white lead), and not the final original paint-layer, which is what we see with the naked eye. It is the first blocking-in, or underpainting, that is revealed because it is so much more dense than the final layer and not because it is different in chemical character.[77] As a simple illustration of this point we may look at the head of the young mother on the left of the *Healing of the Lame Man* (*Pls.* 15, 18). It is characteristic of many other heads in that the most heavily impasted areas, the strongest highlights, have flaked, and in this case the flaking amounts to a total loss on the forehead and nose; the losses have been compensated by seventeenth-century (and possibly eighteenth-century) repainting which is invisible in the X-ray photograph.[78] Fortuitously, as will be explained in the next Chapter, the final outlines of all forms were pricked at a later date, and the pricking shows as strings of black spots on the X-ray; but the final painted surface of a form, where it differs considerably from the underpainting, does not register except very faintly in certain cases. In the head in question the hair was much extended at the back (*Pl.* 15), and its final outline may be read in the pricked line but the body of the painted form itself cannot be seen. An even clearer case is the head, perhaps that of Leo X, to the left of *Paul preaching at Athens* (*Pl.* 46); the eventually invisible ear of the underpainting is much in evidence in the radiograph whereas the large *pentimenti*, the addition of the long flap to the cap and the broadening of the profile to the right are barely discernible as painted forms and the final shape of the head is principally marked by the pricking. In other cases even quite prominent highlights visible to the naked eye are invisible in the X-ray, not because they have flaked or been restored but because they belong only to the thin final layer of paint and were not envisaged at the moment of the first blocking-in.[79]

Looking through this material, which is, then, substantially a wholly new experience of the Cartoons, one is very forcibly reminded that when a discussion turns to differentiating 'hands' it does in fact deal with minds. There are a number of minds at work here, and they have distinct capacities, quantitatively and—partly as a consequence—qualitatively, which allow some degree of classification. There is first of all an outstanding, indeed breathtaking painter who has an extraordinary range of expression. He has no single, uniform style but a spectrum of style, marked always by absolute assurance, clarity in the instantaneous translation of idea into image, and sensitivity of such amplitude, and so essentially visual, that it is better seen than described. There was only one artist in the workshop of this stature and that was Raphael himself. He paints women, like the two mothers in the *Healing of the Lame Man (Pls.* 15, 19), with a sense of noble and substantial beauty (both ideal and real), with emotion in his mind and the capacity to describe it in his hand; he paints them, too, with great sensitivity to light, and by light he describes the subtlest movement of skin-surfaces and the liquid flow of their hair. In an altogether different frame of mind he characterizes with ferocious acuity the cripples in the same Cartoon and Ananias in the next one, distorting their features with a wholly convincing freedom born of absolute control and a sovereign imagination. One of these vivid heads is that of the cripple seized in a moment of ecstatic faith in the *Sacrifice at Lystra (Pl.* 37); on such occasions the immediacy of Raphael's vision is expressed in brushwork so loaded and so fluent that the paint drips down the paper, and where the drip stops, and dries, it flakes. The spectacular fury of creative energy in such underpainting marks another extreme of his range. Then in the same fluent vein but with contrasting, tender, feeling he paints Barnabas on the left of the *Conversion of the Proconsul (Pl.* 31): a less sensational performance, but a study of the profile of the head reveals on the one hand the rapidity of realization and the economy of means, on the other hand the remarkable complexity and completeness of the information, insistently descriptive of situation, form and expression.

On the opposite side of the *Conversion of the Proconsul* the head of the blinded Elymas *(Pl.* 27) marks the extreme of sharpness and boldness: simple at first sight, it is nevertheless the product of a mind deeply informed of physiognomy and concentrated with marvellous sculptural effect upon the shaping of the eye-socket. Where the light is direct and strong the contrasts are stark; but where the light glances over the temple, or the cheek, the modelling is as *pastoso* as that of the women in the *Healing of the Lame Man (Pls.* 15, 19). Around Elymas, however, are hands of contrasting appearance and quality; they are inarticulate in form, tedious in technique, minimally informative of light or texture, and they are the product of a mind the simplicity of which was involuntary. One of these hands belongs to the background group on the right, and within the heads of this group there is undoubtedly a certain variety of technique *(Pls.* 32, 33), but it seems that they are all by the same artist, and the capacities and range of this man are very different from Raphael's. His power to describe structure, light, emotion or anything else is inadequate to the task and—as if he knew it— his approach is timid. We find the same weakness in the heads next to the young mother by Raphael on the left of the *Healing of the Lame Man (Pl.* 17) and again in the deacons distributing alms on the left of the *Death of Ananias (Pl.* 25).[80] The artist may be Raphael's senior assistant Penni, for his shortcomings are like those we see in the flaccid grisailles under *Parnassus* in the Stanza della Segnatura and in the subsidiary, less expressive and sometimes ridiculous parts of the *Repulse of Attila*.

Another, more impressive, character is revealed in the heads of Dionysius and Damaris *(Pls.* 42, 43) in *Paul preaching at Athens*. This man had a capacity for describing solid structure almost comparable with Raphael's; but the result is not a sensitive and complex structure, with regard to outline or to

80. These heads are not, in fact, the worst revealed by the X-rays. The background head on the left of the *Conversion of the Proconsul*, against the oblique pier, is by an artist (Pellegrino da Modena?) who attempted bold blocks of light and shade but was quite unable to make them describe a coherent form, or even an effect of light itself.

surface, but it is simple. Simple, also, is the expression, and very limited the capacity to describe an effect or even a direction of light, as if the construction of form monopolized all his attention and exhausted his talents. The measure of his limitations, certainly less disastrous than those of the colleague who might be Penni, is clear when we compare these two heads with the final results in the Cartoon (*Pl.* 44). The head of Damaris acquires grace and coherence (the transformation of the rather ugly mouth and jawline of the underpainting is remarkable) and, what is more important, it acquires a trembling subtlety of surface and emotion and a continuous rhythmical energy in the hair which combine wonderfully into an expressive unit and which together make the underpainted head look wooden. The transformation of the head of Dionysius is essentially similar: a slightly less obvious accession of emotion, rather a refinement and greater precision, but a more extensive reorganization of the effect of light which becomes a great deal more descriptive of situation, texture and form. These are qualitative differences of a kind that are not found in the heads begun and finished by Raphael. The capacities of this second principal assistant are like those of the executant of the *Battle of Ostia* in the Stanza dell'Incendio, painted at about the same time and generally attributed to Giulio Romano.

The elevation of quality in the finished result is also illustrated by the two heads on the left of the *Death of Ananias* (*Pl.* 25), underpainted most probably by Penni. On the other hand this situation is far from universal. The subsidiary heads in the *Healing of the Lame Man* (*Pl.* 18) and in the *Conversion of the Proconsul* (*Pl.* 28) are not much improved in the completed Cartoons. What we may say is that the sample of sixty radiographs provides no instance of a drop of quality as work progressed; on the contrary they suggest most strongly that Raphael's share in the work was greater at the end of the executive process than at the beginning, or in other words that he took over the finishing of some of the more important parts which had been blocked-in by his assistants. There are even a few cases where his intervention can be seen during the underpainting itself: a more complex situation and necessarily more difficult to assess but nevertheless logically related to the previous conclusion. An example is the head of John in the *Charge to Peter* (*Pl.* 10). It should, perhaps, be stressed again that the final paint-layer is barely recorded in this plate (only the ghost, for instance, of the hair dropped to the shoulders), and that the modifications that are clearly visible are made in the underpainting; and it may be remembered that this is one of the heads the inclination of which was slightly changed between the *modello* and the final stage of the Cartoon. In the radiograph there seems to be a real contrast between the timid shaping of the eye-socket or the pedantic drawing of the hair, on the one hand, and the bold correction of the profile and the subtle, *pastoso*, modelling of cheek and ear on the other. The first blocking-in of this head may have looked very like what one sees in the right background of the *Conversion of the Proconsul* (*Pl.* 32), while the repainting has the same quality as the mother on the right of the *Healing of the Lame Man* (*Pl.* 19).

The radiographs illustrate changes of a different kind, arising from problems left unresolved in the drawings. A most interesting example occurs in the *Healing of the Lame Man* (*Pl.* 12). Just beyond the left-hand foreground column is a group of three male heads, one covered with a hooded cape, one almost in profile looking down at the miracle, one behind and turned towards Peter; this last head, the nearest to the column, appears in the copies of preliminary drawings (*Figs.* 55, 56, 58), but turned this way and that, once wearing the hood, and never with the form or posture shown in the Cartoon. The X-ray of this area (*Pl.* 16) shows the nearer head, which had never been a problem, underpainted in a masterly manner by Raphael himself, but it shows no trace of underpainting of the background head against the column; it is landscape that we see in its place, and the pricking of the outlines and the ghost of the final painting of this head, improvised in the finishing process. There was a different kind of indecision over the head of the lower and nearer lictor to the left of the throne in the *Conversion of the Proconsul*; in the *modello* (*Fig.* 65) the head was lit from the left, in the Cartoon (*Pl.* 30) it is cast in shadow and lit by reflected light from the right. The X-ray (*Pl.* 29), which shows in a most dramatic way the firm, commanding and expressive technique of Raphael, shows also a total confusion of lighting which is the result of the change in its direction made during the execution of the underpainting.

The X-rays also reveal one very general change during the progress of the work. The underpainted heads are frequently strongly characterized in physiognomy and expression, yet the characterization becomes more acute, and also more refined, in the final painting. It is a centrifugal tendency away from compactness and consistency and towards variety and particularization; the women become more feminine, more delicate in feature, while the men acquire creases and wrinkles of flesh, they sprout warts and whiskers and eyebrows. Hair and beards throughout become strikingly more luxuriant, whether the underpainting is by Raphael (as in the cripple in the *Sacrifice at Lystra*, *Pl.* 37) or by an assistant (as in the case of Dionysius, *Pl.* 42). The process may be defined as a polarization of each head towards the ideal of its type, for the heads of beggars are just as ideal as those of Christ, or of the young women. The idealism and simultaneously—by some kind of pictorial magic—the realism and the variety are more richly described than in the underpainting, and the difference is not simply due to different degrees of finish but above all to an amplification, improvised with great painterly freedom, of the more constrained characterization and sculpturally more compact form of the underpainting. The latter is in general closely related to the form invented in the drawings.[81]

The sample of areas radiographed is insufficient for detailed and definitive conclusions as to the extent of the responsibility of this hand or that one, and the insufficiency may appear a blessing when we remember that connoisseurship heads the table of inexact sciences. They do, however, provide evidence which is as conclusive as visual evidence is ever likely to be that there are several hands at work. If the one here isolated as Raphael's is correctly identified they show his presence in about equally extensive measure in each Cartoon, and they show him responsible—or taking over responsibility—for the most prominent or expressively most essential parts. They provide no comfort for the very common view that his personal contribution was more restricted in some Cartoons than in others, and they make utterly redundant the extremist view that there were some Cartoons among those that survive which he left wholly in the charge of his assistants. On the contrary the sample suggests a remarkably unrelaxed involvement; to this extent the evidence of the X-rays supports the judgement of many, made with the naked eye in front of the finished works, but puts that judgement on a more secure base. The greater clarity of the evidence of the X-rays is almost certainly due to the fact that they record a simpler situation, of independent responsibility for different areas more nearly exclusive in the underpainting than in the finished Cartoons. It must be regretted that we are not better informed about those parts where the assistance of the brilliant

81. This is particularly true of a comparison between the X-rays of the *Death of Ananias* and the two prints after what appears to have been the *modello* (see above, p. 100); it is not the case, however, with the head of Dionysius in *Paul at Athens*, where the final painting restores the extent of the beard decided upon in the *modello* (*Fig.* 72) but restricted in the underpainting (*Pl.* 42).

82. Since Passavant, op. cit. in n. 4, ii, p. 231, and J. Hübner, 'Qui a colorié les Cartons de Raphaël pour les fameuses Tapisseries?', *Revue universelle des arts*, xxii, 1865–66, p. 316, there have been repeated references to a passage in Vasari's *Vita* of Giovanni da Udine in which Giovanni is said to have worked on the Cartoons; I can find no such passage, and I think that Passavant must have misread Vasari's statements (*Vite*, vi, p. 555) about Giovanni's cartoons for two other sets of tapestries woven in Flanders, the *Giuochi de' putti* and the *Grottesche*. Nevertheless the suspicion that he did assist Raphael in, for example, the *Miraculous Draught of Fishes* (already voiced by Quatremère de Quincy, *Histoire de la vie et des ouvrages de Raphaël*, Paris, 1824, p. 316, and Platner-Bunsen, op. cit. in n. 73, II, ii, p. 403) seems well founded and is reinforced by the drawing published here, *Fig. 40*. It is worth considering Pellegrino da Modena as a fourth assistant at work on the Cartoons (see, for example, n. 80, above); the possibility is suggested by the similarity in handling between the small background groups of figures in the *Miraculous Draught* (*Fig. 33*) and in Pellegrino's *Repentance of Hermogenes* in the Serra Chapel, S. Giacomo degli Spagnoli (c. 1518–20). This artist was in Rome by February 1515 and in later work shows himself specifically familiar with the Cartoons (see B. F. Davidson, 'Pellegrino da Modena', *The Burlington Magazine*, cxii, 1970, pp. 78 ff.).

83. The Twelfth Discourse (ed. R. Fry, London, 1905, p. 336).

84. The Sala di Costantino, on the decoration of which Raphael had made considerable progress before his death, was a ceremonial room that offered comparable challenges and opportunities; and in my view his conception of that decoration was as dense and rich in texture as that of the Cartoons.

specialist Giovanni da Udine is particularly to be suspected, in the animals, birds and fish, and perhaps in some minor sections of landscape.[82]

In this discussion of attribution and quality the necessity for particularization, that is to say the recognition of the uniqueness of the problem under examination, is perfectly obvious. The same guiding principle should be observed in the discussion of another major issue to which we must now turn: the visual sources of the Cartoon-designs. For this problem is indeed highly particularized, not only by the personality of Raphael himself but also by the nature of this unique commission.

The ever-quotable Joshua Reynolds said that Raphael's 'known wealth was so great, that he might borrow where he pleased without loss of credit'.[83] But this formula, however neat, is still a disguised apologia which covers the embarrassment felt by many of those who most love Raphael's work. In any case he did not borrow: he plundered, selfishly. It would be better to follow Reynolds's reasoning farther, and to say that Raphael's riches included the accumulated capital of a vast range of visual experiences, and that he had no inhibitions, not even that of being found out, against investing this capital for profit in his own enterprises. There is no mistaking, thereby, the essential novelty of those enterprises. The point is clearest when the exploitation is most ruthless, or unashamed, as in the Brera *Sposalizio* of 1504; the confrontation of this painting with its prototypes in Perugino's paintings and Francesco di Giorgio's architectural studies reveals first of all an utterly new artistic personality whose ambitions of aesthetic and expressive perfection did not happen to embrace novelty of form with great enthusiasm. At this early date Raphael may already have sensed that a solution to the problem of communication was facilitated by the use of established forms. But the allusive value of quotation, in the manner of poetry, is not the only intention; one may feel in such a case as the *Sposalizio* that he intends to surpass his models, and this necessarily entails, again in the manner of poetry, their recognition. At other times he may use a motif as so many other artists will— including Michelangelo—precisely because it is unsurpassable as a solution to his present problem; and it must also be admitted that he will plunder, at times, to supply a lack in his own capacities, or simply in order to learn how to do things. If the impression that his dependence upon precedent was exceptional is a true one, to put it into just perspective it is only necessary to recall that no artist's works were more profitably plundered by others.

And yet it is still insufficient to attempt to define the unique personality in such a way. There is no such thing as a typical work by Raphael, and no such thing as a typical approach on his part to artistic problems. His strength is largely derived from a peculiar and immensely flexible pragmatism. And the commission for the Cartoons presented him with opportunities, circumstances and obstacles unlike those of any other of his tasks. He could not fail to be struck by the implications of the destination of his designs, the *Capella papalis*; for in his world there could be no more critical and informed audience for his performance and it was, moreover, a captive audience to an unusual degree, with a lot of time on repeated occasions for scrutiny and interpretation.[84] The character of the place makes plausible an unusual sophistication, a kind of layered depth, in programmatic meaning; similarly he had every incentive to demonstrate on the one hand his command of tradition, which one might call the state of mind of the *Capella papalis*, and on the other his virtuosity in the positive use of quotation—a demonstration the more effective and functional if its complexity revealed itself only through long familiarity. It is a fact, at least, that this is the way in which his performance does work. To suggest that its apparent inexhaustibility was carefully planned may seem ambitious within the terms of the visual arts of his period, but that idea may be taken for granted in literature and in Raphael's case it would be absurd to imagine a barrier between the ideas of one art and the other. It would also be absurd in Michelangelo's case. And thus it is not accidental that the only painted work of the Renaissance comparable with the Cartoons in depth of programmatic meaning and formal reference is precisely Michelangelo's ceiling-decoration in the Sistine Chapel.

In order to illustrate these points for the Cartoons it is not necessary to force comparisons with potential sources; the difficulty with formal reference as with programmatic meaning is rather to make the right choice among the rich material that presents itself. In some cases, here again, it may be wrong to make a choice; we may be nearer the truth, if apparently less precise, when we set a design against a whole tradition, or a motif against a long sequence of repeated use, for it would be arrogant to assume that Raphael was less aware of these things than we are. Let us consider as an example the *Conversion of the Proconsul* (*Pl.* 26). The action is cast in a pattern which is already exemplified by Giotto's *Trial by Fire before the Sultan* in the Bardi Chapel in S. Croce;[85] but among the many derivatives of that composition there is one that comes closer to Raphael's, that is Ghirlandaio's fresco of the same Franciscan subject in the Sassetti Chapel in S. Trinita. The near-identity of floor-pattern between the Cartoon and Ghirlandaio's fresco may suggest that the latter was an effective prototype, but this conclusion does not exclude the probability of Raphael's knowledge of and reference to an established tradition in which Giotto's and Ghirlandaio's are only two outstanding examples. From a judgement-formula which is primarily Tuscan his mind seems to have passed to a particular painting in a related Venetian tradition, Sebastiano del Piombo's *Judgement of Solomon* now at Kingston Lacey (or, just conceivably, to a common prototype), from which he took one of the lictors who stands on the steps to the left of the throne.[86] And yet at the same time Raphael's subject prompted a recollection of another Florentine fresco, Filippino's *Saint Philip exorcizing a Devil* in the Strozzi Chapel in S. Maria Novella. A relationship in this case is less evident in the general cast of the composition than in individual ideas: the reactions of the group of onlookers, their placing against a pier (deep in space but also framing it) and against an enfilade of three columns, and perhaps in the gesture of Paul too. However, Raphael, when he conceived his Paul, was probably as clear as we are that he was inspired by a sequence of such powerfully gesturing columnar saints in the work of Giotto (the *Raising of Drusiana* in the Peruzzi Chapel), Masaccio and Filippino (both in the Brancacci Chapel). Similarly we cannot, and probably should not, isolate one particular precedent for the figure behind Elymas, turning forward with hands raised, from a sequence that runs from Giotto (the *Raising of Drusiana* again) through Leonardo (the *Adoration of the Magi*) to Michelangelo (the *Battle of Cascina*); on the other hand the context of the motif, in relation to the figure affected by the miracle and to the one that performs it, suggests that he did recall, among other things, the work that stands at the head of these sequences: Giotto's *Raising of Drusiana*.

Out of this confusing situation there comes the impression that there is something very positive about Raphael's process of recall; it is controlled by associations of meaning and is selective in a purposive sense. He uses his visual experiences, with the gift, clearly, of an extraordinary memory, as an epic poet uses his reading. The letter which Raphael addressed to Leo X in

85. The comparison was already made by Wölfflin, op. cit. in n. 73, p. 114.

86. Nothing is known of the early history of this painting, which is to be dated *c.* 1510.

87. The letter is reprinted in V. Golzio, *Raffaello nei documenti*, Vatican City, 1936, pp. 78 ff. It must be this text which Vasari acknowledges in the *Conclusione della opera*, or *L'autore agli artefici del disegno* (*Vite*, vii, p. 727): 'mi sono stati ... di non piccolo aiuto gli scritti di Lorenzo Ghiberti, di Domenico Grillandai, et di Raffaello da Urbino'.

88. A group of these scenes is collected and reproduced by C. G. Stridbeck, *Raphael Studies II: Raphael and Tradition*, Stockholm, 1963, pp. 53 ff., Figs. 12–15; to his examples we might add the fresco attributed to Giusto de' Menabuoi in the Paduan Baptistery, and Marco Zoppo's predella in San Clemente, Bologna. Stridbeck's presumed 'prototype' was in a Petrine cycle in the apse of Old Saint Peter's; but there is no evidence that such a scene existed there (see above, p. 74, n. 168).

89. Florence, Biblioteca Laurenziana, MS. Plut. vi. 23, fol. 111v.; *Mostra della Biblioteca di Lorenzo nella Biblioteca Medicea Laurenziana*, Florence, 1949, No. 12; K. Weitzmann, *Illustrations in Roll and Codex*, Princeton, 1947, pp. 87 ff. The book is presumably the 'Testamentum novum liber antiquissimus' in the list of Greek *Sacri* in the inventory compiled for Clement VII (Anon., *Index bibliothecae mediceae*, ed. Florence, 1882, p. 28). I should like to take this opportunity to acknowledge my debt to the Index of Christian Art at Princeton, where I first came across a photograph of this illumination.

90. See the discussion of the Albertina drawing (*Fig. 44*), above, p. 95.

91. For the relationship between Lascaris and Raphael, see above, p. 61; for Lascaris's Greek acquisitions for Lorenzo: B. Knös, *Un ambassadeur de l'hellénisme, Janus Lascaris*, Paris-Uppsala, 1945, pp. 33, 42.

92. Particularly the types represented by a relief on the rear façade of Casino Doria-Pamphilj (G. Wilpert, *I sarcofagi cristiani antichi*, Rome, 1929, i, p. 17, *Pl.* X. 1) and by a *Navicella* from S. Sisto, Rome (G. Stuhlfauth, *Die apokryphen Petrusgeschichten in der altchristlichen Kunst*, Berlin, 1925, p. 10).

93. Repr. Stridbeck, op. cit. in n. 88, Fig. 26 (p. 64 with earlier bibliography on the connection); Stridbeck, pp. 61 ff., suggests several other prototypes, none of which seems to me relevant except in the most generic sense. For the history of the Sixtine Ciborium, see above, p. 74, n. 168); for the latest summary of problems of attribution: G. C. Sciolla, *La scultura di Mino da Fiesole*, Turin, 1970, pp. 122 ff.

1519 is sufficient evidence for the statement that he stands in the historiography of Art History in an important position between the founders Ghiberti and Vasari.[87] The astonishing extent of his knowledge of the history of his own art was one of the reasons why he could not approach any of his subjects in the Cartoons with a mind like a *tabula rasa*. Every one of the Cartoons, with the not unnatural exception of *Paul in Prison*, was cast in the mould of a tradition appropriate to its meaning.

The *Miraculous Draught of Fishes* is not derived, as has been supposed, from a long tradition of representations of the Vocation of the Apostles in which Christ stands on the shore.[88] These several representations all illustrate a different text (Matthew iv. 18–22); and Raphael had a particularly good reason for avoiding that tradition, and the consequent probability of confusion over the text, since an example of it already existed in the Sixtine decorations of the chapel. He was forced, one may imagine, to look elsewhere. His Cartoon has a specific and very interesting prototype in what must have appeared to him a very ancient and authoritative source, a Greek Gospel-book (which is now dated to the eleventh century) then in the private library of Leo X (*Pl.* 1, *Fig.* 73).[89] In the illumination in this manuscript which illustrates three episodes from Luke v. 1–11, the scene in the centre provides the only known precedent for Raphael's Cartoon in which Christ sits in Peter's boat, Peter kneels before Him, and there are two boats, overlapping, containing four Apostles in all; furthermore in this little scene the second Apostle in Peter's boat has an oar, as he appears to have done in Raphael's first draft for the Cartoon.[90] That Raphael should have known and consulted this beautiful manuscript does not strain credibility; any one of a number of Greek-scholars could have drawn his attention to it if Leo did not do so himself, and perhaps one should think first of his friend Janus Lascaris, who had almost certainly acquired the book for Lorenzo *il magnifico* in the first place.[91] The Gospel-book, moreover, would have been conspicuous not only for its antiquity and beauty but also for the sheer quantity of its illustrations; this book undoubtedly offered the most complete cycle of Gospel-scenes available in Rome and here, if anywhere, they might hope to find a precedent alongside this rarely illustrated text. The type of boat—like a slice of melon—represented in this and other illuminations in the manuscript is in fact closer to the one adopted by Raphael (especially in the preliminary drawings) than is the type shown in comparable scenes on Early Christian sarcophagi; nevertheless it is very probable that a knowledge of the sarcophagus-reliefs,[92] together with a memory of a figure reaching down to the water in Michelangelo's *Battle of Cascina*, shaped Raphael's conception of the action of the fishermen in the second boat, a conception substantially different from that shown in the illumination.

94. The former is a study for a subsidiary fresco in the Stanza della Segnatura (Popham-Wilde, op. cit. in n. 4, No. 797 *recto*); the latter, now Fitzwilliam Museum No. 2515, for a bronze relief for the Chigi Chapel in S. Maria della Pace (M. Hirst, 'The Chigi Chapel in S. Maria della Pace', *Journal of the Warburg and Courtauld Institutes*, xxiv, 1961, p. 175).

95. The text (Luke xxii. 38) was taken as an indication of the divine grant of both temporal and spiritual power, as for instance in the Bull *Unam Sanctam*; there is a long definition of this doctrine in Domenico Jacobazzi's *De concilio* (15 ff.), ed. C. Jacobazzi, Rome, 1538, pp. 776

96. For example Fischel, op. cit. in n. 13 (194[8?] p. 257.

97. See for example Torquemada, *Summa ecclesia* (1448–49), Bk. II, v, the third proof the *Primatus*, quoting Ambrose and Augustin ('ipsum enim constituit esse caput eorum, pastor esset gregis dominici'); also, in th Leonine period, Giovanni Francesco Poggi *De potestate papae et concilii* (1511–12), Rom

There can be little doubt that the principal model for the *Charge to Peter* (*Pl.* 6) was the relief of the *Donation of the Keys* from the Ciborium of Sixtus IV;[93] in this relief, for example, Raphael found together the attitudes of Peter and John which he followed when he posed his models for the life-study (*Fig.* 47). At the same time it is clear that Raphael was taking up again an expressive and figurative problem that he had tackled before, notably in drawings for the *Doctrine of the Two Swords* and the *Doubting Thomas* (*Fig.* 50);[94] it is remarkable that these two earlier subjects were related to his new one, the first as an illustration of the powers of the Church conferred by Christ[95] and the second as the penultimate appearance of Christ to His apostles (John xx. 26–29), immediately preceding the last, which culminates in the Charge to Peter. The associative process of recall also brought to mind Donatello's *Ascension* relief now in the Victoria and Albert Museum, which undoubtedly suggested to him some of the reactions and grouping of the Apostles; the relief is an important thematic precedent in that it shows the conflation of the Donation of the Keys and Christ's final appearance. It is less clearly demonstrable, but an impression shared by many, that Raphael also had in mind Masaccio's *Tribute Money*;[96] if the impression is a true one it should be noted that Masaccio's text (Matthew xvii. 24–27) was also a testimony to the *Primatus Petri*, interchangeable, in effect, with the Donation of the Keys.[97] Raphael had the opportunity to refresh his memory of Masaccio's frescoes, and of other Tuscan works, while he was at work on the Cartoons, for he accompanied his patron to Florence late in 1515.[98]

Again in the case of the *Healing of the Lame Man* (*Pl.* 12) the Sixtine Ciborium relief of the same subject (*Fig.* 75) provided a point of departure; Raphael was probably well aware of the Classical origin and meaning (generosity) of the gesture with which Peter raises the cripple by the hand, either from a knowledge of the *Pietas Augusti* medallions[99] or of Roman monumental sculpture.[100] This time, however, the Ciborium relief was not the prototype for the whole scene but only for the centre section. The entire composition, instead, is cast in the pattern of Early Christian sarcophagus-fronts of the 'columnar' type; and of these the one that is most similar in appearance, now at Leyden (*Fig.* 74), was also very probably the most conspicuous to Raphael since it appears to have served as the tomb of Pope Marcellus I in S. Marcello al Corso until about 1519.[101] Four of the five compartments of this sarcophagus-front illustrate miracles of healing, and the exception, to the left of centre, shows the Donation of the Keys; Raphael had good reason, therefore, to think of this particular example. Inspired, very probably, by Dürer's engraving, the *Healing of the Lame Man*,[102] he changed the column-front into a quadruple colonnade, and then he seems quite consciously to have developed the colonnade into a *vestibulum* which expressed perfectly the literal and metaphorical meaning of the subject. The essential reason for the choice of the so-called Salomonic columns in this setting has for long been well understood, and the manner in which they help to characterize the Beautiful Gate as the gate to the Celestial Jerusalem has been discussed in the previous Chapter. It is perhaps interesting to record that while Fuseli still believed that the 'barbaric colonnade, loaded with profane ornament' was put in for 'popular amusement',[103] James Barry, as early as 1774, had already made the correct identification (which may never have been entirely forgotten in Rome) and even went so far as to criticize Raphael's choice on archaeological grounds.[104] In our present context there is little that need be added to Barry's observation, except to point out that Raphael did in fact use the original Constantinian set of columns,[105]

n.d., fols. 42r.–v., 61r. (quoting Ambrose, Augustine and Chrysostom); Domenico Jacobazzi, *De concilio*, ed. cit. in n. 95, p. 676; Cristoforo Marcello, *De authoritate summi pontificis*, Florence, 1521, fol. 8v. (both quoting Augustine).

98. The evidence for this return to Florence appears in a letter of Bandinelli, who in this case must be considered both an informed and an impartial witness (the text in Golzio, op. cit. in n. 87, p. 36).

99. The type is also used with the inscription *Restitutor Reipublicae* (which could as well have caught Leo's eye); see F. Gnecchi, *I medaglioni romani*, Milan, 1912, i, pp. 31, 38, and ii, p. 136, Pls. 13.3–4, 19.8–12, and 131.7.

100. Some examples are discussed by Stridbeck, op. cit. in n. 88, p. 66.

101. J. H. Jongkees, 'De verzameling oudheden van Reinier van der Wolff (*c.* 1660)', *Mededelingen van het Nederlands historisch Instituut te Rome*, xxxi, 1961, pp. 132 ff., who dates the sarcophagus about A.D. 390.

102. From the Little Engraved Passion, B. 18, 1513. With about the same degree of certainty it may be suggested that the boy in the left foreground of the Cartoon was inspired by one in the same position in Dürer's *Rejection of Joachim's offering in the Temple*, B. 77, from the *Marienleben*.

103. *The Life and Writings of Henry Fuseli*, ed. J. Knowles, London, 1831, ii, p. 235. Jonathan Richardson Snr. (*A Theory of Painting*, in the Strawberry Hill edition of the *Works*, 1792, p. 25) had thought the columns a 'prodigiously magnificent' invention of Raphael's, but a justifiable 'piece of licentiousness'.

104. *An Inquiry into the Real and Imaginary Obstructions to the Acquisition of the Arts in England*, 1774 (*The Works of James Barry Esq.*, London, 1809, ii, p. 277): 'the column preserved in St. Peter's, and said to be brought from Jerusalem, did never belong, as is pretended, to any temple of Solomon; and Raffaelle should not have placed it in his cartoon . . .'; he believed it to be post-Constantinian (an opinion already expressed in a letter to Burke from Rome, 1767, in *Works*, i, p. 128), which was going a little too far. Barry was not, of course, the first in Rome to doubt the Salomonic origin of the columns; see above, p. 56, n. 69.

105. J. B. Ward Perkins, 'The Shrine of St. Peter and its Twelve Spiral Columns', *Journal of Roman Studies*, xlii, 1952, p. 25 ('set 1'), and Pls. II, III.3.

106. The copy in Munich (Inv. 2460) from another of the reliefs on the arch is one of the very small group of drawings by Raphael after antique sculpture that survives. In his letter to Leo X (Golzio, op. cit. in n. 87, p. 85) Raphael seems to be the first to make a correct discrimination between the various sculptural styles represented on the monument; the latest and most authoritative statement on this point is by R. Weiss, *The Renaissance Discovery of Classical Antiquity*, Oxford, 1969, p. 88. The Munich drawing was placed by O. Fischel, 'Raphael's Pink Sketch-book', *The Burlington Magazine*, lxxiv, 1939, p. 182, in the so-called 'Roman sketch-book' together with the Windsor landscape (above, n. 68) and a study at Frankfurt for the *Repulse of Attila*.

107. H. P. L'Orange, *Der spätantike Bildschmuck des Konstantinsbogens*, Berlin, 1939, pp. 24, 81 ff.

108. L'Orange, op. cit., p. 88, quotes Ammianus on the *Rostra Augusti*: 'perspectissimum priscae potentiae locum'; some such association would seem very appropriate in the *Death of Ananias*.

109. First suggested, I believe, by Waagen, op. cit. in n. 4, ii, p. 376.

110. The observation was made by H. Grimm, 'Raphael und das Neue Testament', *Preussische Jahrbücher*, li, 1883, p. 19.

111. P. G. Huebner, 'Studien über die Benutzung der Antike in der Renaissance', *Monatshefte für Kunstwissenschaft*, ii, 1909, p. 277, who gives a detailed account of the statue's availability; he also suggests that the figure of the man kneeling opposite Ananias may have been inspired by a *Gaul* now in the Louvre, and this also seems convincing, particularly when modern restorations are subtracted (for these, and a reproduction, see P. R. Bieńkowski, *Die Darstellungen der Gallier in der hellenistischen Kunst*, Vienna, 1908, pp. 52–53, Fig. 63).

112. A detailed account of these restorations is given by Bieńkowski, op. cit., pp. 47–49.

113. Compare especially Marcantonio's engraving of this relief, B. xiv. 275.301.

114. The fall on the wrist rather than the hand was already interpreted in this sense by Quatremère de Quincy, op. cit. in n. 82, p. 308.

115. J. Shearman, 'The "Dead Christ" by Rosso Fiorentino', *Boston Museum Bulletin*, lxiv, 1966, p. 156 and n. 29, with references to Raphael's other adaptations of the relief; his familiarity with it is guaranteed by a letter of Costabili, 30 March 1517 (Golzio, op. cit. in n. 87, p. 54).

which twist like his in both directions and which remained standing before the *Confessio* of Saint Peter's after the erection of Bramante's altar-house in 1513–14.

For an appropriate formula within which to cast the *Death of Ananias* (*Pl.* 21) Raphael turned in quite a different direction. Uniquely attentive student of the Arch of Constantine that he was,[106] he saw the possibilities of the relief on that monument which illustrates the *Oratio Augusti* (*Fig.* 62).[107] It is uncertain, of course, that his archaeological studies were so advanced that he could identify the location of the event at the *Rostra Augusti* in the North-west corner of the Forum,[108] but there is little doubt that he could recognize a rostrum when he saw one and that he knew in general terms where a rostrum should stand. To think along these lines is to be confronted with the possibility that the Constantinian relief occurred to him as a proper formulation for the expression of the exercise of authority in the *Forum exterius*, if that indeed was the theological distinction intended between this and the previous scene; the recognition of the visual source may even be a factor in the iconographical argument. However that may be, Raphael liberated the figure-composition from its late-antique strait-jacket with wonderful imagination; yet there remain enough explicit references: to the gesturing Emperor surrounded by his senators, the open centre of the balustrade, the raised arm of the figure on the extreme right, the crowds on either side on a lower level, to the *vexilla*, perhaps, in the hangings behind the Apostles, and even, in the *modello* (*Fig.* 60), to the columns supporting statues. The spatial liberation, moreover, seems to operate under the guidance of two other reliefs, each again with an open-centred balustrade which may have brought them to his mind: Donatello's *Raising of Drusiana* in the Old Sacristy of San Lorenzo (an exact source for the form of Raphael's balustrade) and Ghiberti's *Solomon and the Queen of Sheba* on the Doors of Paradise. A connection in the second case[109] is not easily proved unless the back-views among Raphael's foreground figures and the half-length at a window in the background of the Cartoon seem sufficiently convincing references; but the *School of Athens* does suggest that he had made careful studies of this relief in Florence.

Two individual figures in this Cartoon are interesting and precise quotations that seem again to have come to his mind by association of their context. Sapphira, counting her money oblivious of the impending catastrophe, repeats the attitude of a woman in a very similar psychological situation in Signorelli's *Antichrist* fresco at Orvieto;[110] and the gesture of the woman on the other side, in the foreground, recoiling from the shock of Ananias's punishment, is extracted from Michelangelo's *Death of Haman* on the Sistine ceiling. These are quite simple cases. The genesis of the figure of Ananias, however, is much more complicated. Its focal position made it naturally a subject for careful thought. But Raphael's preoccupation was perhaps heightened by an awareness that this conspicuous figure set him the problem he was least well equipped to solve, of violent and exposed anatomical movement; and this awareness may account for a peculiarly studied and— it must be admitted—stilted performance. It has been suggested very convincingly that the pose was drawn from an antique *Dying Gaul* which is now

116. For example: fourteenth-century frescoes in the Cappella Pulci-Beraldi, S. Croce, Florence, and in the Cappella della Madonna in the Duomo at Prato; a panel attributed to

Martino di Bartolomeo in the Staedel Instit at Frankfurt; another by Carpaccio at Stuttga Fra Angelico's fresco in the Chapel of Nicho V in the Vatican; and the woodcut in

in Naples but was then in Rome;[111] the three parts of the figures that differ (the right foot, the lower part of the left arm, and the head) all correspond to parts missing from the statue in its Renaissance state.[112] In his completion of the figure Raphael turned to sculpture again: to a dead warrior in one of the Battle-reliefs on the Arch of Constantine for the position and expression of the head,[113] and to the fallen sorcerer in the Sixtine Ciborium relief, the *Fall of Simon Magus*, for the expressive position of the left arm (expressive because only an unconscious man could fall on his wrist in this way).[114] When he came to compose these elements into a single movement with the torso and right arm from the *Gaul* there came into his mind the appropriate example of the sleeping figure on the relief generally known as the *Bed of Policleitus* which was adapted by other artists to the problem of representing death.[115] In addition it seems very probable that the initial choice of the principal source, the *Gaul*, was suggested by Filippo Lippi's fresco at Prato, *Saint Stephen exorcizing a Possessed Man*, where the context and motif of the fallen man are similar to those of Ananias in the Cartoon.

In the *Stoning of Stephen* (*Fig.* 18) Raphael could, and certainly did, refer to a long tradition of representations of the same subject.[116] However, it is not in this case artificial to select from the tradition two frescoes which are in fact the closest in their general configuration to Raphael's design: one in the *Sancta sanctorum* of Nicholas III at the Lateran,[117] the other Filippo Lippi's at Prato. The first suggested itself, perhaps, as an authoritative type because it was part of the decoration of a *Cappella palatina* which was itself a precedent for the Sistine Chapel, the second likewise by virtue of its context in the bottom left corner of a chapel's altar-wall. From his own earlier drawing in the Albertina of the *Stoning of Stephen*,[118] made for some other and apparently unrealized project, Raphael rescued and redeveloped figural ideas for the group of executioners.

In the *Conversion of Saul* (*Fig.* 20), similarly, Raphael could turn to a fairly well-stabilized tradition.[119] It is difficult to be certain of his reference to any particular work of this type with the exception of the illumination in the Bible of Federico da Montefeltro (*Fig.* 84),[120] a book for which he must have felt a personal if not sentimental attachment; in this case the repetition of the triangular relationship between Christ, Saul and the running soldier, and of some details such as the spears, seems to guarantee a real connection. The equestrian group on the right is clearly an addition based upon his earlier studies of Leonardo's *Battle of Anghiari*, while the runaway horse on the left, with its groom, is an adaptation of one of the antique *Dioscuri* groups on the Quirinal which, as we know from a measured drawing at Chatsworth,[121] Raphael studied with particular care. The group of Christ and putti, in principle similar to that in the Urbino Bible, is obviously reshaped under the influence of Michelangelo's frescoes on the Sistine ceiling,[122] but the process was by no means simple; while the relationship between Christ and Saul recalls the *Creation of Adam*, the heavenly group is more similar in its make-up to the *Separation of Earth and Waters* and more similar still to Raphael's own Pantocrator in the Chigi cupola, which had been designed a year or more earlier than the Cartoon. And the idea of the figure bursting through cloud (which is conceived as something so solid that it may be pushed) is one that seems very personal to Raphael; he had used it in earlier drawings for a *Resurrection* and an *Assumption*, just as he used it again in the *Stoning of Stephen*.

The principal sources of the *Conversion of the Proconsul* (*Pl.* 26) have already been mentioned but there remain some lesser sources in the antique. The

second illustrated edition of the Malermi Bible (*Biblia vulgare istoriata*, Venice, 1493, fol. clxii, v.).

117. H. Grisar, S.J., *Die römische Kapelle Sancta Sanctorum und ihr Schatz*, Freiburg-im-Breisgau, 1908, Pl. 12; this fresco is a more convincing prototype than the 'Cavallini' in S. Paolo fuori le mura, a copy of which is reproduced in this connection by Stridbeck, op. cit. in n. 88, Fig. 44.

118. See above, n. 35.

119. For example: a panel attributed to Agnolo Gaddi in the Accademia, Florence; a four-teenth-century Venetian panel in Berlin (L. Coletti, 'Lorenzo Veneziano in neuem Licht', *Pantheon*, ix, 1932, p. 49); a Pollaiolesque *niello* (A. M. Hind, *Nielli . . . in the British Museum*, London, 1936, p. 61, No. 276); Signorelli's fresco at Loreto (which Fischel, op. cit. in n. 13 (1948), p. 265, suggested as Raphael's proto-type); and other fifteenth-century works illustrated by H. van Dam van Isselt, 'Sulla iconografia della conversione di Saulo di Michelangelo', *Bollettino d'arte*, xxxvii, 1952, pp. 315 ff.

120. The connection was first pointed out by E. von Dobschütz, 'Die Bekehrung des Paulus', *Repertorium für Kunstwissenschaft*, i, 1929, p. 102.

121. Chatsworth, No. 657; repr. *Old Master Drawings from Chatsworth* (International Ex-hibitions Foundation, Washington etc.), 1969–1970, No. 56; the style is very close to that of the study for the *Conversion of Saul* also at Chatsworth (*Fig.* 63). W. Pinder, 'Antike Kampfmotive in neuerer Kunst', *Münchner Jahrbuch der bildenden Kunst*, N.F.v., 1928, p. 371, in a valuable survey of the influence of antique equestrian reliefs, suggested that Raphael's tapestry, on the left side, was based upon an Alexander-sarcophagus; on this particular point I find his demonstration unconvincing. Pinder reproduces (p. 365) a miniature of the *Conversion of Saul* from the Queen Mary Psalter, which is clearly derived from classical reliefs and is also startlingly similar in general disposition to Raphael's composition. The MS. can scarcely have been a source for Raphael, but he could have known a related work (in addition to the Urbino Bible) through which he was influenced indirectly by the antique reliefs.

122. Springer, op. cit. in n. 4, ii, p. 270.

123. L'Orange, op. cit. in n. 107, p. 185, Pl. 47.c. The heads of both lictors to the left of the throne reveal the intensity of Raphael's study of the *Laocoön* group.

124. Above, p. 59.

125. G. A. Mansuelli, *Galleria degli Uffizi: Le sculture*, i, Rome, 1958, No. 3 (Inv. 72); J. W. Crous, 'Florentiner Waffenpfeiler und Armilustrium', *Mitteilungen des deutschen archäologischen Instituts, römische Abteilung*, xlviii, 1933, pp. 1 ff. A detailed comparison suggests that Raphael's left-hand relief (in the Cartoon) was based upon a drawing of the lower right side of Uffizi 72 (Crous, Pl. 13, Nos. 561, 558, 563, 564, 567); the hypothetical drawing would fill the rectangle below the top step, the remaining area being filled out with similar motifs. His right-hand relief seems to be derived in the same way from a drawing of the lower front of the same pillar (Crous, Pl. 10, Nos. 383, 387, 398, 395). I am glad to acknowledge that Professor Frank Brommer suggested to me that the Uffizi pillars might provide the answer to this problem.

126. For example by Reynolds, *Discourses*, ed. cit. in n. 83, p. 335, but already by Edward Wright, *Some Observations made in travelling through France, Italy, &c. in the years 1720, 1721, and 1722*, London, 1730, p. 330; the whereabouts of the Uffizi relief in the early Cinquecento remains uncertain (Mansuelli, op. cit., i, No. 149). B. Ralph, *The School of Raphael, or the Student's Guide to Expression in Historical Painting*, London, 1759, p. 20, defined Raphael's source as a relief-scene on Trajan's Column.

127. See, for example, R. Falb, *Il taccuino senese di Giuliano da San Gallo*, Siena, 1902, Pl. xxv. Becatti, in *Raffaello*, cit. in n. 18, ii, p. 539, reviewed a number of sacrifice-reliefs, including those in the Uffizi, at Benevento, and on the Arch of the Argentarii; he singled out the Benevento relief as the single effective source in 'Il classico in Raffaello', *Accademia Nazionale dei Lincei*, Quaderno 132, ccclxvi, 1969, p. 11, and made the deduction, which I think illogical, that Giulio Romano participated in the design of this Cartoon.

128. For the use of these terms, and other details of the sacrificial ritual, see O. Brendel, 'Immolatio Boum', *Mitteilungen des deutschen archäologischen Instituts, römische Abteilung*, xlv, 1930, pp. 198 ff. Detailed interpretations of the ritual represented by Raphael were already given by the Rev. R. Cattermole, *The Book of the Cartoons*, London, 1837, pp. 152 ff., and C. B. Norton, *Analysis of the Cartoons of Raphael*, New York, 1860, pp. 80 ff.

posture and throne of Sergius Paulus are inspired by a relief on the Arch of Constantine, once more, but this time by an Aurelian composition in the attic which represents the seated Emperor before the people.[123] The *Salus* roundel between the two herms has a precise numismatic prototype, as we saw in the previous Chapter.[124] The trophy-reliefs on the steps of the throne are expanded from drawings of the lower part of one of the four-sided trophy-pillars then in S. Sabina in Rome and now in the Uffizi.[125] The leggings of Elymas are clearly (and rather appropriately) imitated from some statue of a *Captive*—but it does not seem possible to distinguish between the many antiques available; and the rinceaux-panels on the piers in the background must be derived from some Roman pilaster such as those on the Arch of the Argentarii but again there are many other examples. These accents of authentic *romanità* are as meaningful as the Salomonic columns in the tapestry designed to hang opposite, since in this episode Paul found himself before a Roman seat of justice.

At first sight the problems that arise in the *Sacrifice at Lystra* also seem insoluble for the existence of too many potential prototypes. It is certain, at least, that the famous Hadrianic sacrifice-relief in the Uffizi, which was believed in the eighteenth century to be Raphael's source, is not the answer.[126] However, even if Raphael profited from the knowledge of many other such reliefs it seems that he did in fact rely particularly upon two. One of these is on the Arch of the Argentarii (*Fig.* 78). A relief on the arch at Benevento, which Raphael could have known through drawings,[127] is almost as close in general composition and in the relationship between *victimarius*, bull and *popa*;[128] but the *popa*'s costume and the line of the bull's back on the Roman arch make that relief a significantly more exact prototype. The conclusive evidence is provided by the manner in which the *victimarius* holds the bull; for in this relief alone we find the horns grasped by the nearer hand, and the nearer arm bent at the elbow (the arm is now broken but the point remains clear), as in Raphael's preliminary drawing (copy, *Fig.* 68) and as in the first painting of the Cartoon. It will be noticed that the Argentarii relief presents the sacrifice in the same direction as the tapestry (which is rare), that the *popa* swings the axe over his left shoulder, and that he carries his knives on the right hip as Raphael's *victimarius* does. The second relief that Raphael studied is on the front of a sarcophagus now in the Uffizi (*Fig.* 79).[129] This example is especially relevant because it shows together, and in the right sequence, scenes of sacrifice (*immolatio*) and salutation (*acclamatio*); the latter represents, perhaps, the return of a victorious general to his family, and it is to be noted that there is a second figure with the attributes of Victory standing with the general on the rock-step as Barnabas shares the step with Paul in the Cartoon. The association of these two separate scenes on the relief seems to have inspired Raphael to his complete fusion of *immolatio* and *acclamatio* which so beautifully embodies the ideas set in motion by his text; for the sacrifice prepared by the people of Lystra for Paul and Barnabas

129. Mansuelli, op. cit. in n. 125, No. 253; he lists the following modern restorations (details different from Raphael's): the axe, the twin pipes, and the tripod. J. D. Passavant, *Rafael von Urbino*, iii, Leipzig, 1858, p. 128, already noticed the relevance of this relief. A drawing in the Codex Escurialensis (ed. H. Egger, Vienna, 1906, p. 91, fol. 28r.) proves that it was

known at an earlier date. For modern inte[r]pretations of the subject, which remains to [be] clarified, see I. Scott Ryberg, 'Rites of th[e] State Religion in Roman Art', *Memoirs of t[he] American Academy in Rome*, xxii, 1955, pp. 164 [ff.]

130. P. P. Bober, *Drawings after the Antique [by] Amico Aspertini*, London, 1957, p. 73.

was in misguided recognition of the *return* of the gods sacred to the place, Mercury and Jupiter.

These two reliefs, then, were the principal guiding precedents for the overall design. Certainly Raphael looked beyond them for supplementary motifs and for the definition of details. The source of the second bull, whose head appears in the crowd, is difficult to define in the Cartoon; but its form in the lost preliminary drawing (copy, *Fig.* 68) repeats that of the bull in the great relief, *Marcus Aurelius sacrificing before the Temple of Jupiter* (*Fig.* 76), which is one of a set of three that stood in S. Martina in the Forum until Leo X presented them to the Palazzo dei Conservatori in 1515.[130] The same relief is still effective in this area of the Cartoon itself in the grouping of the heads of the *victimarii* around the realigned bull's head; and it may also have been Raphael's guarantee of the propriety of accompanying the boy (*camillus*) with double pipes behind the tripod-altar (as in the Uffizi sarcophagus-relief) by another with incense-box (*thurarium*). This propriety, however, could also have been clear from studies of the Column of Trajan, and it may have been from this source, or alternatively from a Flavian triple-sacrifice relief then in the Grimani Collection in Rome,[131] that he took the subsidiary episode, the introduction of the ram. These latter sources, illustrating the preparation for the sacrifice rather than the *immolatio* itself, would have given Raphael some details for the dressing of the bulls, particularly with the *dorsualia*, the broad band over its back; this however is just as conspicuous in the processional frieze of the Arch of Titus and in several other reliefs; the beaded fillet attached to the horns of both bulls is also exactly correct in form.[132]

It is by the inclusion of these details, however, that Raphael committed a mistake. The dressing of the bull is not shown on the antique reliefs of the performance of the sacrifice because the bull should in fact be undressed before it is killed.[133] The issue is clearly an ambiguous one, for even if Raphael could have known from textual sources that this was the rule he could still have taken the less pedantic view that a demonstration of his knowledge of the sacrificial ritual was more complete if the bulls were both dressed.[134] His altar is probably also, strictly speaking, a mistake. Its triangular form follows that of a great many objects which should, it seems, properly be recognized as candelabrum-bases rather than as altars.[135] He copied no single example—or none that survives—but made, rather, an assimilation of details from several, and from rectangular altars, with striking success.[136]

Raphael's sacrifice differs in one other respect from the antique reliefs: his bull is considerably foreshortened. The explanation for this deviation is probably to be found in a text from Pliny's *Historia naturalis*: 'Pausias . . . also painted large pictures, as for example the famous sacrifice of bulls in the Gallery of Pompeius. He devised an innovation which has often been imitated but never equalled. The most striking instance is that, wishing to display a bull's length of body, he painted a front and not a side view ('adversum eum pinxit, non traversum') and yet contrived to show its size.'[137] Emulation as motivation has to be considered seriously in Renaissance art; Raphael's 'imitation' of the *Death of Meleager* reliefs in his Borghese *Entombment* was probably inspired by a provocative passage in Alberti's *Della Pittura*, and Giorgione's *Tempesta* by Pliny's account of Apelles painting the unpaintable, a thunderstorm.

Antique reliefs, in any case, do not provide all the visual sources for the *Sacrifice at Lystra*. The figure of Paul belongs to a tradition of personifications

131. The *suovetaurilia* relief, now in the Louvre; Bober, op. cit., p. 46; another alternative: a relief *In Albano* copied in the Codex Destailleur (Hermitage) A, fol. 1r.

132. See particularly the fragment of the *Ara Pacis Augustae* (Scott Ryberg, op. cit. in n. 129, Fig. 36a; and also Figs. 61a, 70). The *paternoster* at the end of the nearer bull's fillet was a detail included in the dressing of the bulls of the second *carro* of the *Broncone* in the Medicean carnival, February 1513 (Vasari, *Vite*, vi, p. 253). It is interesting to note that the Roman carnival of the same date included a *carro* with a double bull-sacrifice (G. J. Penni, *La magnifica & sumptuosa festa facta dalli S.R. per el Carnovale MDXIII*, Rome, 1513). Some earlier representations are assembled by F. Saxl, 'Pagan Sacrifice in the Italian Renaissance', *Journal of the Warburg and Courtauld Institutes*, ii, 1938–9, pp. 365 ff.; in addition there is a remarkable *immolatio* woodcut in the second illustrated edition of the Malermi Bible, Venice, 1493 (Numbers xix).

133. *Real-Encyclopädie der classischen Altertumswissenschaft*, ed. G. Wissowa and W. Kroll, xvii, Stuttgart, 1914, col. 1128, and Scott Ryberg, op. cit. in n. 129, p. 69.

134. It might be felt that Raphael should be excused on the grounds that he could not show a past action, but I do not think that this argument works; there is much truth in the observation of G. A. Lazzarini, *Dissertazioni sulla Pittura* (*Opere*, Pesaro, 1806, i, pp. 27 ff.), that in this Cartoon above all Raphael did overcome the inherent disadvantage of painting *vis-à-vis* poetry since he described what had happened to the cripple, what was then happening, and to some extent what would happen next.

135. W. Altmann, *Die römischen Grabaltäre der Kaiserzeit*, Berlin, 1905, pp. 9–11.

136. One of these, with little doubt, must have been the so-called *Ara Grimani*, which was much more exactly reproduced in the *Madonna of the Oak-tree*, *c.* 1518 (the best discussion in T. Buddensieg, 'Raffaels Grab', *Munuscula discipulorum* (*Festschrift Hans Kauffmann*), Berlin, 1968, p. 65); compare also, however, the Uffizi candelabrum-base and rectangular altar, Mansuelli, op. cit. in n. 125, Nos. 182, 224, and another altar in the Vatican, Altmann, op. cit., Figs. 40–41.

137. K. Jex-Blake and E. Sellers, *The Elder Pliny's Chapters on the History of Art*, Chicago, 1968, p. 152.

138. The meaning may, naturally, be limited to a simple extension of the text (Acts xiv. 14: 'Barnabas et Paulus, conscissis tunicis suis exilierunt in turbas clamantes', etc.); but it is worth noting a long passage in Aegidius of Viterbo's *Historia viginti saeculorum* (Bibl. Angelica, MS. Lat. 351, fols. 51r.–53r.) in which the bull is taken as a symbol of divine anger, and the sacrifice of bulls, as of animals in general, as a ritual superseded by the *Nova lex.*

139. Op cit. in n. 4, ii, p. 246.

140. E.g. Gnecchi, op. cit. in n. 99, iii, p. 46, Pl. 153.14.

141. J. Pope-Hennessy and R. Lightbown, *Catalogue of Italian Sculpture in the Victoria and Albert Museum*, London, 1964, i, p. 266, No. 282.

142. Above, p. 105.

143. B. 31; see F. Baumgart, 'Biagio Betti und Albrecht Dürer', *Zeitschrift für Kunstgeschichte*, iii, 1934, p. 235.

144. B. 7.

145. Reynolds (*Discourses*, ed. cit. in n. 83, p. 335) and Fuseli (ed. cit. in n. 103, ii, p. 78) were surely right in detecting the spirit of Masaccio in the figure of Saint Paul preaching. However the point is as true of another Saint Paul, in many ways very similar, in Raphael's *S. Cecilia* altar-piece, the execution of which is probably contemporary with that of the Cartoon. These are not strictly quotations; it seems fair to say that throughout the period of the Cartoons Raphael was haunted by his memories of the Brancacci Chapel. The group of apostles in the *Death of Ananias* is another example, unthinkable without the precedent of the *Tribute Money* but not in fact a quotation from it; in this case the reminiscence may have been prompted by the thought that Peter in the Cartoon was particularly in the position of *Vicarius Christi*, for it is Peter's gesture in the centre of this group that recalls Christ's in the *Tribute Money*. I would judge that Springer (op. cit. in n. 4, ii, p. 287) was right in thinking that there were reminiscences of Masaccio's *Donation of Alms and Death of Ananias* in the *Healing of the Lame Man*, which are most nearly specific in the cripple and young mother on the right of the Cartoon.

146. Passavant, op. cit. in n. 4, ii, p. 248; but in fact the observation was already made (1814) in *The Italian Journal of Samuel Rogers* (ed. J. R. Hale, London, 1966, p. 216), and by Platner-Bunsen, op. cit. in n. 73, p. 404; it may have been received opinion among Roman guides.

of Anger,[138] a tradition that encompasses the grisaille by Giotto in the Arena Chapel and a figure in the *Story of Joseph* relief on Ghiberti's Doors of Paradise; the latter may be the effective source. The background, which Passavant surely rightly interpreted as the Forum of Lystra,[139] may reflect Raphael's knowledge of Roman medallions in some of which a circular temple may be found behind a bull-sacrifice,[140] or it may reflect his experience of stage-design, as we shall see later; but in fact it bears a striking resemblance to the architectural setting of a relief by Francesco di Giorgio—now in the Victoria and Albert Museum but then, probably, in Urbino—the subject of which is generally taken to be *Discordia.*[141]

The fusion of an ancient and a modern source in the earthquake-figure of the *Release of Paul from Prison* has already been described.[142] The genesis of the remaining design, *Paul preaching at Athens (Pl. 39)*, is characteristic in its complexity of the set as a whole. The general cast of the composition follows that of fifteenth-century preaching scenes—Fra Angelico's *Sermon of Saint Stephen* in the Chapel of Nicholas V in the Vatican Palace, for example, or Carpaccio's painting of the same subject in the Louvre—some of which in turn are derived from Roman *adlocutio* reliefs. In this tradition there is in fact one example, a small panel in Siena attributed to Spinello Aretino (*Fig. 82*), which is a rare representation of Paul's sermon at Athens; it is unnecessary to believe that Raphael remembered this work, and more realistic to calculate that he had in mind something like it and that he worked consciously within a familiar formula with the intention and the result that through that familiarity the essential nature of his subject could be clear at first glance. Yet the formula is far from being a stifling constraint upon Raphael's thinking, for when *Paul preaching at Athens* is placed within that tradition its essential novelty, particularly of viewpoint, is all the more obvious. The new invention has two points of departure. The first is Dürer's *Christ before Pilate (Fig. 77)* from the Little Woodcut Passion[143] which has already the eccentric distribution of levels, with the haranguing figure in the immediate foreground elevated on steps above the main group towards which he is turned. It is interesting that Raphael thought of this design by Dürer when he was already well advanced in the inventive stages of the Cartoon—at some time after he had made the red chalk life-study in the Uffizi (*Fig. 71*) but before the *modello (Fig. 72)*—and interesting, too, that he turned later still to the print of the same subject in the Little Engraved Passion[144] for a detail of costume added to the Cartoon in a *pentimento*, that is the cap with long knotted ear-flaps on the figure behind Paul which might be a portrait of Leo X. The second point of departure was a frustrated design of Raphael's own: the first draft for the *Mass at Bolsena* made about four years earlier. The grouping of the crowd around the steps in the Cartoon, and especially the positions of Dionysius and Damaris, are redeveloped from the right half of the rejected design (*Fig. 81*) and this redevelopment is a degree more obvious in the *modello (Fig. 72)*, which has additional space on the right, than in the Cartoon itself.[145] Such reworking of earlier frustrated

A complete bibliography of repetitions of this point would be immensely long and a little invidious.

147. Vitruvius, I. ii. 5.

148. E. Rosenthal, 'The antecedents of Bramante's Tempietto', *Journal of the Society of Architectural Historians*, xxiii, 1964, pp. 63 ff.

149. Raphael to Leo X, 1519 (Golzio, op. c͏ in n. 87, p. 86).

150. In the engraving by Hieronymus Coc͏ 1551 (repr. A. Bartoli, *Cento vedute di Ro͏ antica*, Florence, 1911, Pl. XI), the stepped att͏ is covered by a tiled roof.

151. '. . . avegna che a dì nostri l'architectu͏

ideas is a constant feature in Raphael's career; the first draft for the *Mass at Bolsena* was itself based upon an unrealized project for the Stanza della Segnatura.

One of the few sources for Raphael's Cartoons that is generally agreed is Bramante's *Tempietto* at San Pietro in Montorio, which is taken for the model for the round Temple of Mars in the background of *Paul at Athens*.[146] For all its repetition the idea is nonetheless wrong. If we accept that both buildings are round, and peripteral, and Doric, we must also accept that they have in common very little else that really matters; the Doric order, in any case, is as mandatory for a Temple of Mars[147] as it is for a Temple of Peter. Raphael's thinking about circular temples, which had begun at least by 1504, was independent of Bramante's and much influenced by the researches of Francesco di Giorgio;[148] and when this education was supplemented by his own studies in and around Rome his thoughts probably became too complex for us to be able to disentangle them. There is in any case little sense in the notion that he should have *represented* any known building in the Cartoon. What he represented, on the contrary, was an ideal of antique architecture, which would have been in this case of Greek architecture and therefore a lofty ideal indeed: 'Grecia, dove già furono gl'inventori e li perfetti maestri di tutte l'arti.'[149] His representational task was the ultimate test of his power of imagining the perfect antique style, as Paul's sermon to the Athenians was the ultimate test of *his* rhetoric, scholarship and rightness of cause. The result in each case was a set-piece. When we see it in this light the Temple of Mars may be read as an informed criticism of the circular temples of Francesco di Giorgio and Bramante—a criticism directed towards authenticity and expressed first in the suppression of their habitual high drum above the cella and in its replacement by a double attic and low dome (he may have found this form under the roof of the Temple of Romulus in the Forum),[150] and second in the richness of materials, for in his letter to Leo X he expressed the opinion that in this respect modern architects and specifically Bramante had failed to match the standards of the ancients.[151]

Raphael's biblical text said nothing about a Temple of Mars. We saw in the previous Chapter[152] that it would be natural for him to have understood the location of Paul's sermon 'in medio Ariopagi' to be 'in the Agora before the Court of the Areopagus', and not 'on the Hill of Mars'; certainly his Cartoon only makes sense if we read it so.[153] It would be unlike the mature Raphael if he had not made some enquiries about the setting for the Court of the Areopagus. And then two facts would have come to light readily, partly because the sources themselves were not obscure and partly because the constitutional importance of the court (in the trial of Socrates, for example) would have made it a subject of interest to Renaissance humanists. From the testimony of Socrates himself, in Plato's *Theaetetus*, it would be clear that the Areopagus met before the portico known as the Stoa Basileos;[154] from one of the commented editions of Valerius Maximus Raphael could learn that the Court took its name from a nearby Temple of Mars.[155] We cannot reconstruct Raphael's reasoning to the extent that we claim that these were in fact sources that he read; but in principle some such research, perhaps by a friend on his behalf, is probable.[156] Raphael's Areopagus does assemble near a Temple of Mars and before a *stoa*, that is the portico behind Paul. It is an odd accident that he got the relationship of the two buildings right—an accident, however, because their forms are wrong[157] and because it appears impossible that any contemporary traveller to Athens could have

sia molto svegliata et veduta assai proxima alla maniera delli antichi, come si vede per molte belle opere di Bramante, niente di meno li ornamenti non sono di materia tanto pretiosa, come li antichi, che con infinita spesa par che mettessero ad effetto ciò che imaginarno . . .' (Golzio, op. cit. in n. 87, p. 85). The criticism seems to be based upon that by Vitruvius, VII. 17, of Gaius Mucius; but this is perhaps the place to add a point about Raphael's letter that seems to have been overlooked: that a man in his position, when addressing Leo X, told the pope what he wanted to hear. Consequently his appreciation of the perfection of antiquity should also be read as flattery of Leo's taste, which was indeed for material richness (see above, p. 14); and it is probable that the representation of an ideal in the Cartoon is complicated in the same way. The ideal, by the way, is not a reconstruction of a Vitruvian round peripteral temple; the only conformity with Vitruvius's text (IV. viii. 2) is in the probable identity of column-height and internal diameter of cella.

152. Above, p. 71.

153. This is, for example, the way in which M. Dibelius, *Studies in the Acts of the Apostles*, London, 1956, p. 68, interprets the Cartoon, while arguing the opposite interpretation of the text itself.

154. 210. D; see also *Euthyphro* 2. A–B; *Regis porticus*, in each case, in the translation by Marsilio Ficino, Florence, 1484–85.

155. For example, *Valerii maximi factorum ac dictorum memorabilium, cum duplici commentario*, Paris, 1513, fol. lx, r., commentary on *De Ariopago*: 'Ariopagitarum officium erat simile Romanis censoribus. Areopagus vicus erat Athenis sic dictus a templo Martis: quod haud procul inde foret . . .'; and compare Abbot Hilduin of St. Denis, *Passio S. Dionysii* (*P.L.* 106, cols. 25 ff.), who says that the statues of Mars and Hercules, the two gods most worshipped by the Athenians, stood in this area and that from the first the court took its name.

156. See, for example, the alternative reasoning, using texts of Pausanias and pseudo-Plutarch, of R. Martin, 'La Stoa Basileios', *Bulletin de correspondance hellénique*, lxvii, 1943, p. 284.

157. See W. B. Dinsmoor, 'The Temple of Ares at Athens', *Hesperia*, ix, 1940, pp. 1 ff., and H. A. Thompson, 'Buildings on the West Side of the Agora', ibid., vi, 1937, pp. 64 ff. Howard Burns has pointed out to me that the order of Raphael's portico (not, in fact, as

ordinary as it looks at first sight) is identical to that of the Amphitheatre at Nîmes; it is perfectly possible that the connection is a real one, since the legacy of his drawings described by Jacopo Strada (1575 preface to Serlio Bk. VII) included 'una grandissima quantità d'Architettura, tanto di quegli di Roma, quanto di Francia . . .'

158. I have read all published Renaissance descriptions of Athens without finding encouragement for any other conclusion (there is a survey of most of these sources in J. M. Paton, *Mediaeval and Renaissance Visitors to Greek Lands*, Princeton, 1951). It is worth noting that the Medici had themselves been established in the Florentine colony at Athens in the fifteenth century, and that Raphael could have spoken to Greek exiles and to Italians, such as Carlo Tocco, who had returned from Greece (W. Miller, *The Latins in the Levant*, London, 1908, pp. 400, 488); but I think it is unlikely that these visitors would have been so much more curious or informed than those who wrote down what they saw, that they could have answered Raphael's questions accurately, even on the matter of the location of the two monuments. I do not know any literary source, or combination of sources, from antiquity that defines more than their proximity.

159. Above, p. 50.

160. See especially fols. xxiv, v. (*Claudia uxor Augusti*) and xxxvi, v. (*Lollia Paulina*); for the compilation of the *Illustrium imagines* see Weiss, op. cit. in n. 106, pp. 178 ff.

161. See above, p. 50.

162. I am unable, however, to follow Stridbeck in his conclusion (op. cit. in n. 88, pp. 62, 69 etc.) that Raphael deliberately sought 'an archaic effect', re-creating 'the spirit of the Early Christian tradition'; it appears to me that this conclusion is based upon comparisons with 'archaic' sources that are generally forced, particularly in the case of the fresco-cycle formerly in S. Paolo fuori le mura, and hypothetical in the case of the supposed Petrine cycle in the apse of Old Saint Peter's.

163. He makes (loc. cit. in n. 149) a conventional judgement on the Greek (that is, Byzantine) 'maniera di pictura . . . pessima e di niun valore'.

identified the remains of the real *stoa* and the real temple.[158] Their disposition in the Cartoon is probably controlled by the decision to continue in the reversed *stoa* of the tapestry the line of the screen of the Sistine Chapel, abutting on its right, which left for the temple no natural position other than the one it occupies.

This survey of visual and textual sources for the Cartoons has been concentrated upon those that were effective in the compositional sense. It should be brought into balance by taking account of more sources for details. It was pointed out in the previous Chapter that the physiognomies of Raphael's Christ and Paul were adapted from the reputedly authentic 'portraits' on an emerald cameo from Constantinople, probably through the intermediary of one of the bronze medallic copies of the end of the Quattrocento.[159] Even the hair-styles of the women in the Cartoons were not casual inventions; those of Damaris in *Paul at Athens*, for example, or of the young woman on the right of the *Sacrifice at Lystra* can be compared with the results of a contemporary piece of research into ancient iconography, the *Illustrium imagines* of Raphael's friend Andrea Fulvio, which appeared in Rome in 1517.[160] To pursue problems of this kind is to meet again the attitude of mind so attentive to detail that led Raphael to select deep-water fish for Peter's haul in the *Miraculous Draught of Fishes*.[161]

An attitude of mind: it is about this that a survey of Raphael's sources can teach us most, about the attitude adopted in this particular task, challenge and predicament, as well as—more generally—about a moment in the evolution of the mind itself. For it is clear that by this date it was a mind that could select with astonishing agility from supremely rich resources of experience and reference. Exactly the same quality of mind is shown a year or so later in the invention of Villa Madama, which is as complex in the texture of reference, form and meaning as are the Cartoons (because the opportunity and incentive were as great). Raphael, moreover, thought and looked with an almost total lack of prejudice. By 1515 he had moved from his earlier ambivalent positions, of partial sovereignty and partial expedient submission to the contingent influences of a Perugino, a Leonardo or a Michelangelo, on to a plateau from which he surveyed—and raided—the whole history of art presented to his view. We happen to know that he could discriminate between Trajanic and Constantinian reliefs and make value-judgements upon them; yet the value-judgement did not make him blind to the expressive possibilities latent in Constantinian and even post-Constantinian sculpture.[162] When he looked at the little miniature in Pope Leo's Greek Gospels he presumably admired the invention, and perhaps the technique too, but surely not the figure-style;[163] and yet this medieval miniature was as valuable an inspiration to him as a page from the Urbino Bible, which he probably considered the most beautiful of modern books. Nor was there any blindness or prejudice in a parochial sense. He had, perhaps, an advantage like that of Rubens when he sacked Italy: the paradoxical advantage of an artistic primary education which was in several respects under-privileged but for that very reason the freer from *a priori* direction, the more liberating in the long run for its lack of durable allegiances.

The broad spectrum of Raphael's sympathies and experiences is instructive in another way. If he could recall so much from his stock of images the scope of his choice has this particular implication: that as with a really literate epic poet so also with Raphael the choice of the reference, to this rather than that, is made with good reasons, which may also be multiple reasons. It should not be surprising if it seems in some cases that there springs to mind more than one explanation for the option of a certain precedent; in his case, and especially in this work, we can reasonably interpret a reference to a source as an answer to an aesthetic problem and simultaneously as associative, or indicative, of patronage, for example, or context or theme.

It would be vain to imagine that this survey of sources might be entirely accurate or complete; but it does not have to be either of these to sustain two more general conclusions. It is obvious that many of Raphael's references were pointless unless they were identifiable in general if not in particular terms; and we have seen repeatedly the thematic association of a quotation of a compositional pattern or of a motif. It seems to follow that the reference to sources was in these cases purposive and functional, that is to say that they were indicative of meaning, that they carried with them a certain significance inherent in the form. And thus the consideration of Raphael's sources tells us something about his attitude to history-painting, not perhaps in general but in this particular situation where he could pull out all the stops and play to the most receptive, comprehending and captive of audiences. It also brings us back to the problem of artistic free-will. The extent of his accumulated capital of visual experience, and the consequent possibilities of choice, form one dimension of his freedom; the agility and pragmatism of his mind form another. Yet the decisions once taken and the choices once made entail a considerable surrender of subsequent freedom and the acceptance of the discipline that alone will enable the choice to be functionally effective. In other words the positive exploitation of precedent plays a determinant rôle in the final result,[164] and in the whole series leaves a natural residue of variety of design that has nothing to do with chronology. Furthermore there was not even a purely aesthetic incentive to evade this variety and to impose an artificial uniformity; on the contrary, variety is likely to have been as much a consciously expressed aesthetic ideal in the Cartoons as it was in Ariosto's *Orlando furioso*, which was also completed in 1516. Raphael seems even to go out of his way to pursue this ideal in the diversification of settings, incidents, dress and colours.

It is not very easy, nor perhaps very prudent, to define closely the concept of history-painting of an artist such as Raphael. The pursuit of variety, however, is an aspect of his thinking as evident in the Cartoons as in the eight principal frescoes of the second and third of the Vatican Stanze. Vasari was right: Raphael did judge that the composition of *storie* should be enriched with 'the *varietà e stravaganza*' of 'backgrounds of buildings or of landscape, a pleasing treatment of draperies, the management of figures so that they are at times pushed back into shadow and at other times brought forward into strong light, and the making of the heads of women, children, young men and old men, alive and beautiful, with appropriate expression and vigour. He considered also the value of such things as the flight of horses in battle, the bravery of soldiers, the ability to make all kinds of animals, and above all the representation of lifelike and identifiable portraits and an infinite number of other things such as clothing, footwear, helmets, armour, the headdresses of women, hair-styles, beards, vases, trees, caves, rocks, fires, murky or clear atmosphere, clouds, rain, lightning, fine weather, night, moonlight and sunlight and many other things that contribute the necessities of the art of painting.'[165] It is in just such a range of interests that Raphael is outstanding among history-painters of the period, and never more clearly than when his Cartoons are set against Michelangelo's austere histories on the Sistine ceiling. Vasari may not have been right when he

164. The degree of constraint is clearly not uniform; it is perhaps most rigorous in the *Sacrifice at Lystra* or the *Conversion of the Proconsul*, least in the *Death of Ananias*.

165. *Vite*, iv, pp. 375–6.

166. Lodovico Dolce, *L'Aretino*, ed. M. Roskill, New York, 1968, p. 154; L. B. Alberti, *Della Pittura*, ed. L. Mallé, Florence, 1950, p. 91.

167. *Poetics*, ix. The same text was used, to interpret the variety of incident in the *Fire in the Borgo* (1514–15), by K. Badt, 'Raphael's "Incendio del Borgo" ', *Journal of the Warburg and Courtauld Institutes*, xxii, 1959, p. 48; it should perhaps be noted, however, that whereas Badt introduces this text in a stimulating discussion of Raphael's debt to dramatic conventions, Aristotle was in fact talking of epic poetry. It may also be noted that the *Poetics* was known somewhat earlier than Badt indicated, for Nicholas V had a MS., translated from Arabic, (see the copy of *Inventarium Nicolai pape V*, published by E. Piccolomini, *Intorno alle condizioni ed alle vicende della libreria medicea privata*, Florence, 1875, p. 114).

168. In Filarete's *Trattato dell'Architettura*, Bk. XXIII (ed. W. von Oettingen, Vienna, 1890, p. 623) there is already an explicit statement on the necessity of appropriateness of behaviour and dress, so that a Caesar or an Apostle, he says, should not be represented wearing 'li habiti che s'usano oggi'.

attributed this diversification to Raphael's supposed acknowledgement that he could not match Michelangelo's mastery of the human figure; but his instincts were surely correct again when he adapted for his catalogue of Raphael's interests not only a well-known passage in Lodovico Dolce's *L'Aretino* (1557) but also one in Alberti's *Della Pittura* on the *copia et varietà* that contributes *voluptà nella istoria*.[166] It is difficult to digest Alberti's theory of history-painting without acquiring the conviction that Raphael had done the same.

No literate man could read Alberti without being conscious that his theory of *istoria* was made up of ingredients borrowed from the more highly developed criticism of other arts, notably rhetoric and poetry. It is therefore reasonable to suspect that Raphael might enrich his concept of history-painting by adapting ideas from the theory or practice of the sister-arts; and one aspect of his procedure which arouses this suspicion is the licence that he assumes to invent action and the manner in which he invents it. The text for the *Healing of the Lame Man* (Acts iii. 1–10) is not directly the source of the quite prominent actions of the women and children (*Pl.* 12); their presence is to be explained by Raphael's thinking around the subject, for the location of the miracle, the *Porta speciosa*, was also the women's gate of the Temple and women would properly use it—as they do in the Cartoon— for the presentation of sacrifices after childbirth. To a greater or lesser degree this kind of extension of incident—the bolting horse in the *Conversion of Saul*, for example—is present in each design. It may of course be interpreted as an aspect of his habit of thinking realistically, and no doubt that is part of the truth. But the process, including thinking realistically, may also be related to Aristotle's formulation of a theory of *mimesis* proper to epic poetry, which is the licence to describe, beyond the matter of history itself, 'the kinds of thing that might happen, that is, that could happen because they are, in the circumstances, either probable or necessary'.[167]

The probable or the necessary: it was perhaps by thinking within these Aristotelian formulae, rather than by applying an antiquarian ideal, that Raphael developed another aspect of his mature historical style, the appropriateness of detail in costume, objects or setting. What was the probable or necessary difference between the dress of Elymas, the Jew, and that of Sergius Paulus, the Roman proconsul? What was the probable or necessary form and style of the architectural setting of this scene, or of those at Lystra and at Athens? He does not always get the right answers. In his last major fresco before the Cartoons, the *Fire in the Borgo*, the water-pots used by the fire-fighters are not convincingly Carolingian to us; what matters, however, is that they are not Renaissance water-pots, for this fact is evidence that Raphael had taken thought and that his concept of history-painting included a sense of historical distance. The same point is very well illustrated by the Cartoons.

A sense of historical distance is by no means new. It is present in Brunelleschi's *Sacrifice of Isaac*, where the relief on the altar is consciously archaic in style (actually the result is approximately Romanesque), and it appears intermittently throughout the fifteenth century in the work of such artists as Piero della Francesca, who almost certainly did not read Aristotle's *Poetics*.[168] Their thinking was natural enough and there is no need to find a text for them. What is new in the Cartoons is the degree of consistency in the approach to historical authenticity. It is not of course complete—the Gothic Damascus in the *Conversion of Saul* is a lapse—but the fact that these lapses are exceptions is itself an indication of a new point of arrival in history-painting. The

Cartoons mark a significant step towards an ideal fully realized in Raphael's last design in the genre, the *Battle of Constantine*, and at that point the fulfilment of the ideal has the force of a statement in theory. The Cartoons and the *Battle of Constantine* set a standard for subsequent history-painters down to Delacroix.

In our circumstances the conclusion that Raphael had been reading Aristotle is probable rather than necessary; there could be proof that he had read the *Poetics* but there is none. The recent discovery of the text of Raphael's letter describing his project for the Villa Madama[169] teaches us how much we had underestimated his self-conscious ambition in other art-forms—in this case the Plinian letter—and how extensive and effective could be the theoretical and literary foundations of his major works. It is not, then, fanciful to reconstruct a situation in which the hesitant, sporadic and apparently unprogrammatic approaches to an ideal of historical realism in earlier painting and sculpture were realized by Raphael, in Rome, under the influence of a new body of literary criticism. In principle this is what Alberti had intended: that the visual arts should increase in stature by the accession of the intellectual processes established in the other arts. And in so far as we can ever explain a new feature of style we can probably best comprehend another innovation in the Cartoons as the logical fulfilment of Alberti's programme; this innovation is in the characterization of gesture and expression.

Gestures and expressions in the Cartoons often have sources in the visual arts and some of them we have already seen; to these we must now add the general example of Leonardo's *Adoration of the Magi*, which Raphael must have studied most intensively in Florence for he exploited its repertoire from his first to his last days in Rome. Nevertheless all these sources are effective within an ideal which is not the sum of all of them but which, on the con-contrary, controls them. The character of gesture and expression is distinguished by the unique combination of elegance, eloquence and emphasis; it seems that each is exemplary and utterly explicit of actions of mind and body that are susceptible of classification precisely because they have been rationalized and defined by deliberation. The eloquence of gesture is clearest when we take a sufficiently typical case which can be compared with a model already matured in an ideal of grace: the recoil of the woman in the foreground of the *Death of Ananias* (*Pl.* 23) and its prototype in Michelangelo's *Death of Haman*. Like a beautifully turned phrase in prose or music Raphael's movement is continuous, fluent and balanced, it has a beginning and an end and it is perfectly clear; in this way it surpasses not only Michelangelo's, but also examples of graceful gesture from Verrocchio and Leonardo. We can also distinguish between the variety of Raphael's gestures and expressions and the variety of Leonardo's. For Leonardo's variety seems to be impelled (and, to judge from his writings, it was in fact impelled) by a conception of an infinite range of psychological and physical response to dramatic situations, whereas Raphael's seems to be controlled by a conception of the exemplary, more clearly in the Cartoons than anywhere else in his work. It is a fact, at least, that the Cartoons did become exemplary in this sense, providing patterns of expression that could be codified in books of engravings as if he had written the first grammar in this language.[170] A pedagogic intention on Raphael's part is unlikely. His intention was in the first place to create, by means of a certain visual hyperbole, instantly legible images of shock, elation, devotion, authority, submission, reflection and so on, each appropriate to its place and each above all *distinct*. The natural

169. Published by Foster, op. cit. in n. 26. The only known version of the letter is unsigned and undated; there is, however, positive evidence that the author is Raphael, and that the date is before March 1519, in a MS. source as yet unpublished.

170. *Receuil de XC Têtes tirées des Sept Cartons des Actes des Apôtres peints par Raph.l Urbin, qui se conservent dans le Palais d'Hampton-Court, dessinées par le Chev.r Nic: Dorigny et gravées par les meilleurs Graveurs, mis en lumière à Londres l'an 1722 et dedié A Son Altesse Royale la Princesse de Galles*; and Benjamin Ralph, *The School of Raphael, or the Student's Guide to Expression in Historical Painting*, London (Boydell), 1759 (on pp. 23–24 there is an alphabetical catalogue of fifty-three *Passions*, each illustrated by one or more heads from the Cartoons).

171. There is a clear distinction in the definitions given by Giovan Battista Pigna, *I romanzi*, Venice, 1554, pp. 49 ff.; but the two ideas seem to be assimilated under the one term *Energia* by Giovambattista Giraldi, *Discorsi ... intorno al comporre de i romanzi ...*, Venice, 1554, pp. 160–1.

172. Especially Quintilian, *Institutio oratoria*, IV. ii. 63, VI. ii. 32, and VIII. iii. 61; see also Aristotle, *Poetics*, xvii (III. 18 in the edition by Lodovico Castelvetro, *Poetica d'Aristotele vulgarizzata et sposta*, Vienna, 1570, pp. 203 ff.), and Cicero, *Partitiones oratoriae*, vi. 20.

173. Quintilian, *Institutio oratoria*, VIII. iii. 88–89; compare Torquato Tasso, *Discorsi dell'Arte Poetica* (ed. C. Guasti, *Le prose diverse di Torquato Tasso*, i, Florence, 1875, p. 56): 'energia: una accurata diligenza di descrivere la cosa minutamente'. I think it has not been noticed that Lodovico Dolce, *L'Aretino*, 1557 (ed. cit. in n. 166, p. 128) makes Aretino use this technical term somewhat self-consciously about the *Inventione* of history-painting: 'dall'ingegno oltre all'ordine e la convenevolezza, procedono l'attitudini, la varietà, e la (per così dire) energia delle figure'. Dolce's dialogue is full of passages, spoken by Aretino who stresses his personal familiarity with Raphael, which could be cited in support of the contention that the artist's ideas were related to those of the other arts. One example, when Aretino is talking of *Historia*: 'in che Rafaello imitò talmente gli Scrittori, che spesso il giudizio de gl'intendenti si move a credere, che questo Pittore habbia le cose meglio dipinte, che essi discritte; o almeno, che seco giostri di pari ...' (ed. cit., p. 160).

174. Especially *Della Pittura*, ed. cit. in n. 166, p. 89.

175. Cicero, *De oratore*, esp. iii. 215 ff. (including the important analogy with painting at 217); Giraldi, loc. cit. in n. 171.

result was a certain abstraction from the infinite range of human response, as if the latter were material by nature amorphous which had to be given artificial shape and categorized before it could serve his artistic purpose of communication.

There can be no mistaking the hyperbole, the abstraction or the artificiality of Raphael's gestures and expressions, and there is no need to excuse them. It was by artifice, by the application of art, and by no other means that this formalization of natural and aesthetic experience could be made. Nevertheless it is probable that the result in the Cartoons was influenced by particular circumstances, the most significant of which was the total context of aesthetic thinking in Rome. It must be admitted that this total context cannot be securely reconstructed. It so happens that we have no completed High Renaissance statement of pictorial theory and little enough about the other arts with the notable exception of music. However the least plausible deduction from this fact is that there was in this period no discussion of aesthetics; on the contrary it is likely to be the result of the circumstance that this was a period of very active formation of new ideas when these matters were in a state of flux and not yet of codification. Everything we know about Leonine Rome suggests that there was indeed intense discussion, and what we know about Raphael's friendships suggests that he would have had easy access to it. In so far as aesthetic speculation impinged upon painting the safest assumption—it is an assumption—is that it would have been conducted, like the earlier arguments in Alberti's *Della Pittura* and the later ones in Lodovico Dolce's *L'Aretino* (1557), within terms of reference mainly derived from the interrelated theories of rhetoric, poetics and tragedy. Thus the consideration of the qualities of Raphael's style of history-painting in relation to the terms of these other arts is justified in the first place because it is likely to reflect the reality of the situation. To ignore the problem, to isolate the thinking of the artist from such a context, is in fact to run the risk of falsifying our reading of his results even more serious than the obvious risk incurred in speculation. And to relate the style of history-painting in the Cartoons to the terms of the other arts is justified in the second place because it seems to work. This point would certainly be susceptible of elaborate demonstration; but because that demonstration would always remain hypothetical it is more appropriate and perhaps also sufficient to give no more than a few indications of the ground it could cover.

Thus the peculiar nature of Raphael's history-painting can be well defined by the rhetorical and poetic terms *enargeia* and *energeia* which in the Renaissance are not always very clearly distinguished one from the other.[171] The first is an elevated clarity or vividness of expression in placing the event before the eyes,[172] the second is an emphasis or force of detail in the illustration which tends towards hyperbole.[173] Another such concept which seems very appropriate is *decorum*, or the fitness of each illustration to its purpose; this had already been applied to the problem of expression in history-painting by Alberti, for example in the important passage in which he stressed the necessary conformity of each gesture with its *oficio*.[174] Alberti had also raided rhetorical theory and it is conceivable that Raphael followed his lead to look, for example, at what Cicero had to say about the orator's repertory of gesture and facial expression, which is that repertory which Giovambattista Giraldi termed the *eloquenza del corpo*.[175] But by this date in Rome the arts of rhetoric and of theatre were closely intertwined and theatre, too, had a close association with history-painting throughout the Renaissance period.

In Raphael's case we know that at a date later than the Cartoons he was directly engaged in theatrical design.[176] It would be a dangerous assumption that he had had no experience of it by 1515; and the perspective background of the *Sacrifice at Lystra* (*Pl.* 38) suggests as strongly as does that of the *Fire in the Borgo* that he was thoroughly familiar with its conventions, both as to architectural forms and (perhaps more important) to the relationship in scale between figures and setting.[177] However, these connections with theatre, which seem sufficiently definite, lie in the field of scenography. In our present context the question is whether there was a parallel connection between the style of contemporary histrionic practice and Raphael's history-mode (the etymological link had not been overlooked).[178] The practical difficulty which stands in our way is in bridging the gap between chance accounts of the highly polished performances of the school of Pomponius Laetus, on the one hand, and the first published histrionic theory, which belongs to the 1550s, on the other.[179] It is best, then, to leave this issue with the observation that the pupils of Pomponius Laetus such as Raphael's friend Tommaso Inghirami were trained, upon a thorough grounding in rhetorical theory, to act their parts with emphasis, appropriateness and grace.[180] We shall probably never know how closely the *Conversion of the Proconsul* or the *Death of Ananias* (*Pls.* 26, 21) reproduced in performance and in setting what was seen on the Roman stage in the period, but they may have done so very closely. If we do not speculate along these lines we may well overlook one of the features of Raphael's history-painting most distinctive in the eyes of his own audience, and one of the factors most formative for the appearance of the Cartoons. The speculation has one merit at least: that it collects together the several aspects of the character of gesture and expression—which otherwise are left in meaningless suspense—and supplies a purpose for them, which is simply to re-employ in the tapestries that visual language of drama which would be the most familiar.

From this rather general and as it were cultural context of the Cartoons we must now return to the specific and physical context intended for the tapestries, the Sistine Chapel, to examine some remaining factors that affected their appearance. For there are a number of ways in which the composition and style of these works were purposefully related to the Sistine fresco-decoration. By way of introduction to this problem we may make one simple observation about the frames that Raphael designed for the woven histories (*Fig.* 25). These frames are box-like in section, apparently porphyry in material, and decorated on their front face with a running *guilloche* design; the remarkable fact that the *guilloche* unwinds in opposite directions in the two sets of tapestries may be recalled at this point as proof of the careful thought that went into the design of these easily neglected parts. In the shape of these frames, their material and scale in relation to the picture-field, Raphael imitated the frames of the Sistine history-cycle (*Fig.* 29); in the *guilloche* he followed the frames of the niches of the papal portraits in the upper register. This relationship, so deliberately established, is indicative of his thinking along the lines that we now have to follow and of the extent to which he visualized the tapestries as an integral part of the decorative scheme.

Raphael also accepted a system established in the Sistine decoration that had a much more profound effect upon his designs: the three-bay pattern. It will be remembered that this system was expressed, in the fictive tapestries of the lowest zone which his real tapestries were to replace, by the alternation of colour (gold-silver-gold, gold-silver-gold), and in the history-cycle above by the emphatic centralization and internal tripartite design of each central

176. In February and March 1519 he was 'occupato in certo aparato di Comedia di messer Lodovico Ariosto', i.e. *I Suppositi* (Golzio, op. cit. in n. 87, p. 93).

177. The connection between the *Sacrifice at Lystra* and stage-design was seen with particular clarity by Fischel, op. cit. in n. 13 (1948), pp. 212, 236, 270; for the *Incendio* the point has been well demonstrated by Badt, op. cit. in n. 168, but I think he has overestimated the rôle of Peruzzi and underestimated Raphael's own capacity to arrive at the same point independently; the architecture of the *School of Athens* is already in the technical sense a *prospettiva*, and functions as one, before the celebrated and well-documented example of the Capitoline theatre of 1513. It should be noted that the drawing (Uffizi 291A) upon which assessments of Peruzzi's importance are largely based (for example in the important article by K. Neiiendam, 'Le théâtre de la renaissance à Rome', *Analecta romana instituti danici*, v, 1969, pp. 157 ff., and Badt, op. cit., pp. 40 ff.) is not by Peruzzi and its date is much later than is usually supposed (C. L. Frommel, *Baldassare Peruzzi als Maler und Zeichner*, Vienna-Munich, 1967–68, p. 76); this drawing, however, represents the type of architectural backdrop that is already relevant to the *Sacrifice at Lystra*, a type known from literary sources (Urbino, 1513, for example) and probably already in use in the 1480s since it seems to be adapted in Filippino's frescoes in the Strozzi Chapel. It is not easy to find material on the second point, that is the absolute scale of early stage-settings; early woodcuts of stage-scenes with actors suggest that the settings were unrealistically small, and that the relationship of scale between actors and proscenium was approximately the same as that adopted in the Cartoons (see, for example, the woodcuts of the Venetian *Plautus* of 1518, repr. L. Magagnato, 'The Genesis of the Teatro Olimpico', *Journal of the Warburg and Courtauld Institutes*, xiv, 1951, p. 212, Pl. 38a, b).

178. E.g. Durandus, *Rationale*, Proeme.

179. G. B. Giraldi, *Discorsi . . . intorno al comporre de i romanzi, delle comedie, e delle tragedie, e di altre maniere di poesie . . .*, Venice, 1554, esp. pp. 277 ff. (ed. Milan, 1864, ii, pp. 109 ff.), largely inspired by Horace; Leone de' Sommi, *Quattro dialoghi in materia di rappresentazioni sceniche* (1556), ed. F. Marotti, Milan, 1968.

180. D. Gnoli, *La Roma di Leon X*, Milan, 1938, pp. 96 ff.; Neiiendam, op. cit. in n. 177, pp. 105 ff., 130.

132

181. See above, p. 48.

182. Above, pp. 30, 36.

183. It appears to my eye that when the pier-strip is visible the whole composition is co-ordinated by the triangular pattern, but that when the strip is covered the centrality of the remaining part of the design is more emphatically stated by the lictors either side of the throne.

184. The distinction in compositional technique is of the kind for the recognition of which we are mainly indebted to the analytical approach of Wölfflin. I should like to draw attention to the anticipatory and historiographically re-markable observations of K. L. Fernow, 'Ueber Rafaels Teppiche', in *Römische Studien*, iii, Zürich, 1808, pp. 155 ff.; he said that the frescoes in the Stanze in general, and earlier works, seemed to be based upon rules and upon formulae like the pyramid, symmetry etc.; in later works, especially the tapestries and the Logge-frescoes 'findet sich keine Spur einer Komponir- und Gruppirungskunst, son-den blos eine deutliche, kunstlose und doch immer malerisch schöne Darstellung des Gegen-standes', as in *Paul at Athens* and the *Sacrifice at Lystra*; he found such designs as apparently *kunstlos* as Nature itself.

scene of three.[181] The tapestries intended for the central positions below, the *Healing of the Lame Man* and the *Conversion of the Proconsul*, are both emphatically symmetrical in design (*Figs.* 16, 23). The realization of this intention could not be straightforward in the case of the *Conversion of the Proconsul* because the intrusion within the picture-frame of the pier on the right—a solution, as we have seen, to the peculiar problem of the uncertain presence of the *baldacchino*[182]—cast the effective centre of the picture-field appreciably to the left. The perspective, however, is centred on the total frame-width and this draws the architecture of the Proconsul's throne nearer to the centre-line of the bay; the movement of the Proconsul himself brings his head nearer still and this head is the apex of a triangular structural system based upon the full width of the tapestry. Raphael could probably go no further towards a solution of approximate symmetry, effective whether the strip on the right were obscured or not.[183] The triangular system, like that in the *Healing of the Lame Man*, works within a tripartite vertical sub-division which is marked in this case by the twin columns and the lictors by the throne. These two central designs alone are controlled by a static structural system of a kind that is normally associated with Raphael's compositional technique in the years before about 1511–12; their particular position is the explanation for what would appear, in a too-simple analysis of his 'stylistic development', an aberration, and the distinction between these two designs and the rest, once again, has nothing to do with chronology.[184]

There is, however, one notable difference between Raphael's organization of his three-tapestry sequences on each side wall and that which was established in the Sixtine cycle above. In the latter the lateral frescoes are distinguished from the central ones by two-part division; the rhythm is consistent down the whole length of the wall but it is a static system and each unit stands by itself. Raphael's lateral tapestries are not organized with respect to this system but with respect to a still more emphatic organization about the centre of the space, inside the screen, to be decorated; it is a logical modification that reflects the difference in the extent of his sequences that was visible at any one moment. On the right wall the focus of the *Charge to Peter* is thrown to the right, that of the *Death of Ananias* to the left; on the left wall the focus of the *Conversion of Saul* is thrown to the left, that of the *Sacrifice at Lystra* to the right. The same system controls the distribution and balance of described movements within each tapestry and thus it has a dynamic character. The implications of this overall organization, presumably one of the first things to be established, are very considerable. It could have played, for example, a quite effective rôle in the choice of principal proto-types for the *Charge to Peter*, the *Conversion of Saul* and the *Sacrifice at Lystra*. It limited, moreover, the possibilities of vertical compositional relationships between tapestries and frescoes; these relationships could only be precise in the centre of each three-bay unit, and there they are precise. When we see the *Healing of the Lame Man* beneath the *Healing of the Leper* (*Figs.* 15, 16) we notice the alignment of the columns in the one with the trees in the other, the superimposition of pediments of wall-tabernacle and Temple, the broad triangle of the same proportion within each composition, and on the right of each the women with their naked children carrying sacrificial offerings; Peter and the cripple are directly below the High Priest and the acolyte. When we see the *Conversion of the Proconsul* beneath *Moses in Egypt* (*Figs.* 22, 23) we notice how the cluster of architectural forms around the throne in the one echoes the group of trees around the well in the other, how the gesture of Paul repeats that of Moses (which may explain how it comes to be left-handed), and how Raphael's pier on the right stands below Botticelli's eccentric strip of architecture; indeed it may have been this architectural feature in the fresco—itself balanced in the equivalent field in the other half of the chapel—that suggested to Raphael the solution to the problem raised by the *baldacchino* of the papal throne.

The vertical relationships in design are coexistent with the strongest vertical relationships of theme. With this thought in mind it is particularly frustrating that we cannot extend this discussion to the altar-wall, where, as there is good reason to believe, a thematic connection between tapestries and frescoes was once again particularly close. If only to understand the probable impoverishment of our understanding of the *Stoning of Stephen* and the *Miraculous Draught of Fishes* it is worth remembering that both the missing frescoes in the zone above were by Perugino. We have no basis, even for speculation, for visualizing his treatment of the *Finding of Moses*, on the left. But we can guess from several other examples in his work how he might have composed the *Nativity*, on the right; and it could have been in general disposition very similar to the *Miraculous Draught*, with the Shepherds (or Kings) approaching and kneeling before Christ as the first Apostles do.

In one other case it seems fairly certain that the fresco above Raphael's field of action exercised some influence upon his thoughts: not, however, on this serious level but rather by tickling his sense of humour. The earthquake which breaks the frame of the *Release of Paul* (*Fig.* 26) is a joke that soon palls when we look at the tapestry out of its context; some observers miss the joke altogether and see Mannerism in its place, from which point it is but one more humourless step to the conclusion that Giulio Romano's was the mind at work.[185] But this tapestry was to hang under the right-hand end of Cosimo Rosselli's *Worship of the Golden Calf*, which at just this point has its only redeeming feature, a small dog that steps delicately out of the picture on to the stone cornice, breaking the frame in a different sense. One joke inspired the other, and each would have been more durable when seen in combination with the other.[186]

The rest of the space below the *Worship of the Golden Calf*, beyond the interrupting screen, was occupied by *Paul preaching at Athens* (*Fig.* 25). The visual sources that came to Raphael's mind were organized with such dexterity that his Paul stood directly beneath the wrathful Moses, and so that the figure-curve that rises from the bottom left-hand corner echoed a similar shape in the fresco. However, the virtuosity in the exploitation of sources is shown most remarkably in the relationship between the design of this tapestry and its position in the chapel in a more general sense. The line of the portico behind Paul is calculated, as we have seen, to continue that of the screen. Paul stands on the same level as that of the action in the rest of the tapestry-series where it is the ground-level, conventional in history-scenes, that notionally begins at the frame. *Paul at Athens* is exceptional in the tradition of monumental history-painting in the descent of the ground-plane to a second level which is unequivocally below that of the frame. When the tapestry was in position, raised above the stone bench and with its 'picture' raised again above its fictive relief-*spalliera*, the lower ground-plane must have seemed approximately on a level with the floor of the chapel;[187] to the spectator whose place was in this part of the chapel it must have appeared that he completed the half-circle of Paul's audience, that his relation to Paul and his message was the same as that of Dionysius, and that he, the lay-spectator of the modern world, had been made a citizen of the new Athens that was Leonine Rome. This was the extraordinary invention

185. Fischel, op. cit. in n. 13 (1948), p. 266, suggested Giulio as the inventor of this motif.

186. It may be that Raphael was simultaneously making a joke at the expense of his medium; for in fifteenth-century tapestries it is not unusual for the figure-design to break over the border.

187. It is perhaps by deliberate design that the difference of level is not exactly calculable; four steps are visible but there could be more, and the position of Dionysius—on the steps or on the ground—is ambiguous.

188. At the time of writing the *Miraculous Draught*, the *Charge to Peter* and *Paul at Athens* have been cleaned; of these, silver alone was used in the first two, silver and gold in the third. The condition of the rest of the set makes it difficult to be precise about the technique, but it appears that gold and silver were also used together in the *Death of Ananias*, the *Stoning of Stephen* and the *Sacrifice at Lystra*.

189. For example: Gerspach, op. cit. in n. 73, p. 104; E. Camesasca, appendix to R. Salvini, *La Cappella Sistina in Vaticano*, Florence, 1965, p. 139; M. Florisoone, 'Gli arazzi classici', in *Il libro degli arazzi*, ed. J. Jobé, Milan, 1965, pp. 79–80. On the other hand G. F. Waagen, *Die Cartons von Raphael . . .*, Berlin, 1860, p. 11 thought that the use of gold was a sign of Raphael's *good* taste; and more recently Fischel, op. cit. in n. 13 (1948), pp. 150, 251, 263, also gave an enthusiastic interpretation and took the gold to be part of Raphael's intentions.

190. In connection with the possible meanings of the tapestries outlined above, pp. 76 ff., it may be interesting to notice that Augustine (*Sermo LXXIX, P.L.* 38, col. 493), commenting on this text and the similar one in Matthew xvii. 2 (he conflates the two: 'vestimenta ejus facta sunt candida sicut nix') said the shining robe was a figure of the healing of the Church; and this thought could have been an additional reason for the exceptionally precise illustration in the tapestry.

191. Jonathan Richardson Snr., *A Theory of Painting* (Strawberry Hill edition of the *Works*, 1792, p. 68); the same point was made by Quatremère de Quincy, op. cit. in n. 82, p. 316.

192. Raphael is careful to identify the principal figures by consistency of colour and by following tradition; Peter is dressed in yellow and blue, Paul in green and red. This may be the right place to clear up a problem that has given rise to some argument: in the Cartoon of the *Miraculous Draught* (*Pl.* 1) Christ's robe is colourless while its reflection is strongly pink. It has been supposed that one or the other is overpainted, but this is not the explanation; the robe was painted with a lake pigment that has faded, but the fading is only skin-deep and the body of the paint beneath is deep pink; the reflection was painted in a non-fading vermilion (red mercuric sulphide). Thus Raphael's Christ in this scene—in contrast to the *Charge to Peter*—wore the traditional red and blue colours. By a curious accident the blue has entirely faded from the figure of Christ in the Vatican tapestry whereas that of Peter's tunic remains; this is perhaps to be explained by the

that came out of Raphael's mind as he pondered the tapestry's subject and position, and the possibilities latent in the composition on disparate, stepped levels of Dürer's *Christ before Pilate*.

One other aspect of the integration of the tapestries into the decorative scheme of the chapel has become obvious during the current restoration of the Sixtine histories. One may now see the hitherto unexpected and certainly exceptional quantity of gold on their surfaces which is applied as liberally to the picture-fields as to the framing elements; the gold picks out highlights on figures, buildings and landscape and is used with an intention which is not solely decorative, for it accentuates and clarifies the relief of forms. Gold and silver are woven with exactly the same effect into the tapestries; the cleaning of some of the Vatican set has revealed how intelligently the metal threads were used to emphasize both plasticity and detail.[188] The effect was surely stunning when the colours and gilding of frescoes and tapestries were still fresh, and above all when they were seen by candle-light at Vespers. The metal thread in the tapestries, so far from being an arbitrary and superfluous addition by the weavers—in poor taste, as some believe[189]—must have been worked according to Raphael's very precise instructions; the imperative in this statement is justified by the identity of the aesthetic effect of the metal in tapestries and frescoes. This conclusion is most important to the understanding of the *Charge to Peter*, where the white robe of Christ is embellished, in the tapestry, with flashes of silver; the effect, as a result of oxidization, is neither pleasing nor realistic now, but it should have been both of these originally and—what is just as important—meaningful. The tapestry illustrates the description of Christ's robes at the Transfiguration (Mark ix. 3: *vestimenta . . . splendentia, candida nimis velut nix*) which, following the implication of the text itself, was taken by exegetes and painters as a prevision of His appearance after the Resurrection. In Duccio's *Maestà*, for example, the appearance of Christ at the Transfiguration and in all post-Resurrection scenes is distinguished by the striation of His robe with gold; but whereas Duccio painted a blue robe throughout the *Maestà*, the robe in the tapestry conforms in both respects with the text: it is shining and white.[190] This precision is more convincing as an intention of Raphael's than as a liberty taken by the weavers and it was presumably effected by a written instruction from the former to the latter. It demonstrates in another way how Raphael both accommodated the tapestries to the decoration of the chapel and saw even in that accommodation further opportunities to achieve his own expressive intention.

Raphael's world was one in which tapestries were a part of everyday experience and it is absurd to suppose that he might have been ignorant of the peculiar potentialities and limitations of the medium; but on the other hand it is far from clear how much attention he paid to them. It was believed already by Jonathan Richardson that the sumptuous brilliance of the colour in the Cartoons, and its extraordinary variety, were designed by Raphael to show tapestry to its best advantage.[191] Perhaps Richardson was right, but one may doubt the point when looking at a contemporary painting largely by Raphael's own hand, the *Santa Cecilia* at Bologna, or even an earlier one like the *Repulse of Attila*, where the gamut of colour is not appreciably different. In any case the opulent beauty of, for example, the *Healing of the Lame Man* is not constant throughout the Cartoons. There is an abrupt change in the *Death of Ananias* to severity of colour as well as of form, and it seems that Raphael's principal concern with colour, here as elsewhere, was that it should be in the highest degree decorative, descriptive and expressive.[192]

But the question that was rightly in Richardson's mind may be put in its starkest form by asking whether there are *any* respects in which Raphael would have behaved differently had he been painting mirror-images of frescoes or oil-paintings to occupy the same positions in the chapel. At this point it is helpful to recall that he had faced the problem of tapestry-design before. In 1514 he had replaced quadrant-shaped sections of the ceiling of the Stanza d'Eliodoro with frescoed simulations of tapestry;[193] and on that occasion he modified his style appreciably so that the four new history-scenes appear exceptionally linear, schematic and two-dimensional. He did no such thing, however, when he designed the Cartoons, and one may wonder why not. Paradoxically the answer may lie in the very fact that he was designing for real and not simulated tapestry. There was no need, in this case, to imitate tapestry. He seems to have felt, on the contrary, that the weavers should simulate painting, and if this impression is correct it is comprehensible in two different ways. He must have been conscious of an ironic inversion of realities: his tapestries, simulating paintings, were to replace paintings simulating tapestries with astounding brilliance in the Sixtine decoration. And just as his paintings of the period are partly conditioned by a virtuoso ambition for the achievement of the impossible (the imitation of light-effects, for example, in the *Release of Saint Peter*) so it would be logical if he felt that the greatest brilliance in tapestry also lay in the nearest approximation to the impossible, in that case the exact imitation of painting.

Raphael's tapestries were not, of course, the first to aspire to the condition of painting. That is an innovation for which he should be neither credited nor—as some would wish—blamed. An earlier series with this characteristic is the Trivulzio cycle of the *Months*, now in the Castello Sforzesco in Milan, which was made about 1503; and there are several isolated pieces of this kind from the fifteenth century. Nevertheless it appeared to a friend of Raphael's, Pietro Aretino, that the innovation was effectively made in the Leonine tapestries.[194] Vasari made a more subtle point when talking of his friend Francesco Salviati's cartoons for *pitture che si tessono* and of his intelligent response to the medium: an exploitation of those qualities in which it might show to best advantage, such as capricious invention, variety and individuality of objects, relief of figures and gaiety of colour, richness of detail in such matters as costume.[195] If we make a mental adjustment for Vasari's way of thinking, in which the twisted columns of the *Healing of the Lame Man* would certainly be interpreted as *capricciose*, and if we allow also that Vasari's approach is likely to have been somewhat more inclined to caprice for its own sake than Raphael's, his text probably provides us with the most apposite formula for defining Raphael's attitude to the problem: no surrender of his own achievements as a painter but a capitalization of the opportunities that the commission had to offer. With a qualification on the matter of *invenzioni capricciose* Vasari's text could be taken as an accurate, if limited, appreciation of Raphael's Cartoons.

One significant addition might be made, however, to Vasari's text. Raphael so organized his compositions that they were filled out, beyond the figure-groups, towards all margins with the colour and detail of landscape and architecture. An intelligent adjustment to the problem of tapestry-design provoked in turn his virtuosity in pure painting, for there is surely no more beautiful painted architecture or landscape (*Pl.* 11) in his whole career. The style of landscape was for him, in fact, substantially a new one. It was formed partly upon the study of the landscape-conventions in the

use of different blue dyes for the threads with which these draperies were woven.

193. The arguments for this statement are in Shearman, op. cit. in n. 1, p. 175.

194. Letter to Francesco Pocopanno, 24 November 1537: 'Ecco le forbicette mandatemi son piene di trofei rilevati e grandi; veramente si cominciò a mutar verso tosto che si viddero i panni di Leone in Capella lavorati da la seta e da l'oro sopra i cartoni disegnati e coloriti da Rafaello. Non si usano più fiori piccoli in damaschi né in razzi ...'; the context of this passage is a very interesting and general discussion of a change of taste (*Lettere sull'arte di Pietro Aretino*, ed. F. Pertile, i, Milan, 1957, p. 87).

195. *Vite*, vii, p. 28: '... tutta quella diligenza che in simile opera si può maggiore, e che hanno di bisogno le pitture che si tessono: invenzioni capricciose, componimenti varj vogliono aver le figure che spicchino l'una dall'altra, perchè abbiano rilievo e venghino allegre ne' colori, ricche nelli abiti e vestiri'.

196. See the catalogue: *Drawings of Landscape and Trees by Fra Bartolommeo*, Sotheby's, 20 November 1957, esp. lot 33 in relation to the *Charge to Peter*. The farm in the same Cartoon, with its line of washing, may be compared with the one in Fra Bartolomeo's *Vision of Saint Bernard* (1504–7).

Sixtine frescoes (particularly in Perugino's *Baptism*) and partly upon direct study of farms in the Campagna, of groups of trees and outcrops of *tufo*; there may well have been a corpus of his landscape drawings, now lost, very like that by Fra Bartolomeo which so fortunately survives.[196]

There remains still one other feature of the style of the Cartoons which cannot be assimilated within Vasari's formula but which could well have been evolved as a conscious adjustment to the problem. A painter of histories whose work is to be translated into tapestry is somewhat in the position of a speaker who must communicate through an indifferent public-address system; interference, if he is conscious of it, will make him enunciate with more than habitual clarity and deliberation. In fact Raphael's problem, supposing that he was conscious of it, was comparable to that of communicating across an interference more familiar to a painter, that of distance; and this problem he had faced before. When he painted the two principal heads of the Virgin and Child in the *Sistine Madonna*, made about 1512–13 for an altar remote from the spectator in S. Sisto in Piacenza, he enlarged the essential expressive units, eyes, nose and mouth, to a scale unnatural in relation to the outline of the faces themselves; the result, and surely the intention, is that the expressions are legible over an exceptional distance. Giotto had adjusted his physiognomic style in the same way in the case of the vault-paintings of the Arena Chapel. There is a comparable phenomenon to be observed in the Cartoons—in some more than in others—but it applies to whole figures and not now to faces alone. The point is most obvious in the group of Apostles in the *Death of Ananias* (*Pl.* 22), where arms and hands, some heads and feet, are unnaturally large in proportion to total stature; the Apostle with the upward-pointing finger would look very odd nude and it is only a swathe of drapery that ensures the (subjective) integrity of this figure. Correggio, perhaps inspired by these very models, took the same anatomical liberties in his Apostles in his second cupola-painting, in the Duomo of Parma. It is revealing to compare Raphael's painted Paul in the *Sacrifice at Lystra* (*Pl.* 34) with the life-study at Chatsworth (*Fig.* 69), and to see the proportionate increase in the expressively essential head and arms between drawing and Cartoon. In this Cartoon it is generally true that arms are very large in relation to torsos. There is approximately the same degree of adjustment in *Paul preaching at Athens* (*Pl.* 39) and in the *Miraculous Draught of Fishes* (*Pl.* 1); there is rather less, perhaps, in the *Conversion of the Proconsul* and the *Healing of the Lame Man* (*Pls.* 26, 12) and probably none at all in the *Charge to Peter* (*Pl.* 6). The assessment of the adjustment is of course extremely difficult and a matter for individual judgement, but it appears to offer the most sensible clue to a sequence of execution if such a clue is required; for this is a feature of style that may be interpreted as a progressive response, after the inventive process and during the painting itself, to the particular problem raised by the 'interference' in the medium. It could also, however, be interpreted as a progressive realization of a pictorial equivalent of the device called *energeia*, emphasis tending towards hyperbole; and it is of course possible that a pursuit of that ideal was related in Raphael's mind to the problem of communicating through tapestry with his accustomed clarity unimpaired.

Finally: how did Raphael regard his Cartoons? However convinced we may be that they were first and foremost a means to a particular end, that is the tapestries in the chapel, it is a little hard to believe that they were in his eyes fit to be discarded when their primary function had been performed. Did he hope, or even intend, that they should be regarded thereafter as works of art in their own right? There is one almost conclusive indication that he did. At one point above all others in the set the convenience of the weavers and the intelligibility of the Cartoon were in direct conflict and he had to make a choice. This point came in the inscription in the *Conversion of the Proconsul* (*Pl.* 26), and the choice was made in favour of the visual integrity of the Cartoon. To this indication may be added another, less sure. In 1521, already, the now-lost Cartoon for the *Conversion of Saul* was in the house of Cardinal Domenico Grimani in Venice;[197] it is difficult to understand its so rapid return from Brussels unless the Cardinal had pre-empted the work before it left Rome, or unless it had been offered to him. That the Cartoons should have been conceived simultaneously as functioning objects and as independent works of art to be valued as highly as any painting seems to me entirely natural. Raphael poured so much of himself into these works, the expenditure of brilliance, of effort, and in a certain sense of personality was so conspicuous and so final, that it appears psychologically inevitable that he should have conceived a great affection for them. The intention, which I think may be assumed, that we should appreciate the beauty of the Cartoons themselves is not the least of those many factors that conditioned their appearance.

197. See below, p. 139.

V: History

Rogers said he was coming out of the Vatican with W. Lock. Rogers said 'Let us look once more.' 'Why?' said Lock; 'you have finer things at Hampton Court!' 'It is not odd,' said Rogers; 'The Elgin Marbles and Cartoons are finer than any thing abroad.' (Benjamin Robert Haydon)

THE payment closing Raphael's account for the Cartoons was made on 20 December 1516, and the weaving of the tapestries had been begun in Brussels before July of the next year.[1] The weaver chosen by Leo X was Pieter van Aelst, or Pierre d'Enghien.[2] There is a confused note by Francisco de Hollanda in his copy of the 1568 edition of Vasari's *Vite* which may be taken to mean that the execution of the tapestries was supervised by the Bolognese artist Tommaso Vincidor;[3] but this information, or perhaps this interpretation of it, is almost certainly false. Vincidor was still in Rome in 1517,[4] and was sent by Leo X to Flanders to supervise other tapestries, in part designed by Raphael and in part by his pupils, in May 1520.[5] In the seventeenth century it was believed, on the contrary, that the execution was supervised by Bernard van Orley and Michel Coxcie;[6] it is probable that this belief too has a grain of truth which has been misplaced, since Van Orley, at least, is a candidate for the authorship of the new borders of some of the earliest sets of tapestries to be made from Raphael's Cartoons, one of them already completed in the 1520s. It is not very obvious, in any case, that Pieter van Aelst required supervision; and it is more likely that he received with the Cartoons written instructions for the assembly of main scenes with their borders (on which point the instructions would seem to have been insufficient or misinterpreted, as we have seen[7]) and for the distribution of gold and silver (where they would seem to have been very precise). Seven of the tapestries had been delivered in time for their exhibition in the Sistine Chapel on 26 December 1519,[8] and the whole set of ten were entered in the inventory of Leo's tapestries drawn up at his death in December 1521.[9]

The appreciation and influence of Raphael's designs have, of course, been conditioned by the very different histories of the Cartoons on the one hand and of the several sets of tapestries on the other and also by the availability of engravings, the earlier ones made from drawings that approximated to a greater or lesser extent to the finished compositions and the later ones—

1. See above, pp. 3, 42. In most early accounts it was assumed that the tapestries were woven in the town of Arras; A. Henne and A. Wauters, *Histoire de la Ville de Bruxelles*, Brussels, 1845, ii, p. 300, n. 1, gave Brussels as the place of manufacture, and A. Wauters, *Les tapisseries bruxelloises: Essai historique . . .*, Brussels, 1878, p. 101, claimed this as the first correct statement. However I find it already in Johann Jacob Volkmann, *Neueste Reisen durch England*, Leipzig, 1782, i, p. 438, in the report, 1824, of the London exhibition of the 'Henry VIII set' by R. Ackermann (see below, n. 45), and in W. Trull, *Raphael Vindicated by a Comparison between the Original Tapestries . . . of Leo X and the Cartoons at Hampton Court . . .*, London, 1840, p. 2.

2. First established by E. Müntz, 'Les tapisseries de Raphaël au Vatican', *Chronique des arts*, 1876, p. 246; see also W. Bombe, 'Raffaels Teppiche und Pieter van Aelst, auf Grund des handschriftlichen Nachlasses von Eugen Müntz', *Repertorium für Kunstwissenschaft*, i, 1929, pp. 15 ff.

3. A. Raczynski, *Les arts en Portugal*, Paris, 1846, p. 200; J. D. Passavant, *Raphaël d'Urbin*, Paris, 1860, ii, pp. 556 ff.; R. Dos Santos, 'Un exemplaire de Vasari annoté par Francisco de Olanda', *Studi vasariani*, Florence, 1952, pp. 91 ff. The *postilla* comes against the name of Penni, whom Hollanda identifies as 'Bologna' (i.e. Vincidor), and the latter is said to have been sent to Flanders to make the tapestries of Leo X from the designs of Raphael and his pupils. It is not evident that Hollanda did in fact mean the *Acts of the Apostles*; the assumption that Vincidor did supervise them is the basis of a recent suggestion that Dürer saw the Cartoons during his Netherlands journey of 1520–21 (S. Sulzberger, 'Dürer a-t-il vu à Bruxelles les cartons de Raphaël?', *Gazette des Beaux-Arts*, 6ème Pér., liv, 1959, pp. 177 ff.). It seems to me, however, that such a remarkable experience is unlikely to have been omitted from Dürer's *Tagebuch*, and I think that the undoubtedly Raphaelesque qualities of his subsequent *Four Apostles* are better explained by his study of the engraved set of *Apostles* by Marcantonio, after Raphael, B. xiv, p. 74, Nos. 64–76 (compare especially Dürer's Apostle drawings of 1522–23, F. Winkler, *Die Zeichnungen Albrecht Dürers*, iv, Berlin, 1939, Nos. 874–5, for this connection); Dürer seems to have arranged, during his Netherlandish journey, to acquire a complete set of prints after Raphael.

4. On 10 January 1517 he witnessed a notarial document on Raphael's behalf: V. Golzio, *Raffaello nei documenti . . .*, Vatican City, 1936, p. 52.

5. R. Foerster, 'Philostrats Gemälde in der Renaissance', *Jahrbuch der königlich preuszischen Kunstsammlungen*, xxv, 1904, p. 28, interprete the documents, including Hollanda's note, i this way; see also O. Fischel, 'Ein Teppichen wurf des Thomas Vincidor', ibid., lv, 1934 pp. 89 ff., and above, p. 42, n. 107.

6. A. Félibien, *Entretiens sur les vies . . . des plu excellens peintres . . .*, ii, Paris, 1672, p. 349; R de Piles, *Abrégé de la vie des peintres*, Paris, 1699 p. 356.

7. See above, pp. 37, 43.

8. See the account of Marcantonio Michie quoted above, p. 38.

from the early eighteenth century onwards—reproducing the Cartoons themselves.[10] The importance of engravings should not be underestimated. It was, for instance, Agostino Veneziano's engraving after the *modello* for the *Conversion of the Proconsul* that brought about the earliest known case of the influence of any of the Cartoon-designs upon another major work, which was in Andrea del Sarto's fresco-cycle in the Chiostro dello Scalzo in Florence; the engraving is dated 1516 and the fresco—the *Arrest of the Baptist* —was completed by July of the next year.[11] However, we cannot hope to account in detail for the circulation of engravings whereas we can reconstruct with fair precision the histories of the Cartoons and tapestries, and that is worth doing. It is significant, for example, that the two greatest artists whose styles of history-painting were profoundly affected by these designs, Rubens and Poussin, knew them in different ways; the former had seen and copied the Cartoons themselves, while the latter had seen and copied the tapestries (*Figs.* 89, 90),[12] and these different opportunities do much to explain the contrast in the way Raphael's influence worked upon them.

In the history of the Cartoons the difficult period is the sixteenth century; a reconstruction of this early part of their story is largely to be deduced from the circumstances of their apparent use, and for this reason it will be better to consider first the history of the tapestries. However, the first event to be noticed, because the history of the tapestry-manufacture is itself affected by it, is the arrival back in Italy of the Cartoon of the *Conversion of Saul*; it is already recorded under the date 1521 in the collection of Cardinal Domenico Grimani in Venice.[13] This instant return is surprising, and the reference, to a *cartone grande*, does not quite exclude the possibility that the object in question was a large drawing; the entry in the 1528 inventory of his heir, the Cardinal Marino Grimani, which describes 'Un quadro in carta grande conversion di san Paulo'[14] does not dispose of the suspicion. But it seems that all doubt is removed by Marino's holograph version of the inventory, drawn up in 1526, which was known in the nineteenth century, for there it was remarked that the Cartoon was coloured.[15]

This being the case it is reasonable to ask whether Pieter van Aelst had in fact used the Cartoons or copies of them instead. That copies were made in the sixteenth century for the purposes of manufacture of tapestries is certain, as we shall see from documents to be introduced shortly; and it is probably this early set of Flemish copies, rather than any of those made later in England, that explains the pricking round all outlines of the Cartoons (which can have nothing directly to do with the weaving process). However, it can be demonstrated that the surviving Cartoons were indeed used in the manufacture of the Leonine set of tapestries. All the Cartoons have been cut into vertical strips a little over a metre wide for easier management under the looms. And one very precise indication is given by a comparison between the *Charge to Peter* and the corresponding Vatican tapestry (*Pl.* 6, *Fig.* 14). It will be noticed that the weavers took minor liberties in interpreting the grasses and flowers in the foreground, as they surely felt well qualified to do; but they also took the far greater liberty of raising the frieze of distant trees and buildings clear above the heads of Christ and the Apostles. This was done by severing landscape from heads by one continuous undulating cut which is still visible in spite of the restorations of the Cartoon; and it was done for a particular reason: to allow specialists in landscape and in heads to do their work independently (the activities of several differently endowed hands are very clear in the Leonine tapestries). This raising of the landscape led to the omission of a shallow strip of sky along the top in the tapestry, and also to a

9. *Inventarium omnium bonorum existentium in foraria S.^{mi} D. Leonis papae X . . . MDXVIII*, Archivio di Stato, Rome, Archivio Camerale I, 1557, filza 1, fols. 30r.–v. This inventory, begun in 1518, was allowed to lapse from about the autumn of 1519 and was brought up to date after the death of Leo, 1 December 1521; but a marginal interpolation to the entry is dated 17 December 1521. See also above, p. 6, n. 28.

10. I must make it clear that I shall not attempt to trace the history of the appreciation and influence of the Cartoon-designs, but to provide some of the materials for anyone who wishes to do so. I should like to acknowledge at this point the very valuable assistance, in the reconstruction of the provenance of the Cartoons, which I have received from Graham Reynolds, who made available to me notes in the files at the Victoria and Albert Museum, and from Oliver Millar, who led me to the material in the Surveyor's Office and to most of that in the Public Record Office which I shall quote.

11. J. Shearman, *Andrea del Sarto*, Oxford, 1965, i, p. 68, ii, p. 301.

12. For the case of Rubens, see below, p. 147. The drawing at Leningrad (Hermitage, Inv. 5293, attributed to Raphael) may be either a study by Poussin or an exact replica of one, and in either case it is of the greatest interest since there is, strangely, no other graphic evidence of his copying a work by Raphael (it may be noted that the drawing was not made after one of the early prints, *Figs.* 58, 59).

13. T. Frimmel, *Der Anonimo Morelliano*, Vienna, 1888, p. 104: '1521 . . . In casa del cardinal Grimano . . . El cartone grande de la conversione de S. Paulo fo de mano de Rafaelo, fatto per un dei razzi della Capella.' The Cardinal was in fact resident in Venice in 1521 (P. Paschini, *Domenico Grimani, Cardinale di S. Marco*, Rome, 1943, p. 101); he died in 1523. Michiel calls this *cartone* a *dissegno* in 1528 (see below, n. 21).

14. P. Paschini, 'Le collezioni archeologiche dei Grimani', *Rendiconti della pontificia accademia romana di archeologia*, v, 1928, p. 182.

15. I can find no reference to this inventory in modern literature, and I quote from J. D. Passavant, *Rafael von Urbino*, ii, Leipzig, 1839, p. 245: 'In dem eigenhändigen Verzeichniss seiner Kunstwerke vom Jahr 1526 hat der Cardinal und Patriarch zu Venedig noch bemerkt, dass der Carton colorirt ist.'

conspicuous gap in the design above Christ's left hand which was filled with an improvised blasted oak (not in fact, or not intentionally, an instant comment on the changed conditions in Medici-Della Rovere relations in 1517, when this particular piece was made).

The tapestries, then, were delivered in Rome between 1519 and 1521. A marginal note, dated 17 December 1521, in the inventory of Pope Leo's tapestries states that they were put in pawn after his death on 1 December,[16] and a letter from Castiglione, dated 16 December, explains that this was done in order to raise money for the expenses during the *sede vacante*, including those of the new conclave.[17] They were then stolen—if they were the *razi di papa Leon* mentioned by a Venetian correspondent—by the Colonna when they sacked the Vatican Palace on 20 September 1526;[18] Leo's silver *Apostles* were removed on the same occasion. But the tapestries were probably returned almost at once, perhaps as a result of the unusually effective edict of Clement VII on 24 October.[19] Within eight months the Vatican was occupied again, and again the tapestries were removed, but not immediately. The most celebrated casualty of the Sack of Rome in May 1527 was in fact the commander of the besieging forces, the Constable de Bourbon, who lay in state in the Sistine Chapel 'hung with the richest and most beautiful tapestries of His Holiness'.[20] This was probably the last occasion upon which the whole set was hung in the positions that Raphael had planned.

Undoubtedly most, if not all, the tapestries were stolen during this occupation, but the story is far from clear. The *Conversion of Saul* and *Paul preaching at Athens* went to Venice, where they were recorded in the possession of Zuanantonio Venier in 1528. They got there by a curious sequence of accidents, having been acquired by Isabella d'Este during the Sack of Rome,

16. The text in Bombe, op. cit. in n. 2, p. 16, n. 4. The practice of pawning was widespread in the period, even among Emperors, and would have seemed much less scandalous than it does now (see A. Luzio and R. Renier, 'Il lusso di Isabella d'Este', *Nuova Antologia,* lxiv, 16 July 1896, p. 314, who give several examples).

17. The letter is quoted by L. Pastor, *The History of the Popes*, ed. R. F. Kerr, ix, London, 1950, p. 3, n. 3.

18. Letter from Rome, 21 September 1526, in *I diarii di Marino Sanuto*, xlii, Venice, 1895, col. 700; see also the letter of Girolamo Negri to Michiel, in *Lettere di principi*, ed. Giordano Ziletti, Venice, 1564, i, fol. 104v., and Paolo Giovio, *Pompeii columnae cardinalis vita*, Florence, 1548 (unpaginated).

19. Girolamo Negri, letter of 24 October, ed. cit. in n. 18, i, fol. 105v.

20. Letter of 19 June 1527 in *I diarii di Marino Sanuto*, xlv, Venice, 1896, col. 418: 'fu posto nella capella del Papa, quale hanno apparata di quelle riche et più belle tapezarie di Nostro Signore'.

21. Marcantonio Michiel (Frimmel, op. cit. in n. 13, p. 98): '1528 ... In casa de M. Zuanantonio Venier ... Li dui pezzi de razzo de seda et d'oro, istoriati, luno della conversione de S. Paulo, laltro della predicatione furono fatti far da papa Leone cun el dissegno de Rafaelo d'Urbino; uno delli qual dissegni, zoè la conversione, è in man del patriarcha d'Aqleia (Marino Grimani—see above, p. 139), l'altro è divulgato in stampa' (see above, p. 106). A. Luzio, 'Isabella d'Este e il sacco di Roma', *Archivio storico lombardo*, xxxv, Ser. 4, x, 1908, pp. 89 ff., 387 ff.

22. Also the Vatican tapestry inventory of 1555, fol. 102v.: 'Panni d'oro doi della cappella, fatti al tempo di Leone X°, li quali forno robbati al saccho di Roma, lo conestabile di Francia li trovò in Constantinopoli molti rotti, li ha fatti racconciar' et rimandar' a S. Stà., a dì 29 di Septembre 1554' (E. Müntz, in *Histoire générale de la tapisserie*, Paris, 1879–84, ii, p. 21, n. 2, and Bombe, op. cit. in n. 2, p. 17).

23. A similar inscription was formerly on a border attached to the *Conversion of Saul*; see, for example, Edward Wright, *Some Observations made in travelling through France, Italy, &c ...*, London, 1730, p. 272.

24. G. Gaye, *Carteggio inedito d'artisti dei secoli xiv, xv, xvi*, Florence, 1839, ii, p. 222.

25. From the report, dated 14 June 1531, of two weavers upon the new set: 'sono bene et lialmente facte et meglior laborate del tapezaria che quelle de S.to Pietro et sancto Paulo li quali dicto Pietro van Aelst ha fatte luy et consigniate a papa Leone ... et ... sono più ricchi d'oro et di seta ... et quest'iudicamo perche abiamo visti e revisti li sopradicti panni et tapezerie al paragone stese in capella del papa in palatio a Roma l'ultimo dì de marzo 1531' (Bombe, op. cit. in n. 2, p. 25).

26. The letters were published by A. Mercati, *Aneddoti per la storia dei pontefici Pio II, Leone X*, Rome, 1934, pp. 17–18 (extracts reprinted in J. White and J. Shearman, 'Raphael's Tapestries and their Cartoons', *The Art Bulletin*, xl, 1958, pp. 215–16); and Pastor, op. cit. in n. 17, x, p. 507. The letters do in fact allow the possibility that six pieces and a fragment were found in Naples; if that were the case it would exclude the possibility that those at Lyon in 1530 belonged to the set.

27. B. Nogara, 'Un arazzo mutilato di Raffaello', *Illustrazione vaticana*, ii, 1931, 1, pp. 22 ff. (the missing part was at that point replaced by painted canvas). It should be noted, however, that Nogara's explanation of the exceptionally good condition of the fragment—that it was not formerly exhibited with the rest of the set—is not correct (see below, ns. 35, 37, 42); it is perhaps partially to be explained by the diminished weight upon tl vertical threads.

28. For the missing borders see above, p. 4 Padre Resta, in the seventeenth century, ma the following note in one of his copies of Vasar *Vite* against the reference to Raphael's tape tries: 'Io ho un pezzetto del lanificio d'u degli arazzi' (G. Mongeri, 'Postille di anonimo seicentista alla prima edizione del vite ... scritte da Vasari', *Archivio stor. lombardo*, iii, 1876, p. 264; for the identificatio of the *anonimo* see J. Hess, 'On Raphael a Giulio Romano', *Gazette des Beaux-Arts*, 6èr Pér., xxxii, 1947, p. 106).

29. Archivio di Stato, Rome, Camerale I, 155 filza 3, fol. 86r., *Inventarium florerie Apostolici . 1544*; the *Sacrifice at Lystra, Death of Ananias a Healing of the Lame Man* are identified togeth with four others, unspecified, of the same se then on fol. 87v.: 'Item un quarto d'un pan di capella di quelli che fece papa Leone Xm che fù rubato al tempo del sacco, tagliato da soldati, et rimandato per il supradetto vesco di regno di Napoli' (see Müntz, op. cit. in 22, ii, p. 21, and *Les tapisseries de Raphaël* Vatican, Paris, 1897, p. 35n.).

30. '... sono ancora conservati nella cappe Papale ...' (*Vite*, 1550, p. 667).

seized by pirates and taken to Tunisia, and finally brought back to Venice by a sea-captain ('Cazadiavolo') who sold them to Venier.[21] The same two tapestries were returned to the Vatican as a gift from the Constable Anne de Montmorency in 1554, and an inscription then added to their borders announced that he had acquired them in Constantinople.[22] The *Paul preaching at Athens* had been severely damaged (*Fig.* 25); together with the inscription in the lower part of the lateral border it was given simultaneously a new *spalliera*, or fictive relief, below.[23] In 1530 Clement VII was in touch with a certain Giovanfrancesco da Mantova who had offered tapestries then in Lyon; the pope was prepared to pay the 160 ducats demanded, provided that the pieces were those of the story of Saint Peter designed by Raphael.[24] The outcome of this correspondence is not known, and there is no confirmation that the tapestries on offer were the right ones. It is certain, however, that some of the Leonine set were at hand for a comparison in the Sistine Chapel on 31 March 1531 with the new set of the Life of Christ, the so-called *Scuola nuova*, designed by Raphael's pupils and woven by Pieter van Aelst.[25] There are then letters of September and November 1532 between Clement and correspondents in Naples regarding the return to the Vatican of four complete pieces and one fragment; in this case it appears certain that these pieces did belong to the Leonine set and that the negotiations were successful.[26] Thus it seems probable that the whole set except the *Conversion of Saul* and *Paul preaching at Athens* had been returned by the early 1530s. The *Conversion of the Proconsul* was returned as a fragment (*Fig.* 27)[27] and the four—or more probably six—missing vertical borders were perhaps lost on this occasion too.[28] Eight pieces are itemized in the Vatican tapestry inventory of 1544, including the fragment returned from Naples which is presumably the *Conversion of the Proconsul*.[29]

Before the complete set was reintegrated by the Montmorency gift of 1554 the feasibility of hanging the tapestries in their intended positions had been prevented once and for all by the destruction of the original decoration of the altar-wall and its substitution by Michelangelo's *Last Judgement*, unveiled in 1541; the lower limit of the new fresco was well below that of the cornice from which the tapestries were suspended (*Fig.* 1), and in fact a new pair of tapestries, to cartoons by Perino del Vaga, were intended as a *basamento* for this wall. However Vasari, in the 1550 edition of the *Vite*, also before the restitution of the last of Raphael's tapestries, remarked of the set in general that it was kept in the Sistine Chapel;[30] and in another passage, in the 1550 *Vita* of Perino del Vaga, he seems to say more explicitly that they were in use there.[31] Lorenzo Vaccari's engraved view of the interior of the chapel (1578) does in fact show the tapestries hanging and several of them are recognizable;[32] the *Death of Ananias* occupies its rightful position but the *Miraculous Draught of Fishes* hangs on the left wall. Travellers' accounts of the Sistine Chapel late in the sixteenth century and early in the seventeenth continue to refer to works by Raphael there, by which they presumably meant the tapestries;[33] and there are specific testimonies to their exhibition there on feast days in Celio's guide to the paintings in Rome, 1638, and in the account of the English traveller Richard Lassels as late as 1670.[34]

At some time in the seventeenth century, however, there began a new custom which was to make the tapestries a focal point of public life in Rome for two centuries and a vivid experience for many travellers. Since the fifteenth century it had been the custom on the feast of Corpus Christi to decorate the processional route from the Vatican through the Borgo with tapestries hung from the houses, and to this public visual feast was now added the exhibition of the tapestries designed by Raphael.[35] The qualification was

31. Talking of the *basamento* of the *Last Judgement*: 'dove si aveva appiccare una spalliera di arazzi, tessuta di seta e d'oro (i.e. to Perino's design), come i panni che parano la cappella' (*Vite*, 1550, p. 939). Perino's cartoons are now in Palazzo Spada in Rome (H. Voss, *Die Malerei der Spätrenaissance in Rom und Florenz*, Berlin, 1920, i, p. 74 and Figs. 1–2).

32. E. Steinmann, *Die Sixtinische Kapelle*, i, Munich, 1901, Pl. XXXIV.

33. For example (1599) in the *Voyage du Duc de Rohan, faict en l'an 1600* . . ., Amsterdam, 1646, p. 85: 'Sixte fit la chapelle, où est ce tant renommé jugement de Michel l'Ange & autres siens ouvrages: auxquelles ceux du grand Raphael sont joints, pour prendre lustre les uns des autres'; also an account from the pontificate of Sixtus V (1581–90) published by R. Lanciani, 'Il Codice barberiniano XXX. 89', *Archivio della R. società romana di storia patria*, vi, 1883, p. 456: 'sono dalle bande opera dell'altro valentissimo homo Raffaele di Urbino'.

34. Gaspare Celio, *Memoria . . . delli nomi dell'Artefici delle pitture . . . di Roma*, Naples, 1638, p. 103: 'si suole ornare la Cappella in alcune feste principali con l'Arazzi di disegnio di Raffaello Santio di Urbino, sono tessuti con seta, & oro. vi sono gl'atti delli Apostoli, Pietro, e Pauolo . . .'; Richard Lassels, *The Voyage of Italy*, Paris, 1670, ii, p. 51: 'Upon great dayes this Chappell is hung with a rare suit of hangings of the design of Raphael Urbin wrought with gold and silk, containing the Acts of S. *Peter* and S. *Paul*' (Lassels might, of course, have been repeating Celio without independent knowledge).

35. I have not found a definitive date for the first exhibition. Passavant, op. cit. in n. 15, ii, p. 233, quotes F. M. Torrigio, *Le sacre grotte vaticane*, p. 142, as authority for the statement that it was made under Paul III (1534–49); I can find no such statement in Torrigio's book, but on p. 242 of the Rome, 1639, edition one to the effect that Paul IV (1555–59) began the custom of decorating the streets with hangings on the feast of Corpus Christi (which is also untrue). Passavant was evidently misquoting W. Gunn, *Cartonensia, or an Historical and Critical Account of the Tapestries in the . . . Vatican*, London, 1831, p. 14, who gave the same wrong page reference to Torrigio but got the name of the pope and the substance of the passage right, adding the suggestion that this might have been the occasion when Raphael's tapestries reappeared. There is a passage in the *Considerazioni sulla pittura* of Giulio Mancini (1614–1630, ed. A. Marucchi, Rome, 1956, i, p. 19) which seems to apply to exhibition in public rather than in the Sistine Chapel: 'dipinse

Raffaello quelli arazzi per Leone X quali a
certe solennità, esposti in publico, fan correre il
popolo ad ammirarli, o con pianger quel pezzo
che dalla malvagità di un furbo fu mutilato,
del quale però si sa dove sia il cartone et con
facilità si potrebbe havere e rifare'. If Mancini
really meant that the Cartoon could be acquired
this passage must be dated before 1623 (see
below, p. 145).

36. Isidoro Toscano, *Della vita, virtù, miracoli e
dell'istituto di S. Francesco di Paola*, ed. Rome,
1698, p. 604.

37. Wright (1720–22), op. cit. in n. 23, pp.
271–2; he noted that the *Conversion of the Proconsul* was placed over a doorway and was
uncertain whether it was cut or folded. A
painting of the ceremonial opening of the Porta
Santa, 1750, by Giovanni Paolo Panini (Bologna, private collection) shows the portico of
Saint Peter's decorated with tapestries, among
which the *Healing of the Lame Man* is identifiable; F. Cancellieri, *Descrizione delle cappelle
pontificie e cardinalizie . . .*, Rome, 1790, iii, pp.
286 ff., locates the Corpus Christi exhibition in
a 'Galleria' next to the Scala Regia. In his
Storia de' solenni possessi de' sommi pontefici, Rome,
1802, pp. 392, 408, Cancellieri records that
Raphael's tapestries (in the index he specifies
those with the *imprese* of Leo X) were used to
decorate the Sala de' Paramenti in the Vatican
(in 1758) and in the Quirinal (1769) for the
Lateran *possessi* of Clement XIII and Clement
XIV.

38. J. W. Goethe, *Italian Journey*, ed. W. H.
Auden and E. Mayer, London, 1962, pp. 321,
341, 351 ff.

39. K. L. Fernow, 'Ueber Rafaels Teppiche', in
Römische Studien, iii, Zürich, 1808, pp. 118, 130,
207 (observing the reactions of the crowd of all
classes that went to see them, he compared
Raphael with Homer as *Volksdichter*); see also
J. D. Fiorillo, *Kleine Schriften artistischen Inhalts*,
Göttingen, 1806, ii, p. 281.

40. There have been many confused accounts
of this removal; the best documented version,
which may however whitewash the French too
liberally, is by E. Müntz, 'Les tapisseries de
Raphaël pendant la révolution française',
Chronique des arts, 1877, pp. 241 ff., 263 ff.; see
also Bombe, op. cit. in n. 2, pp. 17 ff.

41. G. A. Guattani, *Memorie enciclopediche
romane sulle belle arti*, iv, 1809, p. 27 ('la Roma
delle belle arti ha con ragione esultato di
gioia').

42. E. Platner and C. Bunsen, *Beschreibung der*

interpreted liberally so that the *Scuola nuova* was shown with the Leonine set,
the *Scuola vecchia*, and this circumstance was no doubt the origin of the
general confusion which exists among writers of the seventeenth, eighteenth
and even nineteenth centuries as to the extent of the set that was truly
Raphael's, and which bedevilled calculations as to the number of lost
Cartoons. The custom was surely not consistent during this period. Towards
the end of the seventeenth century one report, for example, says that the
exhibition took place on Corpus Christi and other feast days;[36] whereas
another early in the eighteenth century says 'They are exposed publickly for
three days in one of the Cloysters leading up to S. Peter's Church, at the
Feast of *Corpus Christi* . . . After this they are hung up in some Apartments

Stadt Rom, II, ii, Stuttgart-Tübingen, 1834, pp.
390 ff.; X. Barbier de Montault, 'Les tapisseries de la Fête-dieu au Vatican', *Annales
archéologiques*, xv, 1855, p. 304, n. 1 (he remarks
that after their return from France Pius VII
was unwilling that they should be taken out of
the Vatican even for the Corpus Christ exhibition); C. Fea, *Nuova descrizione de' monu-
menti antichi ed oggetti d'arte contenuti nel Vaticano*,
Rome, 1819, pp. 124 ff. At that time the
Scuola vecchia, including the fragmentary *Conversion of the Proconsul*, was augmented by the
baldacchino of the consistorial throne (the *Three
Virtues*, with the *imprese* of Clement VII), now
exhibited with the *Scuola nuova*; the latter set,
however, had been reduced from 12 to 11
pieces by the loss of the *Christ in Limbo* during
the Parisian journey. Platner and Bunsen, loc.
cit., describe the arrangement in detail, and it is
clear that the two sets were thoroughly inter-
mingled.

43. They were moved by Gregory XVI in 1838
to the west corridor of the Belvedere, and in
1932 to their present positions in the new
Pinacoteca of Pius XI (B. Nogara, *Origine e
sviluppi dei musei e gallerie pontificie*, Rome, 1948,
p. 39; the 1838 hanging is described in *Galleria
degli arazzi al Vaticano*, Rome, 1840, pp. 11 ff.).
'R.', 'Die Tapeten im Vatikan', *Kunstblatt*,
xxiv, 1843, p. 317 ff., recounts that on a visit
to the Vatican in 1840 he had found the
tapestries recently moved to their new position,
and that he thought the new hanging less
satisfactory than the previous one at the end of
the Galleria geografica. He also said that they
had suffered more by the Napoleonic removal
than by the Sack of Rome in 1527, and very
remarkably made a direct comparison between
Leo X's commission and the rich tapestry-gifts
made by Leo III to Saint Peter's (cf. above, p.
6). The tapestries were restored under Pius
VII, again in 1866–70, and again in 1899–
1901.

44. Trull, op. cit. in n. 1, pp. 2, 17.

45. I am much indebted to Margaret Mitch[ell?]
who investigated this problem in a M.A. the[sis?]
presented at the Courtauld Institute, 196[ ]
*Artistic relations between the Papal Court and He[nry]
VIII*. The earliest positive reference to th[e]
tapestries still appears to be the well-kno[wn]
passage in Henry Peacham, *The Compleat Gen[tle]-
man*, London, 1622, p. 137 (1634 ed., p. 15[ ])
'. . . those stately hangings of Arras, containi[ng]
the History of Saint *Paul* out of the *Acts* (th[e]
which, eye never beheld more absolute A[rt]
and which long since you might have seene [at]
the banquetting house at White-hall) we[re]
wholly of his (sc: Raphael's) invention, boug[ht]
(if I bee not deceived) by King *Henry* the eig[hth]
of the state of *Venice*, where *Raphael Urb[in]*
died . . .' The first claim that they we[re]
presented to Henry by Leo X seems to come [in]
the catalogue: *Exhibition of the Arras or Tapest[ry]
for which Raffaello di Urbino designed the Cartoo[ns],
presented by Pope Leo X. to Henry VIII. . . . at [ ]
Egyptian Hall, Piccadilly*, London, 1824; s[ee]
also the reports of this exhibition in *T[he]
Repository of Arts, Literature, Fashions, &c.* (e[d.]
R. Ackermann), 3rd series, iv, 1824, pp. 356–[ ]
and in *The Literary Gazette and Journal of [ ]
Belles Lettres*, 13 November 1824, p. 732.

46. The absence of the mark is interpreted [in]
this sense by E. Kumsch, *Die Apostelgeschich[te],
eine Folge von Wandteppichen nach Entwürfen [von]
Raffael Santi*, Dresden, 1914, p. 12; this bo[ok]
contains a useful but somewhat uncritic[al]
collection of material on sets of tapestries ma[de]
from these Cartoons or later copies; he describ[es]
56 sets, some fragmentary, but even so his l[ist]
is not complete. The effectiveness of the ruli[ng]
on the *BB* mark is well documented by M[ ]
Crick-Kuntziger, 'Marques et signatures [de]
tapissiers bruxellois', *Annales de la société roy[ale]
d'archéologie de Bruxelles*, xl, 1936, pp. 166 ff.

47. W. G. Thomson, *A History of Tapest[ry]*,
London, 1906, p. 264: 'The Tower . . . Han[g]-
ings of Arras . . . 9 peces of the Storye of thac[t]
of thappostles'.

within the Palace, a few days to be seen there; and then they are put up in their Wardrobes, where they continue all the rest of the Year.'[37] An engraving by Francesco Panini, c. 1770, shows the Corpus Christi exhibition with three of the tapestries hanging on Bernini's Scala Regia (*Fig.* 88). It was the anticipation of this splendid event that made Goethe leave Naples, with the greatest reluctance, on 31 May 1787 to be back in Rome in time to see the Raphaels. He did see them, but registered no immediate reaction. The celebrated and indeed very moving passage on the tapestries ('. . . virilely conceived, dominated by a spirit of instinctive nobility and moral seriousness . . .') was written much later, in 1829, and was inspired by a comparison of two engravings of the *Death of Ananias*.[38]

The end of the regular Corpus Christi exhibition came a decade later, in 1797.[39] In the next year, together with the *Scuola nuova*, by devious ways and means the Leonine tapestries began their last journey—this time to France—and six of them were exhibited in the Louvre in 1799.[40] Pius VII Chiaramonti bought them back in 1808, and in 1809 on Corpus Christi they were seen again in Rome in their accustomed position, symbolically and probably finally.[41] A month later Pius VII himself was removed to Paris and the year of his return, 1814, was also the year in which a new room for the tapestries, the Stanza degli arazzi di Raffaello, was opened in the Vatican Palace;[42] since that date, in one part of the palace or another, they have been on permanent exhibition.[43]

Sets of tapestries made from Raphael's Cartoons, like the Cartoons themselves, seem to be unusually peripatetic and accident-prone. The second set to be woven from the Cartoons was probably the one which was reputedly presented by Leo X to Henry VIII;[44] the idea of such a gift is intrinsically credible in the years 1520–21, when Henry earned for himself and his successors the title Defender of the Faith, but there is no direct early evidence to support the attractive legend.[45] All that seems certain is that the set in question was woven before 1528 because it was not marked with the initials *BB* that were mandatory on all tapestries woven in Brussels from that date onwards.[46] They are to be identified with some probability with a set of nine *Acts of the Apostles* listed in the inventory of the tapestries in the Tower of London, 1549 (the *Paul in Prison* Cartoon, understandably, was never used again after the Leonine set);[47] and they are certainly the nine pieces in the Tower valued at nearly £7000 in an inventory drawn up at the death of Charles I, 1649.[48] The remarkable price—the Cartoons were valued at about this date at £300—was undoubtedly due to the fact that, like the Leonine set, they were woven with gold and silver. During the Commonwealth, probably in 1653, they were acquired by the Spanish ambassador in London, Alonso de Cárdenas,[49] on behalf of Don Luis Mandez de Haro, Marquis del Carpio, and in 1662 they became the property of the Dukes of Alba,[50] in whose palace in Madrid they were seen by several eighteenth-century travellers.[51] The British Consul in Catalonia, Mr. Tupper, bought them in 1823 and they returned to London to be exhibited in the Egyptian Hall in the next year.[52] They were exhibited in London again in 1838 and then in the Midlands,[53] but no buyer was found and in 1844 they were acquired for the Berlin Museum;[54] in Berlin they were burnt in 1945.[55]

The third set of tapestries is probably the one now in Madrid; it is to be dated before 1528 because it too lacks the *BB* mark, and like the Berlin set again it was woven with gold and silver and it consists of nine pieces.[56] It is said to have been made for Margaret of Austria, Governess of the Netherlands—which is, however, an idea so reasonable that it might have been

48. Public Record Office, L.R. 2/124, fol. 77; I owe this reference to Oliver Millar, who will publish the inventory in *The Walpole Society*, xliii. He has also found in P.R.O., State Papers, 29/447, fol. 24, a document dated 11 October 1650 of the sale of these tapestries to Robert Houghton.

49. The export permit, dated 24 August 1653, for 24 chests containing pictures and hangings belonging to the Ambassador, is in P.R.O. S.R. Dom., 25/70, p. 276.

50. Trull, op. cit. in n. 1, pp. 17–18.

51. For example, Henry Swinburne, *Travels through Spain in the Years 1775 and 1776*, London, 1779, p. 353; see also Mengs and Pons, cited by G. F. Waagen, *Treasures of Art in Great Britain*, London, 1854, ii, p. 402, and Fiorillo, op. cit. in n. 39, ii, p. 283.

52. See above, n. 45, and additionally: Waagen, loc. cit., and B. R. Haydon, *Diary* (1824), ed. W. B. Pope, Harvard, 1960, ii, p. 500. J. D. Passavant, *A Tour of a German Artist in England*, London, 1836, i, p. 92n., adds that they were on that occasion 'offered to the King at a very high price, and the purchase was never concluded'.

53. Trull (who was the proprietor), op. cit. in n. 1, p. 19.

54. G. F. Waagen, *Die Cartons von Raphael in besonderer Beziehung auf die nach denselben gewirkten Teppiche in der Rotunde des königlichen Museums zu Berlin*, Berlin, 1860; Kumsch, op. cit. in n. 46, p. 12. Eight of the set are reproduced in H. Grimm, *Raffael*, ed. Berlin, 1941, Pls. 274–7, and the exception, the *Conversion of Saul*, by Kumsch, Pl. 16.

55. Another set of tapestries, the one in Dresden, was once believed to have been commissioned by Leo X; W. Buchanan, *Memoirs of Painting*, London, 1824, i, p. 335, believed moreover that there were documents in Rome to support this provenance, and this claim has occasionally been repeated. However, the Dresden set was woven at Mortlake, was acquired in Paris in 1723 from the heirs of Cardinal Egon von Fürstenberg and reached Dresden in 1728 (C. Emmrich, 'Die Raffaelischen Tapeten in der Dresdener Gemäldegalerie', *Dresdener Kunstblätter*, v, 1961, pp. 19 ff.).

56. Waagen, op. cit. in n. 51, ii, p. 406; Kumsch, op. cit. in n. 46, p. 11; E. Tormo Monzó and F. J. Sanchez Cantón, *Los Tapices de la casa del Rey N.S.*, Madrid, 1919, pp. 35 ff.

57. G. Martin-Mery, exhibition catalogue: *Tapisseries des maisons royaux en Espagne*, Bordeaux, 1968, No. 3, with further bibliography. Another mark may be that of Nicolas Leyniers (Tormo Monzó-Sanchez Cantón, loc. cit.).

58. Eight of the set are reproduced in A. F. Calvert, *The Spanish Royal Tapestries*, London, 1921; he also illustrates a later, probably seventeenth-century set which was clearly not made from the same cartoons.

59. Waagen, op. cit. in n. 51, ii, p. 405, and Müntz, op. cit. in n. 29, p. 24, both with further references.

60. A. Luzio, *Gli arazzi dei Gonzaga restituiti dall'Austria*, Bergamo, 1919; M. Viale, *Arazzi e tappeti antichi*, Turin, 1952, p. 48 (with a long but still incomplete bibliography); *La serie mantovana degli arazzi raffaelleschi*, Ente provinciale per il turismo, Mantua, n.d. (1969?), with an excellent set of colour-reproductions.

61. I. Donesmondi, *Dell'istoria ecclesiastica di Mantova*, ii, Mantua, 1616, p. 214.

62. The most obvious case is the early Schiavone in the Pinacoteca Querini Stampalia, Venice (repr. B. Berenson, *Italian Pictures of the Renaissance: The Venetian School*, ed. London, 1957, ii, Fig. 1154); and the most precise quotation (the heads of the soldiers) in Boldrini's woodcut, *The Blinding of Samson*, c. 1540, after Titian (H. Tietze, *Titian*, London, 1950, Fig. 326). Alessandro Ballarin, whom I asked to produce more examples, duly did so in his fine article 'Jacopo Bassano e lo studio di Raffaello e dei Salviati', *Arte Veneta*, xxi, 1967, pp. 96 ff. (Bassano, Sustris, Giuseppe Salviati, Tintoretto). O. Fischel, *Raphael*, London, 1948, p. 265, already pointed to the clear reflection of the design in Titian's *Battle of Cadore* (1538), but in that case the tapestry was perhaps the effective prototype as it was for Giulio Clovio's miniature in the Farnese Breviary. A late reflection of one or the other model is Palma Giovane's painting of the same subject in the Prado.

63. I think this connection was already clear to Fischel; the reference is ambiguous in the English edition, loc. cit., but seems more definite in the German text (ed. Berlin, 1962, p. 198).

64. *The Walpole Society*, xviii, 1930, p. 37. Vertue's notes contain a great deal of confused information about the Cartoons and tapestries, some of which he knew to be false; most of his references to lost Cartoons and to fragments of Cartoons, like others in the eighteenth century, seem to apply to those made for the *Scuola*

invented by an historian—and it bears the mark of the weaver Jan van Tiegen.[57] This set, unlike the one in Berlin, which had simple floriated borders or frames, was provided additionally with a new set of *spalliere*, or lower borders, and was framed on each side with vertical borders partly made up from the Leonine designs and partly from supplementary ones with new subjects; it is for these new cartoons that Van Orley may have been responsible.[58] The next datable set, also of nine pieces woven in Brussels, was ordered by Francis I some time before 1534; it was burnt in 1797 for the sake of its gold.[59] The Gonzaga tapestries, probably the best known of these secondary sets, were perhaps woven towards 1540; they were not made initially for Cardinal Ercole Gonzaga, whose arms they bear but not integrally with the original fabric, but they were perhaps made for stock by the weavers, who in this case were Jan van Tiegen, Josse van Herselle and Claes Leyniers; the date is certainly after 1528 since the *BB* mark is present.[60] They were probably acquired by the Cardinal in 1559 and they were used for the decoration of the choir of the *Cappella palatina*, Santa Barbara, of the Palazzo Ducale at Mantua on feast days;[61] transferred to the State Apartments of the palace in 1776, they were forcibly removed to Vienna in 1866 and were not returned until 1919. They have been restored but, like the Madrid set, their execution is of excellent quality and their state of preservation remarkable (partly, no doubt, because they contain no metal threads); it is occasionally necessary to refer to these sets for the interpretation of passages which are not clearly legible in the Leonine set or in the Cartoons (see, for example, *Fig. 36*).

There is no documentary evidence that these four post-Leonine sets were woven from the original Cartoons; but there is apparently conclusive visual evidence that this was so. We left the history of the Cartoons at the point in 1520–21 when Pieter van Aelst had just finished his work and the *Conversion of Saul* had been extracted from the Cartoon-set and had come into the hands of Cardinal Domenico Grimani in Venice. The subsequent history of this piece is puzzling. There are several reflections of the design in Venetian painting until the time of Palma Giovane, late in the sixteenth century, and Titian evidently studied it with profit and attention to detail;[62] it is not always possible to distinguish between the influence of the Cartoon and that of the tapestry, which was also in Venice at least momentarily in 1528, but Raphael's painting seems to be what Titian had looked at most recently when he designed the *Bacchus and Ariadne* (unfinished in 1522, delivered in 1523).[63] The last reference to Raphael's Cartoon seems to be a remark in George Vertue's notebooks (1716) that it was 'said to be in Spain'.[64]

The extraction of the *Conversion of Saul* should have been compensated by a copy if the remaining Cartoons continued to be used in the production of the secondary tapestry-sets; alternatively, of course, those tapestry-sets could have been made from a complete set of Cartoon-copies. If the original Cartoons were still used by Jan van Tiegen and his associates after 1521 one would expect this use to be evident, if at all, in some significant difference in the case of the *Conversion of Saul*; and in fact there is such a difference. The point is complicated by the liberties that these weavers took with foreground

nuova. The present case is exceptional in that he specifies the subject.

65. I do not feel competent to express an opinion on the authorship of the Henry VIII-

Berlin set, which in any case I know only fro[m] photographs; but so far as I can see there [is] nothing to contradict the natural conclusi[on] that, since the frames have the same floriat[ed] design as those of the Madrid and Mantua[n]

vegetation, liberties bolder than those taken by Pieter van Aelst. On the other hand Jan van Tiegen and his team followed Raphael's background landscape in the *Charge to Peter*, for example, with impressive fidelity and did not feel the need, as Pieter van Aelst had done, to separate this part of the Cartoon from the figures; in general one may say that while their interpretation of the Cartoons was in a few details bolder they were, nevertheless, more successful in the faithful reproduction of Raphael's designs. The exception is their *Conversion of Saul* (*Fig.* 21). We have no Cartoon with which to compare it, but the Vatican tapestry (*Fig.* 20) is entirely convincing in detail—particularly in the landscape background—as a reproduction of its model as faithful as the rest of the set; it may serve as an approximate reproduction of the Cartoon in all respects except in its dimensions, for the figure-design seems to be cut awkwardly. The Van Tiegen tapestries, on the other hand, are more convincing in showing a larger area and thus a complete figure-design, but there is a general lack of detail (in armour, for instance) and above all the landscape background, which is so fine in the Vatican tapestry, is entirely omitted; these are both procedures very uncharacteristic of Van Tiegen. Thus it seems that in the secondary sets the *Conversion of Saul* was indeed woven from a cartoon different, and inferior in quality, compared with the rest; the natural conclusion is that these sets were woven from the original Cartoons among which there was, by necessity, a substitute for the one in Venice.

The deduction to be made from this examination is that the Cartoons—reduced to nine originals, or perhaps eight if the *Paul in Prison* had been discarded at once—passed in the 1520s from the workshop of Pieter van Aelst to that of Jan van Tiegen and his associates;[65] this is not difficult to understand, since the former workshop was engaged, probably from 1524, on a still larger task for Clement VII: the tapestries of the Life of Christ, the *Scuola nuova*, designed by Raphael's followers. And from the Mantuan set we have an indication that the Cartoons were in the Brussels workshop of Jan van Tiegen until about 1540.[66] At this point it seems appropriate to express surprise that such conspicuous objects should have been so little noticed in Flanders in the sixteenth century and that it should be so difficult to follow their history; their neglect may of course be due to the fact that they remained cut up in vertical strips, in which condition they may well have made little sense to anyone other than a weaver. The next trace of them comes in a group of letters from Brussels, 1573, to the Cardinal Granvella; the cardinal had expressed to his agent an interest in obtaining a set of tapestries of the Acts of the Apostles, and he was told that at that time production was being effected from a set of copies, the original Cartoons—still in Brussels—being too much damaged for further use.[67] These copies, which may have been made much earlier, cannot be identified with certainty; but it is possible that from this set came the two—the *Healing of the Lame Man* and the *Conversion of the Proconsul*—which Reynolds acquired during his tour of the Low Countries and which are now in the National Gallery in Dublin.[68] These Dublin copies are severely damaged but of sound quality and convincingly Flemish authorship, and they bear such a precise dimensional relationship to the originals that they could have been produced by pouncing, a process which would explain the pricking of the originals.[69]

The next indication of the whereabouts of Raphael's Cartoons comes after another gap of about thirty years, but in order to understand it we have to move still farther forward, to 1623. On 28 March of that year Charles,

sets, the workshop is likely to have been Van Tiegen's too; the style of weaving in general looks consistent with those sets and distinct from that of the Leonine one.

66. Claes Leyniers, one of the weavers of the Mantuan set (which appears to be the last of this group), died in or before 1548. A. Wauters, *Les tapisseries bruxelloises: Essai historique*, Brussels, 1878, p. 107, states that the Cartoons remained in the hands of the family of Bernard van Orley (d. 1541); his source appears to be M. F. Goethals, *Histoire des lettres, des sciences et des arts en Belgique . . .*, iii, Brussels, 1842, p. 52, who made the more modest suggestion that the Cartoons—the weaving of which he believed Van Orley to have supervised at the request of Adrian VI—might have followed the same course as Van Orley's collection of drawings.

67. M. Piquard, 'Le Cardinal de Granvelle, amateur de tapisseries', *Revue belge d'archéologie et d'histoire de l'art*, xix, 1950, pp. 113, 124.

68. For the provenance see *National Gallery of Ireland: Catalogue of Pictures of the Italian Schools*, Dublin, 1956, Nos. 171–2.

69. The Dublin pair are in fact slightly larger than the equivalent originals, but this is because the latter have been trimmed at the edges (see below, p. 167). Superimposition of X-ray photographs of the London pair on those at Dublin demonstrates such fidelity of scale and detail that the relationship between originals and copies cannot be casual. I have been unable to find traces of pouncing on the Dublin cartoons, but perhaps one should expect it to be covered by the black chalk underdrawing, which is prominent enough; however, they could also have been produced by tracing, and the pricking of the London set could have been done on another such occasion. The Dublin pair are at present being examined for the possibility of a thorough restoration. I am most grateful to Michael Wynne for his patient assistance in studying them. It should be noted that the author of the Dublin *Conversion of the Proconsul*, unlike Raphael, reversed the inscription for the greater convenience of weavers; there are very slight differences in this inscription, presumably made free-hand, which are however sufficiently marked for a positive conclusion that these copies were not the models used for the ex-Berlin, Madrid or Mantuan tapestries. They have, nevertheless, been used in manufacture since they are cut into vertical strips, like the originals, and it seems reasonable to believe that they were the ones used in Brussels production towards the end of the sixteenth century.

Prince of Wales, wrote from Madrid to request that money be put aside for the delivery of 'certaine patterns to be brought out of Italy, and sent to us into England for the making thereby a Suite of Tapestry. wch drawings (as we remember) are to cost neir uppon the poynt of Seaven hundred pounds'; for the date of arrival the Council are referred to Sir Francis Crane, the manager of the Mortlake tapestry-factory which had been established by King James four years before. But negotiations for the purchase had begun earlier, for Sir Francis Crane, in a letter of about the same date to the King, refers to an order given by Prince Charles before his journey to Spain 'to send to Genua for certayne drawings of Raphaell of Urbin, which were

70. The first letter is in a volume in the Duchy of Cornwall Office, *Affairs of Charles, Prince of Wales*, p. 4 (the date has been checked by Oliver Millar). The second letter, now untraced, was in the mid-eighteenth century in the hands of R. Harding, Rector of Ashton, who had married into the Arundel family; it was first published by the Rev. Peter Whalley, *The History and Antiquities of Northamptonshire*, Oxford, 1762–91, i, p. 328 (from the MS. notes of John Bridges) and again anonymously (but probably by Whalley) in *The European Magazine*, x, 1786, p. 285; this letter is undated, but Mr. Millar has found a report of action taken upon it in *Calendar of State Papers, Domestic* (1619–23), p. 623, under the date 28 June 1623. Both letters were already known to Thomson, op. cit. in n. 47, pp. 296–7; see also M. D. Whinney and O. Millar, *English Art 1625–1714*, Oxford, 1957, p. 3. For the foundation of the Mortlake tapestry factory see Thomson, op. cit., pp. 291 ff., and Whinney-Millar, op. cit., pp. 124 ff.

71. The drawing (Uppsala, University Library Inv. 39, black chalk, 278 × 405 mm.) was first mentioned by J. Q. van Regteren Altena, 'Rubens as a Draughtsman I: Relations to Italian Art', *The Burlington Magazine*, lxxvi, 1940, p. 199, n. 6; for the most recent discussion of this and other copies attributed to Rubens see M. Jaffé, 'Rubens and Raphael', *Studies in Renaissance and Baroque Art presented to Anthony Blunt*, London, 1967, p. 102. The first scholar to suggest that this material might help in tracing the history of the Cartoons was J. Müller Hofstede, 'Some Early Drawings by Rubens', *Master Drawings*, ii, 1964, p. 5, and 'Beiträge zum zeichnerischen Werk von Rubens', *Wallraf-Richartz-Jahrbuch*, xxvii, 1965, pp. 275 ff.

72. This statement is first found, I believe, on the frontispiece (1720) of Gribelin's set of engravings (*Fig.* 85) and in Dorigny's dedication of his engravings to George I, 1719; one or the other of these was presumably the source for the many authors in the eighteenth and nineteenth centuries who repeated this tradition which, since it first appears in a semi-official context, deserves to be taken seriously.

73. Whinney-Millar, op. cit. in n. 70, p. 126. A remark in the 1639 inventory of Van der Doort (ed. cit. in n. 76, p. 172) that some of the Cartoons had been sent 'to M^r ffranciscus Cleane at Moore clapp to make hangings by' may be taken to mean, on the contrary, that they were to be the very models used by the weavers; but it may also be interpreted in another sense, that they were for Cleyn's use, i.e. as models for his cartoon-copies, and this seems to me the more probable meaning.

74. One attributed to Daniel Mytens was presented by Charles I to Lionel Cranfield, First Earl of Middlesex, and is now at Knole (V. Sackville-West, *Knole*, London, 1950, p. 32); if the attribution is correct the set was probably completed within ten years of the Cartoons' arrival, since Mytens is generally believed to have returned to the Low Countries c. 1634–35. The other, on a much smaller scale and drawn with the pen, also of much higher quality, was made by Cleyn's sons and bears dates between 1640 and 1646; the earliest reference (1648–1650) is in Edward Norgate's *Miniatura, or the Art of Limning*, ed. M. Hardie, Oxford, 1919, p. 82; see also John Evelyn, *Sculptura: or the History and Art of Chalcography*, London, 1662, p. 111; they are now exhibited in the Print Room of the Ashmolean Museum; for provenance see Evelyn, loc. cit., Gunn, op. cit. in n. 35, p. 17, F. J. B. Watson, 'On the Early History of Collecting in England', *The Burlington Magazine*, lxxxiv–vi, 1944, pp. 225–6, K. T. Parker, *Catalogue of the Collection of Drawings in the Ashmolean Museum, II: Italian Schools*, Oxford, 1956, p. 352, and A. F. Blunt, *A History of the Royal Collection of Drawings*, preface to E. Schilling, *The German Drawings . . . at Windsor Castle*, London, 1971, p. 6. The copy of the *Conversion of the Proconsul*, unlike the original Cartoon but like the Dublin copy, shows the inscription reversed, which suggests that this set was made not merely as reproductions but to serve some practical purpose; they are far too large to be models for engravings, but too small to be cartoons for tapestries.

75. The detail in question is in the lower left corner of the Cartoon. The crutches discarded by the cripple were rearranged by Pieter van Aelst in the Leonine tapestry (*Fig.* 24) because —for a reason that is still to be elucidated— the lower edge of this piece was set somewhat higher than that of the Cartoon (*Pl.* 38). The Mantuan tapestry appears to be once again a more accurate reproduction of Raphael's design. Both the Leonine and Mantuan tapestries show a knee-crutch, in slightly different positions, which is missing from the much damaged and repainted area of the Cartoon, and all that remains of it is the strap,

also altered in form. The repainted state : reproduced in both sets of copies, and ver exactly in the more trustworthy Cleyn copy a Oxford.

76. *Abraham van der Doort's Catalogue of th Collections of Charles I*, ed. O. Millar, *Th Walpole Society*, xxxvii, 1958–60, pp. 172, 179 Against the first entry the provenance-note i the margin reads: 'bacht bij te king bij so franzis krans means'; this is consistent with th letters of 1623 quoted above and is not neces sarily in conflict with the tradition of Rubens intervention.

77. P.R.O., L.R. 2/124, fol. 9v.; the entr comes at the end of a list of 'Pictures of y privie Lodgings & privie Gallery at Whitehall one of several lists of works from the Roya Collection then in the care of Henry Brown at Denmark House.

78. I hesitate because of a puzzling printe sale-notice, unfortunately undated, bound i Daniel Lysons's *Collectanea* (British Museum 1881. b. 6, ii, fol. 226v.); the objects for sal are mostly furniture, 'The whole to be seen a Mortlake, and shewn by Mr Watson, Gardener' but the last item is: 'the four original *Cartoon* by Raphael'. I should be surprised if the type face were as early as c. 1650, but that woul appear to be the last occasion upon which an of the Cartoons could have been at Mortlake if it is to be taken at its face-value it is the onl known printed sale-notice connected wit Charles I's possessions.

79. There is evidence that in 1651 alread attempts were made to revive the Mortlak factory as a going concern; and in 1653 it wa decided that Mantegna's *Triumph of Caesar*, the at Hampton Court, should be sent to Mortlak for use as cartoons for tapestries (Thomson, op cit. in n. 47, pp. 311–12).

80. F. P. G. Guizot, *Histoire de la républiqu d'Angleterre*, Paris, 1854, i, p. 411, and le Comt de Cosnac, *Les richesses du Palais Mazarin*, Paris 1884, p. 414: 'Estat de quelques tableaux exposés en vente à la maison de Somerset, May

desseignes for tapistries made for Pope Leo the Xth, and for which there is 300 l. to be payed, besides their charge of bringing home'.[70] In fact it seems very likely that the Cartoons had been in Genoa for some time, for there is a drawing by Rubens after *Paul preaching at Athens*—the Cartoon, not the tapestry or any engraving—which seems to have been made early in his Italian years, and Rubens was in fact in Genoa in 1604 if not before (*Fig.* 89).[71] There is no great difficulty in imagining how the Cartoons travelled from Brussels to Genoa, for by the end of the sixteenth century the Genoese merchants formed the largest foreign colony in Antwerp. Rubens had clearly seen the Cartoons—in fact he made, but not necessarily so early, a set of painted copies which is lost—and he was painting for Prince Charles and discussing the project for painting the ceiling of the Banqueting House in Whitehall as early as 1621; since these contacts with the English court came so soon after the foundation of the tapestry-factory at Mortlake there may well be some truth in the opinion current early in the eighteenth century that it was he who recommended their purchase.[72]

The Cartoons, in any case, were acquired so that they might perform once more their original function, and the preparations for the first of the Mortlake sets of tapestries were under way in 1629; Raphael's own Cartoons were not used, but copies made from them by Francis Cleyn.[73] At least two other sets of copies were made during the reign of Charles I, and these survive;[74] they suggest that the several strips of the Cartoons were reassembled, if only momentarily, or that they were hung up together for some time, as they must have been earlier when Rubens saw them in Genoa. The copies, moreover, provide evidence of otherwise unrecorded restoration and repainting of the Cartoons since they show with perfect clarity the alteration of a detail in the *Sacrifice at Lystra* and they show it in the state in which we see it now (*Fig.* 87);[75] it may be that much more of the repainting of the Cartoons—most of which is normally assumed to have been done c. 1698–99—should be referred back to this early date.

However, Abraham van der Doort makes it clear in his inventory of Charles I's Collections, 1639, that at that time only five of the Cartoons were at Mortlake and that two—the *Death of Ananias* and the *Conversion of the Proconsul*—were in store at Whitehall.[76] After the death of Charles I a list was made of pictures taken from the Privy Lodgings and Gallery at Whitehall, dated 13 September 1649, and among them were 'The Cartoons of Raphaell being yᵉ Acts of yᵉ Appostles. vallued at 300' (pounds);[77] it is probably safe to assume that the seven Cartoons were then together again,[78] and that the valuation was based upon the original purchase price of 1623. For reasons that are still a matter for speculation the Council of State did not allow their sale with the rest of Charles I's Collections; Mantegna's *Triumphs* were reserved at the same time. It seems most likely that both series were retained for future use at the Mortlake factory.[79] After two references to the Raphael Cartoons at Somerset House in the early 1650s[80] there is a long gap in our knowledge of their history, perhaps for the good reason that nothing notable happened to them.[81] Jonathan Richardson has a story, very circumstantial and probably true, that Charles II was prepared to sell them to Louis XIV and was only dissuaded by the entreaties of his Treasurer, the Earl of Danby.[82] Celia Fiennes, in the first years of the eighteenth century, had heard independently that 'the King of France offer'd 3000 pound apiece for them, or indeed any money'; the customary inflationary effects upon such stories, particularly when told to impress foreigners, had raised Louis's offer to £300,000 for the set when a German visitor was shown them in

1650 ... Les cartons de Raphaël des Actes des Apôtres' (valued at £300). Secondly, a list of the late King's goods including those reserved from sale (MS. in House of Lords Library), under the heading: 'Goods Reserved viz: By an order of the Counsell of State dated the 27° of September 1651 ye particular goods hereafter named are reserved from Sale untill the pleasure of ye Parliam.ᵗ be further known thereon ... The Cartoons of Raphaell being the Acts of the Apostles valued at⸺ 0300.00.00' (marginal notes: 'At Somersett House', and a cross-reference to an earlier inventory of goods in the Privy Lodgings at Whitehall). It is to be noted that the Cartoons were not *bought* by Cromwell.

81. It is difficult to be sure how much we can rely upon the account of this period in the Cartoons' history given by George Bickham, *Deliciae Britannicae, or the Curiosities of Hampton-Court ...*, London, 1742, p. 105, who says that Cromwell was 'too much a Connoisseur in Painting to part with these inestimable Pieces; but they were carefully preserved in Deal Boxes, in the Banquetting-House at Whitehall; some of them being in four, and others in five Pieces, and there they remain'd till after the Revolution when King *William* rebuilt *Hampton-Court ...*' This account appears to be dependent upon that given by the Richardsons (see below), but projecting circumstances back into the period of the Commonwealth.

82. Jonathan Richardson Jnr., *Description de divers fameux tableaux*, in J. Richardson, Père et Fils, *Traité de la peinture*, Amsterdam, 1728, iii, p. 459: 'Louis xiv. fit un jour proposer à Charles II. par son Ambassadeur Barillon, de les lui vendre; & ce Prince l'auroit fait, s'il n'en avoit été dissuadé par le Grand-Tresorier d'alors, qui étoit le Compte de Danby, & qui fut dans le suite fait Duc de Leeds: c'est-la ce que mon Père a apris de la bouche même de ce Seigneur.' The Earl of Danby, who died as late as 1712, was Treasurer 1673–79; Paul de Barillon d'Amoncourt was appointed ambassador in London in May 1677 (A. Browning, *Thomas Osborne, Earl of Danby*, i, Glasgow, 1951, pp. 235, 246 ff.); thus Louis's bid would have been made in the late 1670s at a time when Charles II was in a particularly weak position as his pensioner, and when Danby, still pursuing his generally anti-French policies, nevertheless became impeachably involved in the dealings over the French subsidy. Richardson's story seems entirely credible.

83. *The Journeys of Celia Fiennes*, ed. C. Morris, London, 1947, p. 355 (*c.* 1701–3); *London in 1710: from the Travels of Zacharias Conrad von Uffenbach*, ed. W. H. Quarrell and M. Mare, London, 1934, p. 155. On the other hand D. Defoe, *A Tour through England and Wales*, 1724 (ed. London, 1928, i, pp. 177 ff.), in his account of the Cartoons, put the offer at 100,000 louis d'or (rather less than £10,000) for the set. No doubt the house-keepers at Hampton Court, like modern guides everywhere, adjusted their stories to their measure of the visitor's gullibility.

84. *Diary of Viscount Percival, afterwards First Earl of Egmont*, i, London, 1920, pp. 218–19: 'My Lord (Pembroke) had this account from old Sir Edward Nicolas, who was Secretary of State to King Charles the First, and told my Lord that he read this in the old Council Book of King Henry's reign.' Sir Edward Nicolas (1593–1669) had indeed been Secretary of State to Charles I and Charles II, and had filled several other posts in the Civil Service; if he was correctly quoted he ought to have known better; but it is not impossible that at some point in the fabrication of this story the Cartoons were confused with Henry's tapestries and—excepting the ornament about Columbus —that it was some reference to the purchase of the tapestries that appeared in the Council Book. George Vertue (in 1716) had heard a story similar to Lord Pembroke's from 'a certain Old Gentleman', but he was quite clear that it was 'false'; see two passages in *The Walpole Society*, xviii, 1930, pp. 36, 37.

85. Probably Thomas Povey, a prominent civil servant under Charles II, former treasurer of James II when Duke of York; a man of substance and (according to Pepys) of cunning, he is quite likely to have accepted Royal goods in pawn but less likely to have attempted to sell them; however, 1685 is the year of his death and the offer to Lord Pembroke was perhaps made by his heirs.

86. Jonathan Richardson Jnr., *Description . . .*, ed. cit. in n. 82, iii, p. 457 (see also Bickham, quoted above, n. 81); for the entry in Huyghens's diary see Watson, op. cit. in n. 74, p. 227.

87. 'I have this day my Lord (Christopher, Viscount Hatton) been at Hampton Court . . . But ye sight best pleased me was ye Cartoons by Raphael which are far beyond all ye Paintings I ever saw they are brought from ye Tower and hung up ther and are copying for my Lord Sunderland . . .': *Correspondence of the Family of Hatton*, ed. E. M. Thompson, London, 1878, ii, p. 229, with unimportant differences of reading; quoted, without date, in *The Wren Society*, vii, Oxford, 1930, p. 197; I have checked

1710.[83] The tallest story ever told about the Cartoons is undoubtedly the one that Lord Pembroke retailed to Viscount Percival in 1732; like many tall stories it was said to be backed by documentary evidence (in this case 'old Council Books'), that they had been bought directly from the weavers by Henry VIII, and that the King of Spain had offered to give in exchange for them all the lands discovered by Columbus.[84] The one part of this account that may not be untrue is Lord Pembroke's reminiscence that in 1685 he could have bought them when they were in pawn to a certain Mr. Povey.[85]

So far the history of the Cartoons—including, in all probability, the bid by Louis XIV—seems to be dependent upon a sequence of practical intentions hyphenated by long periods of neglect. It will be remembered that the Leonine tapestries also continued to serve their practical uses until the seventeenth century, but also that by the end of that century their function had changed and they had become artistic treasures to be exhibited. A similar change occurred in the case of the Cartoons. The public history of the Cartoons began after the accession of William III (1688). Jonathan Richardson the Younger, relying upon his father's memory which may have stretched back into the 1680s, said that the Cartoons remained in strips, in boxes, until after William's accession and that on the rare occasions upon which they were seen the strips were put together in the Banqueting House in Whitehall; this was still the arrangement in 1690, when Constantine

the date (the letter is British Museum, Add. MS. 29575, fol. 82r.), which is undoubtedly correct; the fact that the Cartoons were moved out of Whitehall between 1690 and 1697 may mean that they had a lucky escape from the Whitehall fire of 1698; and the fact that they were at Hampton Court before the latter date suggests that King William's intention to use them in the decoration of Hampton Court was not, as might otherwise be supposed, directly connected with his renewed interest in this palace following the fire at Whitehall. The copies, made for Lord Sunderland, were perhaps those which Vertue said were made 'in small' by C. Jervaise *c.* 1698 (*The Walpole Society*, xxii, 1934, p. 15). A set of copies made at this time by Henry Cooke (d. 1700) 'in turpentine oil, in the manner of distemper, a way which he invented' (Gunn, op. cit. in n. 35, p. 20), was presumably made for William III, who sent them to Holland (Blenheim MS., F1/56, *List of Pictures and Hangings sent into Holland*, Nos. 26–32). A third set of about this date was made for the King by Antonio Verrio (*Illustrated and descriptive Catalogue of the magnificent Copies of the celebrated Cartoons of Raffaelle, at Hampton Court, painted by order of William the third, by Antonio Verrio . . .* (London, 1864?); and *Loan Museum of Art Treasures*, Industrial Exhibition Palace, Dublin, 1873, Nos. 196–202).

88. Vertue, in *The Walpole Society*, xviii, 1930, p. 94; xxii, 1934, p. 43, talking of a small set of

copies made by James Thornhill 'wherein he will take the liberty to add the parts or Capital that was Cutt off. & some parts at the ends a he can demonstrate was discoverd by him to be done. to fit them to the places intended when they were repaird or joynd together in K Williams reign. by M.ʳ Cooke. painter. & th Surveyor of the pictures M.ʳ Walton father o the present M.ʳ Walton'. The trimming to which Vertue refers may be exemplified by the losses on the right and below in the *Healing o the Lame Man*, and on the right and above in the *Conversion of the Proconsul*, which are revealed by a comparison between the Cartoons and their Dublin replicas, or early tapestries. The copie by the Cleyn brothers at Oxford suggest tha the major marginal losses throughout the se occurred after *c.* 1650 (see above, n. 74; p. 210 below). Cooke and Walton were presumably responsible, at the same time, for adding the strip at the top of the *Charge to Peter* which bring the height of this Cartoon exactly to th average of all the rest save the *Miraculou Draught*; the latter was left unequal because i was to be hung in the central position, over fireplace (*Fig.* 85). It should be noted, how ever, that it is not entirely certain that th Cartoons were never cropped again. Vertue specifically says that Thornhill's small set o copies will show the full original extent of th designs; but in fact his full-sized copies (th property of the Royal Academy since 1800 also show slightly more of the original desig at some points, for example on the right of th

Huyghens records such an opportunity in his diary.[86] However, a letter of Charles Hatton, dated 2 September 1697, tells us that he had seen the Cartoons at Hampton Court, where they were hung up so that copies could be made, and that they had been brought there from the Tower.[87] It may have been at this time that the strips were definitively reintegrated in the first recorded restoration, which was carried out by the Surveyor Parry Walton and the painter Henry Cooke.[88] This restoration was directly connected with the scheme of permanent presentation devised for William III by Christopher Wren and William Talman in 1699, which entailed remodelling the former King's Gallery in the part of Hampton Court Palace that Wren had built between 1689 and the death of Queen Mary in 1694.[89]

The arrangement produced by Wren and Talman is shown with admirable clarity in the frontispiece to Simon Gribelin's engravings, the first of many sets made from the Cartoons (*Fig. 85*). It is interesting from a number of points of view, of which the first concerns the order of presentation. It is clear that no attention was paid to subjects and that no attempt was made to show them as parts of a consecutive narrative. The sequence of display was governed, on the contrary, by the desire to arrange the varying shapes of the Cartoons into a rhythmically ordered pattern. They were all of about the same height except for the *Miraculous Draught of Fishes*, which was placed centrally over the fireplace. The four longest were separated by the *Miraculous Draught* and again by the two other shorter ones, the *Conversion of the Proconsul* and *Paul preaching at Athens*, so as to produce a regular alternation of long and short Cartoons. It seems clear that the intention to display with the greatest decorative effectiveness a series of masterpieces of painting overrode any considerations as to their meaning.

The second interesting aspect of the presentation of 1699 is that it conforms to a tradition of room-decoration which is characteristic of the Renaissance; to put the point in another way, it may be supposed that if Cardinal Grimani had acquired all the Cartoons in the 1520s and had displayed them in a long room the system would have been similar in principle, with the paintings raised well above head-level, and above panelling and doors. This tradition for the placing of figurative paintings in room-decoration was well established, in fact, long before Raphael's lifetime, but it is not to be suggested that the author of the Hampton Court scheme saw the problem down such a long historical perspective; it seems more probable that his system was derived, with a proper sense of style, from knowledge of one of the great Renaissance decorative schemes exemplified by Rosso's Galerie François Premier at Fontainebleau, and it might be natural to think across to Fontainebleau from Hampton Court. It is worth remembering that Wren, who appears to have been responsible for the specifications for the Cartoon Gallery, had in fact been to Fontainebleau in 1665.

A third point of interest about this display is that it was designed with more than a passing thought for the best preservation of the Cartoons. In his estimate for remodelling the Gallery Wren particularly remarked that the panelling was to be continued behind them 'to preserve them from the walls', that is, to minimize the effects of damp. And it appears from a much later report that Wren (or Talman) had even provided an effective fireproof barrier between the Gallery and the apartments above.[90] This care for preservation was taken a step farther a few years later—unless Gribelin omitted to include the precaution in his engraving—when the Cartoons were provided with green silk curtains to protect their colours from the light; and a fire was kept alight throughout the winter to reduce humidity.[91] A set

Sacrifice at Lystra. If Vertue meant that the large copies would show the Cartoons as they were around 1728–31 (the date of Thornhill's work —see Vertue in *The Walpole Society*, xxii, 1934, pp. 43, 53) then it is possible that further cropping occurred after that date (for an occasion, see below, n. 116). Vertue also records that Thornhill made a third set of copies, medium-size.

89. Wren's estimate for the remodelling of 'The Gallery to be fitted for the Cartoones' is dated 28 April 1699; a letter from William Talman, in which he says 'The Gallery for the Cartoones of Raphell is so forward that I shall fix up the pictures in a week', is dated 12 September 1699; these documents are in E. Law, *The History of Hampton Court Palace*, ii, London, 1891, pp. 65, 84, and *The Wren Society*, iv, Oxford, 1927, pp. 59, 60.

90. P.R.O., L.C. 1/531, No. 87, J. C. Robinson to Sir Spencer Ponsonby Fane, 20 August 1890; he says that Wren had put 'shell gravel between the joists' of the ceiling of the Gallery, and that this had proved its effectiveness in two recent fires in the apartments.

91. Jonathan Richardson Jnr., ed. cit. in n. 82, iii, pp. 456–7; see also Giuseppe Piacenza's long footnote in his edition of Filippo Baldinucci, *Notizie de' professori del disegno*, Turin, 1770, ii, p. 348, in which he says: 'Infinite diligenza si usava per conservarli, tenendoli coperti con una tenda di drappo verde, e mantenendovi il fuoco tutto l'inverno per cacciarne l'umidità'; Piacenza goes on to explain that his information about the Cartoons came from English friends in Rome, and he uses the past tense because he knows that at the time of writing the Cartoons have been removed from the Gallery. In the eighteenth century the dangers of excessive light should have been clear since the major damage had already occurred; the 'Mytens' copy (see n. 74) of the *Miraculous Draught* shows that the superficial fading of Christ's robe was already complete by c. 1630. Law, op. cit. in n. 89, iii, p. 85, thought that the omission of an upper row of windows in the Gallery, the presence of which would have been logical from the point of view of the exterior elevation, was Wren's intention, having in mind the dangers of strong light. This can hardly be correct, since the elevation in question was constructed (1689– 1694) before the project for installing the Cartoons (but see below, n. 100); it could be that an awareness of the problem was one factor in the choice of the system of display, with the Cartoons on the higher and darker parts of the walls, or indeed in the choice of this room for their exhibition. Wren, or whoever else was

of 'fine carv'd & gilt frames' described by George Vertue, in 1750, which again are not evident in Gribelin's plate, may be early Georgian additions too.[92]

It is far from clear that the first display of the Cartoons at Hampton Court was ever intended to be a means of sharing the greatest set of paintings in England with the public. That, at least, is not the deduction to be made from the accounts of the earliest visitors, Celia Fiennes and Zacharias Conrad von Uffenbach, because these people could not be kept out of any promising interior;[93] Jonathan Swift happened to see the Cartoons in 1710 because he was invited to dine at Queen Anne's table.[94] It appears, in fact, that from 1702 the Privy Council used to meet in the Cartoon Gallery.[95] The *Privy Council Registers*, being even more business-like than Paris de Grassis's *Diarium*, do not record the Archbishop of Canterbury's reaction to the *Charge to Peter* or the *Death of Ananias*, which is perhaps a great loss; this little known function of the Cartoons nevertheless makes a satisfying footnote to Alexander Pope's *Rape of the Lock* at the point where he mentions Hampton Court:

> Here thou, great ANNA! whom three realms obey,
> Dost sometimes counsel take—and sometimes tea.

Sir Richard Steele remarked of the Cartoons in 1711 that 'These invaluable Pieces are very justly in the Hands of the greatest and most pious Soverain in the World; and cannot be the frequent Object of every one at his own Leisure.' Steele, however, had seen them.[96] And in fact as early as 1703 the new presentation of the Cartoons at Hampton Court had been celebrated

---

responsible, showed more sense than G. F. Waagen, *Works of Art and Artists in England*, London, 1838, ii, pp. 88–89, who complained of the gloom of the Gallery. Vertue, in 1729, was well aware of 'the Casualties by Time the damage by repairs, unskillfully done, colours changing . . .', and so was Thornhill (*The Walpole Society*, xxii, 1934, p. 39).

92. George Vertue, inventory of Hampton Court (1750: MS. in Surveyor's Office), fol. 4r. The Cartoons are there listed in the same order as in the Queen Anne inventory of Hampton Court, *c.* 1710 (MS. in Surveyor's Office), fol. 33r., which is also the order shown in the Gribelin plate. Jonathan Richardson Jnr., ed. cit. in n. 82, iii, p. 456, mentioned that the Cartoons were 'guarnis de bons quadres, mais qui sont simples, & qui n'arrêtent pas la vue . . .'

93. See above, n. 83; Celia Fiennes rather oddly referred to 'a noble gallery with curious pictures of the Scriptures painted by the Carthusion'.

94. *Journal to Stella*, 2 October 1710 (quoted by Law, op. cit. in n. 89, iii, p. 180).

95. The point was made by Law, op. cit. in n. 89, iii, p. 171; I am uncertain, however, of his authority, for his footnote leads to a number of pages in Narcissus Luttrell, *A Brief Historical Relation of State Affairs 1678–1714*, v, Oxford, 1857, none of which specifies that the Council met in the Gallery and one of which, indeed, refers to a ship called *The Hampton Court*. However, Luttrell does say that the Privy Council met in the palace on Thursdays when Queen Anne was in residence at Windsor. The custom of meeting in the palace goes back at least to the reign of James I, and was continued by Cromwell, and Charles II, as well as by Queen Anne, and it is to be noted that the membership, which between 1700 and 1760 averaged about sixty, did require a very large room (E. R. Turner, *The Privy Council of England in the Seventeenth and Eighteenth Centuries*, Baltimore, 1927, i, pp. 88, 318, 382, ii, pp. 20–21, 46–48, 200). In practice attendance was about a third of the membership at the summer meetings, which were those sometimes held at Hampton Court. In the *Privy Council Registers* the location is merely noted as 'At the Court of Hampton Court' (for meetings of 6 August 1702, 10 June–12 August 1703, and 15 June–21 September 1704, see P.R.O., P.C. 2/79, pp. 189, 397, 405, 414, 428, 436, and P.C. 2/80, pp. 126, 175). But it seems reasonable to agree that the Council did meet in the Gallery since in Vertue's inventory of 1750 (loc. cit. in n. 92), the room is referred to as 'The Cartoon Gallery, or Great Council Chamber'; and it is still called the 'Council Chamber' in C. Knight, *A Compendious Gazetteer . . . to the Royal Palaces*, Windsor, 1801, p. 16.

96. *The Spectator*, No. 226, 19 November 1711, an article under the Horatian text: *Pictura Poesis erit*, which gives notice that the Queen has commissioned Dorigny to engrave the Cartoons; the account includes appreciations of the emotions described in *Paul at Athens* and the *Charge to Peter* (without sectarian bias), and as the first (and almost the last) description of the Cartoons which deserves to be considered as literature it has considerable importance; I think that a finer prose style has never been applied to these works (unless it is Goethe's), and it is sad that the appreciations are so brief.

97. Anon., *A Hymn to the Light of the World, with a Short Description of the Cartons of Raphael Urbin, In the Gallery at Hampton-Court*, London, 1703, p. 16. The descriptions are not, in fact, short; their sequence corresponds to that of the hanging order, beginning with the *Death of Ananias* and ending with the *Charge to Peter*. This publication appears to be extremely rare; there is a copy in the Bodleian Library at Oxford.

98. This would seem to be the natural deduction from the publication of such works as Defoe, op. cit. in n. 83 (1724), Bickham, op. cit. in n. 81 (1742), and the collection of Richardson Snr.'s notes as *A description of the Cartoons at Hampton Court*, edited by Horace Walpole and published with *A Catalogue of the . . . Pictures of George Villiers, Duke of Buckingham . . .*, London, 1758, pp. 67 ff.; also the description (again largely based on Richardson) in R. J. Dodsley, *London and its Environs Described*, London, 1761, iii, pp. 154 ff.; all of these were written to be used as guides.

99. See above, n. 39.

100. See, for example, the sarcastic reference in Giovanni Bottari's edition of Vasari's *Vite*, Rome, 1759, ii, p. 124n., and, most recently, F. Mazzini, 'Fortuna storica di Raffaello nel sei e settecento', *Rinascimento*, vi, 1955, p. 159. The operation of national pride working in the other direction may in fact be sensed in Bottari's amusing misinterpretation of the story of the restoration and exhibition of the Cartoons (which he seems to have taken from Bickham's *Deliciae Britannicae*): 'E quindi fu fabbricato il palazzo di Amptoncourt per distendervegli.' Jonathan Richardson Jnr., too, was probably, though less certainly, mistaken in thinking that the Gallery was expressly built for the Cartoons (ed. cit. in n. 82, iii, p. 456); it is possible that Wren realized in 1699 the decoration of the King's Gallery already intended in 1689.

in verse-descriptions of each of them appended to an anonymous *Hymn to the Light of the World*; for the moment we need to notice only the terms of the introduction which imply that the author, at least, expected visitors:

> Stay, Stranger, here, in this Apartment stand,
> And view the Wonders of great *Raphael's* Hand.
> His Skill does all the Sons of Art controul,
> They only Paint the Body, he the Soul.
> Such Admiration will thy Eyes possess,
> As none, but *Raphael's* Pencil can express.[97]

It is surely true that by the middle of the century access to the Cartoons was relatively easy[98]—as easy as access to any private collection but also as difficult without the right connections; it was not until the nineteenth century that Raphael, through the Cartoons, became a *Volksdichter* to the English as he had been to the Romans through the medium of the tapestries since the seventeenth century.[99]

Nevertheless it was in this period that the first steps were taken towards the installation, which is now forgotten, of Raphael as an honorary Englishman. These steps were taken by the Richardsons, father and son, who were the first to rank the Raphael of the Cartoons above the Raphael of the Stanze. Their remarks caused instant irritation in Italy, as they still do,[100] and it is hard to believe that they anticipated any other reaction to their spectacularly insular appreciation of the Vatican, 'qui, après Hampton-Cour, est le plus riche trésor des Ouvrages de ce divin Peintre'.[101] One may sense while reading the context of such remarks that they were provoked by a prior irritation on the Richardsons' part on finding the Cartoons so little valued outside England; they speculated upon the esteem in which these works would be held if they had happened to be in Rome, which was a speculation much to the point through which they touched upon the serio-comic effects of location and nationalism upon judgements of works of art. But while this point was cogent in their own argument they provided another illustration of it, for one must also sense that they themselves were partly motivated by national pride: partly, but not by any means entirely.

When reading some of the Richardsons' English followers one may feel that the Continent had been isolated by a blanket of cultural fog in the Channel. But the Richardsons themselves cannot be so dismissed, and could not be at the time. Their arguments were sometimes thoroughly misleading,[102] but generally they were humanist, informed and persistent to a degree that could command European respect, chiefly because they held a natural place in international academic discussions of history-painting; and if the prime intention was to draw greater attention to the Cartoons there is no doubt that they succeeded.[103] The Richardsons' exaltation of these works was for that effect perfectly timed. It followed immediately upon a remarkable appreciation of two of them, the *Charge to Peter* and *Paul preaching at Athens*, in one of the central literary works of the academic tradition, the *Reflexions critiques sur la poësie et sur la peinture* (1719) of the Abbé Jean Baptiste Dubos; in a discussion of the distinct provinces of the two arts Dubos came to the problem of defining the area of common ground and in order to illustrate 'le Peintre, en opérant comme Poëte' he chose first these two Cartoons and analysed at length their conformity with Horace's formula *Ut pictura poesis*.[104] However the Richardsons not only placed the Cartoons in the full limelight of academic criticism, which was largely the achievement of the father; the body of 'catalogue' information (and sometimes misinformation) which they

101. Op. cit. in n. 82, i, p. 83; see also Jonathan Richardson Jnr., *An Account of the Statues, Bas-reliefs, Drawings and Pictures in Italy, France, etc.*, London, 1722, pp. 201–2, 251–6 (also republished, amplified, as *Description*, ed. cit. in n. 82, iii, pp. 440 ff.), and Daniel Webb, *An Inquiry into the Beauties of Painting*, London, 1760, pp. 177 ff. The Richardsons had made tracings of the Cartoons (Vertue, 1723, in *The Walpole Society*, xxii, 1934, p. 13). Their insult to the Stanze was eventually avenged in the anonymous *Guida della Pinacoteca Vaticana*, Vatican City, 1933, p. 142: 'Quanto ai così detti cartoni conservati nel "Victoria and Albert Museum" di Londra, siamo propensi a ritenerli come delle mediocri derivazioni eseguite forse nei primi anni del secolo xvii e tratte dai cartoni originali, andati poi distrutti e dispersi. Certo, posti a confronto cogli arazzi, appaiono troppo meschini di esecuzione, sordi di colore, goffi di disegno (sono evidenti e pronunciati barocchismi) per supporre che si tratti di opere di Raffaello; tanto più che, oltre indubbie ragioni di stile, non si spiegherebbe come mai su cartoni tanto mediocri, fossero stati eseguiti degli autentici capolavori.'

102. As, for example, when contrasting the *obscurité* of the Stanze with Hampton Court: 'tout y est riant; tous les Tableaux sont ... placés dans un grand Jour' (ed. cit. in n. 82, iii, pp. 446–7; in general the special pleading of this amplified version of the younger Richardson's *Account* of 1722 is unimpressive and tendentious beside his father's arguments in the main part of the *Traité*, vols. i and ii, passim).

103. Occasionally one finds on the Continent explicit agreement with the Richardsons' judgement, for example by Fernow, op. cit. in n. 39, p. 119, and by Quatremère de Quincy, *Histoire de la vie et des ouvrages de Raphaël*, Paris, 1824, p. 298 (who had, in fact, seen the Cartoons several times). And we should notice the similar appreciation of the tapestries by Platner, op. cit. in n. 42, II, ii, p. 390 (1834): 'Wir erkennen ihn (Raphael) in diesen Werken auf dem Gipfel seiner Grösse, in Composition und Zeichnung. Sie zeigen unstreitig einen noch höheren Styl als seine vaticanischen Fresco-gemälde...'; and similarly E. Förster, *Raphael*, Leipzig, 1867, p. 98. Reynolds, on the other hand, was one of many English who settled for a draw (*Discourses*, ed. R. Fry, London, 1905, p. 296).

104. Paris, 1719, i, pp. 88 ff.; he was talking specifically of the Cartoons, which he knew to be at Hampton Court, and not of the tapestries; he was presumably using the engravings of Gribelin.

105. Signed 'N.B.'; I found this poem in a set of six volumes of press-cuttings in the Victoria and Albert Museum Library, which are a rich mine of information on the arts in England in the eighteenth and nineteenth centuries.

106. *The Parliamentary History of England*, xix, London, 1814, cols. 190 ff.

107. Wilkes may have relied upon the Richardsons' account (ed. cit. in n. 82, iii, p. 458) where it is said that at the sale of Charles I's goods 'Cromwell donna ordre d'acheter les Cartons; & c'est ainsi qu'ils nous ont été conservés.' It is curious to find an echo of Wilkes's sentiments (but with much less provocation) in M. D. Conway, *Travels in South Kensington*, London, 1882, pp. 61–62, where great exception was taken to notices beneath each Cartoon, *Lent by the Queen*: 'The last individual who clearly owned them was Oliver Cromwell, who paid what was supposed a large sum (£300) for works which no amount could purchase from the Protector's true heirs—the English Nation.'

108. The 'Great Room' was the former Saloon of Buckingham's house, and is the present Green Drawing-Room. Several different dates are given in the literature for this and for later translations. In this case the primary source-material exists in the form of press-reports, of which the earliest I know is under the date 30 December 1763 in a series of brief news-items in *The Gentleman's Magazine and Historical Chronicle*, xxxiv, January 1764, p. 42: 'The celebrated cartoons have lately been removed from Hampton-Court to the Queen's Palace.' On the other hand the payments to the Surveyor for the expenses of the removal fall in the year beginning 10 October 1763 (O. Millar, *Zoffany and his Tribuna*, London, 1966, p. 28, n. 3).

109. *Description of the Cartons of Raphael Urbin in the Queen's Palace*, London, 1764; the text (already on sale by 28 March 1764) was a reprinting of Benjamin Ralph's introduction (heavily indebted to the Richardsons) to *The School of Raphael, or the Student's Guide to Expression in Historical Painting*, London, 1759. See also T. Martyn, *The English Connoisseur*, London, 1766, ii, p. 3, who somewhat casually puts gleanings from the Richardsons (or perhaps from Ralph) under the heading 'The Queen's House'; there is no reason to believe that he had been inside.

—but particularly the son—collected has also been the single most influential contribution to the bibliography of these works.

Obviously it was the display of the Cartoons at Hampton Court that set off these and other historical and critical studies; but it was also a most decisive step in what might be called the social history of the Cartoons. It is always difficult to measure the penetration of a work of art into a national consciousness, and particularly difficult in the case of the English. But the penetration achieved by the Cartoons through the literate classes must have been both rapid and widely effective. As evidence of this point we may resurrect a poem *Upon the late Bishop of Rochester Preaching* which was published in *The True Briton* of 3 January 1724;[105] the significant fact is that the author did not feel that he had to explain his peroration:

> So ATHENS once upon her Preacher hung,
> Transported by the Precepts of his Tongue:
> So stood great PAUL; so skilful RAPHAEL drew;
> And as in HIM another PAUL we view,
> Another RAPHAEL may we find in you.

William III, Wren, Talman and the Richardsons each contributed in their different ways to the resurrection of the Cartoons, but their progress from that first period of their after-life has been astoundingly devious. We can perhaps best approach the next and successive stages in this progress by descending *in medias res* to hear Wilkes speaking in the House of Commons on 28 April 1777 on a motion for referring the petition of the Trustees of the British Museum to the Committee of Supply. He is, as one might expect, baiting George III but also urging more support for the purchase of printed books and paintings: 'Such an important acquisition as the Houghton Collection, would in some degree alleviate the concern, which every man of taste now feels at being deprived of viewing those prodigies of art, the Cartons of the divine Raphael. King William, although a Dutchman, really loved and understood the polite arts. He had the fine feelings of a man of taste, as well as the sentiments of a hero. He built the princely suite of apartments at Hampton-Court, on purpose for the reception of those heavenly guests. The English nation were then admitted to the rapturous enjoyment of their beauties. They have remained there until this reign. At present they are perishing in a late baronet's smoky house at the end of a great smoky town. They are entirely secreted from the public eye; yet, Sir, they were purchased with public money, before the accession of the Brunswick line, not brought from Herrenhausen. Can there be, Sir, a greater mortification to any English gentleman of taste, than to be thus deprived of feasting his delighted view with what he most desired, and had always considered as the pride of our island, as an invaluable national treasure, as a common blessing, not as private property? The Kings of France and Spain permit their subjects and strangers the view of all the pictures in their collections; and sure, Sir, an equal compliment is due to a generous and free nation, who give

110. Letter to Burke from Rome (1766) in *The Works of James Barry Esq.*, London, 1809, i, pp. 68–69: 'they are (even in the prints, which is only what I have seen) without contradiction, beyond anything here . . .' The contrast is particularly relevant with the case of Benjamin West, who arrived in London in August 1763,

and who made his first journey outside the city (just in time) to Hampton Court to see the Cartoons (J. Galt, *The Life, Studies and Works of Benjamin West, Esq.*, London, 1820, ii, p. 5).

111. *Neueste Reisen durch England*, Leipzig, 1782, ii, p. 361.

112. Letter dated 12 September 1787 i[n] *Tagebuch einer Reise durch Holland und Englan[d]* 2nd ed., Offenbach-am-Main, 1791, pp. 296[–]297; she seems to have had the run of th[e] whole house.

113. In 1783 or thereabouts even Horac[e]

their prince an income of above a million a year, even under the greatest public burthens.'[106]

It would be as difficult to separate truth from untruth in Wilkes's speech as to separate its sincerity from its malice. But while it clearly was not true that the Cartoons had been 'purchased with public money'—they had been reserved from sale[107]—it was true that they were no longer at Hampton Court. The 'late baronet' was Sir Charles Sheffield and his 'smoky house at the end of a great smoky town' was the Queen's Palace, that is, Buckingham House, which George III had bought for Queen Charlotte in 1761; and the Cartoons had indeed been moved there in December 1763, to be hung in the Great Room.[108] That enterprising publisher John Boydell brought out an exegetical guide in the spring of 1764, and in his *Advertisement*, or preface, expressed all his optimism if not all his prescience: 'The Cartons having very lately been removed to her Majesty's Palace in the Park, it is to be presumed, that a greater Number of Persons will have an opportunity of viewing these celebrated Works of Raphael, than when they were at Hampton Court; and as many may be desirous of having a fuller Explanation of those inimitable pieces, than the Leisure of those who usually attend to shew them, can possibly permit, it is hoped the following little Piece may prove useful and acceptable to the Public.'[109] But 1764 was also the year of James Barry's arrival in London, and it is surely indicative of some obstacle (perhaps, in his case, a social one) that when he went to Rome two years later he had not yet seen what he nevertheless had 'not the least scruple about pronouncing . . . the best of Raffael's works'.[110] When Wilkes said that they were entirely secreted from the public eye he himself was not, and he could not have said something that was entirely and obviously contrary to common and contemporary experience. Since Queen Charlotte was German it might be supposed that her fellow-countrymen would enjoy some privilege, but by about 1780 even the admirably inquisitive Johann Jacob Volkmann was turned away; he remarked that at first Buckingham House had been accessible to visitors who wished to see the pictures but it was now forbidden to do so.[111] Sophie von la Roche, who had all the right connections, wrote triumphantly in 1787 that she had seen 'die berühmten Cardons des Raphaels';[112] but Sophie was a very special case. There can be little doubt that in this period the Cartoons were indeed rarely seen,[113] and this is a fact to which some significance may be attached; for this was the ripe moment—not later, in the nineteenth century, when in spite of continued optimism it was clearly too late—when the powerful presence of Raphael's greatest history-cycle might really have exercised a stimulating, and sobering, influence upon English history-painting. They were not forgotten, of course; but academic criticism so rarely touched upon those qualities in a work of art that distinguish the experience of the original from that of an engraving.

Undoubtedly the translation of the Cartoons to Buckingham House was sanctioned by George III, at least in part, because he wished his Queen to enjoy them.[114] On the other hand Richard Dalton, who was the King's librarian, said that they had been moved from Hampton Court 'on their suffering from damps', and this seems wholly credible too.[115] In the Royal Library at Windsor there is a set of drawings which shows the disposition of the paintings hung in Buckingham House early in the reign of George III. The drawing of the Great Room shows the Cartoons in position and their lighting. They fitted in remarkably well, with the three short ones on the long wall opposite the windows, and two long ones on each end-wall;[116] in

Walpole could have only 'a slight view'; he noticed that 'the Cartoons are in the great room, hung on light green damask' (*Journal of Visits to Country Seats, &c.*, in *The Walpole Society*, xvi, 1928, p. 78). P. J. Mariette, *Abecedario*, in *Archives de l'art français*, viii, 1857–58, p. 296, had information from Walpole that the Cartoons had been moved to Buckingham House 'où il est fort difficile de pénétrer. Le plus grand mal, c'est que, dans le transport, on assure que les cartons ont souffert, que plusieurs parties des couleurs se sont détachées, qu'il a fallu y suppléer, et, pour peu qu'il faille y travailler encore, il est à craindre que le pinceau de Raphaël ne disparoisse tout à fait.'

114. In fact John Watkins, *Memoirs of . . . Sophia Charlotte, Queen of Great Britain*, London, 1819, p. 178, was uncertain whether 'this removal was at the desire of Her Majesty, or of the King'.

115. 'R.D.', 'Remarks on the whole number of the Sacred Historical Designs of Raphael d'Urbino', *The Gentleman's Magazine*, lvii, Part 2, October 1787, p. 853; the Rev. Matthew Pilkington, *A Dictionary of Painters*, 1770 (ed. H. Fuseli, London, 1805, p. 498) already complimented the King on his wisdom in moving the Cartoons from Hampton Court 'where they were evidently in danger of perishing, to place them under his own royal care and inspection'. A set of engravings by James Mitchell and W. Buchanan, published in Glasgow in 1773, is entitled *The Seven Cartoons of Raphael formerly at Hampton-Court, now, for their better preservation, in the Queen's Palace.*

116. The Rev. James Dallaway, *Anecdotes of the Arts in England*, London, 1800, p. 501 says 'In 1763, they were removed, and doubled up to fit the pannels of a room at Buckingham-house, but have been lately emancipated, and are now in excellent preservation at Windsor Castle . . .' He seems to mean that they were folded, and that does not seem to have been the case. The Windsor drawing of the Great Room, exceptionally, has detailed measurements of the frames of the Cartoons from which it would appear that folding would not have been necessary if the Cartoons then had their present dimensions; in fact the frames may be those still in use today, but there is conflicting evidence on this point (see below, n. 124). Even so it should be noted that Dallaway's assertion is partly consistent with two press-reports of 1819 (Courtauld Institute, *Press-cuttings*, ii, pp. 140–1) in which it is said that the Cartoons were 'curtailed' or 'abridged' to make them fit the 'pannels' in Buckingham House, and with a similar assertion already made in a poem attributed to Peter Pindar, 1788 (Victoria and Albert Museum, *Press-*

cuttings, p. 413). If it was meant that they had been cut, rather than folded, there may be some truth in these statements; the evidence of the Thornhill copies of *c.* 1730 (see above, n. 88) may be interpreted as an indication that the Cartoons were cut again to their present size after that date and not only in the restoration of 1699; and it is a fact that the framed Cartoons were very tightly fitted into the Great Room at Buckingham House, particularly on the side walls. But if there was some loss at this time it could only have been a matter of a few centimetres.

117. Dalton, loc. cit. in n. 115, October 1787: 'They are now at Windsor Castle, and open to public inspection' (in implied contrast to conditions at Buckingham House; he also commented that they were much damaged, and cut through by tracing). That the removal continued into 1788 is proved by a newspaper report, provoked by the fact that the workmen engaged on packing the Cartoons at Buckingham House were working on Sundays (Victoria and Albert Museum, *Press-cuttings*, p. 413); another, undated, cutting which is presumably earlier states that three had been taken to Windsor for the embellishment of the Queen's Drawing-Room to replace other pictures carried from the Castle to the Queen's Lodge (ibid., p. 340), and this also suggests that the move was made in two stages. It should be noted that while Sophie von la Roche said that she saw the Cartoons at Buckingham House in September 1787 (see above, n. 112) she also remarked rather hurriedly of Windsor that there were some Raphaels there too. And late in 1787 Romney went to Windsor to refresh his memory of the Cartoons (W. Hayley, *The Life of George Romney Esq.*, London, 1809, p. 132; I owe this reference to John Sunderland); it is not clear how many he saw, but the painting for which he felt he needed Raphael's assistance, *Prospero and Miranda*, suggests that he had studied in particular the *Sacrifice at Lystra* (T. S. R. Boase, 'Illustrations of Shakespeare's Plays in the Seventeenth and Eighteenth Centuries', *Journal of the Warburg and Courtauld Institutes*, x, 1947, p. 98, Pl. 27a). According to *The General Evening Post*, 27–29 November 1788, Benjamin West had been summoned to Windsor to 'repair, recolour and amend the Cartoons' (D. Irwin, *English Neoclassical Art*, London, 1966, p. 105).

118. *England, Wales, Irland und Schottland: Erinnerungen ... aus einer Reise 1802–3*, iv, Dresden, 1805, pp. 24, 193 ff. His account was in fact followed by Waagen, op. cit. in n. 51, ii, p. 402.

119. The *Charge to Peter*, *Death of Ananias*, *Conversion of the Proconsul*, and *Paul preaching at*

addition to the main windows there was, on the same side, top lighting in a coved ceiling. The presentation was simple and probably very impressive.

In 1787 and 1788 the Cartoons were moved again, this time to Windsor.[117] The period that follows is one of the most confusing in their history, because of a direct conflict in the evidence. On the one hand we have an apparently informed account from another German traveller, Christian August Gottlieb Goede, who was a most intelligent and observant forerunner of Passavant and Waagen.[118] He was at Hampton Court and Windsor in 1802–3, and said that from Buckingham House the Cartoons had been taken to Windsor, then to Frogmore (the Queen's House, remodelled by Wyatt in 1792), then to Windsor again 'where they wandered from one room to another and were finally displayed separately, some to remain in the old Castle and others to be set up as the decoration of the Queen's Drawing-Room in the so-called Queen's Lodge'; he himself had seen four in the King's Presence-Chamber in the Castle,[119] but two others in the Queen's Lodge he was unable to see. On the other hand we have a number of sources—guides and one undated entry in an inventory—which specify that from 1792 onwards three Cartoons were hung in the Queen's Presence-Chamber and four in the King's (the same four that Goede saw).[120] It is possible that the German visitor was confused, and understandably so, by the distinction between the Queen's apartments and the Queen's Lodge, which was a separate part of the Castle; and he could have been led astray by a reference to Cartoons that were indeed in the Queen's Lodge but which were, in fact, copies by Benjamin West.[121] But even with these emendations to his account of the situation at the time of his visit, 1802–3, there remains to be explained his tale of earlier wanderings around the Castle and to Frogmore, which is not irreconcilable with other sources known so far.[122]

Goede also remarked on the poor state of preservation of the Cartoons, specifying that some heads in *Paul preaching at Athens* were practically unintelligible; nevertheless he thought that the Cartoons he saw were the greatest of Raphael's works and sufficient on their own to place him above all modern artists. This otherwise unhappy state of affairs was very soon, however, to be changed; and at first sight it would appear that the change was for the better, since George III decided in 1804 that the Cartoons should be returned to Wren's Gallery at Hampton Court.[123] This migration was

Athens; W. H. Pyne, *The History of the Royal Residences*, London, 1819, i, p. 172, confirms that four Cartoons were formerly hung in this room. A set of full-size engravings of details, *Essays after the Cartoons of Raphael at Windsor*, by A. Cardon after J. Ruyssen, illustrates the *Miraculous Draught*, *Charge to Peter*, *Healing of the Lame Man*, *Death of Ananias* and *Sacrifice at Lystra*; the plates are dated between 1798 and 1801 and each specifies that the subject is at Windsor.

120. George III inventory of Windsor Castle (*c.* 1790, MS. in Surveyor's Office), fol. 69v., Queen's Presence-Chamber, pencil addition: '3 Cartoons', and fol. 99v., King's Presence-Chamber, similarly, '4 Cartoons'. C. Knight, *The Windsor Guide*, Windsor, 1792, pp. 17, 34 (ed. 1796, pp. 17, 34–36), Queen's Presence-Chamber and King's Presence-Chamber, list-

ing subjects. Dallaway, loc. cit. in n. 116 (1800) D. Lysons, *An Historical Account of those Parishe in the County of Middlesex which are not describe in The Environs of London*, London, 1800, p. 68 and Knight, loc. cit. in n. 95 (1801), all mention that the Cartoons are at Windsor Castle, bu unspecifically.

121. Knight, loc. cit. in n. 95.

122. The 'wanderings' recall the press-repor of 1787–88 (see above, n. 117) that three of th Cartoons had been taken to the Queen' Drawing-Room at Windsor Castle.

123. *The Farington Diary*, ed. J. Greig, ii, London 1923, p. 280 (30 August 1804); Courtauld Institute, *Press-cuttings*, i, p. 226 (1804); both make it clear that the decision was the King' own.

not simply a restoration of the installation of 1699. The Cartoons were now set in the so-called 'Carlo Maratta' gilt frames that had been provided for them in the meantime (the frames that are still used in the present display in the Victoria and Albert Museum),[124] and the sequence was changed with a rather startling result. In this new arrangement the two surviving pairs that had been planned by Raphael as pendants (the *Healing of the Lame Man* and the *Conversion of the Proconsul*, the *Death of Ananias* and the *Sacrifice at Lystra*) were once more hung as pendants; and moreover the compositions designed by Raphael to terminate the groups inside the screen, *Ananias* and *Lystra*, again terminated this scheme, mirrorwise as they should. It was an odd result if it was accidental, since it could not have arisen from taking into account obvious factors such as subject, dimensions or even light—indeed it was notably untidy from all these points of view. If, on the other hand, it must be doubted that any of the characters concerned with the re-installation of 1804, above all the Surveyor Benjamin West, had the visual intelligence to arrive at it by using his eyes and his head, it is not impossible that a greater mind—Reynolds's, for example—had previously worked out an ideal scheme in the years since the Cartoons had last been at Hampton Court. The very frequency of their movements in those years could have prompted the question: what goes best with what? And the suggestion of Reynolds's name, although it is hypothetical, is not quite casual, for he owned the full-scale copies, now in Dublin, of the *Healing of the Lame Man* and the *Conversion of the Proconsul*; and owning them he might have reflected that—within the whole sequence—these two made excellent pendants. However that may be, reflection upon the original order is not impossibly out of character with historical thinking of the period; in 1834 Carl Bunsen was to produce the first reconstruction of the hanging-order of the tapestries in the Sistine Chapel.

The arrangement of 1804 is recorded in an engraving (*Fig.* 86) published in Pyne's *History of the Royal Residences* (1819), which can only be criticized as a document of conditions of viewing in the Cartoons Gallery for its omission of the notorious gloom. But it must not be imagined that the return effected in 1804 inaugurated a long period of peace for the Cartoons like that which began in 1699. All the Cartoons were taken down in 1817 so that a new set of engravings could be made from them by Holloway;[125] and, what is worse, all the Cartoons were brought up to London again for exhibition at the British Institution between 1816 and 1819,[126] and the *Charge to Peter* was at Somerset House, on loan to the Royal Academy for copying, in 1823.[127] It must be one of the major miracles of the history of art that they survived all this moving around, for the manner of their handling was more brutal than the imagination, unaided by a document, would conceive. The document was drawn up by one of the great characters in the history of the Royal Collection, Richard Redgrave, who was appointed Surveyor in 1857. In his *Report* of 1865[128] Redgrave said that he had 'found these valuable works liable to serious injury and suffering great delapidation'; there was the danger of fire from kitchen flues beneath the floorboards, and there was the dust of two hundred thousand visitors who tramped each year through the Gallery, but most frightening of all there was the constant rolling and unrolling of the paper whenever the Cartoons travelled. 'The frames also', he adds, 'have been made to fold horizontally, and they have been so folded (of course with a great loop, but necessarily), to the great injury of the dry and fragile paper on which the Cartoons are painted. Tracing was allowed, and I have seen large sheets of tracing paper pinned on to the Cartoons, and a hard pencil used to trace the lines . . .' Copying was also allowed, of course, and

124. Pyne, op. cit. in n. 119, ii, pp. 76 ff., describes the move of 1804 and with it he associates the making of the frames at a cost of £500. I have been unable to check a report of a statement in J. Williams, *A Schizzo on the Genius of Man*, 1793, that new frames had already been made by that date; and I think it is possible that Pyne was mistaken and that the frames had been made for Buckingham House (see above, n. 116).

125. Anon., *The Hampton Court Guide*, Kingston, 1817, p. 20 (Holloway had in fact begun his work at Windsor by 1800: Dallaway, op. cit. in n. 116, p. 500n.). Haydon, however, was able to see the Cartoons in 1805 and again in 1812 (*Diary*, ed. cit. in n. 52, i, p. 231, v, pp. 175, 435). In the Farington Diary (the greater part of which remains unpublished—I have used the typed transcript in the Royal Library at Windsor), under the date 28 August 1814, there is an account of a visit to the Cartoons in the company of West, Smirke, Lawrence and Holloway. 'Here we remained two hours. Many of the Country People and from London dressed in Sunday attire came in large parties to see the Palace and passed through the Apartments attended by Persons appointed to shew the pictures . . . many essential remarks were made by West.' Farington thought the Cartoons the 'most perfect' of Raphael's works; 'Lawrence said admitting His "School of Athens", He thought as I did, and West concurred in it.'

126. 1816: The *Miraculous Draught* and *Paul preaching at Athens*; 1817: The *Conversion of the Proconsul* and the *Death of Ananias*; 1818: the *Healing of the Lame Man* and the *Charge to Peter*; 1819: The *Sacrifice at Lystra*.

127. William Hazlitt, *Criticisms on Art . . .*, London, 1843, p. 82. Lawrence had in fact negotiated this loan with the Prince Regent as early as 1816 (Farington Diary, source as in n. 125, 24 November 1816). The large Thornhill copies (see above, n. 88) were hung in the Great Room of the Academy and used for demonstration in lectures (the Rev. R. Cattermole, *The Book of the Cartoons*, London, 1837, p. 17; W. T. Whitley, *Art in England 1800-1820*, Cambridge, 1928, p. 14).

128. *Report on the state of the Cartoons on their Removal from Hampton Court Palace in April, 1865, and the nature of their accommodation at Hampton Court, and in their new locality* (privately printed sheets, n.d.); see below, n. 144.

129. Redgrave also felt that the Gallery was damp, and not properly heated in winter; after he took office in 1858 he had extra precautions taken against fire and glazed the Cartoons which 'ill seen and ill lighted before, have, from their glazing, become so many mirrors'. The glazing was begun in 1861 (P.R.O., L.C. 1/96, No. 3). In Redgrave's inventory of October 1858 (MS. in Surveyor's Office, Nos. 625-31) he noted severe damage to the *Sacrifice at Lystra*, including water-damage and rotting paper, and in 1860 he added that some of the paper was hanging loose; he made similar observations in 1858 and 1860 of *Paul at Athens* and in 1860 of the *Healing of the Lame Man*. In a generally rather rude review of the British Institution exhibition of 1816 (Victoria and Albert Museum, *Press-cuttings*, p. 1228; see above, n. 126) the two Cartoons then shown were called 'these torn and faded washed-drawings'. From documents of the removal of the Cartoons to London, 1865, it appears that a recent and very expensive innovation had been heavy machinery in the Gallery to allow the Cartoons to be lowered from their frames and moved out in case of fire; this was also, probably, a precaution of Redgrave's (P.R.O., L.C. 1/152, Nos. 51, 59). Redgrave's *Report* of 1865 inspires trust, but it may nevertheless give a false impression. His predecessor in the office of Surveyor, Thomas Uwins, had not been negligent but on the contrary much concerned, and soon after his appointment (in 1845) he had also deposited a *Report* with the Office of Woods and Forests which had not been acted upon except that Lord Carlisle, then First Commissioner, had promised a Committee on the subject; Uwins had also wanted the Cartoons glazed, and it should be noted, in contrast to Redgrave's account, that he remarked that very little copying was done at Hampton Court (see his unsolicited statement to the Select Committee on the National Gallery, in *House of Commons, Reports from Committees*, 1850, British Museum series xv, pp. 14 ff.).

130. *Diary*, ed. cit. in n. 52, ii, p. 502; in 1827 there was a project in the air to transfer all the larger pictures from the Royal Collection to the National Gallery (Victoria and Albert Museum, *Press-cuttings*, p. 1704).

131. Victoria and Albert Museum, *Press-cuttings*, p. 1686. On 18 December 1833 he had a private conversation with Lord Grey which, not unnaturally, did not go well: 'Are the Cartoons coming?' 'No,' said he, 'they are better off at Hampton Court!'; they discussed the matter again a few days later with the same result (*Diary*, ed. cit. in n. 52, iv, pp. 145-6).

132. Victoria and Albert Museum, *Press-cuttings*, p. 1654: 'The Cartoons of Raphael,

Redgrave had seen paint thrown upon them, they were touched with brushes and mahl-sticks, and they even suffered water-damage, but perhaps on account of a leaking roof.[129] The 'great loop' of unsupported Cartoon is perhaps the part of this account that bears least contemplation; yet fire was not simply a potential danger—it was an actuality. The editorial of *The Art-Union* for 15 April 1841, sarcastically entitled 'The Worthless Cartoons', announced that they 'have lately had an escape from destruction by fire, little less than miraculous. A policeman on duty within the palace of Hampton Court, being alarmed by smoke rising in the gallery, discovered, upon examination, that it proceeded from a part of the skirting-board, which was in a state of ignition.' Although 'the progress already made by the fire being inconsiderable, it was speedily extinguished', the editorial justly pointed out that actual combustion of the paper was not essential for their destruction: radiant heat alone would be equally effective.

It was a disturbed period in the history of the Cartoons in another, quite different, sense. It will not have been forgotten that in 1777 Wilkes wanted them on public display. When the National Gallery was founded in 1824 Benjamin Robert Haydon immediately felt that that was where the Cartoons belonged; since his enemy Benjamin West, Surveyor to George III, was by then dead, Haydon was conceivably motivated by the highest principles and not by spite.[130] His next step came with the publication of an open letter to the Prime Minister, Lord Grey, in which he was arguing that the projected new building in Trafalgar Square, designed to house the Royal Academy as well, would not be big enough; and in this letter, of 26 April 1833, he asked 'Will any gallery which excludes the cartoons of Andrea Mantegna and Raffael be a National Gallery? and they alone will occupy the space.'[131] In the meantime there had been a proposal in 1829 to construct for their display a new octagonal Private Chapel in Buckingham Palace, as it was then called, in effect a *Cappella palatina* for the head of the Anglican Church;[132] and this, if one recalls their original programme, would have been a diverting change of function for the Cartoons. It is true that 1829 was a year of tolerance, the year of Peel's Emancipation Bill and also the year in which the first Roman Catholics were readmitted to Parliament, but it may be suspected that the proposal was not ecumenical, and least of all ironical, but a serious attempt to do something constructive about the Cartoons and even to make them more readily accessible; at all events it is an indication that George IV or his advisers appreciated the unsatisfactory situation at Hampton Court.

While the National Gallery was still housed in Pall Mall Haydon's proposal was not, surely, very practical. But when Wilkins's new building was begun in 1833 it was probably inevitable that the future of the Cartoons should be discussed again; Haydon's open letter of that year ensured that it

which were removed from Windsor Castle to Hampton Court, for the convenience of the late amiable Mr Holloway, who has executed from them a series of engravings in the highest style of the art, will shortly be transferred to the New Private Chapel, appended to the Royal Palace, late Buckingham House, which is built in an octagon form, and so constructed as to exhibit, in the best possible light, those inimitable productions. We trust students and amateurs in art, as well as the public generally,

will, at all proper times, be permitted to see them.' The Chapel, probably one of the la of Nash's ideas for the new Palace, was to hav top lighting and was to be formed out of th octagonal library of George III; see W. I Leeds, *Supplement* to (J. Britton and A. Pugin *Illustrations of the Public Buildings of Lond* London, 1838, p. 118, where it is said that th Chapel 'is not yet completed', perhaps : indication that the project of 1829 was st alive.

was. In 1836 a distinguished group of connoisseurs and artists (including Haydon) was summoned to give evidence before a Select Committee of the House of Commons and they were asked, among other things, to express an opinion upon the proper future for the Cartoons; none took the view that the subject was *ultra vires*—which is in itself quite an interesting reflection of the assumed position of the Cartoons in the texture of national life—and opinion was generally in favour of their transfer to the National Gallery where, said the architect Wilkins, room could be found for them.[133] And on 15 September 1839 *The Art-Union* came out with an editorial that asked rhetorically, and rather tendentiously: 'Why are they allowed to moulder on the walls of Hampton Court useless and unproductive in their effects, when, if removed to the National Gallery, they would produce better results upon Art than the Elgin Marbles?' Pollution in Trafalgar Square was admitted as an obstacle but it was suggested, at this early date already, that they could be glazed.[134] The Hampton Court fire of 1841 led not only to another editorial, which we have already noticed, but also to another House of Commons Committee. The evidence given before this Committee by the Surveyor Seguier was somewhat complacent about conditions at Hampton Court, and he was strongly, even possessively, against sending the Cartoons to the National Gallery; but the compromise that he suggested, Kensington Palace, where the air was then clean, is interesting and perhaps important with respect to later developments.[135]

It is also interesting to notice changes in viewing conditions occurring at Hampton Court itself. Since 1838, the year after Queen Victoria's accession, entry had been free to the public and apparently quite unrestricted, and there were guided tours around the Cartoons.[136] And thus the annual visitation rose to the extraordinary figure of two hundred thousand attested by Redgrave in 1865. It was another change in the social history of the Cartoons and, by such universal exposure of the obvious inadequacies of their conservation at Hampton Court, it must have contributed to their eventual removal to London. The fact that the exhibition at Hampton Court did become in this period a truly popular spectacle is proved by two local reactions when it became known, from a leaked press-report in the spring of 1865, that the decision upon their removal had been taken: the inhabitants of Hampton Court drew up a petition of protest, which was presented in the House of Lords, and the innkeepers were alarmed by the anticipated loss of trade.[137]

The full story of the decision upon the removal to London will probably never be known because in part, at least, it matured in private and perhaps principally in the ever-active mind of the Prince Consort. It is a fortunate accident that in 1851 Prince Albert mislaid a private submission, addressed to him, on the dangers of the situation at Hampton Court since we learn, from a scrap of correspondence in which another copy was requested, that he was sympathetic and wanted to make an urgent personal report on the matter.[138] However, the Prince Consort immediately became involved in his great plans for the disposal of the profits of the Great Exhibition of 1851, leading eventually to the foundation of the South Kensington Museum which was opened by Queen Victoria in 1857; and action upon the Cartoons was probably delayed too by his project of November 1851 to transfer the National Gallery to the new site in South Kensington, a project which was still alive in 1856.[139] The final formulation of his plans for the Cartoons is described by Charles Ruland who, as the executant of Prince Albert's remarkable documentary project, the 'Raphael Collection' in the Royal

133. The Select Committee on Arts and Principles of Design, in *House of Commons, Reports from Committees*, 1836, B.M. series ix, pp. 1 ff., esp. p. 149 (Edward Solly and Haydon); there is a summary of evidence in an editorial in *The Art-Union*, 1 September 1841, p. 154.

134. The editorial, p. 130, is entitled 'On the present state of the Fine Arts in Great Britain'.

135. I have used the summaries of this Committee's evidence in the editorial cit. in n. 133.

136. Editorial, *The Art-Union*, 1 December 1841, p. 202; Trull, op. cit. in n. 1, p. 4.

137. Lord St. Leonards in the House of Lords, 31 March 1865 (Hansard, series 3, clxxviii, col. 556); and a letter of 25 March from the housekeeper at Hampton Court, reporting local reactions to a leaked report in *The Surrey Comet* (P.R.O., L.C. 1/152, No. 59, 1/150, No. 86).

138. The submission to the Prince was made by Miss Susan Horner, who later became the author of a number of books, mostly on Italian subjects. A letter from her brother-in-law, Sir C. Lyell, dated 14 July 1851, passed on, in the Prince's own words, his request for a duplicate: 'Tell her if she will only put the *facts* fully it will do ... to ensure a report I must put the affair in hand before I leave town' (Victoria and Albert Museum, English MSS., Box 86. BB). In the second edition of his *Works of Art and Artists in England*, London, 1854, i, p. 324 and ii, p. 410, G. F. Waagen suggested once more that the Cartoons should be moved to the National Gallery and drew attention—objectively and prominently—to their neglect at Hampton Court and their exposure there to damp and cold. Waagen had given the same advice to the Select Committee of 1850 (*Report*, cit. in n. 129, pp. 39 ff.); it is clear from his questioning on that occasion that as Director of the Berlin Gallery his views were accorded great respect.

139. Sir Henry Cole, *Fifty Years of Public Work*, London, 1884, i, pp. 314, 318, 320; and the summary of these and related proposals in the speech of W. Cowper (First Commissioner in the Office of Works), 6 June 1864 (Hansard, series 3, clxxv, col. 1298). A Select Committee of the House of Commons voted in favour of the translation of the National Gallery in 1851, but this decision was finally reversed by a Royal Commission of 1856.

140. C. Ruland, *Notes on the Cartoons of Raphael now in the South Kensington Museum . . .*, London, 1867, p. 8. Henry Cole, in *The Morning Star*, 9 January 1860, proposed a radical rearrangement of Hampton Court whereby *all* the paintings should be brought to London, which he would probably not have dared to suggest unless he knew that the Prince Consort would agree.

141. On 6 March 1865 the Lord Chamberlain wrote to the First Commissioner for Works (Cowper) concerning a motion to be put to the House of Commons that Raphael's and Mantegna's Cartoons should go to South Kensington, pointing out that these works were not at the disposal of Parliament, but were the private property of the Queen; the motion was never put to the House. On 15 March Henry Cole, on behalf of the Lords of the Committee of the Council on Education, wrote to the Lord Chamberlain requesting the Queen's consent for the loan of the Raphaels to South Kensington 'in galleries that are fireproof' (which they were not); on 16 March Sir Charles Phipps (who was not officially the Queen's Private Secretary but seems to have acted as such) communicated her consent to the Lord Chamberlain; Cole was informed the next day and was sent, for his signature, a form of guarantee for their safe removal and custody, and return when required. On 27 March, as a result of a telegram from Windsor, Eastlake, at the National Gallery, was told that his Trustees' request for the loan had been turned down since the Queen had already given her consent that they should go to South Kensington and wished this arrangement adhered to (P.R.O., L.C. 1/150, Nos. 74, 76, 88, 138; L.C. 1/152, Nos. 39, 46, 49, 56). Details of the transport to South Kensington are contained in Captain E. R. Festing's *Memorandum on the Removal of the Cartoons from Hampton Court to the South Kensington Museum*, a privately-printed sheet dated 8 May 1865 (a copy is in the Victoria and Albert Museum with Redgrave's *Report*); the operation was conducted with impressive care, the case containing the Cartoons being suspended in its van 'by india rubber springs'. Before the move the Cartoons were examined by Faraday (Victoria and Albert Museum, Conservation Department, docs. 6267, 8679); and Richard Redgrave also wrote *Suggestions for the conservation of Raphael's Cartoons, now at the South Kensington Museum* (printed, as above), which were mainly practical: the loose paper should be laid down, the glass sealed, the backs covered with painted cloth, the top lighting restricted and curtains to be placed over each Cartoon; he also made recommendations about ventilation and heating and regular hygrometric and temperature tests, but was adamant that no 'repairs' should be attempted: alto-

Library at Windsor, was in a good position to know the truth; he says that the eventual loan to the South Kensington Museum in 1865 was made 'with a view of carrying into effect a suggestion made by the Crown Princess of Prussia, in remembrance of a plan of His Royal Highness the Prince Consort, viz., to assemble together, if possible, all Raphael's works now existing in England'.[140] It is reasonable to suppose that the National Gallery was the destination initially envisaged by the Prince Consort (who died in December 1861), and that this plan was modified by the Crown Princess, his eldest daughter, and also by Queen Victoria. For whereas the Queen gave to the National Gallery in 1863 a number of the Prince's earlier Italian paintings as an outright gift in deference to his wishes, it is clear from Redgrave's *Report* of April 1865 that her attitude to the Cartoons was in all respects different: 'Her Majesty was graciously pleased to allow of their exhibition for a time at South Kensington'; and her private secretary made it very clear at that time that they were to be returned whenever she might 'desire to resume possession of them'. The Trustees of the National Gallery made a last-minute request for the loan but they were too late. The Queen had already given her consent on 16 March that the Cartoons should go to the South Kensington Museum and they travelled to London at the end of April.[141]

Redgrave's *Report* was initially drawn up in response to a query from the First Commissioner of Works (in other words a Government initiative) 'if there would be serious danger in removing the Cartoons to the National Gallery in Trafalgar Square'.[142] The final choice of South Kensington rather than the National Gallery might have reflected the short-sighted supposition that atmospheric conditions would be better westwards from Trafalgar Square, since that consideration—even with specific reference to the hanging

gether an astonishingly advanced approach. It appears from a memorandum of the Lord Chamberlain, 13 April 1865, that Faraday was being quoted as having advised against the move, but that he had no recollection of having done so (P.R.O., L.C. 1/152, No. 65); Faraday's concern is probably the result of his residence at Hampton Court, since 1858, in a house belonging to the Queen (B. H. Jones, *The Life and Letters of Faraday*, London, 1870, ii, p. 398).

142. See above, n. 128, and below, n. 144.

143. See, for example, the 1850 Select Committee *Report*, above, n. 129.

144. P.R.O., L.C. 1/531, No. 87, letters of 11 May 1864 from Cowper (Office of Works) to Sir Charles Phipps, and 17 May 1864 from Redgrave to Phipps commenting on the first. Cowper wrote in advance of the Government motion which he introduced in the Commons on 6 June 1864, in fact concerning a proposal (which was defeated) for the removal of the National Gallery to the Burlington House site; during the speech he said that 'The Cartoons might, if it was thought fit, be brought up from Hampton Court; and, for his own part, he should desire that, as London already possessed

the greatest works of sculpture—the Elgin Marbles—it should also have the greatest work in drawing—the Cartoons of Raphael' (Hansard, series 3, clxxv, col. 1318). These events led directly to Redgrave's *Report* and explain why it answered the First Commissioner's query about the National Gallery.

145. Similarly his predecessor, Thomas Uwins, would seem to have combined his two interests as Surveyor and as Keeper of the National Gallery when, giving evidence to the Select Committee of 1850 (loc. cit. in n. 129), he said that he would have no objection to the transfer: 'If another site were found for the National Gallery, a little removed from town, then I think it would be a glorious thing indeed to have the Cartoons in it; it would make such a National Gallery as no other country in the world could present.'

146. The visit and its purpose are recorded in her *Journal*; she returned on 10 March 1866 when she remarked that the Cartoons were placed 'where they are seen to the greatest advantage'. I am grateful to Miss Jane Langton for telling me of these entries, which are quoted with the gracious permission of Her Majesty the Queen.

of the Cartoons—had been applied to the slightly earlier proposals to move the National Gallery to Kensington.[143] But it seems still more probable that the Queen's decision was principally influenced by the advice of Richard Redgrave, who had been made Inspector General for Art at South Kensington in the same year, 1857, as his appointment as Surveyor. For the question had been raised in 1864 and then Redgrave had already agreed with a proposal to the Queen that the Cartoons should be preserved in a place safer than Hampton Court; but he had not agreed with the hint that they should go to the National Gallery but felt that they would be 'more appropriate at South Kensington as designs for Tapestries'.[144] Redgrave's opinion is rather clearly influenced by the combination of his two responsibilities, and his reasoning looks like special pleading.[145] If Queen Victoria did follow Redgrave's advice in 1865 she took, nevertheless, a personal interest in the future of the Cartoons; she visited the Museum to inspect their destination on 6 April 1865, that is to say after she had given her consent to their translation but before it was put into effect.[146]

The removal of the Cartoons to South Kensington probably was instrumental in arresting their further deterioration, and now we may be grateful for it. But in other respects and for the time being it was a disaster such as Eastlake would never have perpetrated if he had had his way and got them for the National Gallery. For the first display of the Cartoons in the Museum must have been a dreadful illustration of the importance of being earnest about works of art. The late Prince Consort's dream of a Raphael Museum was reduced to an educational programme conducted at a depressingly low level. A full-sized eighteenth-century copy of the *Transfiguration*, also from the Royal Collection, was hung with them, together with a tapestry of the *Charge to Peter*, which was more sensible; but there were also drawings after the Stanze frescoes, and small oil-copies of them too, sixteen lunettes and some grotesque pilasters copied from Raphael's Loggia, and a Gobelins tapestry after a *Holy Family* in the Louvre.[147] In 1883, to mark the fourth centenary of Raphael's birth, three full-size copies of the missing tapestry-designs were commissioned and in due course added to the collection of mummies.[148] With the possible exception of this addition it was not an educational display that could be justified as illuminating the Cartoons themselves; on the contrary the Cartoons were reduced to the status of documents and they were given yet another new function: to serve the cause of Art History. The intentions may well be thought admirable, and sociologically interesting, but they were made too obvious. And most of us would now view with revulsion the idea that works of art should be made to serve the art-historian's limited purposes. From another point of view this High-Victorian display was the most brutal and insensitive ever devised for the Cartoons, for it differed from all previous ones, and from the present one, in denying simultaneously two of the principal intentions of Raphael himself: that they should be seen to mean something in the programmatic sense and that they should give pleasure.[149]

However the purely visual conditions of viewing had to become worse before they were improved. The problem of the fading effects of light had been a worry for a long time, as we have seen, and to some extent they must have been held in check by the gloom, which may have been intentional, of the Gallery at Hampton Court. By about 1890 it was held in some quarters that further damage of this kind had become perceptible since the Cartoons had been moved from Hampton Court.[150] Scientific research produced a startling solution in 1889, which was put into effect two years later: the

147. The display is described in the *Guide to the South Kensington Museum*, 1868, pp. 59–60. The *Transfiguration* copy is by Casanova, 1760, and it had been hung in a small room next to the Cartoons at Hampton Court (P.R.O., L.C. 1/152, No. 65). In view of the Prince Consort's project, as reported by Ruland, it is interesting that the proposal to assemble these copies, which seems to have come from the South Kensington authorities, was at first thought to be tactless; Sir Charles Phipps wrote to the Lord Chamberlain, 12 April 1865: 'I will ask the Queen about the copy of the Cartoon (i.e. the *Transfiguration*) and let you know. I doubt whether it would do to let the Science and Art Department form a Raphael Collection'; nevertheless Henry Cole made a formal request for the *Transfiguration* on 20 April 'in order that it may be placed in the Gallery which it is proposed to devote to the Exhibition of Raffaelle's works' (P.R.O., L.C. 1/150, Nos. 103, 119). The material assembled in the South Kensington Cartoon Gallery was rearranged in 1918–19, and again in 1925.

148. The copies were made by W. M. Palin in 1884.

149. A strongly worded critique of the display appeared in the *Pall Mall Gazette*, 1 October 1867; the anonymous author was very rude about the 'authorities' at South Kensington: 'They are destroying the cartoons of Raffaelle, which were, after long-continued pressure, brought from Hampton Court . . . These priceless pictures are now hung on the walls of a dismal and badly lighted room, and subjected every evening to the fumes of London gas . . .'; he was perhaps genuinely concerned about the danger of fire from the system of gas-lighting, which does—in his account—sound alarming, and held that 'if the Government were to do its duty, not a day would be lost in transferring the Cartoons to Trafalgar-square'. It was not, however, a matter for the Government but for Richard Redgrave, who drew up a report on the *Gazette*'s charges for the Lord Chamberlain (P.R.O., L.C. 1/182, No. 367) in which he defended the installation at South Kensington; his main points were that the Cartoons were more carefully looked after than they had been for centuries, that the light was deliberately kept low by a covering of calico under the skylight, that the gas-lighting had been approved by a committee of eminent chemists, that he had had each Cartoon 'hermetically sealed' with glass in front and painted cloth behind (cf. n. 141, above), and that the fire-precautions in the Museum were excellent.

150. This is the impression given by Law, op. cit. in n. 89, p. 85 (1891); but his remark may

have been more personal and more partisan than he admitted, and it was certainly polemical since he counselled that the Cartoons should be 'removed once more to the purer air of Hampton Court (so that) they may yet remain for many generations unimpaired, which they certainly will not, if subjected much longer to the gassy, smoke-laden, and corroding atmosphere of London'. J. C. Robinson stated in 1892 (see below, ns. 152–3) that until a short time previously direct sunlight had fallen on the Cartoons in the gallery at South Kensington.

151. This solution was devised by Sir William Abney; see J. A. Macintyre and H. Buckley, 'Protection of pictures and Museum Pieces from Fading', *International Illumination Congress,* Saranac Inn, N.Y., 1928, p. 7, and N. S. Bromelle, 'The Russell and Abney Report on the Action of Light on Water Colours', *Studies in Conservation,* ix, 1964, p. 148, who describes the context of preceding controversy on the more general issue of fading, out of which grew the particular solution applied to the Cartoons.

152. *Report of the Commission appointed to inquire into the Question of the Housing of the Raffaelle Cartoons,* London, 1892.

153. His opinion was consistent with that of Ernest Law (above, n. 150) and of the Queen's Private Secretary, Sir Henry Ponsonby (expressed in a letter to Miss Susan Horner from Osborne, 11 February 1892, in the Victoria and Albert Museum, English MSS., Box 86. BB; he claimed to be impartial on the matter, but his feelings are quite clear). The proposal was revived in an editorial in *The Burlington Magazine,* lxxxi, 1942, p. 263, which followed a correspondence in *The Times.* The Royal Commission of 1891–92 was in fact set up as a result of a number of reports produced between 1886 and 1890 by Robinson; in the earliest of these (P.R.O., L.C. 1/473, No. 83) he referred to the new system he was installing at Hampton Court for the rapid removal of the Mantegnas in case of fire, which could also be provided there for the Raphaels, he expressed his worries about environmental conservation-problems at South Kensington, and suggested that the Queen might be asked to instruct the Department of Science and Art to set up a Commission of Enquiry; there were counter-reports by other parties, and more memoranda by Robinson (L.C. 1/473, Nos. 22, 35, 66, 69) but it was agreed that action should await the Russell and Abney Report (above, n. 151). Robinson produced yet another very long report on 20 August 1890 (L.C. 1/531, No. 87) in which he argued ingeniously for the return of the Cartoons to Hampton Court; he felt

top-lighting of the gallery was filtered through sheets of orange and green glass, the intention being that these would produce an artificial daylight free from harmful ultraviolet light.[151] And it is this macabre environment, yellowish and sepulchral, that remains in the memory of those who saw, or tried to see, the Cartoons before the Second World War.

A visually insignificant modification was the provision in 1893–94 of a fireproof roof; this was the practical result of a Royal Commission appointed by Queen Victoria in May 1891 to enquire into the safety of the Cartoons from fire and atmospheric pollution (by then a serious matter in South Kensington), and to see if they would not be better preserved at Hampton Court once more.[152] There was evidently weighty support for their restitution, and in many ways the most interesting part of the Commission's *Report* is the minority submission of the Surveyor, J. C. Robinson, who could argue persuasively in favour of that solution;[153] his case included the melancholy observation that the accessibility of the Cartoons to art-students was no longer a reason for keeping them in London, because no students paid any attention to them. Since he was himself a scrupulous scholar whose catalogue of the Raphael drawings at Oxford (1890) was the last sane contribution to that subject for many years, Robinson might have added that art-historians were not paying much attention either; for this was just the moment at which critical appreciation of the Cartoons entered what is known as the dustbin phase.[154] No doubt the dispiriting conditions at South Kensington made any appreciation of them an act of almost totally blind faith, but while that may be an explanation of the long absence of any more positive scholarly reaction it does not explain the initial misjudgement. The dustbin phase affected the history of Renaissance art generally and was itself an act of faith, misplaced in two directions: it reflected the quite unwarranted trust in the new tool, photography, as a substitute for the personal appraisal of the work of art, and it was a kind of hubris born of satisfaction with pseudo-scientific analytical method.

The Cartoons, in any case, were due for resurrection once more. This came about in two stages. First came the critical reappraisal, which was performed in the 1930s by that great Raphael scholar, Oskar Fischel; his excitement, at what was for him a personal rediscovery of a level of quality in many areas of the Cartoons that could be Raphael's alone, led him to the intention to write a monograph on these works.[155] The project was never realized, but the passages on the Cartoons in his posthumous book on Raphael, assembled from notes, communicates at least the level of his excitement if not its full extent.[156] The second stage came with the re-hanging of the Cartoons in 1950. During the war they had been taken down from the notorious upper gallery in the Victoria and Albert Museum and now a more spacious gallery was provided which approximated to the scale of the Sistine Chapel; the light was better and the miscellaneous copies were discarded.[157] There remained two serious inhibitions to enjoyment, the caulked joints between the three strips of plate-glass by which each was protected, and obtrusive restorations and lacunae. These inhibitions were removed in 1964–65 in a campaign of discreet restoration, during which the glazing problem was also finally solved.[158] They may now be seen under better conditions, probably, than ever before—the possible exception is the Buckingham House period—and they may also communicate to the agile mind more of Raphael's programmatic intentions, since the hanging-order is for the first time as near as possible a mirror-image of the arrangement intended for the tapestries. But one cannot say that on an ordinary day there is much seeing or communicating actually going on. This is the latest irony in a story that is in fact full of ironies from that very first moment when it was decided that Pope Leo X, of all people, should look across from his throne to his predecessor healing the cripple with the words: 'Silver and gold have I none . . .' The Cartoons have served many purposes and there is perhaps one sense in which they now serve in a way approximating to that which was originally intended for the tapestries and which might please at least Pope Leo. Occasionally, at appointed times and for hours on end, they have captive audiences; and it is probable that then, from concert-audiences, they receive most attention. There is a certain artistic justice in this. For as great music serves so many of us in the later twentieth century as aural wallpaper so it is perhaps not unfair that these great paintings should serve—if this is the right phrase—as a visual baffle which traps the wandering minds of music-lovers.

George III's librarian, Richard Dalton, made a very bold statement about the Cartoons which was, however, probably true in every particular in the late eighteenth century: 'And if they are seen without sensibility by the greater part, few will dare to own that they are not properly affected by performances which have received such universal applause.'[159] The burden of obligatory admiration was most effectively lifted by Ruskin when in 1856 he published the fourth part of *Modern Painters*; for Ruskin then showed in a sensational manner that it was possible to be both English and rude about the Cartoons, which were his point of departure for an undoubtedly stylish attack upon the general 'poison of the art of Raphael'. At first sight it seems odd that Ruskin was finally brought to the boil not by his aesthetic convictions but by a correct understanding of the iconography of the *Charge to Peter* —'that infinite monstrosity and hypocrisy . . . Note first the bold fallacy— the putting *all* the Apostles there, a mere lie to serve the Papal heresy of the Petric supremacy, by putting them all in the background while Peter receives the charge, and making them all witnesses to it . . .'[160]

And yet it was inevitable that the accident that brought these pre-eminently Popish works to Protestant England should produce reactions as comic as Ruskin's—so long, that is, as people remained interested in the meaning of works of art. Monsignore Farabulini, writing in 1884, consoled himself for the exile of these works from Rome with optimism that was, alas, absolutely false, with respect both to the future and to the past: 'Raphael's Cartoons have been of the greatest service to the English in the progress of their national art, which was practically extinguished by Protestantism; it is, therefore, a real benefit that that nation has received from Papal Rome, which fulfils its sublime mission in the world also through masterpieces of Catholic art.'[161] He utterly misjudged the ability of English artists to profit by them, and he could not conceive the stubbornness—occasionally relieved by ingenuity—of the Anglican reaction. It is not essentially because this situation is funny that it is worth illustrating this reaction—and a Marxist one—but rather because the issue brings us back to a serious point which we have touched upon when examining the methodological problems of interpreting meaning. The capacity of works of art to sustain a plurality of meanings may justify the hypothesis that more than one, or a certain flexibility of choice, was intended in the first place; but in the after-life of such a work as the Cartoons that same capacity allows the accretion of new meanings which could never have come out of the context in which they were produced.

Ruskin was not especially percipient when he recognized the essential programmatic meaning of the *Charge to Peter*. Even the English had shown

that at South Kensington their prestige had been lowered and that they had no logical connection with the rest of the collections there: 'the majority of visitors in fact now pass them by with languid indifference'; however he somewhat injudiciously added that the Treasury was unlikely to vote money for what needed to be done to the gallery at South Kensington because a future reorganization of 'National Collections' would allocate the Cartoons to the National Gallery as 'Fine Art', and this produced a sharp reaction from Balmoral: 'The Queen is rather taken aback by the idea that the Cartoons are slipping out of her grasp. At any rate she approves the proposed commission being suggested. But would like to consider the names rather further' (Sir Henry Ponsonby to the Lord Chamberlain, 5 September 1890: L.C. 1/531, No. 89). It may be noted that Robinson's list of names (ibid., No. 94) included Ernest Law (cf. above, n. 150), who was not appointed.

154. Beginning with Dollmayr, 1895 (see above, p. 111, n. 73); see also n. 101, above.

155. This project is described by A. P. Oppé, 'Right and Left in Raphael's Cartoons', *Journal of the Warburg and Courtauld Institutes*, vii, 1944, p. 82.

156. *Raphael*, London, 1948, esp. pp. 250 ff.

157. The editorial in *The Burlington Magazine*, xcii, 1950, p. 337, celebrates this event and contrasts the opportunities for a just assessment afforded by the new display with those of the old.

158. See above, p. 112. At the same time a system for the rapid emergency removal of the Cartoons was installed for the first time at South Kensington.

159. Op. cit. in n. 115, p. 853.

160. *Modern Painters*, ed. L. Cust, London, 1906, iii, pp. 52 ff.

161. Mgr. D. Farabulini, *L'arte degli arazzi e la nuova Galleria dei Gobelins al Vaticano*, Rome, 1884, p. 32.

162. See above, n. 97.

163. *Traité*, ed. cit. in n. 82 (1728), i, pp. 32, 83, iii, pp. 232, 449.

164. M. Kitson, 'Hogarth's "Apology for Painters" ', *The Walpole Society*, xli, 1966–68, p. 81.

165. Op. cit. in n. 127, p. 73.

166. *The Athenaeum*, 13 January 1838, pp. 25 ff. This very witty review—even more unkind than modern anonymous reviews—makes formidable demands upon an author of a monograph on the Cartoons, and it should be read by anyone who writes on this subject.

themselves constantly aware of it, and that awareness was manifest at the earliest moment in the public history of the Cartoons. Let us return to the verse-descriptions appended to the *Hymn to the Light of the World*, 1703, and read carefully an extract from the one devoted to the Cartoon which the author disingenuously entitles *Our Saviour and his Twelve Apostles* (which is, by the way, notably the shortest of these poems):

> See holy *Peter*, on his bended Knees,
> From his great Master's Hand receives the Keys,
> That open wide high Heav'n's Immortal Gate
> To all pure Souls that for Admission wait:
> But lock it fast against the impious Train,
> Doom'd to the Seats of Death and endless Pain.
> Thus the Redeemer did the Saint invest
> With Pow'r Divine, but not above the rest.
> For all the Sacred Tribe, as well as he,
> Have Pow'r to bind, and set a Sinner free.
> Much less this Grant did Sov'raign Right convey,
> Obliging all th'Apostles to obey
> Their Monarch *Peter*'s universal Sway.
> But do not ask what Raphael's Notions were,
> His Judgement might, his Pencil cannot err.[162]

It is clear that the poet did not see, or did not want to see, that Raphael's subject in fact conflated two texts, from Matthew xvi and from John xxi; but it is equally clear that he knew the first of these very well, and that he saw the point. His answer, however, was but a paraphrase of the one produced by pre-Lutheran anti-monarchic or conciliar theologians and subsequently revived at the Reformation; and it was an answer that would have exasperated Leonine theologians—even such a patient polemicist as Domenico Jacobazzi—who like many before them had argued most elaborately against this interpretation of Matthew xvi, and specifically by citing this text together with the Charge to Peter in John xxi.

The Richardsons, on the other hand, saw not only the point of the *Charge to Peter* but also the conflation of the two texts—but one has to look not in the English but in the French edition of their works for the really explicit (and very carefully phrased) statements.[163] They overlooked only one of the finer theological points when they took the fact that Peter already holds the Keys as Raphael's determination to preserve, like a good academic theorist, the Unity of Time. And Hogarth—the only English artist whose response to the Cartoons was truly personal and creative—made a private and rather moving acknowledgement of their moral content when he wrote that he would rather have been the author of the *Four Stages of Cruelty*, for the good they might do, than of the Cartoons 'unless I lived in a roman Catholic country'.[164] On this tradition of acknowledgement, if not of sympathy, is based the straight Anglican reaction of the nineteenth century. The Reverend Richard Cattermole, for example, deplored the 'sectarianism' that led Raphael to put the Keys in Peter's hands;[165] and if that remark was typical of him it shows that he would have been hopelessly outclassed even by Jacobazzi's chaplain, Cyprian Benetus. Cattermole's monograph on the Cartoons, published in 1837, was corrosively and anonymously reviewed in the *Athenaeum*,[166] and there the approach was more ingenious. The reviewer contrasted the *Charge to Peter*, dramatic and real, with Perugino's *Donation of the Keys*, more abstract: 'religious pictures like the Cartoons, having no tendency to produce image or saint worship in ignorant votaries, are of a less Romish nature' (he admitted, however, in a footnote that Raphael was a Papist). The same reviewer took exception to the superstitious introduction of the Salomonic columns in the *Healing of the Lame Man*; but he preferred to blame an interfering cardinal for this 'sole example of decidedly impure taste throughout the works of Raffael Sanzio'.

Reynolds observed that he had come across several varied readings of the expressive actions in the Cartoons, and his characteristically imaginative interpretation of this result was that Raphael himself encouraged it 'and . . . by an indistinct and imperfect marking, left room for every imagination, with equal probability to find a passion of his own'.[167] He was undoubtedly right about the latitude of readings of the *Charge to Peter*, but if he was also right about Raphael's intention, which is less sure, the latitude was to be exploited to a degree that neither artist could have foreseen. The Abbé Dubos, in 1719, had thought not unnaturally that the expression of Saint John showed his enthusiasm for the just choice of Peter by Christ.[168] About a hundred years later, however, we find quite a different interpretation of the whole scene by an anonymous Anglican commentator who seems determined not to see the point;[169] Peter, this writer thought, is singled out for the crime of his threefold denial and shows his guilt, while John 'seems as if he was about to assure his Lord, that his love was at least equal to Peter's', and James, between them, seems surprised 'at the affectionate manner in which Peter's crime was noticed by his Lord'. This reading brings us near the extreme Anglican position which was adopted by the Reverend William Lisle Bowles when preaching in 1837 in the chapel at Bowood, which had recently been embellished with stained-glass copies of the Cartoons presented by William IV.[170] This prolific parson knew his theology, knew also how to use it, and had some experience of polemics. He recognized that the Donation of the Keys represented 'the peculiar creed of the Vatican', and that Raphael had described accurately in this sense the position of Peter 'as if to him the plenitude of apostolic power was exclusively given'; but the sense should in fact be inverted, he said, for the threefold charge had the effect of restoring Peter, after his denial, to *equal* authority with the other apostles—even Matthew xvi. 19 is invoked to prove the point—and after an excursionary study of *Revelation* Raphael's design is eventually adduced as a demonstration of Christ's foundation of the Protestant faith. There are, of course, a number of reasons (not all of them creditable) why this particular perversity would not be produced today, and instead we have to turn to Marxism to find an equally wilful, creative and passionate response to the Cartoons. Quite recently there has come out of East Germany a new interpretation of them which would again make Raphael an anti-papal hero, but in a different sense; the Cartoons and tapestries, it is believed, are a monument to international cooperation and they express an historical moment of humanist liberty and social felicity before the neo-feudalism of the Counter-reformation.[171] But it is just as hard to agree; as it happens the evidence proves more conclusively that Raphael was at heart a capitalist than that he was a Papist.

Tempora mutantur et nos mutamur in illis. We can perhaps best conclude this survey by reflecting very briefly upon the history of a slightly different question, the standing of the Cartoons as works of art. When the Elgin Marbles came to England in 1808 it was inevitable that the two series of masterpieces should be compared, and the comparison itself has an interesting evolution. Remarkably, one finds it anticipated by Jonathan Richardson the Elder, who had already paired Raphael not (as one might have expected

167. *Discourses*, ed. cit. in n. 103, p. 115; the same observation, but not the conclusion, already appears in Webb, op. cit. in n. 101 (1760), p. 195. Reynolds's interpretation appears to be borrowed from literary criticism and it recalls, for example, justifications of the obscurities in Tasso's *Gerusalemme liberata*.

168. *Réflexions critiques sur la poësie et sur la peinture: Ut pictura poesis*, Paris, 1719, i, pp. 88 ff.

169. This is the letterpress published with Holloway's engraving (Victoria and Albert Museum, Box VIII, 107.G).

170. *A Series of Discourses preached in Bowood Chapel on Subjects from the Cartoons of Raphael*, 2nd ed., Salisbury, 1838, pp. 3, 14, 114.

171. C. Emmrich, 'Die Raffaelischen Teppichkartons und ihre Beziehungen zu Zeitverhältnissen und Auftraggeber', *Dresdener Kunstblätter*, v, 1961, pp. 94 ff.

172. Op. cit. in n. 82, i, p. 144; his point was
in fact that no artist had the capacity of visualizing the Divine: 'Le Colosse de *Phidias*, les
peintures de *Raphaël* ne sont que de foibles
ombres de cet Etre Infini & Incomprehensible';
but in its context the sense is: 'not even
Phidias or Raphael . . .', and the 'peintures'
in Richardson's mind would be, in the first
place, the *Transfiguration* and the Cartoons.

173. An undated Discourse to the Royal
Academy, *c*. 1800 (Galt, op. cit. in n. 110, ii,
p. 153); he was discussing patronage and
remarked that Raphael found 'as animated a
protector in Leo X as Phidias experienced in
Pericles'.

174. *Diary*, ed. cit. in n. 52, i, p. 233; and a
review, May 1817, of the Cartoons exhibited
at the British Institution (Victoria and Albert
Museum, *Press-cuttings*, p. 1016).

175. Trull, **op.** cit. in n. 1, p. 14; *Inventaire de
tous les meubles du Cardinal Mazarin*, ed. Henri
d'Orléans. London, 1861, p. 14.

176. A. Springer, *Raffael und Michelangelo*, Leipzig, 1878, ii, p. 284.

of an author in the humanist tradition) with Apelles but with Phidias;[172] and
Benjamin West, in another context, had done the same.[173] Haydon, writing
in his Diary in 1812, seems to be the first to isolate the Elgin Marbles and the
Cartoons as the purest sources for a future great style in art (hopefully his
own) and he put the idea into print five years later;[174] thereafter the comparison in these rather general terms became a commonplace in the first half
of the nineteenth century in England. There were variations; William
Trull, in 1840, made it in the sense that both would have been better left
unrestored, and Henri d'Orléans, in 1861, made it again when saying that
these were the most beautiful works of art in England.[175] There was,
therefore, nothing surprising in the fact that Anton Springer should set them
side by side in 1878. What was new in Springer's much-quoted passage was
the meaning he attached to their equation: that these were absolutes,
paradigms of Greek and Renaissance art respectively, by which all other
works of their periods must be judged.[176] To say that was to say in a particularly memorable way what others had felt for some time, that the
Cartoons represented a peak of achievement not only within Raphael's work
but also within post-antique art as a whole. Of course this had never been a
universal opinion; but the question that lies behind this answer or any other
is as interesting as the answer itself, because it is a question to which there is
no conceivable answer today.

I think that we would not now say that the Cartoons are the Parthenon
Sculptures of modern art, and I doubt whether we could agree that they are
the greatest of Raphael's works. For myself, I would not know how to
evaluate them against, for example, the Villa Madama. There is no need to
complain that they are underestimated, and it is unnecessary to re-write the
Richardsons' eulogies. Our unwillingness to make hierarchical judgements is
founded upon a wary disbelief in absolutes. Perhaps criticism will re-cycle
itself so that the question may be asked again, but for the time being it has no
reality because its premises seem to us too simple. We have acquired a kind of
aesthetic agnosticism which may be justified on moral grounds for its tolerance
and for the freedom of universal enjoyment that it allows. Yet there remains
a distinction which we value between the great works of art and the less great,
and just as clearly the intellectual, imaginative and visual beauty of the
Cartoons makes Raphael's achievement there one of his greatest, and one of
the greatest in the whole history of art.

PLATES

1. *The Miraculous Draught of Fishes.* Victoria and Albert Museum. (Reproduced by Gracious Permission of Her Majesty the Queen.)

2. Christ. Detail from Plate 1.

3. Saint Peter. Detail from Plate 1.

5. Detail from Plate 1.

4. Crane and fish. Detail from Plate 1.

6. *The Charge to Peter*. Victoria and Albert Museum. (Reproduced by Gracious Permission of Her Majesty the Queen.)

7. The Apostles. Detail from Plate 6.

8. Landscape. Detail from Plate 6.

9. Saint John and three other Apostles. Detail from Plate 6.

10. Saint John (X-ray photograph). Detail from Plate 9.

12. *The Healing of the Lame Man.* Victoria and Albert Museum. (Reproduced by Gracious Permission of Her Majesty the Queen.)

13. Saint Peter, Saint John, and the Lame Man. Detail from Plate 12.

14. Detail from Plate 12.

15. Detail from Plate 18 (X-ray photograph).

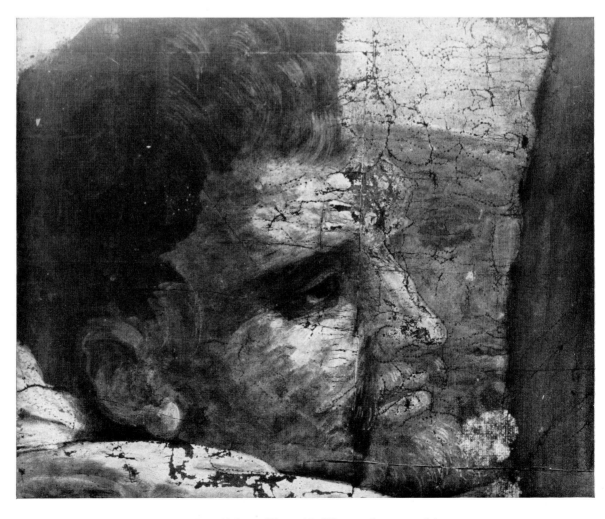

16. Detail from Plate 18 (X-ray photograph).

17. Detail from Plate 18 (X-ray photograph).

18. Detail from Plate 12.

19. Detail from Plate 20 (X-ray photograph).

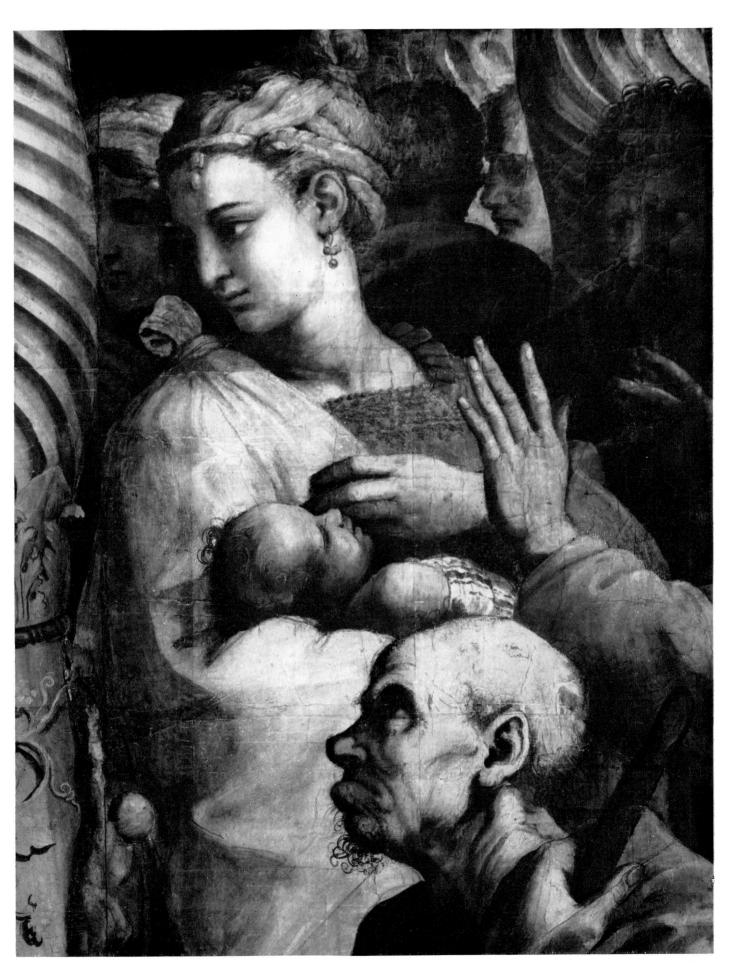

20. Detail from Plate 12.

21. *The Death of Ananias.* Victoria and Albert Museum. (Reproduced by Gracious Permission of Her Majesty the Queen.)

22. The Apostles. Detail from Plate 21.

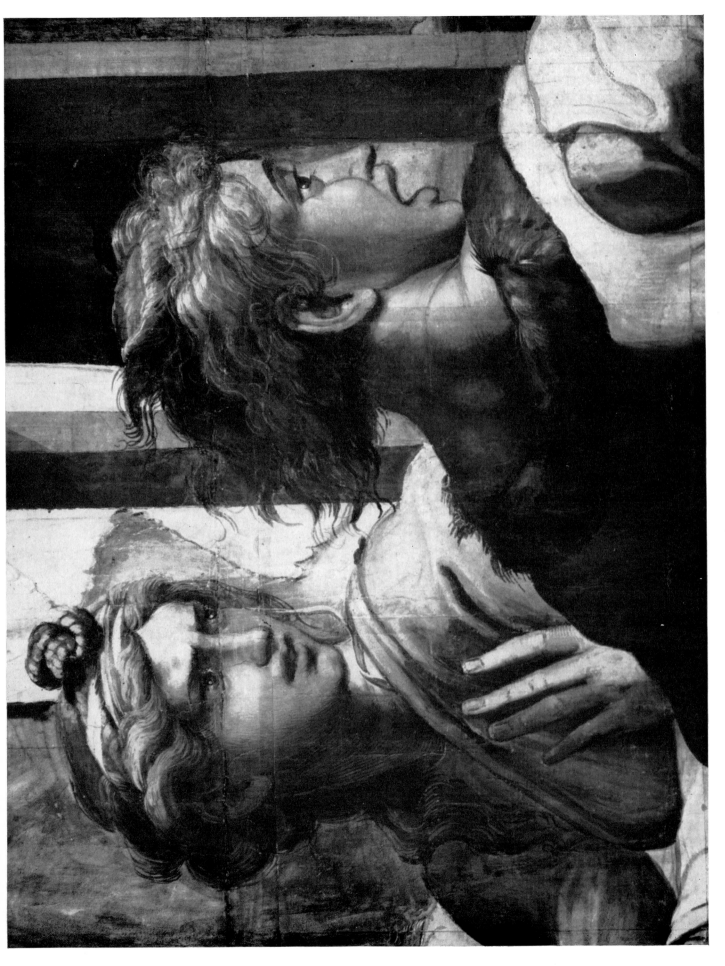

24. Detail from Plate 23.

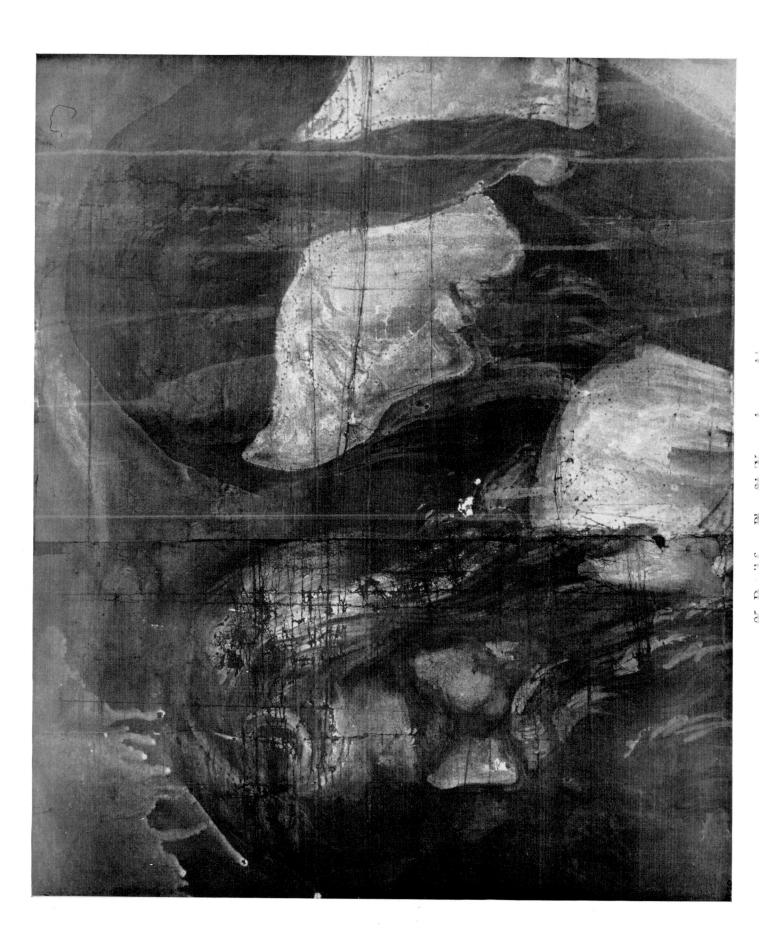

L·SERGIVS·PAVLVS·
ASIAE·PROCOS·
CHRISTIANAM·FIDEM
AMPLECTITVR·
SAVLI·PRÆDICATIONE

26. *The Conversion of the Proconsul (The Blinding of Elymas).* Victoria and Albert Museum. (Reproduced by Gracious Permission of Her Majesty the Queen.)

27. Elymas (X-ray photograph). Detail from Plate 28.

28. Elymas. Detail from Plate 26.

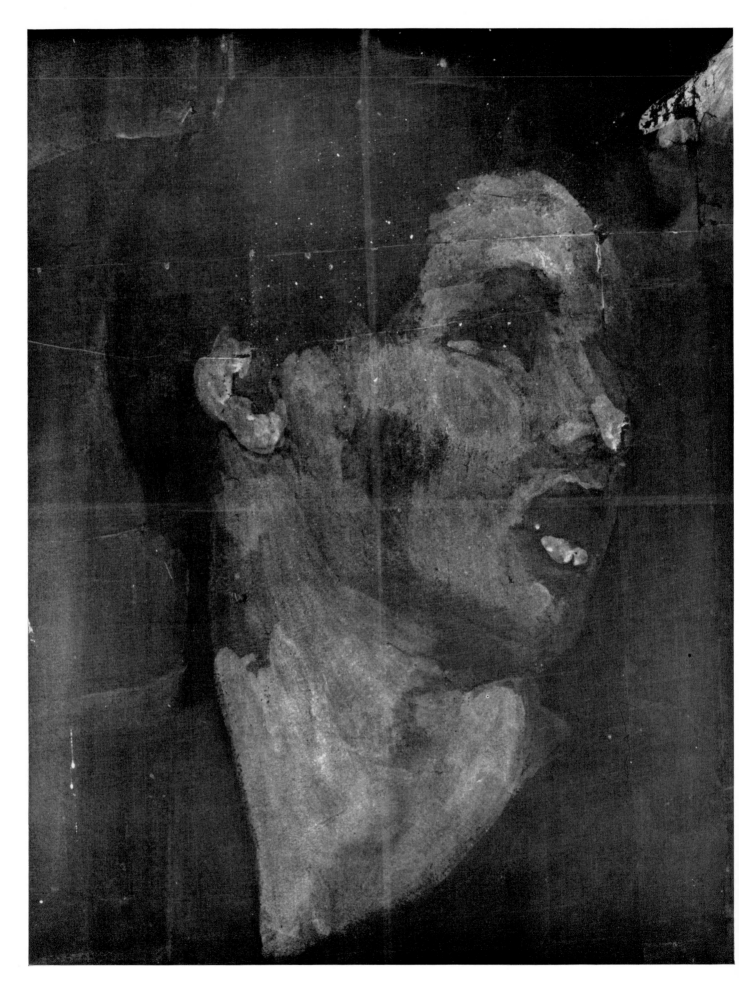

29. A Lictor. Detail from Plate 30.

30. Saint Paul. Detail from Plate 26.

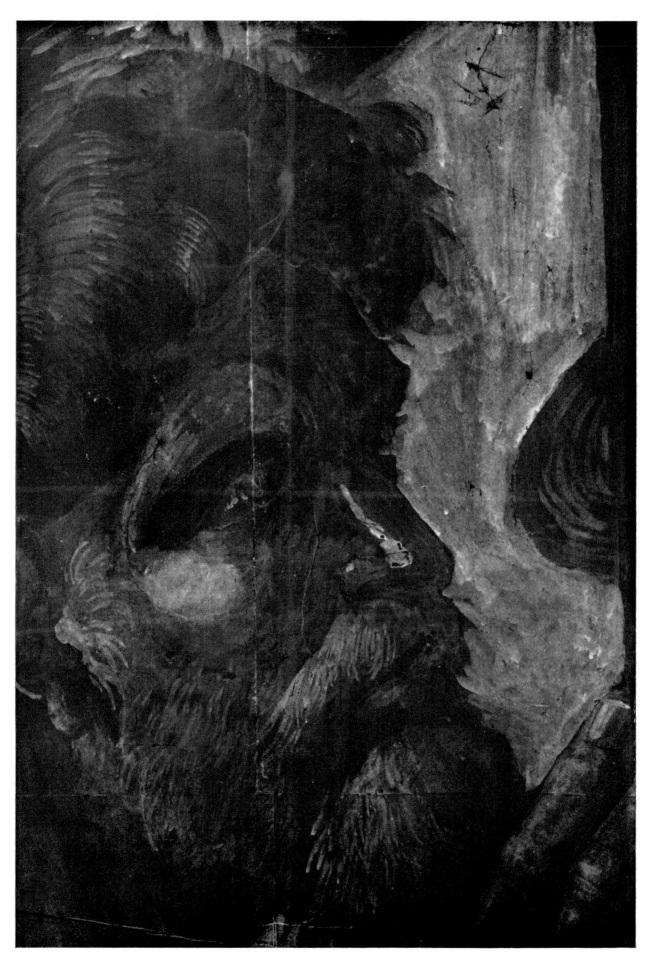

31. Barnabas (X-ray photograph). Detail from Plate 30.

32. Detail from Plate 28 (X-ray photograph).

33. Detail from Plate 28 (X-ray photograph).

34. *The Sacrifice at Lystra*. Detail from Plate 38.

35. *The Sacrifice at Lystra*. Detail from Plate 38.

36. The *popa*. Detail from Plate 34.

37. The Healed Cripple (X-ray photograph). Detail from Plate 35.

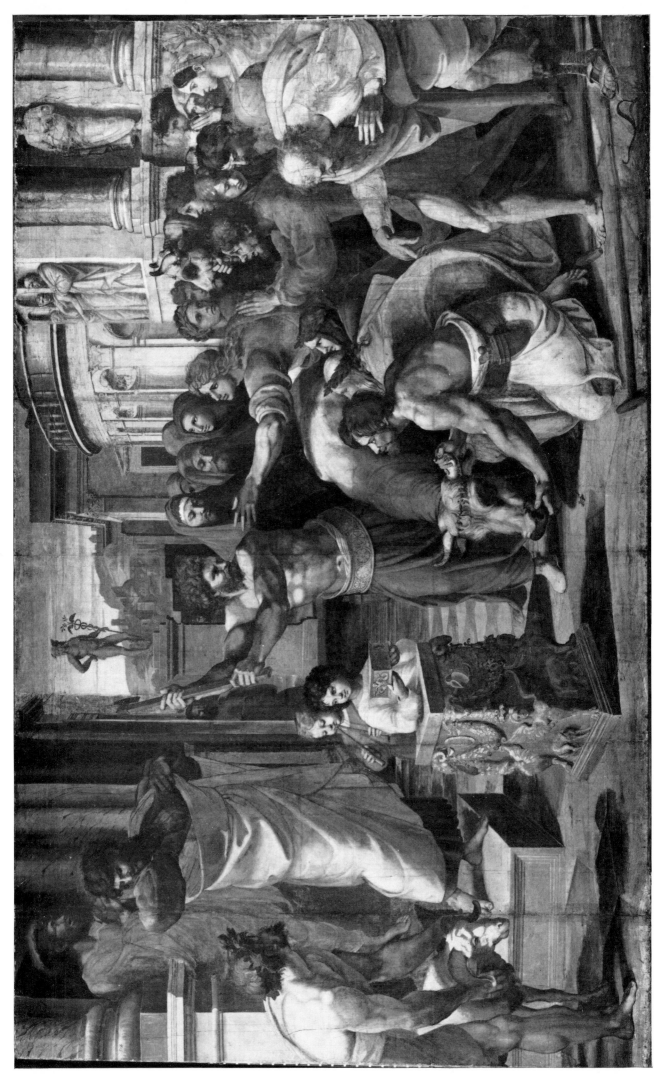

38. *The Sacrifice at Lystra*. Victoria and Albert Museum. (Reproduced by Gracious Permission of Her Majesty the Queen.)

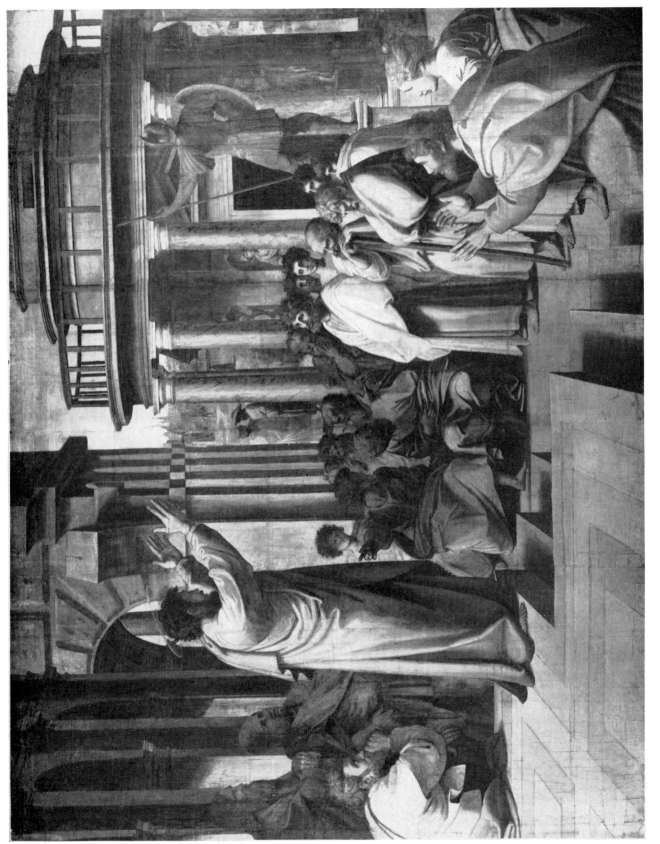

39. *Saint Paul preaching at Athens.* Victoria and Albert Museum. (Reproduced by Gracious Permission of Her Majesty the Queen.)

40. Saint Paul, with possible portraits of Lascaris and Leo X. Detail from Plate 39.

41. The Athenians, with Dionysius and Damaris. Detail from Plate 39.

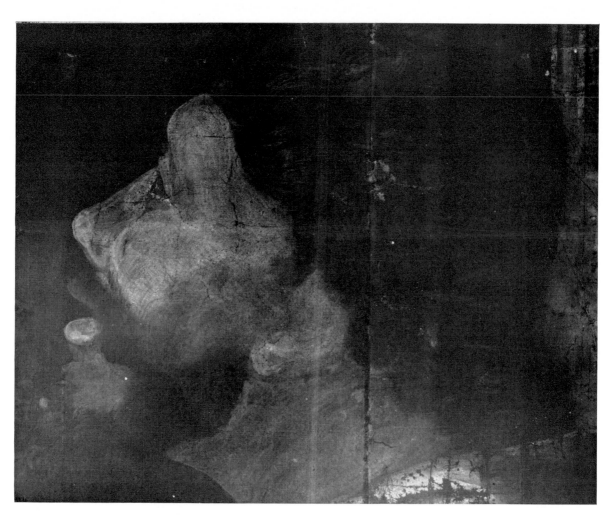

42. Dionysius (X-ray photograph). Detail from Plate 44.

43. Damaris (X-ray photograph). Detail from Plate 44.

44. Dionysius and Damaris. Detail from Plate 39.

45. Two Athenians. Detail from Plate 39.

46. Portrait, possibly of Leo X (X-ray photograph). Detail from Plate 40.

CATALOGUE NOTES

Catalogue Notes

PHYSICAL COMPOSITION

Each Cartoon is constructed of a large number of sheets of tough paper, each *c*. 43 × 29 cm., glued together and overlapping. The original Cartoon appears to have been made of one thickness of paper only, which has been reinforced in some places by a further thickness at a later date. All the Cartoons are laid upon a canvas lining, presumably —but not demonstrably—*c*. 1698 when they were set up at Hampton Court (see above, p. 149); and the canvas is stretched upon wooden frames. The technique may be described as a kind of gouache or body-colour; the pigments —mainly mineral—are bound with an animal glue.

CONDITION

In general the state of the Cartoons may be described either as miraculously good or as very worn, depending upon the point of departure—their eventful history (Chapter V, above), or comparison with most surviving paintings by Raphael (or, indeed, other famous Renaissance cartoons). A detailed account in words of each Cartoon's condition is not practicable, and no diagram could convey adequately the complexity of degrees and kinds of damage and restoration. X-ray photography is the best starting-point for an understanding of condition, and the plates reproduced here give a reasonable impression of the extent of damage typical of most of the surface (see p. 112), without illustrating the worst passages; but the limited radiographic survey also shows that any attempt to describe the state of a Cartoon would remain largely guesswork until the survey could be completed. Obviously damage is particularly serious around edges, and along joins between the vertical strips ('slips', of widths varying around 1 metre), into which the Cartoons were cut for weaving; the results are most serious in the *Charge to Peter*, where there is distortion by misalignment, and false interval, as well as much painted restoration, along the joins.

Equally obviously there is a considerable amount of repainting throughout the Cartoons, even where the support is sound, some justifiable as compensation for total losses of original pigment but much of it unnecessary. During the restoration of 1964–65 some of this repainting was removed, with particular benefit in the case of the *Miraculous Draught*, where, in the landscape background, the previous almost total overpainting of sky and water had concealed incidentally several small birds in the distance (and false ravens had been supplied); now most of the original swans and ravens have been revealed, but some distortion still remains, most notably in the townscape on the right (see p. 51). Another significant distortion of Raphael's intentions remains in a severely damaged area in the foreground of the *Sacrifice at Lystra*, where the crutches have been altered; the disappearance of the knee-crutch makes it impossible to understand the manner or extent of the cripple's cure; in this instance the repainting can be dated *c*. 1640 (see p. 147).

Apart from damage by avoidable neglect, and by clumsy restoration, there have been natural changes characteristic of the ageing process of paintings which, in this case, are most significant where fading of pigments has occurred. A well-known peculiarity of the Cartoons, to be explained in this way, is the colourless appearance of the robe of Christ in the *Miraculous Draught*, where the reflection of the robe is red (see *Pl.* II, p. 134). A less familiar but equally striking example occurs in the *Sacrifice at Lystra*, where the old man on the extreme right wears a shirt with yellow-green highlights but colourless shadows (*Pl.* 35); tapestries woven from the Cartoon show that this passage of drapery was originally painted with yellow-green highlights and rose shadows.

Naturally to these distortions of the original painted surface there is to be added the deterioration of the primary support, the paper, which is cut, torn, wrinkled and patched to a degree that is dispiriting for the close observer; but, on the other hand, this damage may be thought providentially limited if the vulnerability of the structure of the works is considered in relation to their history of use and abuse.

A detailed account of the restoration of 1964–65, and of the technical findings on that occasion, is to be published in *Studies in Conservation* by Norman Brommelle.

DRAWINGS

All known preparatory drawings, or records of drawings, are listed and discussed in Chapter IV, pp. 94 ff.

ENGRAVINGS

Prints of all subjects except the *Stoning of Stephen*, the *Conversion of Saul*, the *Sacrifice of Lystra* and *Paul in Prison*, were issued more or less immediately; none of these prints, however, was made from a Cartoon or tapestry, but they were probably all made, directly or indirectly, from preparatory drawings (for the *Miraculous Draught*, see above, pp. 95–96, ns. 6, 7, 10, and *Figs.* 42, 45; *Charge to Peter*: pp. 96–97, ns. 18, 19, and *Fig.* 80; *Healing of the Lame Man*: p. 98, ns. 21, 23, and *Figs.* 58, 59; *Death of Ananias*: p. 100, ns. 31, 32, and *Figs.* 60, 61; *Conversion of the Proconsul*: p. 102, n. 41; *Paul preaching at Athens*: p. 106, n. 57).

The earliest engravings after the Cartoons themselves are the set by Simon Gribelin (1707, but the frontispiece, *Fig.* 85, added 1720). Gribelin's modest and rather coarse set was followed immediately by the much more ambitious one by Nicolas Dorigny (1711–19), which was commissioned by Queen Anne. For lists of prints after Cartoons, tapestries and preliminary drawings see J. D. Passavant, *Rafael von Urbino und sein Vater Giovanni Santi*, ii, Leipzig, 1839, pp. 236 ff., G. F. Waagen, *Treasures of Art in Great Britain*, London, 1854, ii, pp. 379 ff., and C. Ruland, *The Raphael Collection in the Royal Library at Windsor Castle*, Weimar, 1876, pp. 243 ff. I do not repeat these lists because I have not checked all the material they contain; they are not complete (even when taken together), but omissions appear to be of little interest with the possible exception of an early set of copies after Gribelin's which was published as a booklet (undated) by Thomas Bakenell, London.

TEXTS

The *Miraculous Draught of Fishes*: Luke v. 3–10.
The *Charge to Peter*: Matthew xvi. 17–19 and John xxi. 15–17.
The *Healing of the Lame Man*: Acts iii. 1–11.
The *Death of Ananias*: Acts v. 1–11.
The *Stoning of Stephen*: Acts vii. 54–60.
The *Conversion of Saul*: Acts ix. 1–7.
The *Conversion of the Proconsul*: Acts xiii. 6–12.
The *Sacrifice at Lystra*: Acts xiv. 7–18.
Paul in Prison: Acts xvi. 23–26.
Paul preaching at Athens: Acts xvii. 16–34.
For the subjects of the lower and lateral borders of the tapestries, see above, pp. 37, 84, 43.

PROVENANCE

The history of the Cartoons is described in detail in Chapter V; for convenience a summary is included here:
1516 (?), Rome to Brussels, workshop of Pieter van Aelst.
c. 1525, to workshop of Jan van Tiegen and associates.
1573, Brussels, unspecified workshop.
c. 1580–1600, Brussels to Genoa.
1623, acquired in Genoa by Charles, Prince of Wales.
1639, *Death of Ananias* and *Conversion of Proconsul* in store at Whitehall, the rest at Mortlake.
1649, entire set at Whitehall.
1650–51, Somerset House.
1685, in pawn in London.
1690, Banqueting House, Whitehall.
1697, Hampton Court (recently brought from the Tower?).
1699, Hampton Court, set up in former King's Gallery (then Cartoon Gallery, or Great Council Chamber).
1763, Hampton Court to Buckingham House.
1787–88, Buckingham House to Windsor.
1792, Windsor, King's and Queen's Presence-Chambers.
1804, Windsor to Hampton Court, Cartoon Gallery.
1865, Hampton Court to South Kensington (now Victoria and Albert) Museum.

DIMENSIONS

The dimensions of both Cartoons and tapestries require careful scrutiny and full tabulation; the present ones do not correspond in either case with Raphael's intentions. In each case there is one distorting factor that is unquantifiable and can only be expressed as a margin of error, and another that can be fairly accurately assessed and applied as a correction.

The Cartoons were measured by the Surveyor Richard Redgrave for his inventory of 1858 (see above, p. 156, n. 129), and his measurements have been used ever since. They themselves are not, in fact, in need of revision; during the recent restoration they were found to be accurate to $\frac{1}{4}$ in. (6 mm.), which is well within the tolerance necessitated by the broken and uneven edges of the paper, and indeed by the use of different tapes. Redgrave's measurements are very accurate, but at the same time accidental. The uncontrollable factor is the contraction of area caused by the marked wrinkling of the paper, the effect of which might be a reduction of between 5 and 10 cm. in linear dimensions; it is unlikely, however, to be consistent. An approximately calculable correction is the restoration of cut paper; the amount to be restored to any given edge can be ascertained from comparison between the Cartoons in their present state and early tapestries woven from them, and the very precise Cleyn copies now in the Ashmolean Museum (see above, p. 147). The results are set out below.

A similar explanation is required of the dimensions assumed for the tapestries in the reconstruction shown in the scale drawing, p. 25, where the present dimensions are not used. No correction has been made for the distortion of the tapestries by stretching, since this seems to be a factor that cannot be precisely controlled; it may be assumed that the vertical extension is considerable, but it must also be as unequal between separate tapestries as it is along the length of single pieces. For structural reasons (the warp in this tapestry-technique being horizontal), the lateral variation is likely to be much less important. The corrections that can, and should, be made to the present dimensions arise from a comparison, edge by edge, between the Leonine tapestries on the one hand and the Cartoons or other early sets of tapestries on the other; for the comparison reveals that Raphael's dimensional intentions were seldom exactly respected, and that the weavers in the workshop of Pieter van Aelst made, in some cases, very considerable changes. One may guess that, like mediaeval masons faced with the new architecture of the Renaissance, they were not fully aware of the unprecedented importance of metrical accuracy entailed by Raphael's architectonic approach to his task. Approximate readjustments can be made to their errors, and these are explained below. The diagram on p. 25 is based upon these adjusted measurements, with the exception that the *Healing of the Lame Man* and the *Sacrifice at Lystra* have been slightly reduced in height to make them fit between the hooks in the cornice and the bench; it may be assumed that they have stretched exceptionally. No subtraction for stretching has been made in calculations of 'intended dimensions' set out below. Height precedes width.

The Miraculous Draught of Fishes
(*Plates* II, 1–5, *Fig.* 13.)

Cartoon: Redgrave 1858: 10 ft. 5½ in. × 13 ft. 1 in.;
    metric: 3·19 × 3·99 m.
    Losses: left, *c*. 2 cm.; right, *c*. 7 cm.; above, *c*. 6 cm.;
    below, *c*. 14 cm.
    Reconstruction: *c*. 3·39 × 4·08 m.
Tapestry, including one lateral border: 4·92 × 5·12 m.
    No corrections to be made.

The Charge to Peter
(*Plates* III, 6–11, *Fig.* 14.)

Cartoon: Redgrave 1858: 11 ft. 3¼ in. × 17 ft. 5¾ in.;
    3·43 × 5·32 m.
    Losses: left, *c*. 2 cm.; right, *c*. 6 cm.
    Gain: present height includes addition above, *c*. 13 cm.,
    probably 1698–99; upper limit of original part probably
    slightly trimmed (Cleyn copy shows a little more); hence
    subtract *c*. 8 cm. from present measurement.
    Reconstruction: *c*. 3·35 × 5·40 m.
Tapestry, including one lateral border: 4·84 × 6·32 m.
    Van Aelst seems to have added a little foreground to
    compensate for loss of sky above (see text, p. 139), but
    probably did not quite make good the loss; the tapestry
    may be *c*. 5 cm. less high than Raphael intended. An
    additional border of *c*. 70 cm. is likely on the left (see
    p. 43); planned dimensions probably *c*. 4·90 × 7 m.

The Healing of the Lame Man
(*Plates* IV, 12–20, *Fig.* 16.)

Cartoon: Redgrave 1858: 11 ft. 3 in. × 17 ft. 6¾ in.;
    3·42 × 5·36 m.
    Losses: left, *c*. 2 cm.; right, *c*. 10 cm.; above, irregular,
    c. 5–2 cm. (left to right); below, irregular, *c*. 2–6 cm.
    Reconstruction: *c*. 3·49 × 5·48 m.
Tapestry, with no borders: 5·00 × 5·66 m.
    In this case the upper limit of the picture-field as woven
    by Van Aelst corresponds precisely with that shown in
    the Cleyn copy of the Cartoon, and with that in the Berlin
    tapestry, whereas that in the Mantuan tapestry is *c*. 6 cm.
    lower; the latter must be (uncharacteristically) inaccur-
    ate. A border of *c*. 70 cm. was probably intended on the
    right, making the planned dimensions *c*. 5·0 × 6·35 m.

The Death of Ananias
(*Plates* 21–25, *Fig.* 17.)

Cartoon: Redgrave 1858: 11 ft. 2¾ in. × 17 ft. 5½ in.;
    3·42 × 5·32 m.
    Losses: left, *c*. 5 cm.; right, *c*. 9 cm.; above, *c*. 4 cm.;
    below, *c*. 7 cm.
    Reconstruction: *c*. 3·53 × 5·46 m.
Tapestry, including one lateral border: 4·90 × 6·31 m.
    No corrections to be made.

The Stoning of Stephen
(*Figs.* 18, 19.)

Cartoon: lost.
Tapestry, with no borders: 4·50 × 3·70 m.
    Variations (see text, p. 31): in the Van Aelst tapestry the
    Cartoon-design was cut in width by *c*. 25 cm. (from the
    left side of the tapestry); and additionally the red frames
    were reduced on all sides by the omission of the inner
    'receding' faces; it appears that a vertical border was
    originally woven on the left; thus the intended dimen-
    sions for the tapestry would have been *c*. 4·55 × 4·70 m.
    The dimensions of the lost Cartoon should, by the same
    reasoning, have been *c*. 3·05 × 3·65 m.; this calculation
    is made from the dimensions of the Van Aelst tapestry,
    allowing for a vertical stretch in the latter of *c*. 5 cm., as
    in the *Miraculous Draught*.
    It should be noted that the proportions of the lost Cartoon
    would be identical with those of the *Miraculous Draught*
    (before trimming), i.e. 1 : 1·2; for an explanation of the
    difference in absolute dimensions see text, p. 36.

The Conversion of Saul
(*Figs.* 20, 21.)

Cartoon: lost.
Tapestry, with no borders: 4·65 × 5·30 m.
    Variations: as in the case of the *Stoning of Stephen* Van
    Aelst reduced the width of the Cartoon-design (mostly on
    the left of the tapestry) by *c*. 25 cm., and additionally the
    inner edges of the red frames were omitted. It is uncertain
    whether the height was also reduced; the Mantuan
    tapestry shows appreciably more foreground and slightly
    more above; the variation is associated with different
    positions for Paul's sword (*Figs.* 20, 21); but in this case
    it is not possible to argue from the completeness of the
    figure-design that the Mantuan vertical extension is also
    more reliable (except, perhaps, above) and it may be felt
    that the additional foreground space is superfluous. The
    Mantuan tapestry was not made from the original
    Cartoon. Thus the vertical loss in the Vatican tapestry
    may be slight (*c*. 10 cm. for frame-edges and the comple-
    tion of Christ's drapery) or considerable (*c*. 27 cm. if the
    Mantuan picture-field is also correct below). The
    intended dimensions of the tapestry would have been
    c. 4·75 (or 4·92) × 5·58 m. (without borders; see above,
    p. 37, n. 73).

The Conversion of the Proconsul
(*Plates* 26–33, *Figs.* 23, 27.)

Cartoon: Redgrave 1858: 11 ft. 2¾ in. × 14 ft. 7½ in.;
    3·42 × 4·46 m.
    Losses: left, *c*. 114 cm.; right, *c*. 17 cm.; above, *c*. 2 cm.;
    below, *c*. 11 cm.
    Reconstruction: *c*. 3·55 × 5·77 m.

Tapestry, with no borders: 2·20 (cut) × 5·79 m.
  Reconstruction: *c.* 5·0 × 5·80 m. (without borders); a
  border is perhaps to be added on the left, making
  c. 5·0 × 6·50 m.

The Sacrifice at Lystra
(*Plates* 34–38, *Fig.* 24.)

Cartoon: Redgrave 1858: 11 ft. 4½ in. × 17 ft. 9½ in.;
  3·47 × 5·42 m.
  Losses: left, *c.* 10 cm.; right, *c.* 15 cm.; above, *c.* 6 cm.;
  below, none.
  Reconstruction: *c.* 3·53 × 5·67 m.
Tapestry, with no borders: 4·82 × 5·71 m.
  Variations: woven by Van Aelst with losses of *c.* 7 cm.
  above, *c.* 13 cm. below. The intended dimensions of the
  tapestry would have been *c.* 5·0 × 5·70 m. (without
  borders; see above, p. 37, n. 73).

Paul in Prison
(*Fig.* 26.)

Cartoon: lost.
Tapestry, with no borders: 4·78 × 1·30 m.
  Reconstruction: it appears that this piece was originally
woven with a border on its right (see above, p. 37, n. 73);
in that case the dimensions would have been *c.* 4·78 ×
2·0 m.

Paul preaching at Athens
(*Plates* I, 39–46, *Fig.* 25.)

Cartoon: Redgrave 1858: 11 ft. 3¼ in. × 14 ft. 6 in.;
  3·43 × 4·42 m.
  Losses: right, *c.* 2 cm.; above, *c.* 3 cm.
  Reconstruction: *c.* 3·46 × 4·44 m.
Tapestry, including one lateral border: 4·94 × 5·35 m. No
  corrections to be made; but the vertical measurement
  includes the substitute 'relief' added 1554–55.

COPIES

  Some of the more important early copies after the Cartoons are mentioned in the text, pp. 139, 144–9, 154–5, 163;
but no systematic collection has been attempted. The Royal
Collection includes a set by Heathcote, at present at Holy-
rood House.

COMPARATIVE ILLUSTRATIONS

2. Raphael: *Leo X and the Cardinals Giulio de' Medici and Luigi de' Rossi*. Oil on panel. Florence, Uffizi.

1. The Sistine Chapel.

3. The Sistine Chapel.

4. Florentine miniaturist *c*. 1470-80: *The Mass of the Capella papalis*. Chantilly, Musée Condé.

5. *Giulio* or *Leone* of Leo X. Silver.
London, British Museum.

6. *Triplice Giulio* of Leo X. Silver.
London, British Museum.

7. *Giulio* of Leo X. Silver. London, British Museum.

8. Dish of Leo X. Silver-gilt, crystal, rubies and sapphires.
Munich, Residenz, Schatzkammer.

9. Workshop of Perugino: Copy of the *Assumption*, formerly the
altarpiece of the Sistine Chapel. Silver-point, pen and wash,
white heightening. Vienna, Albertina.

10.-11. Roman miniaturist *c.* 1517: Frontispiece and Title-page to Giovanni Francesco Poggio, *De veri pastoris munere.* Biblioteca Apostolica Vaticana.

12. Raphael: *Leo the Great and Attila.* Fresco. Palazzo Vaticano, Stanza d'Eliodoro.

13. Pieter van Aelst after Raphael: *The Miraculous Draught of Fishes*. Tapestry.
Musei Vaticani.

14. Pieter van Aelst after Raphael; *The Charge to Peter*. Tapestry. Musei Vaticani.

15. Botticelli: *The Healing of the Leper*. Fresco, before restoration. Sistine Chapel.

16. Pieter van Aelst after Raphael: *The Healing of the Lame Man*. Tapestry. Musei Vaticani.

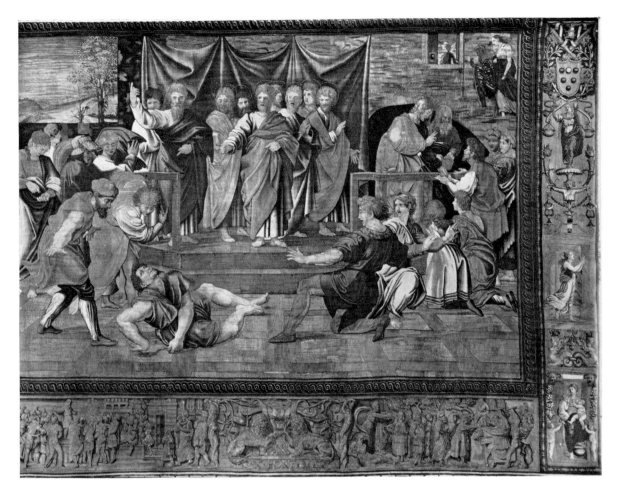

17. Pieter van Aelst after Raphael: *The Death of Ananias*. Tapestry. Musei Vaticani.

18. Pieter van Aelst after Raphael: *The Stoning of Stephen*. Tapestry.
Musei Vaticani.

19. Jan van Tiegen and associates after Raphael: *The Stoning of Stephen*. Tapestry. Mantua, Palazzo Ducale.

20. Pieter van Aelst after Raphael: *The Conversion of Saul*. Tapestry. Musei Vaticani.

21. Jan van Tiegen and associates after Raphael: *The Conversion of Saul*. Tapestry. Mantua, Palazzo Ducale.

22. Botticelli: *Moses in Egypt*. Fresco, after restoration. Sistine Chapel.

23. Jan van Tiegen and associates after Raphael: *The Conversion of the Proconsul*. Tapestry. Mantua, Palazzo Ducale.

24. Pieter van Aelst after Raphael: *The Sacrifice at Lystra*. Tapestry. Musei Vaticani.

25. Pieter van Aelst after Raphael: *Paul preaching at Athens*. Tapestry, after restoration.
Musei Vaticani.

26. Pieter van Aelst after Raphael:
Paul in Prison. Tapestry.
Musei Vaticani.

27. Pieter van Aelst after Raphael: *The Conversion of the Proconsul*. Tapestry, fragment. Musei Vaticani.

8. Jan van Tiegen and associates: Tapestry borders: (a) *Hercules I*, (b) *Liberal Arts I*, (c) *Liberal Arts II*, (d) *Cardinal Virtues*, (e) *Four Elements*, (f) *Hercules II*. Mantua, Palazzo Ducale.

29. Botticelli: *The Punishment of Corah*. Fresco, after restoration. Sistine Chapel.

30. J. C. Le Blon after Raphael: *Head of Christ*. Tapestry.
London, Victoria and Albert Museum.

31. Roman artist,
c. 1500:
*Medallion Portrait of
Christ*. Bronze.
London,
British Museum.

32. Roman artist,
c. 1500:
*Medallion Portrait of
Saint Paul*. Bronze.
London,
British Museum.

33. Raphael: *The Miraculous Draught of Fishes*, detail. Tapestry-cartoon, size-colours on paper. London, Victoria and Albert Museum, on loan from Her Majesty the Queen.

34. Pieter van Aelst after Raphael: *The Miraculous Draught of Fishes*, detail. Tapestry. Musei Vaticani.

35. Marten van Heemskerck: *View of Saint Peter's under construction*. Pen and ink. Berlin, Kupferstichkabinett.

36. Jan van Tiegen and associates after Raphael:
The Sacrifice at Lystra, detail. Tapestry.
Mantua, Palazzo Ducale.

37. Anonymous: *Portrait of Janus Lascaris*.
Milan, Biblioteca Ambrosiana.

38. Roman artist *c.* 1520-30: *A Crane*.
Woodcut, from I. Santa Fiore,
In la creatione di Paulo III.
Biblioteca Apostolica Vaticana.

39. Raphael: *Portrait of Leo X*. Black chalk. Chatsworth.

40. Giovanni da Udine (or copy): *Studies of Birds*. Pen, bistre wash, watercolour. Present location unknown.

41. G. F. Penni after Raphael: *Study for the Miraculous Draught of Fishes*. Black chalk, pen and brown ink, sepia wash, white heightening. Windsor Castle, Royal Library.

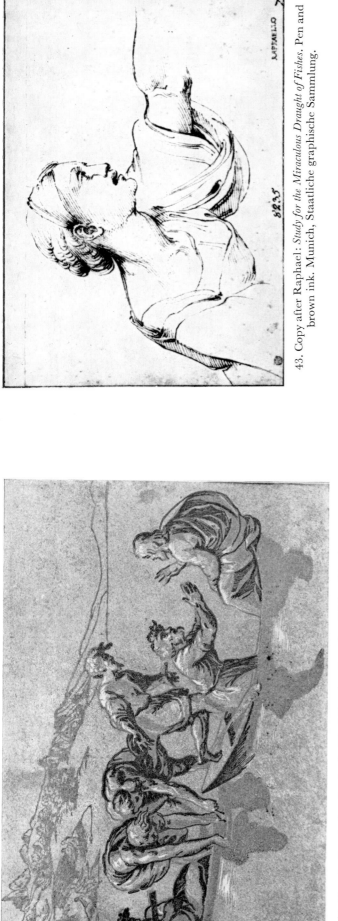

43. Copy after Raphael: *Study for the Miraculous Draught of Fishes*. Pen and brown ink. Munich, Staatliche graphische Sammlung.

45. Anonymous, after Giulio Romano (?): *The Miraculous Draught of Fishes*. Etching.

42. Ugo da Carpi after Raphael: *The Miraculous Draught of Fishes*. Woodcut. Windsor Castle, Royal Library.

44. Giulio Romano after Raphael (?): *The Miraculous Draught of Fishes*. Black chalk, pen

46. Raphael: *Study for The Charge to Peter.* Red chalk, fragment. Paris, Louvre.

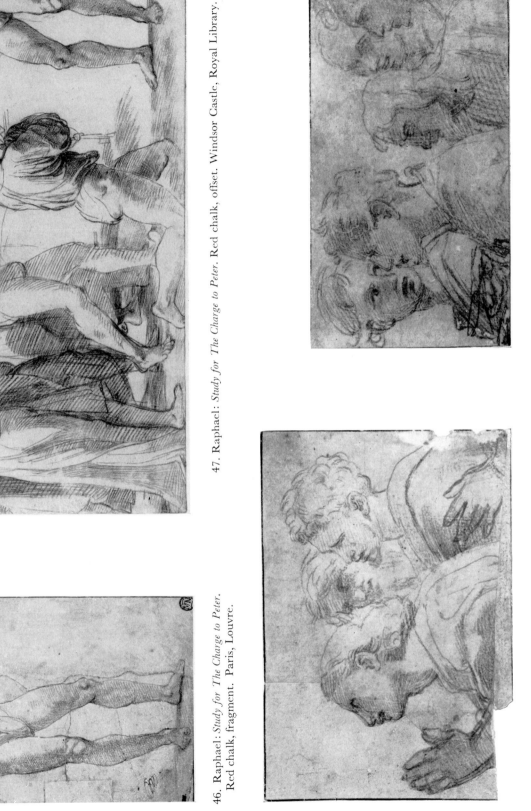

47. Raphael: *Study for The Charge to Peter.* Red chalk, offset. Windsor Castle, Royal Library.

49. Raphael: *Study for The Charge to Peter.* Red chalk, fragment. Paris, Private Collection.

48. Raphael: *Study for The Charge to Peter.* Red chalk, fragment. Paris, Private Collection.

50. Raphael: *Study for The Doubting Thomas*. Pen and ink. Cambridge, Fitzwilliam Museum.

51. Raphael: *Modello for The Charge to Peter*. Black chalk, pen and bistre wash, white heightening. Paris, Louvre.

52. Girolamo Genga: *Vestibulo* of Villa Imperiale, Pesaro.

53. Raphael: *Study for Parnassus*. Black chalk. Florence, Uffizi, Horne Collection.

54. Raphael's workshop (copy): *Study for The Entry of Cardinal Giovanni de' Medici into Florence*. Black chalk, sepia wash, white heightening. Vienna, Albertina.

55. Copy after Raphael: *Study for The Healing of The Lame Man.* Black chalk, sepia wash, white heightening. Paris, Louvre.

56. Copy after Raphael: *Study for The Healing of The Lame Man.* Pen and brown wash, white heightening. Present location unknown.

57. Copy after Raphael: *Study for The Healing of The Lame Man.* Pen and brown wash, white heightening. Nürnberg, Germanisches Nationalmuseum.

58. Parmigianino (?) after Raphael: *The Healing of The Lame Man*. Etching. Windsor Castle, Royal Library.

59. Battista Franco after Raphael: *The Healing of The Lame Man*. Engraving. London, British Museum.

61. Agostino Veneziano (?) after Raphael: *The Death of Ananias*. Engraving. London, British Museum.

60. Ugo da Carpi after Raphael: *The Death of Ananias*. Woodcut. London, British Museum.

62. *Oratio Augusti* relief, Arch of Constantine, Rome; detail.

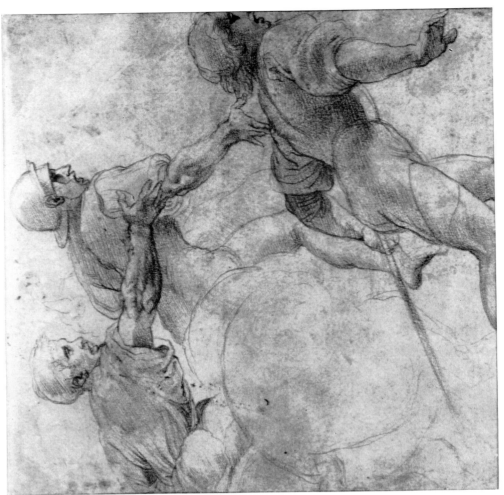

64. Copy after Raphael: *Study for The Conversion of Saul.* Red chalk. Haarlem, Teyler Museum.

63. Raphael: *Study for The Conversion of Saul.* Red chalk. Chatsworth.

65. Raphael: *Modello for The Conversion of the Proconsul*. Silver-point, white heightening, brown wash, pen and brown ink. Windsor Castle, Royal Library.

66. Raphael: *Study for a Caryatid*. Silver-point. Oxford, Ashmolean Museum.

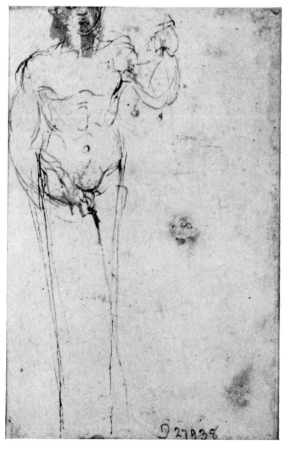

67. Raphael: *Study for a Herm*. Pen and brown ink. Oxford, Ashmolean Museum.

68. Copy after Raphael: *Study for The Sacrifice at Lystra*. Pen and brown ink, white heightening. Florence, Uffizi, Santarelli Collection.

69. Raphael: *Study for The Sacrifice at Lystra*. Silver-point, white heightening. Chatsworth.

70. Raphael: *Study for Paul in Prison* (?). Silver-point, white heightening. New York, Janos Scholz Collection.

71. Raphael: *Study for Paul preaching at Athens*. Red chalk. Florence, Uffizi.

72. G. F. Penni (?): *Modello for Paul preaching at Athens*. Black chalk, pen and brown wash, white heightening. Paris, Louvre.

73. *The Miraculous Draught of Fishes*. Eleventh-century Greek Gospel Book. Florence, Biblioteca Laurenziana, MS. Plut. vi. 23.

74. Late fourth-century Columnar Sarcophagus. Marble. Leyden, Rijksmuseum van Oudheden.

75. Roman sculptor *c.* 1475: *The Healing of The Lame Man*. Marble. Rome, Saint Peter's, Grotte Vaticane.

76. Aurelian Sacrifice relief. Marble. Rome, Palazzo dei Conservatori.

77. Dürer: *Christ before Pilate*. Woodcut, from The Little Passion.

78. Sacrifice relief. Arch of the Argentarii, Rome.

79. Sarcophagus. Marble. Florence, Uffizi.

80. Bonasone after Raphael (?): *The Charge to Peter*. Engraving. London, British Museum.

81. Copy after Raphael: *Study for The Mass at Bolsena*,
detail. Pen and brown wash, white heightening.
Oxford, Ashmolean Museum.

82. Spinello Aretino: *Paul preaching at Athens*. Tempera on panel.
Siena, Pinacoteca.

83. Florentine miniaturist *c.* 1518: *Portrait of Leo X*, from Piero Cattaci, *Genealogia medicea*.
Florence, Biblioteca Laurenziana.

84. Florentine miniaturist *c.* 1480: *The Conversion of Saul*, from the Urbino Bible.
Biblioteca Apostolica Vaticana.

85. Simon Gribelin: Frontispiece to engravings of Raphael's Cartoons. London, British Museum.

86. J. Stephanoff and W. J. Bennett: *The Cartoon Gallery at Hampton Court*. Lithograph, coloured.

88. F. Panini: *The Scala Regia*. Engraving.

90. Poussin (or copy) after Raphael: *The Healing of The Lame Man*. Pen and ink. Leningrad, Hermitage.

87. J. and F. Cleyn, copy after Raphael: *The Sacrifice at Lystra*. Pen and ink. Oxford, Ashmolean Museum.

89. Rubens, copy after Raphael: *Paul preaching at Athens*. Black chalk. Uppsala, University Library.

INDEX

Index